Excavations at Caldicot, Gwent: Bronze Age Palaeochannels in the Lower Nedern Valley

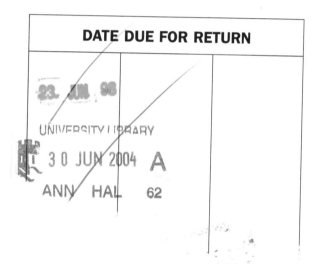

Excavations at Caldicot, Gwent: Bronze Age Palaeochannels in the Lower Nedern Valley

Nigel Nayling and Astrid Caseldine

with contributions by
S Aldhouse-Green, C Barrow, M Bell, R A Brunning,
N Cameron, J Compton, C Earwood, S Hamilton-Dyer, J Hillam,
S Howe, S Johnson, F McCormick, S McGrail, R Morgan,
E Murphy, P Northover, P Osborne, A O'Sullivan,
E Robinson, M Taylor, D F Williams,
A B Woodward

and line drawings by
C Earwood, B Garfi, P Jones, A O'Sullivan,
S Railton and C Seabright

CBA Research Report 108
Council for British Archaeology
1997

Published 1997 by the Council for British Archaeology
Bowes Morrell House, 111 Walmgate, York YO1 2UA

British Library Cataloguing in Publication Data
A catalogue for this book is available from the British Library

ISSN 0141 7819

ISBN 1 872414 79 6

Typeset from authors' disks by Archetype, Stow-on-the-Wold
URL http://ourworld.compuserve.com/homepages/Archetype

Printed by York Publishing Services Ltd., York

This book is published with the aid of a grant from
Cadw: Welsh Historic Monuments

Front cover Aerial photograph of the site during excavation and its immediate environs in the Nedern
Valley, including Caldicot Castle

Back cover Pegged mortised plank (24837) and the remains of the associated upright (24605) at its right
hand end: a possible repair to the Late Bronze Age bridge (structure 22441)

Contents

List of figures

List of tables

Acknowledgements

The project was largely funded by Cadw: Welsh Historic Monuments and the joint managers of the Caldicot Castle Country Park, Gwent County Council (GCC) and Monmouth Borough Council (MBC). Jeremy Knight, and subsequently Rick Turner as the relevant Inspectors of Ancient Monuments contributed much to the project as did Tim Bradfield, Peter Johns and Mike Longford (MBC) and John Palmer and Gordon Probert (GCC). Andrew Helme (Museums Officer: Monmouthshire Museums Service) represented the local authorities on the steering committee which monitored progress and continues moves towards the display and interpretation of the site. Annie Raynesbury (Curator, Chepstow Museum) provided facilities for the initial safe storage and cataloguing of finds. Bryony Coles (University of Exeter) and Gareth Dowdell (Director, Glamorgan-Gwent Archaeological Trust) also sat on the steering committee. Additional support was provided by Stephen Aldhouse-Green (National Museum of Wales), Francis Lynch (University College of North Wales, Bangor) and Bill Manning (University of Wales, Cardiff) as the archaeological sub-committee of the Ancient Monuments Board.

The site's discovery owes much to the initial observations of Derek Upton of Caldicot, Dennis Manning (Country Park Warden, Caldicot Castle Country Park) and Bob Trett (Curator, Newport Museum). Sean Brewer (Curator, Caldicot Castle) and the rest of the staff in the castle accommodated our requirements for storage and study space and accepted with good grace the endless mud we brought with us.

An integral part of the project was public access to the site and an on-site exhibition. Through considerable effort on the part of Trust staff, a topical exhibition was created and maintained. Numerous individuals and parties visited the excavations either during the working week or on open days. None of this would have been possible without the kind support and enthusiasm of the Caldicot Trust, in particular the Cliffe, Turner and Strong families.

Up to the end of the 1990 season, the project was jointly directed by Stephen Parry and Jonathan Parkhouse for the Glamorgan-Gwent Archaeological Trust: thanks are due for their dedication in producing the record inherited by the writer in 1991. Pete Wright assisted greatly in ordering and computerising much of this and subsequent data. The field staff employed by the Trust worked relentlessly in trying and very uncomfortable working conditions on a site which required consistently thoughtful excavation and keen observation. Pete Lennox as supervisor (1991–2) bore much of the responsibility whilst Joyce Compton's rigorous approach to finds recording kept us all on our collective toes. The extensive environmental sampling strategy was co-ordinated by Alison Rutherford and subsequently by Belinda Allen, in liaison with Astrid Caseldine. Caroline Earwood ordered and assessed the wood held in store after the 1988–90 excavation before Richard Brunning and Aidan O'Sullivan took on responsibility for the recording of wood as on-site specialists. Caroline also arranged for students from University College Dublin and Exeter University to assist on the excavations as part of their European Social Fund post-graduate course in wetland archaeology.

Post-excavation analysis required ordering and grouping of a substantial and sometimes disparate data set. Belinda Allen, Pete Lennox, Pete Wright and Adam Yates as post-excavation assistants carried out much of this work. Mari Pambianchi produced the majority of the inked archive drawings which formed the basis for many of the final illustrations. We are grateful to Bryony Coles, Edith Evans, James Rackham and Rick Turner for commenting on the draft text, and to Kate Sleight for final editing.

Assistance with the production costs for this volume were received from Cadw: Welsh Historic Monuments, the Caldicot Trust, Monmouth Borough Council and Gwent County Council.

Some specialist contributors would like to acknowledge those who assisted them in their endeavours. Astrid Caseldine and Kate Barrow would like to thank Martha Hannon for assistance with the pollen preparation and plant macrofossil sorting during the early stages of the project, and are also grateful to Professor Michael Walker for his helpful comments on an early draft of the report. Su Johnson acknowledges Kate Phillips' initial wood identifications. Nigel Cameron wishes to thank Roger Flower for his original diatom assessment of material from the site and to Simon Patrick for organisation. Martin Bell and Su Johnson are grateful to Shannon Fraser who did some preliminary work on sample 3012. Su would also like to thank Dr Peter Gasson of the Royal Botanic Gardens, Kew, for his help with the identification of the problem *Cornus* samples. Jennifer Hillam is grateful to Mike Baillie, Bernd Becker, Dave Brown, and Janet Neve for providing unpublished tree-ring chronologies; Ian Tyers for unpublished computer programs, and Dave Brown for checking the original Caldicot oak chronology against unpublished Irish chronologies.

List of Contributors

Stephen Aldhouse-Green, Department of History and Archaeology, Gwent College of Higher Education, Caerleon Campus, PO Box 179, Newport NP6 1YG

Kate Barrow, Department of Archaeology, University of Wales, Lampeter, Ceredigion SA48 7ED

Martin Bell, Department of Archaeology, University of Wales, Lampeter, Ceredigion SA48 7ED

Richard Brunning, Environment Department, Somerset County Council, County Hall, Taunton TA1 4DY

Nigel Cameron, Environmental Change Research Centre, University College London, 26 Bedford Way, London WC1H 0AP

Astrid Caseldine, Department of Archaeology, University of Wales, Lampeter, Ceredigion SA48 7ED

Joyce Compton, Glamorgan-Gwent Archaeological Trust, Ferryside Warehouse, Bath Lane, Swansea SA1 1RD

Caroline Earwood, Clwyd-Powys Archaeological Trust, 7A Church St, Welshpool, Powys SY21 7DL

Sheila Hamilton-Dyer, 5 Suffolk Avenue, Shirley, Southampton, Hampshire, SO1 5EF

Jennifer Hillam, Dendrochronology Laboratory, Research School for Archaeology, University of Sheffield, 2 Mappin St, Sheffield S1 4DT

Steve Howe, Department of Geology, National Museum of Wales, Cathays Park, Cardiff CF1 3NP

Su Johnson, Department of Archaeology, University of Wales, Lampeter, Ceredigion SA48 7ED

Finbar McCormick, Queen's University Belfast, Palaeoecology Centre, Queen's University Belfast, Belfast, Northern Ireland BT7 2NN

Sean McGrail, Bridge Cottage, Chilmark, Salisbury, Wiltshire SP3 5AU

Ruth Morgan, 128 Psalter Lane, Sheffield, South Yorkshire S11 8YU

Eileen Murphy, Queen's University Belfast, Palaeoecology Centre, Queen's University Belfast, Belfast, Northern Ireland BT7 2NN

Nigel Nayling, Glamorgan-Gwent Archaeological Trust, Ferryside Warehouse, Bath Lane, Swansea SA1 1RD

Peter Northover, University of Oxford, Department of Materials, University of Oxford, Parks Road, Oxford OX1 3PH

Peter Osborne, The Yett, Hopton Bank, Cleobury Mortimer, Nr Kidderminster, Worcester DY14 0PB

Aidan O'Sullivan, Discovery Programme, 13–15 Lower Hatch Street, Dublin 2, Republic of Ireland

Eric Robinson, Department of Geological Sciences, University College London, Gower Street, London WC1E 6BT

Mark Taylor, School of Geography, University of Leeds, Leeds LS2 9JT

David Williams, Department of Archaeology, University of Southampton, Southampton SO9 5NH

Ann Woodward, 17 Great Western Road, Dorchester, Dorset DT1 1UF

Summary

The site at Caldicot is located on the floodplain of the river Nedern, a small tributary of the Severn Estuary close to the coastal wetlands known as the Gwent Levels, which fringe the northern shore of the estuary on the South Wales coast. During the construction of a lake in the grounds of the Caldicot Castle Country Park, waterlogged timbers were observed and work halted to permit archaeological investigations. Trial excavations indicated the presence of silted palaeochannels of the Nedern containing well-preserved spreads of wood, stone and artefactual material including a Wilburton style chape, suggesting a Bronze Age date for the site. An integrated programme of environmental and archaeological investigation of this complex sequence of palaeochannel sediments followed, the results of which form the subject of this report. The taphonomic processes, inherent in the incorporation of various biota and artefactual material into fluvial sedimentation, were taken into consideration during the interpretation of the eight major phases identified. These phases are briefly described here.

During Phase I, the valley bottom of the Nedern was steadily infilling with fine sands, clays and silts, interrupted occasionally by the formation of peats and organic clays. Limited excavation and auger survey suggested that these horizontally-bedded sediments did not occupy a constrained channel, but rather represented deposition across much of the valley bottom, leading to substantial infilling of a deep, glacial channel. Environmental indicators suggested a strong marine influence and the presence of salt-marsh nearby. Organic clays, dated by radiocarbon to the Neolithic period, contained plant remains indicating the development of reed swamp for brief episodes, reflecting periods of relative stability in relation to sea level, and fresher water conditions. On the surrounding valley sides, mixed deciduous forest dominated during the Neolithic, initially consisting largely of oak but later with lime playing a significant role. The evidence for woodland clearance and agriculture suggested only a low level of activity.

A significant change in the valley had occurred by Phase II. For the first time there was evidence for the presence of a constrained palaeochannel within the site. The construction of a revetment or weir of finely-cut hazel piles is dated by radiocarbon to the earlier Bronze Age. Contemporary environmental indicators point to a continuing but less marked estuarine influence, along with changes in woodland composition and some suggestion of cereal cultivation on higher land.

Phase III sees a radical change in the nature of the river channel and its fills. Highly organic basal sediments contained spreads of worked wood (including a massive oak plank interpreted as a strake from a sewn plank boat), stone and domesticate bone fragments. Environmental indicators imply a predominantly freshwater river, subject to occasional estuarine influences, an open grassy floodplain, and scrub and secondary woodland on drier ground accompanied by continuing agricultural activity. Calibration of eight of the radiocarbon dates place this phase in the 2nd millennium BC, mostly in the first three quarters of that millennium, ie the Middle Bronze Age.

Phase IV, seen as a period of relative inactivity, is characterised by the absence of evidence for channel down-cutting and the presence of highly organic fills with low artefact content. Palaeoenvironmental evidence suggested the channel was more susceptible to drying out at this time. Phase V comprised a period of active channel down-cutting and migration with freshwater channels of relatively narrow proportions filled with inorganic silty clays containing limited artefactual assemblages. Activity may have shifted away from the site but pollen records indicate on-going agricultural activity in the area.

Phase VI sees a major change in riverbed form to a broad (c 7m wide), flat-bottomed channel containing dense spreads of dumped stone, wood and bone. A cross-channel line of driven uprights and associated dumps of stone may have acted as a ford, weir, hard or a combination of these functions. Initially the channel was freshwater but through time there were increasing indications of marine influence. Radiocarbon dates and a tree-ring date of 998/7 BC place this phase in the Late Bronze Age. Throughout this and the following phase, agricultural activity and clearance continues on drier ground.

During Phase VII, in a period of increasing marine influence, sediment continued to accumulate in this large channel. A double line of oak and ash piles built across the channel, probably soon after 990/989 BC on the basis of dendrochronological dating, is interpreted as a bridge. The function of intermediate, slighter rods of hazel is unclear; this structure may also have operated as a cross-channel fish weir. An associated rough 'trackway', consisting of a spread of woodworking debris and stone may have temporarily consolidated the riverbed to facilitate construction of the bridge. A small channel in the east half of the lake and the near-complete skeleton of a dog are also assigned to this phase. Tree-ring dates suggest activity was limited to decades rather than centuries. There appears to have been fairly rapid sedimentation at this time until Phase VIII, possibly at the Late Bronze Age/Early Iron Age transition, when rapid accumulation of sediment, possibly the result of increased over-bank sedimentation and marine inundation, mark the end of human activity within the excavated area.

Approximately 5000 pieces of wood from the site were examined in detail. The site assemblage contained a broad range of species dominated by hazel, blackthorn and hawthorn-type roundwood interpreted as the by-products of scrub woodland clearance. Oak, ash and alder had been preferentially selected for woodworking/carpentry. Worked timbers included driven piles, mortised planks, woodworking debris and a range of artefacts including containers and boat fragments.

Analysis of the faunal assemblage, one of the largest collections from Bronze Age Wales, indicated predominance of sheep amongst the domesticates, as well as exploitation of wild species. The bone, often fractured, is suggestive of discarded food refuse. A number of canid bones, including the skeleton of an aged and diseased individual, are identified as domestic dog. A small number of bones had been worked to form both utilitarian and 'decorative' artefacts. Other artefact groups comprise metalwork, a single amber bead and a largely residual collection of flint.

Comparison with pollen data from elsewhere in the region enables the environmental, structural and artefactual data from the site to be placed in a broader context of vegetational history and environmental change, and combined with other archaeological data permits an assessment of the site's importance within regional prehistory and the development of the cultural landscape.

Crynodeb

Lleolir y safle yn Caldicot ar orlifdir afon Nedern, sef isafon fechan yn aber afon Hafren yn agos at leithdir arfordirol Morfa Gwent, sy'n amgylchu glan ogleddol yr aber ar arfodir De Cymru. Yn ystod y gwaith o wneud llyn yng ngerddi Parc Gwledig Castell Caldicot, sylwyd ar brennau llawn dŵr ac ataliwyd y gwaith er mwyn cynnal ymchwiliadau archeolegol. Dynodai'r cloddio rhagbrofol bresenoldeb paleosianelau llawn llaid y Nedern a hwythau'n cynnwys mannau â lledaeniad o ddeunydd pren, carreg a gwneuthurbethau wedi'u cadw mewn cyflwr da, gan gynnwys amgarn yn arddull Wilburton, a oedd yn awgrymu dyddiad o Oes yr Efydd ar gyfer y safle. Yn dilyn, cafwyd rhaglen gyfunedig o ymchwiliadau amgylcheddol ac archeolegol ar y dilyniant cymhleth hwn o waddodion paleosianelaidd, a chanlyniadau'r ymchwil hwnnw yw testun trafod yr adroddiad hwn. Yn ystod y dehongli a fu ar yr wyth is-gyfnod o bwys a ddynodwyd, cymerwyd i ystyriaeth y prosesau taffonomig sy'n hanfodol cyn y caiff deunydd amryw fiota a gwneuthurbethau ymgyfuno â gwaddodiad afonol. Yn dilyn, ceir disgrifiad byr o'r wyth is-gyfnod.

Yn ystod is-gyfnod I, yr oedd llawr dyffryn Nedern yn graddol mewnlenwi â thywodydd mân, cleiau a llifwaddodion ond, o bryd i'w gilydd, torrid ar draws hyn gan ffurfiant mawndiroedd a chleiau organig. Awgrymai cloddio cyfyngedig ac arolwg tyllu nad llanw sianel gyfyng yng ngwely'r afon yr oedd haenau llorweddol y gwaddodion ond, yn hytrach, eu bod yn cynrychioli dyddodion ar draws cryn dipyn o lawr y dyffryn, gan arwain at fewnlanw sylweddol ar sianel ddofn, rewlifol. Yr oedd dangosyddion amgylcheddol yn awgrymu dylanwad morol cryf a phresenoldeb morfa heli gerllaw. Yr oedd cleiau organig, a ddyddiwyd yn ôl trwy radio carbon i Oes Newydd y Cerrig, yn cynnwys olion planhigion a ddynodai ddatblygiad gwernydd cawn am ysbeidiau byr, ac adlewyrchai hyn gyfnodau cymharol sefydlog o ran lefel y môr, ac amodau dŵr mwy croyw. Hyd ochrau'r dyffryn oddi amgylch, coedwig gollddail gymysg oedd drechaf yn ystod Oes Newydd y Cerrig, coedwig dderw'n bennaf i gychwyn ond, yn fwy diweddar, daeth coed pisgwydd i chwarae rhan mwy amlwg. Dim ond lefel isel o weithgaredd a awgrymid gan y dystiolaeth a gafwyd o ddigoedwigo ac amaethu.

Erbyn is-gyfnod II yr oedd newid o bwys wedi digwydd yn y dyffryn. Am y tro cyntaf yr oedd yna dystiolaeth o bresenoldeb paleosianel gyfyngedig y tu mewn i'r safle. Trwy radio carbon, dyddiwyd adeiladwaith cynhalfur neu gored, a wnaed o byst coed cyll wedi'u hollti'n fain, yn ôl i'r Oes Efydd gynharach. Mae dangosyddion amgylcheddol cyfoes yn awgrymu dylanwad aberol parhaus ond llai amlwg, ynghyd â newidiadau yn nghyfansoddiad y coetir a rhyw awgrym o amaethu grawn ar dir uwch.

Yn ystod is-gyfnod III, gwelir newid sylfaenol yn natur sianel yr afon a'i llenwadau. Yr oedd gwaddodion gwaelodol organig iawn yn cynnwys mannau â lledaeniad o bren gweithiedig (gan gynnwys astell dderw anferth a ddehonglwyd fel un o'r planciau oddi ar gwch 'styllod gwniedig), cerrig a darnau o esgyrn anifeiliaid byd amaeth. Mae'r dangosyddion amgylcheddol yn awgrymu fod yma afon o ddŵr croyw gan mwyaf, gyda dylanwadau aberol yn effeithio arni weithiau, gorlifdir agored glaswelltog, a phrysgwydd a choetir eilaidd ar y tir mwy sych, gyda gweithgaredd amaethu'n parhau. Trwy raddnodi wyth o'r dyddiadau radio carbon lleolir yr is-gyfnod hwn yn ystod yr 2il fileniwm CC, gan mwyaf yn ystod tri chwarter cyntaf y mileniwm hwnnw, h.y. Canol Oes yr Efydd.

Y mae is-gyfnod IV, a ystyrir yn gyfnod cymharol dawel o safbwynt gweithgarwch, yn cael ei nodweddu gan absenoldeb tystiolaeth o dyrchu sianelau a chan bresenoldeb llenwadau organig iawn sy'n cynnwys lefel isel o wneuthurbethau. Yr oedd tystiolaeth paleoamgylcheddol yn awgrymu fod y sianel yn fwy tueddol o sychu i fyny yn ystod yr amser hwn. Yr oedd is-gyfnod V yn cynnwys cyfnod gweithredol o dyrchu sianelau a mudo gyda sianelau dŵr croyw o faintioli cymharol gul yn llawn cleiau llifwaddodol anorganaidd a gynhwysai gasgliadau cyfyngedig o wneuthurbethau. Hwyrach i'r gweithgarwch symud i ffwrdd oddi ar y safle ond dengys cofnod y paill weithgarwch amaethu'n digwydd yn yr ardal.

Gwêl is-gyfnod VI newid mawr yn ffurf gwely'r afon a drowyd yn sianel lydan (c 7m o led) â gwaelod gwastad, gan gynnwys mannau a ledaenwyd yn drwch â dadlwythiad o gerrig, pren ac esgyrn. Hwyrach i'r llinell ar draws y sianel o ystlysbyst a ffustwyd i mewn i'r ddaear, gyda phentyrrau cysylltiedig o gerrig, weithredu fel rhyd, cored neu war galed neu fel cyfuniad o'r swyddogaethau hyn i gyd. I gychwyn, sianel o ddŵr croyw oedd hi ond, gyda threigl amser, yr oedd yna arwyddion cynyddol o ddylanwad morol. Mae dyddiadau radio carbon a dyddiad cylchoedd coeden o 998/7 CC yn gosod yr is-gyfnod hwn yn Oes Ddiweddar yr Efydd. Trwy gydol yr is-gyfnod hwn a'r is-gyfnod dilynol, mae gweithgarwch amaethyddol a chlirio'n parhau ar dir mwy sych.

Yn ystod is-gyfnod VII, mewn cyfnod o ddylanwad morol cynyddol, yr oedd y gwaddodion yn dal i grynhoi yn y sianel fawr hon. Codwyd llinell ddwbl o byst deri ac ynn ar draws y sianel, yn fuan wedi 990/989 CC yn ôl pob tebyg ar sail dyddio dendrocronolegol, a'r dehongliad a roddir ar yr adeiladwaith yw mai pont ydoedd. Nid yw'n eglur beth yn hollol oedd swyddogaeth y rhodenni llai eu maint o bren cyll sydd yn y canol; gallai'r cyfanwaith fod wedi cael ei ddefnyddio'n ogystal fel cored bysgod ar draws y sianel. Hwyrach i 'sarn' arw gysylltiol, a wnaed o ledaeniad shwrwd gwaith coed a cherrig, gael ei bwriadu ar gyfer sadio gwely'r afon dros dro er mwyn hwyluso'r gwaith o adeiladu'r bont. Priodolir i'r is-gyfnod hwn hefyd sianel fechan yn hanner dwyreiniol y llyn, yn ogystal ag ysgerbwd sydd ymron â bod yn gyfan o gi. Mae dyddiadau cylchoedd coeden yn awgrymu bod y gweithgaredd yn gyfyngedig i ddegawdau yn hytrach na chanrifoedd. Ymddengys i ddyddodi gwaddodion ddigwydd yn eithaf cyflym yr adeg hon tan is-gyfnod VIII, yn ystod y trawsnewidiad o Oes Ddiweddar yr Efydd i Oes Gynnar yr Haearn, efallai, pan geir arwydd yn y crynhoi cyflym ar y gwaddodiad, o ganlyniad efallai i'r dyddodi cynyddol tros y glannau a llifogydd o'r môr, bod diwedd wedi dod ar weithgarwch dynol y tu mewn i safle'r cloddio.

Cafodd oddeutu 5000 o'r darnau o bren a gafwyd ar y safle eu harchwilio'n fanwl. Yr oedd casgliad prennau'r safle'n cynnwys amrywiaeth eang o rywogaethau gyda'r trechaf yn eu plith yn lwyni coed cyll, a drain du a drain gwynion o'r mathau a ddehonglid yn sgîl-gynnyrch digoedwigo prysgwydd. Arferai coed deri, ynn a gwern â chael eu dethol yn arbennig ar gyfer gwaith coed/ gwaith saer. Yr oedd prennau gweithiedig yn cynnwys pyst wedi'u ffusto, estyll morteisiog, shwrwd gwaith coed ac amrywiaeth o wneuthurbethau gan gynnwys llestri a darnau o gychod.

Dynodai'r dadansoddiad a wnaed o'r casgliad milodol, un o'r casgliadau mwyaf a gafwyd o Oes yr Efydd yng Nghymru, mai defaid oedd fwyaf niferus ymysg anifeiliaid byd amaeth ac, yn ogystal, bod yna ymelwa ar rywogaethau gwyllt. Mae'r asgwrn, toredig yn aml, yn awgrymu gweddillion bwyd a daflwyd o'r neilltu. Dynodwyd nifer o esgyrn cŵn, gan gynnwys ysgerbwd un hen gi afiach, yn esgyrn ci dof. Saernïwyd nifer fechan o'r esgyrn yn wneuthurbethau defnyddiol ac 'addurnol'. Yr oedd grwpiau o wneuthurbethau eraill yn cynnwys gwaith metel, un glain gwefr sef glain o ambr, a chasgliad callestr (neu fflint) gweddillol gan mwyaf.

Mae cymhariaeth â data paill o fannau eraill yn y cyffiniau yn galluogi gosod data amgylcheddol, adeileddol a gwneuthurbethau'r safle yng nhyddestun lletach hanes llystyfiannol a newid amgylcheddol, a thrwy gyfuniad â data archeolegol eraill yn caniatáu llunio asesiad o bwysigrwydd y safle oddi mewn i gynhanes yr ardal a datblygiad y tirwedd diwylliannol.

Résumé

Le site de Caldicot est situé sur la zone inondable de la rivière Nedern, un petit affluent de l'estuaire de la Severn, près des Gwent Levels, les zones humides du littoral au bord de la rive nord de l'estuaire, sur la côte du sud du pays de Galles. Pendant la mise en oeuvre d'un lac artificiel dans les terres du Parc rural du château de Caldicot, on remarqua la présence de bois de construction imprégné d'eau et on arrêta les travaux pour effectuer des fouilles archéologiques. Les sondages indiquèrent la présence d'anciens lits envasés de la rivière Nedern, contenant des concentrations bien préservées de bois, pierre et matériel provenant d'objets façonnés, y compris une chape de style Wilburton, suggérant que le site datait de l'âge du bronze. Y fit suite un programme intégré d'enquêtes archéologiques et liées à l'environnement portant sur cette suite complexe de sédiments des anciens lits, programme dont les résultat forment le sujet de ce rapport. On tint compte des processus post-sédimentation inhérents dans l'incorporation de divers biotes et matériaux façonnés dans la sédimentation fluviale lors de l'interprétation des huit grandes phases identifiées. Une brève description de ces phases se trouve ci-dessous.

Pendant la phase I, le fond de la vallée de la Nedern s'était progressivement rempli de sables fins, d'argiles et de vases, interrompus de temps en temps par la formation de tourbes et d'argiles organiques. Des fouilles limitées et des forages ont suggéré que ces sédiments en couches horizontales n'occupaient pas un lit restreint mais plutôt qu'ils représentaient un dépôt au travers d'une grande partie du fond de la vallée, menant à un considérable remplissage d'un profond lit glaciaire. Les indices liés à l'environnement suggéraient une importante influence maritime et la présence d'un marais salin à proximité. Des argiles organiques datées au carbone 14 à la période néolithique et contenant des restes de plantes indiquait le développement épisodique d'un marécage de roseaux, reflétant des périodes relativement stables par rapport au niveau de la mer et des conditions d'eau plus douce. Sur les versants de la vallée, une forêt composée de divers feuillus dominait pendant le néolithique et se composait au départ de chênes, auxquels s'ajouteront par la suite de nombreux tilleuls. Les indices de défrichement des bois et d'agriculture ne suggéraient qu'un faible niveau d'activité.

Un important changement s'était produit dans la vallée avant la phase II. Pour la première fois, on trouvait des indices révélant la présence d'un ancien lit à l'intérieur du site. La construction d'un revêtement ou barrage de pilotis en noisetier coupés avec précision est datée au carbone 14 au début de l'âge du bronze. Des indices contemporains liés à l'environnement indiquent que l'influence estuarienne continue mais est moins marquée, que la composition de la forêt change et qu'on cultivait des céréales sur les terrains plus élevés.

La phase III témoigne d'un changement radical du lit de la rivière et de ses matériaux de remplissage. Les sédiments du fond, de haute teneur organique, contenaient des concentrations de bois façonné (y compris une planche de chêne massif, qu'on pense être la virure d'un bateau en planches suturées), de pierre et de fragment d'os d'animaux domestiques. Les indices liés à l'environnement laissent supposer une rivière principalement d'eau douce, soumise de temps à autre à des influences estuariennes, une zone inondable ouverte et couverte d'herbe, de la broussaille et une forêt secondaire sur les terres plus sèches, avec une activité agricole qui se poursuivait.

La moyenne de huit des dates au carbone 14 situe cette phase au second millénaire av. J.-C., principalement dans les trois premiers quarts de ce millénaire, c'est-à-dire le milieu de l'âge du bronze.

La phase IV, vue comme une période relativement inactive, est caractérisée par l'absence d'indices de percée d'un lit et par la présence de matériaux de remplissage de haute teneur organique et de faible teneur en matériaux façonnés.

Les indices paléo-écologiques suggéraient que le lit avait davantage tendance à s'assécher à cette époque. Le Phase V comprenait une période de percée active de lits et de migration, avec des lits d'eau douce relativement étroits et remplis d'argiles vaseuses non organiques ne contenant que de petits ensembles de matériaux façonnés. L'activité s'était peut-être éloignée du site mais les traces de pollen indiquent que l'activité agricole continuait dans la région.

La Phase V voit un important changement de la forme du lit de la rivière, qui se transforme en lit large (environ 7m de largeur) à fond plat contenant de denses concentrations de pierre, bois et os déchargés. Une rangée de montants enfoncés au travers du lit et de pierres déchargées associées servait peut-être de gué ou de barrage ou de ces deux fonctions. Au début, c'était un lit d'eau douce mais, au fil des ans, il y a de plus en plus d'indices d'influence maritime. Les dates au carbone 14 et une date de 998/7 av. J.-C. obtenue par la dendrochronologie situent cette phase à la fin de l'âge du bronze. Pendant toute cette phase et la phase suivante, l'activité agricole et le défrichement continuent sur les terrains plus secs.

Pendant la phase VII, une période d'influence maritime croissante, les sédiments continuèrent à s'accumuler dans ce grand lit. On pense qu'une double rangée de pilotis en chêne et en frêne construite au travers du lit, probablement peu après 990/989 av. J.-C. sur la base de la datation par dendrochronologie, était un pont. La fonction de plus fines tiges intermédiaires en noisetier n'est pas claire ; cette structure servait peut-être aussi de barrage à poissons au travers du lit. Une "piste" rudimentaire qui s'y rattachait, composée d'une concentration de débris de menuiserie de pierre avait peut-être servir à une consolidation temporaire du lit de la rivière afin de faciliter la construction du pont. Un petit lit dans la partie est du lac et le squelette presque entier d'un chien sont également attribués à cette phase. Les dates par dendrochronologie suggèrent que l'activité ne dura que quelques décennies plutôt que des siècles. Il semble que la sédimentation ait été relativement rapide à l'époque et jusqu'à la phase VII, peut-être au moment de la transition entre la fin de l'âge du bronze et le début de l'âge de fer, moment auquel l'accumulation rapide de sédiments, peut-être le résultat d'une sédimentation accrue par dessus la berge et de l'inondation maritime marque la fin de l'activité humaine à l'intérieur de la zone fouillée.

Environ 5000 morceaux de bois du site furent étudiés en détail. L'ensemble découvert sur le site contenait une grande variété d'espèces, dominée par les noisetiers, les bois d'amourette et divers types d'aubépine ; on estime que c'était les dérivés du défrichement des bois et broussailles. Le chêne, le frêne et l'aune avaient été choisis de préférence pour la menuiserie. Le bois d'oeuvre comprenait des pilotis enfoncés, des planches mortaisées, des débris de menuiserie et un éventail d'objets façonnés comprenant des récipients et des fragments de bateaux.

L'analyse de l'ensemble de la faune, l'une des plus grandes collections de l'âge du bronze au pays de Galles, indiquait la prédominance des ovins parmi les animaux domestiques ainsi que l'exploitation d'espèces sauvages. Les os, souvent brisés, suggèrent que ce sont des déchets alimentaires. Un certain nombre d'os de canidés, y compris le squelette d'un vieil individu malade, sont ceux de chiens domestiques. Quelques os avaient été façonnés pour former des objets à la fois utilitaires et décoratifs. D'autres groupes d'objets façonnés comprennent des objets en métal, une seule perle d'ambre et une collection de silex, en grande partie résiduelle.

Une comparaison avec les données de pollen d'autres endroits dans la région permet de placer les données liées à l'environnement, aux structures et aux objets façonnés du site dans un contexte plus général d'histoire de la végétation et de changement de l'environnement ; lorsqu'on joint ces données à d'autres données archéologiques, on peut évaluer l'importance du site dans le contexte de la préhistoire de la région et du développement du paysage culturel.

Zusammenfassung

Das Gelände bei Caldicot liegt an der Schwemmebene des Flußes Nedern, ein kleiner Nebenfluß des Severn Estuary (Mündung), in der Nahe der Marschlände, die als Gwent Levels bekannt an dam nördlichen Ufer der Mündung am Rande der Südküste von Wales liegen. Bei der Konstruktion eines Sees in den Anlagen des Caldicot Kastells im County Park wurden voll mit Wasser angesaugte Planken gefunden und um archäologische Nachforschungen zu ermöglichen, wurde die Arbeit eingestellt. Testausgrabungen ließen darauf schließen, daß sich hier prähistorische Kanäle des Flußes Nedern befanden, die verschiedene gut erhaltene Holz und Steinarten und Kunstgegenstände, insgesamt eine in Wilburton Stil gearbeitete Scheidespitze, enthielten. Aus diesem Grunde nimmt man an, daß das Gelände aus dem Bronzezeitalter stammt. Ein einheitliches Programm von Recherchen in die Umgegend und archäologische Untersuchungen dieser komplexen Reihenfolge der prähistorischen Kanalablagerungen folgte und dieser Bericht schildert diese Vorgänge. Die nach der Beerdigung stattgefundenen Vorgänge, die sich bei dieser Integration biologischer Reste manifestierten, wurden bei der Interpretation dieser acht bedeutenden Phasen identifiziert und hier kurz geschildert.

In der 1. Phase wurde das Talende des Flußes Nedern ununterbrochen mit feinem Sand, Lehm und Schlick angefüllt. Nur gelegentlich wurde dieser Ablauf durch die Formung von Turf und organischem Lehm unterbrochen. Befristete Ausgrabungen und Bohrvermessungen ließen daraus schließen, daß diese waagrecht gelegenen Ablagerungen nicht in eingeengten Kanäle vorkamen aber eher eine Deponie durch fast das ganze Talende darstellten. Die Folge dessen war, daß ein tiefer Gletscherkanal erheblich gefüllt wurde. Die Umgegend ließ darauf schließen, daß diese Gegend stark vom Meer und von der Gegenwart eines naheliegendem Salzsumpfes beeinflußt wurde. Organischer Lehm, durch Radiokarbonmethode bis zum Neolithikum datiert, beinhalteten Pflanzenreste, die auf die Fortbildung von Schilfschlumpf in kurzen Episoden hinwiesen, die wiederum Perioden relativer Stabilität im Verhältnis zum Meeresspiegel wiederspiegelten, und sußere Wasserbestände. Im Neolithikum dominierte gemischter Laubwald die Umrandung des Talgebietes. Anfangs bestand dieser Laubwald aus Eiche, aber später spielten Linden eine wichtige Rolle. Beweismaterial für die Entfernung von Laub und Resten der Lanwirtschaft ließen darauf schließen, daß es nur ein niedriges Niveau an Betätigung gegeben hatte.

Bis zum Eintreffen der 2. Phase geschah eine bedeutende Veränderung im Tal. Zum ersten Mal gab es Beweismaterial für die Anwesenheit prähistorischer, eingeengter Kanäle in dieser Gegend. Der Bau eines Uferschutzes oder Wehr aus dünn geschnittenen, aufgestapelten Haselnußgerten wird durch die Radiokarbonierungmethode in die Frühbronzezeit datiert. Zeitgenössische Hinweise aus der Umgebung lassen darauf schließen, daß, gesamt der Veränderungen in der Zusammenstellung der Waldlandschaft und einige Vermutungen, die auf Getreideanbau in den höher gelegenen Gegenden schließen, die Mündung einen fortwährenden, jedoch geringer ausgeprägten Einfluß ausäbte.

In der 3. Phase erkennt man eine radikale Veränderung in der Beschaffenheit des Flußkanals und seinem Schüttmaterial. Höchst organische Grundablagerungen enthielten verbreitet gearbeitetes Holz (insgesamt eines riesigen Eichenbrettes und als riesiger Plattengang eines zusammengehefteten Bootes interpretiert), Gestein und Knochenfragmente domestizierter Tiere. Hinweise aus der Umgegend lassen darauf schließen, daß ein vorherrschend Süßwasserfluß vorhanden war, der gelegentlichen Mündungseinflüssen, einer offenen übergrasten Schwemmungsebene, Gestrüpp und zweitrangiger Waldgegend auf trockenem Grund zusammen mit fortwährenden Landwirtschaftsbetätigungen ausgesetzt war. Die Kalibrierung acht radikarbonierten Daten versetzen diese Phase in das 2. Jahrtausend v. Chr., vor allem in das 1. Dreiviertel dieses Jahrtausends in die Mittelbronzezeit.

Die 4. Phase wird als eine Periode relativer Untätigkeit betrachtet und ist durch die Abwesenheit von Beweismaterial für die Bildung von Kanalfurchen und durch die Anwesenheit höchst organischen Schüttmaterials mit wenig vorkommenden Artefakten gekennzeichnet. Prähistorisches Beweismaterial aus der Umgegend ließen annehmen, daß der Kanal in dieser Zeit mehr Gefahr lief, auszutrocknen. Die 5. Phase war eine Periode aktiver Bildungen von linienmäßigen Kanalfurchen und schneller fließenden Süßwasser in Kanälen relativer enger Proportionen, die mit unorganischem schlickigem Lehm angefüllt waren und der befristete ArtefaktenAssemblage enthielt. Es ist möglich, daß sich die Betätigung auf diesem Gelände verschob, jedoch lassen die BlütenstaubVerzeichnisse darauf schließen, daß in dieser Gegend weiterhin Landwirtschaft betrieben wurde.

Die 6. Phase verzeichnet eine Veränderung des Flußbettes in einen breiten, flachbodigen Kanal (ca 7m breit), der verbreitet deponierte Steine, Holz und Knochen enthielt. Eine Kanallinie aus eingerammten Pfalzen und die damit assoziierten deponierten Steine könnten als Furte, Wehr, Küstenvorland oder als eine Kombination dieser funktioniert haben. Anfangs führte der Kanal Süßwasser, aber mit verstreichender Zeit gab es zunehmende Anzeichen, die auch auf einen späteren Meereseinfluß schließen ließen. Radiokarbonierte Daten und eine DendrochonologieDatierung 998/7 v. Chr. versetzen diese Phase in däs Spatbronzezeitalter.

Die 7. Phase, in der der Meereseinfluß zunahm, verlief mit der Fortsetzung der Ansammlung von Ablagerungen in dem großen Kanal. Eine Doppellinie aus Stapeln von Eichen und Eschenholz, die über den Kanal gebaut war, wurde aufgrund einer Dendrochonologie wahrscheinlich bald nach 990/989 datiert, wird als Brücke interpretiert. Die Funktion der gelegten mittelgroßen, leichteren Haselnußger-

ten war unklar. Es könnte sein, daß diese Konstruktion als KanalfischWehr gedient hatte. Ein damit assoziierter 'Spurweg', der aus einer Streuung aus Holzteilen und Steinstücken bestand, könnte vorübergehend das Flußbett verstärkt haben, um dabei den Bau der Brücke zu erleichtern. Ein kleiner Kanal in der Osthälfte des Sees und ein fast komplettes Skelett eines Hundes gehören auch in diese Phase. DendrochonologieDatierungen lassen annehmen, daß Betätigungen sich eher auf Jahrzehnte als auf Jahrhunderte begrenzten. Es scheint eine ziemlich schnelle Sedimentation von dieser Zeit bis zur 8. Phase gegeben zu haben – wahrscheinlich geschah dies beim Übergang von der Spätbronzezeit zur Frühsteinzeit – als scnelle Anhäufung von Ablagerungen und vielleicht das Resultat einer aus dem Ufer getretenen Sedimentation und einer Meeresüberschwemmung, das Ende menschlicher Betätigungen innerhalb dieser ausgegrabenen Gegend markieren.

Ungefähr 5 000 Holzstücke aus diesem Gelände wurden gründlich untersucht. Die GeländeAssemblage beinhaltete eine große Auswahl von Holzarten, die hauptsächlich aus Haselnuß, Schwarz und Hagedornen bestand und die als Nebenprodukt von Gestrüppentfernungen interpretiert werden. Für Holzverarbeitungen und Tischlerarbeiten wurden hauptsächlich Eiche, Esche und Erle bevorzugt. Zu den gearbeiteten Holz gehörten eingerammte Pfalzen. Ausgestemmte Bretter und gearbeitete Holzstücke und eine Reihe von Artefakten, insgesant Behälter und Bootfragmente. Die Analyse der FaunaAssemblage, eine der größten Sammlungen aus der Bronzezeit in Wales, deutete darauf hin, daß, unter den domestizierten Tieren, das Schaf den Vorrang hatte, wie auch die Ausbeutung wilder Tiere. Die oft gebrochenen Knochen lassen darauf schließen, daß sie teils weggeworfenem Abfalls waren. Eine Anzahl von Hundeknochen zusammen mit einem Skelett eines alten und kranken Individiums sind die eines domestiziierten Hundes. Eine geringe Anzahl von Knochen wurde gearbeitet um sowie nützliche als auch 'dekorative' Artefakten herzustellen. Weitere ArtefaktenGruppen beinhalten Metallarbeiten, eine einzelne Bernsteinperle und einer zum größten Teil Restsammlung von Feuerstein.

Vergleiche mit den Blütenstaubdaten von anderswo in der Region ermöglichen die Daten der Strukturen und Artefakten aus diesem Gelände in einen weiteren Kontext vegetarischer Geschichte und Veränderung der Umgebung zu setzen und zusammen mit anderen archäologischen Daten bieten sie eine Einschätzung der Wichtigkeit des Geländes innerhalb der lokalen Vorgeschichte und der Entwicklung der kulturellen Landschaft.

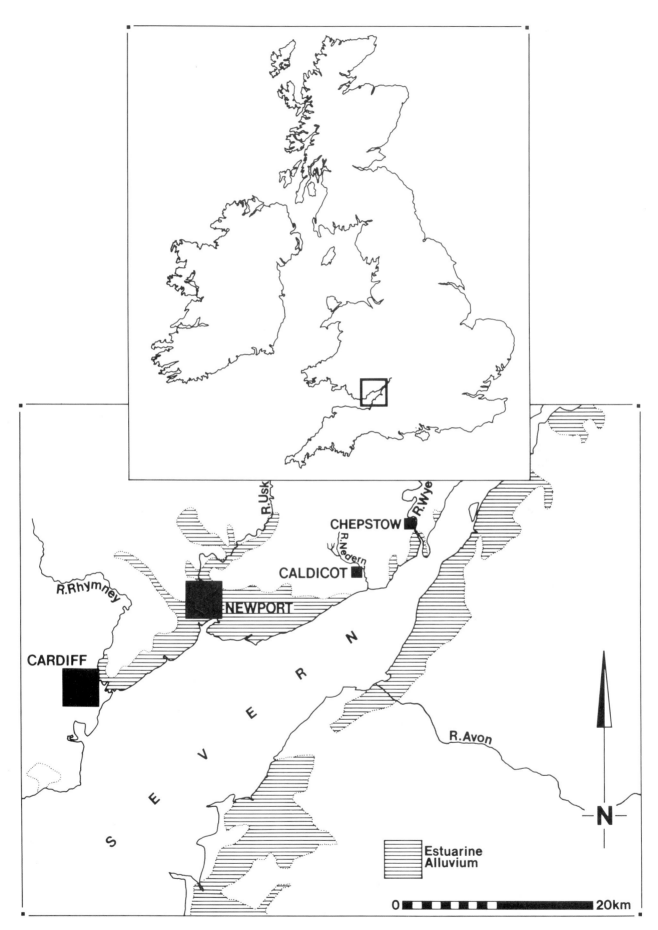

Fig 1   Location map: location of the town of Caldicot and the River Nedern in relation to the British Isles and the Severn Estuary

Introduction

During the late 1980s, renewed interest in the archaeological potential of the low-lying coastal plain in South Wales known collectively as the Gwent Levels, partly in response to proposals for a tidal barrage across the Severn, concentrated on exposures in the intertidal zone. Here, the complex succession of Holocene estuarine deposits and intercalated peats associated with fluctuating sea level rise over the last 8000 years were clearly visible. Whilst archaeological finds had been recovered from the foreshore for decades, the organic component of the archaeological resource had only recently begun to be appreciated with limited excavation of prehistoric sites associated with eroding peat surfaces on the foreshore (Whittle 1989). The formulation of geological models for the development of these Holocene sequences (eg Allen and Fulford 1986; Allen and Rae 1987) encouraged fieldwork within a stratigraphic framework. On the landward side of the sea wall protecting the Levels, prehistoric sequences were seen as essentially invisible, too deeply buried to permit systematic investigation, and the degree of Roman and post-Roman sedimentation remained a subject of debate. Hence the archaeological potential and sensitivity of the coastal plain and the alluviated river valley bottoms which enter it from the north were unclear.

The initial archaeological response to a proposal to excavate an amenity lake in the valley bottom of the Nedern Brook, directly east of the small town of Caldicot on the edge of the Levels, should be seen against this uncertain appreciation of the archaeological resource. The exposure of prehistoric timbers was not anticipated, and the subsequent excavations which this volume describes and assesses took place against a background of limited but growing awareness of the importance of the prehistoric evidence encapsulated within the Gwent Levels.

Site location

The modern town of Caldicot is located some eight kilometres west of Chepstow, Gwent, on an eroded plateau of Triassic sandstone overlain by gravels of the Second Severn Terrace. The southern limit of this plateau defines the edge of the Caldicot Level, the major eastern element of the Gwent Levels between the River Usk at Newport and the River Wye in the east (Fig 1). To the east of the town, the hard geology is bisected by the Nedern Valley, an infilled deep channel created during the last glaciation and now carrying the much canalised Nedern Brook, one of a series of small tributaries entering the Severn from the north via the Gwent Levels (Fig 2). Geologically,

Caldicot is situated on the southern side of the Caerwent Basin, a down-folded structure of Carboniferous rocks overlain, unconformably, by Mesozoic and younger sediments (Welch and Trotter 1961). The setting of the archaeological site at Caldicot can best be described by considering the geomorphology and topography of the catchment of the Nedern Brook.

The course of the Nedern rises at 220m above Ordnance Datum (OD) in a prominent line of hills, outliers of the Old Red Sandstone of the Brecon Beacons, which run from Wentwood in the west through Shirenewton to Chepstow Park Wood in the east (Fig 3). Upon entering the area of rolling hills of Carboniferous limestones and sandstones, which form the northern exposure of the Caerwent Basin, the brook cuts a deep gorge before flowing out into the wider floodplain of the Vale of Caerwent. Topographically this upper 8.9km of the Nedern, which comprises some 70% of the catchment and descends to 50m OD, contrasts markedly in terms of gradient with its lower reaches.

In the lower half of the catchment, the remainder of the hard geology comprising pink, yellow and conglomeratic Triassic sandstones (10.8% by surface area of the catchment), is bisected by a deep, buried channel. This is the probable result of lowered sea levels during Pleistocene glaciation and subsequently increased melt-water flows at the end of the Ice Age. Little is known of the extent or maximum depth of the buried channel of the Nedern Brook although it is likely to be at least 9m below present river levels (Howe pers comm). Raised sea levels, notably at the end of the Pleistocene, led to the deposition of river terraces, mainly composed of gravels, within the catchments of the rivers Wye and Severn. Within the Severn river system, five terraces are recognised, three of which occur within the Caldicot area. The Second Severn Terrace is the most extensive, occurring under a large part of the town, along the lower reaches of the Nedern Brook and in the Caerwent area. Some 18% of the catchment area comprises head or terrace deposits.

The most recent deposit within the catchment area is the postglacial alluvium that occupies the flood plain on the floor of the Nedern Brook, and merges with the alluvium making up the Caldicot Level. The fine, silty nature of this deposit produces generally poorly drained soils which are liable to flooding. By the time the Nedern reaches Caldicot, the floodplain alluvium is some 200m in width (Fig 2), reflecting infilling of the deep glacial channel rather than the erosive capabilities of the present river. The Nedern's present course here is, in part, the result of canalisation aimed at reducing flooding. Its course across the

Caldicot Level to its mouth at Caldicot Pill on the Severn Estuary is probably the result of post-medieval diversion (Rippon 1996, 77–8); its more ancient course is fossilised as the parish boundary and its former mouth is located west of Sudbrook Camp at the east end of Caldicot Level.

Caldicot Castle, occupying a spur of sandstone protruding eastward from the town of Caldicot into the flood plain, now acts as the focal point of a country park which encompasses part of the river valley bottom and the gravel terraces on both sides. Jointly managed by Monmouth Borough Council and Gwent County Council, the park and castle fulfil a variety of functions including a museum, banqueting hall, and venue for fairs and other gatherings in addition to providing open space for recreational use. A proposal to enhance the habitat and aesthetic value of the park through the creation of a lake was put forward in 1986, leading to submission in January 1987 of a planning application by Monmouth Borough Council for the construction of a lake of 3600 m^2 in the river valley bottom within Caldicot Castle Country Park, east of the present course of the Nedern Brook and opposite the castle at ST488886. Accompanying plans indicate that the initial design

proposed removal of up to 2.3m depth of floodplain deposits in the lake's construction. As a result of archaeological advice from the Glamorgan-Gwent Archaeological Trust, as part of the planning process, informal arrangements were made for the Country Park Warden, Dennis Manning, to watch the excavations.

Site discovery

During mechanical excavation of the modern lake, timbers were observed by both Dennis Manning and Derek Upton of Caldicot, a seasoned observer of wetland archaeology in the intertidal zone of the Gwent Levels. The latter informed Bob Trett, curator of Newport Museum, who visited the site on the 29th April, confirmed the presence of wooden posts and brushwood including cut pieces, and took notes, photographs and wood samples (Trett pers comm). Initial investigation by a small field team from the Glamorgan-Gwent Archaeological Trust, led by Stephen Parry, commenced on 3rd May. Observations of the widespread presence of waterlogged wood in the lake bottom, including possible structural

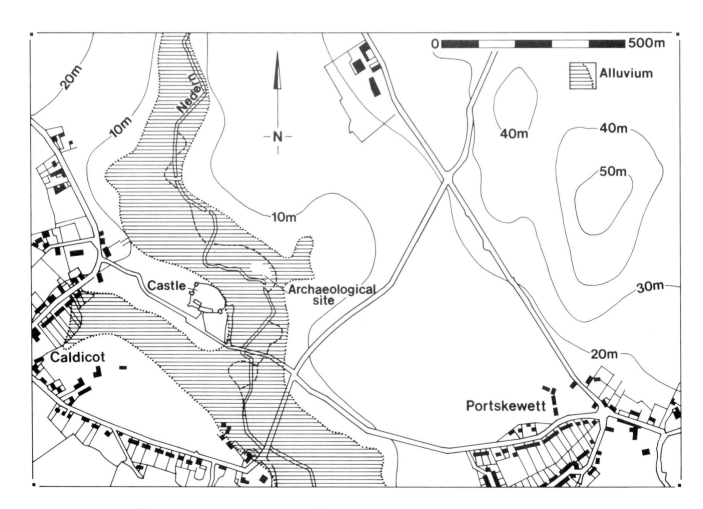

Fig 2   Location of the excavations in relation to the Nedern Valley. The location of former courses of the river, evident from aerial photography are marked in dashed line on the floodplain. Based on the Ordnance Survey 1:10,000 series. © Crown copyright

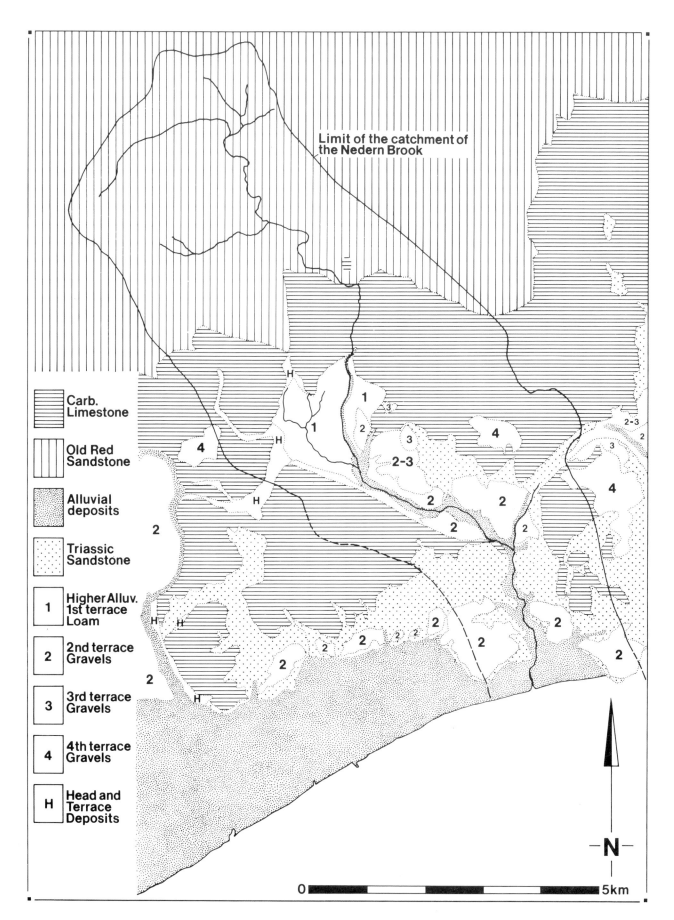

Fig 3   Geology of the Nedern catchment and the surrounding area. Based on Geological Survey of Great Britain sheet 250. © Crown copyright

4

Fig 4   Wilburton chape in situ. Object length 172mm

groups, and the recovery of a Wilburton style chape (Fig 4) following a metal detector sweep, both indicated the need for extensive evaluation.

Evaluation

Discussions between the Glamorgan-Gwent Archaeological Trust, Monmouth Borough Council, Gwent County Council and Cadw: Welsh Historic Monuments led to a programme of field evaluation, directed by Jonathan Parkhouse and Stephen Parry, from mid-July to the beginning of September, 1988. The machine excavation of the proposed lake had created a wet, muddy, shallowly-sloping, kidney-shaped depression with a relatively level base at *c* 3.6m OD. The primary objective of the evaluation was to define the extent and nature of the palaeochannel deposits exposed within this depression, to enable an informed strategy of excavation and/or protection for the site to be developed. Work concentrated in three 'sondages' which later developed into areas A, C and F (Fig 5). An excavation strategy was employed in which wood and artefactual material was recorded spatially but assigned to only very generalised stratigraphic units (Parry 1989).

Through the winter of 1988/9, discussions tended to favour recording and recovery of the most vulnerable material in selected areas of the lake bed followed by protection of the remaining archaeological features by plastic pond-liner, prior to completion of the lake, to reduce potential root damage to unexcavated deposits. Limited auger survey of deposits outside the limits of the lake was carried out in March 1989 with assistance from students undertaking a post-graduate wetland course funded by the European Social Fund. Fieldwork, which recommenced in mid-August, 1989, was initially focused on selective excavation in advance of completion of the lake. However, continuing doubts about the efficacy of the proposed liner, and concerns about the stability of the exposed, formerly anaerobic palaeochannel fills, prompted two postponements to the completion of the lake which had been timetabled for mid-September. On 13th November, Sir Wyn Roberts, then Minister of State for Wales, announced a programme of 'measured exploration' at the site to be funded jointly by Cadw: Welsh Historic Monuments, Gwent County Council and Monmouth Borough Council to consist of three seasons of excavation followed by two years of post-excavation. Excavations were concluded for the year and the site was flooded for the winter (Parry and Parkhouse 1990).

Excavation

The initial project design envisaged total excavation of the palaeochannel deposits observed in the base and sides of the modern lake bed over three seasons.

Evaluation areas

Organic palaeochannel deposits

Findspot of Wilburton style chape

0 _____ 20m

SITE GRID
NORTH

Fig 5   Plan of lake and evaluation trenches

The first season was to concentrate on areas A, B and C (Fig 6), aiming to complete excavations in the western third of the lake bed by removing the palaeochannel fills in spits and taking representative samples for environmental studies. It was recognised that methodologies would need to be reviewed and developed and a steering group was established to assist in this process and to monitor progress. The uncovering, *in situ* recording and lifting of a substantial boat strake found towards the end of the 1990 season not only affected the project design by requiring reallocation of resources, but also showed that the site was more complex stratigraphically, and covered a longer period of time than had been expected. A pile structure encountered south-west of the main palaeochannel deposits tended to confirm this.

In 1991, the writer took over direction of the excavation and an updated project design was produced. This recognised that, in the light of the unexpected complexity and extent of archaeological deposits exposed within the lake-bed, selective excavation should focus on clarifying the full sequence of palaeochannel development, linking previously exca-

vated assemblages to this sequence, and taking additional environmental samples to cover this sequence. This strategy was implemented in a five-month field season from May to September, 1991, through the excavation of a diamond-shaped trench within Area A to examine strata predating the main phase of activity; a south-west to north-east oriented trench extending Area B to the south-west of the find spot of the boat strake; Area E, a west-north-west to east-south-east oriented trench measuring 17m by 2m to examine the fullest sequence possible in the east half of the lake-bed; and Area G, a 3m by 3m trench to test for the presence of a midden suggested by the recovery in 1990 of a small number of artefacts in the vicinity. It also proved possible to excavate a trench in the south-east edge of the lake (Area H) where channel deposits were less truncated by modern machining and contemporary ground surfaces might have survived.

The primary objectives of the final season of excavation in 1991 were to record the remaining structural elements and correlate the previously excavated sequences. This was achieved through an extension in Area A to the deep diamond-shaped

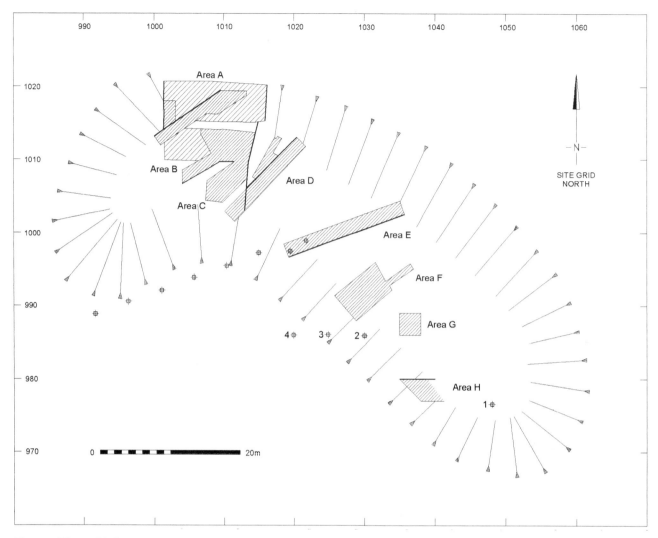

Fig 6   Plan of lake, excavation areas, boreholes, and published sections. Numbered points relate to boreholes (see Fig 12 for section). The positions of published sections (see Figs 10 and 11) are indicated in thicker lines along the edge of the excavation areas. The site coordinate system is used on plans of palaeochannel groups

trench to the south-west, where bends in earlier channels were anticipated, and correlations with a major sampling site in the east facing section were required; further excavation in Area C to complete the removal of an early pile structure and clarify its stratigraphic relationships; and the excavation of a long trench, Area D, to examine a group of piles initially seen in 1988 and to ensure correct correlation between sequences excavated in the east and west halves of the rescue area.

During the final season, unexcavated archaeological deposits deemed particularly vulnerable to damage were protected by a combination of polythene covers and spoil tipping. In September 1992, completion of the lake's construction was begun to a design adapted to minimise impact on remaining archaeology. Machine works were watched by staff of the Glamorgan-Gwent Archaeological Trust staff and exposed sections briefly recorded (Lennox 1992). Survey stations destroyed in the process were replaced by permanent reference points set in concrete.

Methodology, strategy and approach

The initial project design drafted in advance of the first major season in 1990 anticipated excavation of one third of the palaeochannel deposits exposed in the modern lake-bed in each season. At the time, the presence of only the later phases was suspected and the complexity of the stratigraphic sequence was underestimated. This imperfect appreciation of the situation led to the promotion of an 'open area' strategy in which the sediments were excavated in spits. Individual pieces of wood, stone, bone, pottery and flint were three-dimensionally recorded either by triangulation or, more commonly, by use of a total station theodolite, within a site grid with grid north some 3.25° west of Ordnance Survey National Grid North. Levels were recorded on site relative to Ordnance Datum. Subsequent attempts to assign artefacts and structural groups to contexts recorded in section on the basis of the material's spatial location were often of limited success, although linkage to major palaeochannel phases has proved possible in most cases. The limitations of this approach were further highlighted by the discovery of the boat strake towards the end of the 1990 season in a complex stratigraphic position, predating most of the archaeology previously encountered.

From 1991, there was a radical change both in excavation strategy and process (Harris 1989, 15–21) in order to meet the major objective of recovering artefactual and environmental material from phases of sedimentation associated with changes in channel morphology. It had become clear that without a change in approach, material would not be associated securely with these phases and that a comprehensive suite of environmental samples would not be forthcoming. Narrower trenches, sited at right angles to the presumed palaeochannel axis were excavated stratigraphically, where possible, with the sections enabling continuous verification of the perceived sequence to be carried out. Artefactual material was assigned to context during excavation, with any alterations or refinements made following detailed examination of adjacent sections. Correlation between trench sequences was a progressive process, in part assisted by the provision of radiocarbon dates and interim results of environmental studies between seasons.

The difficulties of deciphering the lithostratigraphy on the site should not be underestimated. Considerable disturbance from machining had resulted in churning, shearing and compression of the uppermost surviving sediments. During excavation, oxidisation and desiccation further obscured the stratigraphy. Compared with the contexts more usually encountered in an archaeological setting, sediments exhibited very restricted differences in particle size, generally consisting of clays or silty clays with occasional silt laminae or rare fine sand laminae. All observed deposits were waterlain through natural processes of sedimentation rather than through human action. Contexts could usually only be differentiated by colour change reflecting variation in organic content, and the presence of coarse components such as clasts of sediment, visible plant macrofossils, mollusca and laminae. Less organic upper fills were particularly difficult to differentiate. With the exception of the earliest and latest units observed during excavation, these sediments generally occupy unconformities resulting from natural channel downcutting or migration followed by periods of siltation. Although stratigraphically these interfaces have many similarities to vertical feature interfaces as defined by Harris (1989, 59), and offer useful subdivisions for the construction of stratigraphic sequences, they are not necessarily the result of single, short-lived, localised events but often part of gradual, continuing processes of channel migration /downcutting and infilling/aggradation. Consideration has also had to be given to the problems of post-depositional movement of material in a semi-liquid matrix far less resistant to intrusion than dryland deposits.

Cultural material is presented in this report in association with these channel cuts and their fills as palaeochannel groups. In some cases, material is linked to specific fills of a palaeochannel whilst elsewhere, where fine resolution of the stratigraphy did not occur (either because of the prevailing methodology or the diffuse nature of sediment boundaries), material is associated with the palaeochannel alone or subdivided on the basis of depth. Due to the proximity of excavation areas, it has often been possible to correlate palaeochannel groups, or even specific contexts, between areas. Within excavation areas, palaeochannel groups have been grouped as phases on the basis of position in the stratigraphic sequence, and similarities in channel profiles and the broad nature of their fills. These phases, correlated between areas, have more in common with Needham's concept of alluvial parcels (1992, 260) than traditional notions of phase, although broad contemporaneity is implied through independent dating (radiocarbon and dendrochronology), biostratigraphic similarities, channel morphology and relative dating through stratigraphic correlation and equation.

Structure of the report and relation to the archive

The first section of the detailed report on the site begins with a summary of the stratigraphic sequence, an outline of the nature of the eight main phases identified and the published section drawings. Each of the eight phases is then described in more detail with a brief introduction followed by standardised information on palaeochannel groups within that phase. In the case of the first and last phases, where sedimentary units do not appear to be confined within palaeochannels, a less standardised approach is taken. Extensive reference is made to subsequent sections where appropriate, as well as drawing on data held both on computer and paper record. Unique context numbers, assigned in the field to a range of entities including excavation areas, layers, interfaces, stratigraphic units or groups, structures, samples, individual finds, and pieces of wood, are used throughout this section to facilitate cross-referencing to the archive.

The paper archive is supplemented by a variety of databases which were created and developed for most categories of material during the excavation and 'post'-excavation (often carried out between seasons of fieldwork) phases of the project. These usually began as little more than indexes of contexts, samples, wood and other artefact types, and site records such as plans and photographs. The wood database developed initially as a management tool to assist in curation and location of material in store, facilitating the process of sampling and prioritisation of material for more detailed technological study, illustration and conservation. As wood samples and items were dispatched to specialists and interim results returned, additional related databases were created to provide updated information to specialists and enable synthesis as post-excavation analysis progressed. Similar development of other databases for artefactual and environmental data occurred assisting liaison with relevant specialists and promoting an holistic view of the site.

In the site section of the report, plans, at a standardised scale of 1:40, of palaeochannel groups illustrate the text, identifying items of particular note and the location of independently dated material. Clear structural groups are discussed in relation to wider parallels and their function.

The second major section presents the results of individual specialist studies following an introductory discussion on issues of taphonomy and site formation. The environmental data, derived from analysis of seven columns of monolith tins and contiguous bulk samples, is presented first helping to define the context of subsequently discussed material. The spatial location of major phases of sedimentation, and varying levels of truncation by fluvial action and modern machining necessitated extensive sampling in the field followed by subsequent selection of samples for analysis. In excess of 400 samples were taken of which 117 are reported on within this report. Further samples were analysed but are not presented here. This includes phosphate analysis of transects of samples from Area B which was inconclusive, and additional sediment analysis by Mark Taylor which do not significantly add to the results. Similarly, results of experimental archaeomagnetic dating by Cathy Batt, as part of a PhD at the University of Durham, are included in the site archive. The waterlogged conditions, combined with a relatively neutral pH, resulted in the preservation of a wide range of environmental indicators. This is reflected in the diversity and extent of the specialist reports. In addition to providing an essential environmental context for the artefactual assemblages

recovered, these data also help to counter the limitations of the site-specific data which are the result of an arbitrary sampling area (the base of a modern lake excavation) dictated by a rescue need. The value of the individual studies was significantly enhanced by Astrid Caseldine's considerable input in co-ordinating the environmental approach.

The subsequent two sections deal with cultural material seen primarily as a product of anthropogenic deposition. Such a division is clearly artificial and individual reports are often dependent upon the results of other studies. This is particularly true for analyses of the wood assemblage which has clear environmental implications: just as the assemblage itself is a reflection of human/environment interactions within a cultural landscape, so these reports reflect interaction between specialists with the data they have generated being utilised by others from various perspectives.

The report concludes with a synthesis of the combined datasets with reference to the wider context, particularly of the wetland archaeology of the Severn Estuary. Investigations in the Severn Levels in the last decade have radically changed our perception of the importance of these low-lying regions to prehistoric populations. The Caldicot Project has played its part in emphasising the considerable potential of these areas for continued study at a time when both natural erosion and rapidly increasing modern development threaten this valuable cultural resource.

Approximately 10% of the excavated wood has now been conserved and along with other artefact types, site records, archive reports and database records will be deposited with the Monmouthshire Museums Service. Hopefully in the relatively near future, the site data and finds will provide the basis for an innovative display, possibly in Caldicot Castle, where the evidence from the excavations could be viewed in context.

Section A: The Site

Summary of the stratigraphic sequence and associated radiocarbon dating

The stratigraphic sequence encompasses sediments observed from auger cores at levels of 1.5m below Ordnance Datum, to topsoil at the present ground surface of c 5.5–6m OD. This sequence has been subdivided into eight main phases on stratigraphic grounds, supported by radiocarbon and dendrochronological dating of associated organic material. The dendrochronological dates are largely confined to later phases, and are detailed in the relevant specialist report (see Hillam, p 190) and stratigraphic sections. The radiocarbon dates are summarised here with more detailed information on the provenance of the samples given in subsequent phase sections. The generation of a suite of radiocarbon determinations was seen as an integral part of the project design, providing an independent check on the construction of stratigraphic sequences and a dating framework for inter-site comparisons. The sampling strategy targeted well stratified, young roundwood: 23 of the 27 dates obtained are derived from immature wood with bark edge (see Table 1).

All the dates were produced by Dr Quentin Dresser (now based at the Department of Geography, University of Wales, Swansea) with the exception of a single high precision date from the boat strake provided by Dr Gerry McCormac at the Radiocarbon Laboratory, Department of Geosciences, Queens University of Belfast. The dates are presented graphically using the Oxcal programme, kindly supplied by Dr C Bronk Ramsey of the Oxford Radiocarbon Accelerator Unit, with the exception of one date (CAR-1409) which is discussed below. The δ13-corrected dates are ordered by stratigraphic phase and uncalibrated value (unless grouped by structure), and the results of calibration to two standard deviations using the 1986 high precision calibration curves (Pearson and Stuiver 1986, Stuiver and Pearson 1986) are shown as non-Gaussian probability distributions (Figs 7 and 8).

Phase I comprises horizontally bedded sediments varying from sand at –1.5m OD, to clays and silty clays up to c 4.2m OD. These have not been investigated in great detail as they predate direct evidence of human activity at the site. Comparison with the stratigraphic succession on the Gwent Levels suggest that much of this material accumulated in the Mesolithic and Neolithic periods. Radiocarbon dates from an organic horizon at c 2.7m OD, calibrated to two standard deviations, fall within the range 3750–2750 BC, dating this deposit culturally to the Middle to Late Neolithic. Associated diatom and pollen analyses point to marine influences in the valley bottom with a wooded landscape on higher ground.

The subsequent Phase II is marked by the first evidence of a constrained channel within the excavation area, filled with minerogenic silty clays. In the latter part of this phase, a revetment of driven hazel uprights (structure 472), dated by radiocarbon to the Early Bronze Age, gives the first direct evidence of human activity. Contemporary environmental indicators point to a continuing but less marked estuarine influence, along with changes in woodland composition and some suggestion of cereal cultivation on higher land.

Phase III sees a radical change in the nature of the river channel and its fills. Highly organic basal sediments contain spreads of worked wood, stone and domesticate bone fragments including a massive oak plank interpreted as a strake from a sewn plank boat. Environmental indicators imply a predominantly freshwater river, subject to occasional estuarine influences, an open grassy floodplain, and scrub and secondary woodland on drier ground. Calibration of eight of the radiocarbon dates place this phase in the 2nd millennium BC, mostly in the first three quarters of that millennium, ie the Middle Bronze Age. A single wood sample from Phase III deposits in Area A (CAR-1409), gave a raw date of 2210 ± 60 BP which calibrates, at two standard deviations, to 394–160 BC and 140–121 BC. This result is not presented in Fig 7 as it would have made the rest of the probability curves unreadable. Although there is some evidence for disturbance of overlying Phase VI deposits, there is no obvious explanation for this very late determination compared with all other results from the site: the roundwood stem was horizontal and securely stratified at 2.49m OD, over a metre below the level of modern machine truncation and half a metre below the base of the overlying Phase VI channel base. The sample from the boat strake dated at Belfast was taken from approximately 15 consecutive heartwood rings. Given the absence of sapwood or a sapwood/heartwood boundary on this timber, the date of tree death relative to the sample cannot be accurately determined. One might anticipate at least 50 years of further tree growth until the date of tree-felling. In addition, the strake was presumably in use for some time before being discarded. Hence there is likely to be some considerable period of time between the date of the sampled tree rings and the date of deposition of the plank.

A single radiocarbon date from Phase IV (CAR-1406), is somewhat later than might be expected, given dates from subsequent phases (see Fig 8). This phase, seen as a period of relative inactivity is marked by highly organic sediment with low artefact content much of which probably derives from earlier deposition. Palaeoenvironmental evidence suggests the channel was more susceptible to drying out at this time.

Phase V is characterised by a period of active channel downcutting and migration with freshwater channels of relatively narrow proportions filled with inorganic silty clays containing limited artefactual assemblages. No radiocarbon dates are available for this phase.

Phase VI sees a major change in riverbed form to a broad, flat-bottomed channel containing dense spreads of dumped stone, wood and bone. A cross-channel line of driven uprights and associated dumps of stone (structure 9014) may have acted as a ford, weir, hard or a combination of these functions. Initially the channel is freshwater but through time there are increasing indications of marine influence. Some sediments, particularly upper fills between 3.25 and 3.5m OD are assigned to Phase VI/VII. This

is recognition of the fact that no very clear division is possible between Phases VI and VII particularly in the west half of the lake. Material thus assigned could date to either Phase VI or Phase VII. Radiocarbon dates and a tree-ring date of 998/7 BC place this phase in the Late Bronze Age. Calibration of the radiocarbon dates suggest activity within an approximate range of 1500–800 BC: the duration of this phase could however be considerably more constrained.

During Phase VII, in a period of increasing marine influence, sediment continues to accumulate in this large channel although modern machining has removed much of this phase in the base of the lake. A rough trackway (structure 473) and possibly associated bridge or jetty (structure 22441) are con-

Table 1 Details of samples submitted for radiocarbon determination

Laboratory Code	Wood number	Palaeochannel Group/(Structure)	Species	Description
CAR-1214	11	D.7.1 (22441)	*Quercus* spp.	Substantial driven pile with dendrochronological date of 1032+ BC
CAR-1215	22	A.7.1		Totally sampled. No wood records
CAR-1216	135	A.6/7.1 (9014)	*Corylus* sp.	12 year old roundwood with chisel point
CAR-1217	157	A.6/7.1 (9014)	*Corylus* sp.	23 year old roundwood with chisel point
CAR-1314	886	C.2.1 (472)	*Corylus* sp.	28 year old roundwood pile with pencil point
CAR-1315	20646	G.6/7.1	*Corylus* sp.	Immature roundwood
CAR-1316	24023	E.7.2	*Corylus* sp.	Immature roundwood
CAR-1317	893	C.2.1 (472)	*Corylus* sp.	26 year old roundwood pile with pencil point
CAR-1318	20650	G.7.1	*Corylus* sp.	Immature splitwood with axe marks
CAR-1319	24193	E.6.1	*Corylus* sp.	Immature roundwood
CAR-1320	24464	E.3.1	*Corylus* sp.	Immature roundwood: possible stake
CAR-1321	20785	E.3.1	*Corylus* sp.	Immature roundwood
CAR-1322	N/A	G.1	N/A	Organic sediment
CAR-1323	N/A	G.1	N/A	Organic sediment
CAR-1405	24643	D.7.3	*Corylus* sp.	Immature roundwood with chisel point
CAR-1406	24896	A.4.1	*Corylus* sp.	Immature roundwood
CAR-1407	24936	C.3.4	*Corylus* sp.	Immature roundwood
CAR-1408	25033	D.7.1 (22441)	*Corylus* sp.	9 year old roundwood with chisel point
CAR-1409	25293	A.3.1	*Corylus* sp.	Immature roundwood
CAR-1410	25377	D.6.1	*Corylus* sp.	Immature roundwood with pencil point?
CAR-1411	25417	C.3.3	*Corylus* sp.	8 year old roundwood with chisel point
CAR-1412	24427	E.3.1	*Taxus baccata L.*	Part of spread of split and cut yew twigs aged up to 12 years
CAR-1413	25747	C.3.1	*Corylus* sp.	Immature roundwood with chisel point
CAR-1414	25864	C.3.1	*Corylus* sp.	16 year old roundwood with removed sidebranches
CAR-1415	25888	C.2.1	*Corylus* sp.	Immature roundwood with removed sidebranches
CAR-1416	735	B.7.1 (1401)	*Corylus* sp.	5 year old roundwood with chisel point
UB-3472	6001	B.3.3 (Boat plank 6001)	*Quercus* spp.	Oak heartwood

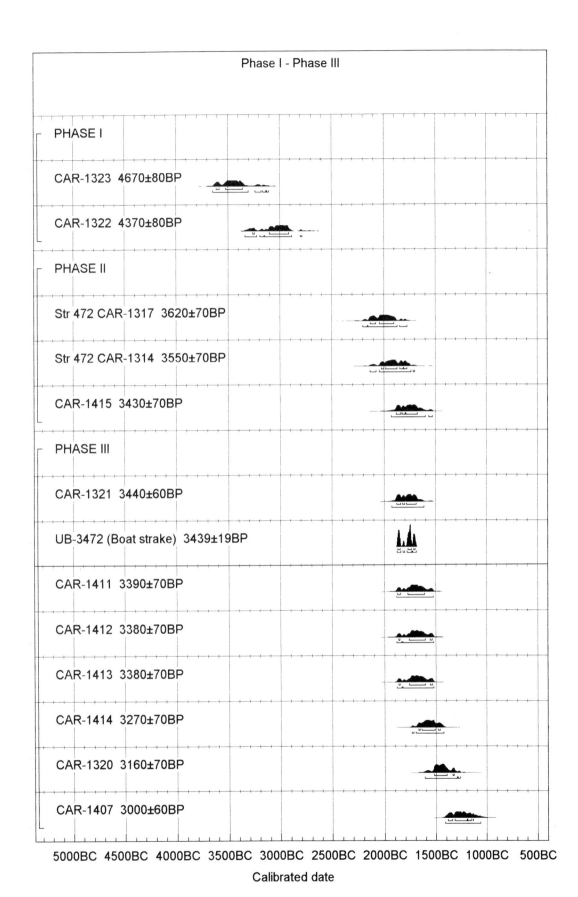

Fig 7   Radiocarbon probability curves, Phases I–III. Produced using OxCal v2.12. Calibration curves Pearson and Stuiver 1986, Stuiver and Pearson 1986

14

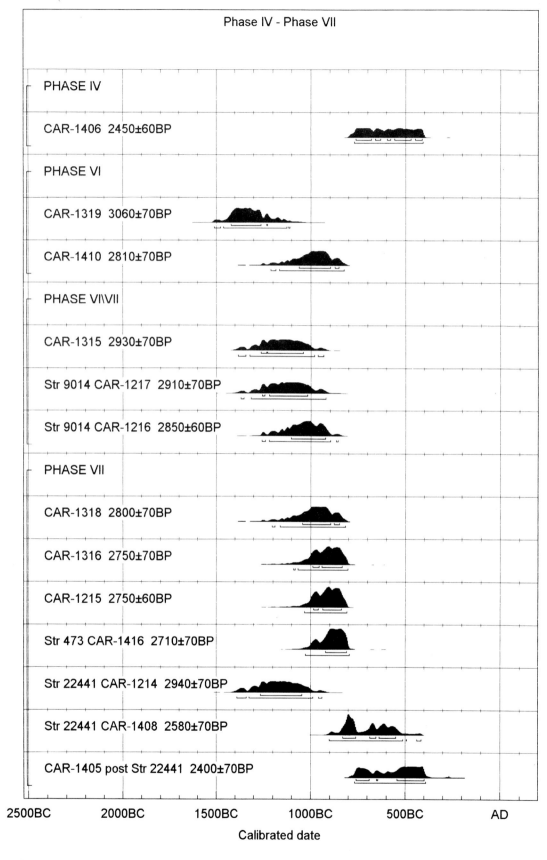

Fig 8   Radiocarbon probability curves, Phases IV–VII. Produced using OxCal v2.12. Calibration curves Pearson and Stuiver 1986, Stuiver and Pearson 1986

structed, probably soon after 990/989 BC on the basis of dendrochronological dating. The calibrated radio-carbon dates are compatible with this when one considers that the apparently early result from one sample (CAR-1214) is derived from oak heartwood which probably formed between ten and one hundred years before the date of tree death. Tree-ring dates from this phase suggest activity was limited to decades rather than centuries, highlighting a limitation of radiocarbon dating's ability to identify brief periods of occupation/construction. A small channel in the east half of the lake and the skeleton of a near-complete dog are also assigned to this phase.

There appears to have been fairly rapid sedimentation at this time until Phase VIII, possibly at the Late Bronze Age/Early Iron Age transition, when rapid accumulation of sediment, possibly the result of a combination of increased over-bank sedimentation and marine inundation, mark the end of human activity within the excavated area.

Presentation of the stratigraphic sequence

In order to provide the reader with a coherent account of the complex succession of palaeochannel deposits recorded, and their associated artefactual and structural material, data is presented by phase, rather than by stratigraphic sequences within discrete excavation areas, followed by subsequent arguments for correlation. Each phase is introduced by a brief description of its main stratigraphic, structural, artefactual and environmental characteristics. Then the data from separate excavation areas are presented from west (Area A) to east (Area H) as palaeochannel groups. These groups are coded according to excavation area, phase and relative stratigraphic position and labelled on the main illustrated sections. Each group is described in terms of its stratigraphy and artefactual and structural content.

Details of palaeochannel interface morphology and associated sedimentation are given using context numbers assigned during excavation. Where clearly-defined channels have been identified, information on their extent, orientation and level compared to Ordnance Datum (OD) are presented. The direction of water flow within channels is implied by the description of channel sides as left or right edges or sides, assuming the reader to be facing downstream. Fills are described by colour, organic content, particle size and coarse components (eg observed macrofossil content, mottling, laminae and clasts). Although Munsell notations were recorded for each layer in the field, often for both fresh and oxidised states of the sediment, these usually fell within a restricted range of hue, value and chroma (around 10YR 4/1) and are not cited in these sections. The colour descriptions given do not strictly adhere to the corresponding Munsell 'color names' but give a more subjective indication of appearance as seen by the field recorder.

This was felt to be helpful in highlighting observed differences between adjacent deposits. During the 1991 and 1992 seasons, sediment descriptions were recorded by either the site supervisor or the environmental assistant to promote consistency in context description. Artefactual and structural material associated with these stratigraphic units are then described.

Wood assemblages from the palaeochannel groups are described by indicating the dominant species, less commonly occurring species and highlighting the nature of the woodworking evidence. Common names are used throughout this section and a number of assumptions have been made. Wood of the genus *Prunus* which has not been positively identified as cherry or bird cherry is assumed to be blackthorn and described as such in the text. Similarly wood identified to the Pomoideae group is described as hawthorn on the basis of limited contemporary plant macrofossil evidence and likely habitat preferences for this species. Items of particular note are labelled on plan but wood species is not indicated on the drawings. During post-excavation analysis, species distribution was examined but generally only highlighted instances where two or more pieces could then be seen as fragments of the same original piece.

Both the bone and stone assemblages have not been considered in great detail from the perspective of spatial patterning of species or geology respectively. Distribution where deemed significant is indicated in the text and illustrated in plan. Bone artefacts are noted individually and also marked on the plans, as are flint, pottery and metalwork (Fig 9).

Before describing the phases in detail, a selection of the sections drawn in the field are illustrated, grouped as 'downstream' (ie east, south-east and south facing) and upstream (ie west, north-west and north facing) sections to provide an overview of the palaeochannel groups and phases described in the subsequent section (Figs 10 and 11). The locations of the published sections are indicated on Fig 6.

Phase I

During Phase I, the valley bottom of the Nedern was steadily infilling with fine sands, clays and silts, interrupted occasionally by the formation of peats and organic clays. Limited excavation and auger surveys suggest that these horizontally-bedded sediments do not occupy a constrained channel, but rather represent deposition across much of the valley bottom, leading to substantial infilling of a glacial deep channel. Organic clays, dated by radiocarbon to the Neolithic period, occur at *c* 2.5–3.0m OD and suggest sedimentation in the valley, mirroring the accumulation of estuarine sediment on the Gwent Levels characterised by the Wentlooge Formation (Allen 1987, 161–3). These deposits extended across the valley on the northern and eastern sides of the site but could not be traced to the west where later palaeochannels had removed them. A strong marine influence is indicated by the diatom assemblage, and the pollen record suggests the presence of salt-marsh nearby. Plant remains in the peats demonstrate the development of reed swamp for brief episodes, reflecting periods of relative stability in relation to sea level, and fresher water conditions. On the surrounding valley sides, mixed deciduous forest dominated during the Neolithic, initially consisting largely of oak but later with lime playing a significant role. The evidence for woodland clearance and agriculture suggests only a low level of activity.

Investigation of the deposits predating the archaeologically rich palaeochannels, exposed during the lake's construction in 1988, did not form part of the initial 1990 project design. Only with the change in approach resulting from a growing appreciation of the stratigraphic complexity of the site was more emphasis placed on their recognition, and limited examination. Most exposures occurred where trenches had been excavated slightly beyond the base of palaeochannels. These are supplemented by a limited auger survey carried out by students from Exeter University and University College, Dublin as part of a course in wetland archaeology supported by the European Social Fund. Details of an initial auger survey carried out in 1989 which demonstrated that the upper organic deposits extended across the valley to the north are held in archive. A further survey in 1991 consisted of two lines of boreholes taken with a gouge auger, running from excavated exposures in areas G and H to the south-west and west respectively (Fig 6). Detailed interpretation of the earliest deposits is not possible as samples from these were not prioritised for analysis.

The most detailed and complete picture of alluvial build-up in the valley bottom can best be achieved by combining data from borehole 1 with the excavated sequences in areas G and H (Fig 12). Less complete sequences encountered in other excavation areas, which had been substantially truncated by later fluvial action or modern machining, are then described and correlated.

From −1.5m OD to 0.5m OD the sediment graded from medium sand through progressively finer sand to silty sand. This was succeeded by 0.9m of increasingly organic silty clay which in turn was overlain by 0.12m of humified phragmites peat with a surface level of 1.31m OD. A succession of inorganic clays and silty clays then accumulated before the development of a group of clays and silty clays of higher organic content between 2.45m and 3.05m OD in borehole 1. This group was paralleled in Area G by very dark grey/brown peaty clay 22273, heavily organic dark olive-grey silty clay 22272, organic mottled clay 22269 and very dark greyish-brown organic clay 22268 (Fig 13, also see Fig 65) between 2.7m and 3.06m OD. Radiocarbon samples from the upper and lower limits of the peaty clay 22273 gave dates of 4370 80 BP (CAR-1322) and 4670 80 BP (CAR-1323) respectively, indicating a Neolithic date for their formation. This organic horizon was sealed by dark grey clay 22257 which survived to a height of 3.55m OD where it had been truncated by the lake's construction. This is equated with clay 22284/22419 in Area H where it underlay a greyish-brown creamy silt 22283 and subsequent silty clay 22279 (Fig 10d). The latter survived to a height of c 4.3m OD, being cut both by modern machining and the Phase VII palaeochannel, 22288.

Whilst deposits 22283 and 22279 are interpreted as part of Phase I, the possibility that they represent over-bank sedimentation by later fluvial systems, particularly of Phase VI, does need brief consideration. Diatom and pollen analysis of monolith samples 23309 and 23310 (see Fig 66) provide some admittedly limited information. Although diatoms are absent in 22279 and only fragments were recovered from 22283, Cameron (p 122) concludes that 'the low concentrations of diatom valves and marine origin of those identified are consistent with the archaeological interpretation of this material as pre-channel (Wentlooge) deposits'.

Area A

Pre-channel deposits were exposed in the diamond-shaped central trench and its extension to the south-west, in a north–south slot linking this to Column 1, and in localised trenches cut to remove driven uprights. The most complete sequence, visible in sections of the diamond-shaped trench (Figs 14 and 10b), comprised a

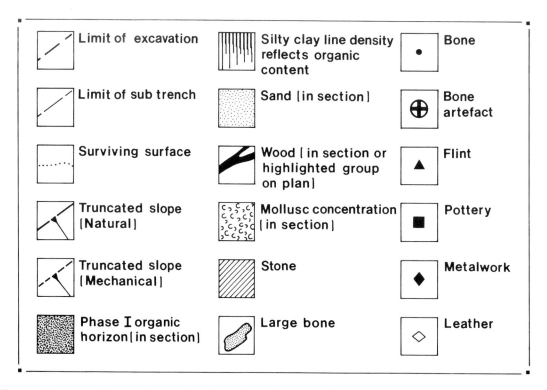

Limit of excavation	Silty clay line density reflects organic content	Bone
Limit of sub trench	Sand (in section)	Bone artefact
Surviving surface	Wood (in section or highlighted group on plan)	Flint
Truncated slope (Natural)	Mollusc concentration (in section)	Pottery
Truncated slope (Mechanical)	Stone	Metalwork
Phase I organic horizon (in section)	Large bone	Leather

Fig 9   Conventions used in sections and palaeochannel group plans

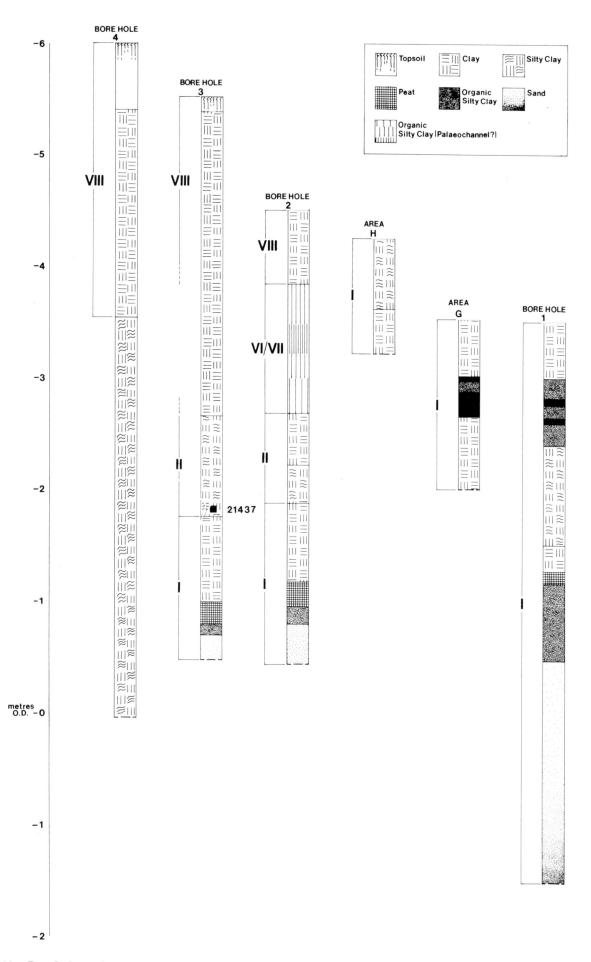

Fig 12   Borehole and section profiles. Phases are indicated along the left side of each sequence. Note the location of pottery sherd 21437 within borehole 3

Fig 13   Area G: Phase I deposits in section. View to south. Scale 2m. Phase VI–VII palaeochannel deposits are visible in the uppermost portion of the facing and right-hand sections – darker, more organic sediment with basal stone spread

Fig 14   Area A: Phase I deposits in section in sub-trench. View to north. Scale 1m

Fig 15   Area B: Phase I deposits in section and Phase II channel cut. View to south-east. Scale 2m. Cf Fig 11b

partially excavated grey clay 22186, overlain by a succession of highly organic sediments (dark grey clay 22253, dark grey peaty clay 22236 and very dark greyish-brown organic clay 22214) between *c* 2.4m and 2.9m OD. A red deer antler tine (21151) from 22253 is interpreted as *in situ* but a flint (21152) from 22236 may well derive from the Phase III channel 22406. This organic group was sealed by the relatively inorganic 22213, which was truncated by Phase V and Phase VI channels, surviving to a maximum height of *c* 3.05m OD.

At the south-west end of this section, and also in the east-facing section (Fig 10a), only a much more limited sequence of blue-grey clay 22536 and overlying dark greyish-brown, organic clay 9033/22509 (*c* 2.3 to 2.6m OD) survived erosion by Phase II and later channel cuts.

A small trench excavated unstratigraphically between the south-east corner of Area A and Area B to verify correlations (Fig 11a) exposed a clean blue clay 22591, cut by the Phase VI channel, with a top height of *c* 3.0m OD into which numerous medium-small stones, pieces of wood and a single bone (21479) had penetrated. The cultural material is associated with the basal deposit of the Phase VI channel, but the blue clay is correlated with 22213 (see above) and directly overlay more organic sediment in Area B.

Further less complete exposures in this area were recorded during the removal of Phase VI/VII driven uprights (see Fig 35).

Area B

Pre-channel deposits were not extensively excavated in this area but were exposed in a small trench in the east (Fig 11a). Dark grey organic silty clay 7075, not bottomed at 2.28m OD, was overlain by an organic unit comprising dark greyish-brown, organic silty clay/clayey peat 7074, between 2.55m and 2.70m OD, and dark grey, organic, silty clay 7073 which underlay the clean, blue clay 22591, linking this unit with Phase I deposits in Area A.

In the north-facing section, where a slot was excavated to facilitate environmental sampling (see Fig 11b and Fig 15), a dark grey/olive-grey, organic, clay 22221, not bottomed at 2.26m OD survived to a maximum height of 2.58m OD, having been cut by Phase II channel action and truncated by Phase III channels.

Less complete exposures of this highly organic unit were recorded in the main south- and east-facing sections where it survived to maximum heights of *c* 2.8m and 2.65m OD respectively.

Area C

A dark grey silty clay 22597, exposed down to 1.8m OD during investigation of the Phase II channel, underlay a more organic unit, a very dark grey/brown, organic, silty clay 22566, which survived to *c* 2.8m OD. Neither of these deposits were extensively excavated (see Fig 16).

Area D

Pre-channel deposits observed in this area were encountered during excavation of Phase VI palaeochannels, removal of the driven uprights of a Phase VII double post alignment (22441), and in a linear trench cut along both sections to confirm completion of excavation of Phase V deposits (see Fig 10c). These comprised a sticky, blue clay with common plant macrofossils and mineral staining (22460), exposed during removal of upright 7001, overlain by an organic horizon (22459). This unit, with a base level of *c* 2.2m OD and top height of *c* 2.95m OD, consisted of three bands of clay/silty clay of varying organic content, the middle band being heavily organic and the uppermost band containing mottles of the overlying sticky, blue clay 22450/22469. This latter deposit was truncated, and in places completely eroded, by later palaeochannels, surviving at its highest level of 3.10m OD below the Phase VI channel 22448, where both stone and pieces of bone had sunk into its surface.

Area E

The stratigraphically earliest pre-channel deposit observed within this trench was encountered during excavation of the Phase II palaeochannel (22376) and consisted of a blue-grey clay, rich in plant macrofossils, with a diffuse boundary with the overlying organic-rich clay (22355). This was first observed where it had been truncated by Phase V palaeochannels, overlain by a deposit (22349/22359) characterised by organic laminations and occasional patches of silt in a clay matrix. In the east, some of the Phase III yew withies (24427) were partially situated within the uppermost surviving parts of this layer. A layer of blue-grey clay (22309/22310) overlay the latter deposit and was substantially truncated by the Phase VI channel. In the west half of the trench some of the stone, and less commonly, wood at the base of the Phase VI channel had penetrated this layer. A single bone find (21238), and twelve stones had probably sunk into this layer at the interface with the Phase VII palaeochannel (22319).

Area F

No controlled excavation of Phase I deposits occurred here, although a clean, blue clay (22198) was noted at the northern end of the trench, apparently cut into by a late Phase VI or Phase VII channel.

Phase II

A significant change in the valley had occurred by Phase II. For the first time there is evidence of a palaeochannel within and to the south and west of the site, down-cutting into Phase I sequences. During rapid infilling of this channel with inorganic silty clays, dumps of stone and bone waste and the construction of a revetment or weir of driven hazel piles provide the first direct evidence of Bronze Age activity on the site. Diatoms suggest the channel was subject to a strong tidal influence. This is supported by the presence of articulated fish skeletons (probably flounder) and pollen which continues to indicate salt-marsh in the area. Other biota also contain taxa indicative of an estuarine environment.

Outside the immediate confines of the channel a floodplain had started to develop with a wet grassland flora. Beyond the floodplain, woodland continued to prevail. However, a marked change in the woodland environment had occurred: lime once again formed a comparatively minor component and oak dominated, presumably having colonised the areas where lime had previously been growing. There is some evidence for clearance of the oak woodland and that both pastoralism and cultivation were taking place. Cattle bones from the site confirm the former activity.

This phase is characterised by the earliest occurrence of a clearly-defined erosive interface, cutting Phase I deposits. This interface was quite distinct from later channel cuts in being straight-sided and

steep, and only seen to cut phase 1 deposits. Relatively little can be said about its size as, with the exception of excavation in Area C around pile structure 472, the channel was not bottomed, and only the left slope (ie north-east edge) was encountered. Fills were generally low in organic content, had high silt fractions, and were apparently little eroded by later channel development. It would appear that as the channel infilled, it migrated to the east or north-east during Phase III, in the process eroding part of the Phase II slope and the Phase I deposits behind it. The absence of the highly organic Phase I horizons in many of the western boreholes, and in a machine-cut test pit to the west of Area B, suggests the presence of this channel to the south and west of the excavation area, although no firm conclusions can be made regarding the original channel width. The find of a single featureless body sherd (21437, see Woodward p 243) of possible Early or Middle Bronze Age date in borehole 3 at a depth consistent with the presence of a Phase II channel lends weight to this supposition.

Area A

A.2.1

The straight-sided cut 22520, only partially excavated in this area, sloped steeply at *c* 40° from the horizontal, cutting Phase I deposits 22536 and 22509 (see Figs 10a and 10b). The interface, interpreted as the left slope (ie north-east edge) of the channel was truncated by Phase III channel migration, surviving to a height of 2.3–2.4m OD. The earliest fill excavated, a pale grey, very silty clay with distinct silt laminae 22530 was overlain by a sticky, blue-grey clay with silt laminations, 22521. Excavation in the south-west end of the extension to Area A recovered a single piece of split hazel roundwood.

Area B

B.2.1

The channel cut, 22181, was seen at an oblique angle in the east-facing section with a top surviving height of 2.6m OD. It was truncated by Phase III channels and contained grey clay 22251 with some stone and wood which was not removed. This material may have sunk from overlying Phase III channels. The channel was more clearly visible in the north-west facing section (see Fig 11b and Fig 14) as a straight-sided left (ie north-east edge) slope 22222, cutting Phase I unit 22221, and truncated by Phase III channel 22223 at a height of 2.6m OD. Exposed fills comprised dark grey/grey clays 22220 and 22218/22044 and, possibly following an erosion event 22405, dark grey/olive-grey clays 22240, 22241 and grey, silty clay 22242. The latter episode of downcutting may relate to localised increase in flow rates, and hence erosion, caused by the construction of the pile structure 472 further downstream. Again, some stone and wood appeared to have penetrated the uppermost deposits from Phase III channels. Bone extracted from bulk samples 23059 and 23061 were identified as eel, field vole tooth and frog/toad (see Hamilton-Dyer p 234). A single cattle bone (21125) was recovered from context 22218.

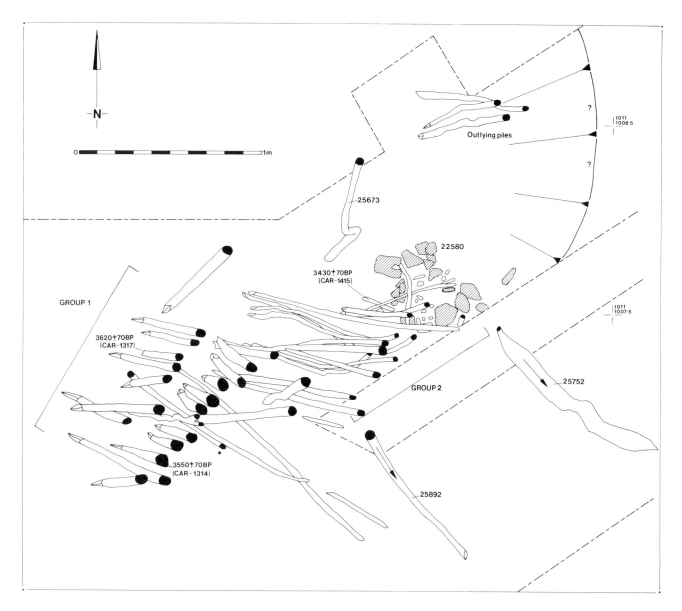

Fig 16   Pile structure 472, stone and wood concentration 22580, and possible location of later Phase II channel edge (left edge)

Area C

C.2.1

Phase II was most extensively excavated in this area in order to complete removal of structure 472 (see below). The depth of deposits created some logistical difficulties. As a result, many of the features described here were visible only within a 1m wide slot. Again, the truncated, left slope (ie north to north-east edge) of the palaeochannel (22569) was encountered: a steeply-sloping interface surviving up to *c* 2.8m OD. A change in the direction of slope suggests the channel was curving to a more east–west orientation. There was a gradual change of slope to a near-flat base dropping to below 1.80m OD. No indications of a right (ie west) bank were recorded, even in the sections south-west of structure 472. The fills of this channel, especially in close proximity to structure 472, were often mixed and disturbed, causing problems in interpretation and obscuring the exact stratigraphic relationship between these deposits and the structure.

A thin basal lens of light-grey, silty clay (22581) with abundant calcareous inclusions and articulated fish skeletons was partially overlain by a small spread of medium to small stones in a matrix of gritty, slightly silty, grey clay (22595). This feature may be the earliest suggestion of structural activity on the site, although the small extent exposed permits little interpretation. To the south-west, a clean, blue-grey clay (22594) sloped down from the south suggesting substantial infilling. Both this fill and the stone spread were overlain by a succession of grey, fine, silty clays (22596, 22593 and 22583 and 22584). Their organic component included small, highly-organic clasts reminiscent of Phase I horizons. This unit was partially overlain by a dense, steeply-sloping deposit of stone, wood and bone (22580) (see Fig 16) which gave a radiocarbon determination of 3430 ± 70 BP (CAR-1415). The wood assemblage was small, comprising just four pieces of apparently unworked roundwood (hazel and blackthorn). Three cattle bones including a skull were also recovered. This deposit either represents a dump, placed on the right slope (ie south-east edge) of a narrowing channel, or was forced down through the riverbed behind the piles of structure 472 at a later date and was therefore intrusive.

Subsequent infill was represented by a distinctive, grey, very silty clay (22568) in the east and silty clays 22585–22587 in the west to a height of over 2.75m OD. The latter contained

Fig 17   Structure 472: pile group 1 with some group 2 piles visible in the left background. View to south-east. Scale 1m. The near horizontal forked wood on the left is interpreted as later Phase III debris

gently-sloping silt laminations suggesting an eastward migration of the channel. It would appear that at some stage during this process, structure 472, or at least some elements of it were constructed presumably on the right bank (ie south-west edge) of this channel.

Structure 472

This structure comprised a linear group of 41 roundwood piles oriented south-west to north-east forming a line *c* 3m long including outlying piles (Figs 16 and 17). The majority of piles were concentrated in an irregular 1.5m line with the piles progressively less vertical towards the north-east. Two additional piles south-east of this line sloped steeply to the south-east in opposition to this main group, whilst a lone pile, 25673, and an outlying cluster of three piles, were situated to the north-east. Many of the piles were severely distorted (possibly as a result of compression rather than damage during driving, as they had not been driven into any hard substrata). Subsequent Phase III erosion appeared to have truncated many of the piles towards the north-east, in contrast to those in the west which survived to the height of modern machining. All the identified piles were hazel with the exception of one

example of dogwood and one of willow, and all were derived from straight stemmed trees.

The wood utilised was not entirely homogenous either in type or in toolmark evidence: Brunning and O'Sullivan (p 169) detect a trend for shallower-cut, more carefully pointed piles in the south-west where two parallel rows approximately 1m in length (group 1, see Fig 17) were cut from thicker, more mature trunks (see Morgan, p 195). Wood diameter and pointing technique may be linked variables here, but the spatial distribution should be seen against a background of eastward channel migration, and the more slender and simply-cut piles (group 2, Fig 18) could equally well reflect later extension of the pile frontage to the north-east in response to channel infilling and migration. Radiocarbon determinations of 3620 ± 70 BP (CAR-1317) and 3550 ± 70 BP (CAR-1314) were derived from the south-western group.

Two north-west to south-east oriented, near-horizontal hazel stems at 2.6–2.75m OD, both with cut north-west ends, may have been parts of the structure as the density of the western piles (group 1) between which they ran would have precluded their later deposition here. At the very least they are an indication of contemporary sediment level when the western group of piles was driven. Morgan (p 195) highlights the fact that these have more in common

with the north-eastern piles (group 2) in terms of
growth pattern, age and diameter than the piles with
which they are placed.

Two opposing piles, 25892 and 25752, driven to
c 2.0m OD, sloped up to the north-west at approximately 45°. The more substantial of the two, 25752,
was unusual both in being cut from a willow type tree
and also in retaining tooling detail at its top, where
reduction in diameter may be the result of woodworking (see Fig 95). If still approximately *in situ*, they could
have acted as bracing elements for the pile frontage
for the slighter north-eastern piles (group 2).

The structure's temporal relationship to the deposits through which it was driven is problematic.
Adjacent sediments are generally low in organic
content and do not exhibit the compression and
distortion seen in sediments associated with larger
driven piles, encountered in later phases. This is
particularly true of the south-western piles (group 1),
mostly lifted in 1990, where the main indications of
contemporary sediment surface are the two horizontal elements and the relatively shallow driving depth
of some of its piles (Fig 19). The stratigraphy
upstream (north) of the north-eastern piles and
around the outlying piles comprised an unusually
loose blue-grey silty clay with occasional organic
bands (22578) within an irregular interface 22582
(see C.2.2 on Fig 19) which suggested localised
downcutting of the riverbed to as low as 1.85m OD.
Such erosion could have been the result of the
structure's presence, which must have caused an
artificial narrowing of the water course. Indeed the
outlying piles, driven significantly lower than others,
may be remnants of a more complete pile line. The
surviving top heights of these piles and those in
group 2 suggest that the structure remained partially exposed in the river bed/side in early Phase III,
although possibly derelict. The willow pile 25752 was
partially exposed in the right (ie south-west) bank
during earlier Phase III (C.3.1 and possibly C.3.2).

Function Whether the surviving elements of structure 472 represent two phases of construction or just
one, singly or together they appear to have formed a

*Fig 18 Structure 472: group 2 piles, outlying piles,
and early Phase II channel base. View to north-
east. Scales 0.5m*

revetment which protruded into the channel restrict-
ing the flow. The north-eastern piles (group 2) may
have been braced. The function of the outlying piles
is less clear: they may be remnants of a cross-channel
line largely removed by later erosion or alternatively
may have secured nets or baskets for fishing.
Environmental indicators from contemporary deposits in Area B point to stronger estuarine influences
during this phase than in later periods. This would

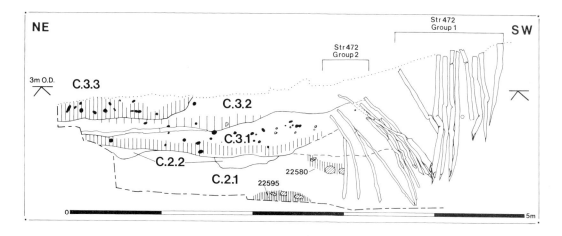

Fig 19 Area C: composite section of structure 472 and associated Phase II and III deposits

Fig 20   Area E: Phase II channel during excavation. View to south-east. Scale interval 0.5m. The steeply-sloping channel interface had been truncated by the later, Phase VI palaeochannel (left). The section acted as one of the major sampling sites (Column 4): see Figs 11c and 63 for sections)

make the location particularly suitable for exploitation of spring runs of migratory fish. More recent examples of river fish weirs are generally constructed of lines of hurdles secured by more widely spaced uprights, often in V-shaped configurations (eg Salisbury 1991). Interpretation is hindered by the small area of contemporary riverbed investigated and the modern and ancient truncation of the piles. Hence alternative functions cannot be dismissed. McGrail (1985) has argued against the need for wharves in the prehistoric period, based on present knowledge of the known range of contemporary boat types, whilst recognising the need for a solid bottom on which boats could rest at low tide in estuarine and marine locations.

Area D

D.2.1

The channel cut 22477 was observed only in section (Fig 10c) as a straight-sided, steeply sloping interface forming the truncated north-eastern edge (left slope) of a north-west to south-east oriented palaeochannel surviving to a height of *c* 2.85m OD. This feature was only partially excavated. Fills observed in section

comprised sticky clays with generally low organic content (22478, 22479, 22481 and 22482).

Area E

E.2.1

In the west end of the trench, a north-west to south-east oriented interface, cutting Phase I deposits was only partially excavated owing to logistical problems. This steep, slightly-convex slope was not bottomed at *c* 2.35m OD and was truncated by a Phase III palaeochannel at *c* 2.9m OD (Fig 20, also see Fig 11c). It contained a succession of partially excavated fills including a restricted area of organic, blue-grey clay interpreted as slumped Phase I sediment (22396); slightly silty, blue clay (22395); very silty, grey clay (22356); a darkly-stained, sticky clay with faint, diffuse boundaries (22393); and a clean, grey clay with faint thin laminae (22398). The uppermost surviving fill (22391) comprised heavily-stained, blue clay with occasional bands of silt. These fills were excavated as a single unit with more detailed recording following examination of the sections. No artefactual material was recovered.

Phase III

Limited downcutting and marginal palaeochannel migration mark the beginning of Phase III. Basal fills in particular were markedly different from those encountered in Phase II, comprising finer, clayey sediments with distinctly higher organic content. Where channel fills were extensively excavated in Areas A, B and C, dense spreads of wood were encountered in stark contrast to earlier phases and overlying Phase IV deposits. In addition to the wood assemblages (which contained apparently unworked and worked roundwood, woodworking debris and wooden artefacts), other materials were present on the contemporary riverbed including bone (primarily from domesticates), stone and, less frequently, pottery and flint. No *in situ* structures were recorded, although a substantial oak timber fashioned to form a strake for a sewn plank boat were recovered from the latest palaeochannel group of this phase in Area B.

The channel environment was essentially one of fresh water, although there continued to be a brackish/marine element in the background, indicating the site was not totally beyond the influence of the occasional high tide, storm surge, wind-blown salt spray or the re-working of older marine sediments. There was also a brief episode, recorded in deposits from below the boat plank, when there was an increased estuarine/marine influence. Generally, the aquatic biota suggest a slowly-flowing, freshwater river.

The environment on the floodplain and beyond is indicated by the plant and insect remains, suggesting the importance of grassland. This conforms with the limited faunal assemblage with its predominance of sheep among the domesticates. A decline in oak pollen along with an increase in ribwort plantain reflects the creation of pasture on the terraces and valley sides as well as on the floodplain. Although pastoralism appears to dominate, the occasional cereal-type pollen grain suggests some arable activity in the area. An increase in shrubby species, apart from hazel, in the pollen record and in the wood record suggests a spread of scrub into recently cleared and abandoned areas or even, possibly, the development of hedges. There seems to be a slight expansion in alder woodland towards the end of the phase. There is also a little evidence for beaver activity during this phase in the form of a small number of beaver-chewed pieces of wood.

Area A

Deposits assigned to this phase were encountered only in the south-west extension where, owing to the oblique angle of some of the channels and the narrowness of this trench, excavation and interpretation proved difficult.

A.3.1

The earliest interface assigned to this phase, 22522 (Fig 21, top) was considerably reduced by later channel action, but appears to have been oriented north-west to south-east, with the truncated left slope (ie north-east edge) running down to *c* 2.2m OD at the limit of excavation in the south-west. It contained mottled, grey,

sticky clay 22524, and greenish-grey, organic, silty clays 22519 and 22518. The density of wood, stone and bone in this area was high in the south-west with a lighter scatter of material up slope to the north-east. The wood assemblage was dominated by hazel (46%) and blackthorn (28%) with lesser quantities of willow and hawthorn roundwood. The substantial hazel stem, 25077, exhibited both pencil and chisel cuts and forked branches. The only other clear evidence of woodworking was a single unidentified roundwood stem with a chisel point. The artefactual assemblage included a flint flake, 21568, and two bone artefacts: an awl/pin (21566) and a gouge (21577). A horizontal stem of immature roundwood at 2.49m OD (25293) from 22519 gave an alarmingly late radiocarbon determination of 2210 ± 60 BP (CAR-1409). This is discussed in the dating section (p 11).

A.3.2

The subsequent channel (22511) survived to a width of *c* 4.5m with a relatively flat base at *c* 2.45m OD and gently sloping concave sides (Fig 21, middle, also see Figs 10a and 10b) and appeared to be oriented north-west to south-east. Fills comprised a grey/brown, organic clay with commonly occurring charcoal and lighter blue-grey laminae of sticky clay, 22517/22539, overlain by a blue-grey clay with organic mottles 22508/22516. The wood assemblage (45 pieces), quite closely aligned with the assumed channel direction, was again dominated by hazel (27%) and blackthorn (20%) with lesser quantities of hawthorn, elder, alder and willow. Five of the stems had chisel or wedge points including a branching stem of dogwood, 25074. A single alder woodchip may be indicative of woodworking and one hawthorn stem exhibited the characteristic teeth marks of beaver. Three fragments of bone were recovered and a flint flake (21152), although found within the underlying Phase I deposit 22214, may have sunk from this channel.

A.3.3

The latest channel of this phase, 22523 (Fig 21, bottom), was again restricted to the south-west extreme of the trench and had suffered from considerable post-depositional, and possibly modern distortion/disturbance such that details of its morphology were unclear. Its apparent restriction to the south west may be a result of truncation by the Phase IV interface although there was little other evidence for downcutting at the onset of Phase IV. Fills consisted of an organic, greenish-grey clay, 22515, overlain by a less organic, blue-grey clay with organic mottles, 22514. A small wood assemblage of hazel, alder, hawthorn and willow included an unidentified roundwood stem with trimmed side-branches, an alder roundwood stem with a chisel point and a radial hawthorn woodchip.

Area B

The bulk of Phase III and later deposits encountered in this area were excavated in 1990 and plans of erosion interfaces are largely non-existent. Where cultural material had not been associated with particular contexts in the record, spatial information has been used to phase it in conjunction with relevant section drawings. Given the close proximity of Phase IV and V deposits, the possibility that some of the wood assemblage, particularly those pieces resting on the boat strake 6001, has been incorrectly assigned to Phase III cannot be excluded. An extension to the south-west in 1991, and partial removal of baulks linking stratigraphic sequences in areas B and C in 1992, were excavated stratigraphically.

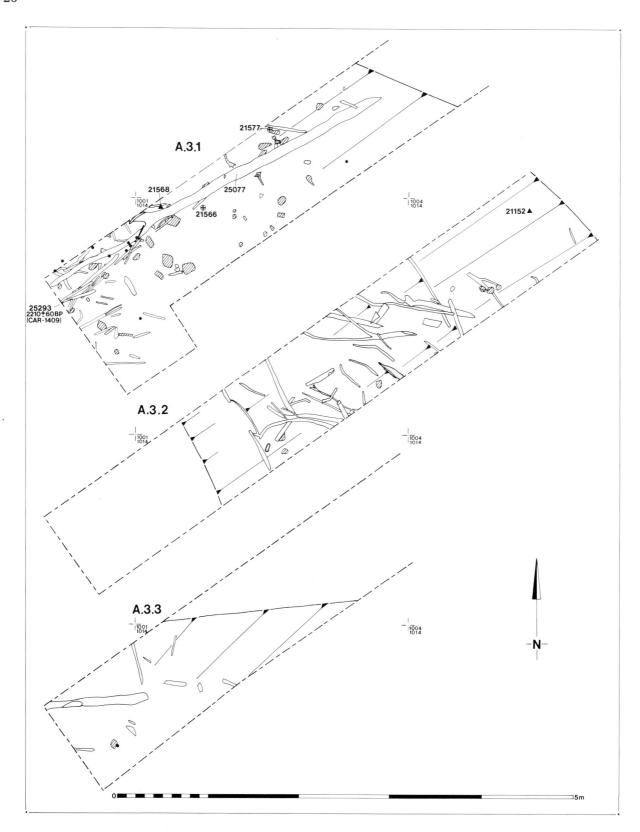

Fig 21   Area A: plan of Phase III palaeochannel groups

B.3.1

The earliest channel was encountered in the south-west extension as a shallowly-sloping, irregular interface (22176) with a gradual change of slope to a rounded base at 2.5m OD. The basal fill, a dark-grey clay with laminations of very organic, dark olive-grey,

silty clay (22041), containing three stems of hazel roundwood was overlain by further dark-grey clay with less frequent but more distinct organic laminae (22043), containing a piece of hazel and a rare example of privet.

B.3.2

The latter group was partially truncated by the subsequent erosive interface (22177) which was similar in profile and bottom depth but located c 1m further to the east. The basal fills of dark-grey, silty clays 22246 and 22170, the latter interdigitated with 22169, a lens of very dark, silty clay extremely rich in mollusca were overlain by a less organic, mottled dark-grey, silty clay 22042. This channel and its fills are correlated with palaeochannel group C.3.1 (see Fig 24). The wood assemblage from this channel included a concentration of ash woodchips (20323), three individually numbered ash woodchips and seven pieces of trimmed or cut roundwood. The other common species were hazel and blackthorn. Rarely encountered species were represented by single examples of possible privet and dog rose.

B.3.3

The subsequent channel was most extensively excavated in the east half of Area B in 1990, during the lifting of the boat strake 6001 with further limited excavation and sampling especially around the north-facing section (Fig 22). This feature comprised a gently-sloping, right slope (ie south-west edge), with a gradual change of slope to a rounded base at c 2.6m OD. Fills identified in the north-facing section, recorded in 1991 (see Fig 11c), consisted of basal, olive, richly-organic clay 22166, grey clay 22239 and a richly-organic, grey clay 22165, all interdigitated with upper fills 22216, a dark-grey clay and 22217, a dark-grey silty clay. Context records from 1990 identify three major contexts from this phase: 7090, 7089 (both greenish-grey clays with abundant plant macrofossils and molluscan remains) and 7019, a greenish-grey silty clay with abundant plant macrofossils and moderate mollusca. 7089 and 7090 correlate with the basal fills 22165 and 22166, although no context records from 1990 closely parallel the intermediate 22239. No left slope (ie north-east edge) of this channel survived presumably owing to subsequent channel migration to the north-east during Phases IV and V. The basal fills were progressively thinner towards the north, either because of less active sedimentation during this phase or as a result of later channel action.

Given the uncertainty of assigning contexts to wood and finds which were not assigned contexts in the field, those appearing in Fig 22 in Area B are assigned to Phase III, rather than to any specific deposit. The spatial distribution of material for which context data is available does however suggest slight eastward migration of a north-west to south-east oriented channel, a pattern seen in contemporary sequences in Area C.

The most important item recovered from this palaeochannel group, a substantial half-split mature oak (6001) interpreted as a boat strake from a sewn plank vessel (Fig 23), lay with its upper surface at between 2.75m and 2.95m OD within basal organic sediment 7089 at a slight angle to the prevailing palaeochannel orientation, sloping up slightly from north to south. The strake was not sealed by the Phase III deposits, and would probably have protruded into the riverbed, contemporary with the overlying Phase IV sediments. Its surface was highly eroded: this is probably a result of use rather than post-depositional abrasion, given the well-preserved nature of adjacent wood and environmental indicators suggesting relatively slow flow rates. Furthermore, the strake exhibited a number of major cracks, particularly at its north end which was incomplete. This damage extended along the central ridge to join a crack running inwards from a stitch-hole. The three cleats were all incomplete, and a substantial piece (20684), originally part of the west side of 6001, was detached and lay adjacent to the north end of 6001. High precision radiocarbon determination of a sample of heartwood from the boat strake gave a date of 3439 ± 19 BP (UB-3472). Wood items possibly associated with the boat strake included an oak handle? (8440) and two split lengths of yew (8441 and 8442) which may be remnants of

stitching. All these items are described in more detail by McGrail (p 210).

The rest of the wood assemblage from this palaeochannel group (133 pieces) was very varied, and included a group of very straight-stemmed hazel rods in the south-west, reminiscent of those from 22567 in Area C. Of the material retained for study, 65% was hazel, 15% blackthorn, 8% oak and 6% hawthorn. Although the majority of the assemblage was immature roundwood, an unusually high proportion (31%) was clearly cut. Less frequent species included ash, alder, lime and elder. Three hazel stems exhibited the characteristic teeth marks of beaver.

In addition to 36 pieces of bone, a serrated mammal rib (5285), a flake from a polished axe (5275), a scraper (5288) and the medial segment of a burnt blade or flake (21106) were also recovered.

Area C

Excavation of Phase III deposits in this area in 1992 resulted from the desire to ensure complete excavation of structure 472. The results refine the stratigraphic sequence in Area B and provide additional artefactual material. The upper fills of these palaeochannel groups, being relatively inorganic, were difficult to separate, whilst the high density of wood in basal fills often complicated context definition.

C.3.1

The first channel in this area assigned to Phase III, a north-west to south-east oriented interface with an undulating concave base and gently sloping south-west edge (22579) cut Phase II deposits down to 2.25m OD. Some of the north-eastern elements of structure 472 remained exposed in this channel edge. Fills of sticky, grey, organic clay with organic laminations (22577); a highly-laminated, greenish, organic, silty clay with lenses of cleaner, sticky, grey clay (22576) and a relatively-inorganic, hard, grey, silty clay (22575), contained a small wood assemblage dominated by hazel roundwood, two with chisel cut ends and one exhibiting the characteristic marks of beaver (Fig 24, shaded). Small quantities of blackthorn and alder were also recovered. Many of the hazel stems were substantial poles only partially exposed within the trench limits. Additional artefactual material comprised unworked bone and a flint flake (21768). Radiocarbon samples from wood 25747 and 25864 gave age determinations of 3380 ± 70 BP (CAR-1413) and 3270 ± 70 BP (CAR-1414) respectively.

C.3.2

The succeeding fill, a pale, bluish-grey clay with organic mottling (22574) extended slightly further to the east but there was no evidence of significant channel migration. Again the wood assemblage (Fig 24, unshaded, and Fig 25) was dominated by hazel roundwood (62%), much of it exhibiting evidence of intentional removal of side-branches, and five pieces having cut ends. Lesser quantities of blackthorn, oak, ash, dogwood, willow and hawthorn occurred. Further evidence of woodworking included single cut stems of dogwood and blackthorn, and three pieces of debris (oak and ash). In addition to unworked bone, a single flint (21745) was recovered. Much of the hazel roundwood consisted of substantial poles including a large forked piece (25430) which lay across the right (ie south-west) slope of this channel, with the cut, forked end apparently caught up in the bank close to piles from the north-eastern group of structure 472 and the pointed, but eroded, lower end snagged in wood from 22574. Its stratigraphic position was somewhat uncertain and it may have lain proud of the riverbed leading to localised deposition of a homogenous, blue-

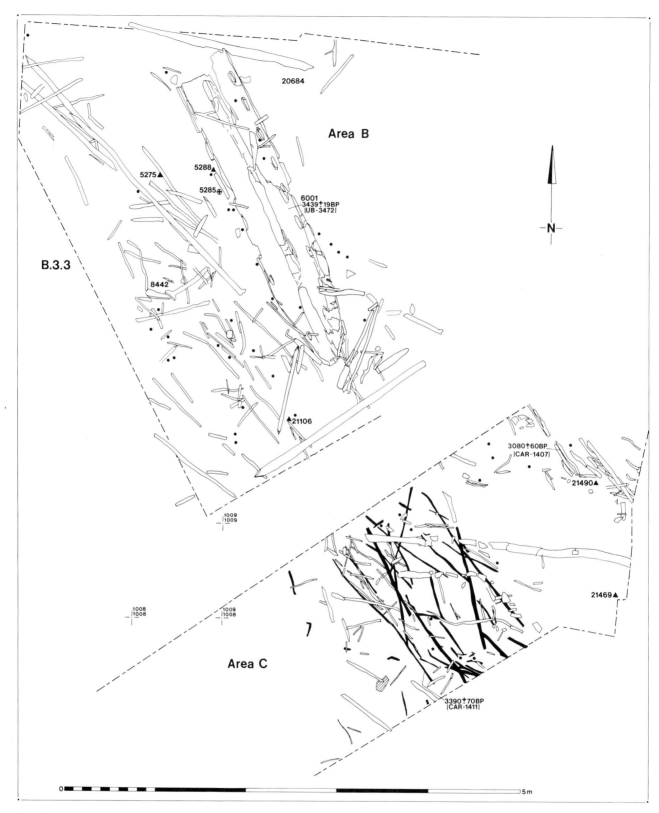

Fig 22   Areas B and C: plan of late Phase III. Wood from palaeochannel group C.3.3 is shaded, and that from C.3.4 is unshaded

grey, slightly-silty clay (22572) along the south-west side of the channel. This deposit contained a small number of yew twigs, one with a chisel-cut end.

Although structure 472 was probably in ruin by this time, some of its western piles may have been partially exposed in the right bank allowing some of the longer roundwood on the east side to become entangled.

C.3.3

The subsequent channel fill of greenish-grey, silty clay (22567) with clasts of extremely-organic, olive-green, silty clay and a thin lens of blue-grey clay contained an assemblage of very straight-stemmed hazel oriented north-west to south-east, six of which exhibited clear axe marks including four with cut ends (see Fig 22,

Fig 23   Boat strake 6001 during excavation. View to north-west

shaded). One of these gave a radiocarbon determination of 3390 ± 70 BP (CAR-1411). Single pieces of elder and elm were also recovered, along with a single tooth.

C.3.4

Interpretation of the artefactual assemblage associated with the latest basal fill assigned to this phase in Area C, an organic, grey clay (22562) was complicated by two main factors: the apparently low density of material in the south-east, probably a function of its partial excavation in 1989 when recording and recovery strategies were less stringent; and a dense group of wood (22561) located at the interface with both Phase IV and V deposits which may be partially incorrectly phased. Even given these problems, it is clear that the channel was both migrating to the north-east and also turning towards the east at this point. The roundwood assemblage exhibited little evidence of woodworking with only six pieces of cut hazel and a single piece of cut blackthorn. Ash, oak and alder woodchips were present however. Single examples of purging blackthorn and spindle tree along with three pieces each of willow type and elder roundwood were also recovered. Two flints (21469 and 21490) and a small group of bone, all from 22562, were retrieved. A single radiocarbon determination of 3000 ± 60 BP (CAR-1407) was derived from 24936, a piece of hazel roundwood from 22561.

Area D

D.3.1

Restricted time and the reallocation of resources to the excavation of the Phase VII structure 22441 meant that only the uppermost fills of this phase were excavated with some lower fills being exposed in section, as was the case in Area E. The previous excavation of area 182 had removed the uppermost fills where the two areas overlapped, resulting in the isolation of deposits 22451

and 22454 in the south-west end of the area, although the north-east facing section of was continuous.

The uppermost deposit of this phase in the south-west corner (22451), a mixed, brownish-grey clay with organic laminations, merged towards the north-east with 22447, a mottled, blue clay with frequent plant macrofossils. Both these deposits were directly sealed by the Phase IV deposits. The close proximity of the excavated wood to this interface caused some difficulties during excavation: some of this material could conceivably have derived from Phase IV. The wood assemblage of 31 pieces (70% hazel with lesser quantities of hawthorn, ash and oak) included a radial oak woodchip, a finely worked hazel pencil point, three hazel chisel-pointed roundwood stems and a hazel stem with a wedge point. Finds comprised three fragments of bone.

The underlying deposits comprised a grey, silty clay with frequent plant macrofossils and distinct silt laminations (22454) which merged with a mixed, grey, silty clay (22452) with common mollusca and plant macrofossils. The small assemblage of wood from 22454 comprised blackthorn and hazel roundwood and a single piece of elder. Although one piece of hazel was a quarter split, no incontrovertible evidence of woodworking was recovered. A single bone (21556) was recovered.

Area E

Phase III deposits were not totally excavated along the full length of this area. Following partial removal of deposits directly underlying Phase IV sediments, excavation was not continued in the westernmost 2.6m of the area but limited to a zone some 2m in length where Phase III deposits overlay the Phase II interface (see Figs 11c and 20). The resulting profile acted as a major sampling site (Column 5).

No clear unconformity between these deposits and the underlying fill of the Phase II channel was observed, although channel migration appeared to have truncated Phase I sediments to the east. The earliest Phase III deposit recorded here, dark olive-grey, silty clay 22392, was rich in mollusca and stained with manganese

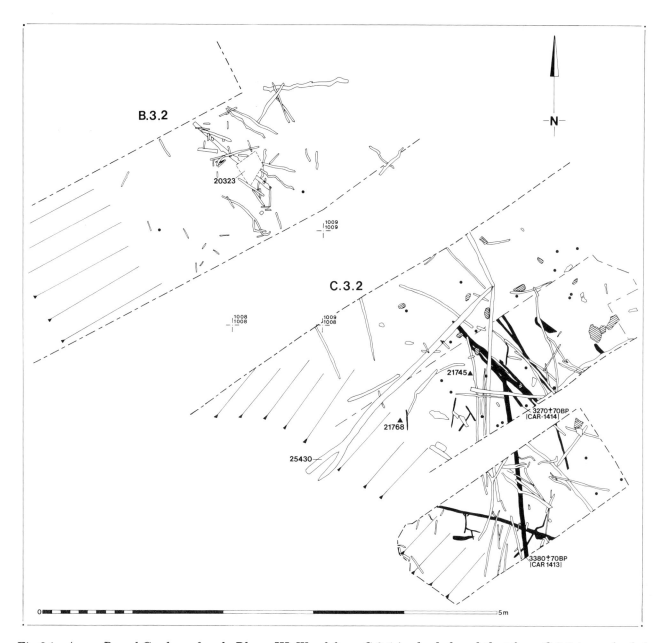

Fig 24   Areas B and C: plan of early Phase III. Wood from C.3.1 is shaded and that from C.3.2 is unshaded

and fine charcoal, had a base height of *c* 2.6m OD and contained a mottled, organic lens of slightly-darker, silty clay 22386. These underlay a dark-grey, organic silty clay 22379 with similar coarse components but locally with extremely rich lenses of mollusca, one of which was sampled and analysed (bulk sample 23166). This layer in turn underlay a highly-organic, dark-grey/brown, silty clay 22347. The density of wood within these deposits made understanding of the stratigraphic sequence difficult during excavation, and wood and stone was assigned to a single number (22375). This material has been subdivided on plan (Fig 26) for clarity. It is worth noting here that three of the oak woodchips from Phase III in this area cross-match dendrochronologically with relatively high t-values to produce a short floating chronology (Hillam p 190).

E.3.1a

The underlying group (Fig 26 top) comprised a total of 152 pieces of wood, of which 93 were from a spread of fine yew stems (24427). At least 21 of these had been cut/pointed at one end, many of which

exhibited splitting at the other end. Often side-branches had been removed, and many had been bent. Their function is unclear although use of yew withies for stitching boat planks at other sites, and the presence of twisted yew pieces adjacent to the boat strake, suggest they may have been waste from production of fibre rope (see Brunning and O'Sullivan p 171, and McGrail p 214). One of these stems gave a radiocarbon determination of 3380 ± 70 BP (CAR-1412). The remainder of the wood assemblage was dominated by hazel roundwood. Worked items included oak woodchips, a possible oak plank fragment, three hazel stems with cut points, a dogwood stem with a wedge point, and an alder woodchip. The wood assemblage provided two further radiocarbon dates of 3160 ± 70 BP (CAR-1320) and 3440 ± 60 BP (CAR-1321). Other material from this group consisted of thirteen pieces of bone, a single flint flake (21444) and a light scatter of subangular stone.

E.3.1b

The later group (Fig 26 bottom) comprised 68 pieces of wood, dominated by hazel roundwood (56%), three pieces of bone and a

Fig 25   Area C: early Phase III during excavation. View to south-west. Scales 0.5m (background) and 1m (foreground)

small number of stones. Worked material included a willow/poplar bole with numerous branches with a single chisel point, hazel roundwood with a pencil point, a substantial piece of alder roundwood with a pencil point, a radially-split oak timber which passed beyond both sides of the trench, and radial and intermediate oak wood chips.

Phase IV

This phase comprised a distinctive group of deposits, which appeared very rich in organic content during excavation, often giving off an odour reminiscent of cess deposits, yet contained very little artefactual material. There was no evidence of substantial downcutting; rather it was this characteristic nature of the fills that encouraged their separation from other groups/phases. In the field, the distinctive nature of these fills proved a most useful aid in correlating sequences between excavation areas. Problems were encountered at the base of this phase where wood lay close to the interface with Phase III deposits, making assignment of these wood assemblages to a particular phase difficult. On balance, the stratigraphic evidence suggests that much of the material found in this situation, including the boat strake 6001, was dumped into the river during Phase III, but remained partially exposed in the bed of the river until changes in conditions led to the accumu-

lation of the highly organic sediments of Phase IV. No major episode of downcutting or channel migration occurred between these events.

Environmental conditions do not appear to differ significantly from the previous phase. The channel environment was predominantly freshwater in character, though again there is a background element reflecting brackish conditions and the presence of salt-marsh in the area. However, there is some evidence, notably molluscan, to suggest the channel was silting up and marshy conditions existed, perhaps rather less favourable conditions for human activities than in the previous phase. A reduction in weedy plants, which grow on disturbed ground, is in agreement with the archaeological evidence for reduced activity at the site. In contrast the pollen record indicates that agricultural activity in the area continued at a similar level to that of Phase III. The woodland seems to have changed little, with a further slight reduction in oak suggesting an increase in cleared ground.

Area A: A.4.1

The oblique angle at which the channel interface passed through the south-west extension of Area A complicated excavation of this palaeochannel group. In addition, erosion by Phase V channel action had partially removed the gently-sloping fill (dark, green-

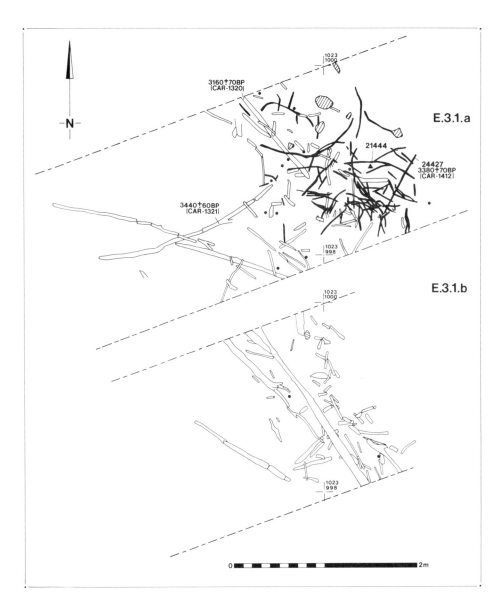

Fig 26   Area E: plan of partially excavated Phase III. The palaeochannel group has been subdivided for clarity. The shaded wood is a spread of fine yew withies, 24427

ish-brown, organic, silty clay 22506) in the south-west end of the trench. This is shown in the south-east facing section of the extension (Fig 10a). The palaeochannel appeared to be turning rapidly here from a west–east to a north-west to south-east orientation with a bottom level of *c* 2.5–2.6m OD. Evidence for erosion of Phase III sediments here was equivocal. The associated fill was highly organic, containing laminae rich in mollusca and decayed plant material. A particularly mollusc-rich lens of greenish-brown, silty clay (22507) was contained within the main fill.

Of the 35 pieces of immature roundwood recovered from this palaeochannel group, all were identified as either hazel or blackthorn with the exception of two stems of oak and three of hawthorn. Only one piece of hazel exhibited clear signs of working in the form of a chisel-cut end. Another hazel stem (24896) gave a surprisingly late radiocarbon determination of 2450 ± 60 BP (CAR-1407). There seems no simple explanation for this result as the piece was securely stratified and horizontally oriented at 2.94–2.97m OD, was sampled within 24 hours of initial exposure and was packaged following standard procedures.

Area B: B.4.1

As this group was excavated in 1990, there is little information available on the morphology of its interface although the channel does appear to be oriented west-north-west to east-south-east. Profiles in section suggest little erosion of underlying Phase III deposits, and substantial truncation by the Phase V interface. The bottom of the channel appeared to be at a slightly higher level than in Area A, at *c* 2.9m OD. It is possible that some of the wood overlying boat strake 6001 (see Fig 22) was deposited during this phase and that some parts of the strake protruded into the channel from the contemporary riverbed. Fills comprised a basal, dark olive-grey, organic, silty clay with dark grey mottling (7016) containing abundant brash, diffuse lenses of greenish-grey, silty clay and occasional sand lenses. Plant macrofossils were common as were mollusca, increasingly so with depth. The overlying deposit (7011) comprised a slightly less dark olive-grey, organic, silty clay with dark-grey and greenish-grey mottling containing numerous lenses and laminations of blue-grey clay (see Fig 11b).

The only faunal remains securely associated with this palaeo-channel group were eel and stickleback bones recovered from

Fig 27   Area C: Phase IV interface and organic fills in section. View to north. Scale 1m. The Phase V cut and less organic fills are also visible in section directly above the scale

residues prepared for molluscan analysis from Column 3 (Hamilton-Dyer, pers comm).

including one field maple and one ash woodchip) and two bone fragments.

Area C: C.4.1

The greater part of this group was excavated in 1990 and recorded only in section. The interface showed no unconformity with underlying Phase III deposits pointing to little or no channel downcutting here. The fills comprised a basal deposit of dark grey/greyish-brown, organic clay (329) with some sand and crushed mollusca towards its base, an overlying slightly-lighter and less-organic, grey-green/brown, organic clay with distinct laminae (324), and an uppermost, dark-grey, slightly-silty, organic clay (323) with dense concentrations of mollusca towards its base. This unit is equated with 22558 which consisted of the remaining part of this group within Area C, south of the baulk between this area and Area B. This was excavated stratigraphically in 1992. It consisted of a succession of highly organic, dark grey-brown, silty clays and clays with distinct laminae and mottles of cleaner, bluish clay occupying a heavily-pitted interface (22559) sloping down to the north-east (Fig 27). Whilst the upper slope was generally well-defined, as the concave slope levelled out to a near-flat base at c 2.95m OD, the distinction between the organic fills 22558 and the underlying Phase III deposits was far more difficult to define.

The small artefactual assemblage recovered consisted of fourteen pieces of wood (including immature blackthorn, hazel, and hawthorn roundwood, and four pieces of woodworking debris

Area D: D.4.1

This group was characterised by gently-sloping, laminated, organic, silty clays with low wood and artefactual content occupying a north-west to south-east oriented palaeochannel which exhibited no unconformity with the underlying Phase III deposits (22447) and had been cut by later Phase V features. These deposits were excavated as a conflated unit (22445) and subdivided following detailed examination of the resulting sections. The interface (22446) survived as a north-west to south-east oriented slope dipping towards the north-east with an imperceptible break of slope to a near level base at c 2.85m OD (Figs 10c and 28). No part of the north-east side of the channel had survived Phase V erosion and channel migration. The basal fill (22474), a dark brown-grey, silty clay, contained dense bands of decayed plant macrofossils visible in section as fine laminations and was overlain by a clearly-defined, paler band of finely-laminated, silty clay (22473), a further dark, organic, silty clay (22472) and a mixed, mottled, sticky clay (22442) which merged with 22472. The surface of 22442, the uppermost surviving Phase IV layer, had been truncated by modern machining and all fills were truncated by the earliest Phase V palaeochannel cut encountered in this area (22444).

Only relatively small quantities of faunal material (eight pieces of bone) and wood were recovered. The wood assemblage, in

Fig 28   Area D: Phase IV interface and laminated, organic fills in section. View to north-west. Scale 2m

particular, was unusually sparse and comprised two pieces of unworked hazel roundwood, two unworked stems of hawthorn, a tangential oak woodchip with partial sapwood and a north-west to south-east oriented oak with an eroded wedge point. The latter ran into the north-west facing section and was only partially lifted. The lifted section was very compressed and the dendrochronological sample was rejected for measurement (see Hillam p 189).

Area E: E.4.1

This group comprised laminated, organic, silty clays with low wood and artefactual content with charcoal visible in some deposits (see Fig 11c). The sediments sloped gently towards the east, apparently occupying a north-north-west to south-south-east oriented palaeo-channel with a base level of c 2.8m OD. These deposits were excavated as a conflated unit (22306) and subdivided following detailed examination of the resulting sections. The basal deposit (22382) darkened with depth but contained little in the matrix of slightly-silty clay except for manganese staining, and merged with overlying, silty clay (22378) with occasional roundwood fragments and charcoal flecks which to the west merged with slightly-silty clays (22387/22388) subject to iron staining. 22378 was overlain by a thick band of very organic, dark grey/brown, silty clay (22377) rich in plant macrofossils, which was in turn overlain by a thin clay lamination with clear, distinct boundaries (22389) and a laminated, heavily-organic layer (22384) of very silty clay, rich in plant macrofossils which underlay a further lamina of blue clay with distinct mottles of silty clay and rare charcoal flecks (22381). These deposits were capped by a highly organic, mixed layer of silty clay (22383) with abundant plant macrofossils, common

manganese and iron staining and generally diffuse boundaries especially with overlying 22372.

No artefacts or substantial pieces of wood were recovered from the whole of this group.

Phase V

This phase was characterised by fills that are markedly less organic than in the preceding phase, and by clear unconformities suggesting a period of more active downcutting. The channel continued to migrate slightly towards the north and east. Particularly in areas D and E, where channel profiles were examined in most detail, the channel appeared to re-cut its course repeatedly producing a more steep-sided and round-bottomed profile than previously encountered. This process was less clear in Area A, where the deep south-west extension was not well aligned with the turning course of the channel, and in Area B where there appeared to have both been some confusion as to the stratigraphic sequence during excavation, and more substantial truncation by Phase VI than seen elsewhere. Artefact densities were higher than in Phase IV but considerably lower than those associated with Phases VI and VII.

The channel environment continued to be largely freshwater. There are occasional indicators which point to estuarine conditions further downstream but

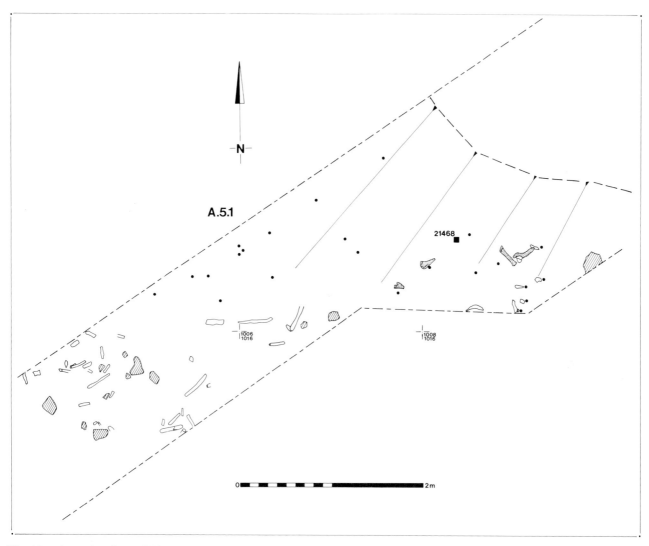

Fig 29   Area A: plan of Phase V palaeochannel group. The eastern concentration of bone probably derived from a single bovine

the site itself was probably generally above the high water mark. Although the extent of woodland beyond the floodplain seems to have remained much the same as in Phase IV there appears to be a brief expansion in alder woods, perhaps reflecting a rising water table and an increase in wetland habitats. Agricultural activity in the immediate area of the site was dominated by pastoralism but there is evidence for cultivation on higher ground. The faunal record suggests that sheep were more prolific than cattle.

Area A

A.5.1

The Phase V interface 22510 was clearly defined in the south west extension, cutting the underlying Phase IV deposits (see Fig 10a), with a base height of *c* 2.6m OD. As in earlier phases, the channel appears to be turning from a west–east orientation towards the south-east, although the oblique angle of the channel in relation to the trench sections and disturbance (probably modern) precluded detailed assessment of the channel development. The fills here, assigned unit number 22504, consisted predominantly of

bluish-grey clays with thin, organic laminae, some containing abundant mollusca. As the channel infilled, there was a tendency for the deposit to become slightly more organic towards the north and east, where it is equated with olive-grey, laminated, silty clay 22168 and was overlain to the east, within the diamond-shaped trench, by a laminated, olive-grey clay 22230, dark grey clay 22184 and a more organic, dark grey, silty clay 22211 rich in mollusca and plant macrofossils. The boundary between 22230 and underlying Phase I sediment 22213 was diffuse and a number of artefacts appear to have 'sunk' into the Phase I sediment when it was exposed in the riverbed. No erosive interface was noted between the later, more organic fills and the earlier unit, 22504. In comparison with contemporary channel profiles further downstream, the channel appears here to be migrating more to the north and east rather than downcutting.

Artefactual material from the contexts of this group was fairly restricted spatially, and was concentrated in later deposits (Fig 29). A small assemblage of wood (32 pieces) from 22504 was dominated by hazel (70%) with ash, alder, hawthorn, blackthorn, oak and willow/poplar also present. A single sherd (21468) was also recovered. Twenty-four pieces of bone were derived from contexts 22230 and 22213, and a further 19 pieces from 22111. Fourteen of the latter were thought during excavation to derive from a single individual. Analysis indicates these are large cattle bones comprising fore-limbs from the same animal and hind-limbs and pelvis fragments, probably from the same individual. Many

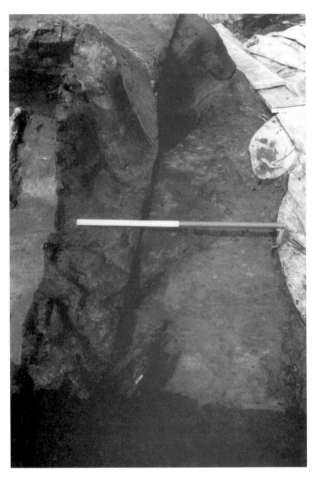

*Fig 30   Area B/C: Phase V interface 22557
following excavation of fill 22556 during
stratigraphic excavation of the baulk between areas
B and C. Scale 1m*

of the bones show clear evidence of breakage for marrow removal
and one piece exhibits a chopping mark and slight evidence of
burning. It is clear, therefore, that the group represents discarded
food refuse, probably of a single bovine.

Area B

The stratigraphic situation was particularly complex in the north
part of this area where the Phase VI channel appears to have
truncated Phase V deposits more extensively than elsewhere.
Context records for this group, excavated in 1990, are somewhat
contradictory and do not appear to accord with the stratigraphic
sequence visible in section. In the north-facing section (see Fig
11b), the Phase V channel was quite clear and was excavated
during removal of the temporary baulk between areas B and C
(Fig 30). Here, the channel survived as a clearly defined erosive
interface 22557 with an irregular concave slope with a gradual
change of slope to a near-flat base at c 3.05m OD. Its fill, a mixed
bluish grey clay 22556 was clearly distinguishable from the
underlying Phase IV sediment.

Area C

This palaeochannel group was totally excavated, apparently
rapidly, in 1990 and the only record survives in the west-facing
section (Fig 11a), where it was recorded as a grey/greenish clay
with organic bands (328) occupying a well-defined interface (327)
with a base height of c 3.00m OD. No artefactual material was
securely associated with these deposits.

Area D

Five palaeochannel cuts with associated fills, oriented north-west
to south-east, were recorded in this phase. Generally the south-
west slope survives but the north-east edge had been eroded by
later channel migration and recutting, with a trend for migration
towards the north-east (Fig 31 and see Fig 10c).

D.5.1

The stratigraphically earliest and most south-westerly channel of
this phase (22444) was clearly defined where it cut the organic
fills of the Phase IV palaeochannel fills. From the 'surface' where
it had been truncated by machining, the north-west to south-
east oriented interface sloped concavely to the north-east with
an irregular and pitted appearance to a sharp break of slope
from which the base gently slopes down to the north-east where
it had been truncated by later Phase V channel action. The basal
fill (22471), a pale grey, silty clay with darker, more organic
mottling, was notable for the abundance of mollusca. It merges
with the overlying grey, slightly silty clay (22467) which
contains a lens with abundant mollusca. A small spread of hazel
and blackthorn roundwood and four pieces of bone were
recovered.

D.5.2

The subsequent interface (22466), also north-west to south-east
oriented, comprises a poorly defined slope, with no unconformity
between its upper fills and those of the earlier cut 22444, with a
gradual change of slope to a rounded base, which cut Phase I
deposits at c 2.72m OD. The slope on the north-east side had
almost completely been eroded by later channel action. The basal
fill (22470), a bluish clay with darker, organic laminae, contains
a scatter of fourteen fragments of bone and interdigitates with the
upper fill (22465) which comprised a slightly silty, clean, blue-grey
clay with mottles and laminae of grey-brown, silty clay rich in
plant macrofossils.

D.5.3

The third identified channel (22464) was again oriented north-
west to south-east with the south-west edge surviving as a convex
slope with a gradual change of slope to a near level base at c 2.81m
OD. The north-east edge did not survive. The basal fill (22468),
a mixed grey, silty clay with mottles of greenish silty clay with
commonly occurring mollusca and dark grey, silty clay with
abundant mollusca and common plant-macrofossils, underlies a
blue-grey clay with silty laminae (22463). A scatter of generally
subangular stone, ten fragments of roundwood (including alder,
hazel, dogwood, ash and blackthorn), and nine pieces of bone were
recovered.

D.5.4

Little of the fourth north-west to south-east oriented channel
interface (22461) of this phase survived: just the concave south-
west slope and part of the concave base at c 2.90m OD. The greater

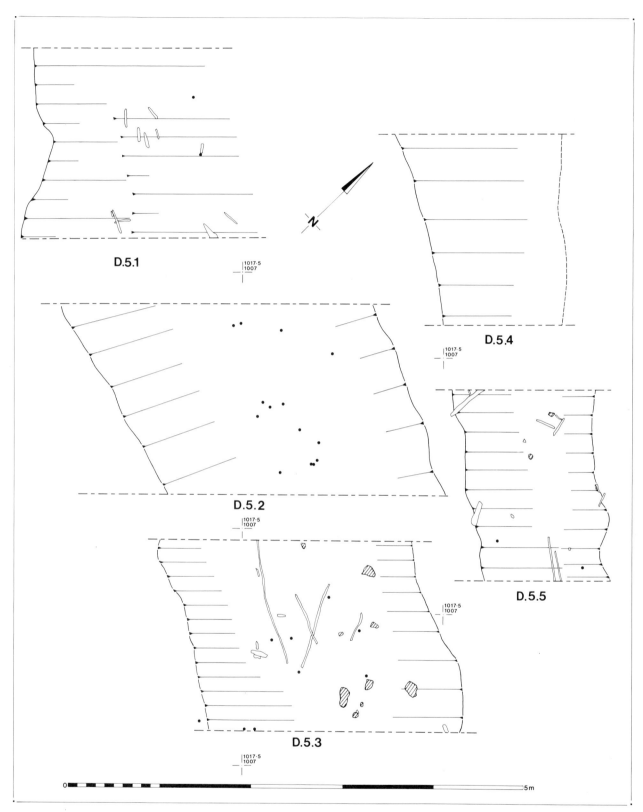

D.5.1

D.5.4

D.5.2

D.5.5

D.5.3

Fig 31   Area D: plan of Phase V palaeochannel groups

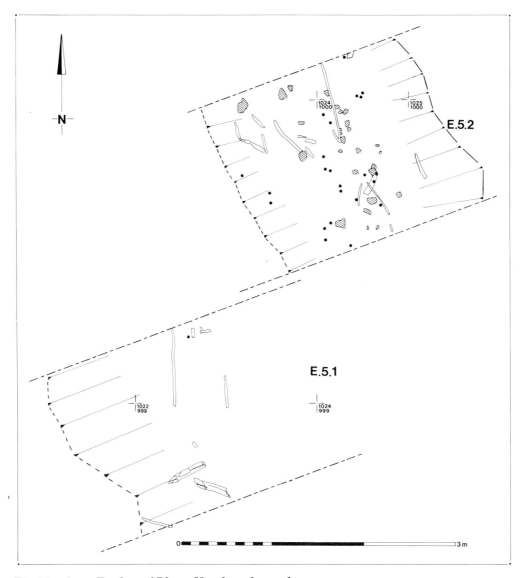

Fig 32   Area E: plan of Phase V palaeochannel groups

part of its base and all of the north-east side have been eroded along with the grey, silty clay fill (22462). No artefactual material was recovered.

D.5.5

The final channel group assigned to this phase was not typical, as the channel (22458), with a steeply-sloping, concave south-west side and concave base at 2.90–2.95m OD, contains a highly-mottled, dark grey-brown, silty clay rich in plant macrofossils (22457) more reminiscent of the fills usually associated with Phase VI. The wood assemblage comprises six hazel roundwood stems, a field maple woodchip, an oak heartwood woodchip, and two oak roundwood stems, one with an eroded chisel point. Two fragments of bone were recovered.

Area E

Phase V is characterised in this area by a succession of palaeochannel cuts suggesting channel migration towards the east through time. The channel profiles were often largely truncated on their eastern sides. Basal fills were usually relatively inorganic and contained artefactual material.

Two contexts (22372 and 22385) cannot be confidently ascribed to either Phase IV or V and are notable for their very diffuse and disturbed boundaries. 22372, a very organic clay, is reminiscent of the underlying organic, silty clay 22383 but has a more swirled, marbled appearance and, like the overlying, less organic 22385, was heavily stained.

E.5.1

The earliest channel cut from this phase (22346/22371) clearly truncated the organic Phase IV deposits on its right (ie west-south-west) slope (Fig 32). The opposite slope did not survive, having been cut by the subsequent channel (22350/22352/22354). The basal fill, a thin lamination of clean, grey clay, rich in plant macrofossils 22370, underlay a laminated, slightly silty clay 22353 and pale grey clay 22345 with occasional bands of organic, silty clay 22373.

The wood assemblage from this group comprised five pieces of hazel roundwood, a piece of bark and a piece of blackthorn roundwood. Three of the hazel stems had pencil points. The number of facets on the two larger pieces argues for their possible use in a structural context rather than being the result of clearance or other non-functional working (see Brunning and O'Sullivan p 167). They did not appear to be *in situ*. A single bone fragment was also recovered.

E.5.2

The subsequent channel (22350/22352/22354) survived as an irregular, north-north-west to south-south-east oriented feature with a rounded base at *c* 2.8m OD (see Fig 32). The basal fill (22358/22360), a grey clay was very rich in mollusca but artefactual material was concentrated in the overlying fills 22357 and 22348. The lower fill 22357, a mixed brownish-grey clay, later subdivided by detailed examination of the sections into a number of contexts (22364/22365/22366/22399), contained subangular stone, seven pieces of wood (including a split and charred piece of blackthorn, a split piece of hawthorn and four pieces of hazel roundwood, one with poorly preserved cut marks), eleven pieces of bone and a single flint flake (21419). The upper fill (22348), a silty clay with abundant charcoal and other plant macrofossils, contained eight pieces of wood including hazel, blackthorn and oak roundwood and an unidentified half split stem with a chisel point and twelve fragments of bone.

E.5.3 (not illustrated)

A poorly defined interface (22328) may have been a palaeochannel cut although there is no clear unconformity between 22348, which it may have cut, and its 'fills' (22312, 22329, 22332) which were silty, grey clays with thin, organic laminations containing charcoal flecks and dense plant macrofossils and mollusca. No artefactual material was recovered from this feature.

Phase VI and VI/VII

Phase VI saw a radical change in contemporary palaeochannel size and profile to a flat-bottomed broad cross-section with the riverbed at *c* 3.0–3.1m OD. The density of artefactual material within the channel was matched only by some of the more concentrated spreads of material encountered in Phase III. A unique characteristic of this phase was the quantity of stone which had been dumped into the channel. Freshwater conditions appear to have been maintained from the previous phase and, in response to a higher water table, there seems to have been a further expansion in alder, perhaps nearer to the site. However this was short-lived before there was a marked decline in alder. Although initially there seems to be a reduction in pasture this could be a filtering effect of local alder woods, and after a relatively short period there is strong evidence for grassland communities. An increase in buck's horn plantain, a plant of coastal habitats, as well as ribwort plantain, suggests an increasing maritime influence. Slightly later the diatoms also indicate an increasing brackish/marine influence, although within a predominantly freshwater environment, and that once again the site suffered periodic tidal inundation.

The faunal record from this phase and Phase VII reflects not only the domesticates, with sheep being of major significance, but also the wild birds which would have favoured these riverine and estuarine habitats. Similarly, the conditions would have been suitable for beaver, which was also present.

Area A

A.6.1

This and later phases were more extensively excavated in this area than the preceding palaeochannel groups, which were only encountered in more restricted, deeper cuttings. Much was excavated unstratigraphically in 1990 or before and cannot therefore be assigned to specific contexts, although broader phasing and association with general stratigraphic units has proved possible. The sloping sides of palaeochannels were not generally encountered: the channel at this time is seen as a broad feature (see Area E below) oriented approximately west-north-west to east-south-east. The channel interface (173/22513/22546) was approximately level at *c* 3.0–3.2m OD with the exception of a partially excavated north–south oriented shallow depression (Fig 33). This is not seen as a separate channel but rather a result of two main factors: partial erosion of less consolidated underlying Phase V deposits and artificial constriction of the channel flow by the construction of structure 9014 to the east. West of this depression, whilst similar stratigraphy was observed, the density of cultural material dropped off significantly. Although this was in part due to localised truncation by modern machining, there was a clear reduction in the occurrence of all types of material indicative of concentrated dumping/deposition in the eastern half of the area.

Basal fills (170/9016/9017/9045/9051/9052/22004/22066/22187/22191/22194) were characterised by dark grey colour, silty clay-clayey silt particle size with thin lenses of fine sand, high organic and mollusc content and occasional laminae of relatively clean paler grey silty clay. Cultural material was concentrated in these sediments. Overlying fills (9013/9015/9022/9050) were less organic, generally lacked sand lenses, contained less dense artefact spreads, and either interdigitated with or were partially truncated by 9025/9027/9042/9043, slightly organic grey silty clays concentrated in the north–south depression or to the west.

Both within this north–south depression and to the east there was a dense concentration of subangular stone generally at 3.0–3.2m OD, much appearing to predate deposition of wooden elements, although it should be stressed that only some of this stone spread was totally excavated (Fig 33). In some instances, small concentrations of stone appear to have been deposited as a unit, perhaps representing a single load. This stone was predominantly Triassic conglomerates and sandstones, and Carboniferous limestones, some of the latter showing signs of heat damage. Outcrops of similar geology occur at the edges of the floodplain within a few hundred metres of the site (Howe p 246).

Structure 9014

In the eastern concentration of stone, an irregular line of at least fourteen uprights ran approximately north-north-east to south-south-east, perpendicular to the channel, from the north-east corner of the excavated area (Figs 33 and 34). The uprights, driven into the underlying Phase I deposits and surviving to heights of 3.7–3.9m OD, were predominantly hazel in the round, although two more substantial piles were oak (one tangentially split) and one was alder

Fig 34   Area A: structure 9014 during excavation. View to south. Scale 1m

(Fig 35). Where driving depth was recorded, it suggests that the uprights could be contemporary with the basal deposits of stone. A tangential ash plank (197) with two mortise holes, the northernmost apparently pegged with a length of hazel roundwood (see Fig 34), may have formed an integral part of this structural group. Associated timber elements included a half split charred oak log (991), a radial split oak plank with a mortise (332) dated to 998/7 BC by dendrochronology, and a further split oak plank with a mortise (049).

Whilst, in common with the majority of wood assemblages from the site, the bulk of the wood from this palaeochannel group consists of immature roundwood there was a relatively high proportion of timber offcuts and woodworking debris. There was a high proportion of hazel and oak debris and relatively little ash debris which may point to in situ woodworking of the driven uprights. Hazel dominated the assemblage, with lesser quantities of oak, ash, alder, hawthorn and blackthorn. The nature of this assemblage is discussed in more detail by Brunning and O'Sullivan (p 171) but it is worth noting here that, even in a context where there can be little doubt that this was the result of intentional deposition, six pieces of roundwood, including a substantial piece (1014) exhibited beaver teeth marks. Their presence within this structural group suggests that even beaver-gnawed wood was being brought to the site by human agency rather than purely natural processes. Immature roundwood (135 and 157) provided radiocarbon dates of 2850 ± 60 BP (CAR-1216) and 2910 ± 70 BP (CAR-1217) respectively.

Wooden artefacts comprised an alder stave

(20074), an oak 'beater' (256), a possible oak cleat (8331), an oak 'beater' (8209) and an oak, sword-shaped object (8457) although the latter two have no spatial information recorded.

A substantial quantity of other artefactual material is associated with this structure including 439 bone fragments, one of which was an awl (21060). Fifteen flints, four sherds (5073, 5105, 5368 and 21774) and a possible ceramic weight (5004) can be associated confidently with this palaeochannel group. A small scrap of leather (5001), the only piece found on the site, was also recovered. A flint knife (21541) was found during excavation of a slot between Area B and the south-east corner of Area A to test correlations.

Function Dendrochronological and stratigraphic data indicate that this structure predated the bridge 22441 (see D.7.1, p 49). The surviving heights of the uprights imply that they would still have been present and visible at the time of 22441's construction. There was no evidence to suggest the presence of the hurdle panels which one might expect in a cross-channel fish weir. Nonetheless, the line of uprights could have held nets: the find of a ceramic weight (5004) provides very limited support for this interpretation. Alternatively, the intention may have been to consolidate the riverbed to facilitate fording and the grounding of boats. In this model, the uprights may have functioned as markers indicating the location of the ford or as mooring posts for small vessels. The total artefactual assemblage suggests that the structure was maintained by dumping food and wood waste including scrub clearance, and

Fig 35   Area A: uprights 013 and 014, structure 9014, driven into underlying Phase I deposits. Scale 1m

Fig 36   Area A: upright 8151: only the Phase I and earliest Phase VI deposits show disturbance by the pile's insertion. The dark, later Phase VI deposits are undisturbed. View to north. Scale 1m

additional stone. Such maintenance may have continued in Phase VII (see A.7.1).

It should be stressed that none of these functions are mutually exclusive. Furthermore, less prosaic implications need some consideration. The symbolism of divisions/demarcations in Bronze Age landscapes may be pertinent here, especially against a background of rising sea level and water tables and possible concomitant restriction of grazing resources out on the coastal wetlands mirroring proposed models for Flag Fen (Pryor 1992, 521).

A.6/7.1

West of the palaeochannel group A.6.1 the stratigraphy was similar, with the channel interface (175/22513/22546) at c 2.95–3.1m OD and basal fills (9032/22541–22544/22547) comprising highly organic dark grey brown silty clays often with fine sand lenses. Overlying fills (9031/9040/9043/22503) were slightly less organic, greenish-grey, silty clays, with lower densities of artefactual material. In the extreme north-west corner of the area a lone pile (8151) had disturbed the basal fill 22544 but not the overlying deposits 22543 and 22542, suggesting that it may have been driven at an early stage in the siltation of the channel (Fig 36). Deposit

22542, restricted to the north-west quadrant, was particularly abundant in charcoal of which a representative sample has been identified (Johnson p 161). The species proportions are broadly comparable with those from contemporary waterlogged assemblages. The very low density of material in the south-west quadrant of this area may be a function of modern disturbance, as levels taken at the beginning of excavations in 1988 indicate that this area had been truncated down to c 3.2m OD, presumably by modern machining. Material density, particularly of stone and bone (50 pieces) was significantly lower throughout the west half of the area. Wood distribution was also sparser with approximately 420 pieces being recovered in the west. A substantial proportion of these (30%) was either unidentifiable or not sampled. The remainder was dominated by hazel (60%) of which 12% had been clearly cut. Less prolific species include oak (10%), blackthorn (8%), ash (6%) and hawthorn (4%) with rare or single occurrences of elm, willow, honeysuckle, wild rose, ivy and holly. Pieces of particular interest included a fragment of a possible boat plank (8143) (see McGrail p 216), a very substantial tangential ash plank (1104) and a half-split, oak plank with two mortises (1066). A single flint (5003), an ogival leaf arrowhead, was recovered near the north section from basal sediment.

Area B

B.6/7.1

The stratigraphic complications pertaining to Phase V in this area also apply to some extent to Phases VI and VI/VII. The morphology of the Phase VI channel interface was not recorded in detail in 1990 and it is possible that at least some of the material described below derived from Phase V deposits. Later material was also difficult to separate from that associated with Phase VII structure 473 (see B.7.1 and Fig 43). It is clear that the channel extended from Area A, running across Area B towards the east-south-east and was clearly defined in the west-facing section (see Fig 11a). For the purposes of analysis and description, material falling outside the boundary defined for structure 473 on Fig 43 is associated with the Phase VI channel. Contemporary palaeochannel fills were described as dark grey, organic, silty clays with occasional lenses of pale bluish-grey clay. Relatively little stone was recovered from the base of the channel in contrast to Area A.

The wood assemblage was sparse in comparison with contemporary assemblages from areas A and D. A total of 126 pieces are assigned to this palaeochannel group, and 44 of these are unidentified. The remainder was dominated by hazel roundwood (66%) of which 14 pieces had cut ends, with less frequent occurrences of blackthorn, ash, alder and hawthorn roundwood. Single examples of spindle, yew, and willow were also recovered. Five relatively immature hazel piles had been driven into underlying Phase I deposits but formed no clear pattern. They may be a continuation of the line of piles forming part of structure 9014 (A.6.1) or relate to structure 473 (B.7.1). All had been truncated by modern machining with the exception of the northernmost of the piles (128/008) which lay within the slope of the modern lake development and survived to a height of 4.08m OD.

A single wooden artefact, a finely worked hooked piece of cherry (1161) was recovered along with 156 pieces of bone (including a finely worked point 5135), 12 sherds of pottery (5039, 5040, 5050, 5051, 5052, 5069, 5071, 5122, 5130, 5250, and 5292) and six pieces of flint (5070, 5116, 12745, 12766, 12767 and 12904).

Area D

D.6.1

An approximately north-west to south-east oriented channel (22456), some 2.8m wide with a base height of c 2.86m OD, had only partially survived as a concave-sided and smooth-based feature with gently-sloping, lower sides (Fig 37). The basal fill (22455), 10–40mm in depth comprised patches of very fine sand at the interface, overlain by an organic rich, greenish-brown, silty clay with commonly occurring mollusca and plant-macrofossils. This was overlain by a dark greenish-brown, silty clay (22453). again rich in mollusca and plant-macrofossils, which survived to a maximum depth of 120mm. Its upper boundary, at the interface 22448, with 22443 was clearly defined.

The channel contained a scatter of small to large subangular stone, 64 pieces of bone, four flints (21578, 21579, 21610, 21621), a single sherd (21607), and 43 pieces of wood. The wood assemblage was dominated by hazel (74%), with small quantities of oak, hawthorn, blackthorn and elder present. Worked material comprised five hazel roundwood stems with worked points or side-branches removed in antiquity, an elder roundwood stem with side-branches removed and an eroded chisel point, and a tangential, oak woodchip. A single piece of hazel roundwood exhibited gnaw-marks on two side-branches, consistent with beaver activity. A radiocarbon date of 2810 ± 70 BP(CAR-1410) was derived from one of the worked hazel roundwood stems (25377).

D.6.2

The above channel fill had been truncated by a more substantial feature (22448), apparently a north-west to south-east oriented palaeochannel extending beyond the northern limit of excavation, with a poorly defined south-west edge adjacent to 22457/22458 and to the upper fills of earlier Phase V channels (Fig 38 and see Fig 10c). The irregular, slightly-concave base extended for c 5.8m from the north-east end of the trench towards the south-west, cut Phase I clays 22450 and 22469, the earlier Phase VI channel 22456 and its fills, and possibly Phase V fill 22457.

The basal fill (22443), comprised laminations of very organic brown clay with fine sand lenses at the base overlain by laminae of relatively-inorganic, blue clay. These were overlain by further organic, silty clay with fine sand lenses. This deposit merged indistinctly into the overlying sediments (22440, 22439 and 22438) and was rich in plant-macrofossils, charcoal and mollusca.

A scatter of subangular stone, bone (60 pieces), a single flint (21541), and 114 pieces of wood occupied the base of the channel. Some of the stone and bone had apparently sunk into the riverbed on deposition. This was most clearly demonstrated where the channel had cut into the Phase I clay 22450. Much of the stone and seven pieces of bone were partially within 22450 but have been associated with this phase. The wood assemblage was dominated by hazel (56%) with lesser quantities, in diminishing order, of oak, ash, blackthorn (5–10%), alder, hawthorn, dogwood, spindle, willow/poplar, elder and bark. Worked material made up approximately 20% of the assemblage and included cut roundwood of hazel, ash, alder, spindle, hawthorn, willow and oak; and oak, ash and alder woodchips. An alder roundwood stem (25176) had four side-branches removed and a chisel point which had been damaged during driving when it hit a stone. In addition to the simple chisel-cut ends seen on much of the small roundwood, indications of felling were apparent on larger pieces. A substantial straight-grained stem of spindle exhibited possible felling marks forming a pencil point with large flat facets (25120). Hawthorn stem (25115) had possible felling marks made with a large, flat axe with a facet width of 46mm. The most substantial piece of wood (25130), the bole of a straight-grained 57-year-old oak tree partially exposed in the trench, had a chisel cut at its south-west end and one face had been split away tangentially. It is possible that the cut end records the original felling of the tree and that one side had been split away to produce a tangential plank before the remains of the bole had been placed in the river. From a modern perspective this seems like profligate waste of good timber but its function within the river is unclear especially as it was only partially excavated.

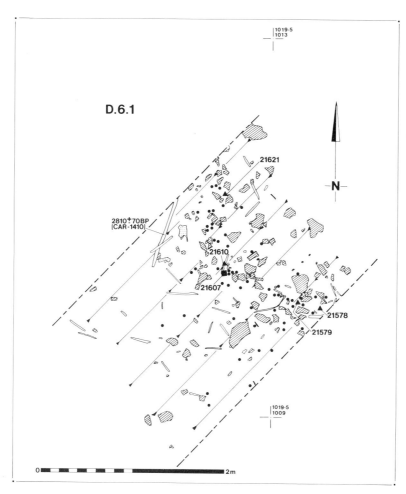

D.6.1

2810⁺70BP
[CAR-1410]

21621

21610

21607

21578

21579

1019·5
1013

1019·5
1009

-N-

0   2m

Fig 37   Area D: plan of early Phase VI palaeochannel group D.6.1

D.6/7

The upper fills of the main channel were relatively poorly defined, merging into one another with indistinct boundaries. For logistical reasons, fills to the east of the eastern line of uprights of structure 22441 (see p 49) were excavated in isolation and separately numbered as 22437 to 22439. These were correlated with 22433 and 22440 during removal of the temporary baulk which had protected these uprights from desiccation.

The sediments 22438–22440 comprised mixed silty clays with common plant macrofossils and mollusca with occasional lenses of highly organic silty clay and less common lenses of clean, blue-grey clay. Artefactual material was distributed as a sparse scatter of wood (40 pieces) and bone (8 pieces). Hazel dominated (67%) with small quantities of alder, dogwood, spindle, ash, hawthorn, oak and lime occurring. Worked material included two hazel stems with chisel points, three pieces of axed oak debris and a very poorly preserved piece of oak which may have been part of a handle (25047).

This material was overlain by a relatively inorganic, mixed deposit of pale- to mid-grey clay with silty clay lenses richer in plant macrofossils and mollusca (22433/22437). Much of it had been truncated by modern machining at c 3.5m OD although it survived at the north-east end of the trench within the slope of the modern lake, where it was overlain by 22436. Excluding a concentration of material associated with structure 22441 (see p 54), the artefactual material (64 pieces of wood and one bone) was thinly spread over c 8m of the north-east end of the trench. Hazel dominated the wood assemblage (55%) with lesser proportions of ash, oak, alder, hawthorn, and dogwood occurring along

with single or rare occurrences of elm and field maple. Clearly worked material included one cut hazel stem, seven hazel woodchips, two ash woodchips and single woodchips of oak, lime and dogwood. A gently-curving roundwood stem of dogwood (24878), 1.44m long, had been stripped of its bark and exhibited narrow, thin flat facets over the whole of its surface. It may have been a tool handle or staff.

Area E

E.6.1

The channel interface (22307) was the broadest encountered in this area with a surviving width of c 6.5m (Fig 39). Its eastern edge had been partially truncated by the Phase VII channel 22319, although there were some indications of a slope at this end. This suggests that only the very extreme edge of this channel and its fills had been removed by later river action, especially as no channel deposits occurred to the east of 22319. The channel base was irregular but relatively flat at 3.1–3.2m OD, and was covered by a dense spread of wood, stone and bone. The interface was mixed and basal artefacts were assigned to context 22326, a mixture of the dark grey, organic, silty clay 22325 and the underlying pre-channel clay 22309. Wood and stone, from both 22325 and 22326, were defined as context 22330. A patchy deposit, comprising pure coarse sand with occasional charcoal flecks and mollusca (22351), was found at this interface, often concentrated around wood or stone.

The wood assemblage (303 total) was dominated by hazel

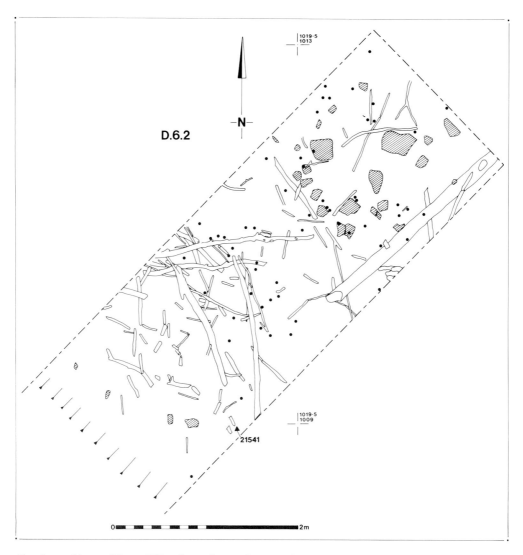

Fig 38   Area D: plan of later Phase VI palaeochannel group D.6.2

roundwood (61%) with significant proportions of alder, blackthorn, oak, hawthorn and dogwood and rare occurrences of spindle, ash, privet, ivy, elder, lime and mistletoe. Ten percent of the assemblage showed clear evidence of woodworking including cut or pointed roundwood of hazel, hawthorn, and alder; a single oak stake and oak, ash, alder and hazel woodworking debris. A further 10% exhibited more equivocal features suggestive of working. Three hazel stems exhibited the distinctive marks caused by beavers. Two of these (24239, 24248) may originally have formed a single stem. An immature roundwood stem gave a radiocarbon determination of 3060 ± 70 BP (CAR-1319).

Artefactual material from this horizon comprised 63 pieces of bone, two flint flakes (21405 and 21415) and a decorated coil of tin (21289, see Northover p 250).

In the western half of the channel, the basal group was overlain by a dark olive grey, laminated, silty clay (22314) with few charcoal flecks, plant macrofossils and mollusca. The wood assemblage (48 pieces) was less dense than the basal spread and again dominated by hazel (62.5%) with the remainder comprising oak, blackthorn, alder, ash and elder. Twelve pieces exhibited clear indications of woodworking including a large oak timber (20846) which may have acted as a timber upright in a standing building (Fig 40, also see Fig 108 and Brunning and O'Sullivan p 184); a large piece of split, oak woodworking debris (24092); hazel, oak, ash, and alder woodchips and hazel stems with cut points; and a radially split and axed piece of alder which had been

charred before deposition but after working. Thirteen pieces of bone were recovered from this horizon.

E.6/7.1

The upper fills of this channel (22302/22327) comprised olive-grey, silty clays with fine, organic laminations with some iron staining and relatively low concentrations of artefactual material. The deposits had been truncated by machine during the modern lake's construction. Of the 50 wood items recovered 56% were hazel. Lesser proportions of ash, bark, blackthorn and alder were recovered along with single items of hawthorn, oak and possible willow/poplar. Worked material included two ash woodchips, a large oak split offcut, a trimmed and chisel-cut hazel stem, a charred piece of bark and a split and chisel-cut piece of alder.

A single bone was recovered from this group.

Area F

F.6/7.1

This area was partially excavated during 1988 and 1989 as part of the evaluation. Completion of excavation within this area did

E.6.1

N

1028
1002

21405

21289

21415

3060±70BP
[CAR-1319]

20846

1025
1001

0 5m

Fig 39   Area E: plan of Phase VI palaeochannel group

Fig 40   Area E: timber 20846 in situ. View to south. Scale 100mm

not subsequently form part of any project design. A limited record was made of the observed stratigraphy and exposed wood lifted in September 1989 (Fig 41). The main features identified in the record were Phase I clay (179) cut by a broad channel (173) which contained a dense spread of subangular stone (178) overlain by organic, silty clays with frequent sand lenses (177). This was in turn overlain by organic, silty clays which closely paralleled those encountered in Area A. Further recording implies the presence of a subsequent channel cut, although its exact location was unclear. It is assumed that this refers to the area of higher finds recovery north-east of the stone strew (178). It seems most probable that this reflects the presence of a smaller channel and its fills, similar to those encountered in areas E and G which are assigned to Phase VII. No attempt was made here to subdivide this material. The retrieved wood assemblage (80 pieces) was relatively sparse and of this less than 70% has been identified. Seven of the 33 hazel stems exhibited cut ends. Other species present were ash, oak, hawthorn, field maple and willow. The most notable timber (7003) was a massive, split, oak plank with opposing notches. Forty-two pieces of bone were recovered including a lightly-polished smoother/polisher (12945) along with four flints including a scraper (12969, see Fig 156/3) and a retouched flake fragment, possibly the butt of a chisel arrowhead (12976, see Fig 156/8). During drainage of this area, a diminutive chape 12821 (see Northover p 252 and Fig 159) was recovered unstratified. It is reasonable to assume that it was derived from an exposed section and must therefore date to Phase VI or later.

Area G

G.6/7.1

During machine clearance of spoil east of Area F in 1990, a group of finds comprising two potsherds (5407 and 5409), a birch ladle (5406), and three pieces of bone were recovered. This led to speculation that a midden might exist in the locality which might yield more concentrated artefact distributions than had previously been encountered. The 1991 project design included excavation of

Area G, a 3m-square trench, just south-east of the find spot. In the event, artefact concentrations were not unusually high, and machine truncation had left only basal fills of two poorly separated palaeochannel groups (see Fig 57). During excavation, no clear separation of the two groups could be made, although differences in fills could be observed, until detailed examination of the fully exposed sections was possible. The latter of the two groups is assigned to Phase VII (see G.7.1).

The earlier of the two groups, confined to the western extreme of the area, comprised a well-defined channel base (22270) sloping down to the west, cutting into underlying Phase I deposits (see Fig 13). At and below this interface at *c* 3.3m OD, a concentration of small–medium subangular stone (22275) is reminiscent of the density of stone encountered at the base Phase VI channels to the north-west. The basal fill, a dark olive-grey, silty clay (22266) was overlain by an olive-grey, silty clay (22256). Boundaries with the subsequent group are unclear.

Twenty-three pieces of wood (hazel, blackthorn and hawthorn roundwood and ash and oak woodworking debris) at the west edge of the area are assigned to this group. Other artefactual material comprised four bones and single pot sherd (21156). One of the eleven hazel roundwood stems gave a radiocarbon determination of 2930 ± 70 BP (CAR-1315).

Phase VII

Silting of parts of the main channel in the west continued during this phase although machine truncation may have removed much of this horizon in the base of the lake. A rough trackway and a bridge were constructed, and downstream a smaller channel was present. Although the environment of the channel was essentially freshwater, the trend towards estuarine conditions persisted. Away from the channel, grassland communities and pastoralism continued to dominate but there is also some evidence for woodland regeneration. Beech occurs for the first time in the pollen record.

Area A

A.7.1

No clear evidence for renewed downcutting or channel migration was recorded in this area in the deposits between *c* 3.5 and 3.7m OD. The sediments here had diffuse boundaries and generally comprised slightly-organic, grey, silty clays with occasional laminae (9010/9011/9013/9034). Artefactual material was sparse and concentrated in the east half of the area (Fig 42). This distribution may in part be a function of more intrusive machining in the west half of the area. Alternatively, it may reflect continuing dumping in the vicinity of structure 9014. This group comprised a small quantity of small–medium subangular stone, 47 pieces of wood, 28 bone fragments and a small flint spall (12823). The wood assemblage was dominated by hazel roundwood and ash woodworking debris and offcuts with lesser quantities of alder, oak and lime. Two mortised planks, both in poor condition were recovered. The larger plank (128:036) is a trimmed tangential split oak with a single mortise whilst the other (128:038.1) is a half split hazel with two mortises, one only partially present. Neither was pegged so they may be discards following damage in antiquity or possibly remnants of the superstructure of 22441 (see D.7.1 below). A fragment of an alder bowl (128:009) was recovered and a radiocarbon determination of 2750 ± 60 BP (CAR-1215) derived from the underlying piece of roundwood. An ash woodchip (128:092) at 3.48+m OD gave a tree-ring date of 991+ BC.

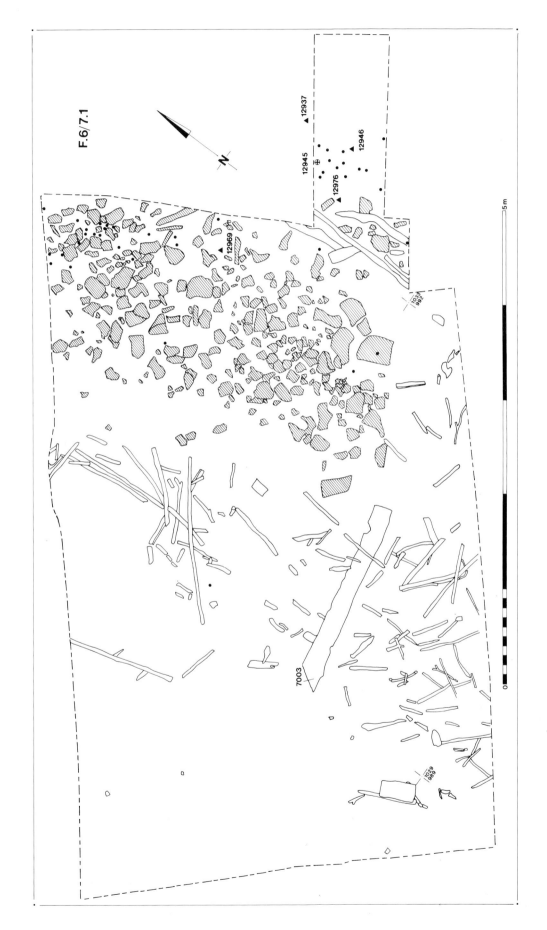

F.6/7.1

12937

12945

12946

12976

12969

7003

1039
1369

1034
902

5 m

Fig 41   Area F: plan of Phase VI/VII palaeochannel group. The concentration of finds in the eastern extension may reflect the location of a later, Phase VII, channel

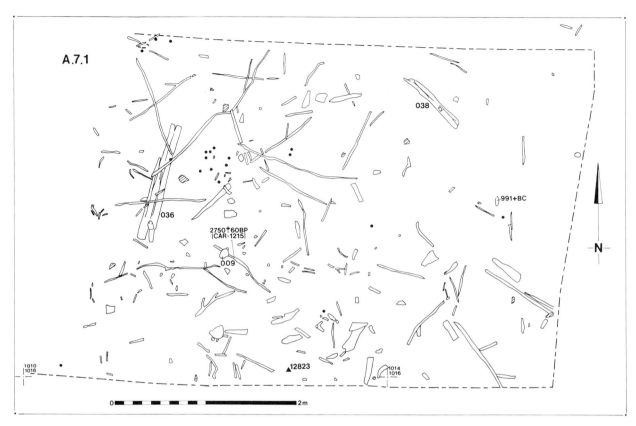

Fig 42   Area A: plan of Phase VII palaeochannel group in the eastern half of the area

Area B

Structure 473 (B.7.1)

An irregular linear spread of driven and dumped wood, a fragmentary hurdle, stone slabs and bone waste survived just below the level of machine truncation at *c* 3.5m OD running west-east apparently initially near the right edge of the contemporary channel before turning slightly towards the north-east towards its centre (Fig 43). Partially overlain by a pale grey, silty clay (7070/22501) with a relatively low organic content, the laid material appears to have been placed following partial silting of the broad channel first encountered in Phase VI. A cluster of truncated uprights at the west end of this group included a field maple pile with a pencil point which appears to have been used as a chopping block prior to driving (see Brunning and O'Sullivan p 181 and Fig 103), an oak pile with pencil point and removed sapwood, dated by dendrochronology to 1023++ BC, and an apparently discarded field maple pencil point. In addition to a small number of immature roundwood stakes in this vicinity, a fragment of worked oak (477) interpreted as part of a sewn plank boat (see McGrail p 216) was also recovered. Four metres to the east, a fragmentary hazel hurdle (1401) had been overlain by a cluster of stone slabs (Fig 44). Although disturbed and partially desiccated, the weaving of rods around the sails was clear, adjacent to the stone

slabs. To the west, the relationship between the small roundwood and the larger north–south oriented elements is less clear. This may have been part of the hurdle or represent dumps of brushwood overlying bearers of more substantial roundwood. There is no definitive evidence for any pegging of this group but the high percentage of hazel (greater than 90%), and the concentrated age range (see Morgan p 197) imply careful selection, possibly of managed woodland, using more mature stemwood for bearers/sails and immature roundwood, generally 4–5 years old, for brushwood/rods. One of the bearers/sails, (735), has produced a radiocarbon date of 2710 ± 70 BP (CAR-1416). To the north, a 'sword-shaped' oak object (541) was recovered. Two stone slabs to the east may mark the line of this structure although distinguishing wood at the east end from Phase VI/VII material is problematic given poor stratigraphic and spatial separation. Hazel and oak uprights in the vicinity of these slabs may be associated but are described along with the rest of palaeochannel group B.6/7.1 (see p 42).

Of the 491 pieces of wood assigned by the excavator to this structural group, just over 50% were retained or sampled for identification. Consideration of the species make-up and technology therefore requires a degree of caution, although it is clear that the assemblage was dominated by immature hazel with oak and ash woodworking debris making up a substantial proportion of the remainder. If anything, the hazel roundwood is most likely to be

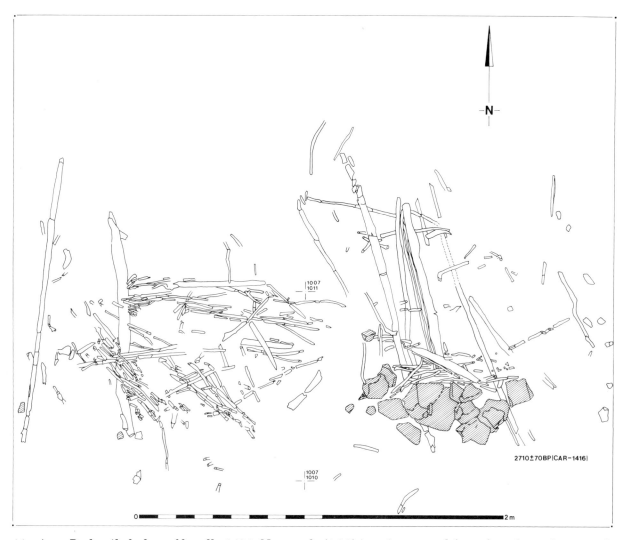

Fig 44   Area B: detailed plan of hurdle 1401. Note scale (1:20) is twice normal for palaeochannel group plans

under-represented. Minor species/genera making up less than 5% each of the identified material include blackthorn, hawthorn and dogwood roundwood and offcuts or woodchips of lime. The small alder assemblage (6%) was more mixed including roundwood, splitwood and debris. In addition there are single identifications of willow/poplar, yew and possible birch. The ash wood chips are of particular interest as they provide dendrochronological dates of 1022+ BC, 1006+ BC, 994+ BC and 991+ BC (Hillam below).

An alder/hazel peg (1136), and a bent stick or handle of hazel (1254.1) form part of the structure. A single wall sherd (5049) is confidently associated with this group as are a flint 'chunk' (12766) and an exhausted blade core (5059). Other artefacts which cannot be securely linked are considered above in Phase VI/VII. A polished cattle mandible, used as a smoother/rubber (5037) was also recovered.

The high proportion of woodworking waste, the spatial relationship between this group and structure 22441, and the close parallels in date, point to both functional and chronological links with 22441. It is tempting to see the group as a rough trackway made up in part from woodworking debris generated

by the preparation of the driven piles used in structure 22441, providing a temporary consolidation of the contemporary riverbed to facilitate access during construction. There are similarities between this group and the concentration of material around structure 22441 at a similar level of *c* 3.5m OD.

B.7.2

A thin scatter of wood was recovered from sediment between 3.6 and 4.0m OD in the north-east corner of the area where truncation by machining was not so severe. No detailed sediment description is available for this group and most of the thirteen pieces of wood were not studied in detail. Three pieces are identified as hazel, oak and ash.

Area D

Structure 22441 (D.7.1)

The recovery of part of an oak pile (7001) from this area in May 1988 by Bob Trett of Newport Museum

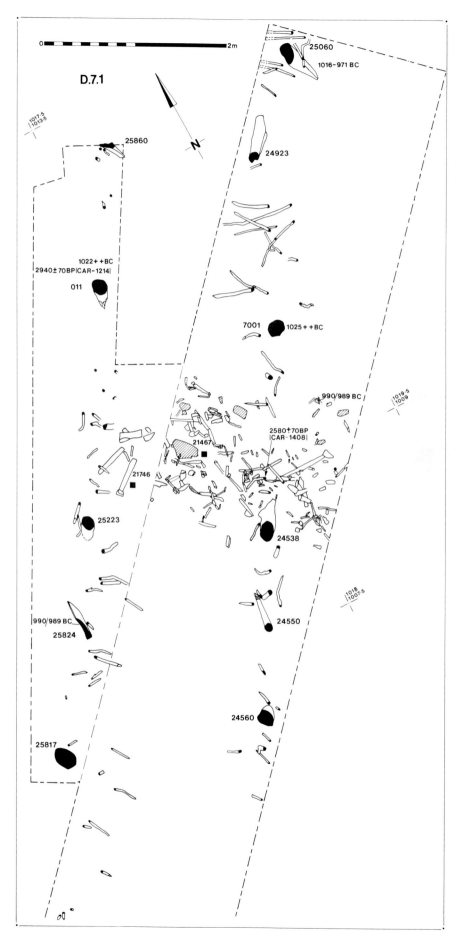

Fig 45   Area D: structure 22441 and its associated palaeochannel group

Fig 46   Structure 22441: the partially exposed
uprights of the western row

Fig 47   Structure 22441: the partially exposed
uprights of the eastern row. View to north-north-
east. Scales 1m

provided an early indication of the archaeological
potential of the site. A poorly preserved concentration of brushwood (006) exposed by machining in
the south edge of the lake, south of this pile, at
c 3.9m OD was briefly described in 1988 as a
discrete layer of laid brushwood, and located directly
south of this pile's position. An additional substantial
oak pile, exposed in the north slope of the lake (11)
was lifted during the evaluation and provided a
radiocarbon date of 2940 ± 70 BP (CAR-1214).
Together, this partial evidence suggested the presence of a substantial structure in the vicinity. One of
the major objectives of the 1992 season was to
identify and excavate any such structural remains in
this area.

Initial cleaning and removal of redeposited sediment revealed the presence of numerous roundwood
uprights running from the north corner of the area
towards the south-south-west, and a parallel line
some 2m to the west (Fig 45). Uprights were located

up to 9m from the northern limit of excavation. The
uprights in the easternmost line were not excavated
in phase but left in temporary baulks or on plinths of
sediment, until excavation of Phase V and VI
deposits had been completed (Fig 47). The uprights
of the westernmost line were partially exposed by
excavating an extension to the area down to c 3.4m
OD, sampling the less substantial uprights and
excavating localised trenches around the more substantial piles to permit their total removal (Fig 46).

In each line, the uprights consisted predominantly
of thin roundwood stakes 20–80mm in diameter,
usually of hazel, with more substantial oak or ash
piles at irregular intervals of c 2m. The eleven piles
appeared to be roughly paired and extended south of
the Phase VI interface, where they had been driven
into Phase IV and V sediments (Fig 48). These were
driven to variable depths in the range 2–3m OD
although the majority had base heights of 2.2–2.7m
OD. Pile 24923 (Fig 49) was one of the least deeply

Fig 48   Structure 22441: part of the western row, with uprights to the south (left side of picture) driven into Phase IV and V deposits. View to west. Scales 0.5m and 1m

Fig 49   Structure 22441: oak piles 24923 (left) and 25060 at the northern exposed end of the eastern row. The point of pile 24923 had encountered a stone during driving and was almost 0.6m above the base of its neighbouring pile. View to west. Scales 0.5m and 1m

driven with a base height of 2.88m OD. The point had come into contact with stone associated with basal fills of the Phase VI channel (see Fig 10c) and may have been particularly unstable as, in contrast to the other piles, it sloped markedly to the south. There is some later evidence for an attempt to remedy this structural weakness (see D.7.2) The thinner round-wood stakes tended to be less deeply driven, usually within the range 2.8–3m OD with occasional depths of c 2.5m OD. The top heights of most of the uprights is a function of their truncation by machine to c 3.6m OD, but the northernmost piles (eg 25060, see Fig 49) and reconstruction of pile 7001 (from the length recovered in 1988 and its point, excavated in 1992) show that uprights had survived to heights in excess of 4.2m OD. Even some of the stakes here survived to 3.8–3.9m OD. Many of these were very distorted, either through damage during driving or as a result of post-depositional compression, and also sloped by up to 30° from the vertical. Those in the east row tended to slope to the east whilst those in the west row, where totally exposed by excavation, often exhibited a slope to the west. This could reflect partial collapse of the structure prior to its alluviation, which must have occurred relatively rapidly to permit preservation of the stakes.

Characterisation of the wood making up the structure suggests careful selection and usage of woodland products (Morgan p 197, Brunning and O'Sullivan, p 174). The 90 stakes associated with the structure were consistently very fast-grown, and restricted in size and age range. Seventy-six (84%) were identified as hazel, six as ash, two as oak, four as willow and one as hawthorn. There does not appear to be any spatial patterning to stakes of the less common species. Frequently, these stakes had been driven 'cap down' with trimmed side-branches

Fig 50 Structure 22441: split ash upright 25824. The mortise close to its driven point serves no clear function in the structure as it was deeply buried in Phase I deposits. View to west. Scale 1m

clearly pointing downwards, possibly to reduce the rate of decay.

The piles were more mature and derived from either ash or oak trees. Those of the east line were exclusively oak in the round, whilst two of the five piles in the west line were ash. Two piles in the latter line (one each of oak and ash) were split. Comprehensive age information is not available as complete sapwood was not present on the majority. Pile 24550 was the most immature at twelve years old followed by the split pile 25860 at thirty-two years although the pith had been removed during tooling of the feather edge produced by splitting. The rest of the oak piles retain between 30 and 77 rings suggesting exploitation of trees aged approximately 50–150 years old. Both of the ash piles were winter felled although they were otherwise very different in character with one, 25223, an immature stem in the round, and the other, 25824, split from a mature tree of 177+ years .

Woodworking analysis indicates that most of the stakes were simply cut, often receiving no sharpening subsequent to the felling cuts. In contrast, the roundwood piles were finely-sharpened to pencil points. Given the excellent preservation of the thin stakes and bark edge on the ash and immature oak piles, the lack of sapwood on the more mature roundwood oak piles is unlikely to be the result of differential preservation. Either the sapwood was intentionally removed prior to use as a pile, or there had been some pre-use in circumstances that led to decay of most of the sapwood. The question of reuse is also pertinent to the split ash pile 25824 where an apparently afunctional mortise was located at the pointed end (Fig 50). Unless this perforation was designed to assist in man-handling the timber, then reuse seems the most probable explanation. However, the timber was in excellent condition with full bark surviving along its outer face suggesting that any pre-use would have been of limited duration.

The absolute dating evidence for the structure is summarised on Fig 45. In addition to the initial radiocarbon date from pile 011, a further date of 2580 ± 70 BP (CAR-1408) was obtained from one of the immature stakes (25033). Dendrochronology has produced a far better dating resolution from both ash and oak piles (Hillam, p 192). Although possibilities of reuse as mentioned above give cause for a degree of caution, none of the dates are inconsistent with construction in the first quarter of the 10th century BC.

The relative date (ie stratigraphic position) of the structure poses a potentially more intractable question: the problem of identifying the contemporary surface associated with driven piles is a perennial one. In this instance, there are a number of indicators which point to the level of the riverbed. The stakes may not all be contemporary: some could have been additions or repairs. The proportion that are probably summer cut (c 25%, see Morgan p 197) is unusually high. Nevertheless, the majority are not driven below 3.0m OD which strongly suggests that deposition of the Phase VI and at least some of the Phase VI/VII contexts must have occurred beforehand, if the stakes were securely driven into the riverbed. The split oak pile 25860 (Fig 51) exhibits differential preservation of the sapwood: the bottom 0.55m (2.69–3.25m OD) was perfectly preserved, the next 0.31m (3.25–3.55m OD) was partially preserved, and above this no sapwood survived. This pattern could be taken as a reflection of differential exposure of the upright to decay processes during the structure's usage prior to alluviation.

Marked discoloration of the uppermost 35–100mm of split ash pile 25824, with a top height of 3.56m suggests the contemporary riverbed here was at c 3.46–3.52m OD although this could be the result of recent disturbance of the wood's environment. Data from the structure itself therefore points to construction at a period when the riverbed was at a level of 3.25–3.5m OD.

The clearest evidence for riverbed level comes from

Fig 51   Structure 22441: split oak pile 25860. Differential sapwood preservation may be a reflection of contemporary water and riverbed levels. View to north. Scale 0.5m

a concentration of wood, stone and other artefactual material (178 pieces of wood, 9 bones and 2 sherds of pottery) in a north-west to south-east oriented zone c 1.2m wide within context 22433 (Fig 45). Hazel dominated the wood assemblage (45%) with pointed roundwood (eight pieces) and four woodchips indicating some woodworking. An unusually high percentage of ash (30%) reflects the frequent occurrence of ash woodworking debris. These were predominantly radial pieces (30) with lesser numbers of tangential (15) and intermediate (2) pieces. One of the woodchips (24852) produced a winter felling date of 990/989 BC, suggesting that much of the material within this spread was contemporary

with both structure 22441 and structure 473. All the oak pieces show signs of working and included six radial and four tangential woodchips of oak and a piece of oak roundwood with a pencil point at one end and a chisel point at the other. Alder, hawthorn, blackthorn and dogwood occurred along with single pieces of elm, field maple, lime (a single piece of woodworking debris), willow/poplar and possible privet. The two sherds of pottery (21467 and 21746) were both body sherds (see Woodward p 243).

The greater part of this group lay between 3.45m and 3.55m OD supporting the evidence from the structure itself for a contemporary riverbed level at c 3.5m OD. This accords well with the levels of both structure 473 (see B.7.1) and the dated ash woodchip from Area A (see A.7.1).

The useful life span of the structure is more difficult to define. Most uprights had been truncated by machining but, as mentioned above, those at the edge of the lake construction survived to higher levels. It is notable that the oak uprights here survived to the limit of machining but the tops of the thinner stakes were sealed by context 22429, the earliest Phase VIII deposit in this area. Not a great deal can be read into this as at this level preservation of organic material was poor and less robust wood could have decayed as a result of later dewatering.

Function of Structure 22441   The paired arrangement of the piles running into or across the channel points to a function for the structure as a bridge or jetty. The absence of consolidated material such as stone slabs, layers of brushwood, or pegged planking within the confines of the uprights argues against interpretation as a causeway. Given the environmental background of increasing estuarine influence and stratigraphic evidence for continuing and possibly accelerating infilling of the channel, it may be that previous methods of consolidating the riverbed by dumping stone and wood as seen in Phase VI, were no longer viable. Similarly, a causeway in these circumstances would not have been an effective solution.

Parallels from the Late Bronze Age are rare in Britain. The post alignments at Fengate/Flag Fen/Northey are not paired. Indeed emerging evidence suggests that the posts of the Fengate landfall may have been constructed as single rows (Pryor 1992, 524). The presence of mortised planks in association with the Fengate alignments are suggestive of a causeway which fossilises the 2nd millennium droveway system. The presence of Bronze Age structures at Northey encourages interpretation of this complex as a delineation of the mouth of an embayment in the Fen on a different scale of magnitude to a localised river crossing as found at Caldicot.

On the basis of the evidence so far available, the paired post alignment at Fiskerton, dated by dendrochronology to between 457/6 and 339 BC (Hillam

1985) may be a bridge, a jetty or a causeway. Field (1985) describes pegged mortised planks within the post alignment which are suggestive of a causeway. Two parallel lines of ash, alder, and oak stakes (structure 873) running parallel to the channel edge at Anslow's Cottages in the Kennet Valley, dated to 2570 ± 70 BP (HAR-9168), are interpreted as a landing stage but do not run out into the contemporary river channel (Lobb 1992, 88–9). The two lines of oak piles at Runnymede Bridge, initially seen as a double row of closely-set piles along the south-west edge of the contemporary river channel, are interpreted as successive waterfronts with radiocarbon means of 2742 ± 28 BP and 2655 ± 30 BP (Needham 1991, 83–91). Perhaps the closest parallel for structure 22441 comes from excavations at Whitecross Farm, Cholsey in the Upper Thames basin (Lambrick 1992, Fig 20.5, 217). Here a Late Bronze Age occupation site is located on a long thin eyot bounded to the east by the present course of the River Thames and to the west by a silted palaeochannel with a possible palisade trench along its edge. A pile structure, running out into the channel for at least 5m, comprises piles at 1.5–2m intervals in two rows with two further closely-spaced rows of piles running at right angles from this alignment to the south. Interpreted as a jetty, the structure has four associated radiocarbon dates suggesting a calibrated probability range within 1000–800 BC. Associated organic palaeochannel fills contain a varied wood assemblage with similarities to Caldicot assemblages (Bradley pers comm). Also in the Upper Thames basin, excavations as part of the Yarnton Floodplain Project, recovered evidence for a timber platform or bridge within a silted palaeochannel associated with a mat of roundwood and debris including burnt stone, pottery and flint (Hey pers comm).

On balance, given prevailing sedimentation, the absence of consolidation between the uprights and the clear pairing of the major piles, interpretation as a bridge is favoured. The function of the thinner stakes remains unclear although dual function as a netted fish weir could be possible. The location of the Wilburton chape (see Northover p 250) only some 4m downstream (south-east) at a compatible level (3.52m OD) is to some degree reminiscent of finds of similar chapes in association with the Fengate post alignment and the Flag Fen site (Coombs 1992, 504–9) and its deposition could be interpreted as the result of ritual activity. Its presence could also reflect navigability of the Phase VII river encouraging transport and exchange.

D.7.2

At the north-east end of this area approximately 2.5m of the trench's length had been far less severely truncated during the initial stages of lake construction with deposits surviving to c 4.1m OD (see Fig 10c). Grey clay (22437) survived to a height of c 3.65m OD here. Partially within but not sealed by this deposit, a

north–south oriented ash plank (24837) with two mortises had been pegged down directly south of pile 24923 of structure 22441 (Figs 52 and 53). The radial plank was secured by three roundwood pegs of hazel. It was in excellent condition apart from some modern damage at its south end, and a crack at the north end where a poorly preserved upright (24605) appeared to have been driven onto it. The upright was also damaged: it did not survive fully in the round and only 0.2m of its length survived to a height of 3.81m OD.

This group could be interpreted in a number of ways. If the plank was seen as predating structure 22441, then the upright 24605 could be part of the east line of stakes and piles. Given other evidence for riverbed level (see D.7.1), it is probable that the plank was placed at or after the time of structure 22441's construction. If contemporary with initial building, it may have provided temporary secure footing, a technique not observed elsewhere on the site. On balance an interpretation of this group as a repair is favoured. With a top height of 3.59–3.61m OD, the plank is 0.1–0.2m higher than other possible indicators of riverbed level when structure 22441 was first built. Its proximity to the leaning pile 24923 is seen as significant: the plank could have acted as a secure anchor for wedging the upright 24605. This upright, which slopes up at an angle to the north and exhibits no cut marks normally associated with driven uprights, could then have acted as a prop at a point of weakness in structure 22441.

The plank and its pegs were sealed by an homogenous greenish-grey, organic, very silty clay (22436) which contained a small assemblage of wood (18 pieces), predominantly hazel roundwood with lesser quantities of ash and oak woodchips. A wooden tie of twisted hazel (Fig 54) was partially exposed just inside the north-east end of the area. The physical and chronological association with possible repairs to structure 22441 point to its use either in initial construction or repair (see also Brunning and O'Sullivan, p 184).

D.7.3

The subsequent deposit, a dark grey, organic, very silty clay (22435) with distinct organic laminae deepened slightly towards the south-east down to 3.72m OD and contained common though poorly preserved wood, concentrated within these organic laminae. The assemblage was large (72 pieces) given the small area exposed and is unusual in that 60% is categorised as debris and ash was the commonest species at 37.5% compared with 29% for hazel. Although poor preservation and subsequent fragmentation may partly explain the high proportion of debris, the quantity of ash does suggest that the assemblage contains woodworking debris rather than purely 'natural' fragments. Less common species comprise alder, oak, blackthorn and elm. A piece of hazel roundwood (24643) gave a radiocarbon determination of 2400 ± 70 BP (CAR-1405).

This was overlain by an intermittent, highly organic, dark greyish-brown sand (22432) at 3.77–3.83m OD containing common desiccated wood. Only four stems of hazel roundwood (two with chisel cuts) were recorded in detail due to the very poor preservation of the remainder. A single, possibly naturally-damaged flint (21461) and one sherd (21460) were recovered. A patchy lens of bluish-grey clay (22434) with mixed organic laminae overlying this survived locally to 3.85m OD and contained very poorly-preserved wood which was not recorded in detail.

Area E

E.7.1

Near the west end of the Phase VI channel 22307, a poorly defined interface 22340/22343, c 1.2m wide with a base height of c 3.45m

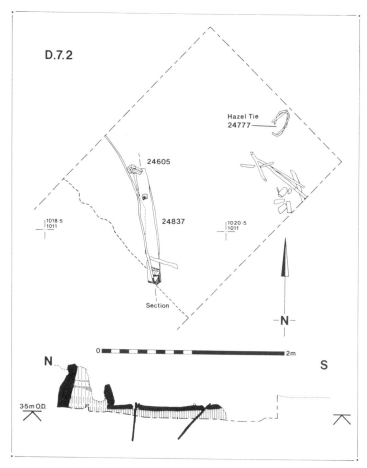

Fig 52 Area D: plan and section of mortised ash plank 24837, its pegs and the remains of a possible upright 24605. This group is tentatively interpreted as a repair to address a structural weakness in structure 22441 (see Fig 49). Note also the twisted wooden tie 24777

Fig 53 Area D: pegged mortised plank 24837 and the remains of the associated upright 24605 at its northern (right hand) end. View to west. Scale 1m

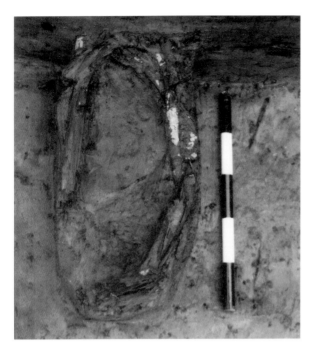

Fig 54   Area D: twisted hazel tie 24777. The hazel extended outside the area of excavation and was only partially exposed. Scale 0.5m

OD, contained a male dog skeleton (22313/22335) and a few pieces of wood in a matrix of organic, silty clay (22334/22341) (Fig 55). This channel and its fills had been truncated by machining in 1988 and was isolated stratigraphically from the other Phase VII palaeochannel group in this area. The distribution of the bones suggests that the animal was deposited as an articulated carcass which underwent some disturbance, presumably through river action and later compression/distortion of the sediments. For a detailed discussion of this find, see Murphy (p 227). A total of 14 pieces of wood were recovered comprising 6 hazel (including 3 woodchips), 3 ash (including one piece of woodworking debris), 2 oak (both woodchips) and single occurrences of elm and holly roundwood. The presence of the last two species and the relatively high proportion of worked material are both unusual characteristics of this small assemblage.

E.7.2

The east end of the Phase VI channel had been cut by a narrower channel (22319) which had a maximum surviving width of *c* 3.0m with a base height of *c* 3.15m OD. Its basal fills comprised thin layers of contrasting organic content with artefactual material concentrated in the more organic sediments. The lowest clearly defined fill (22322), a thin lamination of grey, granular silt, rich in mollusca, contained sixteen bones and a burnt chip of flint (21277). This was overlain successively by a lamination of grey, silty clay (22323), from which no artefactual material was recovered, a dark-grey, granular, silty clay (22324) which contained 20 pieces of wood and 3 bones and a patch of very dark grey, organic, silty clay (22318), a lamination of olive-grey, silty clay with patches of pale yellow silt (22321) which contained a single alder woodchip, a dark grey silty clay (22317) with 5 bones and 5 sherds of pottery (21239–21243), 19 pieces of wood and 18 subangular stones, an organic, silty clay, rich in mollusca, and plant macrofossils (22315) with 130 pieces of wood and 4 bones and a single burnt flint flake (21237), and a grey silt (22320) with

5 bones and 9 pieces of wood. The wood and finds from these basal fills are considered as a sub-group but presented on plan along with the overlying material (Fig 56).

A total of 182 pieces of wood are included in this sub-group of which 50% were hazel, 10% alder, 9% ash and 8% oak. Less prolific species included dogwood, privet, blackthorn, willow/poplar and lime. Clearly worked material included four roundwood hazel stems with chisel points, ten hazel woodchips including a cluster of four to the north of oak 20909 and a coppice heel; alder, ash and oak, willow and lime woodchips; a split and burnt oak timber (24007) and the worked oak stake 20909. Sixty-five pieces (36%) showed some form of working from single cut marks possibly associated with clearance to the woodworking skill apparent on stake 20909. This latter piece is interesting both technologically (see Brunning and O'Sullivan p 184, Fig 109) and stratigraphically. Its point had been driven through the interface of its associated channel (22319) into the underlying deposits, and at some later date had collapsed, disturbing the deposits into which it had been driven, before becoming buried by deposition of wood and sediment. Its location, towards the surviving west edge of the channel, along with the presence of a worn 'tang' at its tip, suggest it may have held some structure within the channel, possibly acting as a mooring post or a stake to hold a fish trap. A radiocarbon determination from immature roundwood provided a date of 2750 ± 70 BP (CAR-1316).

The upper fills of channel 22319 consisted of a dark-grey, silty clay with common plant macrofossils and common charcoal flecks (22316) overlain by a slightly paler silty clay (22308) with less frequent occurrence of charcoal. The later, uppermost deposit had been partially removed by machining in 1988. With the exception of a single hazel stem, all the wood derived from 22308. The combined assemblage comprised 56 pieces of which 63% was hazel, 9% alder, 7% ash and 5% oak with lesser quantities of dogwood, hawthorn and lime. Sixteen pieces (29%) exhibited evidence of working including cut stems of alder, hazel and alder; oak, ash and lime woodchips; and two wooden artefacts. A poorly-preserved alder trough (20836) overlay the collapsed oak stake. Part of an oak peg/handle (20836) was also recovered along with a single bone and a small number of subangular stones.

Five sherds were discovered in a cluster in context 22317. Two decorated, bevelled rim sherds (21239 and 21243) come from the same jar. A further decorated body sherd (21240) has incised and grooved decoration very similar to that found on sherds of the same fabric in Area G (see G.7.1).

Area G

G.7.1

The majority of the palaeochannel deposits and their associated material in this area are assigned to this group. It consisted of a north–south oriented channel interface with a base level of *c* 3.35m OD (Fig 57). It was poorly defined on its west edge but clearly defined in the east where it cut Phase I sediment (22257) and contained a basal fill of dark grey, sandy and silty clay (22262) with frequent charcoal and ash, and subangular stone. A radiocarbon date of 2800 ± 70 BP (CAR-1318) was derived from one of seven stems of hazel which formed part of a small wood assemblage which also included a hawthorn stem and a piece of oak debris. The greater part of the artefactual material was recovered from the overlying dark grey, very silty, organic clay (22259). The wood assemblage (158 pieces), dominated by hazel roundwood (54%) contained lesser proportions of hawthorn (10%), alder, ash, oak, spindle and willow. Twenty-eight percent showed clear signs of working including five pointed hazel stems, two pointed hawthorn stems and numerous cut marks evident on woodchips of ash, oak and alder. A linear north–south concentration of hazel roundwood was poorly preserved but did

58

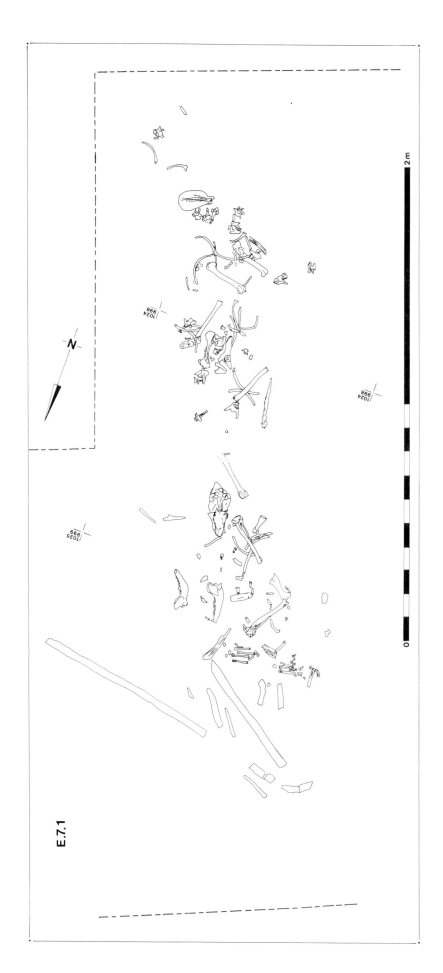

Fig 55   Area E: plan of Phase VII articulated dog skeleton and associated wood spread

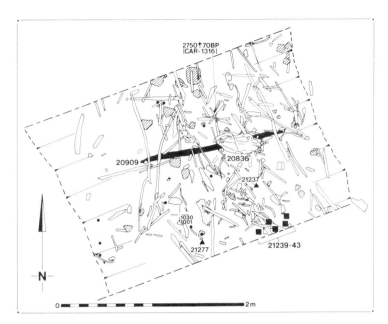

Fig 56   Area E: plan of Phase VII palaeochannel. Note cluster of decorated pottery sherds, collapsed oak stake 20909 and alder trough 20836

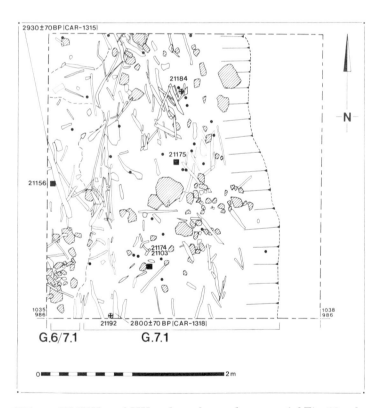

Fig 57   Area G: plan of Phase VI / VII and VII palaeochannel groups (cf Fig 13: photograph of these deposits in section)

not appear to contain any driven pegs which might suggest the presence of a wicker frontage to the palaeochannel edge. The bone assemblage (32 pieces) included two possible bone amulets; a pierced horse incisor (21192) and a utilised pig canine (21184). Three sherds from a finely finished jar (21103, 21174 and 21175) exhibited distinctive decoration. The uppermost surviving fill, grey-brown, very silty clay (22260) contained no

artefactual material and was both truncated and disturbed by machining.

Although separation from palaeochannel group G.6/7.1 is not well defined, the channel morphology, and base level of this group support its allocation to Phase VII as do the radiocarbon determination, and the close parallels between pottery from this group and one sherd from E.7.2.

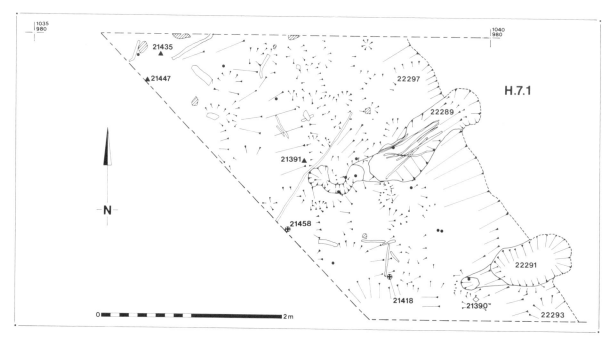

Fig 58   Area H: plan of Phase VII palaeochannel group

Fig 59   Area H: Phase VII palaeochannel group. Note the heavily rutted interface and the features, one containing roundwood stems. Scale 2m

Area H

H.7.1

This area, located on the slope of the artificial lake, was excavated in order to identify the uppermost extent of survival of palaeochannel features and organic material, and if possible to identify any contemporary ground surface. After initial cleaning and removal of mixed sediment redeposited during construction works on the lake, it became clear that a palaeochannel interface survived to a height of 4.2–4.4m OD where it was truncated by machining. No contemporary ground surface survived.

A complete transect of the north-west to south-east oriented palaeochannel interface (22288) was not exposed, only part of the left slope (Fig 58) down to a level of 3.25m OD. This interface was heavily rutted and pock-marked (Fig 59) as if trampled by livestock and in places palaeochannel fills had mixed with underlying Phase I deposits (22415). The interface was also interrupted by four apparent features. Two of these (22293 and 22297) were subcircular depressions whilst the remaining two were enigmatic features surviving as sloping voids. The latter appeared to have been open within the channel as they were filled with sediments identical to those which accumulated throughout the channel. One of these voids (22289), with a surviving length of *c* 3.4m and an irregular internal diameter of 0.1–0.3m, contained seven pieces of roundwood, six identified as hazel with one exhibiting a chisel cut. The function of these features is unclear. The presence of cut roundwood stems in 22289 suggests these were not 'natural' phenomena such as tree root disturbance or animal burrows (unless the wood had flooded in), but rather the result of human activity. The fact that they appeared to silt up with the same deposits which occupied the channel as a whole suggest they were water filled hollows. Perhaps they carried out some function associated with wood processing.

The earliest channel fills encountered comprised a dark grey, very silty clay rich in charcoal and poorly preserved brash (22298), from which five pieces of bone were recovered, and two lenses of highly organic, olive-brown, silty clay (22417/22418), the latter producing a bone gouge or chisel (21458).These were overlain by a dark greyish-brown, silty clay (22295/22414), with less frequent charcoal and decomposed wood fragments containing four pieces of hazel roundwood, one of blackthorn, a radial oak offcut, a single piece of bone, and two flint fragments (21435 and 21447). This deposit also partially filled the four features described above. In the extreme north-west corner of the trench, it was overlain by slightly paler silty clays (22403/22401), whilst throughout the area these deposits were sealed by dark grey–dark olive/grey clay (22278) which also filled the four features. It contained eight pieces of bone including an awl/needle (21418), a flint flake (21391), an amber bead (21390), and nine pieces of poorly preserved wood including one alder and one oak offcut, and five hazel stems.

Phase VIII

This phase comprised clays and silty clays above *c* 3.8m OD which survived in the sloping sides of the lake, sealing Phase VII palaeochannel fills. They did not appear to occupy palaeochannels and are tentatively interpreted as alluviation resulting from over-bank sedimentation and/or tidal flooding. Although the conditions for the preservation of environmental evidence are generally poorer than in earlier phases, there is evidence to suggest that the increase in estuarine conditions, evident in the previous phases, continued. A slight decrease in woodland indicates some renewed clearance in the area and this is accompanied by evidence for both pastoralism and cereal cultivation.

Area A

Between *c* 3.75m and 4.8m OD, a grey/grey-brown silty clay with manganese staining and increasing iron staining was recorded as 9000/9001/9005. This overlay Phase VII 9010, but did not appear to occupy any definable channel and there was no evidence for downcutting. Occasional lenses of dark grey silty clay (9002/4/6/7/8) are evident in the west-facing section (see Fig 11a) between 3.8m and 4.05m OD but otherwise organic content was low and little artefactual material was recovered. A single utilised flint flake fragment (12804) was recovered at 4.07m OD. Some of the driven uprights in structure 9014 (see A.6/7.1) survived to heights of 3.9m OD suggesting that it may still have been partially visible at the onset of this phase of sedimentation.

Area D

Excluding modern re-depositions, sediment observed in this area which post-date Phase VII are confined to the north-east end of the trench where machine truncation was less severe. Bluish-grey clay 22429 with heavy iron and manganese staining overlay Phase VII deposits 22434 and 22432 at *c* 3.8m OD and was overlain by pinkish-grey slightly silty clay 22427 at 3.9–4.0m OD. The latter deposit, surviving to a maximum height of 4.4m OD in the excavation area was heavily iron stained, oxidised and desiccated. Stakes from structure 22441 did not survive within these deposits but piles 011, 24923 and 25060 survived to the height of machine truncation. A single, probably natural, rolled pebble (21462) was recovered at a height of 3.92m OD from 22429.

Area H

Phase VII deposits were overlain by a succession of increasingly inorganic and oxidised clays from *c* 4.05m OD to *c* 5.2m OD where machine truncation has removed the uppermost sediment and subsoil. A poorly-defined, grey clay with some iron staining (22287) was overlain by greyish-brown clay with iron and manganese staining (22277), grey clay with iron staining (22282) and a heavily-stained greyish-brown friable clay (22281). The latter deposit, much disturbed by modern machining, contained a fragment of a Roman *imbrex* (21262) (Compton p 253).

Watching Brief

During the final construction of the lake, following completion of the excavations, machine trenches cut to take a vertical water-proof membrane from surface level to *c* 4.7m OD were watched and a sample section recorded in detail (Lennox 1992). A creamy, grey-brown clay with heavy iron staining (22553), recorded up to 5.4m OD, is correlated with the uppermost recorded contexts in areas A, D and H. It was overlain by a heavily oxidised and iron stained, pale grey, crumbly clay (22552) up to 5.7m OD and a blue-grey, iron stained, silty clay (22551) to 6.1m OD before a poorly developed soil horizon of dark rusty-brown, friable silty loamy clay was encountered with a surface level of 6.3m OD.

Section B: Environmental and Artefactual Analysis

Issues of taphonomy and site formation

Taphonomy, site formation processes and environmental interpretation

At any site, the cultural and environmental records that survive are dependent on the taphonomic and site formation processes that have operated in the past and some of which may be still operating. Within the fluvial sediments at Caldicot a wide range of environmental and archaeological evidence, not mutually exclusive, was preserved and consideration needs to be given as to how this material became incorporated and the interpretative implications.

Taphonomy is concerned with the formation processes which lead to the transformation of the original living environmental assemblage into the subfossil assemblage, and in particular with the post-mortem history of the organism. The likelihood of an individual becoming incorporated in the subfossil record is dependent on a number of factors including the reproductive and survival capacity of the organism involved. This includes the number of individuals produced and their success or failure to perform their function in life, for example in the case of seeds their success or failure to germinate, for pollen grains to find the appropriate stigma and animals to survive predators. The methods by which they are transported and dispersed, their resistance to decay and the diagenic processes operating in the sediment in which they are ultimately deposited will all help to determine whether or not the organism concerned is preserved in a subfossil assemblage. For example fragile salt marsh diatom valves may be destroyed by fragmentation and dissolution and therefore be under-represented in comparison to allochthonous marine littoral species (Sherrod *et al* 1989). Inevitably asymmetries arise between the living and death assemblages and between the death and subfossil assemblages.

The methods by which the plant and animal remains are transported and dispersed and the size of area from which they are likely to be derived are particularly relevant, especially at a site like Caldicot where material is incorporated within channel sediments which formed within active channels. These are discussed in more detail in individual contributions but given general consideration here. In channel deposits, depending on flow rates, either a greater or lesser amount of the assemblages will be allochthonous, that is transported to the site from elsewhere, rather than autochthonous – originating at the site. Some remains will float, for example seeds of duckweed and celery-leaved buttercup are particularly adapted to do so, and will be carried on the surface or in suspension while other remains may

sink rapidly. As a result some remains may originate some distance, from the site. Flood events may transport material from an even greater distance and at a site such as Caldicot, which is relatively close to the Severn Estuary, tides and storm surges may also affect the assemblages, introducing remains from downstream rather than upstream. This, in particular, has implications for the diatom assemblage. Diatoms which are autochthonous *sensu stricto* are those which are benthic or, in a low-energy environment; epiphytic and planktonic diatoms which live just above the bottom of the channel and have not been transported are considered to be autochthonous *sensu lato* (Vos and de Wolf 1988). In such a situation the influx of allochthonous diatoms is small. In contrast, in tidal environments the allochthonous component may exceed the autochthonous component. In coarse river channel deposits all the biological remains are likely to be allochthonous whereas in finer sediments, deposited in still or slowly moving water, much of the aquatic assemblages are likely to be autochthonous. The terrestrial component is, of course, allochthonous. At Caldicot the sediments generally indicate a low energy depositional environment and therefore that the aquatic remains are mainly autochthonous, with the possible exception of the diatoms, but coarser silts and sand in some phases may indicate a slightly higher proportion of allochthonous material. Changes in flow rate in fine-grained sediments are difficult to identify based on sediments alone.

Within channels, however, water is not the only method by which plant and animal remains are dispersed. Aerial transport also plays a part, particularly as far as seeds, pollen and insects are concerned. Various models have been put forward for the incorporation of pollen into sediments (see Caseldine p 100). Animal and bird remains, apart from being washed onto the site, may be present because they died at that particular point or because of being brought there by other animals or humans. The latter may also be responsible for carrying pollen, seeds, insects and molluscs to the site and clearly much of the wood and bone at Caldicot is there because of human agency.

The bone assemblages in a channel may provide some clue as to flow rates. The anatomical elements of the assemblage present may indicate whether or not the assemblage has been acted upon by fluvial processes (Coard and Dennell 1995). The bone assemblage present may in terms of post-mortem taphonomic processes be considered to be autochthonous, ie locally derived having not been moved far after entry into the channel. Alternatively the assemblage may be allochthonous, ie derived from upstream during periods of high flow rate or downstream during periods of high tides and/or storm conditions. Certain skeletal elements have a higher transportable potential than others, hence their presence along with elements indicative of low transport potential suggests little movement locally and therefore low flow rates.

In the same way that the bone assemblage can be considered to be autochthonous or allochthonous in terms of post-mortem taphonomic fluvial processes within the channel so can the wood assemblage. Wood which displays working almost certainly has moved only a short distance over the activity area of the site after initial deposition. Small wood chips which are likely to be easily transported were encountered in tight clusters. Their presence and distribution suggests a slow rate of flow during deposition. The presence of contemporary vegetation, particularly emergent species, would have assisted the incorporation of more buoyant materials into riverbed sediment. Wood which shows no sign of working presents a greater interpretative problem, and some may be derived from upstream. However, as with other plant material, the allochthonous element is likely to be diluted by local material (Spicer 1989). Comparisons between the worked and unworked wood support the view that the assemblage is predominantly the result of human activity in the immediate environs of the site rather than flood dispersal (see p 158).

Denser materials, notably flint and stone, will not have been subject to depositional fluvial transport as such. There can be little doubt that much of the stone encountered within the channel sediments lay where it had been dumped. However, in the presence of processes such as channel down-cutting and lateral migration, the incorporation of material originally deposited on the dry banks and floodplain is possible. Indeed these natural processes can explain the presence of flint artefacts interpreted as residual on typological grounds (see Aldhouse-Green, p 246). Erosion and re-working of older sediments has therefore had some effect in introducing residual material into artefact assemblages otherwise relatively unaffected by fluvial transport.

In contrast, many of the environmental indicators preserved within the palaeochannel deposits came from variable distances from the site. Their interpretation requires an assessment of the areas from which they originated.

Catchment areas

In any sediment it is usual to find that any one category of remains will contain taxa which originate from a range of source areas, thereby reflecting a range of environments and habitats. Moreover, different types of biota will derive from different areas and different environments. Some of the biological remains will be derived from the immediate area of the site or close to it and may be termed a local component. In the case of Caldicot this would be the palaeochannels and the banksides. An extra-local or intermediate component is that beyond the immediate bounds of the site but in the vicinity. At Caldicot this would include remains from either further upstream or downstream, from the floodplain and, depending on the proximity of it, from the nearest dryland. The final component, the regional, encompasses a much wider catchment and could include remains from, at least in theory, the source of the Nedern and its tributaries, from the estuary, from fen and raised bog deposits known to have existed in the area at the time and from dryland beyond the extra-local area. In addition on an archaeological site humans may have accidentally or deliberately introduced plant or animal material onto the site, material from both nearby and further afield and even from beyond the natural catchment of the site. It has been proposed that in a riverine situation the major land biological groups would have the following catchment areas with 50% of the group deriving from this catchment, assuming there was no significant human interference (Evans 1991, 364–5):

Pollen – 2km upstream and 100m each side of the river
Beetles – 0.5km and 50m
Waterlogged seeds – 0.5km and 10m
Molluscs – 0.2km and 2m

However, it is pointed out that extensive flooding or dumping of organic material by humans would negate the figures. At Caldicot a downstream dimension also needs to be added because of a possible tidal influence and events such as storm surges. Another complication is the possible erosion and reworking of older deposits which may result in the incorporation of older material into the fossil assemblages. Nevertheless, the actual evidence from Caldicot is broadly in agreement with the above suggested figures, or at least the different catchment areas for the various groups. The molluscs mainly reflect the channel environment, the waterlogged seeds the channel, banksides, and floodplain nearest to the channel, the beetles the aforementioned environments but a greater area of floodplain and possibly a small area of dryland, and only the pollen especially demonstrates the environmental conditions on the surrounding dryland.

Environmental Remains

Environmental sampling

Introduction

The discovery of Late Bronze Age waterlogged wood preserved within palaeochannel deposits at Caldicot provided an opportunity for an integrated programme of archaeological and environmental investigations. The site was visited at least once by most of the specialists and progress/co-ordination meetings were held twice. Analytical work commenced while excavations were still taking place and interim results were taken into account in the later seasons when sampling strategies were revised and priorities for analytical work were formulated.

A large number of samples – more than 400 – were taken, from which, given the time-consuming nature of the analyses and the time constraints, a subset was selected for investigation. The aim of the analysis has been, given the nature of the site, to provide as complete an environmental record as possible within the time available. A single set of samples was taken from Area A in 1990 but as excavation proceeded it became apparent that there was a series of palaeochannels and that no one section encompassed the whole site sequence (see p 7). This necessitated the taking of multiple columns and the selection of samples to ensure that environmental evidence was recovered for each phase; a process requiring close liaison between archaeological and environmental project team members. Inevitably parts of the environmental record have been lost through erosive events and, in the case of Phase II, the deposits were not fully sampled. However, even though there are gaps, the results do provide a record of environmental change in the area stretching from the Neolithic through to the Late Bronze Age/ Early Iron Age.

Samples for pollen, diatom and sediment analyses were recovered using monolith tins of galvanised steel. The pollen and diatom samples were taken from the same tins, whereas separate sample tins were used for the sediments. Apart from Column 1 where a separate adjacent column of bulk samples was taken for insects, a single set of bulk samples was taken for plant macrofossil, mollusc, ostracod and beetle analyses and subdivided in the laboratory. For the most part the samples were processed by the individual specialist concerned, however in the case of the molluscs and plant macrofossils, one set of samples was processed and used for both analyses. Samples taken from the stitch holes in the Phase III boat timber (6001) were processed for examination of plant remains alone. Details of the methods used to process the samples are given in the specialist reports.

Location of sampling columns (Fig 60)

Column 1: Area A monoliths 2330, 2331, 2332, 2333, 2335, 2340, 2342, 2343, 2344, bulk samples 2050–2078, insect samples A2–A26.

This series of samples included Phase I pre-channel intercalated clay and organic deposits. Phase II, III, and IV palaeochannel deposits have been eroded and hence there is a marked discontinuity between Phase I and the later palaeochannel deposits belonging to Phases V, VI, VI/VII, VII and VIII. Phase VI includes the stone platform and Phase VII the bridge structure.

Column 2: Area B monolith 23010 and bulk samples 23053–23061

These samples covered palaeochannel deposits from Phases II and III. Phase II included the pile structure and Phase III the boat plank.

Column 3: Area B monolith 23004/5 and bulk samples 23017–32.

These samples included some Phase I pre-channel deposits but consisted mainly of Phase III and Phase IV deposits. The samples were from close to the boat plank. Phase II deposits had been removed by erosion.

Area B: Stitch hole samples

These samples were removed from the stitch holes of the plank-sewn boat timber (6001) belonging to Phase III.

Area C: spot sample 3012

One spot sample from Phase III deposits was analysed for molluscs.

Column 4: Area E monolith 23195, monoliths 23196–8 and spot sample 23166

The samples from these columns covered Phases II, III, IV, V and VIII. The spot sample was from Phase III.

Column 5: Area E monolith 23188/9 and bulk samples 23251–60.

These samples included Phase I pre-channel deposits and much later Phase VI and VII palaeochannel deposits.

Column 6: Area G monolith 23168

This column was taken for pollen analysis through the Phase I pre-channel organic layer from which radiocarbon dates of 4670 ± 80 BP (CAR-1323) and 4360 ± 80 BP (CAR-1322) were obtained.

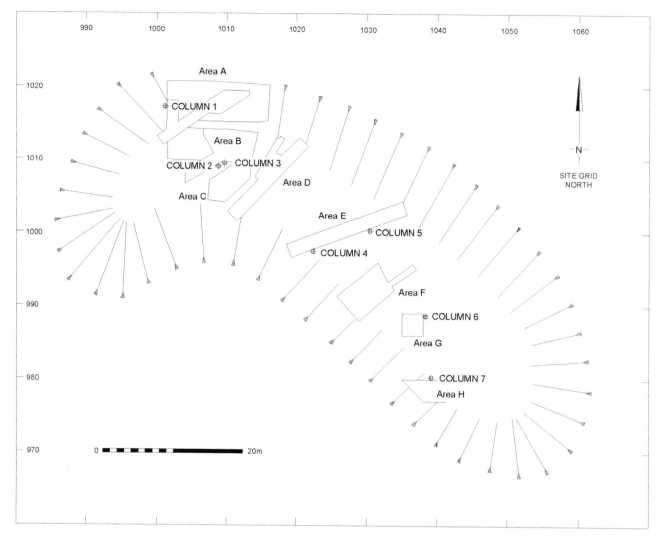

Fig 60   Location of environmental sampling columns

Column 7: Area H monolith 23309/10

This column was taken from Phase I deposits outside of the palaeochannels and therefore represent deposits which have been removed elsewhere on the site.

Contexts

Details of the contexts and lithostratigraphies examined are as follows. Depths are given for contexts in the pollen/diatom columns. 0cm = the top of the column, which does not necessarily start at the top of the context. Where a context occurs in the sediment or bulk sample columns but not the pollen/diatom column the details are inserted at the appropriate point in the sequence. A few bulk samples incorporated material from more than one context in which case the bulk sample number occurs more than once. Details of the stitch hole contexts are in the site archive. Table 2 lists the bulk samples examined for the different types of analyses and the contexts involved.

Column 1: Area A. Sediment monoliths 2330, 2331, 2332, 2333, 2335 and pollen/diatom monoliths 2340, 2342, 2343, 2344 and bulk samples 2050–2078 and A2–A26 (Fig 61)

Context 9005 (Bulk samples 2050 and A2)
0–11 cm Grey, 5Y 5/1, silty clay. Heavy iron staining. Manganese streaks decreasing in frequency with depth. Faint organic laminations. Occasional charcoal .

Context 9010 (Bulk samples A2 and A3)
11–13 cm Slightly organic grey, 5Y 5/1, silty clay with greenish grey mottles. Iron staining rare. Manganese staining. Diffuse laminations. Fine distinct organic laminations.

Context 9034 (Bulk samples 2054 , 2056, A3, A6 and A7)
13–32 cm Slightly organic grey, 5Y 5/1, laminated silty clay. Silty clay bands increasing in frequency with depth. Iron staining. Brash present. Monocot. plant remains and wood frags. common. Molluscs rare.

Context 9031 (Bulk samples 2056, 2058, 2062, A7, A10, A11, A12, and A14)
32–68 cm Dark grey, 5Y 4/1, laminated very silty clay (organic), slightly lighter grey above 53cm. Iron staining. Brash increasing with depth. Wood common. Molluscs and insects rare. Monocot. plant remains present.

Context 9032 (Bulk samples 2066, 2067, 2068, A16, A18 and A19)
68–88 cm Dark greenish-grey, 5G 4/1, laminated fine sandy silty clay. Abundant brash, plant macrofossils and molluscs. Decrease in sand, brash and plant remains with depth. Wood rare.

Context 22168 (Bulk samples 2068, 2069, 2070, A19, A20, A21 and A23)

Table 2 Bulk samples used for mollusca, ostracod, plant macrofossil and insect analyses (+ indicates analysis, – no analysis, A indicates specialist's sample code)

Column 1: Area A

Sample	Phase	Context	Mollusca	Ostracods	Plant macros.	Coleoptera
2050	VIII	9005	+	−	+	−
	VIII VII	9005, 9010	−	−	−	A2
	VII	9010	−	−	−	A3
	VII	9034				
2054	VII	9034	+	+	+	−
	VII	9034	−	−	−	A6
2056	VII VI/VII	9034, 9031	−	+	−	A7
2058	VI/VII	9031	+	+	+	−
	VI/VII	9031	−	−	−	A10
	VI/VII	9031	−	−	−	A11
	VI/VII	9031	−	−	−	A12
2062	VI/VII	9031	+	+	+	−
	VI/VII	9031	−	−	−	A14
	VI	9032	−	−	−	A16
2066	VI	9032	+	+	+	−
2067	VI	9032	+	−	−	A18
2068	VI V	9032, 22168	+	−	+	A19
2069	V	22168	+	−	−	A20
2070	V	22168	+	+	+	A21
	V I	22168, 9033	−	−	−	A23
2074	I	9033	+	+	+	A25
	I	9033	−	−	−	A26
2078	I	9033	+	+	+	−

Column 2: Area B

Sample	Phase	Context	Mollusca	Ostracods	Plant macros.	Coleoptera
23053	III	22216	+	−	−	−
		22217				
		22042				
23054	III	22217	+	−	−	−
		22042				
		22169				
23055	III	22169	+	+	+	+
23056	III	22170	+	−	−	−
23057	III	22170	+	+	+	−
		22246				
23059	II	22241	+	+	+	+
23061	II	22240	+	+	+	−

Table 2 (cont.)

Column 3: Area B

Sample	Phase	Context	Mollusca	Ostracods	Plant macros.	Coleoptera
23017	IV	22254	+	+	+	+
23019	IV	22219	+	+	+	+
23021	IV	22100	+	+	+	+
23023	IV	22100	+	+	+	+
		22238				
		22171				
23026	III	22165	+	−	+	+
23027	III	22165	+	+	+	+
23028	III	22165	+	+	+	+
23030	III	22239	+	+	+	+
23032	III	22166	+	+	+	+

Area C

Sample	Phase	Context	Mollusca	Ostracods	Plant macros.	Coleoptera
3012	III	326	+	−	−	−

Column 4: Area E

Sample	Phase	Context	Mollusca	Ostracods	Plant macros.	Coleoptera
23166	III	22379	+	+	+	+

Column 5: Area E

Sample	Phase	Context	Mollusca	Ostracods	Plant macros.	Coleoptera
23251	VII	22320	+	+	+	+
23253	VII	22317	+	+	+	+
23257	VII	22322	+	+	+	+
23258	VI	22325	+	−	+	−
23259	VI	22351	+	−	+	+
23260	VI	22309	+	−	+	−
	I	22325				

88–125 cm Olive-grey, 5Y 4/2, laminated silty clay. Some organic staining towards base.
Context 9033 (Bulk samples 2074 , 2078, A23, A25 and A26)
125–129 cm Dark reddish-brown, 5YR 3/2, highly organic peaty clay. *Phragmites* and woody plant macrofossils.
129–137 cm Very dark greyish-brown, 10YR 3/2, organic silty clay becoming less organic with depth.
137–152 cm Dark greyish-brown, 10YR 4/2 organic silty clay. Clay increasing towards base.

Column 2: Area B Pollen/diatom monolith 23010 and bulk samples 23053–61 (Fig 62)
Context 22216 (Bulk sample 23053)
0–3 cm Dark grey, 5Y 4/1, slightly silty clay. Plant macrofossils and molluscs present. Manganese.
Context 22217 (Bulk samples 23053 and 23054)
3–7 cm Dark grey, 5Y 4/1, clay. Plant remains present. Manganese. Molluscs abundant.
Context 22169 (Bulk sample 23055)

7–10 cm Very dark grey, 5Y 3/1 clay. Mollusca very abundant and plant remains frequent.
Context 22042 (Bulk samples 23053 and 23054)
10–12 cm Dark grey, 5Y 4/1, silty clay. Mottles, 5Y 5/1, and fine laminations very dark grey (5Y 3/1). Iron staining towards top.
Context 22169 (Bulk samples 23054 and 23055)
12–18 cm Very dark grey, 5Y 3/1 silty clay. Mollusca very abundant and plant remains frequent.
Context 22170 (Bulk samples 23056 and 23057)
18–23 cm Dark grey, 5Y 4/1, and dark olive-grey, 5Y 3/2 moist and 5Y 4/1 dry, laminated clay.
Context 22246 (Bulk sample 23057)
23–32 cm Dark grey, 5Y 4/1, silty clay. Manganese common. Wood, molluscs and plant remains present.
Context 22241 (Bulk sample 23059)
32–40 cm Olive grey, 5GY 4/1 moist and 5Y 5/2 dry, clay. Streaks of manganese common. Plant macrofossils throughout. Wood, stone and mollusca present.
Context 22240 (Bulk sample 23061)

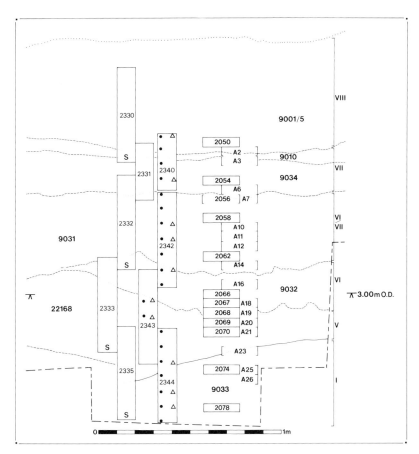

Fig 61   Section of environmental Column 1. Also see section 10a. Spot samples for pollen and diatoms indicated by dots and triangles respectively

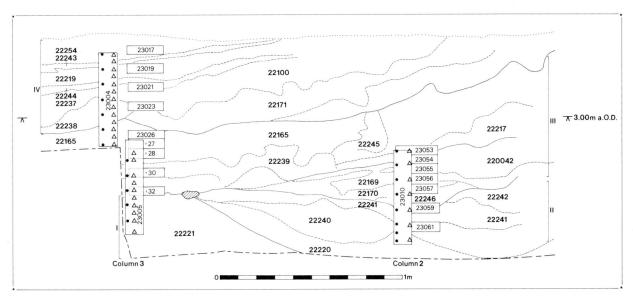

Fig 62   Section of environmental Columns 2 and 3. Also see section 11b

40–45 cm Dark grey, 5Y 4/1, clay. Manganese prominent. Monocot. plant remains present.
Context 22220
45–50 cm Grey, 5Y 5/1, fine sandy silty clay. Fine sandy lenses. Manganese streaks. Mollusca occasional.

Column 3: Area B Pollen/diatom monolith 23004/5, and bulk samples 23017–32 (Fig 62)
Context 22254 (Bulk sample 23017)

0–5 cm Very dark greyish-brown, 2.5 Y 3/2, very silty clay. Diffuse dark grey, 5Y 4/1, laminations. Iron staining. Monocot. plant remains present.
Context 22243
5–7 cm Grey, 5Y 4/1, dark grey, 5Y 5/1, silty clay. Iron staining. Mollusca and plant remains throughout.
Context 22219 (Bulk sample 23019)
7–15 cm Very dark greyish-brown, 2.5 Y 3/2, very silty clay. Wood and monocot. plant remains.

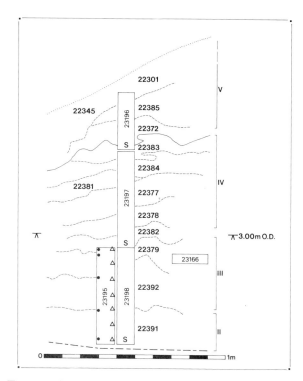

Fig 63   Section of environmental Column 4. Also see section 11c

Context 22244
15–18 cm Olive-grey, 5Y 4/2 moist, dark olive-grey, 5Y 3/2 moist, silty clay mottled with organics. Oxidised to dark grey, 5Y 4/1. Faint diffuse mottles, 5Y 4/1–5Y 5/1. Plant macrofossils and molluscs throughout.
Context 22100 (Bulk samples 23021 and 23023)
18–24 cm Very dark grey, 5Y 3/1, slightly silty clay. Mollusca and plant macrofossils frequent.
Context 22238 (Bulk sample 23023)
24–37 cm Olive-grey, 5Y 4/2 moist, silty clay oxidised to dark grey, 5Y 4/1. Grey, 5Y 5/1, mottles. Wood, molluscs and monocot. plant remains.
Context 22171 (Bulk sample 23023 and sediment column)
Dark grey, 5Y 4/1, silty clay. Many grey, 5Y5/1, mottles. Plant remains and wood.
Context 22165 (Bulk samples 23026–8)
37–60 cm Dark grey, 5Y 4/1, clay becoming lighter grey, 5Y 5/1, with increasing depth. Mollusca and wood frequent. Large wood fragment c 60cm. Plant macrofossils present.
Context 22239 (Bulk sample 23030)
60–66 cm Grey, 5Y 5/1, clay oxidised to dark grey, 5Y 4/1. Laminations. Plant macrofossils.
Context 22166 (Bulk sample 23032)
66–76 cm Olive, 5Y 4/3, very organic clay oxidised to dark olive grey 5Y 3/2. Rich in monocot. plant remains and mollusca abundant.
Context 22221
76–97 cm Very dark grey, 5Y 3/1, dark olive-grey, 5Y 3/2 organic clay. Abundant plant macrofossils, monocot. remains, increasing with depth.
Large pieces of wood c 90–7cm.

Area C. Spot sample 3012
Context 326
Greenish-grey, 5G 5/1, with darker organics, 5Y 5/1 and 5Y 4/1, silty clay. Abundant plant macrofossils and molluscs and frequent insect remains.

Column 4: Area E. Sediment monolith 23196–8 and pollen/diatom monolith 23195 (from context 22382) and spot sample 23166 (Fig 63)
Context 22345
Dark grey, 5Y 4/1 sticky clay-bands of silty clay. Faint organic bands (5Y 3/2). Manganese, charcoal and plant macrofossils.
Context 22385
Grey, 5Y 5/1, silty clay. Manganese. Heavy iron staining. Plant remains few. Bands of silt.
Context 22372
Dark grey, 5Y 4/1, organic laminated silty clay. Mottles 5Y 5/1. Iron, manganese and plant remains present.
Context 22383
Very dark grey, 10YR 3/1, organic laminated silty clay. Iron staining common. Manganese. Plant macrofossils abundant.
Context 22384
Black 5Y 2.5/1, very silty clay. Laminated organic layer. Iron staining common. Manganese present. Plant macrofossils abundant.
Context 22381
Dark grey, 5Y 4/1, silty clay. Laminations. Mottling, 5Y 3/1, slightly silty. Iron and manganese. Charcoal flecks rare. Mollusca and plant macrofossils common.
Context 22377
Very dark grey, 5Y 3/1, organic silty clay. Plant macrofossils, seeds, beetles, wood, molluscs present. Manganese.
Context 22378
Very dark grey, 5Y 3/1, organic silty clay, with abundant mottles of grey/ dark grey, 5Y 5/1–5Y 4/1, clay.
Context 22382 Pollen/diatom monolith 23195
0–3 cm Dark grey / dark olive-grey, 5Y 4/1–5Y 3/2, organic sticky clay, slightly silty. Silt in laminations. Abundant mollusca, monocot. plant remains and wood.
Context 22379 (Bulk sample 23166)
3–9 cm Dark grey, 5Y 4/1, organic silty clay. Manganese streaks. Charcoal present. Abundant mollusca and plant macrofossils and roundwood present.
Context 22392
9–32 cm Dark olive-grey, 5Y 4/2–3/2 silty clay. Frequent greenish-grey, 5GY 5/1–4/1, mottles. Charcoal, manganese, plant remains present and abundant mollusca.
Context 22391
32–51 cm Olive-grey, 5Y 4/2, sticky clay. Heavily streaked with manganese. Fine silty laminations. Becoming siltier towards base. Roundwood, monocot. plant remains and stones.

Column 5: Area E. Pollen/diatom monolith 23188/9 and bulk samples 23251–60 (Fig 64)
Context 22308
0–7 cm Dark grey, 5Y 4/1, silty clay. Grey, 5Y 5/1, clay mottles. Iron staining. Charcoal, molluscs and plant macrofossils. Few stones.
Context 22316
7–12 cm Dark grey, 5Y 4/1, organic silty clay with firmer silty clay 5Y 4/1: 5Y 5/1. Laminations present.Charcoal, wood, stones and molluscs present. *Phragmites* frequent.
Context 22320 (Bulk sample 23251)
12–16 cm Grey, 5Y 5/1, dark grey, 5Y 4/1, silt. Plant remains present.
Context 22315
16–23 cm Dark olive-grey, 5Y 3/2, silty clay. Grey, 5Y 5/1, clay. Mollusca, plant macrofossils and wood frequent. Insects present.
Context 22317 (Bulk sample 23253)
23–29 cm Dark grey, 5Y 4/1, silty clay. Occasional plant remains, mollusca and stone. Manganese.
Context 22321
29–30 cm Olive-grey, 5Y 5/2, with pale yellow, 5Y 7/3 silt, very silty clay.
Context 22324
30–32 cm Dark grey, 5Y 4/1, silty clay–granular. Roundwood, molluscs and monocot. plant remains.

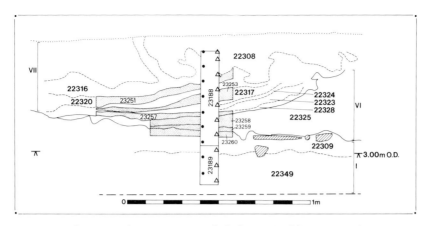

Fig 64   Section of environmental Column 5. Also see section 11c

Context 22323
32–33 cm   Dark grey, 5Y 4/1, silty clay. Lens of light grey silty clay. Monocot. plant remains.
Context 22322   (Bulk sample 23257)
33–35 cm   Dark grey/ grey, 5Y 4/1–5/1, silty clay with yellow patches, 5Y 7/3, of granular silt – aggregates *c* 5mm diameter. Monocot. plant remains and wood fragments.
Context 22325   (Bulk samples 23258 and 23260)
35–44 cm Dark grey, 5Y 4/1, silty clay. *Phragmites* plant remains, beetles, molluscs, ostracods present.
Context 22351   (Bulk sample 23259)
44–48 cm   Dark olive-grey, 5Y 3/2, silty clay. Charcoal, wood, plant macrofossils and molluscs.
Context 22309   (Bulk sample 23260)
48–54 cm   Grey, 5Y 5/1, clay with some silt. Plant macrofossils throughout. Manganese, iron, desiccated wood.
Context 22349
54–60 cm   Dark grey, 5Y 4/1, organic clay with patches of silt , 5Y 4/1–5/1 Monocot. plant remains increasing with depth. Wood, stone, manganese.

60–72 cm   Very dark greyish-brown, 10YR 3/2 increasingly organic clay. Monocot. plant remains.

Column 6: Area G. Pollen monolith 23168 (Fig 65)
Context 22272
0–3 cm   Very dark greyish-brown, 2.5Y 3/2, organic lens.
3–6 cm   Dark olive-grey, 5Y 3/2, organic silty clay. Molluscs present. Plant macrofossils abundant.
Context 22273
6–17 cm   Very dark greyish-brown, 2.5Y 3/2, well humified peat. Abundant *Phragmites* remains.
17–20 cm   Dark grey, 5Y 4/1, clay becoming less organic with increasing depth.

Column 7: Area H. Pollen/diatom monolith 23309/10 (Fig 66)
Context 22279
0–43 cm   Greyish-brown, 2.5Y 5/2, slightly clayey silt. Some iron staining.
Context 22283
43–61 cm   Greyish-brown, 2.5Y 5/2, dark greyish-brown, 2.5Y 4/2, laminated silty clay. Laminations decreasing with depth. Some iron staining. Molluscs and plant macrofossil rootlets.
Context 22284
61–82 cm   Olive-grey, 5Y 4/2, clay.

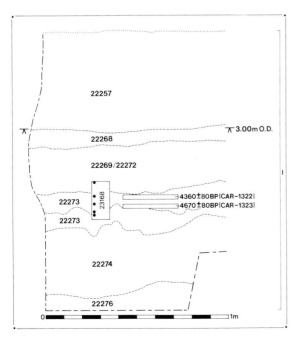

Fig 65   Section of environmental Column 6

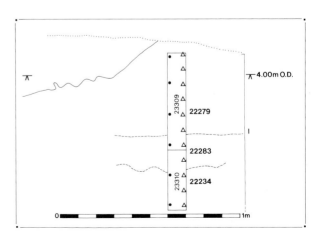

Fig 66   Section of environmental Column 7

Alluvial sedimentation and environmental change
Mark Taylor

Introduction

This report considers the nature of alluvial sedimentation of the Nedern Brook. The field site lies close to the Severn Estuary (see Figs 1–3) and has a catchment area of only 44.72km². This report assesses the character of the alluvial sediments.

Catchment morphology and the modern floodplain of the Nedern Valley

Welch and Trotter (1961) have suggested that the present direction of the Nedern Brook was diverted from flowing through the dry valley in the south-western corner of the Caerwent basin to St Bride's Netherwent (ST 429 896). Here, the small stream which occupies the wide valley, where the village of Magor lies, has the appearance of a misfit stream. Welch and Trotter (1961) suggest that ice may have dammed the Caerwent basin, forming a lake, which escaped along the line of the present Nedern Brook. Borehole evidence does indicate the presence of a buried channel in the Nedern valley, with the base of the alluvium being found at 10m below OD (Richardson 1887). In addition to the buried channel of the Nedern, other similar features are also known to exist in the lower Severn Valley and in the valleys of South Wales, which were formed by earlier phases of down-cutting during low sea level stands (Codrington 1898; Beckinsale and Richardson 1964; Williams 1968; Anderson and Owen 1979; Culver and Bull 1979).

The floodplain between Caerwent and Llanvair Discoed is overlain with a brown sandy loam which contains abundant Old Red Sandstone debris (Welch and Trotter 1961).These workers suggest the loam is of local origin and was deposited across the valley floor when the Cas Troggy Brook, as the Nedern is known in its higher reaches, was dammed. According to the present 1:50,000 geological map (British Geological Survey 1981) the Nedern Brook has now cut through this material to form a series of higher, older alluvial surfaces (see Fig 3). The current floodplain of the Nedern has an extremely low gradient after the channel emerges from the gorge at Earlswood Common, Llanmellin where it falls from 0.021m m⁻¹ (metres per metre) to 0.0042m m⁻¹. The low gradient combined with the loss of surface flow underground into the limestones at Llanmellin, plus the reduction of the base flow as a result of the tapping of the spring at Sudbrook during the building of the Severn Bridge in the 19th century (Welch and Trotter, 1961), now means that the present channel of the Nedern Brook is largely incapable of eroding its floodplain.

Sampling

The location (see Figs 60–6) and context details of the sediment samples reported on here are given in the environmental sampling introduction. Discussion is concentrated on the results obtained from Column 1 which included the deposits from the substantial Phase VI channel. The sediments analysed cover the height range of 4.198m OD to 2.327m OD and contain the deposits associated with Phases I, V, VI, VII, and VIII (see Fig 61). Phases of sedimentation not present in Column 1 were sampled in Column 4 (Area E, monoliths 23196–8). The results of a more limited range of analyses undertaken on samples from columns in areas B, E and H are held in the site archive.

Laboratory methods

Sediment samples were analysed for their wet and dry bulk densities, organic and carbonate contents using the methods proposed by Bengtsson and Enell (1986). Grain size analysis was carried out using a Micromeritics Sedigraph 5100. Grain size distributions were analysed for their characteristics using Moment Measure statistics (after Lindholm 1987). Sub-samples of the <4φ fraction were analysed for their heavy metal contents using an Inductively Coupled Plasma Mass Spectrometer (cf Thompson and Walsh 1983). Munsell soil charts were used to obtain the colour of the sediments immediately the monolith tins were opened for sedimentary analysis. Logging of structures, mottling, bioturbation features and organics inclusions were also carried out before the sediments were allowed to dry. These details were recorded schematically, and are held in the site archive.

Sedimentological results from Column 1

The analyses carried out on the sediments from Column 1 include logging and description of the sediments, wet and dry bulk density measurements, organic and carbonate contents, grain size characteristics and heavy metal concentrations of selected samples.

Laboratory analyses

The results of all the sediment density, organic and carbonate content data along with mean grain size data are shown in Fig 67a–e. These results demonstrate that sediments are not uniform in character and although five phases of sedimentation are represented in the Column 1 (I, V, VI, VII, VIII) there appear to be four main lithostratigraphic units present, with Phases VII and VIII being indistinguishable on the basis of the laboratory analyses presented. Table 3 shows the relationship between

CALDICOT Column 1
Monoliths 2330, 2331, 2332, 2333, 2335

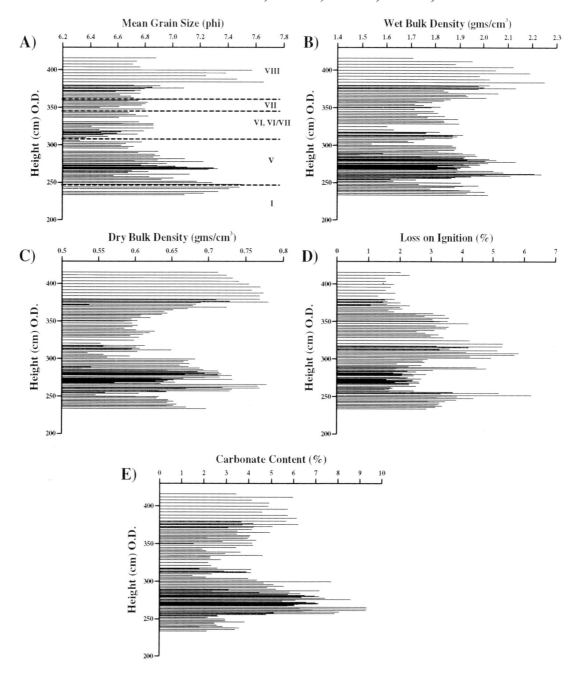

Fig 67   The results of laboratory analyses carried out on Column 1 sediments

the sedimentation events identified, the stratigraphic phases and their heights OD. Each sedimentation phase will be considered separately, with the exception of Phases VII and VIII which will be considered together.

Sedimentation Phase I

The deposits associated with Phase I sedimentation are characterised by blue-grey clays. Augering (Fig

12) has shown that these sediments can be found to a depth of at least –2m OD. The sediments in the lower section are composed largely of mottled grey clays with darker more organic horizons towards the top of the phase. These organic horizons have yielded radiocarbon dates demonstrating that they were deposited during the Neolithic period (p 11). Laboratory analyses show that the wet and dry bulk densities are higher at the base of the phase (Figs 67b, 67c) and gradually reduce towards the top as the organic content increases (Fig 67d). This sedimenta-

Table 3 Heights (OD) of the sedimentation events and their associated phases for Column 1

Sedimentation Event	Phases	Height OD (m)
A	I	2.33–2.53
B	V	2.53–3.00
C	VI, VI/VII	3.00–3.515
D	VII, VIII	3.515–4.20

Table 4 Pearson's product correlation coefficient matrix for the laboratory analysis carried out on Column 1

	Depth	Wet bulk density	Dry bulk density	Loss on ignition
Wet bulk density	0.157			
Dry bulk density	0.158	0.537		
Loss on ignition	–0.194	–0.779	–0.625	
Carbonate content	–0.114	0.666	0.434	–0.687

tion period is also characterised by some of the lowest carbonate contents in the sediments with values in the range of 2–4%. Figure 67a shows that mean grain size tends to increase towards the top of Phase I. X-ray radiography did not reveal any sedimentary structures from sedimentation Phase I except the presence of vertical 'tubes' or burrows (see p 77 for more discussion) in a rather dark homogeneous sediment matrix.

Sedimentation Phase V

The sediments associated with this phase were located from 2.53m to 3.00m OD (Table 3). The logged sections indicated a definite change in the nature of sedimentation, from one largely devoid of structures, to one where frequent laminations of darker material were separated by light grey clays. Laminations at the bottom section of the sediments, (c 2.53m OD to 2.64m OD) were generally coloured light grey 10Y 7/1, while the intervening clays were slightly darker (grey, 7.5Y 5/1). At 2.64m OD to 2.70m OD, sediments between the grey laminations were darker (5Y 3/2, olive-black, wet sediment). Here the laminations were wavy and coarser (medium silts) than the intervening fine silts and clays. Sediments between 2.70m OD and the top of the event at 3.00m OD were unlaminated, mottled and were truncated by darker grey sediments at the base of Phase VI.

X-ray radiographs from monolith tin 2335 clearly revealed laminations in the upper part of the sediment section. Thin sections taken from the monolith tin 2335, covering the range 2.715m OD to 2.672m OD, and from 2.627m OD to a depth of 2.622m OD

showed that the majority of the sediments were finer than 63μm, with only occasional larger grains. Finer fractions between the aforementioned laminations were darker due to the presence of ferric oxides. Other minerals present included biotite, muscovite, mica, orthoclase feldspar, chloritic clays and diagenetic rhombs of calcite, with the most abundant being quartz. The occurrence of laminations suggest that there may have been intermittent incursions of coarser particles into what was generally a low energy depositional environment where finer clays were being deposited as background sedimentation from suspension load materials.

The wet and dry bulk density values (Fig 67b–c) of Phase V are slightly higher than those from Phase I. Strong negative correlation coefficients of –0.78 and –0.63 between the wet and dry bulk density measurements and organic content (see Table 4) probably reflect closer packing of the grains and the reduction of pore space for the infiltration and accumulation of organic materials. The percentage carbonate contents of Phase V (Fig 67e), are the highest recorded in the Column 1 sediments with values up to 9.5%. Higher concentrations could result from increase in sediment supply from the limestone areas of the catchment or from the effect of rising ground waters enriched in calcium carbonate.

Sedimentation Phases VI and VI/VII

This phase begins at a depth of approximately 3.00m OD and has its upper limit at around 3.515m OD. This period of deposition is associated with the substantial Phase VI channel and has yielded substantial deposits of stone, wood and associated artefactual materials. The log of the sediments shows that Phase VI is initiated by a band of dark grey sediment, overlain by several lighter grey (7.5Y 4/1) laminations each approximately 30mm thick. At 3.09m OD the sediments are an homogenous mottled grey clay which are overlain by 0.12m of laminations at 3.26m OD The depositional mechanism was likely to have been similar to that proposed for similar units in Phase V.

Laboratory analyses for Phase VI indicate that the contemporary channel contained some of the coarsest sediments in the whole of Column 1 (Fig 67a), with mean grain sizes as large as 6.29 (medium silts). Associated with these coarser grain sizes are the lowest density values and carbonate contents of the whole master column (see Fig 67b, c, e). Low carbonate percentages may have been caused by variations in the sediment source, indicating that there was a reduction in erosion from the limestone areas of the catchment (see Fig 3).

Sedimentation Phases VII and VIII

These sedimentation phases occur between 3.515m OD and 4.20m OD, the top of Column 1. Figures 67, a–e do not show any obvious discontinuities between these two phases of sedimentation, although in cross-sectional exposures they clearly represent separate periods. Most of the sediment contained in the upper portion of the monolith tins is related to Phase VIII with approximately 80mm belonging to Phase VII.

Sediment logs indicate that these upper phases contain several laminations within an otherwise mottled light grey silty clay. These are visible in monolith 2331 at 3.755m, 3.71m and 3.67m OD. Cross cutting through these laminations are some vertical features or 'tubes' of about 3mm in width. These appear to postdate the laminations and are probably formed by either vegetation growing through the sediments, or by organisms burrowing into them. These burrows may have been formed by *Skolithos*, an intertidal dweller which tends to create vertical burrows with a structureless infill (Collinson and Thompson 1989). However, these organisms are more common in sandy rather than muddy environments like Caldicot, suggesting that vegetation is primarily responsible for bioturbation. Similar bioturbated laminations are also visible in monolith 2330 at 4.14–4.16m OD, and at 3.76–3.85m OD.

The sediments associated with Phase VIII comprise mixed consolidated pinkish-grey silty clays. The sediments analysed in the monolith tins 2332–2330 (sedimentation event D, Table 3) were mainly light grey with organic inclusions and some iron staining, with grain sizes of 6.62 to 7.65φ (medium to fine silt). Iron staining may have been more extensive in the exposed section, giving rise to the description of pinkish-grey sediments. The upper part of the sequence is not associated with any palaeochannels, but a similar silty red-brown sequence up to 3m in depth has been reported from borehole exposures across the catchment. The occurrence of this unit may indicate a catchment-wide sedimentation event which occurred sometime after the Late Bronze Age.

Bulk density results indicate that the sediment associated with Phases VII and VIII have some of the highest densities (Figs 67b, c) and some of the lowest loss on ignition values in the whole of Column 1 (Fig 67d). The grain size analysis for Phases VII and VIII show a decrease in the mean grain size at around 3.80m OD from medium to fine silts, with a return to medium silts at the top of the section (Fig 67a). Similar variations in mean grain size are also reflected by changes in the bulk density measurements (Figs 67b, c), probably reflecting differences in grain packing. The density of calcium carbonate is 2.71g/cm^3 which is very similar to that of quartz (2.65g/cm^3) (Whitten and Brookes 1972); therefore changes in the bulk density measurements must be due to some factor other than that of mineral composition. The strong negative correlation coefficient between organic content and the wet and dry bulk densities (see Table 4) indicates that variations in the percentage concentrations of organic matter are responsible for variations in the density of the sediment.

Grain size analysis for Column 1

The results of the moment measure analyses are presented in Fig 68a–f. The mean grain size results, already discussed, have also been included in Fig 68. The results in Figs 68b–d indicate that the sediments are, by and large, uniform in their grain size characteristics. For example, sorting values (Fig 68b) are predominantly poorly-sorted with values between 1.3φ and 1.7φ (after Folk and Ward 1957) indicating that despite being 'fines' they possess a polymodal grain size distribution. A cluster of five values around 4.00m OD are distinctly different in that they have lower sorting values by up to 0.7φ. These sediments also possess different skewness and kurtosis values than those recorded for the remainder of the profile (Fig 68c–d); they are negatively skewed and are extremely leptokurtic as opposed to the overall pattern which shows near symmetrical, positively skewed and very leptokurtic distributions. In addition, they are also composed of the finest grain sizes of the whole sediment profile (Fig 68a). Differences between this group of five samples and the remainder of the sediments is demonstrated by the bivariate plots of Fig 68e and in particular, that of Fig 68f which show the two separate groups. These deposits equate to sedimentation Phase VIII, representing deposition since the development of the palaeochannels. A possible explanation for their differing nature is that they represent a very fine distal over-bank sedimentation event (cf Hughes and Lewin 1982, Magilligan 1992, Marriot 1992).

Sorting, skewness, and kurtosis values indicate the general uniformity of the sediments. However, the variations in mean grain size that are shown to exist between the sedimentation phases, do imply that slightly variable hydrodynamic conditions operated in each of the palaeochannels. Explanations for this variability are not readily apparent, but the fact that Phase VI is characterised by coarser grains than that of Phases I, V, VII and VIII may be due to the fact that sedimentation in this phase relates to the 'main channel'. This feature is recognised as the largest surviving palaeochannel, which has an approximate channel width of c 6.5m. The other palaeochannels exposed at the site may have been at least as wide, but cross-sectional evidence does not support this. As Phase VI represents the largest recorded palaeochannel it seems probable that deposits contained within this feature have the coarsest grain sizes.

Heavy metal analyses on Column 1

The heavy metals analysed for Column 1 sediment were nickel, copper, zinc, cadmium, barium and lead. The results of the analyses are presented in Fig

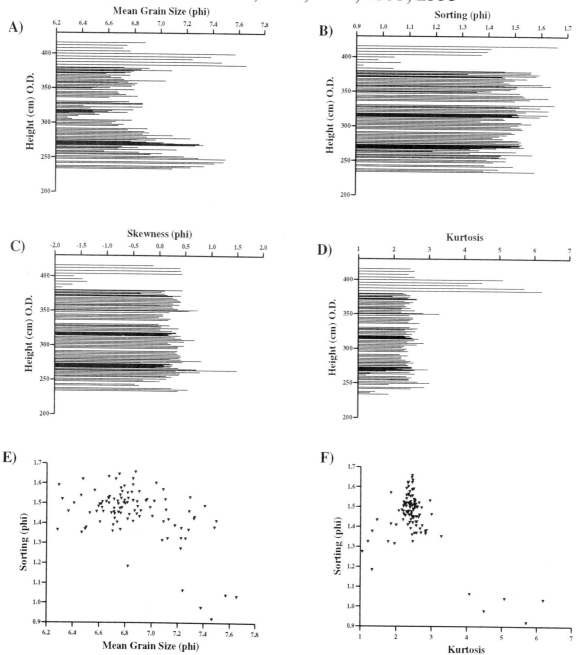

CALDICOT Column 1
Monoliths 2330, 2331, 2332, 2333, 2335

Fig 68   Grain size data for the Column 1 sediments

69a–f. The results show that the sediments all have low values and that they are very uniform throughout the profile. Exceptions to these results are occasional samples from the nickel, copper, zinc and cadmium analyses. These data compare well with those obtained by Allen and Rae (1986) who found the Late Flandrian sediments from the Severn Estuary had mean zinc values of 205.3 ppm, copper values of 39.9 ppm and lead values of 60.4 ppm. Some of the sediments analysed by these workers included

sediment which has been contaminated by recent industrial activity, hence the slightly higher mean lead and copper values.

Column 4: Area E monoliths 23196–8

Additional analyses were undertaken to provide coverage of those phases not represented in Column 1, particularly Phases II–IV. The results from mono-

CALDICOT Column 1
Monoliths 2330, 2331, 2332, 2333, 2335

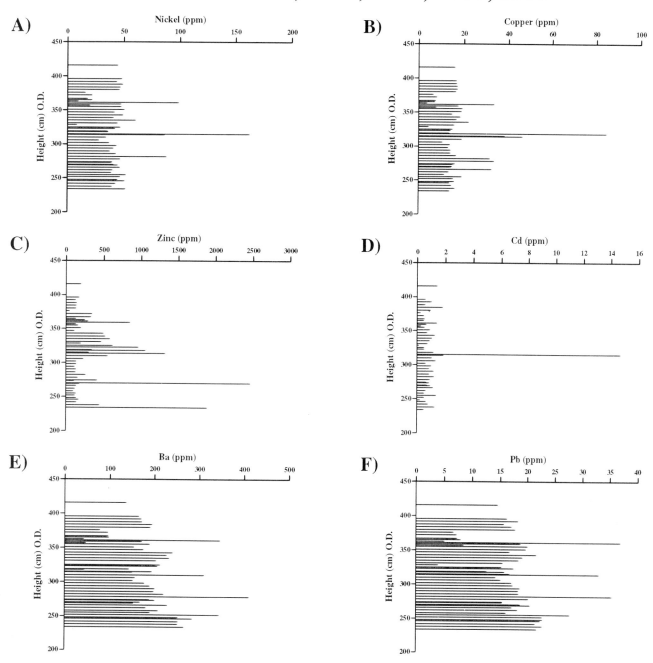

Fig 69   Heavy metal analyses of the fine sediments obtained from Column 1 sediments

liths 23196–8 are presented here, whilst results from the other sample columns, which do not add significantly to the site's interpretation, are held in the site archive. These sediments were logged, photographed and analysed for their wet and dry bulk densities, loss on ignition and percentage carbonate contents. No grain size, heavy metal or x-ray radiography analyses were undertaken. This section of sediments, excavated in Area E (Column 4), covered an exposure of 1.33m and contained sediments from Phases II to V and VIII.

Phase II

Only a small proportion of the total exposure (0.19m) includes sediments from Phase II. Nevertheless, laboratory analyses show that there is a distinct contrast between this phase and the overlying Phase III (Figs 70a–d). This is particularly pronounced in the loss on ignition and the percentage carbonate content results. The sedimentary logs show that the deposits are mottled with a number of organic inclusions and have a greyish-olive hue (5Y 4/2). The

CALDICOT Column 4
Monoliths 23196, 23197, 23198

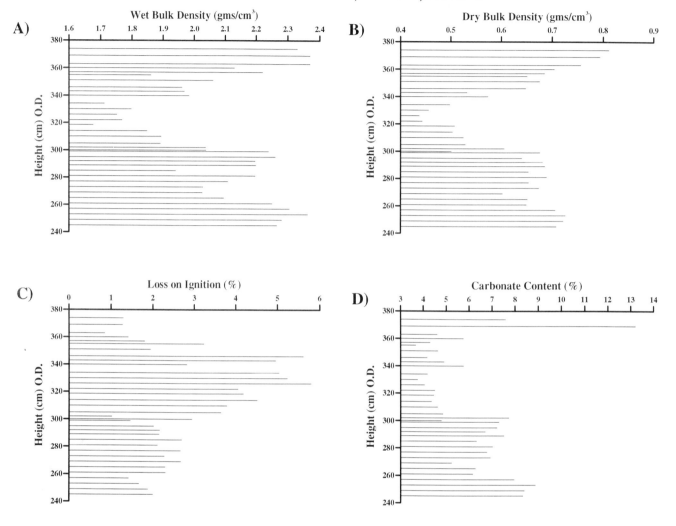

Fig 70   The results of laboratory analyses carried out on Column 4 sediments

loss on ignition results show that Phase II has low values (<2%) compared to the remainder of the profile (Fig 70c).

Phase III

This sedimentation phase covers some 0.31m of the exposure in Area E (Table 5). The logging of the sediments in the monolith tins showed that they appeared to be a largely homogeneous unit which consists of a grey (5Y to 10Y 4/1) sediment, with intermittent organic inclusions. The loss on ignition values are relatively low (less than 3%) while the percentage carbonate values range from 5.3 to 7.8% (Figs 70c–d).

Phase IV

This phase occurs between 3.46m OD and 2.92m OD and shows the most significant variation of all the

Table 5   Relative heights (OD) of phases present in monoliths from the second phase of sediment analysis

Monoliths	Phases	Height OD (m)
23196–8	VIII	3.75–3.71
	V	3.71–3.46
	IV	3.46–2.92
	III	2.92–2.61
	II	2.61–2.42

profiles in Figs 70a–d. From around 3.00m OD to around 3.40m sediment bulk densities are significantly lower than elsewhere in the sediment section, whilst loss on ignition values are as high as 5.8% with percentage carbonate values between 4 and 5% (Figs 70c–d). These changes correspond to organic deposition during Phase IV. The sediment log shows that this phase is very mottled and has undergone a variable amount of oxidation. A reduction in the length of time the sediments are in anaerobic conditions will increase the amount and rate of oxidation compared to gleyed waterlogged environments and lead to mottling, a feature which is particularly common to this phase of sedimentation as well to others.

Phase V

This phase is characterised by a darker more mottled sediment (black, 2.5Y 5/1) in the lower section (3.45m OD to 3.60m OD), whereas the overlying sediments from 3.60m OD to 3.75m OD have a hue which is a grey (2.5Y 7/1), and are significantly less mottled. Loss on ignition analyses show that this change is related to decreases in organic content above 360cm (see Fig 70c). Decreases in loss on ignition values are closely mirrored by increasing bulk density values for the sediments towards the top of the exposure and are probably a function of the different densities of the organic and mineral components of the sediments.

Phase VIII

Phase VIII in this profile is limited to an exposure of 40mm. Therefore any inferences about changes in the physical characteristics of the sediments is of little value. Details of this unit are discussed in the section covering Column 1.

Interpretation and discussion

Assessment of the importance of Caldicot

Accelerated floodplain alluviation in the Lower Severn and across southern Britain as a whole during the late Holocene appears to have been a more or less synchronous event (eg Brown 1983, 1987a, 1987b; Burrin and Scaife 1984; Burrin 1985; Limbrey 1978; Macklin and Lewin 1993; Robinson and Lambrick 1984; and Shotton 1978). The stratigraphy and alluvial chronology of the alluvial valley fills in South Wales have received much less attention than the actual nature of over-deepened bedrock channels in this region: Al-Saadi and Brookes (1973); Anderson (1968, 1974); Anderson and Blundell (1965); Anderson and Owen (1979); Beckinsale and Richardson (1964); Codrington (1898); Culver and Bull (1979); Welch and Trotter (1961); Williams (1968); Wills (1938), with the exception of Saunders *et al* (1986, 1989) who reported on the valley fill of the Ilston River, on the Gower. The present study therefore fills a gap in the published literature by examining the alluvial history of a small tributary of the River Severn in the late Holocene within the context of human interactions with the developing landscape.

Interpretation of the data

Physical analyses of the sediments retrieved from Caldicot demonstrate that the sediments do not display homogeneous physical and chemical characteristics. Thin section analysis and x-ray radiographs reveal laminations which are indicative of intermittent flood inundation which transported slightly coarser silt particles. These laminations probably formed as a result of flooding and rapid infilling of former channel zones, increasing the preservation potential of any sedimentary structures. Increases in sediment yields from within the catchment, probably led to inchannel sedimentation and a reduction of width-depth ratios (cf Brown, 1987b). This would have increased the number of flows exceeding bankfull capacity, thereby accelerating the infilling of the abandoned channels on the floodplain. The finer silts and clays were probably deposited as backwater sedimentation in slack water zones formed by lateral channel migration or in alluvial cut-offs, while the slightly coarser medium silts were added during flood inundation. A second possibility is that the coarser layers are the product of weak density currents flowing close to the bed, with the finer clays representing the background sedimentation (Collinson and Thompson 1989). The sediments which are bioturbated indicate periods of relative stability, allowing biota to colonise and homogenise the deposits.

The grain size characteristics, show that the sediments are typical of fine grained palaeochannel infills. They are poorly sorted and have very leptokurtic distributions; similar results were obtained by Lewis (1982) for alluvial cut-offs in mid Wales and those by Rotnicki and Borowaka (1985) from cut-offs on the Prosna river, Poland. However, at Caldicot skewness tends to be largely positive, which contrasts data from palaeochannels at Welshpool which are dominated by negative or near symmetrical distributions (Taylor 1993). This may be due to the fact that a greater proportion of the deposits consists of coarser material at Welshpool than at Caldicot, thereby resulting in a more negative skewed (coarsely skewed) distribution.

Most of the environmental data suggest that the environment of deposition in these palaeochannels is predominantly quiet water lacustrine-type conditions or slowly moving water. However, the mollusc data conflicts with these results, as the dominant species found towards the bottom of the palaeochannels is *Valvata piscinalis* whose most common habitat is a moving freshwater environment (Bell p 139). Periods of channel cutting and erosion are punctuated by periods of channel infilling conditions, both of which must have created particular fluvial environments in which certain species were able to flourish. *Valvata piscinalis* was perhaps most likely to have occupied the Nedern Brook during periods of down-cutting while there was a constant flow of water. Subsequent lateral channel migration or alluvial cut-off forming slack water zones leading to the development of quiet water environments. The final silting-up and drying-out of former channel areas would have produced conditions suited to the mollusc *Anisus leucostoma* (Bell p 135). Periodic drying-out of the sediment phases is also indicated by the presence of ferric oxides in the thin sections. Mottling and the occurrence of ferric oxides probably formed due to the conversion of ferrous to ferric compounds during aerial exposure to oxygen (Leeder 1982). Oxidation occurring near the sediment-water interface, forms variable shades of light grey and brown colours, whereas reducing conditions which tend to form below the interface develop black sediment colours (Nichols and Biggs 1985).

Towards a possible model for the alluvial history of Caldicot

One of the main considerations for the Caldicot site is why so much sediment accumulated near the mouth of the fluvial system and why it was not dispersed into the estuary. Allen's (1990) fine sediment budget model shows that the Severn Estuary has undergone a marine transgression during the Holocene. Foraminifera data from sediments within the estuary (Murray and Hawkins 1976) support this model. Nichols and Biggs (1985) argue that submergence by rising sea level increases estuary water depth and length, hence favouring entrapment of estuarine sediments, producing typical marine transgressive sequences in which the marine element of sedimentation becomes dominant over time. However, the sediments at Caldicot at the base of Phase I (and to a lesser extent Phase II) appear to have a marine origin (inter-tidal to supra-tidal environments) (p 124) and are overlain by Phases III–VIII, a series of units containing a predominantly freshwater ecology, though with some evidence for an increasing marine influence again in VII and VIII (p 126).

If sea level rises that have been identified in the post-glacial period for the Severn Estuary are exceeded by local increases in the net rate of sedimentation from within the catchment, then the estuary will fill and fluvial sediments will prograde across marine sediments (Nichols and Biggs 1985). Roy *et al* (1980) proposed a model for the evolution of a drowned valley when incoming sedimentation exceeds the rate of local relative sea level rises (Fig 71). At Caldicot the stratigraphic evidence suggests that a similar sequence of events has occurred, where local increases in the catchment sediment yield has resulted in the erosion of the estuarine clays and the subsequent deposition of 4–4.5m of fluvial sediments. Radiocarbon dating, the presence of the Bronze Age boat strake and other archaeological artefacts from the same period, suggest that the palaeochannel infills and the alluviation of sediments over estuarine deposits at Caldicot coincides with a period of accelerated alluviation identified throughout the Severn basin (Pannett and Morey 1976; Shotton 1978; Brown 1983, 1985, 1987a,b;

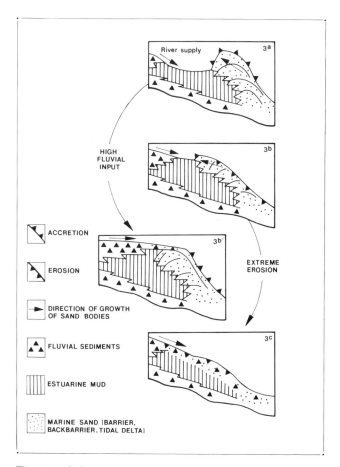

Fig 71   Schematic sections showing progressive stages in the evolution of a drowned valley (after Roy et al 1980)

Brown and Barber 1985; Barber and Twigger 1987, Taylor and Lewin 1996) and across Britain as a whole (Macklin and Lewin 1993). Although research has shown that there has been a progressive sea level rise during the Post Glacial period, the stratigraphic sequence at Caldicot suggests that at the mouth of the catchment, local sea level rises (eg Heyworth and Kidson 1982; Shennan 1983; Shennan *et al* 1983) were negated by an influx of sediments from the Nedern catchment. This led to valley infilling and the progradation of fluvial sediments over an estuarine sequence.

The uppermost phase (VIII) seen at Caldicot comprise some 2m of consolidated pinkish-grey silty clays (p 61). Although no radiocarbon dates exist for this phase, it is possible that it is contemporaneous with Iron Age and later sea level rises identified by Allen (1991). Such rises in sea level would have reduced the channel gradient of the Nedern Brook, its competency to transport suspended sediments in flood discharges, leading to the deposition of fines across the Nedern Brook floodplain.

Summary

The sedimentary sequences exposed at Caldicot show that there are two main phases of aggradation;

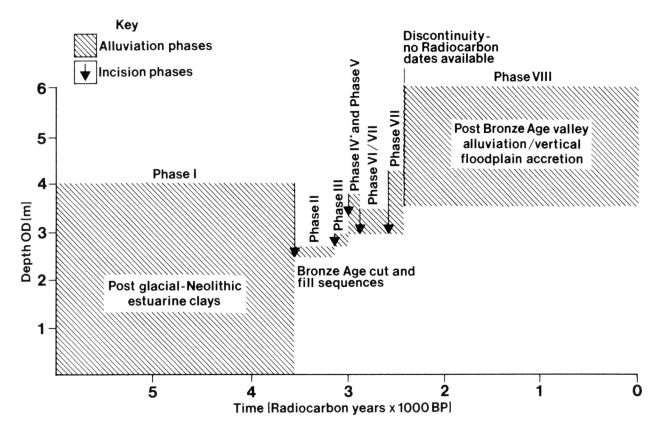

*Fig 72   Schematic diagram illustrating the two main periods of alluviation separated by a series of cut and fill events. The shaded areas which represent the periods of alluviation are plotted according to the maximum and minimum heights that were identified in the sediment samples analysed in this section. *Sedimentation phase with no radiocarbon dates*

estuarine silty-clays that occur at the base of the section (Phase I) which have been dated to the Neolithic period and a later sequence of fluvial deposits, punctuated by a series of cut and fill structures associated with Bronze Age occupation (Fig 72). The flora and fauna analyses indicate that the sediments from the Caldicot palaeochannel, are typical of those found in abandoned channels or slack water zones formed by alluvial cut-offs or lateral migration of the channel thalweg (the line following the deepest part of the channel). During the Bronze Age period, increases in sediment yields to the mouth of the Nedern Brook resulted in fluvial deposits prograding over estuarine sediments, leading to widespread infilling of the valley floor.

The palaeobotanical evidence
Astrid Caseldine with Kate Barrow

Introduction

The palaeobotanical evidence demonstrates the range of vegetation communities surrounding Caldicot, both in the immediate area and the wider region. Together the pollen and plant macrofossils complement each other, the pollen providing a regional as well as a local picture whilst the plant macrofossils

provide a more detailed largely local picture. However, this is to some extent an over-simplistic view and needs to take account of taphonomic processes and interpretative problems which are discussed in more detail later. The vegetation communities, based on the pollen, plant macrofossil and wood evidence from the site, that may have existed in the area are considered first, followed by the environmental sequence and vegetational history.

Methods

Pollen

Pollen samples were collected from seven sequences (see Figs 60–6). Details of the lithostratigraphy are given on pp 68–73. In the majority of cases sub-samples were analysed at every 8cm but in two sequences, Columns 4 and 7, a broader framework of 16cm intervals was used. Additional samples, notably in Column 6, were examined at a closer interval. Samples were analysed from every phase, although not from every context.

Samples of 1ml were prepared using established procedures (Moore *et al* 1991), including disaggregation in 10% NaOH, followed by micro-sieving and boiling in HF (because of the highly minerogenic nature of the samples), and then Erdtman's acetolysis. Stockmarr tablets containing *Lycopodium* spores were added to enable pollen concentrations to be calculated. Concentrations (unpublished) were generally quite low, frequently less than 40,000 grains/ml, with the highest concentration *c* 80,000 grains/ml and the lowest less than 10,000 grains/ml. The pollen was mounted in silicone oil and counted using a Leitz Laborlux microscope. A magnification of ×400 was used for general counting and ×630 and ×1000, the latter with phase contrast, for more critical determinations. In most cases 300 total land pollens was achieved but where concentrations were particularly low the count was stopped after 1000 *Lycopodium* spores.

Identification was by reference to type slides of modern material and identification keys, including Moore *et al* (1991), Moore and Webb (1978) and Faegri and Iversen (1989). Diagrams (Figs 73–9) have been prepared using Tilia and Tilia.Graph (Grimm 1991). Following the publication of Stace (1991) and recent discussions on pollen nomenclature (Bennett *et al* 1994), the nomenclature largely follows that outlined by Bennett (1994).

Plant macrofossils

Plant macrofossil remains were examined from four sequences and one spot sample (Figs 60–6). Context details are given on pp 68–73. The same procedure as that for the recovery of molluscs was used, ie the samples were allowed to soak in dilute hydrogen peroxide and then washed through a stack of sieves (2mm, 1mm, 500micron and 250micron). Samples of 1kg were analysed from sequence 2050–2078 and 250g samples from the other sequences. Samples from the stitch holes were variable in size (details in Table 68). Apart from the stitch-hole samples, the coarser fractions were analysed in detail and the 250micron fractions were scanned and the remains recorded on an abundancy scale. All fractions of the stitch-hole samples were scanned and the remains recorded on a presence/absence basis. Identification was by comparison with modern reference material and the use of standard identification texts, including Bertsch (1941), Beijerinck (1947), Berggren (1969, 1981) and Schoch *et al* (1988). Nomenclature mainly follows Stace (1991). The results are summarised by phase in Table 6 and detailed results presented in appendix Tables 64–8.

Pollen zonation

Because of the nature of the site, with earlier sediments eroded by later channels, no single diagram covers the full sequence and therefore the results from all the diagrams will be discussed together. However, the zonation for each of the diagrams will be outlined first. Inevitably stratigraphic discontinuities occur in the sequences because of the erosion of older deposits. Where there is a discontinuity, a pollen zone boundary normally coincides but sometimes possible mixing of sediments has blurred the distinction. Initially, local pollen assemblage zones have been defined for each diagram but comparison of the diagrams has allowed a site zonation to be established (Fig 73, Table 7). The following local pollen zones have been recognised. Percentages are of Total Land Pollen except aquatics which are of aquatics + TLP, spores which are of spores + TLP, indeterminables which are of indeterminables + TLP and *Pediastrum* which are of *Pediastrum* + TLP.

Column 6 monolith 23168 Area G

Two zones have been identified (Fig 74)

CA.1: 18–17cm This zone is limited to only one level. It is defined by having low arboreal and high Cyperaceae values (> 60%). *Tilia* values are *c* 2%, *Ulmus* is *c* 1% and *Quercus* less than 5%. Shrubs are dominated by *Corylus avellana*-type (<10%). *Plantago lanceolata* and Chenopodiaceae are present at more than 1%. *Polypodium* spores are frequent. Total concentrations are *c* 30,000 grains/ml.

CA.2: 17–0cm The zone is characterised by high arboreal values (>70%) and coincides with a lithostratigraphic change to an organic deposit. *Tilia* values reach a maximum of *c* 12%. *Pinus* and *Ulmus* are consistently greater than 1%, *Quercus* is *c* 15–25%, and *Alnus c* 15%. *Corylus avellana*-type percentages vary between 15–25%. Poaceae values are low, generally less than 10%, while Cyperaceae values vary between 10–25%. Chenopodiaceae pollen is consistently present. *Plantago* is absent. Aquatics are scarce. *Polypodium* is reasonably well represented and *Pteridium* and Pteropsida (monolete) indet. values are low. Concentration values vary between 30,000–40,000 grains/ml.

Column 7 monolith 23309/10 Area H

One zone has been distinguished (Fig 75). Above 32cm pollen was too sparse and poorly preserved to count.

CB.1: 80–32cm Arboreal pollen dominates the assemblage. *Quercus* is most abundant (25–35%), whilst *Alnus* values are relatively low (<10%). *Tilia* is quite well represented *c* 5%. *Pinus* and *Ulmus* are generally more than 1%. *Corylus avellana*-type pollen is *c* 15%. Herbaceous pollen is dominated by Poaceae (5–15%) and Cyperaceae (10–15%). *Plantago lanceolata* and Cerealia-type pollen are present. Chenopodiaceae pollen reaches over 10%. Aquatics are poorly represented. Spores are quite frequent, mainly *Pteridium aquilinum* (> 20%). Concentration values are *c* 10,500–12,500 grains/ml.

Column 2 monolith 23010 Area B

Two zones have been recognised, with the former zone divided into two sub-zones (Fig 76).

CC.1a: 48–36cm Arboreal pollen predominates but decreases steadily. *Quercus* (25–40%) is dominant but declines during the zone. *Alnus* values vary and *Tilia* and *Ulmus* are both present. *Pinus* occurs consistently at more than 1%. *Corylus avellana*-type pollen is *c* 10–15%. Poaceae pollen increases while *Plantago lanceolata* and Cerealia-type decrease. Chenopodiaceae pollen is also present. Cyperaceae pollen is low. Aquatics are sparse. *Polypodium*, *Pteridium* and Pteropsida (monolete) indet. are quite

Table 6 Plant macrofossils from Phases I-VIII

Phase	I	I-VI	II	III	IV	V	V-VI	VI	VI/VII	VII	VIII	Habitat preferences
Sample size	1kg	1kg	1kg	1kg	1kg	1kg	1kg	1kg	1kg	1kg	1kg	
RANUNCULACEAE												
Ranunculus repens type (Creeping buttercup)	–	–	4	12	10	5	4	7	20	1	–	M,Gd,D,Da,W,Cst
R. bulbosus L. (Bulbous buttercup)	–	–	–	–	–	–	–	–	–	–	–	G,Cst
R. sceleratus L. (Celery-leaved buttercup)	69	64	12	51	49	16	23	42	5	8	5	B,A
R. cf. *flammula* L. (Lesser spearwort)	–	–	–	–	–	–	–	–	2	–	–	A
R. Subgenus *Batrachium* (DC) A. Gray (Crowfoots)	2	64	2	217	44	1	32	54	3	4	+	B,A
Ranunculus spp. (Buttercups)	–	–	–	5	–	–	–	3	2	–	–	B,A,M,Gd,D,Da,W,Cst
PAPAVERACEAE												
Papaver rhoeas / dubium (Common/long-leaved poppy)	–	–	–	–	–	–	–	–	–	1	–	D,Da
URTICACEAE												
Urtica dioica L. (Common nettle)	85	76	10	25	107	9	22	60	19	16	4	M,G,D,Da
U. urens L. (Small nettle)	–	–	–	–	–	–	–	–	1	–	–	D,Da
BETULACEAE												
Betula spp. (Birch)	–	8	–	1	3	–	1	2	1	–	–	M,W
Alnus glutinosa (L.)Gaertner (Alder)	1	100	2	9	10	2	11	34	15	1	–	Bs,M,W
A. glutinosa (L.) Gaertner cone-scale	–	12	2	1	1	–	–	1	–	–	–	D,Da
Corylus avellana L. frags. (Hazel)	–	–	4	–	–	1	–	–	–	–	–	H,S,W
CHENOPODIACEAE												
Chenopodium rubrum L. (Red goosefoot)	–	–	–	–	1	–	–	1	–	+	–	B,D,Da
C. polyspermum L. (Many-seeded goosefoot)	–	–	–	–	–	–	–	2	1	1	–	D,Da
C. ficifolium Smith (Fig-leaved goosefoot)	–	–	–	1	1	–	–	1	–	1	–	D,Da
C. cf. *ficifolium* Smith	–	–	–	1	–	1	–	–	–	–	–	
C. album L. (Fat-hen)	–	16	–	23	1	11	3	10	8	9	–	D,Da
Chenopodium sp. (Goosefoots)	–	–	–	–	1	–	–	–	–	–	–	B,D,Da
Atriplex prostrata Boucherex DC. (Spear-leaved orache)	–	–	–	1	1	–	–	–	–	–	–	B,D,D
A. patula L. (Common orache)	–	–	4	21	1	–	–	–	–	–	–	B,D,Da
Atriplex spp. (Orache)	1	36	10	50	5	43	16	25	8	11	–	B,D,Da
Salicornia spp. (Glassworts)	–	–	–	1	–	–	–	–	–	–	–	B
Suaeda maritima (L.)Dumort. (Annual sea-blite)	1	–	–	1	–	–	–	2	–	–	–	B

Table 6 (cont.)

Phase	I	I-VI	II	III	IV	V	V-VI	VI	VI/VII	VII	VIII	Habitat preferences
Sample size	1kg	1kg	1kg	1kg	1kg	1kg	1kg	1kg	1kg	1kg	1kg	
Chenopodiaceae indet.	–	–	6	1	1	–	–	–	–	–	–	
PORTULACEAE												
Montia fontana L. (Blinks)	–	4	–	1	–	–	–	1	1	–	–	Bs,Gd,Da
CARYOPHYLLACEAE												
Moehringia trinervia (L.)Clairv. (Three-nerved sandwort)	–	–	–	1	–	–	–	–	–	–	–	W
Stellaria media (L.) Villars (Common chickweed)	–	–	2	3	1	1	3	5	2	2	–	B,G,D,Da
S.holostea L. (Greater stitchwort)	–	–	–	1	–	–	–	–	–	–	–	H,W
S. palustris Retz. (Marsh stitchwort)	–	–	2	3	–	1	–	–	1	–	–	M
S. cf. palustris Retz.	–	–	–	–	–	–	–	1	–	–	–	
S. uliginosa Murray (Bog stitchwort)	–	–	2	1	–	–	2	2	5	1	–	Bs,W
Stellaria sp. (Stitchworts)	–	–	–	2	–	–	1	–	1	–	–	B,Bs,M,G,D,Da,H,W
Cerastium sp. (Mouse-ears)	–	–	–	–	–	+	–	+	+	+	–	G,Cst,Da
Sagina sp. (Pearlworts)	–	–	–	–	–	+	+	–	+	+	–	B,Bs,G,D,Da,Cst
Spergularia sp. (Sea-spurreys)	+	–	–	–	–	–	+	–	+	+	–	B,Cst
Lychnis flos-cuculi L. (Ragged robin)	1	20	–	–	–	–	1	14	1	1	–	M,Gd,Wd
Silene sp. (Campions)	–	–	–	–	–	–	–	–	1	–	–	B,Bs,G,D,Da,H,W
Caryophyllaceae indet.	–	–	–	–	–	–	+	–	1	–	–	
POLYGONACEAE												
Persicaria maculosa Gray (Redshank)	–	–	–	–	–	–	–	–	1	1	–	A,D,Da
P. lapathifolia (L.) Gray (Pale persicaria)	–	–	–	–	–	–	–	–	1	–	–	A,D,Da
P. hydropiper (L.) Spach (Water-pepper)	–	4	–	1	4	4	–	1	–	–	–	A
P. laxiflora (Weihe) Opiz (Tasteless water-pepper)	–	–	–	1	–	–	–	–	–	–	–	A
Persicaria spp. (Knotweeds)	–	–	–	–	5	–	–	1	1	1	–	
Polygonum aviculare L. (Knotgrass)	–	–	2	6	2	6	1	1	1	5	1	B,D,Da,Cst
Rumex acetosella L. (Sheep's sorrel)	–	–	2	5	3	–	–	1	1	6	–	M,G,Da,Ht
R. hydrolapathum type (Water dock)	–	4	18	34	1	3	–	–	–	1	–	A,Bs,G,M
R. cf. crispus L. (Curled dock)	–	–	8	18	–	–	1	1	–	–	–	B,G,D,Da,Cst
R. conglomeratus Murray with perianth (Clustered dock)	–	–	2	51	13	–	4	3	5	6	–	Gd,W,Bs
R. cf. conglomeratus	–	8	22	75	8	8	5	5	3	5	–	

Table 6 (cont.)

Phase / Sample size	I 1kg	I-VI 1kg	II 1kg	III 1kg	IV 1kg	V 1kg	V-VI 1kg	VI 1kg	VI/VII 1kg	VII 1kg	VIII 1kg	Habitat preferences
R. sanguineus L. (Wood dock)	–	–	–	–	–	2	–	1	–	–	–	G,D,W,H,Bs
R. cf. obtusifolius L. (Broad-leaved dock)	–	–	–	2	–	–	–	–	–	2	–	D,H,G
R. cf. palustris Smith (Marsh dock)	–	–	4	3	–	1	–	–	1	–	1	A,Gd
Rumex spp. (Docks)	–	4	8	47	10	4	19	11	2	6	3	B,A,Bs,G,Gd,D,Da,H,W
Rumex sp. perianth frags.	–	–	–	5	3	–	3	–	–	3	–	
CLUSIACEAE												
Hypericum sp. (St. John's-worts)	–	+	+	1	+	+	+	+	+	+	–	Bs,G,Wd,Bs,W,Ht
MALVACEAE												
Malva sylvestris L. (Common mallow)	–	–	–	2	1	1	3	–	17	3	–	D
Althaea officinalis L. (Marsh mallow)	–	–	–	1	–	1	–	4	14	4	–	B,Bs,G,Cst
BRASSICACEAE												
Rorippa nasturtium-aquaticum (L.) Hayeck (Water-cress)	–	–	–	+	5	–	1	–	–	–	–	A
Rorippa cf. nasturtium-aquaticum (L.) Hayeck	–	+	+	+	+	+	–	+	–	+	–	A
R. palustris (L.) Besser (Marsh yellow-cress)	–	4	2	1	8	–	–	1	–	–	–	A,Dd
R. cf. amphibia (L.) Besser (Great yellow-cress)	–	–	–	–	–	–	+	+	1	–	–	A
Brassicaceae indet	–	–	–	–	–	–	–	–	1	–	–	
PRIMULACEAE												
Anagallis minima / Samolus valerandi (Chaffweed/Brookweed)	–	–	+	+	+	–	–	+	–	–	–	B,Bs,Ht,W,Cst
Glaux maritima L. (Sea-milkwort)	–	–	–	2	–	1	1	1	2	–	–	G,Cst,B
ROSACEAE												
Rubus fruticosus L. agg. (Bramble)	2	8	–	34	8	8	5	6	1	4	–	Ht,D,H,S,W
R. cf. idaeus L. (Raspberry)	–	–	–	–	–	–	–	1	–	–	–	Ht,D,W
Rubus sp. (Brambles)	–	4	6	12	1	2	1	2	–	1	2	Ht,D,H,S,W
Rubus sp. thorn	–	–	–	5	8	–	–	–	–	–	–	
Potentilla anserina L. (Silverweed)	–	–	2	7	5	1	9	2	16	12	–	B,Gd,D
Potentilla sp. (Cinquefoil)	–	–	–	1	–	–	–	–	–	–	–	B,M,Ht,Gd,D,Cst,H
Aphanes arvensis L. (Parsley piert)	–	–	–	1	–	1	2	–	–	–	–	D,Da
A. inexspectata Lippert (Slender parsley-piert)	1	–	–	2	–	–	–	–	1	3	–	D,Da

Table 6 (cont.)

Phase	I	I-VI	II	III	IV	V	V-VI	VI	VI/VII	VII	VIII	Habitat preferences
Sample size	1kg	1kg	1kg	1kg	1kg	1kg	1kg	1kg	1kg	1kg	1kg	
Rosa sp. (Rose)	–	–	–	–	1	–	–	–	–	–	–	H,S,W,Cst
Prunus spinosa L. (Blackthorn)	–	–	2	7	–	1	1	2	–	–	–	H,S,W
Prunus spp. (Cherries)	–	–	–	2	–	–	–	–	–	–	–	H,S,W
Crataegus monogyna Jacq. (Hawthorn)	–	–	–	1	–	–	–	–	–	–	–	H,S,W
C. monogyna Jacq. thorn	–	–	–	3	–	–	–	–	–	–	–	
Rosaceae thorn	–	–	–	3	3	–	+	–	–	–	–	
cf. Rosaceae	–	–	–	–	–	+	+	–	–	–	1	
LYTHRACEAE												
Lythrum sp. (Purple-loosestrifes)	+	4	–	+	+	–	+	+	1	+	–	Bs,M
ONAGRACEAE												
Epilobium hirsutum type (Great willowherb)	1	4	–	6	34	+	3	4	+	+	+	Bs,M
APIACEAE												
Berula erecta (Hudson) Cov. (Lesser water-parsnip)	–	–	–	–	–	–	–	–	–	1	–	A,Bs,M
cf. *Berula erecta* (Hudson) Cov.	–	–	–	–	–	–	–	–	–	–	–	
Conium maculatum L. (Hemlock)	–	–	–	1	–	–	–	–	–	–	–	Bs,d,D
Apium graveolens L. (Wild celery)	–	4	–	12	25	–	2	4	–	1	–	B,A
A. nodiflorum (L.) Lag. (Fool's water-cress)	–	–	–	6	1	1	1	–	1	–	–	A,Bs,M
A. nodiflorum / inundatum (Fool's water-cress/lesser marshwort)	–	–	–	–	2	2	5	–	–	–	–	A,Bs
A. repens (Jacq.) Lag. (Creeping marshwort)	–	–	–	2	4	–	–	–	–	–	–	A,Bs
Apium spp. (Marshworts)	–	–	–	4	7	–	–	2	–	–	–	A,Bs,M
Peucedanum sp. (Hog's fennels)	–	–	–	–	–	–	–	–	1	–	–	B,Bs,M
Apiaceae indet.	–	+	–	2	+	–	–	+	1	+	–	A,Bs
SOLANACEAE												
Solanum nigrum L. (Black nightshade)	–	4	–	2	–	2	–	1	–	3	–	D,Da
S. dulcamara L. (Bittersweet)	2	8	2	3	–	–	2	4	3	1	–	D,H,W,M,Cst
BORAGINACEAE												
Myosotis sp. (Forget-me-not)	–	4	–	1	1	–	–	–	–	–	–	A,Bs,M,Gd,Cst
LAMIACEAE												
Stachys cf. *palustris* L. (Marsh woundworts)	1	–	–	–	–	–	–	1	–	–	–	Bs,D

Table 6 (cont.)

Phase Sample size	I 1kg	I-VI 1kg	II 1kg	III 1kg	IV 1kg	V 1kg	V-VI 1kg	VI 1kg	VI/VII 1kg	VII 1kg	VIII 1kg	Habitat preferences
Prunella vulgaris L. (Selfheal)	–	–	–	1	–	–	–	–	1	–	–	G,D
cf. *Clinopodium acinos* (L.) Kuntze (Basil thyme)	–	–	–	–	–	–	–	–	1	–	–	G
Lycopus europaeus L. (Gypsywort)	1	20	2	3	–	–	5	8	–	2	–	Bs,M,Gd
Mentha arvensis/aquatica (Corn/water mint)	57	72	–	9	18	7	19	36	1	1	–	A,Bs,M,Da,Wd
Mentha sp. (Mint)	–	–	–	–	–	–	–	–	–	1	–	A,Bs,M,Da,Wd
HIPPURIDACEAE												
Hippuris vulgaris L. (Mare's-tail)	–	4	–	1	–	–	–	5	–	1	–	A
CALLITRICHACEAE												
Callitriche sp. (Water-starworts)	–	24	–	17	60	2	11	6	1	13	–	A
cf.*Callitriche* sp.	–	–	–	1	–	–	–	–	–	–	–	
PLANTAGINACEAE												
Plantago major L. (Greater plantain)	3	8	20	109	9	18	38	6	1	8	–	D,Da
P. lanceolata L. (Ribwort plantain)	–	–	–	–	1	–	–	–	–	–	–	
SCROPHULARIACEAE												
Veronica beccabunga L. (Brooklime)	+	+	+	+	+	+	+	+	+	+	+	A,M,Bs
Veronica sp. (Speedwell)	–	–	–	–	1	–	–	–	–	–	–	Bs,M,G,Gd,H,W
RUBIACEAE												
Galium palustre L. (Common marsh-bedstraw)	–	–	–	–	1	–	–	–	–	–	–	M,Gd,Bs
CAPRIFOLIACEAE												
Sambucus nigra L. (Elder)	1	16	4	8	2	1	8	13	1	1	1	S,W,H
ASTERACEAE												
cf. *Carduus* sp. (Thistles)	–	–	–	1	–	–	–	1	–	–	–	Bs,G,D,Cst
Carduus/Cirsium	–	–	–	1	–	–	–	–	–	–	–	
Cirsium cf.*vulgare* (Savi) Ten. (Spear thistle)	–	–	–	–	1	–	–	–	–	–	–	G,D,Da
C. cf. *palustre* (L.) Scop. (Marsh thistle)	–	–	2	6	1	–	1	2	–	–	–	Gd,H,W,M,Bs
C. cf. *arvense* (L.) Scop. (Creeping thistle)	–	–	12	16	1	1	16	6	1	4	–	G,D
Cirsium sp. (Thistles)	–	4	2	4	1	–	–	2	–	1	–	G,Gd,D,H,W,Da
Lapsana communis L. (Nipplewort)	–	–	–	1	–	–	–	1	1	1	–	D,Da,H,W
Picris hieracioides L. (Hawkweed oxtongue)	–	–	–	1	–	–	–	–	–	–	–	G
Sonchus cf. *palustris* (Marsh sow-thistle)	–	–	–	–	1	–	–	–	–	–	–	Bs,M

Table 6 (cont.)

Phase Sample size	I 1kg	I-VI 1kg	II 1kg	III 1kg	IV 1kg	V 1kg	V-VI 1kg	VI 1kg	VI/VII 1kg	VII 1kg	VIII 1kg	Habitat preferences
S.arvensis L. (Perennial sow-thistle)	–	–	–	1	–	–	3	–	–	–	–	Bs,Da,Cst
S. oleraceus L. (Smooth sow-thistle)	–	–	–	1	–	–	–	–	–	–	–	D,Da
S. asper (L.) Hill (Prickly sow-thistle)	–	4	2	21	4	2	–	6	2	1	–	D,Da
Sonchus sp. (Sow-thistles)	–	–	2	–	–	–	–	–	–	–	–	Bs,M,D,Da
Taraxacum sp. (Dandelions)	–	–	–	–	2	–	–	–	–	–	–	G,Cst,Gd,M
Aster tripolium L. (Sea aster)	–	–	–	1	–	–	–	–	–	–	–	B
cf.*Chamaemelum nobile* (L.) All. (Chamomile)	–	–	–	1	–	–	–	–	–	–	–	G
Senecio sp. (Ragworts)	–	–	–	1	–	–	–	–	–	–	–	M,G,D,Cst
Eupatorium cannabinum L (Hemp agrimony)	39	–	4	4	8	1	3	–	–	1	–	Bs,M,G
Asteraceae indet.	–	–	–	–	–	–	+	–	–	1	–	
ALISMATACEAE												
Alisma spp. (Water plantain)	18	20	6	13	34	3	10	9	2	2	–	A
POTAMOGETONACEAE												
Potamogeton lucens L. (Shining pondweed)	–	–	–	–	1	–	–	–	–	–	–	A
P. praelongus Wulfen (Long-stalked pondweed)	–	–	–	1	–	–	–	–	–	–	–	A
P. berchtoldii Fieber (Small pondweed)	–	4	–	–	1	–	–	12	103	–	–	A
P. cf. *berchtoldii* Fieber	–	–	–	–	–	1	1	–	–	–	–	A
Potamogeton sp. (Pondweed)	–	4	–	1	1	1	1	–	4	–	–	A
cf. *Potamogeton* sp.	–	–	–	–	–	–	–	–	2	–	–	A
ZANNICHELLIACEAE												
Zannichellia palustris L. (Horned pondweed)	–	–	–	2	–	–	1	1	–	4	–	B,A
LEMNACEAE												
Lemna gibba L. (Fat duckweed)	3	4	–	1	5	–	–	–	2	1	–	A,B
L. cf. *gibba* L.	–	–	–	–	–	–	–	–	–	–	–	
L. minor L. (Common duckweed)	–	–	–	–	1	–	–	–	–	–	–	A
L. trisulca L (Ivy-leaved duckweed)	–	–	–	–	1	–	–	–	1	–	–	A
Lemna spp. (Duckweeds)	–	–	–	–	+	–	–	+	–	–	–	A
JUNCACEAE												
Juncus spp. (Rushes)	+	+	+	+	+	+	+	1	+	–	+	Ht,G,D,d,M,B,Cst
Luzula sp. (Wood-rush)	–	–	–	1	–	–	–	–	–	–	–	Bs,Ht,H,W,G

Table 6 (cont.)

Phase / Sample size	I 1kg	I-VI 1kg	II 1kg	III 1kg	IV 1kg	V 1kg	V-VI 1kg	VI 1kg	VI/VII 1kg	VII 1kg	VIII 1kg	Habitat preferences
CYPERACEAE												
Eleocharis palustris /uniglumis (Common/slender spike-rush)	–	8	–	21	8	–	5	6	1	3	–	B,M,Bs
Bolboschoenus maritimus / *Schoenoplectus lacustris* (Sea/Common club-rush)	–	8	12	5	2	1	1	2	1	–	–	B,M,A
S. tabernaemontani (C. Gmelin) Palla (Grey club-rush)	–	8	2	3	1	2	2	3	1	1	–	B,M,A
Schoenoplectus sp. (Club-rush)	–	–	–	1	–	–	–	–	–	–	–	B,M
Cladium mariscus (L.) Pohl (Great fen-sedge)	–	–	–	–	–	–	–	–	1	–	–	Bs,M
cf. *Cladium mariscus* (L.) Pohl	–	–	–	1	–	–	–	–	–	–	–	Bs,M
Carex paniculata L. (Greater tussock sedge)	–	12	2	3	1	–	1	4	1	1	–	M,Wd,Bs
C. otrubae Podp. (False fox-sedge)	3	8	6	11	6	–	4	8	5	1	–	B,Bs,Gd
C. pseudocyperus L. (Cyperus sedge)	–	–	–	1	–	–	–	2	–	–	–	Bs,M
C. cf. *rostrata* Stokes (Bottle sedge)	–	–	–	–	–	–	–	–	1	–	–	Bs,M
C. cf. *vesicaria* L. (Bladder sedge)	–	–	–	–	–	1	–	1	–	–	–	Bs,M
C. cf. *distans* L. (Distant sedge)	–	20	–	2	3	–	–	4	1	–	–	B,M
C. cf. *extensa* Gooden. (Long-bracted sedge)	–	–	–	1	–	–	–	2	–	–	–	B
C. cf. *hostiana* DC. (Tawny sedge)	–	–	–	2	–	–	–	–	2	–	–	B,M
C. cf. *pallescens* L. (Pale sedge)	–	–	–	1	–	–	1	10	2	1	–	Bs,Gd,S,W
C. cf. *digitata* L. (Fingered sedge)	–	–	–	–	–	–	–	1	–	–	–	W,S
Carex spp. - biconvex (Sedges)	–	–	–	–	–	–	–	2	–	–	–	
Carex spp. - trigonous	–	–	–	–	–	2	–	1	–	–	–	
Carex spp.	–	4	6	1	7	–	–	1	4	1	–	B,Bs,M,Gd,S,W
Carex spp. utricle	–	–	–	1	1	–	–	–	2	–	–	
POACEAE												
cf. *Festuca* sp. (Fescues)	–	–	–	4	2	–	–	1	–	–	–	B,G,W,H
Poa annua L. (Annual meadow-grass)	–	–	2	1	4	–	–	–	1	1	–	G,D,Da
Poa cf. *annua* L.	–	–	2	1	–	–	–	–	1	–	–	G,D,Da
Poa spp. (Meadow grasses)	–	–	–	4	–	–	–	–	–	–	–	G,D,Da,Cst
cf *Poa* sp.	–	–	–	1	–	–	–	–	–	–	–	
Phalaris arundinacea L. (Reed canary-grass)	–	–	–	9	3	1	–	–	27	5	–	B,Bs,M,Gd,D

Table 6 (cont.)

Phase	I	I-VI	II	III	IV	V	V-VI	VI	VI/VII	VII	VIII	Habitat preferences
Sample size	1kg	1kg	1kg	1kg	1kg	1kg	1kg	1kg	1kg	1kg	1kg	
Phalaris cf. *arundinacea* L.	–	–	–	1	–	–	–	–	–	–	–	
Agrostis sp. (Bents)	–	–	–	1	–	–	–	–	–	–	–	G,Gd,D,Da,M,Cst
Phragmites australis (Cav.) Trin. ex Steudal (Common reed)	–	–	–	1	2	–	–	–	3	3	–	B,Bs,M
Poaceae indet. <2mm	2	48	8	36	19	–	10	11	12	1	–	
Poaceae indet. >2mm	–	4	12	37	16	4	7	5	12	7	–	
cf. Poaceae indet. >2mm	–	–	–	1	1	–	–	–	2	–	–	
SPARGANIACEAE												
Sparganium cf. *natans* L. (Least bur-reed)	–	–	–	1	1	–	–	2	–	–	–	A,Bs,M
Sparganium sp. (Bur-reed)	–	96	2	7	6	–	1	30	13	–	–	A,Bs,M
OTHER REMAINS												
Bud scales	–	8	–	11	4	1	–	2	–	–	–	
Tree buds	–	–	8	47	4	–	–	2	–	1	–	
Leaf scars	–	–	–	2	–	–	–	–	–	–	–	
PTEROPSIDA												
Pteridium aquilinum (L.) Kuhn leaf frags (Bracken)	–	4	10	7	2	–	6	2	–	–	–	Ht,W
BRYOPHYTA												
Moss leaves (Stoneworts)	–	–	*	*	*	–	–	–	–	–	–	M,G,D,Da,H,S,W
CHAROPHYTA												
Chara sp.	*	*	–	*	*	*	*	*	–	–	–	A
POLYZOA												
Plumatella sp. statoblasts	–	*	–	*	*	*	–	*	*	*	*	A
CLADOCERA												
Daphnia sp. ephippia	*	–	–	–	–	–	*	*	*	*	*	A
No. of items/kg	294	876	270	1259	653	181	349	544	390	195	18	

Habitat preferences: B = brackish; salt-marsh; A = Aquatic; Bs = Bankside; M = fen,swamp, marsh; Ht = heathland; G = grassland; D = disturbed; Da = disturbed agricultural; H = hedges; S = scrub; W = woodland; d = damp; Cst = coastal.

+ = Present only in 250µm fraction (see tables 59–62)

* = present in all fractions (not quantified)

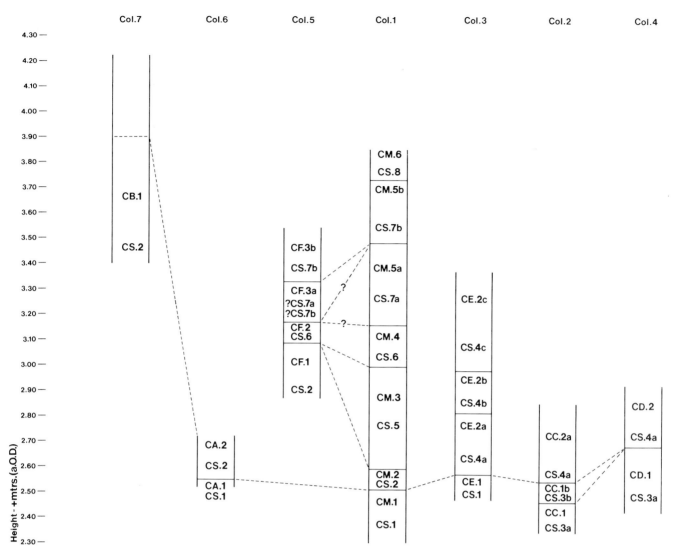

Fig 73   Correlation of pollen zones between sample columns plotted against depth

CALDICOT Column 6 Monolith 23168

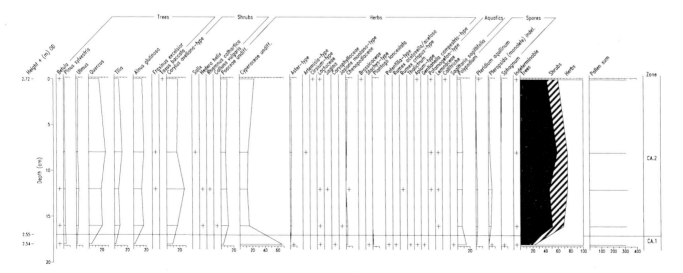

Fig 74   Percentage pollen diagram from Column 6 monolith 23168 in Area G

94

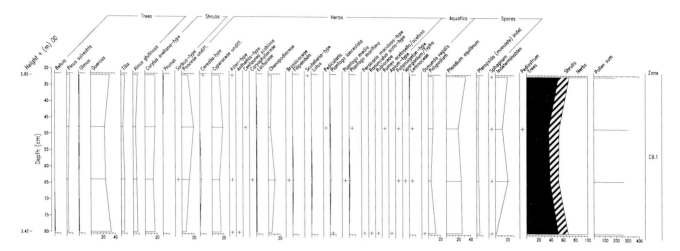

Fig 75   Percentage pollen diagram from Column 7 monolith 23309/10 in Area H

Table 7 Correlation of Caldicot pollen zones

Phase	Site zone	Description	Column 1	Column 2	Column 3	Column 4	Column 5	Column 6	Column 7
I	CS.1	Cyperaceae-*Quercus - Corylus avellana*	CM.1		CE.1			CA.1	
	CS.2	*Quercus-Tilia-Corylus avellana*	CM.2				CF.1	CA.2	CB.1
II	3a	*Quercus*-Poaceae		CC.1a		CD.1			
	3b	*Quercus*-Poaceae-*Plantago lanceolata*		CC.1b					
III	4a	Poaceae-*Quercus-Corylus avellana-Plantago lanceolata*		CC.2	CE.2a	CD.2			
	4b	Poaceae-*Quercus-Alnus-Corylus avellana-Plantago lanceolata*			CE.2b				
IV	4c	Poaceae-*Alnus Corylus avellana-Plantago lanceolata*			CE.2c				
V	5	*Alnus*-Poaceae *Plantago lanceolata*	CM.3						
VI	6	*Alnus*-Poaceae	CM.4				CF.2		
?VI	7a	Poaceae-*Plantago lanceolata-P. coronopus*	?CM.5a						
or ?VII			?CM5.a				?CF.3a		
VII	7b	Poaceae-*Plantago lanceolata-P. coronopus-Alnus-Corylus avellana*	CM.5b				?CF.3a CF 3b		
VIII	8	Cyperaceae-*Quercus-Plantago lanceolata-P. coronopus*	CM.6						

CALDICOT Column 2 Monolith 23010

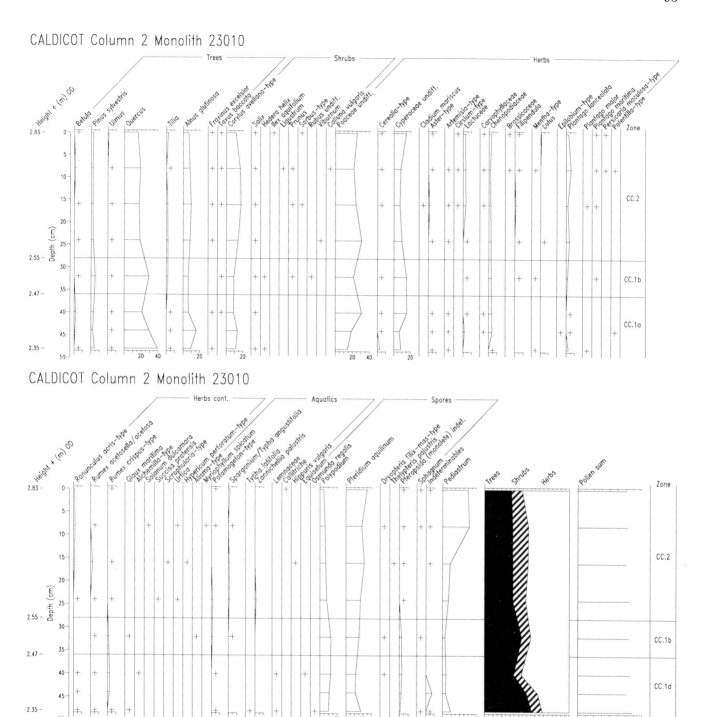

CALDICOT Column 2 Monolith 23010

Fig 76   Percentage pollen diagram from Column 2 monolith 23010 in Area B

well represented. Total concentrations vary between 12,000–15,500 grains/ml.

CC.1b: 36–28cm This sub-zone is distinguished by a slight increase in arboreal pollen, mainly *Quercus* and to a lesser extent *Alnus, Tilia, Pinus* and *Corylus avellana*-type. *Ulmus* is sporadic. A much greater diversity of shrubs occurs. Poaceae values are quite high, Cerealia-type is occasional, while *Plantago lanceolata* increases marginally. Chenopodiaceae pollen is quite well represented. *Potamogeton* is consistently present. *Polypodium, Pteridium* and Pteropsida (monolete) indet. spores increase very slightly. *Pediastrum* is present at low levels. The concentration is around 15,000 grains/ml.

CC.2: 28–0cm A slight decline in tree pollen marks the beginning of this sub-zone. *Quercus* and *Pinus* decrease but *Alnus* and *Corylus avellana*-type show a small increase. *Ulmus* and *Tilia* are present. Poaceae maintain quite high values (>20%) throughout the zone. Cyperaceae are generally low. Other herbaceous pollen, particularly *Plantago lanceolata*, Lactuceae, *Ranunculus* and *Rumex* spp. increase in frequency. Cerealia-type pollen is sporadic. Chenopodiaceae are consistently more than 1%. *Potamogeton* and *Sparganium/Typha* are present. *Polypodium* and Pteropsida (monolete) indet. decrease while *Pteridium* increases steadily. *Pediastrum* rises slowly then sharply in mid-zone to over 30%. Concentrations vary between 20,000–25,000 grains/ml.

CALDICOT Column 4 Monolith 23195

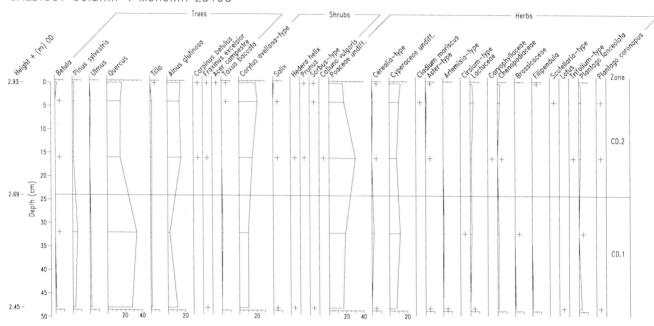

CALDICOT Column 4 Monolith 23195

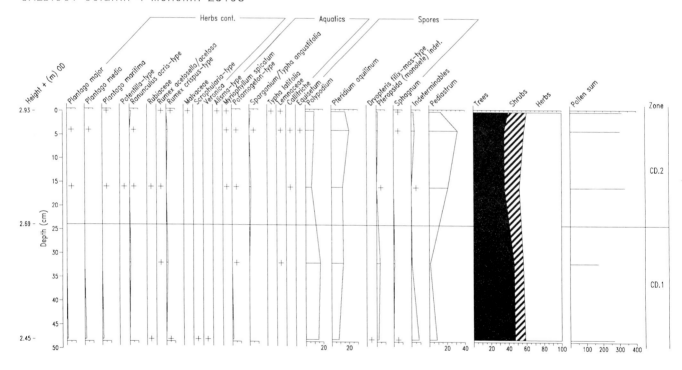

Fig 77   Percentage pollen diagram from Column 4 monolith 23195 in Area E

Column 4 monolith 23195 Area E

Two zones are delimited (Fig 77)

CD.1: 48–24cm Arboreal pollen dominates the assemblage. *Quercus* (20–35%) is most abundant. *Alnus* declines to less than 5%. *Tilia, Ulmus* and Pinus maintain values of more than 1%. *Corylus avellana*-type, Poaceae and Cyperaceae values remain fairly constant. *Plantago lanceolata* declines. Cerealia-type pollen is relatively frequent. Chenopodiaceae pollen is over 1%. Aquatic pollen is sparse. Spores are quite frequent, largely *Polypodium* and *Pteridium*. *Pediastrum* declines to a very low value. Total concentrations are c 10,000 grains/ml or less.

CD.2: 24–0cm The zone is marked by a reduction in *Pinus, Ulmus* and *Quercus* and a rise in *Alnus* (c 15%). *Carpinus betulus* and *Acer campestre* are recorded. *Corylus avellana*-type pollen increases as does shrub diversity. Poaceae and other herbaceous taxa increase in frequency, especially *Plantago lanceolata* and Lactuceae. Cerealia-type pollen occurs. *Sparganium/Typha* pollen is quite frequent. *Polypodium* are lower. *Pediastrum* reaches a peak of more than 30%. Concentrations range from 14,000–28,000 grains/ml.

CALDICOT Column 3 Monolith 23004/23005

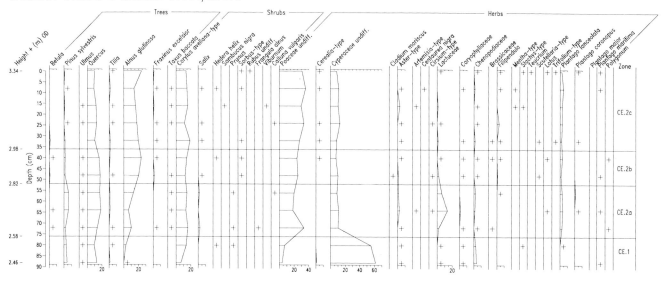

CALDICOT Column 3 Monolith 23004/23005

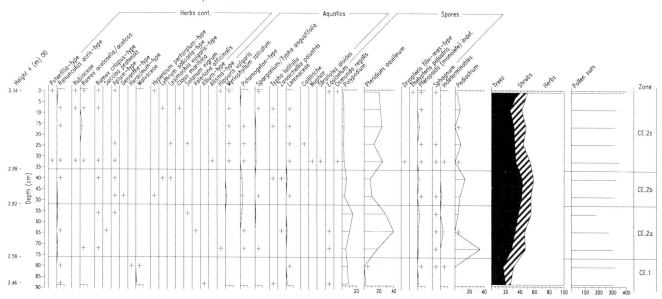

Fig 78   Percentage pollen diagram from Column 3 monolith 23004/5 in Area B

Column 3 monolith 23004/5 Area B

Two zones are recognised (Fig 78). The second zone is subdivided into three sub-zones.

CE.1: 88–76cm This zone is characterised by relatively low arboreal pollen percentages and abundant Cyperaceae pollen (>50%). *Quercus* (10–15%) dominates the tree pollen whilst *Alnus* values are very low (<5%). *Pinus, Ulmus* and *Tilia* are represented continuously. *Corylus avellana*-type pollen increases slightly. Poaceae values are low. Cerealia-type pollen and *Plantago lanceolata* are recorded. Chenopodiaceae (>1%) are quite well represented. Aquatics are scarce. *Polypodium* is the most frequent of the spores. Total concentrations vary from 18,000–28,000 grains/ml.

CE.2a: 76–52cm Arboreal values are higher, notably *Quercus, Alnus* and *Pinus. Tilia* and *Ulmus* occur consistently. *Corylus avellana*-type (c 15%) remains fairly constant. *Salix* is quite frequent. Poaceae pollen is much more plentiful. Cyperaceae decline abruptly to c 10%. *Plantago lanceolata* and Lactuceae

show a distinct increase. Cerealia-type pollen is absent. Chenopodiaceae occur. Aquatics are present. Both *Polypodium* and *Pteridium* increase, the latter markedly. *Pediastrum* is abundant before declining sharply. The total concentration declines from 18,000–9,000 grains/ml.

CE.2b: 52–36cm This sub-zone is distinguished by lower *Pinus* and higher *Alnus* values. *Quercus, Tilia, Ulmus,* and *Corylus avellana*-type values are similar to the previous sub-zone. *Fraxinus* is more frequent and *Salix* less frequent. Poaceae and Cyperaceae remain much the same. *Plantago lanceolata* declines briefly and Lactuceae declines sharply. Cerealia-type pollen is present. Chenopodiaceae are present. Aquatics, notably *Potamogeton* and *Myriophyllum*, increase marginally. *Polypodium* and *Pteridium* both decline. *Pediastrum* is quite frequent. Total concentrations are c 24,000–34,000 grains/ml.

CE.2c: 36–0cm The final sub-zone is characterised by a slight decline in tree pollen, largely *Quercus* and *Alnus,* though the latter does recover at the end of the zone. *Ulmus* is sporadic while *Pinus, Tilia* and *Fraxinus* are present continuously. *Corylus avellana*-

98

CALDICOT Column 5 Monolith 23188/23189

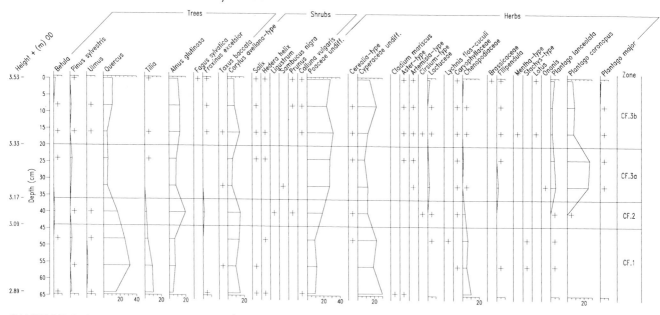

CALDICOT Column 5 Monolith 23188/23189

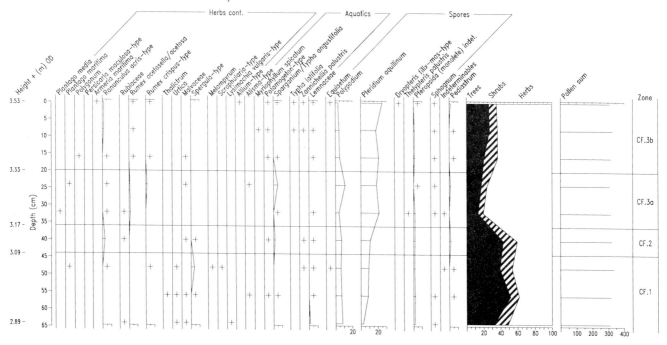

Fig 79   Percentage pollen diagram from Column 5 monolith 23188/89 in Area E

type values are similar to the previous sub-zone. Poaceae and Cyperaceae increase very slightly. *Plantago lanceolata* continues to be reasonably well represented. Chenopodiaceae pollen continues to be present at low levels. *Sparganium/Typha* is the most frequent of the aquatics. *Polypodium* spores decrease further while *Pteridium* spores increase sharply. *Pediastrum* values fluctuate throughout the zone. Total concentrations are relatively high (35,000–83,000 grains/ml.).

Column 5 monolith 23188/89 Area E

Three zones have been defined (Fig 79). The third zone is subdivided into two sub-zones.

CF.1: 64–44cm High arboreal values characterise this zone. *Quercus* (15–30%) values dominate. *Tilia* values are as high as 10%. *Ulmus* and *Pinus* are present. *Alnus* values are relatively low. *Corylus avellana*-type is c 10–15%. Poaceae remain constant at c 10%. Cyperaceae pollen is quite abundant. *Plantago lanceolata* and Cerealia-type pollen is present. Chenopodiaceae pollen is particularly abundant (up to 10%). *Spergula*-type peaks later in the zone. Aquatics are scarce. *Polypodium* is c 5–10% while *Pteridium* increases to c10%. Concentrations range from 18,000–22,000 grains/ml.

CF.2: 44–36cm This zone is distinguished by lower *Quercus* and *Tilia* and an increase in *Alnus*. Poaceae values are higher while Cyperaceae values are less. *Plantago lanceolata* and *Plantago coronopus* are present. Chenopodiaceae decrease slightly. *Sparganium/Typha* pollen is present at more than 1%. Spore values

CALDICOT Column 1 Monoliths 2340, 2342, 2343, 2344

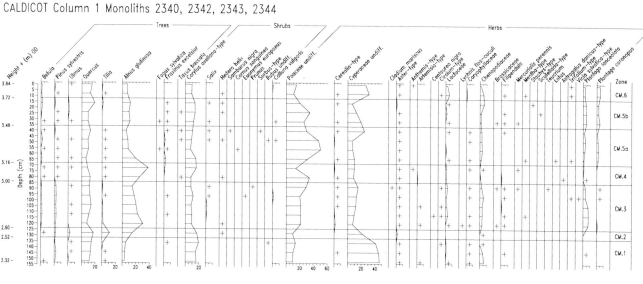

CALDICOT Column 1 Monoliths 2340, 2342, 2343, 2344

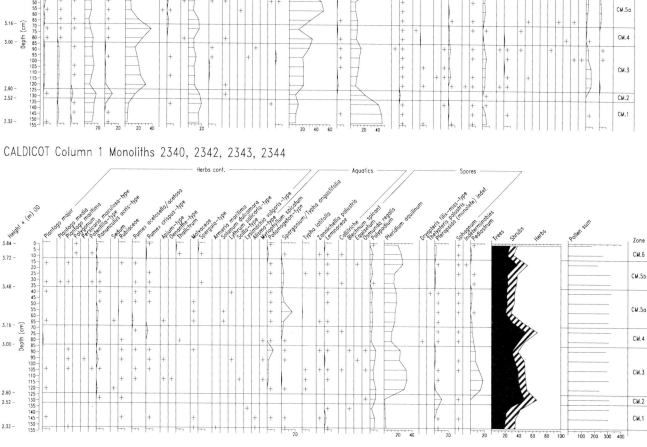

Fig 80   Percentage pollen diagram from Column 1 monoliths 2340, 2342, 2343, 2344 in Area A

are similar to the previous zone. *Pediastrum* is more than 1%. Total concentration is *c* 15,000 grains/ml.

CF.3a: 36–20cm This zone is marked by a decline in arboreal pollen and a sharp rise in herbaceous pollen, notably *Plantago coronopus*. *Quercus*, *Alnus*, *Tilia* and *Corylus avellana*-type all decrease. *Ulmus* is absent. Herbaceous pollen is well represented. Poaceae pollen increases to *c* 25%. *Plantago lanceolata* increases to *c* 5% and *Plantago coronopus* exceeds 25%. Lactuceae are more than 1%. Chenopodiaceae are less frequent. Cyperaceae remain at *c* 10–15%. *Sparganium/Typha* is quite frequent. *Polypodium* and *Pteridium* values rise slightly. *Pediastrum* is present. Concentrations vary from 19,000–33,000 grains/ml.

CF.3b: 20–0cm The sub-zone is characterised by a slight increase in *Quercus*, *Alnus* and *Corylus avellana*-type and distinct decline in *Plantago coronopus*. *Tilia* and *Ulmus* occur sporadically. *Fagus* is present at the end of the zone. Poaceae values are similar to the previous zone. Cyperaceae increase. *Plantago lanceolata* (<5%) and *Plantago coronopus* (5–10%) values are less. Aquatics are scarce. *Polypodium* spores are low while *Pteridium* remains relatively constant. *Pediastrum* is sparse. Concentrations range from 23,000–38,000 grains/ml.

Column 1 monoliths 2340, 2342, 2343, 2344 Area A

Six zones have been defined with one zone subdivided in two (Fig 80).

CM.1: 152–132cm Comparatively low arboreal pollen and abundant Cyperaceae characterise the zone. *Quercus* (<15%) dominates the tree pollen, *Alnus*, *Pinus*, *Ulmus* and *Tilia* are represented at low levels. *Corylus avellana*-type is *c* 15–20%. Poaceae are *c* 10–15% whilst Cyperaceae exceed 40%. *Plantago lanceolata* and Cerealia-type are present. Aquatics are scarce, apart from Lemnaceae. Spores are not very frequent. Total pollen concentration increases from 8,000–36,000 grains/ml.

CM.2: 132–124cm This brief zone coincides with a lithostratigraphic change to a peaty clay. It is distinguished by an increase in arboreal pollen, notably *Tilia* to more than 10%. *Quercus*, *Alnus* and *Ulmus* values are also higher. *Corylus avellana*-type and Poaceae are similar to the previous zone but Cyperaceae decline markedly. *Plantago* is absent. Chenopodiaceae are present. Aquatics are absent. Pteropsida (monolete) indet. increases to over 10%. The concentration is *c* 23,000 grains/ml.

CM.3: 124–84cm The beginning of this zone is marked by a

decrease in *Quercus*, *Tilia* and *Ulmus* pollen and an increase in *Alnus*, initially to over 30%. *Betula* and *Pinus* are consistently present at more than 1%. *Corylus avellana*-type pollen is slightly less frequent. *Salix* is present in noticeable amounts. Poaceae pollen increases to over 20%. Cyperaceae pollen decreases further. *Plantago lanceolata* shows a sharp rise, reaching almost 10%. Lactuceae are quite frequent. Chenopodiaceae are reasonably well represented. Aquatics are quite frequent, especially *Potamogeton* at the end of the zone. *Pteridium* increases abruptly, initially to over 30%. *Pediastrum* also shows a marked rise. Total concentrations range from 10,000–15,000 grains/ml.

CM.4: 84–68cm. This short zone is marked by an increase in arboreal pollen, largely attributable to *Alnus* (maximum c 40%). In contrast, *Betula*, *Pinus*, *Quercus* and *Tilia* all decrease in frequency. *Corylus avellana*-type increases slightly. Poaceae decline sharply during the zone. Cyperaceae are less frequent. *Plantago lanceolata* values are low. Cerealia-type pollen continues to be quite well represented. Lactuceae maintain values above 1%. Chenopodiaceae pollen is scarcer. Aquatics are less. Spores are not as frequent. *Pediastrum* values are declining. Concentrations are 22,000–24,000 grains/ml.

CM.5a: 68–36cm A further decline in tree pollen, principally *Alnus* and to a lesser extent *Quercus*, characterises this zone. *Tilia*, *Pinus* and *Ulmus* are less frequent. *Fraxinus* is more abundant. *Fagus* is present. *Corylus avellana*-type, after a decline increases steadily. Poaceae expand further. Cyperaceae values are low until the end of the zone. *Plantago lanceolata*, *Plantago coronopus* and Chenopodiaceae are constantly present at more than 1%. *Sparganium/Typha* pollen peaks sharply in mid-zone. Representation of spores is much the same as in the previous zone. *Pediastum* values are lower. Total concentrations range from 18,000–35,000 grains/ml.

CM.5b: 36–10cm This zone is distinguished by marginally higher *Quercus* and *Alnus*. *Ulmus* is slightly more frequent whilst *Fraxinus* is less. *Tilia* is scarce. *Fagus* is present. *Corylus avellana*-type values continue to rise steadily. Poaceae and Cyperaceae decline. *Plantago lanceolata* and *Plantago coronopus* increase marginally. Chenopodiaceae values are slightly less, then increase. *Sparganium/Typha* is quite frequent. Spore values are generally similar to the previous sub-zone. *Pediastrum* is sparse. Total concentration declines from c 28,000 to 9,000 grains/ml.

CM.6: 10–0cm This zone is characterised by a decline in arboreal pollen. After a small rise at the end of the previous zone *Quercus* declines. *Alnus* and *Corylus avellana*-type decrease very slightly. Other trees and shrubs are scarce. Poaceae values fall further whilst Cyperaceae increase. *Plantago lanceolata* is very slightly less and *Plantago coronopus* slightly greater. Chenopodiaceae increases to over 5%. *Potamogeton* is more frequent. *Pteridium* increases. *Pediastrum* is present. Concentrations are relatively low (6,000–11,000 grains/ml).

Taphonomy and interpretation

Before the pollen and plant macrofossil evidence from Caldicot is discussed, some of the taphonomic processes and interpretative problems inherent in the techniques and the implications for environmental reconstruction will be considered.

Pollen

Until comparatively recently (Needham and Macklin 1992) alluvial sediments and palaeochannel deposits have tended to receive less attention as potential pollen sites than lacustrine or mire deposits. One reason for this is that the taphonomic processes leading to the incorporation and preservation of pollen in alluvial sediments are much more complex.

Various models of pollen production, dispersal and deposition have been proposed, largely related to a wooded environment (Andersen 1970, 1973; Tauber 1965, 1967; Moore *et al* 1991; Price and Moore 1984; Jacobson and Bradshaw 1981), while Edwards (1979, 1982) has discussed the registration of anthropogenic activity in pollen diagrams, and in particular in relation to the woodland edge. More recently a model closer to the situation at Caldicot has been suggested by Scaife and Burrin (1992) which considers the sources of pollen in alluvial sediments in a rural anthropogenically affected catchment. However at a site like Caldicot this model is further complicated by a possible tidal influence. A brief summary of the possible sources of pollen found at Caldicot (Fig 81) is as follows:

1) Airborne pollen:
    a) rain component with long distance transport
    b) canopy component
    c) trunk space component
2) Fen carr woodland pollen
3) Local component:
    a) aquatic and mire
    b) wet meadow and tall herb
    c) inundation grassland, ie grassland subject to flooding either by fresh waters or brackish or salt waters
4) Secondary component:
    a) contemporary but from upstream
    b) erosion from older alluvial sediments
    c) erosion of older soils on interfluves
    d) erosion from geological sediments of much earlier age
5) Secondary component (marine):
    a) contemporary but from downstream
    b) erosion from salt marsh
    c) erosion of older marine sediments
6) Pollen from pastoral and arable environments
7) Pollen from secondary anthropogenic sources, eg construction activities, processing activities, goods, refuse, excreta from humans and domestic animals

Particular problems which need to be borne in mind when dealing with alluvial sediments and palaeochannel deposits include the possible reincorporation of older pollen, biological reworking, oxidation as a result of fluctuating water levels, surface weathering where burial is slow, and the pH (especially alkalinity) of the water from the catchment (Scaife and Burrin 1992, 83). Hence preservation of pollen in minerogenic sediments is frequently poorer than in organic deposits, though at Caldicot preservation was relatively good. Despite these difficulties valuable palaeoenvironmental data can be obtained from such deposits, particularly when there are pollen sequences from peat deposits in the area with which to compare the data.

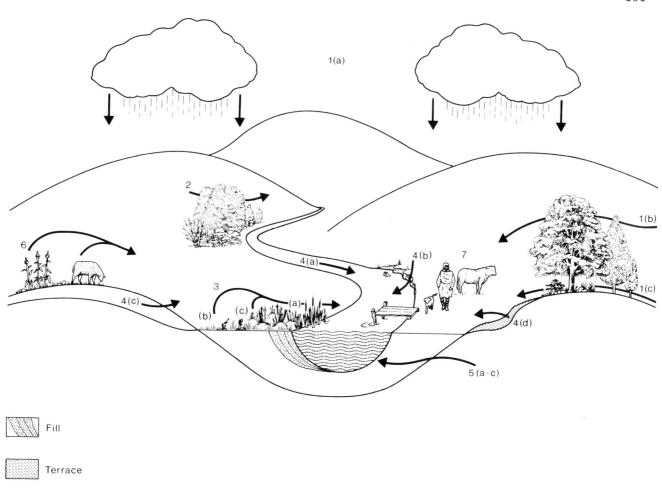

Fill

Terrace

Fig 81 Possible sources of pollen at Caldicot. Drawing by B Garfi

One approach to the determination of the effects of people on the vegetation in an area relies on the recognition of 'indicator' pollen types, ie types which are sensitive to human activity. Attempts have been made to determine the nature of the activity, in particular whether pastoral or arable agriculture was more important, by the formulation of an arable/pastoral index (Turner 1964). Behre (1981) has taken this further, identifying a range of man-managed habitats. However, one problem, particularly at a site like Caldicot, is that inevitably many 'indicator taxa' are not solely confined to man-managed habitats. This can be illustrated, for example, by the occurrence of Chenopodiaceae pollen which could represent salt-marsh, disturbed ground, cultivation or even all three environments. In some instances plant macrofossil evidence can, to some extent, help to resolve problems of interpretation. Another complication that arises is in the case of cereal-type pollen as it encompasses both wild and cultivated grasses (Dickson 1988). The Cerealia-type pollen at Caldicot appears to fall mainly into the *Hordeum* group which includes wild grasses that are found in maritime, wetland and waste ground habitats. Hence while the Cerealia-type pollen may reflect cultivation, the other interpretations are a possibility.

Plant macrofossils

It is generally held that, in contrast to pollen evidence, plant macrofossils provide a largely local picture, but this fails to take into account the efficiency of wind and water in long-distance transport, particularly where large bodies of water are involved. Recent investigations in the Netherlands of drift litter samples from along the Dutch coast and the River Rhine have demonstrated that many species can be dispersed by water over long distances, and that even vegetative remains are no guarantee that the plants were growing locally (Cappers 1993). However, investigations of both modern lacustrine and fluvial environments in southern Britain have shown that, whilst some of the plant remains recovered in samples from point bar samples taken along the river appear to have originated from further afield, the majority probably originated from local sources (Field 1992). It has also been demonstrated that it cannot be taken for granted that the quantitative representation of a taxon in a fossil assemblage reflects its abundance in the past vegetation. The presence of a taxon in the subfossil record will depend on its production, dispersal, germination and preservation characteristics (Fig 82). Hence it is not unusual to find seeds of plants which are not

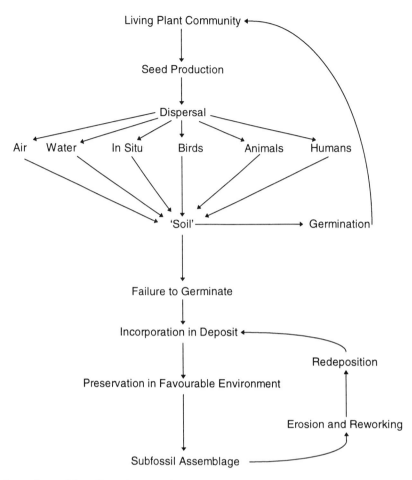

Fig 82   The formation of a subfossil seed assemblage from a living plant community (after West 1972)

represented in the local vegetation, or for seeds to be absent of plants which are present.

Examples of variation in productivity, dispersal and germination of some of the taxa recorded at Caldicot demonstrate the difficulties involved in environmental reconstruction. For example it has been estimated that one *Juncus* plant can produce 1.5–3 million seeds (Salisbury 1976), *Lythrum salicaria* 220,000 seeds/plant, *Plantago major* 30,000 seeds/plant, *Sonchus asper* 23,000, *Solanum dulcamara* 53,459 ± 13,822, *Alisma plantago-aquatica* 36,518 ± 9,766 achenes/plant. In terms of dispersal there is also, for example, considerable variation in the ability of different species to float. According to Praeger (1913) seeds of *Plantago major* sink immediately on contact with water. Similarly *Sambucus nigra* seeds do not float (Praeger 1913) but are a particular source of food for birds and may be dispersed this way. It is also suggested that *Juncus effusus* and *Juncus inflexus* (Praeger 1913) sink within one minute of contact with water, but are supposedly well transported by wind (Salisbury 1976). In contrast *Ranunculus* subgenus *Batrachium* seeds are supposed to be capable of floating 1–12km while seeds of *Chenopodium album* can remain afloat for as long as 4.5 days (Praeger 1913). For some of the species mentioned above, in addition to water transport, the seeds are particularly adapted for

dispersal by wind, animals or birds. Apart from these 'natural' factors, an additional factor as far as Caldicot is concerned is human activity which may not only have transported seeds to the site but also created suitable habitats for certain taxa and thereby aided germination.

The germination rate also has an effect on the likelihood of a seed's becoming a subfossil, ie the greater the germination rate the fewer seeds available to become subfossils. *Solanum dulcamara* (Salisbury 1942) has an estimated 70–90% germination rate and *Plantago major* a 60–90% germination rate (though it may remain dormant for up to 40 years).

Recent work by Field (1992) comparing representation in deposits and abundance in surrounding vegetation has demonstrated that there is not always a direct relationship. He found *Urtica dioica*, *Epilobium hirsutum* and *Veronica beccabunga* to be both well represented and abundant, whereas *Lythrum salicaria*, *Alisma plantago-aquatica*, *Solanum dulcamara* and *Sonchus asper* were poorly represented and *Chenopodium album* and *Plantago major* well represented in comparison to abundance in the vegetation.

Interpretation of the results from Caldicot must be qualified in the light of this data, ie that the majority of remains are probably derived from the local

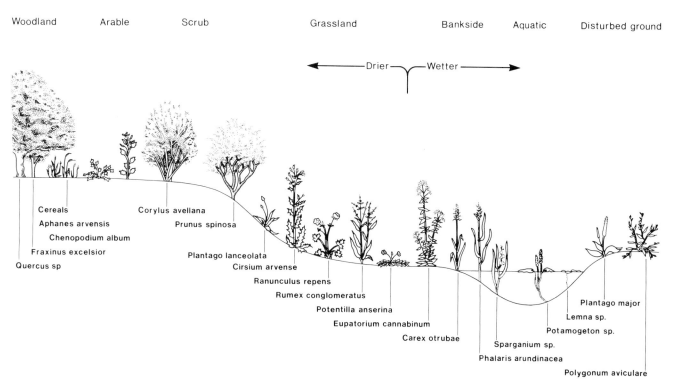

Woodland   Arable   Scrub   Grassland   Bankside Aquatic Disturbed ground

←—Drier—⌄—Wetter—→

Cereals
Aphanes arvensis
Chenopodium album
Fraxinus excelsior
Quercus sp
Corylus avellana
Prunus spinosa
Plantago lanceolata
Cirsium arvense
Ranunculus repens
Rumex conglomeratus
Potentilla anserina
Eupatorium cannabinum
Carex otrubae
Sparganium sp.
Phalaris arundinacea
Polygonum aviculare
Plantago major
Lemna sp.
Potamogeton sp.

Fig 83   Possible types of vegetation and habitat in the Caldicot area. Drawing by B Garfi

environment but that there is the possibility that some taxa were from outside the immediate area and were washed downstream, brought upstream by high tides, or blown in; or dispersed by birds, other animals, or by human activity. In addition the quantitative representation of a taxon does not necessarily reflect its abundance in the past contemporary vegetation. However, it is evident that the plant macrofossil assemblages provide a clear indication of the plant communities growing within the channel environment and on the adjacent floodplains and dry land, if not all from the immediate environs of the site.

Results

The vegetation communities in the Caldicot Region

Any attempt at reconstructing past vegetation communities involves certain assumptions and limitations. In the first place, in attempting to identify communities that exist today the assumption is made that ecological preferences and requirements have not changed. Secondly, the fossil record is, inevitably, only a partial record, distorted by taphonomic processes. In considering the vegetation communities represented at Caldicot, apart from the weed communities where reference is made to Ellenberg (1988), particular reference is made to the communities recognised by the National Vegetation Classification project and published in *British Plant Communities volumes 1–5* (Rodwell 1991a, 1991b, 1992, 1995, forthcoming). However, these communi-

ties may not be strictly comparable to those in the past, and others not recognised today could have existed. For example, the composition of many woodland communities is the result of human interference in the past, as indeed is apparent from the Caldicot evidence. The drainage of swamps and fens has also resulted in changes in composition, particularly of aquatics, even within the recent past (see Rodwell 1995).

A further problem is that individual species are generally not restricted to only one community, and can frequently represent a range of habitats (see Table 6). One particular difficulty in deciphering the evidence from Caldicot is that species indicative of disturbed ground and human activity are also often found in maritime habitats. Nevertheless, by considering the Caldicot evidence in the light of present day communities and their characteristics it is possible to give some indication of the environmental conditions and habitats (Fig 83) which may have prevailed. The vegetation communities at Caldicot seem to have remained much the same in character, but varied in extent throughout the period involved, the main exception being the dry-land woodland communities which appear to have changed in composition.

Freshwater vegetation

Included in this vegetation group are both aquatic and emergent swamp and fen species, as well as both species that might in some classifications be considered as marsh species, and species that in terms of habitat might be referred to as bank-side. Generally, plants characteristic of these communities are well represented both in the plant macrofossil and pollen records from Caldicot. They include floating, floating-leafed, and submerged species such as *Lemna* spp. (duckweeds), *Potamogeton berchtoldii* (small pondweed), *Zannichellia palustris* (horned pondweed), and *Ranunculus* subgenus *Batrachium* (crowfoots), as well as emergent types such as *Sparganium* spp. (bur-reeds), possible *Schoenoplectus lacustris* (common club-rush) and *Alisma* spp. (water plantain), *Eleocharis* sp. (spike-rush) and *Carex* spp. (sedges). The distribution of such species in British rivers is affected by a number of physical, chemical and biotic factors (Haslam 1971, 1978). Physical factors include substrate, rate of flow, depth, clarity and channel width. Hence variations in the frequency of occurrence of species may suggest changes in the channel environment.

Many of the aquatic taxa that are recorded at Caldicot are found within a *Nuphar lutea* (yellow water-lily) community but can equally well be found in others, including *Lemna gibba* (fat duckweed), *Lemna minor* (common duckweed), *Callitriche stagnalis* (common water-starwort) and various *Ranunculus* subgenus *Batrachium* communities (see Rodwell 1995). One characteristic of all these communities is that in general they occur in still or sluggish water, though *Callitriche* can be found in swiftly-flowing water in streams with sandy or gravelly beds and certain of the crowfoots can occur in faster-flowing water. In addition the *Lemna* and *Callitriche* communities are particularly good at re-establishing themselves in recently disturbed habitats and *Callitriche* can tolerate habitats which periodically or seasonally dry up, as can the *Ranunculus* species. The latter are frequently found on moist ground where there is grazing and trampling by stock, which is likely to have occurred at Caldicot, particularly during the later phases. The *Lemna* species also require a certain degree of warmth, favouring waters that are ice-free in winter (Ellenberg 1988, 296). All the aquatic taxa can be found growing with various swamp communities.

A number of swamp and tall-herb fen communities (see Rodwell 1995) may be represented in the pollen and plant macrofossil records. Certain dominant species may have been present as monospecific stands, as well as accompanied by understorey assemblages, in the channels. Gradations between the different communities could have been complex. Physiognomic dominants for which there is evidence at Caldicot include *Phragmites australis* (common reed), *Phalaris arundinacea* (reed canary-grass), various Carices, *Schoenoplectus tabernaemontani* (grey club-rush), *Typha* spp. (bulrushes), *Apium nodiflorum* (fool's water-cress), and *Rorippa nasturtium-aquaticum* (water-cress). Associated understorey species recorded include *Eupatorium cannabinum* (hemp agrimony), *Lythrum salicaria* (purple-loosestrife), and *Potentilla anserina* (silverweed) Some understorey species, like *Rorippa nasturtium-aquaicum*, *Apium nodiflorum* and *Myosotis scorpioides* (water forget-me-not), are also the most prominent vegetation in water-margin vegetation found alongside sluggish streams.

Inferences can be drawn about water depths, flow rates, and salinity at Caldicot by considering the ecology and environmental tolerances of the dominants in the swamp and tall-herb fen communities. There seems to be a crude relationship between the water-depth ranges and the physiognomy of the dominants (Rodwell 1995). Hence *Schoenoplectus lacustris* will penetrate into open water with a maximum summer water depth of up to 1.5m while *Bolboschoenus maritimus* (sea club-rush), *Schoenoplectus tabernaemontani*, *Eleocharis palustris* (common spike-rush) and *Typha latifolia* (bulrush) will extend down to about 60cm. Other species such as *Carex paniculata* (greater tussock sedge), *Cladium mariscus* (great fen-sedge) and *Sparganium erectum* (branched bur-reed) will tolerate a depth of up to 40cm. Finally, smaller plants like *Carex otrubae* (false fox-sedge) and *Apium nodiflorum*, *Veronica beccabunga* (brooklime) and *Rorippa nasturtium-aquaticum* are usually confined to less than 20cm of water. Representatives of the different water depth ranges occur throughout the phases at Caldicot and a succession of vegetation types may have occurred fringing the channels.

The bulk of the vegetation types at Caldicot are found in waters of negligible to slow flow, but some of the emergent aquatics, such as *Schoenoplectus lacustris* and Glycerio-Sparganion species, can tolerate moderately fast-flowing water, whilst the *Phalaris arundinacea* community exhibits the widest tolerance of variation in flow velocity. Once emergents are established they begin to modify their environment, including initiating the accumulation of sediments and affecting flow rates. Velocities in and around the weeds are lower while velocities in the weed-free areas tend to increase (Westlake 1971). Hence the vegetation itself is likely to have created a range of micro-environments at Caldicot.

Generally swamp and tall-herb fen require a certain degree of stability in the pattern of water level fluctuations to persist, but some communities tolerate regular short-term fluctuations such as where there is a tidal influence. One species recorded at Caldicot able to tolerate water-level fluctuations is *Phragmites australis*. Other species which are found in understorey assemblages where there are often fluctuating fresh or brackish waters include *Atriplex prostrata* (spear-leaved orache), *Agrostis stolonifera* (creeping bent) and *Potentilla anserina* are, and *Phalaris arundinacea* is often, associated with the limits of inundation. Several other 'freshwater' communities that may be represented at Caldicot can also occupy brackish water, including *Schoenoplectus tabernaemontani*, *Phragmites australis*, *Carex otrubae*, and *Eleocharis palustris* and may be accompanied by such species as *Aster tripolium* (sea aster), *Glaux maritima* (sea-milkwort), *Ranunculus sceleratus* (celery-leaved buttercup), *Chenopodium rubrum* (red goosefoot) and *Atriplex prostrata*.

Salt-marsh vegetation

A number of the species recorded at Caldicot can form dominants in salt-marsh communities, including *Salicornia* spp. (glassworts), *Suaeda maritima* (annual sea-blite) and *Aster tripolium*. Others which might be represented but where identifications are not to species level include *Spergularia marina* (lesser sea-spurrey), *Sagina maritima* (sea pearlwort), and *Eleocharis uniglumis* (slender spike-rush).

Low-marsh (see Rodwell forthcoming for details) includes communities dominated by *Salicornia*, *Suaeda maritima* and *Aster tripolium* with taxa such as *Glaux maritima* and *Plantago maritima* (sea plantain) often prominent, all species present in either the plant macrofossil or pollen records. The two last species often have a high frequency in mid-marsh communities whilst patches of *Plantago coronopus* (buck's-horn plantain), *Carex distans* (distant sedge) and *C. extensa* (long bracted sedge) may occur throughout and glycophytes like *Potentilla anserina* can be prominent. Hence the presence of the latter species at Caldicot may be attributable to these communities. Other species represented at Caldicot which can be abundant in these communities include *Rumex crispus* (curled dock) and *Atriplex prostrata*. Upper-marsh occurs towards the upper limit of tidal influence and includes two grass-dominated communities, *Elytrigia atherica* (sea couch) and *E. repens* (common couch). Both these grasses produce large cereal-type pollen grains. *Atriplex* (orache) is common in these communities and *Atriplex* seeds are frequent in the plant macrofossil record, as is Chenopodiaceae pollen in the pollen record.

On salt-marshes where there is a small tidal influence and soil salinity combined with a fresh-water influence, a variety of other vegetation types may result. Communities which might be reflected at Caldicot include various mesotrophic grasslands, discussed below, and swamp communities, already mentioned, which occur where there is brackish water. *Phragmites australis-Atriplex prostrata*, and *Schoenoplectus tabernaemontani* are more or less confined to such situations whereas *Phalaris arundinacea* and *Typha latifolia* communities are much more widespread in fresh-water and only marginally halophytic. Whilst salt-marsh communities undoubtedly would have existed downstream from Caldicot the 'salt-marsh' taxa recorded could derive from swamp communities or from inundation grassland communities which were periodically subject to flooding during high tides or storm surges.

Grassland

Many of the pollen and plant macrofossil taxa represented are indicative of grassland, including ill-drained pasture and possibly inundation grasslands. Taxa that could have originated in one or other mesotrophic grassland community (see Rodwell 1992 for details) include *Prunella vulgaris* (selfheal), *Rumex conglomeratus* (clustered dock), *Potentilla anserina*, *Cirsium arvense* (creeping thistle), *Persicaria hydropiper* (water-pepper), *Succisa pratensis* (devil's bit scabious), *Lotus* (bird's foot trefoils), *Trifolium* (clovers), *Plantago lanceolata* (ribwort plantain), and *Plantago major* (greater plantain).

Although the Poaceae seeds have generally not been identified in detail the occurrence of taxa such as *Potentilla anserina*, *Rumex conglomeratus*, *R. crispus* and *Glaux maritima*, may indicate inundation grassland. Three inundation grassland communities have been recognised (Rodwell 1992) any of which could have been present in the Caldicot area. Seeds and pollen which could have originated from such communities occur in samples from Phase II onwards and coincide with the development of the channels and flood plain in the valley. The *Agrostis stolonifera-Alopecurus geniculatus* community typically occurs on silty soils which are subject to periodic flooding by fresh waters. Taxa found in it represented at Caldicot include *Rumex crispus*, *R. conglomeratus*, possible *Mentha aquatica* (water mint), *Persicaria hydropiper*, *Ranunculus sceleratus*, *Potentilla anserina*, *Cirsium arvense*, and *Montia fontana* (blinks). It commonly occurs alongside sluggish streams and rivers and particularly on puddled soil by a pool or stream which is used by stock for watering. Given the known presence of stock in the vicinity of the site it seems quite probable this community was present. Its closest affinities are with another inundation community – the *Festuca rubra-Agrostis stolonifera-Potentilla anserina* – but this community is one that is frequently inundated by brackish as well as fresh water. Seeds of *Rumex* cf *obtusifolius* (broad-leaved dock), *Atriplex prostrata*, *Polygonum aviculare* (knotgrass), *Sonchus asper* (prickly sow-thistle), *Stellaria media* (common chickweed), *Urtica dioica* (common nettle), *Carex distans*, and *Glaux maritima* may all be derived from such a community. Cattle and sheep are often pastured on this community and can lead to local disturbance and eutrophication resulting in a local abundance of nitrophilous species such as *Urtica dioica* and *Stellaria media*. The final inundation community, *Festuca arundinacea*, also receives occasional inundation by tides. It is found on the banks of tidal rivers and on upper salt-marsh and includes species such as *Glaux maritima*, *Carex otrubae*, *Sonchus arvensis* (perennial sow-thistle), *Potentilla anserina*, *Cirsium arvense*, *Rumex crispus*, *Stellaria media*, *Plantago major* and *Galium palustre* (common marsh-bedstraw) recorded at Caldicot.

Weeds of disturbed ground and cultivation

Species typical of ruderal (rubbish tips, waste ground) communities found at Caldicot become more abundant from when there is direct evidence of human activity at the site, particularly from Phase III onwards. Taxa present include *Chenopodium album* (fat-hen), *Urtica dioica*, *Stellaria media*, *Cirsium arvense*, *Lapsana communis* (nipplewort) and *Chenopodium polyspermum* (many-seeded goosefoot). Direct evidence for cultivation in the form of cereal grain is lacking but the presence of the above species as well as others such as *Persicaria maculosa* (redshank), *P. lapathifolia* (pale persicaria), *Sonchus asper*, *S. arvensis*, *Rumex acetosella* (sheep's sorrel) and *R. conglomeratus* could indicate some cultivation taking place in the area. All these species could derive from arable weed communities (see Ellenberg 1988 for details). Cereal-type pollen provides further possible evidence for cultivation in the area.

There are two subspecies of *Plantago major* each of which has a preference for different habitats, *intermedia* preferring slightly saline and *major* disturbed ground, either cultivated or grassy. It is in the latter context that it is considered here. It is typical of footpaths and trampled areas, being able to withstand the mechanical damage caused by the tread of grazing animals or human feet (Ellenberg 1988), and is most abundant during Phases III and V. *Polygonum aviculare* is another species typical of this environment and occurs from Phase II onwards. From a taphonomic point of view, it is worth bearing in mind that where there is the heaviest trampling these plants do not produce seed and that its presence is derived from vegetation in the surrounding neighbourhood. A slight reduction in frequency during Phase VI may, therefore, be attributable to increased activity at the site itself. Usually the seeds are dispersed in the mud adhering to animals' hooves or human feet. Both *Plantago major* and *Polygonum aviculare* require really wet conditions for their seeds to germinate. Hence at Caldicot in the area of the site there would have been favourable conditions, with inevitably some seeds becoming incorporated in the contemporary deposits. These species in this context are assigned to the *Lolio-Plantaginetum majoris* community in which *Poa annua* (annual meadow-grass) is also a regular component (Ellenberg 1988).

Woodland and scrub

Pollen from arboreal taxa and wood from the site provide the main evidence for wood and scrub communities. Other macrofossils are relatively rare, though *Alnus glutinosa* (alder), *Betula* spp.(birch), *Corylus avellana* (hazel), *Prunus spinosa* (blackthorn), *Crataegus monogyna* (hawthorn), *Rosa* sp. (rose) and *Rubus fruticosus* agg.(bramble) are represented. As with the herbaceous plant communities, many of the woodland communities recognised today could have existed in the Caldicot area and surrounding region during the period of the fossil record and it is difficult to be certain from which communities the evidence derives. At the same time, it is apparent that woodland communities have altered as a result of human interference.

In terms of wet woodland communities there is evidence for *Alnus glutinosa-Carex paniculata* woodland (see Rodwell 1991a) in the Caldicot area, both from the range of woody and herbaceous species present in the pollen and plant macrofossil records. Although taxa such as *Salix* spp.(willow), *Ilex aquifolium* (holly), *Betula pubescens* (downy birch), *Quercus robur* (pedunculate oak) and *Fraxinus excelsior* (ash) may be present, it is *Alnus* which clearly dominates the community and the strongest evidence for this community in the pollen record occurs during Phases V and VI. *Alnus* fruits are best represented during Phases VI–VII. It is the distinctive tussocks of *Carex paniculata* which dominate the field layer and *C. paniculata* nuts are present in most phases from Phase II onwards. Other herb taxa recorded include *C. pseudocyperus* (cyperus sedge), *Urtica dioica*, *Filipendula ulmaria* (meadow sweet), and *Eupatorium cannabinum*. Undershrubs include *Rubus fruticosus* agg., and *Rosa* spp. and 'sprawlers' include *Galium palustre* and *Solanum dulcamara* (bittersweet).

Typically, *Alnus-Carex* woodland is characteristic of wet to waterlogged organic soils and is particularly associated with fen peats and flood-plain mires. Such conditions did not exist in the immediate Caldicot area but are known to have occurred nearby, for example, in the Vurlong Reen area (Walker and James 1993). Another community which may have been present in which *Alnus* dominates is *Alnus glutinosa-Urtica dioica* woodland (see Rodwell 1991a). Characteristically, *Alnus* is by far the commonest tree and *Urtica dioica* the commonest herb. The latter is reasonably well represented throughout the plant macrofossil record. On wetter soils there is the strongest representation of swamp and fen species such as *Phragmites*, *Phalaris arundinacea* and *Epilobium hirsutum* (great willowherb), which are present at Caldicot. It is regarded as particularly characteristic of alluvial terraces and mature stretches of river valleys where allochthonous minerogenic sediments are or have been deposited, its occurrence reflecting active alluvial deposition as in the Nedern valley. It can also occur in flood-plain mires and open-water transitions.

The representation of dry-land trees in the wood record at Caldicot is possibly greater than would be expected from a wood assemblage from a palaeochannel where direct human activity was absent. At the same time, this emphasises the problem of identifying ancient woodland communities, as clearance activity and woodland management practices in the past have resulted in communities which are not directly comparable with those of today. Having said that, it is probable that by the time the environmental record starts at Caldicot the woodland communities had already been altered and managed to some extent. The range of species (see Table 22) present in the wood assemblage together with the pollen record from the site points towards two main communities occurring on different soils in the region, the *Fraxinus excelsior-Acer campestre-Mercu-*

rialis perennis community and the *Quercus robur-Pteridium aquilinum-Rubus fruticosus* community and, in particular, the *Hedera helix* sub-community of each of these (see Rodwell 1991a). Both these sub-communities are found in the area today. *Fraxinus-Acer-Mercurialis* woodlands are characterised by *Fraxinus excelsior, Acer campestre* (field maple) and *Corylus avellana,* and by Phase VII at Caldicot the composition of the woodland may have been similar to now. However, *Acer campestre,* whilst present in later deposits, was clearly not a major constituent of the earlier woodland at Caldicot in which *Quercus* played a more significant role. *Quercus* is the next most common tree in this community today, and in earlier modern accounts these woodlands were described as 'oak woodlands'. The *Quercus-Pteridium-Rubus* community is dominated by oak. The latter community occurs on less base-rich soils than the *Fraxinus-Acer-Mercurialis* community and would have been absent from the limestone in the area.

Other trees which occur in both these communities are *Tilia cordata* (small-leaved lime), *Ulmus* (elm) and *Carpinus betulus (hornbeam).* From the pollen evidence it is evident that *Tilia* was a major constituent of the woodland in later Neolithic times in the Caldicot area, whereas *Ulmus* was comparatively minor, and its decline probably attributable to human activity during the early Bronze Age. The present distribution of *Tilia* is influenced by summer temperatures allowing it to set seed (Pigott and Huntley 1980, 1981). *Fagus* (beech) and *Taxus* (yew) are infrequent trees in these communities today and *Fagus,* along with *Carpinus,* is rare in the pollen record, though *Taxus* is more frequent. The appearance of *Fagus* late in the pollen record from Caldicot may reflect a decrease in seasonality in the later Holocene favouring its spread (Huntley *et al* 1989), rather than forest disturbance (Iversen 1973, Birks 1989), or may be caused by a combination of both. *Betula* is usually common in *Quercus-Pteridium-Rubus* woodland, and although generally sparse and infrequent in *Fraxinus-Acer-Mercurialis* woodland, may be temporarily important following clearance (Rodwell 1991a). Therefore, *Betula* pollen might have been expected to be better represented than it is in the pollen record from Caldicot. One possible explanation for this may be that grazing and browsing prevented regeneration (Atkinson 1992). Grazing by sheep can prevent regeneration of birch (Pigott 1983) and red deer can have a similar effect (Miles and Kinnaird 1979).

Corylus avellana is the commonest shrub in both the *Fraxinus-Acer-Mercurialis* and the *Quercus-Pteridium-Rubus* communities and is reasonably well represented in all the pollen zones and dominates the wood record from Caldicot. In these communities understorey shrubs apart from *Corylus,* include the hawthorns, with *Crataegus monogyna* the commonest, accompanied by *Sambucus nigra* (elder) and *Prunus spinosa.* However, whereas *Cornus sanguinea* (dogwood), *Euonymus*

europaeus (spindle) and *Ligustrum vulgare* (wild privet) may be locally prominent in the *Fraxinus-Acer-Mercurialis* community they are rare in the *Quercus-Pteridium-Rubus* community. Diagnostic of the herb layer in the former community is *Mercurialis perennis* (dog's mercury), and *Hedera helix* (ivy) is also quite characteristic, whilst particularly well represented in the field layer of the latter community are *Pteridium aquilinum* (bracken), and *Rubus fruticosus* agg. The occurrence of these taxa in the pollen, plant macrofossil and wood records suggests that both these woodland communities were present at Caldicot. It is also possible that various scrub communities, independent of woodland, existed in the Caldicot area, particularly from around Phase III onwards. These include *Crataegus monogyna-Hedera helix* scrub, in which *Rubus fruticosus* agg. is also a constant, *Prunus spinosa-Rubus fruticosus* scrub and *Pteridium aquilinum-Rubus fruticosus* underscrub, this last being a community in which trees and shrubs make a negligible contribution. The first two communities typically invade neglected ground, particularly grassland where grazing has been relaxed. Of the two communities, *Prunus spinosa-Rubus fruticosus* is more resistant to salt spray and exposure and may have been more prominent closer to the coast. *Pteridium aquilinum-Rubus fruticosus* underscrub is most commonly found in association with woodland, but if the woody cover is removed by clearance activity or coppicing, as may have occurred in the Caldicot area, then the abundance of *Pteridium* can increase greatly.

Heathland

Evidence for heathland comes entirely from the pollen record in the form of the occasional grain of *Calluna* (heather) and *Sphagnum* spores, and presumably was derived from the areas of raised bog which existed in what is today the intertidal area or which occurred inland, such as at Barland's Farm (see Fig 163); both areas are now largely buried by substantial alluvial deposits.

The environmental sequence and vegetational history

Phase I

The earliest evidence comes from pollen sequences from Columns 1, 3 and 6 and plant macrofossil sample 2078 (Column 1). It is pre-palaeochannel and before any known direct activity at the site. At this time, as far as is known from borehole evidence (p 15), sedimentation was occurring across the whole valley floor. The first zone in all three pollen sequences, CA.1, CE.1 and CM.1, can be correlated as site zone CS.1 (see Table 7 and Fig 73). It is dominated by high Cyperaceae (sedge) values, at least 40% TLP, suppressing the values of dry-land taxa. Arboreal taxa are dominated by *Quercus* and *Corylus avellana*-type with *Alnus* relatively poorly represented. *Tilia* and *Ulmus* are also low and *Betula* is very sparse. In contrast, *Pinus* (pine) is consistently present at more than 1% in this and later zones, a situation which might be related to water transport and differential flotation (Hopkins 1950). Overall the evidence suggests a mixed deciduous woodland on the dry land with some alder carr, valley-side or terrace alder woods (see above p 106). Poaceae values are comparatively low but pollen of *Plantago lanceolata* and Cerealia-type is present and suggests some limited agricultural activity at this time. However, as previously mentioned, Cerealia-type includes certain wild grasses such as *Elytrigia repens, E. juncea* (sand couch), *Leymus arenarius* (lyme-grass), and *Ammophila arenaria* (marram), which are found in maritime habitats, and *Glyceria fluitans* (floating sweet-grass) and *G. notata* (floating sweet-grass) which occur in shallow water and wet meadows, any of which might have been found in the Caldicot region. *Plantago lanceolata* also frequents coastal habitats.

Freshwater aquatics are generally scarce in the pollen record, as is the freshwater algae *Pediastrum*, whereas Chenopodiaceae (goosefoots) are abundant in all three instances, indicating salt-marsh. The high sedge values suggest fen communities, some of which are tolerant of brackish conditions (p 104), and therefore along with the Chenopodiaceae evidence could point to a marine influence. This is further supported by the occurrence of *Plantago maritima* and is also in agreement with the diatom evidence (Cameron p 124).

In contrast to the pollen record, the plant macrofossil assemblage from 2078 (appendix Table 64) is dominated by aquatic taxa, notably *Ranunculus sceleratus* and *Mentha arvensis/aquatica* (corn/water mint), with lesser amounts of *Lemna*. *Alisma* is also relatively well represented. Whilst *R. sceleratus* is commonly found in eutrophic (nutrient rich) fresh water, it is also often found in brackish water (Haslam *et al* 1982). It tends to grow in still or slowly moving shallow water and can occur on seasonally exposed mud. *R.* Subgenus *Batrachium* encompasses a number of species, most of which occupy freshwater habitats, but it includes *R. baudotii* (brackish water-crowfoot) which, like *R. sceleratus*, can occur in brackish water. It can exist in water up to a depth of 30cm along with other species in this sub-genus. It is currently recorded from the area along with other species in this sub-genus (Wade 1970). Though most of the aquatics favour still or slow flow rates, some can stand swifter moving water. *Alisma* species tolerate flow from still to moderate and a water depth of up to 75cm, while *Mentha aquatica* can occur in still to fast-flowing water, as can *Rorippa nasturtium-aquaticum* (Haslam *et al* 1982). In comparison *Lemna gibba* is confined to still or slow water and generally the evidence suggests still or sluggish water movement at the site.

The pollen evidence for fen communities is sup-

ported in the plant macrofossil record by the presence of *Lychnis flos-cuculi* (ragged robin), *Urtica dioica, Lycopus europaeus* (gypsywort) and *Epilobium hirsutum* type which could reflect fen (eg *Phragmites australis-Urtica dioica* fen). The last two taxa are also typical of a bankside habitat. In addition, *Urtica* could indicate ground disturbance as could *Plantago major* (greater plantain). Seeds of the latter can be subdivided (Stace 1991) on the basis of size into two subspecies, Ssp. *major* and Ssp. *intermedia*, though there is considerable overlap. As mentioned earlier, Ssp. *major* is found on either cultivated or grassy rough ground whilst Ssp. *intermedia* usually occurs in damp slightly saline situations near the sea. Measurement of *Plantago major* seeds from this and later phases failed to resolve whether or not only one subspecies was present: taken overall it would seem probable that both were present though the absence of particularly large individuals might indicate the population was Ssp. *intermedia*.

Further evidence for a slightly saline environment is provided by nuts of the sedge *Carex otrubae* which, as well as occurring in freshwater conditions, can be found in brackish ditches and on estuarine flats. However, the strongest evidence for a maritime influence is the presence of *Spergularia*. Most species of *Spergularia* occur in coastal habitats and today *Spergularia marina* forms a mid-marsh community with *Puccinellia distans* (Rodwell forthcoming; Adam 1990). This community is especially characteristic of hyper-saline conditions, which can occur where there are shallow pools and high evaporation. Overall the assemblage suggests a fresh-water environment but with evidence for an estuarine influence. Interpretation of this deposit in the field was that it was estuarine/marine in origin, and, as referred to above, this is supported by the diatom evidence (Cameron p 124). The plant macrofossil evidence does not conflict with this as the freshwater element could be derived from upstream, though equally the brackish component could originate downstream and be carried upstream by tides or storm surges.

Plant macrofossil evidence which might reflect human activity is slight. As already mentioned, *Urtica dioica* and *Plantago major* could be present as weeds, indicating ground disturbance. The only tentative evidence for cultivation is a possible seed of *Aphanes inexspectata* (slender parsley-piert). However, it may simply signify disturbed ground, as might *Sambucus nigra*.

To summarise, the evidence suggests a local environment possibly subjected to a tidal influence, while on the surrounding dry land mixed deciduous woodland dominated with limited clearance and agricultural activity. The pollen zone is dated to pre–4670 ± 80 BP (CAR-1323) in Column 6 and therefore this episode of clearance and possible agricultural activity can be ascribed to Neolithic activity shortly after the 'elm decline'.

The following site pollen zone (CS.2) is recognisable in sequences from Columns 1, 6, 5 and 7 (Table

7). In the first two in particular, it coincides with organic-rich horizons, again pre-channel in date. Sequence 23168 was taken through the clearest and deepest organic horizon (context 22273) visible in Area G. Radiocarbon dates suggest this organic deposit developed between 4670 ± 80 BP (CAR-1323) and 4360 ± 80 BP (CAR-1322). Arboreal pollen is quite well represented in this deposit with *Quercus* dominating, *Alnus* more frequent and, notably, *Tilia* values reaching more than 10% TLP. *Ulmus* is also consistently present with values between 2–4% TLP. *Corylus avellana*-type pollen is also frequent. Similar values occur in CM.2, in particular high *Tilia*, although this zone is represented by only one level. The evidence from these two sequences suggests mixed deciduous woodland in the area but with lime now forming a significant proportion of the woodland, indeed probably dominating in certain areas, especially if the correction factor of ×8 for the poor production and dispersal characteristics of *Tilia* (Andersen 1970) is applied. The evidence is consistent with that from elsewhere in the area (Walker and James 1993) and southern England (Greig 1982). In both diagrams herbaceous pollen is mainly made up of Poaceae and Cyperaceae pollen, though the latter is considerably less abundant than in the previous zone, suggesting a contraction in areas of sedge-fen. *Aster*-type is the most frequent of the other herbs and could reflect fen, salt-marsh or dry-land habitats, although abundant *Eupatorium cannabinum* in the macrofossil record indicates the former. Perhaps most noticeable is the absence of any *Plantago lanceolata* and Cerealia-type pollen in CA.2 and CM.2, indicating that in the immediate area human activity might have been minimal at this time. *Pteridium* values are also very low. Reduced amounts of Chenopodiaceae pollen, compared with the previous zone, suggest that whilst estuarine conditions continued to be maintained in the area they exerted a less strong influence at the site. The highest pollen level in CA.2 lies above the main organic band and therefore post-dates 4360 ± 80 BP (CAR-1322). It displays a similar pollen assemblage to that below. Arboreal percentages, including *Tilia*, are comparable and there is no evidence for any human activity on the surrounding dry land. Some slight changes do appear to have taken place in the local environment. Cyperaceae values are higher, indicating an increase in fen while Chenopodiaceae values rise again slightly, suggesting an increasing marine influence.

Plant macrofossil sample 2074 from Column 1 (appendix Table 64), is in agreement with the pollen evidence from site zone CS.2. It differs from the previous sample in being from a much more organic deposit with *Phragmites australis* remains. In comparison to the previous sample there is a reduction in aquatics. The assemblage is dominated by *Urtica dioica* and *Eupatorium cannabinum* which could be derived from local fen (eg *Phragmites australis-Urtica dioica* and *Phragmites australis-Eupatorium cannabinum* communities) and bankside environ-ments. *Lythrum* is present and like *Eupatorium* occurs beside water or in fen. Again, there is a hint of brackish conditions from the presence of *Carex otrubae*, *Suaeda maritima* and possibly *Atriplex* which may reflect salt-marsh communities. Compared to the previous sample there is a little evidence for woodland, namely an *Alnus* fruit.

Site zone CS.2 is also considered to be represented in the basal zone, CF.1, of Column 5 where the sediments become increasingly organic with increasing depth. Stratigraphically, this zone is from pre-channel deposits but from a higher OD level and from above the organic layers examined in the other two sequences and therefore provides a record post-dating them. Again, CF.1 is characterised by high *Tilia* values. However, it differs from CM.2 (Column 1) and CA.2 (Column 6) in that *Quercus* is slightly more frequent, *Alnus* is less frequent and *Pinus* and *Ulmus* are less well represented, perhaps reflecting some minor changes in the composition of the woodland. Poaceae is similar in all three local zones but Cyperaceae marginally more abundant in CF.1, fen communities perhaps becoming slightly more extensive again. Indicators of anthropogenic activity are absent until the end of the zone when *Plantago lanceolata* and Cerealia-type pollen, though scarce, are represented, suggesting a renewal of activity at a low level. A fall in arboreal pollen, notably of *Tilia* and *Quercus* is also recorded at this time. *Pteridium* spores are more frequent, and this might also tend to indicate some interference with the woodland cover. Although this is essentially a regeneration phase it does not preclude agricultural activity along the lines put forward by Göransson (cf 1983,1986, 1987) and termed by Edwards (1993) as the 'forest utilisation model'. In this, it is envisaged that, in the later Neolithic, coppiced woods would be used to their full extent, accompanied by 'forest farming'. Cereal cultivation would take place for one year in axe-cleared coppice and then the woodland would be allowed to regenerate. The coppice would also produce leaf fodder, and regeneration of natural forest would occur in marginal areas. It is possible that such a system was operating in the Caldicot area.

High Chenopodiaceae values occur throughout the zone and towards the end are accompanied by *Plantago maritima* and a peak in *Spergula*-type pollen, pointing towards an increasing marine influence. *Spergula*-type pollen includes *Spergula arvensis* (corn spurrey) which is a weed of cultivation, though it can occur in short turf near the sea, but the other species, *Spergularia* spp., are generally representative of coastal habitats. Whilst the pollen could be derived from *Spergula arvensis*, and therefore provide further evidence for cultivation, the presence of *Spergularia* seeds in Phase I samples tends to suggest a maritime origin. Malvaceae pollen also includes species with a range of habitat preferences. *Malva sylvestris* (common mallow) is found on rough or waste ground whereas *Althaea officinalis* (marsh mallow) occurs near the sea, including in brackish ditches. Also present is the aquatic *Zannichellia palustris* which can be found in either fresh or brackish water. As mentioned previously, the *Plantago lanceolata* and Cerealia-type pollen could be accounted for by taxa inhabiting maritime habitats, but the decrease in arboreal pollen supports disturbance of the forest cover and human activity.

A plant macrofossil sample, 23260 from Column 5 (see Table 6 and appendix Table 67), included Phase VI as well as Phase I sediment and, as the seed assemblage most closely resembles other Phase VI assemblages, is not considered here.

The final sequence which may reflect this zone and pre-channel deposits is from Column 7. This column was taken from silty clays lying well above the organic deposits and outside the later palaeochannels. It therefore clearly post-dates the evidence discussed so far but its relationship to the palaeochannels and precise date is less certain. As in the previous diagrams the zone is characterised by relatively high *Tilia* values and the frequency of other arboreal taxa is broadly comparable to that in CF.1, suggesting a continuation of the 'regeneration' phase. Small peaks in *Plantago lanceolata* and Cerealia-type pollen occur and, with a small but distinct decrease in arboreal pollen, especially *Quercus*, appear to signify further clearance activity in the catchment, perhaps on a slightly greater scale or slightly nearer to the site. *Pteridium* values are noticeably higher which would support this. Concentration values are low, in the region of 10–12,000 grains/ml, suggesting a fairly rapid accumulation rate which would be consistent with clearance taking place in the catchment and increased run-off and sediment load. This may also account for the high *Pteridium* values, as the spores of this species are poorly air-dispersed but have been found to be well transported by water, particularly during flood events (Peck 1973). Relatively abundant Chenopodiaceae and low numbers of freshwater aquatics reflect the maintenance of estuarine conditions, if not directly at the site then not far away. The diatom evidence (Cameron p 122), though scarce, suggests marine conditions. Overall, the assemblage in CB.1 is interpreted as a continuation of that in CA.2, CM.2 and CF.1, rather than contemporary with any of the palaeochannels where representation of *Tilia* is much lower. There is, however, a possibility that *Tilia* is over-represented because of poor preservation conditions and that the zone is later in date.

Pollen preservation is generally poor in Column 7 in comparison to that in the other sequences and was too poor in the upper levels to permit a count. However, the lower levels were at a comparable OD height to those in the upper levels of the palaeochannel deposits of Column 1 where preservation was not a problem, although concentrations declined. This difference in preservation may be because the levels analysed in Column 7, being outside the palaeochannels, had at one time been nearer the 'ground surface' and subject to greater changes in waterlogging and

aeration. The pollen assemblage in Column 7 is clearly different from that recorded at a comparable OD height in Column 1 and, as already discussed, seems most closely to resemble CA.2, CM.2 and CF.1. However, given the OD height and stratigraphic record from the site, it must post-date the other diagrams and, if the evidence from CB.1 represents a continuation of CS.2, then the record is post 4360 ± 80 BP but pre- the earliest of the palaeochannels and the earliest date from them of 3620 ± 70 BP (CAR-1317).

To summarise, the main change during the latter part of Phase I is the increased importance of lime in the woodland community. There is some evidence for human activity on a fairly limited scale but possibly increasing. A marine influence is indicated but interrupted by periods when fresher water conditions appear to have existed and organic clays and peats developed, accompanied by fen and swamp vegetation communities.

Phase II

The earliest pollen record from the palaeochannels comes from Column 2 from Area B and Column 4 from Area E (see Figs 76 and 77). The plant macrofossil evidence from this phase is from samples 23059–23061 (see Tables 6 and 65), adjacent to pollen Column 2. The lowest deposits in these sequences are broadly contemporary with the first archaeological evidence from the site, the pile structure dated *c* 3500 BP. In both CC.1a and CD.1 (site zone CS.3a Table 7) arboreal pollen is reasonably well represented with *Quercus* and *Corylus avellana*-type dominating. It differs from the previous zone, CS.2, by *Tilia* being much less frequent. *Alnus* values are generally quite low. Other trees are scarce, apart from *Pinus*. Essentially, oak appears to dominate the woodland with lime, once again, reduced to a more minor role. A decline in lime, of varying date, is widely recognised in British diagrams during the Bronze Age, and is frequently attributed to human activity, including the use of it for leaf fodder (Turner 1962). However, an alternative interpretation recently put forward for changes in *Tilia* frequencies is paludification, the conversion of dry land to mire through waterlogging and peat formation (Waller 1994). It is suggested that in the same way that *Tilia* representation decreases with distance from source, paludification, by progressively increasing the distance between a site and dry land, can produce an apparent reduction in *Tilia* in a vertical pollen sequence and hence through time. It is argued that *Tilia* representation is particularly likely to be influenced in coastal areas where sea-level rise has promoted paludification and increased the wetland size. However at Caldicot the deposits are generally not peats and the distance of the site from dry land between Phases I and II would have remained more or less constant; there is also some evidence for human activity both towards the end of Phase I and during Phase II. Hence an anthropogenic interpretation for the reduction in *Tilia* seems most likely. Arboreal values remain fairly constant in CD.1 whereas there is more evidence for a decline, and hence clearance, in CC.1. Similarly Poaceae values are comparatively low but show a more marked increase in CC.1. However, in both zones there is further possible evidence for farming. Cerealia-type pollen is present in appreciable amounts. *Plantago lanceolata* is present but declines towards the end of the zones. Other taxa which might be indicative of cultivation include *Artemisia* and Lactuceae. *Pteridium aquilinum* spores are also quite abundant, and in this and later channel deposits, *Pteridium* might owe its relative abundance to clearance activity and increased run-off. Alder carr does not appear to be particularly significant, at least not in the immediate area.

Apart from the differences in the aquatic taxa between Phase I and Phase II in the plant macrofossil record (see below), the most marked difference is the increase in dry-land taxa, a number of which could reflect habitats associated with human activity. Many of the taxa can occur in more than one habitat (see Tables 6 and 67). Hence *Ranunculus repens* (creeping buttercup) type and *Stellaria media* could reflect grassland, disturbed or cultivated ground; *Cirsium* cf. *arvense* grassland or disturbed ground; *Sonchus asper* and *Plantago major* disturbed or cultivated ground. Species such as *Rumex* cf. *crispus* (curled dock) and *R. conglomeratus* , though dry-land taxa, frequently occur in damp grassland, including grassland subject to inundation by either fresh or salt water (see p 105), and their occurrence together with the increase in dry-land taxa generally appears to be consistent with the development of a more restricted channel and floodplain.

A brief pollen sub-zone, CC.1b, has been recognised in the later Phase II deposits in 23010. *Quercus* values are higher and Poaceae values lower than at the end of the previous zone CC.1a and in the following zone CC.2 (Phase III), suggesting possibly a very brief regeneration episode with human activity either further away from or at a lower level in the area of the site. Shrubby species are better represented, as in Phase III, perhaps reflecting either opening up of the woodland or colonisation of previously cleared areas. This sub-zone shows characteristics of both earlier and later zones and it is possible that some erosion (secondary component 4b p 100 and Fig 81) and mixing of the sediments has occurred as the pollen level occurs at the boundary of Phase II/Phase III deposits.

The evidence for woody species is more diverse in the plant macrofossil assemblage from this phase. As in Phase I there is an indication of alder woodland in the area from the presence of a fruit and cone-scale of *Alnus*. However, there is also evidence for dry-land species such as *Prunus spinosa*, *Corylus avellana*, *Sambucus nigra* and *Rubus*, indicating scrub or the understorey in woodland. This is in agreement with the wood record (p 158) and particularly the pollen evidence from zone CC.1b. There is, however, the

suggestion that some wood may be intrusive from Phase III (p 169).

There is some evidence to suggest slight variations in salinity. At the beginning of both pollen zones CC1.a and CD.1 there are noticeable amounts of the freshwater algae, *Pediastrum*, which then decrease. Chenopodiaceae pollen is scarce at the beginning of CC.1 then shows a marked increase, whereas it remains consistently present at over 1% TLP in CD.1. *Atriplex*, which is found in salt-marsh, is present in the plant macrofossil record. Other pollen taxa recorded in these zones which reflect a brackish influence include *Plantago maritima* and *Glaux maritima* and, as in previous zones, taxa which could be indicative of human activity could equally owe their presence to the existence of maritime habitats. The diatoms also suggest tidal conditions at this time (Cameron p 119).

Contrasting with the pollen and diatom evidence, the plant macrofossil assemblage generally indicates freshwater. Most of the taxa in Phase I also occur in Phase II. *Lemna* and *Mentha arvensis/aquatica* are absent but *Rumex hydrolapathum* (water dock) type and *Rumex* cf. *palustris* (marsh dock) are present. *Rumex hydrolapathum*, like many of the others, is a species which signifies water conditions that are still or slowly moving, whereas *Callitriche* (water-starworts) can also withstand rapid flow. *Sparganium* is recorded and *S. erectum* tolerates a range of flow rates (Haslam 1982). As well as occurring in stream margins up to 1m deep it can be found just above mean water level. *Spergularia* and *Suaeda maritima*, indicative of salt-marsh conditions are absent but a small Primulaceae, either *Anagallis minima* (chaffweed) or *Samolus valerandi* (brookweed), both of which can occur in coastal situations, is represented as is *Schoenoplectus tabernaemontani* which is found frequently in brackish water.

From the pollen concentration values (CC.1 c 12–15,000 grains/ml, CD.1 c 7,000–10,000 grains/ml) and depth of deposit, it would appear that fairly rapid aggradation was taking place during site zone CS.3. Two main possibilities may account for this, either singly or together. Clearance elsewhere in the catchment, particularly with cultivation associated, could lead to increased run-off, and sediment deposition. The decline in *Quercus* in CC.1, peaks in Cerealia-type pollen and relatively frequent *Pteridium* in both diagrams provide some corroboration for this. Alternatively some of the sediment could derive from further downstream and the estuary. Support for this is provided by the presence of salt-marsh taxa and the diatom evidence (p 124). Furthermore, some of the pollen was indeterminable because of what appeared to be a manganese-like deposit obscuring the grains. Hence it is possible that the apparent increase in *Quercus* values compared with earlier zones may be because more of the pollen is derived from further away, and possibly includes older pollen (secondary components 4 and 5 p 100 and Fig 81). However, there is evidence from other sites in the area (Walker and James 1993, unpublished) for an increase in *Quercus* for a very brief period around this time, presumably reflecting an expansion of oak into areas from which *Tilia* had previously been cleared.

In summary, one of the main changes in the Caldicot area, which had already occurred by the beginning of Phase II, was the decline in lime which is probably attributable to anthropogenic activity. There is possible evidence for cultivation and pastoralism. By this time there is also evidence for a more restricted channel and the development of a floodplain in the valley. Indicators of brackish water suggest that the site was subject to an estuarine/marine influence at times.

Phase III

Phase III is represented in three pollen diagrams (see Figs 75-7). Zones CC.2 in Column 2 and CD.2 in Column 4 (site zone CS.4) are assigned on stratigraphic grounds to this phase. Also allocated to this phase are zones CE.2a and CE.2b in Column 3 taken from the trench containing the boat strake dated by radiocarbon to 3439 ± 19 BP (UB-3472). The corresponding plant macrofossil sequences are samples 23055-7 and spot sample 23166, and 23026-32 (see Tables 65 and 66). The results are summarised in Table 6. In addition samples (appendix Table 68) were taken from the stitch-holes of the boat strake. Radiocarbon dates for this phase generally lie in the range 3000-3400 BP.

The pollen evidence from Column 3 clearly demonstrates there is a marked discontinuity between zones CE.1 and CE.2 with erosion of a number of deposits, including the later Phase I (site zone CS. 2) and all Phase II deposits (site zone CS.3). This zone is characterised by lower *Quercus* values than in the previous phase, otherwise *Tilia*, *Ulmus* and other trees continue at a similar level, implying little change in the composition of the woodland, but clearance in particular of oak-dominated woodland. *Taxus* is slightly more frequent. One feature common to CC.1b at the end of Phase II and all the Phase III zones is the marked increase in frequency of shrubby species recorded. This, together with the reduction in *Quercus* and increase in herb taxa such as *Plantago lanceolata* and Lactuceae, suggests clearance of oak woodland accompanied by an expansion of shrubby species into cleared areas, or increased representation of these shrubby species because of removal of the oak canopy. *Prunus spinosa* and *Crataegus monogyna* readily colonise neglected areas with *Prunus spinosa* being more tolerant of conditions in coastal areas (Rodwell 1991a). *Prunus* is well represented in the wood record from this phase (Johnson p 160), being second only to *Corylus*, and confirms the probable local occurrence of this pollen. However, it should also be noted that standard pollen models may not apply, as some of the pollen could originate from material brought onto the site because of human activity (anthropogenic com-

ponent 7 p 00 and Fig 81). *Alnus* values remain at a relatively low level and it seems that alder communities were largely unaffected by human activity, although alder is present in the wood record. Basically, it would seem that local clearance of oak towards the end of the previous phase and beginning of this phase favoured an increase in shrubby species which were then used at the site. However, the utilisation of these species, particularly *Corylus*, cannot be detected in the pollen record. The range of woody taxa in the plant macrofossil record is much the same as in Phase II, apart from the absence of *Corylus avellana* and presence of *Crataegus* and *Betula*, and agrees with the pollen evidence for alder woodland and scrubland.

The increase in *Plantago lanceolata* and other herb pollen clearly supports the archaeological evidence for human activity in the area, which is also evident from the plant macrofossil record. Whilst the *Plantago lanceolata* and *Rumex* spp. may indicate grassland and pastoralism, the occasional Cerealia-type grain would suggest limited cultivation. Significant amounts of Lactuceae pollen may also point to cultivation or disturbance and waste ground. In the plant macrofossil samples, dry-land taxa show a distinct increase in abundance. *Rumex conglomeratus* and other *Rumex* spp. possibly reflect damp grassy conditions, presumably near the channel. *Plantago major* increases substantially, and it seems most likely that this is due to an increase in disturbed ground associated with human and animal activity at the site. Disturbance by the latter is considered to be the most important factor governing the distribution of the species and it is regarded as one of the most resistant species to trampling (Sagar and Harper 1964). *Chenopodium album* is present and may also be derived from trampled areas around the site. Alternatively, along with *Sonchus asper*, *Lapsana communis* and *Solanum nigrum*, it may indicate cultivation was taking place relatively nearby. Overall the plant macrofossil evidence appears clearly to reflect human activity at the site and in the immediate area.

Pollen taxa reflecting aquatic, swamp and fen communities are frequent and *Pediastrum* shows some distinct peaks in pollen zone CS.4. Whilst most indicate freshwater environments, *Zannichellia* can occur in brackish environments (see below). Oscillations in the curves for *Pediastrum* could also relate to variations in salinity and are discussed in more detail later (p 262). Possibly of significance is the marked decline in *Pediastrum* at 64cm in Column 3 which coincides with a peak in marine diatoms (Cameron p 120). Indeterminable pollen also increases at this time. It seems that there might have been a very brief episode of more saline conditions. The continued presence of Chenopodiaceae pollen could be attributable to salt-marsh environments, disturbed ground near the site, cultivation, or a combination of all three, as could the Lactuceae pollen and the various *Plantago* spp. Plant macrofossils of taxa belonging to the Chenopodiaceae and

Lactuceae taxonomic groups with a preference for these different habitats suggest that the last interpretation may indeed apply.

Aquatic taxa are more or less the same as in Phase II in the plant macrofossil record but *Zannichellia palustris* and *Hippuris vulgaris* (mare's tail) are present in a few samples. *Zannichellia* is found in both freshwater and brackish streams and rivers, frequently on clay streams and in water up to 2m deep (Haslam *et al* 1982). *Hippuris* will occur in still waters when in sheltered shallow margins and, again in lowland clay streams, where there is slow flow. One difference from previous phases is that, whereas *Ranunculus sceleratus* had tended to dominate the aquatic *Ranunculus* flora, it is now *R.* subgenus *Batrachium* which dominates. Whether this reflects a reduction in a brackish influence or some other factor is unclear. Other taxa such as *Sparganium* and *Alisma* are slightly more frequent. *S. erectum* is regarded as the most widely distributed stream plant (Haslam *et al* 1982). It can tolerate oligo-halinous waters with salinities not exceeding 0.18% Again the presence of *Suaeda maritima*, *Salicornia* and possibly *Atriplex* suggests salt-marsh not far away and the sedges also hint at a brackish influence.

Levels 40cm, 48cm and 56cm in pollen Column 3 are from contexts considered to be contemporary with the boat strake and coincide with the end of sub-zone CE.2a and sub-zone CE.2b. The latter is defined notably by an increase in *Alnus*. *Pinus* and *Salix* also decrease but other arboreal taxa are similar to CE.2a, suggesting little change in the dry-land woodland. Herbaceous pollen, particularly of Lactuceae, is less abundant though *Plantago lanceolata* remains at much the same level, indicating that pastoralism continued to be important. There may have been a slight reduction in arable farming activity in the area, as Cerealia-type pollen is only recorded at the end of sub-zone CE.2b. *Myriophyllum spicatum* (spiked water-milfoil) peaks, *Potamogeton*-type pollen is frequent in all three levels, *Sparganium/Typha* decreases and *Pediastrum* shows a steady increase, perhaps reflecting a reduction in swamp communities and increase in aquatics. Chenopodiaceae pollen also becomes less frequent. One possible interpretation of these changes is a marginal expansion in freshwater environments at this time, including an increase in alder carr nearer to the site. An increase in concentration values from *c* 10–20,000 to *c* 25–30,000 may indicate a decrease in accumulation rates or increased pollen output.

The plant macrofossil assemblage from the stitch holes is essentially the same as that from the other samples with no evidence for plant material that could have been directly associated with the boat, either in its construction or use.

Overall the evidence during Phase III suggests increased activity in the area, with some woodland clearance and an increase in scrubland. The strongest farming evidence is for pastoralism but with limited cultivation taking place elsewhere in the catchment. The channel environment appears to have been primarily freshwater.

Phase IV

Phase IV, a period of little or no activity at the site, is represented by pollen sub-zone CE.2c (site zone CS.4d) in Column 3 (Fig 73) and plant macrofossil sequence 23017–23 (see Tables 6 and 67). This phase is largely undated, but a radiocarbon date exists from wood from the interface of Phase III/Phase IV deposits of 3000 ± 60 BP (CAR-1407). This pollen sub-zone differs only marginally from the previous sub-zones. Further clearance is indicated by a slight decline in the frequency of a number of arboreal taxa including *Pinus*, *Quercus*, *Ulmus* and *Alnus*. A range of shrub taxa continues to be present and could reflect either the understorey in deciduous woodland or scrubland, most probably the latter. However, fruitstones of *Prunus spinosa* and *Crataegus*, which occur in Phase III, are not recorded from Phase IV. Similarly the amount of *Prunus spinosa* and Pomoideae wood from this phase is low, but so is the total amount of wood. The absence of these remains could reflect a change in woodland composition or simply indicate that they owe their presence in the Phase III deposits to deliberate collection and dumping.

Pollen of Poaceae increases marginally and Cerealia-type occurs slightly more frequently. *Plantago lanceolata* continues to be reasonably well represented and *Centaurea nigra* (common knapweed), also indicative of grassland, is present. *Pteridium* values return to a level more comparable to that in CE.2a. Chenopodiaceae pollen is sparser and may reflect a reduction in the level of disturbance at the site, which is consistent with the archaeological evidence, or a reduced marine influence. The dryland assemblage from the plant macrofossil record continues to suggest grassland, waste ground and possibly cultivation but there is a distinct reduction in *Plantago major* which is consistent with the archaeological evidence for reduced activity at the site. Similarly a decrease in *Chenopodium album*, *Sonchus asper* and possibly *Atriplex* spp. and absence of *Aphanes* spp. and *Lapsana communis* may mirror a reduction in activity at the site or cultivation in the area. In contrast, even though only one seed is present, *Chenopodium ficifolium*, which has a similar habitat preference, but is also found around manure heaps, might point to the presence of large herbivores around the site.

Freshwater aquatics also continue to be well represented in the pollen record. *Sparganium/Typha* increases slightly indicating an expansion in swamp. Concentration values (maximum >80,000 grains/ml) are the highest recorded from the site and suggest a period when accumulation rates were slower and conditions relatively stable as the channel gradually silted up and was colonised. Reed stems and seeds of *Alisma* spp., *Sparganium* sp. and *Phalaris arundi-*

nacea support this. Possible changes in the aquatic flora are indicated by a reduction in the frequency of seeds of *Ranunculus* Subgenus *Batrachium* and *Rumex hydrolapathum* type and an increase in *Apium graveolens* (wild celery), *Rorippa nasturtium-aquaticum*, *R. palustris* (marsh yellow-cress), *Alisma* spp. and *Lemna* spp. *Potamogeton lucens* (shining pondweed), frequently associated with *L. trisulca* (ivy-leaved duckweed) and *L. gibba*, is present. *Epilobium hirsutum* type is more abundant. A few species which could indicate a brackish influence persist.

The final level in pollen Column 4 (Fig 77) stratigraphically should belong to Phase IV but there is insufficient evidence to define a separate zone. However, *Carpinus betulus* and *Acer campestre* pollen are present. The former is not recorded in the wood record from the site but is recorded from Goldcliff at *c* 3400 BP (Smith and Morgan 1989). The latter is present in the wood record from the site but not until Phase VI/VII. It also occurs at Goldcliff but all that can be said about the date is that it is after 3130 ± 70 BP (CAR-644).

Essentially, similar conditions to those in Phase III seem to have prevailed during Phase IV, though the slight reduction in arboreal pollen and slightly more frequent Cerealia-type pollen could indicate that, whilst there was a shift in activity away from the site, the level of activity in the region actually increased. The consistent record for *Plantago lanceolata* in this and previous sub-zones belonging to site zone CS.4 demonstrates the continued importance of pastoralism throughout Phases III and IV. Freshwater conditions continued to dominate in the channel itself which was becoming increasingly silted up.

Phase V

A return to human activity at the site is recorded in Phase V and, given the radiocarbon dates for Phases III and VI (p 11), probably dates to *c* 3000 BP. The evidence for Phase V is recorded in zone CM.3 (site zone CS.5) from Column 1 (Fig 80) where again it is clear that there is a marked discontinuity in the environmental record, with deposits contemporary with the pile structure and boat strake clearly absent. The plant macrofossil assemblage is represented in samples 2068–70 (Table 6, appendix Table 64).

Alnus pollen values are greater than in previous zones and for the first time dominate the arboreal assemblage, but show a steady decline throughout the period. Similarly, *Betula*, though present in low amounts, is more frequent than in previous phases and could indicate an increase in fen woodland or regeneration on dry land, most likely the former. An increase in *Salix* is also consistent with an expansion in fen woodland communities. The composition of the woodland on the dry land seems to be much the same as in the previous zones. *Tilia* continues to be continuously represented but *Ulmus*, as in CE.2c, is

present only sporadically. *Quercus* and *Corylus avellana*-type values remain relatively low. The pollen spectrum for *Alnus* seems to indicate a spread of alder woodland in the area, although it remains absent from the site, some of which was then cleared. Alternatively, increasingly wet conditions indicated by an increase in *Potamogeton*, which initially could have favoured *Alnus*, ultimately could have led to a reduction in alder carr.

Fruits of *Alnus* are slightly more frequent, which is in agreement with the pollen evidence for an expansion in alder woodland at this time. Otherwise, woody species in the plant macrofossil record are similar to before, but include *Prunus spinosa* and *Corylus* which were absent from Phase IV; both of which are also more abundant in the wood record (Johnson p 160) and indicate scrubland.

Another marked difference in this pollen zone is in *Plantago lanceolata* which is more abundant than in any of the previous zones. Other grassland weeds again include *Centaurea nigra*, and *Rumex* spp Lactuceae and Chenopodiaceae are also well represented and Cerealia-type is comparatively frequent. *Artemisia*-type, which includes species indicative of waste ground or salt-marsh, is present. *Pteridium* spores are also abundant. Generally, the evidence points to an increased level of human activity in the area of the site with pastoralism predominating, confirmed by the faunal record (McCormick p 220) from the site, but with some cultivation taking place in the area.

The plant macrofossil evidence is very much in agreement with the pollen record. A marginal increase in weedy taxa in the plant macrofossils such as *Plantago major*, *Chenopodium album* and possibly *Atriplex* also seems to support the archaeological evidence for a return to human activity in the neighbourhood of the site. As in the previous phase the occurrence of a possible seed of *Chenopodium ficifolium* could indicate herbivores and pastoral activity as could *Chenopodium album*, which is commonly present on dunghills (Williams 1963). It is readily eaten by cattle and is frequently dispersed in dung and droppings. In contrast to the previous phase, *Aphanes arvensis* (parsley piert) re-appears and along with *Sonchus asper* and *S. arvensis* could indicate cultivation.

Although Chenopodiaceae pollen is well represented, relatively high counts of *Potamogeton* and *Pediastrum* indicate that freshwater conditions prevailed locally. It therefore seems likely that the relatively high representation of the former may relate to ground disturbance in the area of the site, rather than a maritime influence. This is at least to some degree supported by the plant macrofossil evidence. In terms of the channel environment, the taxa represented in the plant macrofossils are largely the same as in the previous phase, apart from *Lemna* is absent and *Zannichellia* is present. The last, along with *Spergularia* and various sedges, does suggest the presence of salt-marsh in the area.

To summarise, the main difference in the woodland

during Phase V compared with earlier phases, is the greater importance of alder. There is also stronger evidence for grassland and pastoralism in the area during Phase V compared with Phase IV. Freshwater conditions continued to dominate.

Phase VI

During Phase VI substantial spreads of stone, wood and associated artefactual remains were deposited. Radiocarbon dates (p 12) suggest this occurred *c* 3000–2800 BP. A mortised plank from structure 9014 in Area A is dated by dendrochronology to 998/997 BC (p 190). The environmental conditions during this phase are demonstrated in pollen Columns 1 and 5 (Figs 80 and 79) and plant macrofossil samples 2066–8 (see appendix Table 64) and 23258–60 (see appendix Table 67) and summarised in Table 6.

Once again, a marked discontinuity is evident in the Column 5 pollen diagram with no Phase II, III, IV or V deposits represented. Both CM.4 in Column 1 and CF.2 in Column 5 (site zone CS.6) reflect a brief episode when *Alnus* dominates the arboreal assemblage, Poaceae values are less than in following zones and *Plantago lanceolata* is poorly represented compared with both later zones and the previous zone (CS.5). The curve for *Alnus*, most clearly represented in Column 1, suggests a renewed expansion in alder and a decline in *Quercus*, *Betula*, *Pinus* and *Tilia*. This could indicate continued clearance of dry-land woodland communities or the development of local alder woodland drowning out representation of the other species. An accompanying increase in *Corylus avellana*-type pollen could relate to increased flowering as a result of removal of the canopy, regeneration of scrub communities and even, very tentatively, some attempt at woodland management. Apart from alder in the plant macrofossil record, evidence for woodland is relatively scarce. *Prunus spinosa* and *Rubus* continue to indicate the presence of scrub on drier land.

Poaceae pollen increases then declines in CM.4. *Plantago lanceolata*, Chenopodiaceae and *Pteridium* are reduced at the beginning of this zone but Cerealia-type remains frequent and increases slightly, as does *Plantago lanceolata*, as *Quercus* declines. Pollen concentration values (unpublished) also reflect these changes. Little difference occurs in the dry-land taxa compared to the previous phase, suggesting that similar conditions continued to prevail, namely trampled areas around the site, wet grassland nearby and possibly some cultivation on dry land away from the site, though the evidence for the latter is slight. However, it is perhaps worth noting the appearance of *Chenopodium polyspermum*, a weed of waste and cultivated ground, for the first time.

Freshwater taxa dominate the plant macrofossil aquatics but there is some evidence, namely *Spergularia*, *Glaux maritima*, *Suaeda maritima*, *Schoenoplec-*

tus tabernaemontani, *Carex* cf. *distans*, *Althaea officinalis* and possible *Bolboschoenus maritimus*, which is indicative of brackish conditions. *Ranunculus sceleratus*, which can occur in brackish water, is slightly less frequent than *R.* subgenus *Batrachium*, most of whose species are freshwater species.

To summarise, compared with the previous phase there is evidence for a further expansion in alder woodland following a gradual decline during the former. Pastoralism appears to continue to predominate but with some cereal cultivation. The presence of salt-marsh habitats is indicated, although freshwater dominates.

Phase VI/VII–VII

Phase VII includes the construction of a bridge, from which a felling date for a split ash upright of 990/989 BC has been produced by dendrochronology. Radiocarbon dates for this phase lie in the range 2750–2400 BP. Pollen zones from two sequences, Columns 1 and 5 (see Figs 80 and 79) relate to this phase, and the corresponding plant macrofossil sequences are 2058–62 (see appendix Table 64) and 23251–7 (see appendix Table 67), summarised in Table 6. There is, however, slight uncertainty as to whether context 9031, corresponding with zone CM.5a (Column 1), belongs to this phase or whether it belongs to Phase VI. CM.5b is definitely assigned to Phase VII as are CF.3a and CF.3b in the pollen sequence from Column 5. CM.5a shares certain characteristics with these zones and all are assigned to site zone CS.7; on that basis, CM.5a is possibly Phase VII. Distinguishing CM.5a and these other zones from earlier zones is the continuous representation of *Plantago coronopus*, although the values are lower in CM.5a than in the other zones. The precise relationship between zones CM.5a and CM.5b from the main channel and zones CF.3a and CF.3b from the minor channel is also uncertain but, apart from exceptionally high *Plantago coronopus* values in CF.3a, the two sets of zones broadly correlate with each other. In comparison to CM.4 and CF.2 arboreal pollen is reduced in both CM.5a and CF.3a, particularly *Alnus*, *Quercus* and *Corylus avellana*-type, although in CM.5a the last two taxa increase again after an initial decline. Poaceae values increase markedly and *Plantago lanceolata* as well as *Plantago coronopus* is reasonably well represented. Chenopodiaceae pollen is present in significant amounts, particularly in CM.5a, and Cerealia-type is present. *Sparganium/Typha* type pollen shows a distinct increase, presumably reflecting a spread in local swamp communities. CM.5b and CF.3b are distinguished from CM.5a and CF.3a, respectively, by a slight increase in *Alnus* and *Corylus avellana*-type pollen. In both CM.5b and CF.3b *Quercus* values also increase towards the end of the zones. However, whereas Poaceae and Cyperaceae decline and *Plantago lanceolata* and *Plantago coronopus* increase slightly in CM.5b, the reverse happens in CF.3b. Alternatively it is possible that CM.5a predates CF.3a, that the comparable deposits are missing, and that CF.3a broadly coincides with the beginning of CM.5b. Indeed deposits assigned to a Phase VI/VII group were present elsewhere in Area E, although they were not necessarily the same as in Area A. The slightly higher *Plantago coronopus* values in CM.5b would support correlation with CF.3a. Chenopodiaceae values are also similar at the beginning of CM.5b to those in CF.3a, and the difference in arboreal values could be accounted for by the high *Plantago coronopus* values in CF.3a depressing the arboreal ones. Radiocarbon dates of 2750 ± 60 BP (CAR-1215) and 2750 ± 70 BP (CAR-1316) from wood from Phase VII deposits in Area A and from the Phase VII lower fills of the later channel (22319) in Area E, respectively, further support the latter correlation.

Plant macrofossil sample 2058 from context 9031 (Phase VI/VII) is relatively rich in plant remains, including the freshwater aquatics *Potamogeton berchtoldii* and *Sparganium* and *Phalaris arundinacea*, although the latter is also found in brackish water. The *Phalaris arundinacea* community is common by rivers. *P. arundinacea* will grow in 40cm or more of water but will not tolerate permanent flooding and to grow well needs the shoots to be above water for at least part of the summer. It can also withstand the turbulence of flood waters and erosion (Haslam 1978). The community can thus survive even where there is sudden and considerable inundation and is frequently found in sites of alluvial deposition (see Rodwell 1995). It often marks the usual upper limit of water-level fluctuation and is the final vegetation type around open-water transitions. Towards open water it may pass directly to swamp or fen or on drier soils which are flooded to inundation grassland, and the increase in *Potentilla anserina* (silverweed) in the Caldicot macrofossil record may support this. Finally, it is a palatable grass and may be summer-grazed by cattle, sheep and horses .

The relationship of the minor channel (22319), containing samples 23251–7, to the main channel, as mentioned, is uncertain. One possibility is that, partly influenced by the construction of the bridge, silting-up occurred on the upstream side of the main channel leading to an increase in colonisation by reed species, while ultimately the structure had a channelling effect which led to erosion of the minor channel downstream. In samples from the latter, *Sparganium* is absent and there is only the occasional seed of *Phalaris*.

Of the most frequent wood types recorded at the site, pollen of *Corylus*, *Quercus* and *Alnus* display a fall, while *Fraxinus* shows minor fluctuations or is absent from the pollen records in CM.5a and CF.3a. It is tempting to see this reduction in arboreal pollen, particularly *Corylus avellana*-type, as associated with local human activity. The absence of *Mercurialis* pollen during CM.5a and reappearance in CM.5b, when *Corylus* values are again higher, is consistent with disturbance of the herb layer brought about by trampling and the development of associated adverse soil conditions during clearance and coppicing activity, followed by recovery during re-growth of the shrubs and trees (Rodwell 1991a). The increased frequency in *Hedera* pollen in CM.5b is also consistent with the development of the shade-tolerant *Hedera* sub-community as canopy cover increases, a situation which is indicated by a peak in *Quercus* pollen as well as higher *Corylus* values. *Prunus* and *Sorbus*-type (Pomoideae in wood record) occur only occasionally and, together with the other changes, could indicate woodland close at hand was being utilised. In the plant macrofossil record fruit-stones of *Rubus* continue to indicate the presence of scrub or waste ground, but *Prunus spinosa* is absent and representation of Prunus in the wood record is much reduced by Phase VII (p 160). The distinct reduction in *Alnus* at the beginning of CS.7 could be a response to rising sea-level and an increasing marine influence, although *Alnus* can withstand a certain amount of flooding by brackish water (Ranwell 1974), rather than be the result of clearance. Fruits of *Alnus* are quite well represented in Phase VI/VII deposits but are sparse in Phase VII deposits. *Fagus* appears for the first time in the pollen record and could be a response to forest disturbance.

The marked increase in *Plantago* pollen at the beginning of CS.7 could be associated with increased pastoral activity at the site, while Cerealia-type pollen indicates some cultivation in the area. However, *Plantago coronopus* is essentially a maritime species and its sudden appearance in comparatively large quantities, particularly in CF.3a, is perhaps significant in this respect. It is frequently found in maritime grassland on cliff tops, but will also occur in areas subject to tidal inundation, including salt-marshes. It is described as preferring soils of a light, sandy or gravelly character and not competing in inland sites except on trampled ground of a sandy or gravelly nature (Dodds 1953). Therefore, trampling by animals may have favoured its establishment in the Caldicot area on the sandy gravel terraces where it may also have been grazed. Soay sheep, goats and ponies have been recorded as grazing on the succulent form on Skokholm Island (Dodds 1953).

The plant macrofossil evidence suggests conditions remained the same around the site as in the previous phase with trampled areas, wet grassland nearby and perhaps cultivation on drier ground. *Urtica urens* (small nettle) and *Persicaria maculosa* (redshank), weeds of waste and cultivated ground, are recorded for the first time.

Chenopodiaceae pollen could relate to either ground disturbance at the site or salt-marsh. A sharp decline in *Sparganium/Typha* pollen halfway through CM.5a coincides with an increase in marine, brackish and halophilous diatoms (Cameron p 124), suggesting a reduction in freshwater habitats and an increasing marine influence. Chenopodiaceae are less frequent during most of CM.5b, CF.3a and CF.3b but increase sharply towards the end of CM.5b and the appearance of *Spergula*-type pollen in CM.5b may again signify a stronger marine influence. Further support for this is provided by *Pediastrum* which is sparse throughout CS.7. Freshwater aquatics dominate the plant macrofossil record but a number, such as *Phalaris arundinacea*, can tolerate slightly brackish conditions. *Ranunculus sceleratus*, which can occur in brackish water, is once again as frequent or more frequent than *R.* subgenus *Batrachium*, most of whose species are freshwater species. *Althaea officinalis*, commonly found in brackish ditches, is present.

To summarise, generally the environment on the dry land seems to have remained much the same throughout CS.7, apart from some woodland regeneration later in the zone. Clearly there was considerable disturbance in the area of the site leading to an increase in species of *Plantago* in particular. Pastoralism appears to have continued to play a major role locally, and this is supported by the faunal evidence (McCormick p 220), but with cultivation more or less consistently present in the area. By the latter half of the period the pollen evidence together with the diatom evidence suggests that estuarine/marine conditions were steadily increasing.

Phase VIII

The remaining phase, Phase VIII, is considered to represent conditions post-channel formation and there is one radiocarbon determination for wood of 2400 ± 70 BP (CAR-1405). The phase is represented by pollen zone CM.6 (Fig 80) and plant macrofossil sample 2050 (Table 6, appendix Table 64). After an increase in arboreal pollen at the end of the previous zone it declines again. *Plantago coronopus* and *Plantago lanceolata* continue to be present at a comparable level to that in the previous zone. Cerealia-type is still present. It therefore seems a similar amount of agricultural activity was taking place. Chenopodiaceae values are high, up to 5%, and *Spergula*-type is more frequent, providing further evidence for a renewed brackish/marine influence during this phase. This is supported by a decrease in freshwater aquatics, notably *Sparganium/Typha*. An increase in Cyperaceae pollen indicates an increase in sedge fen communities, certain of which are tolerant of brackish conditions (p 104). The diatom evidence also suggests an increase in estuarine conditions (Cameron p 126).

Plant macrofossil preservation was poor and remains sparse, apart from *Juncus* (rush) which was frequent, and there is insufficient evidence to draw any firm conclusions about the environmental conditions.

Conclusions

Throughout the period covered by the environmental record, the site seems to have been towards the upper limit of a brackish/marine influence. At times this might have been little more than the occasional storm surge, at others high tides might have reached the site more frequently. During Phases I and II this influence seems to have been stronger and again from around Phase VI/VII, c 2900 BP onwards, the last is in agreement with an overall rise in sea-level recorded at other sites throughout the Severn Estuary (see p 276 for discussion).

Limited clearance and agricultural activity, both pastoral and arable, seems to have been going on in the area during the Neolithic. Towards the end of the Neolithic there was a period of regeneration when *Tilia*, once again on the basis of evidence from other sites in the area as well (see p 273), established itself as a major component of the woodland, but some farming appears to have continued. Early in the 4th millennium BP there was renewed clearance, particularly at the expense of the limewoods. There was a brief period when oak woodland increased but this was followed by more extensive clearance by the middle of the 4th millennium BP which also led to the spread of scrub in areas which were abandoned. Apart from an increase in alder woods around the beginning of the 3rd millennium BP and minor fluctuations, the woodland seems to have remained much the same for the rest of the period although *Carpinus betulinus*, *Fagus sylvatica* and *Acer campestre* appear in the later record. Finally, although pastoralism clearly predominated there seems to have been some limited cereal cultivation throughout the period.

The Diatom Evidence
Nigel G Cameron

Introduction

As part of an integrated programme of environmental archaeological research, diatom (microscopic unicellular or colonial algae) analysis was carried out on deposits from palaeochannels discovered during the excavations. The primary aim of diatom analysis was to determine the salinity conditions under which the sediments accumulated. In addition, it was hoped that other information from the diatom assemblages, for example species lifeform and autecology, would assist in the interpretation of the general environments in which the sediments formed and the taphonomy of deposits.

Battarbee (1988) has reviewed the international literature and archaeological applications of diatom analysis. The technique has been used infrequently at archaeological sites in the UK (eg Battarbee *et al* 1985). An exception is Juggins' (1992) detailed quantitative study of diatom ecology and palaeoecology in the Thames Estuary. The diatom-salinity transfer function developed was applied to sediments from archaeological sites in the City of London (Juggins 1992, 167–82). Diatom analysis continues to be used routinely at wetland, alluvial and coastal excavations in Mainland Europe (eg Jansma 1990;

Table 8 Summary table of diatom sequence in Column 4, monolith 23195

Phase	Context	Height +OD (m)	Depth (cm)	Diatom assemblage	Environment
IV	22382	2.90/2.92–2.93	3/1–0	fresh water	fresh water
III	22379	2.84/2.85–2.90/2.92	9/8–3/1	fresh water	fresh water
III	22392	2.57/2.62–2.84/2.85	36/31–9/8	marine spp. Dominant 32cm decline to 24cm	marine then fresh water
II	22391	2.43–2.57/2.62	50–36/31	mixed assemblage upper part predominantly marine, brackish phase 40cm	mixing of fresh water to marine elements followed by clear marine phase

Straub 1990) and particularly in Scandinavia (eg Gaillard *et al* 1988, Håkansson 1988).

Unpublished assessments and diatom analyses have, however, been carried out at several archaeological sites in Britain during recent years (Cameron unpubl results). In the Severn Estuary work is in progress at associated sites on the Gwent Levels (Barland's Farm) and the approaches to the English side of the Second Severn Crossing. Diatom analyses were carried out on a sequence from Caldicot Pill (Cameron 1993) lying in the present day intertidal zone. The successful use of diatom analysis at these sites suggests that the approach has great potential both on and off site for qualitative and quantitative reconstruction of water quality parameters such as salinity, pH and nutrient levels.

Methods

Wet samples were received in glass sample tubes sealed in polythene bags. Diatom sample and slide preparation followed standard techniques (Battarbee 1986; Renberg 1990). Counting was carried out using a Leitz research microscope (phase contrast ×1000–×1250). Identifications were made with the aid of a range of diatom floras and taxonomic publications held in the collection of the ECRC; UCL. The floras most commonly consulted were: Cleve-Euler (1951–55), Hendey (1964), Hustedt (1930–66) and Werff and Huls (1957–74). Where diatoms were present in sufficient concentrations a total of *c* 200–300 valves were counted per sample. This sum was considered adequate to determine dominant taxonomic composition. Data were entered into the DISCO diatom database at the ECRC; these data, slides and cleaned valve suspensions are available for examination at the ECRC. Data manipulation was carried out using the program TRAN (Juggins 1993) and the diagrams were plotted using TILIA and TILIA.GRAPH (Grimm 1991).

Diatom species' salinity preferences were summarised using the halobian groups of Hustedt (1957, 199):

1 Polyhalobian: >30 g l⁻¹
2 Mesohalobian: 0.2–30 g l⁻¹

3 Oligohalobian – Halophilous: optimum in slightly brackish water
4 Oligohalobian – Indifferent: optimum in freshwater but tolerant of slightly brackish water
5 Halophobous: exclusively freshwater
6 Unknown: taxa of unknown salinity preference.

The principle source of data on species ecology used was the recent survey of Denys (1992).

Results

A total of 69 samples from six sequences (see Figs 61–66, 84–88) were prepared for diatom analysis. Of these a total of 51 samples contained countable diatom assemblages. Only in the eleven samples prepared from Column 7 (monoliths 23309/10) were diatoms more or less absent from the whole sequence. In two samples from the base of the master column and five samples from the base of the Column 3 (monoliths 23004/5) diatoms were not countable. These sections were associated with Phase I prechannel deposits in the respective sequences. A total of 209 diatom taxa were identified from the site.

Area E: Column 4, monolith 23195

A sequence of seven samples, at 8cm intervals, from the 50cm monolith 23195 was analysed for diatoms. A total of 101 diatom taxa were identified in the sequence. A summary diatom diagram (Fig 84) shows species that occurred at abundances of more than 2%, grouped according to salinity preferences. According to the site phasing this monolith cuts across four contexts associated with Phase II–Phase IV (Table 8).

The basal part of the monolith 23195 has a fairly evenly mixed assemblage of freshwater to marine diatom species. It is unlikely that these groups of taxa would grow under similar salinity conditions (p 126). The freshwater element is a predominantly non-planktonic assemblage whilst the marine component is of planktonic or tychoplanktonic species. This mixture of different elements at the base of the sequence could be the result of one or a combination of processes. For example, post-depositional biotur-

CALDICOT Column 4 Monolith 23195

Diatoms occurring at abundances greater than 2%

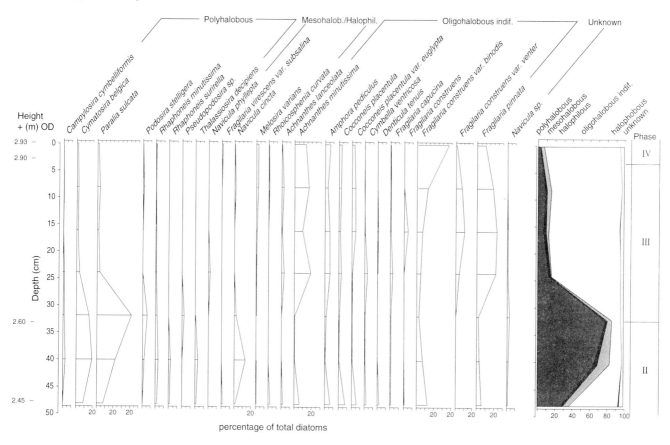

Fig 84   Column 4, monolith 23195: diatoms > 2% and their halobian classification

bation and physical mixing of sediments may have resulted in the time averaging of diatom assemblages. Another possibility is that the assemblage represents the incursion of marine species into a freshwater (or possibly slightly brackish) environment. Alternatively the intrusion of freshwater into a tidal environment may have introduced benthic freshwater species.

However in the upper part of this section of the monolith there is a transition where brackish species, notably *Navicula cincta* (13%), and then marine species such as *Paralia sulcata* (maximum 42%) and *Cymatosira belgica* (maximum 20%), become dominant. At the same time the abundances of freshwater taxa decrease. This part of the sequence, in the upper part of context 22391 and associated with Phase II of the site scheme, represents salinity conditions such as those that might be found in the tidal estuary today. In the uppermost part of 23195, above about 30cm depth and corresponding with Phase III and Phase IV, the assemblages continue to represent a predominantly freshwater environment. There are shifts in the abundances of freshwater taxa in this part of the sequence such as an increase in *Fragilaria construens* var. *binodis* at 8cm. *Melosira varians*, a brackish water species, is present at a maximum abundance of 3%. However, marine taxa are present

in low numbers, probably as a result of reworking of older material by bioturbation or physical mixing.

Area B: Column 2, monolith 23010

The 50cm monolith 23010 was analysed for diatoms at 8cm intervals. A total of 107 diatom taxa were identified in the seven samples counted; a summary diatom diagram (Fig 85) shows species occurring at abundances of more than 2%. According to the phasing scheme the column cuts four contexts associated with Phase II and Phase III (Table 9).

The three samples (48–32cm) analysed from the base of the sequence are dominated by coastal marine species, such as *Paralia sulcata* (max 20%), *Cymatosira belgica* (max 23%), *Rhaphoneis* spp. and *Thalassiosira decipiens*. There is also a significant element of halophilous species, such as *Navicula cincta* which has a maximum abundance of 10% at the base of the sequence.

Marine taxa decline from 32–24cm and oligohalobous taxa become dominant, in particular *Fragilaria* spp. and *Achnanthes minutissima*. Freshwater species continue to dominate the diatom assemblages, although in the uppermost sample there are slight increases in the percentages of polyhalobous taxa

CALDICOT Column 2 Monolith 23010

Diatoms occurring at abundances greater than 2%

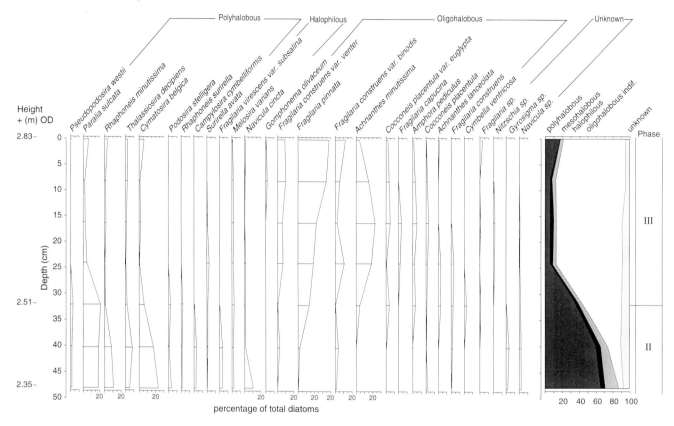

Fig 85   Column 2, monolith 23010: diatoms > 2% and their halobian classification

Table 9   Summary table of diatom sequence in Column 2, monolith 23010

Phase	Context	Height +OD (m)	Depth (cm)	Diatom assemblage and environment
III	22246; 22170; 22169; 22042; 22217; 22216	2.58/2.60–2.90	32/30–0	Freshwater with slight increase in marine/halophilous spp. in 22216
II	22220; 22240; 22241	2.40–2.58/2.60	50–32/30	Marine with halophilous taxa at base

such as *Paralia sulcata*, *Rhaphoneis minutissima* and *Cymatosira belgica*.

Area B: Column 3, monolith 23004/5

A sequence of 24 samples at 4cm intervals was analysed for diatoms from the monolith 23004/5. A summary diagram showing species occurring at abundances greater than 2% is presented (Fig 86). Diatoms were countable in the uppermost nineteen samples of the sequence, but were either absent or present only in very low concentrations in the five basal samples of 23005 (Table 10). These diatom-poor samples were contained within the context 22221 which is related to pre-channel deposits of Phase I. A total of 128 taxa were identified in the nineteen countable samples.

The sparse marine diatoms from the basal section of 23004/5 are, however, consistent with the interpretation of Phase I deposits as related to intertidal Severn Estuary (Wentlooge) deposits (Allen 1987). The appearance of fragments of freshwater species at the top of this part of the sequence may relate to down-mixing of material from the freshwater-deposited sediments above.

The first sample containing countable diatoms is at 72cm depth which corresponds approximately to the lower horizon of context 22166 which belongs to Phase III. Samples at 72 and 68cm have freshwater diatom assemblages, dominated by *Fragilaria* sp. and *Achnanthes minutissima*. A single sample, at 64–5cm, is dominated by marine species including *Paralia sulcata* (22%), *Podosira stelligera* (11%), *Rhaphoneis* spp. and *Cymatosira belgica* (8%). However, although there are minimum abundances of

CALDICOT Column 3 Monolith 23004/23005
Diatoms occurring at abundances greater than 2%

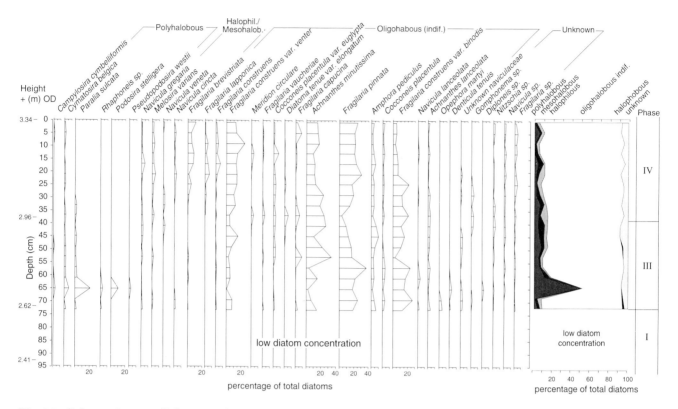

Fig 86 Column 3, monolith 23004/5: diatoms > 2% and their halobian classification

Table 10 Diatom evidence from the five basal samples in Column 3, monolith 23004/5

Depth (cm)	Diatom assemblage	Possible environment
76–77	Fragments of *Fragilaria construens* v. *binodis* & *Meridion circulare*	Freshwater species
80–81	diatoms absent	unknown
84–85	diatoms absent	unknown
88–89	1 *Paralia sulcata* fragment	a coastal marine planktonic sp.
92–93	1 part of *Nitzschia navicularis* & indeterminate fragments	1 identifiable fragment is a brackish to marine estuarine taxon

diatoms such as *Fragilaria construens* var. *venter* and *Achnanthes minutissima*, other oligohalobous taxa, like *Fragilaria construens* var. *binodis* (15%) and *Fragilaria pinnata* (18%), are present in significant abundances. This level must therefore be interpreted as a mixed assemblage containing disparate marine to freshwater elements. It is probable that the record of a marine episode or series of episodes has become mixed with underlying and overlying, predominantly freshwater deposits. This level corresponds to context 22239.

At 60cm marine species decline in importance and freshwater taxa become dominant again.

Above this level marine taxa are present at abundances of less than 2%. Therefore in the contexts above this level the diatom assemblages indicate the dominance of freshwater conditions with a small but significant halophilous element. Notably the diatom assemblages between 58cm and 38/35cm depth corresponding to the context 22165, which contains the boat strake, are of predominantly freshwater species. The beginning of contexts associated with Phase IV at approximately 38cm is accompanied by the establishment of continuous curves for the oligohalobous taxa *Fragilaria brevistriata*, *Fragilaria lapponica* and *Fragilaria construens* (see p 126).

CALDICOT Column 5 Monolith 23188/23189

Diatoms occurring at abundances greater than 2%

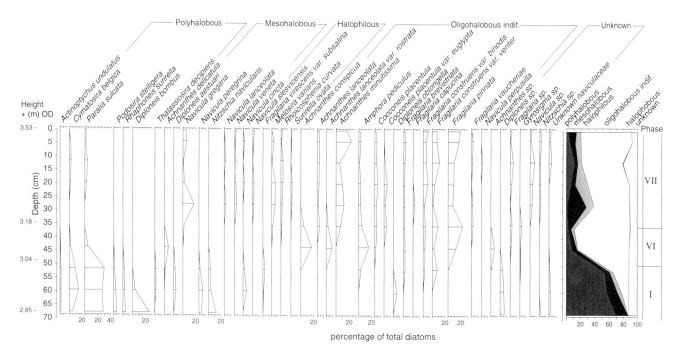

Fig 87 Column 5, monolith 23188/9: diatoms > 2% and their halobian classification

Area E: Column 5, monolith 23188/9

A total of ten samples were analysed from the composite sampling column formed by the monolith 23188/9. One hundred and thirty taxa were identified; a summary diatom diagram (Fig 87) shows taxa occurring at abundances of more than 2%. The base of the sequence, cutting contexts 22349 and 22309, belongs to Phase I. The diatom assemblages in this part of the sequence c 70–50cm, represented by three samples 68–52cm, are consistent with this interpretation. The assemblages of the lower two samples consist entirely of marine and mesohalobous (brackish) taxa typical of the intertidal Severn Estuary. The dominance of *Diploneis bombus* in the basal sample is noteworthy. This is a benthic and often epipsammic (inhabiting the surface of sand grains) brackish/marine species and its abundance suggests that the species was growing *in situ* or that it was deposited with transported sand. *Diploneis bombus* is also a robust heavily silicified species and may have been preferentially preserved.

Between approximately 50–35cm, cutting contexts 22351 and 22325, and associated with Phase VI, the abundances of marine species decrease and oligohalobous taxa such as *Fragilaria pinnata*, *Achnanthes conspicua* and *Amphora pediculus* become dominant.

Freshwater species generally dominate the assemblages to the top of the monolith in the contexts associated with Phase VII. However, there are large variations in the salinity indicated by the assemblages. For example the dominance of *Navicula gregaria* (19%), a mesohalobous species, indicates that estuarine conditions were associated with the depositional environment of context 22321.

Area H: Column 7, monolith 23309/10

Diatom analysis was attempted on eleven samples from the sequence of samples taken from monolith 23309/10. These samples lay at 8cm intervals between 0cm and 80cm in the composite monolith. The top of the sequence (0cm) lay at about +4.22m OD, the base of the sequence was therefore at +3.42m OD. As a result of the absence, or very low concentrations, of diatoms throughout the monolith, detailed diatom analysis was not possible.

Comparing the results of diatom analysis with the stratigraphic record from Area H: diatoms are absent from context 22279; a single fragment of *Podosira stelligera*, a tychoplanktonic marine diatom, was found in the lower level analysed from 22283; and low concentrations of diatom fragments (probably of marine taxa) were found in the three samples from 22284. All three contexts are associated with Phase I on stratigraphic grounds. The low concentrations of diatom valves and marine origin of those identified is consistent with the archaeological interpretation of this material as pre-channel (Wentlooge) deposits.

CALDICOT Column 1 Monoliths 2340,2342,2343,2344

Diatoms occurring at abundances greater than 2%

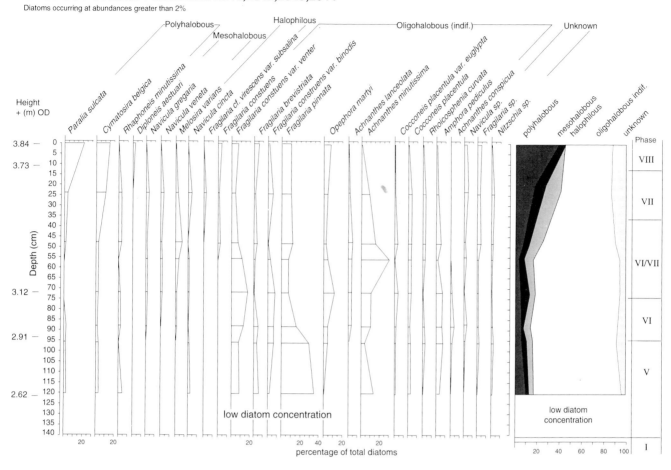

Fig 88   Column 1: diatoms > 2% and their halobian classification

Table 11   Column 1: summary of diatom assemblages by sample height and archaeological context

Phase	Context	Height +OD (m)	Depth	Diatom assemblage and environment
VIII	9001	3.84	0	predominantly marine
VII	9034	3.60	24	mixed marine to freshwater assemblage
VI/VII	9031	3.36	48	freshwater with increased in halophilous element
VI/VII	9031	3.28	56	freshwater with increase in halophilous spp.
VI	9032	3.12	72	freshwater
VI	9032	2.96	88	freshwater
V	22168	2.88	96	freshwater
V	22168	2.64	120	freshwater
I	9033	2.48	136	low concentration
I	9033	2.40	144	low concentration

Area A: Column 1, monoliths 2340, 2342, 2343, 2344

Ten samples from the Column 1 were analysed for diatoms. The sequence ranged from +2.40m OD to +3.84m OD. However, the two basal samples, at +2.40 and +2.48m OD, from context 9033, were found to contain very low concentrations of diatom fragments; diatom counting was not therefore possible.

A diatom diagram showing species occurring at abundances of greater than 2% is presented in Fig 88. The results of diatom analysis relative to the archaeological stratigraphy are tabulated below (Table 11).

The very low concentrations of diatom fragments in 9033 is consistent with the results of analysis of Phase I contexts elsewhere across the site (23189,

Table 12 Diatom assemblages of the six sample columns related to phase and height OD(m)

Phase	Column 1	Column 5	Column 4	Column 2	Column 3	Column 7
VIII	3.73–3.84 inc. marine					
VII	3.16–3.73 fresh/brack. to mar.	3.18–3.53 fresh/brack.				
VI	3.03–3.16 fresh	3.04–3.18 fresh				
V	2.62–3.03 fresh					
IV			2.90–2.93 fresh		2.96–3.34 fresh	
III			2.60–2.90 fresh	2.51–2.83 fresh	2.62–2.96 fresh, marine episode	
II			2.45–2.60 marine, mixed at base	2.35–2.51 marine		
I	2.40–2.62 ?marine	2.85–3.04 marine			2.41–2.62 ?marine	3.42–4.22 marine

23005, 23310). The overlying Phase V deposits are dominated by freshwater species such as *Fragilaria pinnata* and *Achnanthes minutissima*.

Diatom assemblages from Phase VI continue to be dominated by freshwater taxa up to a height of +3.12m OD. In these levels the abundances of some oligohalobous (indifferent) taxa such as *Fragilaria construens* var. *venter*, *Achnanthes minutissima* and *Achnanthes lanceolata* increase whilst the abundance of *Fragilaria pinnata* declines.

In the levels associated with Phase VI/VII, at +3.28 and +3.36m OD, the percentages of halophilous taxa increase, but the assemblages are composed predominantly of freshwater diatoms.

At +3.60m OD the diatom assemblage is a mixed one, with significant marine, mesohalobous, halophilous and oligohalobous (indifferent) components. The top of the sequence at +3.84m OD is dominated by marine taxa such as *Paralia sulcata* and *Cymatosira belgica*.

Discussion

The diatom assemblages of the six sequences, relative to the site phasing and height (OD), are presented in Table 12. Further summary diatom diagrams showing the halobian classification of all taxa identified in each sequence relative to site phasing and heights above OD are shown in Figs 84–8.

It can be seen from Table 12 that there is good correspondence of diatom assemblages during the respective phases. Clearly the absolute heights of the facies depend on the location of the sequences across the site (Table 12). However, where channel features are close, for example in the case of Columns 2 and 4, the phases can be correlated quite well with good agreement between the nature of the diatom assemblages and the heights of associated sediments in Phases II and III. This is supported by palynological evidence (Caseldine pp 93–4). The diatom sequence is discussed below with reference to the site phases.

Phase I

Sediments belonging to Phase I, dated by radiocarbon to the Neolithic, are included in four sequences: the Columns 1, 3, 5, and 7. Diatom assemblages are either marine or marine-brackish or they are poorly preserved/absent. The sediment is considered to be a pre-channel sequence of horizontally bedded blue-grey clays resembling that of the Wentlooge formation (Allen 1987, 1990, 1992; Allen & Rae 1987) observed in the intertidal zone of the Severn Estuary. Phase I diatom assemblages are reasonably well preserved only in Column 5 and are composed of *c* 60–70% polyhalobous taxa (Fig 87) with a significant component (10–15%) of mesohalobous (brackish water) species.

The poor survival of diatoms in Phase I deposits of Columns 1 and 3 broadly equates with the organic horizons at *c* 2.4–2.6m OD. Column 7 lies at the edge of the modern lake and the pre-channel deposits, which contain occasional valves of marine diatom species, survive to above +4.0m OD.

Phase II

Phase II deposits occurred in the lower parts of Columns 2 and 4. The diatom assemblages in both cases are predominantly polyhalobous (60–70%) with 10–20% mesohalobous or halophilous taxa. Only in the basal sample of Column 4 and upper level of Phase II sediments in Column 2 are there mixed assemblages with high proportions of both marine and freshwater taxa. These probably represent transitional, time-averaged assemblages, particularly in the case of Column 2, where sediments dominated by oligohalobous taxa overlie them.

Phase II sediments were associated with the earliest channel identified on the site. They occurred at approximately the same levels, around 2.35–2.6m OD. This channel was straight sided, cutting to *c* 1.7m OD (p 20); three radiocarbon determinations of archaeological material from the base and sides of the channel all give dates around 3500 BP uncalibrated radiocarbon years. The remains of flatfish, possibly flounder (Hamilton-Dyer p 234), and the results of ostracod analysis (Robinson p 141) suggest that the channel was subject to an estuarine influence. Diatom analysis is consistent with this conclusion. There are high percentages of marine tychoplanktonic taxa such as *Paralia sulcata* and *Cymatosira belgica* along with significant abundances of benthic halophilous taxa such as *Navicula cincta* in the sections of both sequences cutting Phase II sediments. It is probable that the benthic species were deposited close to their lifetime habitats and that, as is likely in such a large channel, diatoms of the foreshore and open water were readily introduced by incoming tides (see below, p 127).

Phase III

Phase III sediments occurred in three sequences: Columns 2, 3 and 4; at levels between approximately +2.5–3.0m OD. These consisted of a complex of channel bases which truncated the large Phase II channel. All Phase III sediments are dominated by oligohalobous (indifferent) taxa which are interpreted as indicating freshwater conditions (see discussion of 'oligohalobous (indifferent)' diatom ecology). In the basal levels of Columns 2 and 4 there are significant percentages of marine taxa. This is probably the result of both the coarse interval at which diatom samples were analysed and partly the result of sediment mixing between facies. There is however a separate peak of marine taxa (> 50%) at the base of Column 3 in the transition from context 22166 to 22239 which might be interpreted as the result of an episode, or episodes, of marine incursion or possibly a longer period of tidal conditions. The polyhalobous species are predominantly tychoplanktonic, and therefore readily transported, such as *Paralia sulcata*, *Cymatosira belgica* and *Pseudoposodosira* (*Melosira*) *westii*. However, the scale and duration of this marine episode are uncertain from diatom analysis alone. This 'marine' episode may be archaeologically significant since the context (22165) immediately overlying 22239 contains the boat strake. Diatom analysis would suggest that the environment of deposition was, with the exception of the marine phase in Column 3, usually beyond the influence of tides.

Phase IV

Phase IV deposits occurred in two sequences analysed for diatoms: Column 3 and a short section at the top of Column 4. These were organic channel deposits with low densities of artefacts possibly derived from the earlier channel fills (p 31).

Both the detailed diatom analysis of the Column 3 sequence and the short Phase IV sequence from Column 4 have assemblages consistently dominated by oligohalobous (indifferent) diatom taxa (Fig 86). The concentrations of halophilous to polyhalobous species are low. It is possible that the low but significant background of marine taxa, generally <5%, derives from marine incursions. True halophobous taxa are absent and there are peaks in the abundances of halophilous to polyhalobous taxa. This background of estuarine taxa could equally be derived from time averaging processes. However, like the Phase III deposits diatom analysis shows that the environment was predominantly beyond the range of tides.

Phase V

Phase V sediments consisted of relatively inorganic channel deposits, largely eroded by later channels (p 34). In the sequences analysed for diatoms they survived only in Column 1. The diatom assemblages (Fig 88) are composed of about 75% oligohalobous (indifferent) taxa, marine and brackish taxa constituting 10% or less of the assemblages. The depositional environment is therefore interpreted as generally being above the high water mark.

Phase VI

Phase VI sediments were well-preserved comprising the fill of a wide (*c* 6.5m) flat-bottomed channel with substantial basal spreads of stone, wood and associated artefactual material (p 39). Sediments associated with Phase VI occur in Columns 1 and 5.

Diatom analysis of Phase VI deposits indicates a mainly freshwater oligohalobous assemblage with only a background of marine, and brackish taxa such as *Achnanthes delicatula*. This background of diatoms of different ecology is discussed for earlier Phases.

Notably there are peaks of the oligohalobous species *Amphora pediculus* and *Achnanthes* taxa such as *Achnanthes conspicua* and *Achnanthes lanceolata* var. *rostrata*. The former is a benthic or epontic (firmly attached to a substrate such as sand grains, rock surfaces, or macrophytes) species and the latter are epontic. This suggests that the species are more likely to have been deposited *in situ* or else their habitats (eg macrophytes, sand grains) were transported to the depositional environment. Again it is concluded that the channel was generally beyond the range of tides.

Phase VI/VII–VII

Diatom analysis relating to this Phase was carried out on samples from Columns 1 and 5. The association of part of Column 1, context 9031, with Phase VI or VII is somewhat unclear. In Column 1, initially there is a high percentage of oligohalobous (indifferent) taxa, and then an increasing proportion of marine, brackish and halophilous taxa towards the top of the column (Fig 88). In Column 5, oligohalobous indifferent taxa are generally dominant but in context 22321 (28cm) there are maxima of brackish and halophilous species, notably *Navicula gregaria* (Fig 87). Both Phase VII sections therefore suggest an increasing marine/brackish influence and therefore a return to a periodically tidal environment such as a saltmarsh, although tolerant oligohalobous freshwater taxa remain dominant.

Phase VIII

Diatom analysis of Phase VIII post-channel deposits was carried out only on samples from Column 1. A single sample at the top of this sequence shows an increasing influence of estuarine diatoms compared with Phase VII. Over 40% of the assemblage is composed of polyhalobous taxa and there is a similar proportion of oligohalobous (indifferent) taxa (Fig 88). Whether the marine component of the Phase VIII deposits is derived from contemporary changes in the salinity regime or whether the marine component derives from post-depositional sediment mixing, as the assemblage of diatoms from different environments might suggest, is not clear. The diatom content of overlying material is not known. Alternatively, the increasing marine/brackish influence noted in Phase VII would support the idea that there was a real increase in estuarine diatoms immediately before this time.

Diatom ecology

Fossil diatom assemblages are derived from a mixture of community sources as well as being subject to post-depositional modification. For example the Caldicot material contained planktonic or tychoplanktonic species, epipsammic species, epipelic and epilithic/epiphytic species. The representation of each of these communities by the fossil assemblages is difficult to estimate, but an example of work on the present day ecology of the mudflat diatom communities may provide a useful comparison.

Recent studies have been carried out on epipelic (mud dwelling) diatoms in the intertidal surface sediments of the Severn Estuary (Paterson & Underwood 1990). Some of this work has been concerned with the important role that benthic diatoms have in sediment stabilisation on intertidal estuarine mudflats, where they are often the dominant group of primary producers (Underwood & Paterson 1993a,

b). However, the research programme has also been concerned with diatom taxonomy (Underwood & Yallop 1994) and the seasonal and spatial distribution of epipelic diatoms in the Severn Estuary (Paterson & Underwood 1990; Underwood 1994).

Sites were investigated on the Avon shore of the Severn Estuary, at Sand Bay, Portishead and Aust (Underwood in press). It was shown that diatoms usually comprise more than 95% of algal cells in counts of live cells trapped using lens tissue. Of the 60 diatom taxa identified, twenty or less taxa occurred regularly and twelve species were dominant in the samples. Comparison of the true epipelic diatoms found commonly on the Severn mudflats by Underwood with the estuarine assemblages found at Caldicot shows some disparity. Of the common diatoms that Underwood identified, only *Cymatosira belgica*, *Rhaphoneis minutissima* and *Navicula gregaria* were commonly found in the estuarine assemblages recovered from the Caldicot site, although other of the species were occasionally recorded in the Caldicot sediments. Estuarine or neritic (coastal) species such as *Paralia sulcata* however are not epipelic so this is hardly surprising. This species has a loose association with benthic habitats (tychoplanktonic), but is primarily planktonic. Other authors (Denys 1992; Juggins 1992) have classified taxa such as *Cymatosira belgica* in this group. Diatom assemblages from the sequence taken in the present day intertidal estuary at Caldicot Pill (Cameron 1993) are similar to the kinds of assemblage recovered from Caldicot. This is probably because the assemblages are most heavily influenced by plankton, and also that robust planktonic species occurring in large numbers in the estuary are easily transported and survive abrasion. These may therefore be better represented compared with, for example, benthic intertidal species. Another observation on the Caldicot data is the relative rarity of a dominant component of brackish (mesohalobous/halophilous) taxa which might be expected to occur at least as transitional phases between marine and apparently freshwater conditions. Rarely were high numbers of benthic saltmarsh taxa found in the diatom assemblages, the reasons for this are unclear.

The salinity classification of some diatom taxa is problematic. A particular problem arises with the abundant *Fragilaria* species, generally classified in the literature as oligohalobous (indifferent), but which have been observed to have tolerance to high salinities (eg Denys 1988; Håkansson 1988).

Denys (1988) observed the present day responses of a group of *Fragilaria* species in coastal habitats of the Belgian Plain. The group of species studied included *Fragilaria pinnata*, *Fragilaria brevistriata*, *Fragilaria construens* var. *venter* and *Fragilaria construens* var. *subsalina*. *Fragilaria pinnata* was found to be best-developed under pronounced brackish conditions although the species is well-known from fresh water. On the other hand *Fragilaria brevistriata*, *Fragilaria construens* var. *venter* and *Fragilaria construens* var. *subsalina* were most common in weakly brackish conditions although both can be abundant in fresh water. His general conclusion was that *Fragilaria* species were most abundant in slightly brackish salt-marsh sediments especially in areas with a strong freshwater influence. *Fragilaria* blooms develop mainly in marshy environments with little tidal influence. It seems that environmental instability stimulates the mass development of this group of *Fragilaria* species, an observation also made by diatomists working on late-glacial freshwater sediments and Baltic isolation lakes (see references cited in Denys 1988).

Peaks of *Fragilaria* species were observed by Denys to coincide with increased concentrations of other diatoms (these were not, however, measured in the Caldicot sediments). It was hypothesised that in situations high on salt marshes, nutrients might be available to tolerant colonising/weed species from the salt-water sediments. Alternatively, as a higher tidal level is reached, accretion rates decrease and as a result the diatom component may become greater compared to other sediment components. Generally, however, the largest blooms of *Fragilaria* spp. occurred where there was a considerable supply of fresh water from drainage. Clearly these species are tolerant to short term fluctuations in water chemistry and are well represented because of high cell division rates, competitive advantages (weedy spp.) and perhaps ease of transport.

Some authors, for example Håkansson, have for specific reasons removed *Fragilaria* spp. from the diatom sum. However, it can be argued, as here, that these taxa are informative as indicators of a rapidly changing or unstable environment. At Caldicot, diatom assemblages in which *Fragilaria* spp. are common or dominant also contain significant numbers of other freshwater taxa. In such cases, the inference that the environment is predominantly one of freshwater is supported. In contrast a true estuarine environment would be dominated by marine plankton and/or mudflat species.

Problems of taphonomy

In addition to diatom ecology, consideration of the taphonomy of diatom assemblages is central to their interpretation. The question of diatom taphonomy and the interpretation of diatom assemblages in coastal and estuarine sediments has been addressed in the recent publications of Juggins (1992); Sherrod, Rollins & Kennedy (1989); Vos & de Wolf (1988) and the references cited in these publications. At Caldicot the interpretation of the diatom assemblages is assisted by the integrated results of archaeological analyses and other biostratigraphical investigations, particularly those of ostracod and pollen analyses. In addition, detailed sedimentological analyses should help in the wider interpretation and incorporation of the diatom evidence, for example in elucidating the disparate origin of some contexts, and episodes of erosion which are apparent.

The Caldicot site is in many ways a problematic taphonomic environment for diatom analysis. The conditions of diatom taphonomy in tidal and supratidal channels of varying size, and the effect of anthropogenic disturbance, are unknown; see Allen (1985) for discussion of the drainage and mass-movement of sediments in the tidal creeks of the Severn Estuary Levels. However, the general salinity conditions are clear from diatom analysis of palaeochannel sediments from Caldicot. Where parallel sequences were examined, the results have been shown to be repeatable across the site. However, significant features such as the origin of the background of marine taxa in a freshwater environment are open to interpretation. *Paralia sulcata,* which is often dominant among these 'background' species, has several likely origins. It is possible that the background concentration of this species represents transport of contemporary diatoms by extreme spring tides into a predominantly freshwater or freshwater-brackish environments. The highest cell concentrations of this planktonic species in the autumn would probably coincide with the time of the highest tides and stormiest conditions. It has been suggested by more than one author (eg Kjemperud 1981) that *Paralia sulcata* may be transported in spray during stormy conditions, although experimental evidence for this is not presented. Another likely source is from reworked estuarine sediments from the sides of channels or re-suspended sediment from mudflats.

Comparison with other Severn Estuary diatom analyses

Diatom analyses have been carried out at two other sites in the vicinity of Caldicot: Caldicot Pill (Cameron 1993) and Goldcliff (Esho 1989). A radiocarbon date from a transgressive contact in the core, Oscar 3, at Caldicot Pill of 6360 ± 70 BP (Beta–79887) dates the freshwater muds there to the Mesolithic (note this radiocarbon determination has not been 13 corrected). This may reflect the presence of a barrier bar causing the formation of a lagoon or more probably a temporary reduction in the rate of sea level rise at that time (Scaife and Long 1994, 85). A subsequent increase in marine taxa is in line with indications from the phase 1 deposits at Caldicot of an increase in relative sea level during the Neolithic period.

A single diatom sample was examined by Esho (1989), from an intertidal sequence at Goldcliff site 1 at a depth of 1350mm. The sample was taken from a blue 'buttery' clay with a basal level of approximately +0.25 m OD. The diatom species list presented was without abundances but is interpreted as representing 'estuarine conditions with a considerable freshwater influence'. The species list indicates a mixture of diatoms from freshwater, brackish and marine environments. Conventional radiocarbon dates place this sample between 5530 ± 90 BP (CAR-657) and 5360 ± 80 BP (CAR-656) in Smith and Morgan's zone GC1–2 (calibrated ages for this occasional incursion began at about 6470 BP and the period of marine influence lasted until about 6130 BP). It is suggested by Smith and Morgan (1989) that the (laminated) clay was laid down in a small creek surrounded by alder carr. From the laminated nature of the clay in the vicinity of the diatom sample it is also suggested that the incursion of the sea was sporadic or only occurred at the highest tides.

Conclusions

Diatom analysis of six sediment sequences, together covering Phases I–VIII, show good agreement between diatom assemblages, implied salinities and estuarine/marine influence. Comparisons with other biostratigraphies and archaeology suggest a consistent picture of environmental change.

Phase I deposits associated with Neolithic time (uncalibrated dates of c 4500 BP) have marine (Severn estuary) diatom assemblages which are probably related to the Wentlooge formation. Phase II sediments of c 3500 BP are also of predominantly marine estuarine species. Phases III to VI with dates ranging from c 2500 BP to c 1500 BP are dominated by freshwater diatoms with a single marine episode recorded in 23004/5 during Phase III. The contexts containing this feature immediately underlie the context containing the boat strake. During these predominantly freshwater phases there remains a background of marine species whose origin is uncertain. Most importantly for the archaeological interpretation, this observation might imply at least occasional inundation by spring tides. The oligohalobous taxa – in particular a group of *Fragilaria* species which dominates many of the assemblages – are tolerant, 'weed' species characteristic of changing environmental conditions. However, other hypotheses are put forward for the occurrence of ecologically very different diatom groups in the same assemblages. In Phase VII, saltwater tolerant freshwater taxa are associated with true brackish species and in the Master column marine species increase towards

the top of the Phase VII section. In Phase VIII sediments, recorded only from Column 1, there are further increases in marine taxa, but there are also high percentages of oligohalobous species resulting in a mixed assemblage.

The molluscs
Martin Bell and Su Johnson

Introduction

Molluscs were represented in the sequence by the calcium carbonate impregnated shells, mostly of freshwater species with some land molluscs and a few brackish water and marine species. Analysis was concentrated on four columns of samples from three trenches; for locations see Figs 60–6. Molluscs are largely from that part of the sedimentary sequence comprising a complex of intercutting channels. Each column on its own provides only a partial sequence with hiatuses. Together the series of columns covers the Bronze Age activity represented by Phases II–VII. Table 13 shows the relationship between the columns and the sedimentary phases.

The longest sequence, Column 1, came from the section on the west edge of the excavation in Area A and covers Phases I and V–VIII. Columns 2 and 3 from Area B were analysed; Column 2 spans Phases II–III, Column 3 spans Phases III–IV. Column 5 from Area E includes Phase I sediments at the base overlain by sediments of Phases VI and VII. The column samples are supplemented by spot sample 23166 from Area E and spot sample 3012 from Area C; both were from sediments of Phase III.

Methods

Sample size varied, according to mollusc numbers, between 250 and 1000g. Samples were sieved down

Table 13 The relationship between site phases and the numbers of samples from each column

Phases	Column 1 Area A	Column 2 Area B	Column 3 Area B	Column 5 Area E	Spot samples
VIII	1 sample				
VII	1–3 samples			3 samples	
VI	5–2 samples			2 samples	
V	2–3 samples				
IV	–		4 samples		
III	–	5 samples	5 samples		2 samples = 3012 and 23166
II	–	2 samples			
I	2 samples			? 1 sample	

CALDICOT Column 1 Bulk Samples 2050–2078

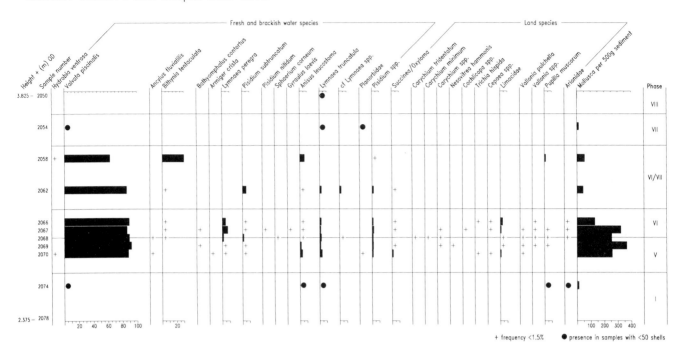

Fig 89   Percentage mollusc diagram, Column 1, Samples 2050–2078

to 0.5mm. Nomenclature follows Kerney (1976a) for freshwater species and Walden (1976) for land species. Valves of *Pisidium* spp. have been identified to species, where the hinge line is complete, but broken shells and tiny juveniles are listed as *Pisidium* spp. In both the tables and Figs 89–91, the number of bivalve valves has been divided by two. The diagrams are on a percentage basis with the species having been divided into fresh/brackish water and land mollusca, without further division into ecological groups, although the aquatic mollusca are ordered from left to right in groups as defined by Sparks (1961): brackish (*Hydrobia, Ovatella, Leucophytia*); moving-water (*Valvata* to *Bithynia*); catholic (*Bathyomphalus* to *Sphaerium*); slow water (*Gyraulus* and *Acrolaxus*) and slum species (*Anisus* to *Pisidium casertanum*). The usual summary diagram has also been omitted. In the case of the land mollusca this is because they were generally so few as to make interpretations based on such groups meaningless. The aquatic assemblage was generally dominated by a single species to such an extent that the other groups were frequently too small to be clearly distinguished on a summary diagram. Where samples contain less than 50 shells the presence of a species is indicated by a black dot. In the histograms showing shell numbers, sample size has been equalised to 500g. The diagrams on Figs 89–91 have been divided by horizontal lines, these reflect site phasing rather than molluscan biozones.

Taphonomic issues

The deposits are predominantly of freshwater origin.

One question therefore concerns separation of autochthonous components, which have lived *in situ*, from allochthonous components which have been washed in. There is, furthermore, the possibility of different types and sizes of shell being sorted because of their differing hydrodynamic properties. This is suggested by samples in Phases V–VII in which numbers of *Bithynia* operculae are very different from the number of apices (Tables 14 and 17). All samples contain mainly aquatic shells, the small terrestrial component is likely to be derived (Evans 1992).

A further issue, given the intercutting channel deposits which characterise the Caldicot sequence, is the likelihood of molluscs being reworked from earlier phases and perhaps reworked material being concentrated by sorting in particular parts of the channel sequence.

Certain horizons within the channel stratigraphy contained quantities of wood, stone and other artefactual material. The possibility needs to be considered that some molluscs could have been introduced to the site by human agency along with these materials.

Column 1

Description (Table 14 and Fig 89)

At the base of the column, deposits of Phase I contain very low numbers of shells, mostly *Valvata piscinalis*. The phasing then indicates a significant hiatus. Deposits of Phase V–VI are much richer in Mollusca. They are closely similar and are considered

Table 14 Column 1 Bulk samples 2050–2078. Land and fresh/brackish water mollusca

	VIII	VII	VI/VII	VI/VII	VI	VI	V/VI	V	V	I	I
Phase	VIII	VII	VI/VII	VI/VII	VI	VI	V/VI	V	V	I	I
Sample number	2050	2054	2058	2062	2066	2067	2068	2069	2070	2074	2078
Depth (cm)	0–5	20–25	40–45	60–65	80–85	85–90	90–95	95–100	100–105	120–125	140–145
Height + (m) OD	3.773 / -3.823	3.573 / -3.623	3.373 / -3.423	3.173 / -3.223	2.973 / -3.023	2.923 / -2.973	2.873 / -2.923	2.823 / -2.873	2.773 / -2.823	2.573 / -2.623	2.373 / -2.423
Sample weight (g)	1000	1000	1000	1000	1000	500	1000	1000	1000	1000	1000
Fresh/brackish water mollusca											
Gastropoda											
Valvata piscinalis (Müller)		27	69	74	219	263	439	666	438	19	
Hydrobia ventrosa (Montagu)			1						1		
Bithynia tentaculata (L)			33	1	2	1	3	11	17		
Lymnaea truncatula (Müller)	2	+		2	5	5	12			1	
Lymnaea peregra (Müller)					11	23	9	10	6		
cf *Lymnaea* spp.				2			1				
Anisus leucostoma (Millet)			7	1	3	2	7	13	18	3	
Bathyomphalus contortus (L)						1		1			
Gyraulus laevis (Alder)						1					
Armiger crista (L)									2		
Planorbidae		1							1		
Ancylus fluviatilis Müller							1		1		
Bivalvia											
Sphaerium corneum (L)							0.5				
Pisidium subtruncatum Malm				4.5	2	0.5	10	8	4.5		
Pisidium nitidum Jenyns						1					
Pisidium spp			0.5	2	4	7.5	8	15	8.5		
TOTAL FRESH/BRACKISH WATER MOLLUSCA	2	28	110.5	86.5	246	305	490.5	724	497	23	0
Land mollusca											
Carychium minimum Müller											1
Carychium tridentatum (Risso)											1

Table 14 (cont.)

Phase	I	I	V	V	V/VI	VI	VI	VI/VII	VI/VII	VII	VIII
Sample number	2078	2074	2070	2069	2068	2067	2066	2062	2058	2054	2050
Depth (cm)	140–145	120–125	100–105	95–100	90–95	85–90	80–85	60–65	40–45	20–25	0–5
Height + (m) OD	2.373 -2.423	2.573 -2.623	2.773 -2.823	2.823 -2.873	2.873 -2.923	2.923 -2.973	2.973 -3.023	3.173 -3.223	3.373 -3.423	3.573 -3.623	3.773 -3.823
Sample weight (g)	1000	1000	1000	1000	1000	500	1000	1000	1000	1000	1000
Carychium spp				+	2	3					
Succinea / Oxyloma spp			10	2		1	3	1			
Cochlicopa spp						1					
Pupilla muscorum (L)		1		1	2	2			2		
Vallonia pulchella (Müller)			1	3	1	1					
Vallonia spp				1	6	4	1				
Arionidae		+			+	+	+				
Nesovitrea hammonis (Strsm)				1							
Limacidae			8	3	6	5	9				
Trichia hispida (L)			3				1				
Cepaea spp			+			+	1				
TOTAL LAND MOLLUSCA	0	1	22	11	19	17	15	1	2	0	0
TOTAL MOLLUSCA	0	24	519	735	509.5	322	261	87.5	112.5	28	2
Bithynia operculae			1	3	45	63	84	2	14	3	1
Marine fragments						1	3				

+ indicates non-apical fragment counts for bivalves = no. of valves divided by 2

132

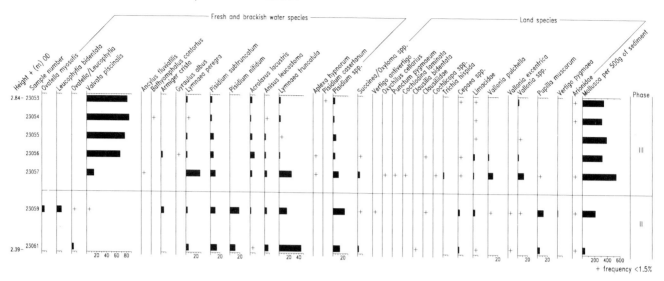

CALDICOT Column 2 Bulk Samples 23053–23061

Fig 90   Percentage mollusc diagram, Column 2, samples 23053–23061

together, the only contrast being a small peak of *Lymnaea peregra* corresponding to Phase VI. *Valvata piscinalis* predominates. The other species consistently present at more than 1.5% are *Lymnaea peregra*, *Anisus leucostoma*, *Lymnaea truncatula* and *Pisidium*. There is a scatter of land species but the numbers are small, only Limacidae are present at more than 1.5%.

The two samples from Phase VI/VII contain significantly lower numbers of shells and a smaller range of species. The general character of the assemblage in the lower sample (2062) is the same as the underlying samples. The upper sample (2058) is distinguished by larger numbers of *Bithynia tentaculata* and *Anisus leucostoma*.

The upper samples are very poor in Mollusca; 2054 being almost totally dominated by *Valvata piscinalis* and 2050 only containing two *Lymnaea truncatula*.

Interpretation

The basal deposits of Phase I have no indication of the marine influence at this stage which is inferred from other sources (p 16). The predominance of *Valvata piscinalis* throughout this column might be interpreted as indicating that all the sediments had accumulated under conditions of moving-water. However, there are only small numbers of other moving-water species such as *Ancylus fluviatilis* and *Bithynia tentaculata* in Phases V–VI. The catholic, slow water and slum groups of Sparks (1961) are almost equally represented. A single apex of *Hydrobia* points to slight brackish influence. This may also be suggested by fragments of marine Mollusca in three samples, the only identifiable pieces being fragments of ? *Littorina* spp. However, these marine molluscs could have been brought to the site by

human agency. Small numbers of land molluscs are interpreted as derived.

The two samples phased as VI/VII have low numbers and species diversity indicating conditions of more rapid sedimentation or those less favourable for molluscan life, although the general character of the assemblages is the same as the overlying deposits. The virtual lack of land molluscs may indicate the absence of a derived component.

Column 2

Description of the sequence (Table 15 and Fig 90)

There is a clear contrast between the assemblages of Phases II, which virtually lack *Valvata piscinalis*, and III in which that species steadily increases. Phase II is characterised by *Lymnaea truncatula*, *Pisidium nitidum* and *P. subtruncatum*. In Phase III *Valvata piscinalis* is accompanied by *Lymnaea peregra*; *Pisidium subtruncatum*; *Acrolaxus lacustris*; *Anisus leucostoma* and *Lymnaea truncatula*. A few land molluscs are present, mostly in the bottom three samples.

Interpretation

Phase II stands out as lacking species of moving-water. During this phase *Lymnaea truncatula* is the most abundant species, and *Pisidium nitidum*, *P. personatum*, *Anisus leucostoma* and *Lymnaea peregra*, would seem to reflect small, probably temporary, wet areas without running water. The presence of *Ovatella myosotis* and *Leucophytia bidentata* in Sample 23059 points to some brackish influence.

Table 15 Column 2 Bulk Samples 23053–23061. Land and fresh/brackish water mollusca

Phase	II	II	III	III	III	III	III
Sample number	23061	23059	23057	23056	23055	23054	23053
Depth (cm)	40–45	30–35	20–25	15–20	10–15	5–10	0–5
Height + (m) OD	2.39–2.44	2.49–2.54	2.59–2.64	2.64–2.69	2.69–2.74	2.74–2.79	2.79–2.84
Sample weight (g)	1000	500	250	250	250	250	250
Fresh/brackish water mollusca							
Gastropoda							
Valvata piscinalis (Müller)		1	27	98	145	132	134
Ovatella myosotis (Draparnaud)		9					
Leucophytia bidentata (Montagu)		15					
Ovatella / Leucophytia	3	1					
Aplexa hypnorum (L.)			1	1			
Lymnaea truncatula (Müller)	35	25	46	3	1	5	5
Lymnaea peregra (Müller)	4	5	51	4	5	2	5
Anisus leucostoma (Millet)	6	7	9	4	5	2	
Bathyomphalus contortus (L)				1		1	
Gyraulus albus (Müller)				1			
Armiger crista (L)		9		5			
Ancylus fluviatilis Müller			1				
Acrolaxus lacustris (L)	+	3	7	13	8	3	7
Bivalvia							
Pisidium casertanum (Poli)							0.5
Pisidium subtruncatum Malm	10.5	16	19	10	13.5	5	6.5
Pisidium nitidum Jenyns	8.5	29.5					
Pisidium spp	11	37.5	20	6.5	12	4.5	6.5
TOTAL FRESH/BRACKISH WATER MOLLUSCA	78	158	181	145.5	189.5	154.5	164.5
Land mollusca							
Succinea / Oxyloma spp	2	3	11	2			
Cochlicopa spp			1				

Table 15 (cont.)

Phase	III	III	III	III	III	II	II
Sample number	23053	23054	23055	23056	23057	23059	23061
Depth (cm)	0–5	5–10	10–15	15–20	20–25	30–35	40–45
Height + (m) OD	2.79–2.84	2.74–2.79	2.69–2.74	2.64–2.69	2.59–2.64	2.49–2.54	2.39–2.44
Sample weight (g)	250	250	250	250	250	500	1000
Vertigo antivertigo (Draparnaud)						1	
Vertigo pygmaea (Draparnaud)						2	
Pupilla muscorum (L)					2	25	4
Vallonia pulchella (Müller)				3	27		
Vallonia excentrica Sterki						1	1
Vallonia spp	4		2	3	33	2	
Punctum pygmaeum (Draparnaud)					1		
Arionidae	+	+			+	+	+
Oxychilus cellarius (Müller)					1		
Limacidae	1	2	1	5	4	8	1
Cochlodina laminata (Montagu)					1		
Clausilia bidentata (Strsm)							1
Clausiliidae				+		+	
Trichia hispida (L)					5		
Cepaea spp	+			+	2	7	2
TOTAL LAND MOLLUSCA	5	2	3	13	88	49	11
TOTAL MOLLUSCA	169.5	156.5	192.5	158.5	269	207	89

+ indicates non-apical fragment counts for bivalves = no. of valves divided by 2

CALDICOT Column 3 Bulk Samples 23017–23032

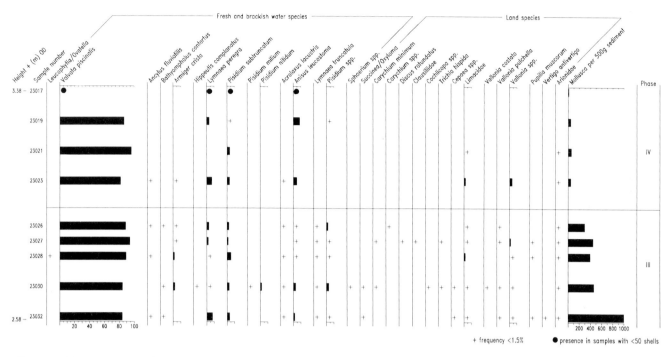

Fig 91   Percentage mollusc diagram, Column 3, samples 23017–23032

Sample 23057 seems transitional between the distinctive communities of Phases II and III with *Valvata piscinalis* increasing and significant numbers of *Lymnaea truncatula*. In Phase III, apart from *Valvata piscinalis*, Sparks' (1961) moving-water group is only represented by one shell of *Ancylus fluviatilis*. His catholic, slow and slum groups are almost equally represented. Land molluscs in the basal two samples of Phase III are probably derived, but this component is almost absent from the upper three samples.

Column 3

Description
(Table 16 and Fig 91)

The column is characterised by abundant molluscs at the base with decreasing numbers upwards in Phase IV. Phase III contains more species and a greater representation of land molluscs. The character of the assemblage remains similar throughout. It is overwhelmingly dominated by *Valvata piscinalis*. The only other species consistently present at levels above 1.5% are *Lymnaea peregra*, *Pisidium subtruncatum* and *Anisus leucostoma*. At the top of the column there is a hint of ecological change in sample 23017 where *Valvata piscinalis* is less abundant than *Anisus leucostoma*, but mollusc numbers at this level are very low.

Interpretation

Samples 23026–8 were from the context which produced the boat strake. The molluscan evidence indicates freshwater conditions at this stage. The presence of *Valvata piscinalis* may imply water movement but no other members of Sparks' moving-water group is abundant. One example of *Ovatella/Leucophytia* points to some slight marine input.

The sediments of Phase IV sealed the boat strake. Mollusc numbers are lower, perhaps indicating increased sedimentation rates but similar ecological conditions are indicated. The paucity of land molluscs and some marsh species in Phase IV is notable and may indicate a much smaller proportion of material derived from neighbouring habitats. The occurrence of *Anisus leucostoma* and fewer *V. piscinalis* at the top could hint at conditions more subject to drying-out.

Column 5

Description (Table 17)

Because only three of the samples produced adequate numbers, the results from this column are not graphed but presented in Table 17. The lower three samples contain low numbers with *Valvata piscinalis* predominant in terms of apices, but *Bithynia tentaculata* represented by more operculae. The Phase VII assemblage is essentially similar but with more *Pisidium*, mainly *P. subtruncatum* centred on

Table 16 Column 3 Bulk Samples 23017–23032. Land and fresh/brackish water mollusca

	III	III	III	III	III	IV	IV	IV	IV
Phase	III	III	III	III	III	IV	IV	IV	IV
Sample number	23032	23030	23028	23027	23026	23023	23021	23019	23017
Depth (cm)	75–80	65–70	55–60	50–55	45–50	30–35	20–25	10–15	0–5
Height + (m) OD	2.58–2.63	2.68–2.73	2.78–2.83	2.83–2.88	2.88–2.93	3.03–3.08	3.13–3.18	3.23–3.28	3.33–3.38
Sample weight (g)	500	500	500	500	500	1000	1000	1000	1000
Fresh/brackish water mollusca									
Gastropoda									
Valvata piscinalis (Müller)	824	375	342	407	256	71	106	79	5
Ovatella / Leucophytia			1						
Lymnaea truncatula (Müller)	2	4	2	2	4				
Lymnaea peregra (Müller)	75	1	3	9	8	6		3	1
Anisus leucostoma (Millet)	18	14	5	1	3	4		8	11
Bathyomphalus contortus (L)	6	2			1				
Armiger crista (L)		10	6	3	1	1			
Hippeutis complanatus (L)		2							
Ancylus fluviatilis Müller	1		1		1	1			
Acroloxus lacustris (L)	8	2	1		1	1			
Bivalvia									
Sphaerium spp.		+							
Pisidium milium Held		0.5							
Pisidium subtruncatum Malm	34	12.5	20.5	6.5	7.5	3	4	1	0.5
Pisidium nitidum Jenyns		7.5							
Pisidium spp	13.5	15	2.5	2.5	6.5			0.5	
TOTAL FRESH/BRACKISH WATER MOLLUSCA	981.5	445.5	384	431	289	87	110	91.5	17.5
Land mollusca									
Carychium minimum Müller		1		2					
Carychium spp					2				
Succinea / Oxyloma spp	2	2							
Cochlicopa spp		1							

Table 16 (cont.)

	III	III	III	III	III	IV	IV	IV	IV
Phase									
Sample number	23032	23030	23028	23027	23026	23023	23021	23019	23017
Depth (cm)	75–80	65–70	55–60	50–55	45–50	30–35	20–25	10–15	0–5
Height + (m) OD	2.58–2.63	2.68–2.73	2.78–2.83	2.83–2.88	2.88–2.93	3.03–3.08	3.13–3.18	3.23–3.28	3.33–3.38
Sample weight (g)	500	500	500	500	500	1000	1000	1000	1000
Vertigo antivertigo (Draparnaud)	1								
Pupilla muscorum (L)	2		1	1					
Vallonia costata (Müller)		1							
Vallonia pulchella (Müller)	2	2		1	3				
Vallonia spp	3	1	2	7		3			
Discus rotundatus (Müller)				+					
Arionidae	+	+	+	+	+	+	+		
Limacidae	4	4	7	5	2	2	1		
Clausiliidae				+					
Trichia hispida (L)		2		1					
Cepaea spp	+	+							
TOTAL LAND MOLLUSCA	14	14	10	17	7	5	1	0	0
TOTAL MOLLUSCA	995.5	459.5	394	448	296	92	111	91.5	17.5

+ indicates non-apical fragment counts for bivalves = no. of valves divided by 2

Table 17 Column 5 Bulk Samples 23251–23260. Land and fresh/brackish water mollusca

Phase	I/VI	VI	VI	VII	VII	VII
Sample number	23260	23259	23258	23257	23253	23251
Height + (m) OD	3.11	3.127	3.20	3.21	3.336	3.466
Sample weight (g)	1000	500	1000	1000	1000	500
Fresh/brackish water mollusca						
Gastropoda						
Valvata piscinalis (Müller)	35	1	13	180	247	285
Hydrobia ventrosa (Montagu)	1					
Bithynia tentaculata (L)			2	4	8	4
Ovatella / Leucophytia						1
Lymnaea truncatula (Müller)	1	1		10	15	6
Lymnaea peregra (Müller)				1	1	
Anisus leucostoma (Millet)	2	1		11	24	8
Gyraulus albus (Müller)						1
Bivalvia						
Pisidium casertanum (Poli)	0.5			2	11.5	4
Pisidium subtruncatum Malm	2.5			8	93.5	22
Pisidium spp	3		1	8.5	101.5	26
TOTAL FRESH/BRACKISH WATER MOLLUSCA	45	3	16	224.5	501.5	357
Land mollusca						
Succinea / Oxyloma spp						
Cochlicopa spp	1	1				
Pupilla muscorum (L)				1	1	
Arionidae	+	+		+		
Limacidae		3	1			
Clausilia bidentata (Strsm)				1		
Clausiliidae			1			
Cepaea spp	1		1	1	+	
TOTAL LAND MOLLUSCA	1	3	2	3	1	0
TOTAL MOLLUSCA	46	4	18	227.5	502.5	357
Bithynia operculae	53	49	57	44	4	2

+ indicates non-apical fragment counts for bivalves = no. of valves divided by 2

sample 23253. Land molluscs are only patchily represented throughout this column.

Interpretation

One *Hydrobia* at the base and one *Ovatella/Leucophytia* in the upper sample indicate some marine influence. The issues here are those already rehearsed in relation to the other *Valvata* dominated assemblages. The occurrence of many *Bithynia* operculae, but few apices of the same species, in the bottom four samples, would seem to support the idea of running water at this stage, assuming that taphonomic factors relating to the differing hydrodynamic properties of shell and operculae account for this contrast. Other members of the moving-water group are poorly represented.

Samples 23258–9 produced numerous larva cases of caddis flies (*Trichoptera*), some of which incorporated *Bithynia* operculae and Limacidae plates in their construction. Caddis fly larvae (Chinery 1986) are aquatic and many construct cases of silk with sand grains, small stones, fragments of vegetation etc, the materials used varying according to species. The larva in its case is able to crawl around in the early stage of its life, then it attaches the case to a stone whilst it pupates, before swimming to the surface to emerge as an adult. Clearly, their incorporation in larval cases would have affected the hydrodynamic properties of the operculae and this is a further reminder of the effect of depositional factors, both water sorting and movement by other organisms, in palaeochannel contexts.

The basal sample (23257) of Phase VII was notable in containing more wood and charcoal than other samples examined. At the time of Phase VII, the late channel with its wooden bridge or jetty, the assemblage is rich in shells but with a restricted range of species. Apart from *V. piscinalis* the main species are the catholic species *Pisidium subtruncatum* and the slum species *Pisidium casertanum*, *Anisus leucostoma* and *Lymnaea truncatula*.

Area E: spot sample 23166

Description (Table 18)

This is a spot sample of Phase III sediment, directly adjacent to Column 4. This sample supplements the results from Column 5, also in Area E, which covered Phases VI–VII. The sample is again overwhelmingly dominated by *Valvata piscinalis* with a significant presence of *Lymnaea peregra*, *Ancylus fluviatilis* and *Pisidium subtruncatum*.

Interpretation

The predominant species *V. piscinalis* is normally found in running water. The second most abundant species *Lymnaea peregra* is found in both slow and standing water. *Ancylus fluviatilis* supports the idea of running water. One shell of *Ovatella/Leucophytia* hints at limited marine influence. The land molluscs are considered in the conclusions.

Area C: spot sample 3012

Description (Table 18)

This is similar to sample 23166 from the same phase, the only contrasts are larger numbers of *Armiger crista* and *Anisus leucostoma* and smaller numbers of *Lymnaea peregra* and *Ancylus fluviatilis*.

Interpretation

As spot sample 23166.

Conclusions

Mollusc numbers vary within and between columns. This could be due to the speed of sediment accumulation, favourability of conditions for molluscan life, water-sorting factors and diagenic factors influencing mollusc survival. In general those deposits which, on other evidence are believed to relate to channel bottoms (eg Phases III and V–VI), contain high numbers. This perhaps reflects conditions favourable for molluscan life with limited sedimentation. These mollusc rich, channel-bottom deposits include both freshwater and land species but the former predominate overwhelmingly and few land species represent more than 1.5%, their occurrence tends to be patchy especially in Column 3. The probable inference is that the small proportion of land molluscs is derived. The sediments overlying the probable channel bottom deposits contain decreasing mollusc numbers (Figs 89 and 91) which may well reflect increased sedimentation and thus smaller numbers of shells per unit of sediment.

The main trends in the sequence from earliest to latest can now be outlined. In Phase I there are few molluscs, suggesting poor conditions for mollusc life or preservation. Other sources of evidence (p 258) suggest greater marine influence during this phase. Phase II is characterised by freshwater conditions represented by the slum and catholic groups of Sparks (1961) with very little evidence of running water.

Phase III is reflected by good conditions for molluscan life, particularly in the two spot samples. The assemblage and indeed all others in Phases III–VII are curiously restricted in terms of species diversity, being dominated by *Valvata piscinalis*. That implies a specialised habitat in which only certain species could flourish. Sparks (1961) included *Valvata* in his moving-water group. It is most abundant in eutrophic ditches, streams and rivers

Table 18 Spot Samples 3012 and 23166. Land and fresh/brackish water mollusca

Area/Column	Area C	Col. 4
Phase	III	III
Sample number	3012	23166
Height + (m) OD		2.85–2.90
Sample weight (g)	1000	250
Fresh/brackish water mollusca		
Gastropoda		
Valvata piscinalis (Müller)	906	962
Ovatella / Leucophytia		1
Aplexa hypnorum (L.)		1
Lymnaea truncatula (Müller)	16	13
Lymnaea peregra (Müller)	37	66
Anisus leucostoma (Millet)	28	14
Bathyomphalus contortus (L)	1	7
Armiger crista (L)	28	2
Hippeutis complanatus (L)	3	
Ancylus fluviatilis Müller	12	37
Acrolaxus lacustris (L)	6	10
Bivalvia		
Pisidium subtruncatum Malm	27	20.5
Pisidium nitidum Jenyns	4.5	2.5
Pisidium spp	14.5	23
TOTAL FRESH/BRACKISH WATER MOLLUSCA	1083	1159
Land mollusca		
Carychium tridentatum (Risso)		1
Cochlicopa spp		1
Vertigo antivertigo (Draparnaud)		2
Vertigo spp	+	
Pupilla muscorum (L)	1	4
Vallonia pulchella (Müller)	8	12
Vallonia spp	20	20
Arionidae		+
Limacidae	5	17
Trichia hispida (L)	1	3
Cepaea spp		+
TOTAL LAND MOLLUSCA	35	60
TOTAL MOLLUSCA	1118	1219

+ indicates non-apical fragment counts for bivalves = no. of valves divided by 2

(Fretter and Graham 1978; Graham 1988, 1971). It is found in lakes but is less common in small bodies of water and those without movement. It has a preference for a muddy bottom and burrows into mud during the winter; during the spring and summer it feeds on detritus on the mud surface and rasps on submerged plants. Eggs are laid on waterweed (Cleland 1954). Fretter and Graham (1978), note plants which it particularly likes, including three represented by macrofossils at Caldicot; *Sparganium*, *Callitriche* and *Rorippa nasturtium-aquaticum*.

At Anslow's Cottages in Berkshire, *Valvata* was very abundant in sediments interpreted as those of a swiftly flowing permanent stream (Evans 1992). At Caldicot, however, other members of the moving-water group, which were abundant at Anslow's, are poorly represented and do not therefore enable confirmation of the moving-water hypothesis. The low diversity of the Caldicot assemblage and the dominance of *V. piscinalis* could relate to its tolerance of brackish conditions up to 0.2% salinity (Fretter and Graham 1978) but this hypothesis is not confirmed by increased occurrence of brackish or marine species during the relevant phases.

Eric Robinson's evidence from the ostracods contrasts with the mollusc interpretation indicating that the water was still or only sluggishly moving. This may relate to differing conditions in microenvironments within the channel. It is also possible that the molluscan and ostracod evidence are not directly associated. The two groups of biological evidence would have different hydrodynamic properties. It is possible that bottom dwelling organisms laid down during minimal sedimentation become associated with organisms laid down during the early phases of sedimentation in the channel bed. Life cycle factors may also be relevant: *V. piscinalis* burrows in winter into the top inch (2.5cm) of mud (Cleland 1954) and might therefore be preserved with ostracod evidence reflecting different conditions.

Phase IV is characterised by a similar *V. piscinalis* dominated assemblage but with low mollusc numbers reflecting either poor conditions for molluscan life or possibly rapid sedimentation.

Phases V and VI have a very similar assemblage to III and IV but with larger mollusc numbers which are thought to reflect a period of reduced sedimentation on the base of a channel. Mollusc numbers are reduced in Phases VI/VII–VII in Column 1; this may relate to reduced water flow and increased sedimentation. Sharply contrasting numbers of *Bithynia* operculae and apices in Phases VI and VII would seem to be clear evidence of moving-water and fluvial sorting at that time. The absence of *Bithynia tentaculata* before Phase VI is puzzling since it is often found in muddy habitats with *V. piscinalis* (Cleland 1954). Salinity, calcium levels or distribution changes at the margins of its Welsh range (Kerney 1976b) are possible explanations. Column 5 (Table 17) has larger numbers in Phase VII perhaps suggesting that it was a more active channel than that in Column 1.

Phase VIII contains virtually no molluscs and there is other evidence (p 126) of greater marine influence at this stage.

Despite the proximity to the coast and estuarine sediments, the mollusc evidence preserved in Phases II–VII indicates freshwater conditions. The only evidence of marine influence is the occasional presence of *Hydrobia ventrosa* and the brackish/estuarine species *Ovatella myosotis* and *Leucophytia bidentata*. Such scattered occurrences might be explained as chance introductions by people or animals. More likely perhaps is that they reflect rare episodic marine flooding events. The molluscs produced only slight hints of the phases of marine flooding which are inferred from other evidence both below and above the Bronze Age sediments, in Phases I and VIII. However, it should be noted that in the Goldcliff sequence 14 km to the south-west,

and closer to marine influence, molluscs are not present in most of the sediments which are inferred to be of marine origin.

The Caldicot samples, with their small proportion of land species are in contrast to the assemblages from Holocene over-bank alluvium discussed by Evans *et al* (1992). At Caldicot the only samples which produced interpretable numbers of land species were samples of Phases II and III in Column 2 and the two Phase III spot samples. *Vallonia* is most abundant, especially *Vallonia pulchella* which is found in wet grassland (Evans *et al* 1992), an interpretation which accords with most of the other species present in these two samples and the more patchy occurrence of land molluscs in other phases. Species of wood or scrub conditions are very poorly represented. That is perhaps surprising in view of the quantity of wood, especially unworked wood (p 158) but a lack of nearby trees is supported by the beetle evidence (Osborne p 150). The very wide range of beetle species present is in sharp contrast to the unusually restricted mollusc assemblage. This must reflect contrasting formation processes and catchment sizes, associated with these different aspects of the palaeoenvironmental record. It may also point to the existence of habitats suitable for beetle but not mollusc life, perhaps because of a lack of calcium or other factors.

The ostracod evidence
Eric Robinson

Introduction

The ostracod fauna, small bivalve Crustacea, was recovered from predominantly silty-clay samples about 250g in weight sieved down to 250m, picked and mounted. Samples were examined from five sample sites: Column 1 (2054–2078); Column 2 (23055–23061); Column 3 (23017–23030); Column 4 (spot sample 23166); and Column 5 (23251–23257) which were also examined for other biota. The location and details of the lithology of the samples are given above (p 67). The results are presented in Table 19.

Discussion

The Caldicot ostracods in general represent an almost wholly freshwater assemblage. The main exception is the series 23055–23061 which includes two samples, 23059 and 23061, from the earliest of the palaeochannels – the channel containing the pile structure 472, (Phase II). The sequence seems to indicate increased marine-intertidal conditions at the base (23061), passing up into lacustrine non-marine (23057, 23055 – Phase III).

Marine influence is represented by the intertidal species *Leptocythere lacertosa*, a form which lives on sea-weeds or in the muds of the edges of estuaries.

Table 19 Ostracoda from Caldicot

Column 1 (samples 2054–2078 (*preliminary samples))

2054

25 *Candona neglecta* Sars	2v A-III, 1v A-I
26 *Cypria opthalmica* (Jurine)	6c

2056

10 *Ilyocypris bradyi* Sars	1v A-V, 2v A-IV, 4v A-III, 5v A-II
11 *Ilyocypris bradyi* Sars	3v A-III, 4v A-1
12 *Ilyocypris bradyi* Sars	3v
17 *Prionocypris serrata* (Norman)	1c 1v A-III
18 *Prionocypris serrata* (Norman)	1v A-II, 2v A-I
21 *Candona neglecta* Sars	12v 1c A-IV, 1c 3v A-III, 1v A-II
22 *Candona neglecta* Sars	4 fragments

*2058

25 *Ilyocypris bradyi* Sars	2v A-I, 2v
26 *Candona neglecta* Sars	4v female
27 *Candona candida* O F Müller	2v
28 *Herpetocypris reptans* (Baird)	fragments

2058

9 *Cypria opthalmica* (Jurine)	1v
10 *Cyclocypris laevis* (Müller)	6v 3c
11 *Ilyocypris bradyi* Sars	2v A-IV, 3v A-III, 4v A-II
12 *Ilyocypris bradyi* Sars	16v A-I
13 *Ilyocypris bradyi* Sars	1v 1c
14 *Ilyocypris biplicata* (Koch)	1v 1c
17 *Candona neglecta* Sars	2v A-IV, 14v 1c A-III, 4v A-II
18 *Candona neglecta* Sars	8v A-I
19 *Candona neglecta* Sars	7v female
20 *Candona neglecta* Sars	1v male
23–24 *Herpetocypris reptans* (Baird)	fragments

*2062

3 *Candona candida* O F Müller	1v
4 *Candona neglecta* Sars	4v female, 2v male
5 *Herpetocypris reptans* (Baird)	4v A-II
6 *Herpetocypris reptans* (Baird)	2v A-I
7 *Ilyocypris bradyi* Sars	2v A-I

2062

9 *Ilyocypris bradyi* Sars	6v A-VI, 9v A-V, 5v A-IV, 5v A-III
10 *Ilyocypris bradyi* Sars	7v A-II, 12v A-I
11 *Ilyocypris bradyi* Sars	8v A-I, 12v
12 *Cypria opthalmica* (Jurine)	2v A-I, 1c
13 *Limnocythere inopinata* (Baird)	1v A-II, 3v A-I, 1c
14 *Cypris pubera* O F Müller	1v A-II
15 *Candona* sp.	4v A-II
16 *Candona neglecta* Sars	4v A-VI, 4v A-V, 12v A-IV, 4v A-III
17 *Candona neglecta* Sars	2v A-II, 7v A-I
18 *Candona neglecta* Sars	8v female
19 *Candona neglecta* Sars	10v 2c female
20 *Candona neglecta* Sars	6v male
22 *Candona candida* (O F Müller)	1v A-I, 1v
24 *Prionocypris serrata* (Norman)	1v
25 *Cyclocypris laevis* (O F Müller)	2v

Table 19 (cont.)

26–27 *Herpetocypris laevis* (O F Müller)	2v A-III, 1v A-II
30 Foraminifera	
*2066	
10 *Herpetocypris reptans* (Baird)	1 fragment
11 *Candona candida* (O F Müller)	3v
12 *Candona neglecta* Sars	4v female 3c
13 *Candona angulata* Müller	4v
14 *Eucypris virens*	1v
15 *Prionocypris serrata* (Norman)	4v A-I, 1v
16 *Herpetocypris reptans* (Baird)	2v A-II
2066	
3 *Herpetocypris reptans* (Baird)	Fragment
4 *Herpetocypris reptans* (Baird)	1v A-II
5 *Herpetocypris reptans* (Baird)	1v
9 *Ilyocypris bradyi* Sars	2v A-VI, 3v A-V, 5v A-IV, 10v A-III
10 *Ilyocypris bradyi* Sars	8v A-II, 10v 1c A-I
11 *Ilyocypris bradyi* Sars	20v 6c A-I,
12 *Ilyocypris bradyi* Sars	11v 1c
13 *Leptocythere* cf. *porcellanea* (Brady)	1c
Foraminifera	2
14 *Limnocythere inopinata* (Baird)	4v A-I, 7v 3c
15 *Ilyocypris biplicata* Koch	3v A-I, 1v
16 *Candona candida* (Müller)	4v
17 *Candona neglecta* Sars	1v A-IV
18 *Candona neglecta* Sars	20v A-III, 3v 4c A-II
19 *Candona neglecta* Sars	6v A-II, 4v 2c A-I
20 *Candona neglecta* Sars	22v female
21 *Candona neglecta* Sars	10v female
22 *Candona neglecta* Sars	4v male
23 *Candona angulata* (G W Müller)	1v A-II, 4v A-I, 2v
25 *Cyclocypris laevis* (O F Müller)	9v
26 *Potamocypris fulva* (Norman)	3v A-I, 2c
27 *Prionocypris serrata* (Norman)	1v A-V, 3v A-IV, 7v A-III
28 *Prionocypris serrata* (Norman)	7v A-II
29 *Prionocypris serrata* (Norman)	8v
30 *Prionocypris serrata* (Norman)	10v
31 Tooth of *Esox* (pike)	
32 Operculae of *Bithynia tentaculata*	
*2070	
18 *Candona candida* O F Müller	3v A-I
19 *Candona compressa* Koch	1v
20 *Candona neglecta* Sars	2v male, 8v female
22 *Ilyocypris bradyi* Sars	1v
2070	
9 *Ilyocypris bradyi* Sars	1v A-VI, 5v A-V, 6v A-IV, 16v A-III, 6v 2c A-II
10 *Ilyocypris bradyi* Sars	12v A-II, 8v 4c A-I, 10v
11 *Ilyocypris bradyi* Sars	12v
12 *Limnocythere inopinata* (Baird)	2v A-II, 8v 2c A-I, 2v 1c
13 *Candona marchica* Hartwig	1c A-III, 2v A-II
14 *Candona candida* (O F Müller)	1v A-III, 2v A-II
15 *Candona candida* (O F Müller)	1v A-I, 9v

Table 19 (cont.)

16 *Candona angulata* G W Müller	1v A-III, 1c 2v A-II, 3v A-I, 6v 1c
17 *Leptocythere porcellanea* (Brady)	2c
18 *Candona neglecta* Sars	2v A-VI, 3c 6v A-V
19 *Candona neglecta* Sars	14v 3c A-IV, 2c A-III
20 *Candona neglecta* Sars	9v A-III, 5v A-II
21 *Candona neglecta* Sars	10v A-I
22 *Candona neglecta* Sars	16v 4c female
23 *Candona neglecta* Sars	12v 1c male
24 *Cypria ophthalmica* (Jurine)	1v
25 *Cyclocypris laevis* (O F Müller)	1v A-I, 15v 1c
27 *Herpetocypris reptans* (Baird)	fragments

2074

9 *Ilyocypris bradyi* Sars	3v A-VI, 3v A-V, 6v A-IV, 12v A-III
10 *Ilyocypris bradyi* Sars	10v A-II, 12v 3c A-I
11 *Ilyocypris bradyi* Sars	8v
12 *Ilyocypris biplicata* (Koch)	2v
13 *Limnocythere inopinata* (Baird)	4v 1c A-I, 3v
14 *Ilyocypris inermis* Kaufmann	1v
17 *Candona neglecta* Sars	1v A-VII, 6v A-VI, 8v A-V
18 *Candona neglecta* Sars	8v 2c A-IV, 9v A-III
19 *Candona neglecta* Sars	5v A-II, 8v A-I
20 *Candona neglecta* Sars	9v male
21 *Candona angulata* G W Müller	9v 1c A-IV, 2v A-III, 1v A-II
22 *Candona angulata* G W Müller	1v A-I, 4v
23 *Candona candida* (O F Müller)	1v A-I, 4v 1c
26 *Cyclocypris laevis* (O F Müller)	4v 1c
27 *Cypria ophthalmica* (Jurine)	1v 1c

2078

Candona neglecta Sars	2v A-III

Column 2 (samples 23055–23061)

23055

9 *Cypria ophthalmica* (Jurine)	1v A-I, 2v
10 *Cyclocypris laevis* (O F Müller)	3v 4c
11 *Limnocythere inopinata* (Baird)	1v A-III, 1v 1c A-II, 12v 3c A-I, 4c
12 *Ilyocypris bradyi* (Sars)	1v A-V, 2v A-IV, 4v A-III, 10v 10c A-II, 7v 9c A-I, 4v 2c
15 *Candona candida* (O F Müller)	3v A-II, 4v A-I, 2c
17 *Candona neglecta* Sars	3v 3c A-III, 5v 4c A-II, 10v A-I female 6v 9c, male 6v 5c
21 *Ilyocypris inermis* Kaufmann	2v 1c A-I, 6v 5c
22 *Potamocypris* sp	1v
23 *Heterocypris incongruens*	1v
28 *Herpetocypris reptans* (Baird)	1v A-IV, 4v A-III, 1v A-II, 1v A-I

23057

4 *Herpetocypris reptans* (Baird)	2v A-IV, 1v A-III, fragments
9 *Leptocythere lacertosa* (Hirschmann)	1c A-I, 1c
10 *Cyclocypris laevis* (O F Müller)	12v 3c
11 *Limnocythere inopinata* (Baird)	1v A-II, 2v A-I, 3v 3c
12 *Cypria ophthalmica* (Jurine)	1v 2c
13 *Heterocypris incongruens*	1v A-I
14 *Candona candida* (O F Müller)	1v A-I, 4v A-II, 2v 3c
17 *Ilyocypris bradyi* (Sars)	8v A-IV, 4v A-III, 5v 3c A-II, 8v 4c A-I, 2v 2c
21 *Ilyocypris inermis* Kaufmann	1v A-II, 2v A-I, 6v 4c

Table 19 (cont.)

25 *Candona fabaeformis* Fischer	1v A-I
26 *Ilyocypris 'gibba'* forms	3c
27 *Candona neglecta* Sars	2v A-III, 5v 8c A-II, 2c A-I, 4v 9c female, 7v 3c male

23059

3 *Leptocythere lacertosa* (Hirschmann)	3c
10 *Candona neglecta* Sars	1v 1c A-IV, 3v 2c A-III, 13v 3c A-II, 8v 1c A-I, 16v 5c female, 12v 4c male
16 *Candona candida* (O F Müller)	6v 3c
18 *Ilyocypris bradyi* (Sars)	2v A-IV, 4v A-IV, 15v A-III, 11v A-II, 8v 6c A-I, 30v 14c
24 *Ilyocypris inermis* Kaufmann	1v 1c A-I, 8v 6c
25 *Potamocypris fulva* (Brady)	2v 2c A-I, 1v 4c
26 *Cyclocypris laevis* (O F Müller)	5v 4c
29 *Herpetocypris reptans* (Baird)	4v A-III-II
Trochaminid foraminifera	

23061

9 Foraminifera	
10 *Leptocythere lacertosa* (Hirschmann)	3v A-II, 10c A-I, 19c
11 *Cypria ophthalmica* (Jurine)	1v
12 *Cyclocypris laevis* (O F Müller)	3v 2c
14 *Candona angulata* (G W Müller)	1v
16 *Candona candida* (O F Müller)	2v 2c
17 *Ilyocypris bradyi* (Sars)	6v A-IV, 4v A-III, 6v A-II, 5v A-I, 5v 5c
21 *Limnocythere inopinata* (Baird)	1v
22 *Ilyocypris inermis* Kaufmann	1v A-I, 10v 9c
25 *Candona neglecta* Sars	1v A-IV, 4v A-III, 12v A-I, 15v, 5c female, 6v 3c male
30 *Herpetocypris reptans* (Baird)	6 fragments A-III-I

Column 3 (samples 23017–23030)

23017

9 *Cyclocypris laevis* (O F Müller)	1v
10 *Cypria ophthalmica* (Jurine)	1v 1c
11 *Candona candida* (O F Müller)	1v A-III
13 *Ilyocypris bradyi* (Sars)	2v A-IV
14 *Ilyocypris bradyi* (Sars)	1v A-II, 5v 1c A-I
15 *Ilyocypris bradyi* (Sars)	2v 1c
17 *Candona neglecta* Sars	1v A-IV
18 *Candona neglecta* Sars	27 1c A-III
19 *Candona neglecta* Sars	5v A-II
20 *Candona neglecta* Sars	4v male
22 *Candona angulata* (G W Müller)	5v A-III, 1v

23019

9 *Cyclocypris laevis* (O F Müller)	1c
11 *Eucypris* sp	1 fragment
12 *Ilyocypris bradyi* (Sars)	5v
16 *Candona candida* (O F Müller)	1v A-II, 1v
18 *Candona neglecta* Sars	17v A-III, 5v A-II
19 *Candona neglecta* Sars	9v A-I
20 *Candona neglecta* Sars	3v
23 *Candona angulata* (G W Müller)	14v A-III, 1v A-II
Herpetocypris reptans	fragments

Table 19 (cont.)

23021

9 *Cyclocypris laevis* (O F Müller)	3c
11 *Cypria ophthalmica* (Jurine)	1v 6c A-I, 10c
12 *Prionocypris serrata* (Norman)	1v A-II, 2v A-I
14 *Eucypris virens* (Jurine)	2v A-I
15 *Candona angulata* (G W Müller)	4v 2c A-III, 1v A-I, 4c 1v
17 *Candona neglecta* Sars	6v 4c A-III
18 *Candona neglecta* Sars	7v 6c A-II
19 *Candona neglecta* Sars	2v A-II, 2v 3c A-I
20 *Candona neglecta* Sars	6v 4c female
21 *Candona neglecta* Sars	2v 2c male
23 *Candona candida* (O F Müller)	4v 1c
25 *Ilyocypris bradyi* Sars	6v A-IV, 4v 2c A-III, 3v 1c A-II
26 *Ilyocypris bradyi* Sars	12v 10c A-II
27 *Ilyocypris bradyi* Sars	10v 13c
28 *Ilyocypris bradyi* Sars	6v 2c
29 *Ilyocypris bradyi* Sars	4c
31–32 *Herpetocypris reptans* (Baird)	3v A-III, 2v A-II, 1v

23023

9 *Cyclocypris laevis* (O F Müller)	8v 3c
10 *Cypria ophthalmica* (Jurine)	2v 1c
11 *Limnocythere inopinata* (Baird)	3v 1c
12 *Ilyocypris bradyi* Sars	1v A-IV, 5v A-III, 4v A-II
13 *Ilyocypris bradyi* Sars	30v 1c A-I
14 *Ilyocypris bradyi* Sars	11v 1c
15 *Ilyocypris bradyi* Sars	5v
17 *Candona marchica* Hartwig	1c A-III
18 *Potamocypris* sp.	1v
19 *Candona angulata* (G W Müller)	1v
20 *Candona neglecta* Sars	13v A-III
21 *Candona neglecta* Sars	22v A-II
22 *Candona neglecta* Sars	4v A-I, 8v female
23 *Candona neglecta* Sars	12v 2c female, 2v male
24 *Candona candida* (O F Müller)	6v

23027

9 *Cyclocypris laevis* (O F Müller)	1v
10 *Potamocypris* sp.	1v
11 *Limnocythere inopinata* (Baird)	3v
12 *Ilyocypris bradyi* Sars	8v A-IV, 2v A-III
13 *Ilyocypris bradyi* Sars	7v A-III, 18v A-II, 2c
14 *Ilyocypris bradyi* Sars	29v 2c A-I
15 *Ilyocypris bradyi* Sars	9v 2c
16 *Ilyocypris biplicata* Koch	1v
17 *Candona neglecta* Sars	18v A-III
18 *Candona neglecta* Sars	7v A-II, 8v A-I
19 *Candona neglecta* Sars	19v A-I
20 *Candona neglecta* Sars	2v female, 2v male
21 *Candona marchica* Hartwig	1v
22 *Candona angulata* (G W Müller)	2v
28 *Ilyocypris inermis* Kaufmann	4v A-I, 4v

Table 19 (cont.)

23028

9	*Cypria ophthalmica* (Jurine)	1v
10	*Limnocythere inopinata* (Baird)	3v
11	*Ilyocypris bradyi* Sars	2v A-III, 7v A-II
12	*Ilyocypris bradyi* Sars	10v A-I
13	*Ilyocypris bradyi* Sars	18v A-I
14	*Ilyocypris bradyi* Sars	12v
15	*Ilyocypris biplicata* Koch	1v
16	*Ilyocypris inermis* Kaufmann	3v A-I, 2v
17	*Cyclocypris laevis* (O F Müller)	1v
18	*Candona neglecta* Sars	2v A-IV, 9v A-III
19	*Candona neglecta* Sars	8v A-II
20	*Candona neglecta* Sars	4v A-I
21	*Candona neglecta* Sars	16v 3c female
22	*Candona neglecta* Sars	9v 3c male
24	*Candona angulata* (G W Müller)	3v
26	*Candona candida* (O F Müller)	1v A-III, 1v A-I, 8v
30	*Eucypris virens* (Jurine)	1v A-II

23030

9	*Cyclocypris laevis* (O F Müller)	1v 1c
10	*Cypria ophthalmica* (Jurine)	1v
12	*Limnocythere inopinata* (Baird)	1v A-II, 2v A-I, 6v 4c
13	*Ilyocypris biplicata* Koch	4v
14	*Ilyocypris bradyi* Sars	6v A-II, 10v 9c A-I
15	*Ilyocypris bradyi* Sars	18v 5c
16	*Ilyocypris bradyi* Sars	2v
17	*Candona candida* (O F Müller)	2v
18	*Candona neglecta* Sars	2v 7c A-III
19	*Candona neglecta* Sars	3v A-II, 5v A-I
20	*Candona neglecta* Sars	11v 4c female
21	*Candona neglecta* Sars	2v male
23	*Candona angulata* (G W Müller)	1v

Column 4 (Spot sample 23166)

23166

9	*Cyclocypris laevis* (O F Müller)	2v
10	*Potamocypris* sp.	1c
12	*Ilyocypris bradyi* Sars	2v A-IV, 5v A-III, 14v A-II
13	*Ilyocypris bradyi* Sars	28v 2c A-I
14	*Ilyocypris bradyi* Sars	17v 2c
15	*Ilyocypris bradyi* Sars	4v
16	*Ilyocypris biplicata* Koch	1v
18	*Candona neglecta* Sars	4v 1c A-IV, 6v A-III
19	*Candona neglecta* Sars	3v A-II, 5v A-I
20	*Candona neglecta* Sars	20v 4c female
21	*Candona neglecta* Sars	10v 2c female
22	*Candona neglecta* Sars	11v 1c male
23	*Candona angulata* (G W Müller)	2v
24	*Candona candida* (O F Müller)	7v 2c
28	*Cyprideis torosa* (Jones)	1v A-I
30	*Ilyocypris inermis* Kaufmann	6v

148

Table 19 (cont.)

Column 5 (samples 23251–23257)

23251

10	*Cyclocypris laevis* (O F Müller)	7v 1c
11	*Cypria ophthalmica* (Jurine)	10v 5c
13	*Candona marchica* Hartwig	2v
13	*Candona neglecta* Sars	3v 2c A-III, 4v A-I. 9v female
14	*Candona neglecta* Sars	11v 4c female, 2v male
15	*Prionocypris serrata* (Norman)	5v A-II, 1v A-I, 1v
16	*Eucypris virens* (Jurine)	1v A-III, 2v A-II, 2v
17	*Ilyocypris bradyi* Sars	6v A-IV, 7v A-III, 4v A-II
18	*Ilyocypris bradyi* Sars	4v A-II, 11v A-I
19	*Ilyocypris bradyi* Sars	11v
20	*Ilyocypris biplicata* Koch	5v A-I, 2v
22	*Candona candida* (O F Müller)	1v A-II, 6v
24	*Candona angulata* (G W Müller)	2v 3c A-II, 2v A-I, 10v
25	*Herpetocypris reptans* (Baird)	9v A-IV
26	*Herpetocypris reptans* (Baird)	3v A-III
27	*Herpetocypris reptans* (Baird)	10v A-II
28	*Herpetocypris reptans* (Baird)	4v A-I
29	*Herpetocypris reptans* (Baird)	2v A-I
30	*Herpetocypris reptans* (Baird)	1v

23253

9	*Cyclocypris laevis* (O F Müller)	9v
10	*Cypria ophthalmica* (Jurine)	2v A-I, 4v
11	*Potamocypris* sp.	1v 1c
12	*Eucypris virens* (Jurine)	2v A-II
13	*Limnocythere inopinata* (Baird)	11v
14	*Ilyocypris bradyi* Sars	4v A-IV, 4v A-III
15	*Ilyocypris bradyi* Sars	14v A-II, 8v 1c A-I
16	*Ilyocypris bradyi* Sars	6v
17	*Candona marchica* Hartwig	1c A-III
19	*Candona candida* (O F Müller)	3v A-III, 4v A-I, 6v
20	*Candona neglecta* Sars	2v A-IV, 17v 2c A-III
21	*Candona neglecta* Sars	5v A-II, 6v A-I
22	*Candona neglecta* Sars	5v female
23	*Candona neglecta* Sars	3v male
24	*Candona angulata* (G W Müller)	15v A-III, 2v A-II
26	*Herpetocypris reptans* (Baird)	1v A-IV
28	*Herpetocypris reptans* (Baird)	2v A-II
29	*Herpetocypris reptans* (Baird)	1v A-I

23257

9	*Cyclocypris laevis* (O F Müller)	1v 1c
	Cypria ophthalmica (Jurine)	1c
10	*Limnocythere inopinata* (Baird)	3v
	Potamocypris sp.	1v
11	*Prionocypris serrata* (Norman)	1v A-II, 1v A-I
	Eucypris virens (Jurine)	1v A-I, 1v
12	*Ilyocypris bradyi* Sars	2v A-IV, 3v A-III
13	*Ilyocypris bradyi* Sars	5v A-II, 17v 2c A-I
14	*Ilyocypris bradyi* Sars	15v 5c
16	*Ilyocypris biplicata* Koch	3v A-I, 1v
17	*Candona neglecta* Sars	1v 1c A-IV, 15v 6c A-III

Table 19 (cont.)

18 *Candona neglecta* Sars	3v A-II
19 *Candona neglecta* Sars	12v A-I, 4v female
20 *Candona neglecta* Sars	7v 4c female
21 *Candona neglecta* Sars	9v male
22 *Candona candida* (O F Müller)	2v
23 *Candona marchica* Hartwig	1v A-I, 1v
24 *Candona angulata* (G W Müller)	5v 2c
27 *Herpetocypris reptans* (Baird)	2v A-IV
28 *Herpetocypris reptans* (Baird)	3v A-III
29 *Herpetocypris reptans* (Baird)	2v A-II

Key: A – adults, A-I pre-adult, A-II younger moult stage, v – valve, c – carapace (2 valves)

Small trochaminid Foraminifera (unicellular micro-organisms) from the same environment lend support to the suggestion that the Caldicot site came into the margins of high-tide flow. In contrast, the freshwater quiet conditions are best indicated by the species *Limnocythere inopinata*, usually taken as an indicator for lacustrine conditions (Klie 1938; Absolon 1973) and unable to flourish in current-moved waters.

In 23061, *Leptocythere lacertosa* represents 30% of the fauna. *Limnocythere* is absent. *Ilyocypris bradyi*, making up some 20% is a freshwater species which can tolerate some saline influx. This is not true of *Candona neglecta*, which makes up 27% of the fauna, which is unable to withstand saline conditions. As this last species is represented by instars as small as A–IV, it is assumed that it was *in situ* and breeding. On these counts, the marine influence was only just registering in the Phase II palaeochannel, and could simply mean that the Caldicot site could be reached by high tide from the Severn Estuary, or by tide surges in abnormal times.

23059 is a sample only some 10cm higher in the sequence, but it already shows differences in the percentages of the ostracod fauna. *Leptocythere* has dropped to 3%, the specimens still being fresh and complete carapaces testifying that they are *in situ* and not washed into association. The percentages of *Candona neglecta* (36%) and *Ilyocypris bradyi* (40%) make up the bulk of the fauna.

In 23057, *Limnocythere* makes its appearance, registering 6% of the fauna while *Leptocythere* is reduced to 2%. The main species are again *Candona neglecta* (33%) and *Ilyocyperis bradyi* (25%). Other freshwater species make a contribution; *Cylocypris laevis*, *Candona candida*, *Cypria opthalmica*, and *Herpetocypris reptans*. This last species is very large and delicate and its survival bespeaks quiet waters at this time in the Phase III palaeochannel.

Sample 23055 shows a marked increase in *Limnocythere inopinata* (13%), a presence of *Herpetocypris* and all the other freshwater species which figure in samples studied from Caldicot.

In the other sequences, which cover the later palaeochannels and Phases (IV–VII), apart from 2078 and 2074 which are from Phase I, the majority of the samples carry the same range of species, predominantly freshwater, with only slight changes in the proportions of one species or another. Two species, *Candona neglecta* and *Ilyocypris bradyi*, dominate the assemblages and together make up as much as 80% of some sample faunas. *Candona neglecta* is represented in every sample and *Ilyocypris bradyi* is present in all but two, 2078 and 2054 (Phases I and VII respectively). Both species speak of quiet, almost still waters, with no salinity, although *Ilyocypris* can stand some saline influx. The *Candona* species are bottom-burrowers on soft mud substrates, or burrowers amongst weed growths. The same is true of *Ilyocypris*, the more ornamented of the species. In 2066, Phase VI in Column 1, there is a higher proportion of shallow-water swimmers/crawlers (*Prionocypris*, *Potamocypris*) than above or below but otherwise there is an equal weighting of *Candona neglecta* to *Ilyocypris bradyi*. Very few of the species recorded are known to be free-swimming forms, *Cypria ophthalmica* is the exception. It requires open water as opposed to sedgey and grassy pools and, though in the minority, is present in most samples. *Herpetocypris* is a large ostracod (up to 2mm long) with very delicate valves. It clambers amongst water weed, being unable to swim in flowing waters. *Limnocythere inopinata*, the indicator for lacustrine or still water conditions as opposed to flowing waters, occurs in a number of samples (2066–2074, 23023–30, 23253–57). *Cyclocypris laevis* and *Potamocypris* in various samples may suggest higher organic content.

Although freshwater lacustrine conditions become more dominant upwards, there are occasional inroads by Foraminifera and the ostracod *Cyprideis torosa*. *Cyprideis* occurs in sample 23166, Phase III, and is the most saline indicator in the later channel deposits; but it is only a single valve and not too much should be made of it. In addition there is also a hint of brackish water from the presence in 2066 (Phase VI) of a possible and in 2070 (Phase V) a certain carapace of the nearshore marine ostracod *Leptocythere porcellana*. Foraminifera are also present in 2062 (Phase VI/VII) and 2066. No traces of

Foraminifera or marine ostracods were recorded in sequences 23017–23032 and 23251–23257 though *Candona angulata* is present. It also occurs in 2066–2074, 23166 and 23061. It can tolerate oligohaline to mesohaline water, thanoligohaline at the most. The salt might be from salt springs from the boulder clays locally but, given the evidence from other biota, more likely reflects estuarine penetration.

To summarise, the samples are dominated by freshwater assemblages with the strongest evidence for marine conditions in 23061, but even then possibly only reflecting the influence of high tides or storm surges. The samples are characterised by ostracod species which testify to sluggishly-moving if not stagnant waters during their deposition – an environment populated by bottom burrowers or weed-living species. The lack of current movement is borne out by the long sequence of small instars for most species recorded. Preservation and the range of juveniles to adults, all sustain the idea that there was little, if any, post-mortem movement of the valves on death; many survive as carapaces, the two valves still locked together. Finally, all species are extant, and would signify temperate climate conditions.

The insect fauna
Peter Osborne

Some 30 samples, from various parts of the site (see Figs 60–6), were processed and examined for insect remains. Their lithologies (p 68) were all fairly similar, consisting of grey silty clay with some plant material included. All were, therefore, processed in the same way, by soaking for a few days in a sodium carbonate solution then washing over a 300 micron sieve through which virtually all the inorganic fraction was able to pass. What was caught on the sieve was then subjected to paraffin flotation and the insect fragments picked out of the floating layer after rinsing with detergent, water and alcohol.

In spite of a rather unpromising appearance to the matrix most samples produced a profusion of insect remains, mostly of beetles but also of some other orders such as Alder Flies (Megaloptera), Caddises (Trichoptera), Bugs (Hemiptera), Dragonflies (Odonata), Earwigs (Dermaptera) and Ants (Hymenoptera, Formicidae).

The large number of samples involved and the abundance of insect material in most of them, together with a shortage of time, has driven the author to agree, rather reluctantly, with the ideas put forward by Kenward (1992) concerning the impracticability of identifying and recording everything found in every sample. In this study, therefore, insects from a number of samples have been identified and enumerated as completely as possible, the method termed 'detailed' by Kenward. The remains from the other samples have been identified as far as the author's experience would allow without pursuing specimens with only limited characters or which

might involve time-consuming comparisons, perhaps at other institutions, a treatment approximating to Kenward's 'Rapid Scan' method. The numbers of sclerites which could be identified in this way were probably augmented by the fact that adjacent samples had often been examined by the 'detailed' method so that insects which might have been hurriedly classified as 'don't know' in an isolated sample had already come to the author's attention.

The same factors, a large number of samples containing a plethora of taxa, makes the presentation of data difficult. An examination of the faunal lists from all the samples shows a close similarity throughout, with the environments depicted being virtually the same in every layer examined so that to publish all the lists would have resulted in many pages of pointless repetition. It is not to be expected, however, that even two samples from the same layer would produce identical lists of contained taxa, in the same way that collecting living insects from the same piece of countryside on two consecutive days would produce similar but not identical lists. It is proposed, therefore, in the interests of economy of space and so as not to produce a completely indigestible mass of names and figures, to present two lists. The first is from what, after protracted deliberation, was considered to be a representative suite of samples. These were the ones from the section near the boat strake in Area B, numbered 23017 (top) – 23032 (bottom) (see Column 3, Figs 60 and 62), covering a depth of *c* 0.80m relating to Phases III and IV. The uppermost samples, 23017–23023 (Phase IV) contained a relatively small number of insects but the other layers (Phase III) all provided substantial faunas, the majority of the taxa being common to several of the samples. An admittedly subjective but very thorough assessment of those species which were not distributed widely through the column, revealed nothing to suggest a deviation from the environments indicated by the majority, and it was concluded that during the period of time over which the samples were being laid down conditions in the area remained substantially the same. For simplicity, therefore, the faunal list from 23017–23032 is presented as though it was from a single collection (Table 20, faunal list 1). The figures on the right of the list are the total numbers of individuals recorded from the five lower-most samples, numbers 23026–23032, as these were the part of the section examined by the 'detailed' method. The small number of taxa from this section not encountered in samples 23026–23032 all came from sample 23021. As the remains from this sample were not counted the figures in the list are replaced by a cross (+). The ratios of numbers of individuals remain roughly the same throughout all the samples investigated.

Taxa found in the other sections but which were not recorded in this first list are tabled in faunal list 2 (Table 21) with the number of the sample from which each came, and are discussed later.

Both lists were compiled using the classification of Kloet and Hincks (1977). Orders other than Coleop-

Table 20 Faunal list 1: Area B, Column 3, samples 23026–32 and 23021 (+)

COLEOPTERA

Carbidae

Nebria brevicollis (F.)	2
Blethisa multipunctata (L.)	1
Notiophilus sp.	1
Elaphrus cupreus Dufts. or *uliginosus* F.	5
Loricera pilicornis (F.)	3
Dyschirius globosus (Hbst.)	11
Dyschirius luedersi Wag.	2
Dyschirius nitidus (Dej.)	1
Clivina fossor (L.) or *collaris* (Hbst.)	15
Trechus obtusus Er. or *quadristriatus* (Schr.)	6
Trechus rivularis (Gyll.)	1
Trechus micros (Hbst.)	3
Trechus sp.	3
Bembidion nigricorne Gyll.	1
Bembidion varium (Ol.)	6
Bembidion assimile Gyll.	3
Bembidion fumigatum (Dufts.)	2
Bembidion harpaloides Serv.	+
Bembidion biguttatum (F.)	4
Bembidion guttula (F.) or *unicolor* Chaud.	12
Bembidion lunulatum (F.)	2
Bembidion spp.	17
Pterostichus diligens (Sturm)	1
Pterostichus gracilis (Deg.)	2
Pterostichus melanarius (Ill.)	1
Pterostichus niger (Schall.)	2
Pterostichus strenuus (Pz.)	5
Pterostichus vernalis (Pz.)	2
Pterostichus sg. *Poecilus* sp.	5
Calathus melanocephalus (L.)	+
Agonum dorsale (Pont.)	1
Agonum mulleri (Hbst.)	1
Agonum obscurum (Hbst.)	2
Agonum sp.	3
Amara sp.	1
Acupalpus sp.	2
Badister unipustulatus Bon.	1
Demetrias monostigma Sam.	1
Dromius linearis (Ol.)	1

Haliplidae

Brychius elevatus (Pz.)	2
Haliplus sp.	1

Dytiscidae

Hygrotus inaequalis (F.)	2
Hydroporus sp.	7
Graptodytes bilineatus (Sturm) or *granularis* (L.)	2
Potamonectes depressus (F.) or *elegans* (Pz.)	7
Stictotarsus duodecimpustulatus (F.)	4
Ilybius sp.	1
Colymbetes ?fuscus (L.)	5
Acilius sp.	1

Dytiscus sp.	2

Gyrinidae

Gyrinus spp. (inc. *natator* (L.))	20
Orectochilus villosus (Mull.)	10

Hydrophilidae

Helophorus aquaticus (L.)	1
Helophorus sp. (small, like *brevipalpis* Bedel)	89
Coelostoma orbiculare (F.)	5
Sphaeridium sp.	1
Cercyon sternalis Sharp	27
Cercyon sp.	3
Megasternum obscurum (Marsh.)	45
Cryptopleurum minutum (F.)	1
Hydrobius fuscipes (L.)	30
Enochrus sp.	16
Cymbiodyta marginella (F.)	20
Hydrochara caraboides (L.)	1
Hydrophilus piceus (L.)	1

Histeridae

Onthophilus striatus (Forst.)	1
Hister sp.	2

Hydraenidae

Ochthebius bicolon Germ.	4
Ochthebius dilatatus Steph.	7
Ochthebius marinus (Payk.)	9
Ochthebius minimus (F.)	59
Ochthebius viridis Peyron	1
Ochthebius spp. (elytra)	170
Hydraena riparia Kug.	2
Hydraena sp.	3
Limnebius aluta (Bedel)	5
Limnebius papposus Muls. or *truncatellus* (Thunb.)	7

Ptiliidae

Acrotrichis sp.	+

Silphidae

Silpha atrata L.	2

Staphylinidae

Lesteva heeri Fauvel	14
Lesteva punctata Er.	1
Lesteva sp.	+
Bledius sp.	3
Platystethus cornutus (Grav.) or *degener* Muls. et Rey	22
Platystethus spp.	6
Anotylus insecatus (Grav.)	1
Anotylus nitidulus (Grav.)	2
Anotylus rugosus (F.)	12
Anotylus sculpturatus (Grav.)	5
Stenus spp.	177
Paederus sp.	2
Lathrobium sp.	17
Rugilus geniculatus (Er.)	1

Table 20 (cont.)

Rugilus rufipes Germ.	1
Rugilus sp.	1
Xantholinus linearis (Ol.) or *longiventris* Heer	28
Philonthus micans (Grav.)	7
Philonthus sp.	7
Staphylinus ophthalmicus Scop.	1
Quedius sp.	1
Tachyporus sp.	2
Tachinus sp.	2
Drusilla canaliculata (F.)	1
Aleocharinae indet.	13
Pselaphidae	
Rybaxis laminata (Mots.) or *longicornis* (Leach)	5
Brachygluta sp.	2
Pselaphus heisei (Hbst.)	1
Geotrupidae	
Geotrupes sp.	4
Scarabaeidae	
Aphodius spp.	13
Onthopagus sp.	2
Phyllopertha horticola (L.)	24
Dascillidae	
Dascillus cervinus (L.)	1
Scirtidae	
Gen. et sp. indet.	24
Byrrhidae	
Byrrhus pilula (L.)	1
Heteroceridae	
Heterocerus marginatus (F.)	28
Heterocerus maritimus Guerin-Meneville	16
Heterocerus sp.	9
Dryopidae	
Dryops sp.	5
Elmidae	
Elmis aenea (Mull.)	285
Esolus parallelepipedus (Mull.)	+
Limnius volckmarii (Pz.)	2
Normandia nitens (Mull.)	1
Oulimnius troglodytes (Gyll.) or *tuberculatus* (Mull.)	116
Elateridae	
Agrypnus murinus (L.)	2
Agriotes sp.	2
Throscidae	
Throscus ?obtusus (Curtis)	1
Cantharidae	
Cantharis sp.	8
Silis ruficollis (F.)	1
Melyridae	
Axinotarsus ruficollis (Ol.)	1
Cryptophagidae	
Atomaria sp.	2

Phalacridae	
Phalacrus caricis Sturm	2
Phalacrus ?coruscus (Pz.)	1
Corylophidae	
Corylophus cassidioides (Marsh.)	1
Coccinellidae	
Coccidula rufa (Hbst.)	1
Tytthaspis sedecimpunctata (L.)	1
Chrysomelidae	
Donacia aquatica (L.)	1
Donacia simplex F.	1
Donacia versicolorea (Brahm)	+
Donacia sp.	3
Lema sp.	1
Chrysolina polita (L.)	1
Hydrothassa glabra (Hbst.)	2
Prasocuris phellandrii (L.)	1
Chaetocnema concinna (Marsh.)	14
Chaetocnema sp.	5
Apionidae	
Apion carduorum Kirby	1
Apion spp.	31
Curculionidae	
Polydrusus pterygomalis Boh.	1
Barypeithes araneiformis (Schr.)	41
Sciaphilus asperatus (Bonsd.)	2
Strophosomus sp.	1
Liophloeus tessulatus (Mull.)	1
Sitona hispidulus (F.)	1
Sitona sp.	26
Hypera sp.	1
Alophus triguttatus (F.)	7
Magdalis ?carbonaria (L.)	1
Tanysphyrus lemnae (Payk.)	7
Notaris acridulus (L.)	4
Notaris bimaculatus (F.)	1
Ceuthorhynchidius troglodytes (F.)	1
Cethorhynchus sp.	5
Anthonomus sp.	3
Curculio sp.	1
Miccotrogus picirostris (F.)	2
Scolytidae	
Scolytus rugulosus (Mull.)	2
Orders other than Coleoptera	
MEGALOPTERA	
Sialidae	
Sialis sp.	+
ODONATA	
Zygoptera	
?Agrion sp.	+
HEMIPTERA	
Gerridae	
Gerris sp.	+

Table 20 (cont.)

Saldidae		Formicidae	
Chartoscirta sp.	+	*Gen. et sp. indet*	+
TRICHOPTERA		DIPTERA	
Gen. et sp. indet	+	Nematocera	
HYMENOPTERA		*Dilophus* sp.	+

Table 21 Faunal list 2, comprising those taxa recorded from samples other than 23017–23032 not in list 1

Taxa	Sample number (phase)	Taxa	Sample number (phase)
COLEOPTERA		*Ontholestes murinus* (L.)	A20 (V)
Carabidae		Pselaphidae	
Cychrus caraboides (L.)	23055 (III)	*Bryaxis* sp.	A18 (VI)
Carabus ?granulatus L.	A19 (V–VI)	*Tychus niger* (Payk.)	A23 (I–V)
Notiophilus palustris (Dufts.)	A10 (VI/VII)	Scarabaeidae	
Bembidion lampros (Hbst.)	A10 (VI/VII)	*Onthophagus ovatus* (L.) or *johannae*	A10 (VI/VII)
Bembidion properans Steph.	23251 (VII)		
Bembidion quadrimaculatum (L.)	23251 (VII)	*Onthophagus ?vacca* (L.)	A10 (VI/VII)
Bembidion gilvipes Sturm	A10 (VI/VII)	*Hoplia philanthus* (Fuess.)	A10 (VI/VII)
Bembidion minimum (F.)	A23 (I–V)	Byrrhidae	
Trachys sp.	A10 (VI/VII)	*Simplocaria semistriata* (F.)	A10 (VI/VII)
Pterostichus (Sg. Poecilus) *cupreus* (L.)	A10 (VI/VII)	Elateridae	
		Agriotes acuminatus (Steph.)	A10 (VI/VII)
Calathus fuscipes (Goeze)	A14 (VI/VII), 23251 (VII)	*Agriotes sordidus* (Ill.)	A10 (VI/VII)
		Throscidae	
Agonum albipes (F.)	23059 (II)	*Throscus* sp.	23055 (III)
Pseudophonus rufipes Deg.	23251 (VII)	Anobiidae	
Panagaeus crux-major (L.)	A18 (VI)	*Anobium* sp.	A6 (VII), A10 (VI/VII)
Chlaenius sp.	23257 (VII), 23166 (III)	Melyridae	
Dromius ?longiceps Dej.	A23 (I–V)	*?Anthocomus* sp.	A10 (VI/VII)
Metabletus foveatus (Fourc.)	23251 (VII)	Nitidulidae	
		Meligethes sp.	23253 (VII)
Dytiscidae		Phalacridae	
Agabus bipustulatus (L.)	A19 (V–VI)	*Phalacrus* sp.	23251 (VII)
Rhantus sp.	23253 (VII)	*Stilbus* sp.	A10 (VI/VII), 23251 (VII)
Hydrophilidae			
Berosus sp.	23059 (II)	Coccinellidae	
Histeridae		*Scymnus frontalis* (F.)	23251 (VII)
Paralister purpurascens (Hbst.)	A10 (VI/VII)	Lathridiidae	
		Enicmus transversus (01.)	A10 (VI/VII), 23251 (VII)
Staphylinidae			
Micropeplus sp.	A25 (I)	*Corticaria* group	A10 (VI/VII)
Olophrum piceum (Gyll.)	A14 (VI/VII), A16 (VI), A18 (VI), A19 (V–VI)	Colydiidae	
		Colydium elongatum (F.)	A19 (V–VI)
Carpelimus sp.	A10 (VI/VII)	Anthicidae	
Platystethus sp.	A23 (I–V), 23055 (III)	*Anthicus antherinus* (L.)	23251 (VII)
Anotylus inustus (Grav.)	23251 (VII)	Chrysomelidae	
Philonthus lepidus (Grav.) or *varius* (Gyll.)	23251 (VII)	*Donacia clavipes* F.	A3 (VII), A6 (VII), A7 (VI–VII), A12 (VI/VII), A14, (VI/VII), A16 (VI), A18 (VI), A19 (V–VI), 23251 (VII), 23253 (VII), 23257 (VII)
Philonthus varius (Gyll.)	A10 (VI/VII)		
Gabrius sp.	A10 (VI/VII)		
Staphylinus olens Mull.	A10 (VI/VII)		

Table 21 (cont.)

Taxa	Sample number (phase)
Donacia semicuprea Pz.	A10 (VI/VII)
Plateumaris sericea (L.)	A10 (VI/VII)
Cryptocephalus moraei (L.)	23251 (VII)
Phyllotreta ochripes (Curtis)	A10 (VI/VII)
Phyllotreta vittula Redt.	A10 (VI/VII)
Phyllotreta sp.	A11 (VI/VII)
Psylliodes sp.	23253 (VII)
Curculionidae	
Barynotus obscurus (F.)	23259 (VI)
Sitona lepidus Gyll.	A10 (VI/VII)
Hypera nigrirostris (F.)	A10 (VI/VII)
Hypera punctata (F.)	A19 (V–VI), 23059 (II)
Tychius pusillus Germ.	A10 (VI/VII)

Taxa	Sample number (phase)
Bagous sp.	23251 (VII)
Tychius sp.	A10 (VI/VII), A21 (V)
Mecinus pyraster (Hbst.)	A7 (VI–VII)
Orders other than Coleoptera	
DERMAPTERA	
Forficulidae	
?Forficula sp.	A6 (VII), A7 (VI–VII), A12 (VI/VII), A18 (VI), A19 (V–VI), A20 (V), 23253 (VII), 23055 (III), 23059 (II)
ODONATA	
Anisoptera	
Gen. et sp. indet.	A10 (VI/VII), 23251 (VII)

tera (beetles), though interesting, were in a minority and are tabled after the beetle lists. Since many of these were of larval forms, having skeletal parts duplicated at each of several instars it was not possible to calculate numbers of individuals with any degree of accuracy so that all the 'other orders' are listed as presence only.

Notes on certain identifications

Gyrinus spp. (inc. natator (L.))

Although some of these specimens could safely be ascribed to *Gyrinus natator* many were fragmentary and defied attempts to identify them further than genus. It was felt safest to list them all as *Gyrinus* spp. with the proviso that at least *natator* (L.) was present and possibly other species as well.

Ochthebius spp. (elytra)

The pronota of members of this genus are fairly readily identifiable to species level and this has been done. The elytra, however, are much less easy to distinguish so they have been counted and listed as *Ochthebius* spp. (elytra) and may belong to any of the species which were identified by the presence of their pronota.

Oulimnius troglodytes (Gyll.) or tuberculatus (Mull.)

Although many pronota of these two species may be readily assigned to one or the other, in a large assemblage a substantial number, particularly if they are flattened or otherwise distorted, are not. Both species were clearly present here but to estimate numbers of each was considered too hazardous so the two have been listed together wherever they occur.

Environmental implications

In terms of numbers of individuals this fauna is dominated by aquatic insects and, as seems to frequently be the case in Flandrian insect assemblages, apparently until quite recent times (Osborne, in prep), it is made up of a mixture of species which today live in still or very slowly-flowing water and a group whose members are found in rapidly running water. Thus in this fauna the dytiscids *Graptodytes, Colymbetes, Ilybius, Acilius* and *Dytiscus*, hydrophilids such as *Helophorus, Hydrobius, Hydrochara* and *Hydrophilus* and the genera *Ochthebius, Hydraena* and *Limnebius* amongst the Hydraenidae all live in still water. The weevil *Tanysphyrus lemnae* was also present whose food plant, the floating duckweed *Lemna*, is a species of ponds, ditches and slowly flowing rivers. In contrast to these the most abundant beetles in the site in terms of numbers of individuals were the Elmids *Elmis aenea* and *Oulimnius troglodytes / tuberculatus* which today are found in water running sufficiently swiftly to keep the bottom scoured more or less free of mud. To these taxa may be added the remaining elmids, the haliplid *Brychius elevatus* and the dytiscids *Potamonectes* and *Stictotarsus*, all species which favour running water.

Many species were recorded which live at the margins of water of various kinds. Amongst the carabid ground beetles *Blethisa, Elaphrus, Loricera, Bembidion assimile* and *B. lunulatum, Pterostichus gracilis* and *Pt. vernalis, Badister unipustulatus* and *Demetrias monostigma* are all most frequently found near water, usually in shaded situations, often with *Carex. Dyschirius luedersi, D. nitidus, Bembidion varium* and *B. fumigatum* on the other hand are species which are predominantly coastal, living actually on the sea shore or alongside tidal estuaries.

The staphylinid *Platystethus cornutus / degener* is found on the muddy banks of ponds and rivers while

Bledius is a fossorial insect, making burrows in sandy or clayey river banks or coasts. A similar lifestyle is followed by members of the genus *Heterocerus*, of which the two species identified from so many of the Caldicot samples *Heterocerus maritimus* and *H. marginatus*, are usually found on the sea shore or at the side of brackish water.

The chrysomelid genus *Donacia* was well represented throughout the site with at least three species being recognised in list 1 and more in list 2. These beetles spend their larval lives at the roots of aquatic vegetation with subaerial leaves, such as *Schoenoplectus, Sparganium, Typha* and *Potamogeton*, which grow at the edges of still or slowly flowing water (see Caseldine, pp 103–4). The adults are found on the foliage of the same plants and it is not unusual to find several species together. *Prasocuris phellandrii* lives on *Oenanthe aquatica* and other aquatic Apiaceae at the edges of ponds and streams.

Apart from beetles the two most frequently occurring insects at Caldicot were the Alder Fly, *Sialis* and the Pond Skater, the bug *Gerris*. The first of these, *Sialis*, was found in every sample examined. Its larvae live as predators at the bottom of slowly running water and the species is dependent on vegetation overhanging the water as the female lays her eggs in situations where the emerging larvae have only to release their hold and fall to find themselves in water. *Gerris*, the familiar Pond Skater lives as a predator running on the surface film, again of still water, often in company with beetles of the genus *Gyrinus*, also well represented here.

Away from the water many of the beetles recognised live in accumulations of vegetable refuse of various sorts. *Geotrupes, Aphodius* and *Onthophagus* are dung beetles which are most often found in the droppings of large grazing animals such as sheep, cattle or horses (see McCormick, p 218). Other species, particularly the histerids *Hister* and *Onthophilus, Sphaeridium, Silpha* and most of the more abundant staphylinids found, particularly members of the genus *Anotylus,* are also found in dung and in other habitats which attract dipterous larvae in large numbers such as carrion, decaying fungi, rotting seaweed and compost. Other very well represented inhabitants of decaying vegetation are the hydrophilids *Megasternum obscurum* and *Cercyon sternalis.*

Apart from the semi-aquatic and waterside vegetation suggested by the *Donacia* species and *Tanysphyrus lemnae* the plant cover indicated by a majority of the remaining fauna is damp grassland (see Caseldine, p 105) or moss on marshy ground. The dung beetles live principally in the droppings of grazing animals whilst the chafer *Phyllopertha horticola*, recorded from many samples, is a grassland species, its larvae living at grass roots level. This habitat is shared by the elaterids *Agrypna murina* and *Agriotes* spp. Amongst the phytophagous beetles noted *Hydrothassa glabra* is found in damp meadowland, usually on Ranunculaceae. *Chaetoc-*

nema concinna lives on *Polygonum, Apion carduorum* on thistles, *Sitona hispidulus* and *Miccotrogus picirostris* on *Trifolium* and *Ceuthorhynchidius troglodytes* on *Plantago lanceolata*, all plants of open grassland. Those found amongst moss are generally predators, like most of the staphylinids and pselaphids, or polyphagous phytophages like the curculionids *Sciaphilus asperatus, Alophus triguttatus* and the most abundant weevil at Caldicot, *Barypeithes araneiformis*. Amongst all these species from different families with diverse life styles there is nothing to suggest the presence of trees locally, with one exception. This is the scolytid *Scolytus rugulosus*, a bark beetle which attacks a variety of deciduous trees with an emphasis on smaller types such as fruit trees of the genus *Prunus* (see Caseldine, p 106 and Johnson, p 158). The beetle was noticed in a number of samples not covered by list 1, and in the absence of virtually any other insect actually needing trees for its survival, it seems most likely that this species was imported onto the site in the cut wood which was so evident in the excavation.

The local environment represented by the insects of list 1, therefore, seems to be a stream without too fierce a current, probably having a clean stony bottom in the centre but with an accumulation of silt amongst the stems of marginal reeds. This, however, appears to conflict with the lithological evidence which in samples 23026–23032 is simply stoneless clay. This problem, of large numbers of Elmids, usually associated with rapidly-flowing water, occurring alongside a fauna of slowly-flowing or still water is one which, in the author's experience, is found in every Flandrian site from early post-Glacial to post-Roman times. It has been postulated (Osborne 1988) that in a natural state, these two components of the fauna are not completely incompatible, but that the Elmids have been to a large extent eliminated from slowly-flowing rivers by the accumulation in relatively recent times of mud and silt washed off the land following deforestation and deep ploughing for agriculture. This group of beetles, therefore, did not so much need a strong current for, say, greater aeration, but a clean river bottom which until recently could exist naturally under even slowly flowing water on account of the small load of silt to be deposited. When, due to the expansion of agriculture, mud began to be washed into watercourses in large quantities, only those streams whose current was strong enough to keep them scoured clean were able to provide a suitable environment for the Elmids. At Caldicot, however, unless the lithological sampling represents extremely local conditions, which does not appear to be the case, they must presumably have come from further upstream. The deposition of these silts and clays certainly presupposes the slowing down of a current which had held the particles in suspension until the proximity of sea level was reached when the flow slowed, and the suspended matter – including Elmid remains perhaps from nearby – was dropped. The stream was close enough to the sea probably for wind-blown salt spray to have an influence, making adjacent standing water brackish, but not so close that the stream itself became so salty with the incoming tide that vegetation, both submerged and marginal, would be inhibited. The waterside reed beds gave way to marshy ground with brackish pools and a covering of vegetation containing mosses, rushes and other wetland plants. Further still from the water this wet ground became damp meadowland with grasses and plants of open grassland on which grazing animals were living.

Trees do not seem to have been growing close to the site but some must have been found at a sufficiently short distance to make the importation of timber economic. The timber suggested by the scolytids need not have been in the form of forest trees of great size but could have come from coppice or hedgerow (see Morgan, p 194; Brunning and O'Sullivan, p 163), as the beetles appear to have a preference for smaller tree species. Unlike many scolytids this beetle is not restricted to dead or moribund trees but will attack healthy wood.

Most members of the fauna would fit into this scenario without difficulty. The species most out of place appears to be *Bembidion nigricorne* which is found on dry, sandy ground, often with *Calluna*. Only one example of the beetle was recorded, however, and it is probable that its presence was adventitious, possibly having been brought from further upstream in flood debris.

Environmental implications from faunal list 2

It will be seen that 66 beetle taxa which were not recorded in the first list appear in faunal list 2. For the most part, however, these are spread over a number of different sections and samples so that almost all are of isolated occurrences which can be put down to accidents of collection. The majority of the taxa in list 2 have much the same environmental requirements as those of list 1 and of those beetles well represented, as numbers of individuals in list 1 a high proportion occur in many other samples in similar abundance. Thus insects such as *Elmis aenea, Oulimnius troglodytes / tuberculatus, Heterocerus marginatus* and *H. maritimus, Megasternum*

obscurum, Hydrobius fuscipes, Ochthebius minimus, Platystethus cornutus / degener, Anotylus rugosus and *A. sculpturatus* and *Phyllopertha horticola* are found in many samples from all sections in equivalent numbers to list 1.

From this it would seem that differences in the environment represented by the various sections and layers within them are in detail only. The most striking of these is the appearance in Phase VI to Phase VII samples from Area A (Column 1) and Area E (Column 5) of the chrysomelid *Donacia clavipes*. This species is principally associated with the reed *Phragmites* so presumably this plant was abundant at the sides of the water in the samples in which the beetles were found. The conditions under which it grows, however, do not differ significantly from those suggested by the host plants of the *Donacia* species recorded in list 1.

The only other insect widely distributed through the list 2 samples but absent from list 1 is the Earwig. These, represented only by pincers, could not be identified further but there is a strong presumption, based chiefly on eliminating some of the other species by size, that they belonged to the common earwig, *Forficula auricularia*. What, however, the apparent absence of such a common insect from one group of samples, and its presence in many others signifies, is a mystery.

Particularly amongst the Carabidae there is a slightly better representation of species of dry open ground, with *Bembidion lampros, B. properans, B. quadrimaculatus* and *Metabletus foveatus* occurring in Phase VI/VII and VII. Again, though, these are all single occurrences and probably, as before, can be construed as oddments scoured from further upstream, perhaps by floodwater.

One further species seems noteworthy here, the colydiid *Colydium elongatum* from Phase V–VI. This is the only species other than *Scolytus rugulosus* which is dependent on trees. Only a single specimen was recorded and as the beetle lives in the burrows of various scolytid species it probably got to the site with *Scolytus rugulosus* in imported timber.

All this points to a considerable degree of consistency between the faunas recorded from the different sections and horizons within them, suggesting a local environment which changed very little over the time of deposition of these deposits.

The Wood Assemblage

Introduction

During the course of the excavations, a total of 4688 individual wood numbers were assigned to wooden items ranging from small fragments of poorly preserved roundwood just large enough to be labelled with a piece of Dymo-tape, to substantial oak piles over 3m in length. Approximately 10% of this material, mostly poorly preserved roundwood fragments or partially exposed items, was neither lifted nor sampled. In rare instances, wood items were assigned duplicate numbers or single numbers were given to concentrations of woodchips. An attempt has been made to rationalise these discrepancies where they have a bearing on the variety of specialist studies which have assessed the waterlogged wood assemblage.

Strategies for the recording, sampling and analysis of wood evolved during the fieldwork phase of the project in response to interim results from specialists and in an attempt to maximise the efficiency of the process of recovery. The task of recording the wood *in situ* was essentially a standard piece of archaeological recording although the stratigraphic removal of the surrounding, often consolidated, fills of silty clays without causing undue damage to the denser scatters of wood was a continual challenge. Maintaining the wood in good condition during the recording process also required considerable care, especially with deeply driven timbers which needed to be protected while surrounding deposits and artefactual spreads were excavated. Frequent spraying with clean water was complemented by the use of plastic covers and/or clingfilm barriers to reduce evaporation.

In the first three years of excavation, no wood specialist was present on site and the vast majority of lifted material was transferred to temporary storage for subsequent study. The wood retained from this period was later assessed by Caroline Earwood, and sampled and analysed by Richard Brunning and Aidan O'Sullivan. In the later seasons of excavation, with one or other of the latter wood specialists present, details of the wood were recorded on site and relevant samples taken before the material was discarded unless additional information (eg toolmark evidence) required recording in more controlled conditions, or material was to be retained for conservation. This change in recording procedures considerably quickened the process and allowed the wood specialists a more intimate knowledge of the contexts from which the material was derived. Storage in covered, water-filled tanks maintained the preservation of the wood once off site.

Basic information was recorded on Wood Record Sheets designed specifically for the Caldicot excavations. Some of the finer attributes recorded were measured by using finely graduated callipers or a gridded template designed for that feature. Other attributes were classified as formal types according to narrowly defined guidelines which will be described in the relevant specialist sections. A representative selection of the worked ends and timbers was also drawn and photographed for archive and publication purposes. A suite of databases was developed to assist in the management of the stored wood assemblage, to provide specialists with relevant site data, and to store specialist results.

Sampling strategies

The strategy for wood identifications aimed at a 100% sampling policy where wood structure appeared sufficiently well-preserved. Mature oak (*Quercus* spp.) was often identified by eye. A total of 4804 identifications of waterlogged wood were made. Of these, a small proportion were partially charred. These are considered separately within Su Johnson's report. In addition, charcoal was occasionally collected from deposits where it was profuse and well-preserved. Samples from two such contexts have been identified for comparative purposes.

The strategy for the collection of ring-count samples evolved during the life span of the project. From the outset, samples were only collected from unconverted roundwood. Splitwood was often too compressed to permit reliable ring-counting. More substantial timbers rarely retain a complete record of wood growth and, if ring-porous, were examined during technological or dendrochronological studies. In the 1991 excavations, tree-ring samples were taken from all numbered pieces of roundwood, but in the next year this was reduced to sampling only from discrete structural groupings.

All items of oak or ash were critically examined for their suitability for dendrochronological analysis. It should perhaps be stressed that, whilst a minimum of fifty annual rings need to be present for dating purposes, small woodchips often proved more productive than large structural timbers. Items selected for conservation which also had sufficient rings for dating purposes were carefully sampled with narrow kerf saws and, following analysis, the cross-sections were delivered to the conservation laboratory to rejoin their parent timbers. The limited damage to the timbers involved was seen as acceptable given their enhanced display potential as a result of having been (in most cases) accurately dated. The dendrochronological analysis provides complementary absolute dating to the radiocarbon results and data on the nature of the parent timber trees being exploited which complements the results of tree-ring counts on the less mature roundwood studied by Morgan.

Taphonomic considerations

Given the potential for post-depositional transport of wood within a fluvial environment, the processes involved in the formation of the wood assemblage need critical assessment before the results of specialist studies can be interpreted. Sedimentological and environmental studies of contemporary channel conditions suggest that flow rates were generally low, and that both the soft riverbed and vegetation within the channel would have tended to mitigate against long distance transport. The Phase II assemblage is dominated by driven piles forming the cross-channel structure, 472. Clearly these remained more or less *in situ* apart from piles which may have been washed out by particularly strong channel flow during episodes of channel incision. The situation is less straightforward in Phase III, with much of the wood forming part of more mixed spreads of debris lying on the contemporary riverbed. Clusters of ash woodworking chips encountered in areas B and C, and the concentration of yew stems in Area E imply very limited fluvial transport. The preservation of wood surfaces were generally very good arguing against significant transport and the presence of emergent vegetation within the channel at this time would have acted as a 'trap' for material which had entered the channel, even if it floated for a period. On the other hand, channel migration is defined by a succession of erosive interfaces which point to downcutting with resultant removal of parts of the artefactual content of the riverbed, along with the sediment into which it had settled. Therefore the possibility that some of the wood assemblage dumped into the channel could have subsequently been eroded out by channel incision cannot be dismissed. This also raises the prospect of wood being washed down to the site from upstream. Such possibilities should not be over-stressed: the infill of these channels are generally of very fine particle size, high in organic content in the basal contexts where the wood is concentrated, and the channel lies in the mature part of the Nedern's catchment (see Taylor p 00). Stratigraphic analysis of the dense wood spreads excavated in areas A and C indicate that the wood assemblages obey the law of superposition (Harris 1989, 30), arguing for orderly deposition and limited subsequent disturbance.

In Phases VI–VII when flow rates could arguably be slightly higher, much of the wood was partially held on the river bed by stones, and emergent vegetation was still abundant. Clearly driven uprights associated with structures 9014 and 22441 had not undergone major transport. Examination of the species distribution and age range of clearly cut

roundwood, and roundwood with no evidence for working from this phase, revealed no significant variation. It is therefore concluded that the vast majority of the wood recovered from the excavations had been deposited by human activity and had undergone relatively little fluvial transport. Even the small number of beaver-chewed pieces could have been collected and subsequently discarded by human populations.

Wood identification
Su Johnson

The cell structure of all the identification samples was examined in three planes under a high power microscope and identified using reference texts (eg Schweingruber 1978) and reference slides.

The preservation of the waterlogged wood was generally very good and obtaining suitable sections for identification presented few problems. There was, however, a small proportion of samples which could not be identified because the cell structure had either deteriorated too far or had been obscured by fungal hyphae.

The majority of the samples could be identified to species level, either anatomically or because only one species of a genus was likely to have been present in the area at the time (ie they were native species). Identification has been taken only as far as genus in cases where there is more than one native species and the cell structure of the wood is not sufficiently different to separate them (eg *Quercus* spp.). Other identifications include more than one genus, again because similarities in the wood structure prevent closer identification (see Pomoideae and *Salix / Populus* below).

A particular problem was encountered with one group of samples where the identification could only be narrowed down to two genera with very similar cell structure – *Cornus* and *Viburnum*. Definite examples of both have been found in the Caldicot samples, but several samples had features which could place them in either genus. The problem could not be resolved using the standard texts and reference material, and use of the GUESS database (Wheeler and LaPasha 1986; Wheeler *et al* 1986) also failed to help. Six samples were therefore submitted to the Royal Botanic Gardens, Kew, with the result that all but one (which remains unidentified) were considered to be *Cornus* (Gasson pers comm).

Bark

Samples consisting only of bark could not be identified since the cell structure of the bark of different species is very similar. Crystals of calcium compounds which may be present in bark and can help with identification were not present in the Caldicot samples.

Unidentified samples

A small proportion of the samples in this category were not identifiable for the reasons outlined above; the remainder were not sampled for identification.

Species present

Acer campestre (field maple): a small tree, found in woods and scrub on a range of fertile soils. May be coppiced.

Alnus glutinosa (L.) (alder): common in marshy places and by streams. In Wales, it also occurs in well-drained woods (Hyde and Harrison 1977,110). May be coppiced.

Betula spp. (birch): both *B. pendula* (silver birch) and *B. pubescens* (downy birch) are native and the wood of the two species cannot be separated. Both are small trees which occur in woods and colonise open ground on all types of soil.

Cornus sanguinea (dogwood): a shrub found in woods and scrub, especially on calcareous soil.

Corylus avellana (hazel): a shrub or small tree, which is often an important part of the understorey of oakwoods. May be coppiced.

Euonymus europaeus (spindle tree): a shrub or small tree found in woods and scrub especially on calcareous soils.

Fraxinus excelsior (ash): a light-demanding tree, found in woods on a wide range of soils, sometimes forming woods with oak (Hyde and Harrison 1977,149). May be coppiced.

Hedera helix (ivy): an evergreen woody climber occurring in woods on most soils.

Ilex aquifolium (holly): a small evergreen tree, tolerant of shade and common in the understorey of oakwoods in Wales on a variety of soil types (Hyde and Harrison 1977,79).

Ligustrum vulgare (common privet): a semi-evergreen shrub which forms thickets in woods and scrub, especially on calcareous soils.

Lonicera periclymenum (honeysuckle): a woody climber which in woodland often twines around saplings and young trees.

Pomoideae: this is a group of trees and shrubs from the Rosaceae family including *Malus sylvestris* (crab apple), *Crataegus* spp. (hawthorn) and *Sorbus* spp.(rowan, whitebeam and service tree). It is not possible to separate these species by microscopic examination of their wood, but it seems likely, given the plant macrofossil evidence (Caseldine, p 83) and soil conditions in the area, that many of the Caldicot samples are *Crataegus*.

Prunus spp.: wood of the genus *Prunus* can be difficult to identify to species. Three species are present and samples which could not be definitely assigned to one of these have been grouped together as *Prunus* spp.

Prunus avium (wild cherry): a small tree found in woods and copses on all soils, but prefers calcareous soils.

Prunus padus (bird cherry): a shrub or small tree, occurring in woods and scrub.

Prunus spinosa (blackthorn or sloe): a thorny shrub found in woods and scrub on all soil types. In a woodland situation it is more likely to occur in clearings and at the woodland edges (Condry 1974, 42), and it can form dense thickets.

Quercus spp.: both *Q. robur* (pedunculate oak) and *Q. petraea* (sessile oak) are native in Wales and their wood cannot be separated microscopically. In semi-natural woodland, pedunculate oak is usually found in lowland woods and sessile oak in the upland woods (Hyde and Harrison 1977, 121). May be coppiced.

Rhamnus cathartica (purging buckthorn): a thorny shrub occurring in woods and scrub on calcareous soils and also on peat.

Rosa spp. (wild roses): several species of often thorny scrambling or trailing shrubs which can not be separated on the basis of their wood.

Salix spp. (willows and sallows): trees and shrubs, of which at least 13 species could be native to Wales (Hyde and Harrison 1977, 134), including *Salix caprea* (goat willow, sallow) and *Salix fragilis* (crack willow). Sallows are shade-tolerant and occur in woodland; other willows are more characteristic of wet woods and streamsides. May be coppiced or pollarded.

Salix/Populus spp: *Populus tremula* (aspen) and *P. nigra* (black poplar) are both probably native in Wales. *P. tremula* occurs in woods, especially on poorer soils, *P. nigra* occurs in wet woods and by streams. The structure of its wood is, however, very difficult to separate from that of *Salix* spp. and in the samples from Caldicot, the identification was not certain.

Sambucus nigra (elder): a shrub or small tree occurring in woods and scrub. It is also characteristic of disturbed, nitrogen rich soil and occurs as a 'weed' around human habitation (Clapham 1975, 35).

Taxus baccata (yew): an evergreen tree occurring in woods and scrub especially on chalk and limestone where it may be found on cliff faces and edges. It also occurs locally on acid sandstone.

Tilia spp. (limes): *T. platyphyllos* Scop. (large leaved lime) and *T. cordata* Miller (small leaved lime) are both native and cannot be separated by their wood structure. Both are trees preferring fertile, especially calcareous, soils.

Ulmus spp. (elms): *U. procera* Salisb. (English elm) and *U. glabra* Hudson (wych elm) are both native and cannot be separated by their wood structure. *U. glabra* occurs in damp woods particularly on limestone. *U. procera* is not generally found in woodlands today.

Viburnum spp.: there are two species which are not separable by their wood structure.

Viburnum opulus (Guelder rose): a shrub found in scrub and woods on damp soils.

Viburnum lantana (wayfaring tree): a shrub of scrub and woodland, especially the woodland edge on calcareous soils.

Viscum album (mistletoe): a parasitic plant occur-

Table 22 Waterlogged wood identifications

Phase	II	III	IV	v	VI	VI/VII	VII	Un-phased	Total
Acer campestre L.			1			4	3	1	9
Alnus glutinosa (L.) Gaertner	1	21	1	3	61	45	46	2	180
Betula spp.						1	1		2
Cornus sanguinea L.	1	15		1	12	12	10		51
Corylus avellana L.	62	414	25	48	745	550	436	26	2306
Euonymus europaeus L.		1			5	5			11
Fraxinus excelsior L.		89	1	4	61	122	99	2	378
Hedera helix L.		1			2				3
Ilex aquifolium L.						2			2
Ligustrum vulgare L.		4			2	1	2		9
Lonicera periclymenum L.						1			1
Pomoideae	1	35	8	3	50	54	13	1	165
Prunus avium (L.) L.					4				4
Prunus padus L.					1				1
Prunus spp.	2	36	6	1	13	10	3	4	75
Prunus spinosa L.		65	6	9	38	42	7	4	171
Quercus spp.	1	27	5	2	98	104	73	9	319
Rhamnus cathartica L.		2			1	1			4
Rosa spp.		1				3			4
Salix spp.	1	14			4	5	7	1	32
Salix/Populus		1		1	1	1			4
Sambucus nigra L.		10			9	2		2	23
Taxus baccata L.		96			1	3	1		101
Tilia spp.		1			8	4	10		23
Ulmus spp.		1				6	1		8
Viburnum spp.					2	1			3
Viscum album L.					1				1
Bark		7	1	3	24	38	24	1	98
Unidentified	5	96	2	6	209	246	221	31	816
TOTAL	74	937	56	81	1352	1263	957	84	4804

ring on a variety of usually deciduous trees, commonly on crab apple, hawthorn etc.

Waterlogged wood
(Table 22, Fig 92)

Twenty-six species/types are present in the waterlogged wood samples from Caldicot most of which are also represented in either the plant macrofossils or the pollen record (see Caseldine, p 83). By far the most commonly occurring was *Corylus* which accounted for around 48% of the assemblage. *Fraxinus* and *Quercus*, the next two most common, only account for around 8% and 6.5% respectively and

Pomoideae, *Prunus spinosa* and *Prunus* spp. together make up a further 8.5%. Fourteen of the 26 species occurred in less than ten samples.

Phases II, IV and V produced small assemblages. Each had fewer than ten species present, *Corylus* being the most common in each phase. In Phase II, there were only one or two examples of other species. In Phases IV and V, Pomoideae and *Prunus spinosa/Prunus* spp. as a group were well represented with only a few occurrences of other species.

The larger assemblages from Phases III, VI, VI/VII and VII had a wider range of species present (15–23 species). Each Phase was dominated by *Corylus*, followed by a group of species which, though much less frequent than *Corylus*, were generally well

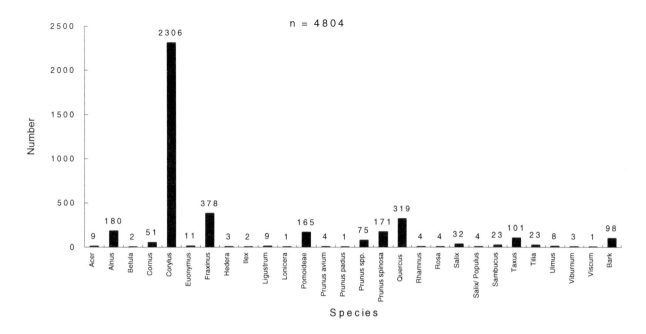

Fig 92   Waterlogged wood identifications: all phases

Table 23   Charred wood identifications

Phase	II	III	IV	V	VI	VI/VII	VII	Un-phased	Total
Alnus glutinosa (L.) Gaertner	1				6		1	1	9
Corylus avellana L.		9		1	13	10	2	1	36
Euonymus europaeus L.					1				1
Fraxinus excelsior L.					1	1	3		5
Pomoideae		1				3	1		5
Prunus spp.							1	1	2
Prunus spinosa L.		1		1	3	2			7
Quercus spp.					4	3	1		8
Salix spp.						1			1
Salix/Populus					1				1
Sambucus nigra L.					1				1
Bark					6	7	6		19
Unidentified		2			1		1		4
TOTAL	1	13	0	2	37	27	16	3	99

represented in each phase, though in slightly varying proportions. This group consists of *Fraxinus, Quercus,* Pomoideae and *Prunus spinosa/Prunus* spp, and *Alnus.* In Phase VII, however, the 'scrub' species *Prunus spinosa/Prunus* spp and Pomoideae became markedly less frequent.

In Phase III *Taxus* was very well represented (96 samples), which all came from a single roundwood spread.

The Charred Wood (Table 23)

The charred wood assemblage was a small subset of the waterlogged wood assemblage (99 samples). The range of species present was much smaller (ten species), but the general pattern was similar to that seen in the waterlogged wood samples (Fig 93). *Corylus* is not so obviously dominant (36%) and the 'scrub' Pomoideae and *Prunus* spp. are relatively

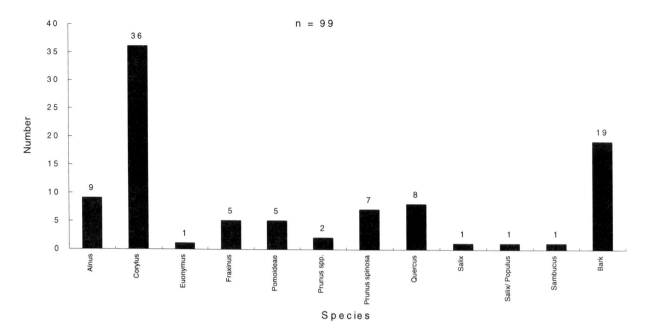

n = 99

Fig 93   Charred wood identifications: all phases

Table 24   Charcoal identifications

Phase	VI	VI/VII	
Context	22542	22440	Total
Alnus glutinosa (L.) Gaertner	6	3	9
Betula spp.	1		1
Corylus avellana L.	37	36	73
Fraxinus excelsior L.	1	1	2
Ilex aquifolium L.		1	1
Pomoideae	3	1	4
Prunus spp.		1	1
Quercus spp.	1	5	6
Salix spp.	1	1	2
Tilia *spp.*		1	1
TOTAL	50	50	100

more common than in the waterlogged samples (*c*14%).

In Phase VII *Fraxinus* was the most commonly occurring species, although the charred assemblage from this phase was very small and this pattern is not reflected in the larger waterlogged assemblage.

The Charcoal
(Table 24)

Identifications were carried out on two samples, one from Phase VI, the other from Phase VI/VII. Fifty fragments were selected at random from each sample. Ten species were present, seven in Phase VI and nine in Phase VI/VII. *Corylus* accounted for over 70% in both samples.

Discussion

The wide range of species present in the Caldicot assemblage includes large trees, understorey trees and shrubs, shrubs of clearings, scrub and the woodland edge, climbers and parasites. The assemblage was overwhelmingly dominated by *Corylus* which was then followed by a group of species (*Quercus, Fraxinus,* Pomoideae and *Prunus spinosa/Prunus* spp and *Alnus)* which, although occurring in differing proportions, were almost always among the five or six most common species in each phase. Phase III was unusual in that, excluding *Corylus,* the most frequent species was *Taxus,* which occurred rarely in other phases. This reflects the recovery of a concentration of yew roundwood (see palaeochannel group E.3.1, p 30).

It is difficult to say how much the species composition of the Caldicot wood assemblage reflects the composition of the local woodland. The species list for Caldicot is, in fact, very similar to species lists for oak woodland (Condry 1974, 44) and oakwood on baserich soil (Tansley 1968, 96), and this is supported by the pollen evidence (Caseldine p 183). However, types of woodland community can vary over a relatively small area (Rackham 1980, 21) and it is possible that more than one type of woodland community is represented in any one phase (see also Caseldine p 00). It is also possible that the Caldicot assemblage reflects only part of the woodland community, since some form of selection, whether for size and/or purpose or for convenience may well have taken place. Wood may have been obtained from different woodland sources at different times, but the tree ring (Morgan p 194) and woodland management evidence (Brunning and O'Sullivan, below) does suggest repeated exploitation of some area(s).

Many of the species present prefer reasonably well drained conditions which, together with the relatively small numbers of *Alnus* and *Salix,* suggests that little of the wood was derived from a wetland or streamside location. It is more likely that most was obtained from woodland growing on higher ground in the area rather than the low-lying land close to the site. Much of it probably grew on the gravels and sandstone near to the site, but given that several species have a preference for calcareous soils, some may well have come from the limestone ridge a little further away.

Wood species selection and woodworking techniques
Richard Brunning and Aidan O'Sullivan

Introduction

Wood species, size and quality

Wood is not a homogenous raw material, but has physical and chemical properties which depend variously on its species, age, size, rate of growth and the local conditions experienced by the growing tree. There can also be significant differences between the wood from different parts of the tree itself. It is well-known that heartwood is more resistant to rot and more difficult to cut than sapwood. Reaction wood and root buttresses provide very dense, hardy raw material, whilst the pliable fibres of bark and bast can be used for textiles or containers. Selection involves the recognition of these differences by the craftsman, leading to the deliberate choice of the species which has the properties that are best suited to the task to be carried out. There is also the possibility that some trees acquired a symbolic meaning which would have led to their wood being used for certain 'ritual' tasks. It needs to be also stated that the presence of differing species in a structure can be an outcome of a relatively casual collection of any available trees. The large scale sampling for identification and tree ring analysis was designed to permit analysis of such factors.

The diameters of the trunks uncovered were measured and in all examples, the maximum cross-sectional dimension is the figure presented. In the case of cleft wood, the measurements taken are maximum width and thickness. The grain of the trunk was subjectively graded from '1' (very knotty) to '5' (very straight). The presence of side branches were also noted and quantified.

Whole roundwood and conversion types

The material can be divided between wood that was used in the round (whole roundwood) and that which was cleft. Split wood can be categorised on the basis of conversion method (in prehistory this was always by cleaving or hewing) and conversion type (the cross-section produced in relation to the original trunk). The initial methods of splitting trunks usually involved hammering wooden or metal wedges into the trunk, preferably along planes of weakness to produce a half-split log. Thereafter this could be halved again to produce a quarter-split, and split again to a smaller radial section. Cleaving across the planes of weakness also occurred producing tangential or intermediate forms. These types were recorded by examining the growth patterns exhibited in the end-grain of the Caldicot timbers.

Point type and cutting angle

The presentation of wood technology studies in archaeology has tended to be somewhat anecdotal, involving textual description supported by illustrations of 'interesting' material. However, it is being increasingly recognised that pieces of worked wood can be assigned formal attributes and analysed as large databases. Such techniques are not considered unusual by archaeologists in the analysis of lithic artefacts and debitage, which have similarities of origin to worked wood assemblages.

The felling, de-branching, bucking (cross-cutting) and sharpening of trunks ultimately lead, deliberately or not, to the production of worked-ends or points. It is often difficult to distinguish between the worked ends produced by sharpening and those produced by felling, although there are some features such as jagged 'slovens' or wide 'kerfs' which can suggest felling techniques. The shape of the points will be classified in this report according to certain established types (Coles and Orme 1985; O'Sullivan 1991). These point types indicate the form of point produced, and indirectly both the style of working and the amount of wood removed during the process. Chisel-ends are cut down one side of the stem only, with the opposing side of the trunk remaining intact. The worked area may be uniformly in one plane or as a chisel-variant with two closely adjacent worked faces. Wedge-ends are cut on opposing sides of the trunk, either directly opposite or as in the case of Wedge Variants on almost adjacent faces. Pencil-ends show the most amount of working, being cut on three or more faces completely around the diameter of the trunk.

The 'cutting angle' denotes the angle of the worked surface to the length of the stem. However a variety of angles can be found on a single piece, so both the minimum and maximum cutting angles were recorded to present the cutting angle range. The means of measuring the angles was by laying the point against a perspex template, graduated into intervals of degrees. A very shallow cutting angle (0–20 degrees) indicates a concern for a sharp point, as well as the ability of the blade to cut into the wood successfully when wielded at steep trajectories. A thin, flat and very sharp blade is required to make successful blows at angles under 10 degrees. Medium to straight cutting angles at timber ends or inside mortises usually result in jam curves, a useful feature of toolmarks to be discussed below. Cutting angles can be referred to in numerical values or as categories. These are 0–20 degrees (very shallow), 21–40 degrees (shallow), 41–60 degrees (medium), 61–80 degrees (steep) and finally 81–90 degrees (straight).

Toolmarks; size and shape

The worked surfaces of a point are composed of one or more individual facets or toolmarks. These can vary in size as successive blows of an axe remove or truncate the traces left by previous blows. The number of facets on each worked surface thus bears little relationship to the number of strokes made, with 50 axe-strokes possibly only resulting in five or six surviving facets, as has been clearly indicated by experimental work (Coles and Orme 1985, 27). The number of facets on each piece is thus not considered an especially useful area of analysis, although it does reflect the greater preparation needed on larger trunks.

The actual shape and size of these facets are likely to be much more informative about the nature of the blade used. Facets can be 'flat', 'slightly concave' or 'concave' depending on the section across the width of the facet. The size of the facets were recorded by means of a callipers graduated to 0.1 cm. The largest facet on each worked end was selected for measurement. The dimensions recorded were the length and width. The length was measured parallel to the direction of the axe blow, whilst the facet width was measured at right angles to this axis.

Jam curves and blade signatures

Jam curves are one of the most informative features to be found on worked ends. They occur when the blade edge becomes briefly embedded in the wood. Subsequent blows may not remove this toolmark feature, leaving a ridge which precisely mirrors the curve of the cutting edge used (O'Sullivan 1991). Jam curves may be concave to straight in plan and their widths can indicate the size and shape of the edge used. These were recorded by placing clear film over the worked surface, outlining the ridge or jam curve with a fine-nibbed marker.

Some of the worked ends were scarred along the length of the individual facets by ridges, grooves and slight striations. These scars derive from faults on the blade edges, the notch leaving a corresponding ridge on the surface of the wood which is termed a 'blade signature'. There are however several problems with blade signatures. When a tool-edge is re-sharpened, fresh nicks and chips are taken from the edge by the grinding stone, while the blemishes that were previously present are polished away and replaced. Thus each re-sharpening would result in a different set of signatures being produced by the same axe on the surface of the wood. Furthermore when the axe is wielded at slightly different angles, a variation probably results in the type of signature produced. On the basis of these potential variables, it would seem that estimations on the number of tools used on the basis of signatures have a fair potential for error.

The Caldicot wood assemblage

Introduction

The wood assemblage recorded in the Caldicot excavations amounts to 4804 pieces of prehistoric wood comprising waterlogged, and waterlogged and charred wood, but excluding charcoal; a usefully large sample, even by wetlands excavation standards. Of that total, 1365 pieces showed evidence of alteration from their natural state. Of that figure, 524 pieces had been split but displayed no further signs of working. The vast majority of these were small items which served no apparent function, and they are likely to have split as a result of natural processes of erosion and decay, and in a small number of cases due to damage during excavation.

This leaves 851 pieces which had unquestionably been worked by humans. This represents almost 18% of the total. This percentage is an underestimate for

Table 25 Most common wood species by wood category: Phase II

Species	Roundwood (no working observed)	Worked roundwood	Splitwood (no observed working)	Worked splitwood	Working debris	Timber	Totals
Hazel	15	43	2	1	1	0	62
Ash	0	0	0	0	0	0	0
Oak	1	0	0	0	0	0	1
Blackthorn	2	0	0	0	0	0	2
Alder	0	0	0	0	1	0	1
Hawthorn	1	0	0	0	0	0	1
Subtotals	19	43	2	1	2	0	67

several reasons. Some wood was numbered but never cleaned or lifted so traces of working may not have been noticed. Because of the relative narrowness of the excavation trenches a significant number of roundwood pieces entered a baulk at one or both ends and therefore the presence of a cut terminal could not have been noted. The same applies to a small number of inclined pieces where the bottom end was not recovered. Roughly 14% of the wood recovered in the 1991–2 excavations was in fact only partially lifted, with a proportion of the piece remaining *in situ*. As the woodworking information for much of the worked assemblage consisted simply of a cut end, this may have resulted in a significant bias. Some of the smaller pieces of wood were also in such poor condition that vestigial traces of working may not have been apparent. In addition the excavated bark fragments may have become detached as a result of purely natural processes, but could also represent waste from the sharpening of stakes or from the early stages of timber preparation.

The material displaying signs of working can be divided into timber, woodworking debris, cut roundwood, and split wood that has also been cut. The *timber* category consists of split planks many of which had notches or mortise holes. The *debris* was the by-product of sharpening stakes and preparing and finishing timber. The boundary of this category is slightly subjective as a large offcut may resemble items categorised as split wood or even the smallest timbers. The *cut roundwood* includes numerous stakes but also a larger proportion of branches and small trunks that have been cut at one, or several, ends. The small numbers of *split and cut wood* that are not classified as timber are almost all stakes that have been cleft to a desired size, or shape. All these categories will be discussed further after the wood assemblage has been analysed by phase, as will the small numbers of charred wood and beaver-gnawed wood. The results of the species identifications can be seen in detail in the section on wood and charcoal identification (see Johnson, p 158). The influence of species in timber selection is discussed below.

Description of the wood by phase

Introduction

The following is an examination of patterns of woodworking within the site's chronological framework. That chronology is broken down into the phases detailed in the introduction. The main groupings of structural wood are then considered in more detail. For the six most commonly encountered tree species a table for each phase shows their breakdown into the categories described above.

Phase II

Virtually all the wood from this phase (Table 25) was derived from context 472, which mainly consisted of the remains of a double row of upright stakes, and which is described more fully as a structure below.

Phase III

Phase III was complex, involving several channels and spreads of wood. The most important discovery was the boat strake 6001, the context and technology of which is described elsewhere (Nayling p 27, McGrail p 210). The phase produced 937 recorded pieces of wood of which 93 were derived from a concentration of cut and bent yew twigs (24427) which is described as a separate group below.

The worked wood ranged in size, measuring between 17–96mm in diameter but typically being 20–40mm in diameter. There was remarkable uniformity in the types of worked points. Most were chisel-ends or basic wedge-ends formed by a few blows at medium angles. This seems to reflect rapid felling or trimming techniques with the points having no apparent function in the deposits. The species identification evidence suggests that this wood is derived from the clearance of scrub woodland mainly composed of hazel and blackthorn (Table 26). The long, relatively branch-free morphology of

Table 26 Most common wood species by wood category: Phase III

Species	Roundwood (no working observed)	Worked roundwood	Splitwood (no observed working)	Worked splitwood	Working debris	Timber	Totals
Hazel	343	52	13	2	2	0	414
Ash	7	0	2	1	78	1	22
Oak	9	0	2	2	8	5	27
Blackthorn	88	11	0	1	0	0	101
Alder	13	1	1	0	4	2	21
Hawthorn	29	4	1	0	0	0	35
Subtotals	489	68	19	6	92	8	620

Table 27 Most common wood species by wood category: Phase IV

Species	Roundwood (no working observed)	Worked roundwood	Splitwood (no observed working)	Worked splitwood	Working debris	Timber	Totals
Hazel	18	1	2	0	4	0	25
Ash	0	0	0	0	1	0	1
Oak	3	1	0	0	1	0	5
Blackthorn	10	1	0	0	1	0	12
Alder	1	0	0	0	0	0	1
Hawthorn	8	0	0	0	0	0	8
Subtotals	40	3	2	0	7	0	52

much of the hazel wood suggests the woodland source may also have had a significant coppiced component and three characteristic coppiced heels have been found from this phase, two of them being hazel. Some very knotty narrow roundwood with several surviving side branches did occur, however, much of it identified as blackthorn.

Three beaver-chewed branches (two of hazel and one of hawthorn) occurred in this phase: potentially significant in that beaver tree-felling and flooding activities can often create adventitious coppiced woodland (see below). Seven pieces of partially charred roundwood were excavated from this phase of which all the identified samples were hazel.

With the exception of the boat strake, there were no large timbers from this phase and no structural wood. There were 22 pieces of converted wood, all but one of which were under 0.35m long. Eleven were simply small half split fragments of hazel, alder, blackthorn and hawthorn. The remainder were small radial or intermediate split fragments of oak and ash which, together with the woodchips, provide possible evidence for other woodworking activities. There were 92 pieces of working debris mostly of ash (78 pieces) and oak (8 pieces). The ash woodchips were predominantly radial as opposed to tangentials, suggesting that timbers of that species were being hewn and finished nearby. Two densely clustered groups of ash woodchips support the hypothesis that such working is taking place on the site, but the

timbers produced by this process were not recovered from the excavations.

Phase IV

Phase IV produced 56 pieces of wood for analysis. Only ten of these showed evidence for working and there were no examples of charred pieces. The unworked fragments had a similar species composition to the previous phase with half the identified wood being hazel and the rest mainly blackthorn and hawthorn, with only one or two examples of oak and alder (Table 27). Seven pieces of woodworking debris were recovered between 150mm and 180mm in length, one of which was oak, four hazel, one blackthorn, and one ash. The ash and blackthorn both had tangential cross sections, while the oak was radial. The other three worked items included branches of oak and hawthorn which had been cut at one end, and were 0.18m and 0.38m respectively in length.

Phase V

Phase V produced 81 pieces of wood for analysis, of which 61 showed no signs of working. The majority of the latter were hazel with some blackthorn and very small numbers of ash, oak, alder and hawthorn

Table 28 Most common wood species by wood category: Phase V

Table 28 Most common wood species by wood category: Phase V

Species	Roundwood (no working observed)	Worked roundwood	Splitwood (no observed working)	Worked splitwood	Working debris	Timber	Totals
Hazel	36	8	2	0	2	0	48
Ash	2	0	1	0	1	0	4
Oak	2	0	0	0	0	0	2
Blackthorn	8	1	1	0	0	0	10
Alder	2	0	1	0	0	0	3
Hawthorn	2	0	0	1	0	0	3
Subtotals	52	9	5	1	3	0	70

Table 29 Most common wood species by wood category: Phases VI and VII

Species	Roundwood (no working observed)	Worked roundwood	Splitwood (no observed working)	Worked splitwood	Working debris	Timber	Totals
Hazel	1218	283	117	37	61	11	1732
Ash	94	14	8	5	137	27	282
Oak	48	27	16	7	112	50	274
Blackthorn	99	6	3	2	3	0	118
Alder	58	10	8	16	53	5	152
Hawthorn	86	18	5	2	4	2	117
Subtotals	1603	358	157	69	370	95	2675

(Table 28). Only eighteen pieces of worked wood were recovered, with a very similar species composition to the unworked material. Two thirds of these pieces consisted of small split fragments between 90mm and 300mm in length, most of which were just half-split except for three radial pieces of blackthorn, hawthorn and hazel, and a piece of ash of intermediate cross section.

Five pieces had been cut at one end, the two smallest (135mm and 290mm in length) exhibiting simple chisel ends. The other three, all of which were hazel, were much longer being between 455mm and 510mm in length, and were all cut to a pencil point with many surviving facets at shallow cutting angles of between 5–8 degrees. The piece with the largest diameter had 28 surviving facets, and in general much more effort was taken in forming these three points, than was the case with the pointed wood from this and other phases which are tentatively interpreted as being non-functional scrub clearance waste. The diameters of these three pieces (35mm, 75mm and 85mm) would not necessarily demand such attention and the point formation technique is generally the same as that used for the hazel poles at the south-west end of structure 472 (group 1) in Phase II.

Phases VI and VII

Roughly three quarters of the excavated wood assemblage from Caldicot is derived from these phases. The poor stratigraphic separation of some of the material from Phase VI/VII, and limited evidence for little absolute chronological separation of Phases VI and VII have encouraged analysis of the wood assemblages from these phases as a single analytical unit. Many structures occur including a possible bridge or jetty 22441 (see palaeochannel group D.7.1), a rough trackway 473 (see B.7.1) and a stone and timber spread with an associated line of wooden uprights 9014 (see A.6.1). All these will be considered in more detail individually. As in previous phases the wood assemblage is dominated by hazel (roughly 65% of the total) with oak and ash occurring in large numbers (Table 29).

Approximately 60% of the wood from this phase was roundwood which had no traces of working. Another 5% was composed of small split pieces of mainly hazel, which displayed no other signs of working and which could in part be a result of natural decay and erosion. Many different factors, outlined in the introduction, mean that the numbers of worked wood may be underestimated, and the

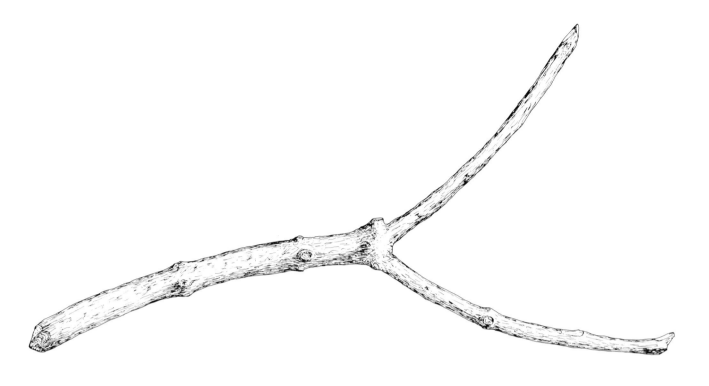

Fig 94   Wood 25809: clearance debris with numerous cut marks and removed side-branches. Scale 1:8

similarity in species distribution between the 'unworked' roundwood and the cut roundwood suggests that they may both be a result of the same process.

The worked roundwood varied in its morphology from trunks which had several side branches still intact to very straight-grained branch-free poles which could have come from coppiced stools. The very branchy material was mainly hazel and blackthorn, and the positions of the surviving axe facets at the base of trunks and on the ends of some side branches suggest that it derived from scrub clearance. One of the largest and best preserved examples of this (25809) is illustrated in Fig 94. The working of the less branchy material was usually limited to simple cutting at one end.

Large numbers of offcuts and smaller woodchips derived from these phases with the majority being oak and ash, with smaller numbers of hazel and alder. Many of these pieces were probably associated with the building of the structures excavated from these phases. The sizes and cross-sections of the woodworking debris support this possibility as many of them were radials which may have been produced from the hewing of radially split planks. Some of the tangential fragments may have come from the formation of mortise holes but this is impossible to prove.

Numerous planks and fragments of planks occur in this phase, many of them displaying mortise holes at one or both ends. The conversion of these planks was varied with radial (eg 24837), tangential (eg 7003), and half-split (eg 128:038) forms all represented.

Oak, ash and hazel were used although the hazel example (128:038) was one of the simplest, being half split with the bark and sapwood left on (see Fig 106). Most of the mortises were unused but one ash plank (24837, see Fig 106) had a mortise at each end both of which were pinned with small pieces of roundwood. A small notch existed on the 'inner' edge of this radial plank near one of the mortises but its use is uncertain. It may be a crude joinery feature or could be designed to assist in the transportation of the unfinished timber using ropes for dragging or towing.

Almost all the partially charred fragments of wood from the excavations came from these phases. The species breakdown is shown elsewhere (Johnson p 160). The broad species range may suggest that any available wood was being used for heating, cooking, or industrial purposes very close to the site.

Several pieces of beaver-gnawed wood came from these phases, the significance of which is discussed below.

Major wooden structures

Structure 472 (Phase II, Area C, palaeochannel group C.2.1)

This structure was a double row of tightly spaced posts, driven into the clays at the edge of a steeply sided estuarine channel which had been infilled with inorganic silty sediments. It can variously be interpreted as the structural elements of a fish-trap or

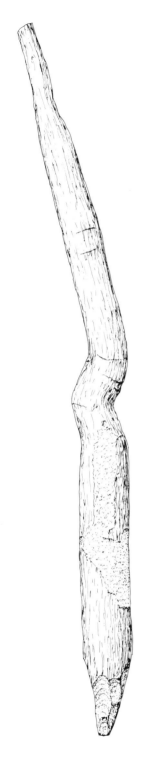

Fig 95 Wood 25752: willow stake with pencil point and trimmed? top. Interpreted as a back-brace in structure 472. Scale 1:8

waterfront. Fifty one pieces of wood were recorded from this context although not all of these were part of the structure itself. All the identified wood was hazel with only two exceptions: two sloping piles tentatively interpreted as possible back-bracing by the excavator (see Nayling p 23 and Fig 95). The wood was very well-preserved at the lower ends, with a range of high-quality working evidence.

No attempt had been made to split these round-

wood trunks and the bark was left intact on the outer surfaces. There seems also to have been a deliberate choice of straight, branch-free roundwood for this post structure, with only the occasional gnarled or branched trunk present. The quality of this roundwood can best be illustrated by a quantification of the 'knottiness' or frequency of side branches, which was recorded in fifty cases. Forty seven (94%) of these could be classified as being medium to very-straight grained. The roundwood trunks seem also to have been chosen for size, with a range of diameters from 25–79mm, with a mean diameter of 50.4mm. It is more difficult to assess the original lengths of these posts, owing to their truncation but the maximum surviving length was 1.81m.

The best evidence for working from structure 472 comes from the sharpened ends of the posts (Fig 96). When this evidence was analysed, there was an unexpected indication of a division of the assemblage into two different 'stylistic' groups. The first group comprised of posts where the worked end had been cut at a steep angle of between 15 and 40 degrees leaving short facets. Chisel-ends and simple wedge-ends had thus been cut rapidly, leaving few individual facets. The second group of posts had, in contrast, been axed with more care, each having a facet with a cutting angle of less than 11 degrees and not more than 30 degrees. The style of worked point produced in this group was predominantly the pencil-end, with more facets surviving on the worked surface. There were very few chisel-ends, while of the seven wedge-ends, five were of the 'wedge variant' type. This type is effectively a pencil-end leaving almost no unworked surface on the wood. The distinction between these styles of point production has a spatial dimension in the structure. The group with shallowly-cut facets is concentrated in the south-west (cf Group 1, Nayling p 22 and Morgan p 195). The group with steeply-cut facets was located in the north-east of the structure, according well with Group 2 as defined in the site description (cf Nayling p 22 and Morgan p 195).

There could be several different reasons for this observed spatial pattern in working styles yet as all the wood bar two was hazel, species is obviously not one of them. The size of the roundwood is perhaps significant as the Group 2 posts were slightly narrower, with an average maximum diameter of 43.6mm. The Group 1 material is larger with an average diameter of 56.8mm. Thus the smaller size of many of the pieces in Group 2 may help to explain the predominance of simple wedge and chisel shaped points, reflecting the fact that smaller poles can be brought to a point with less effort. However, it is unlikely that a difference in average diameter between the two groups of only 13mm could have so influenced the sharpening techniques. There are several relatively thick poles in Group 2 cut with steeply angled blows, while similar sized poles from Group 1 were in contrast brought to a more tapering point with shallower cutting angles.

The toolmarks on the worked ends were generally

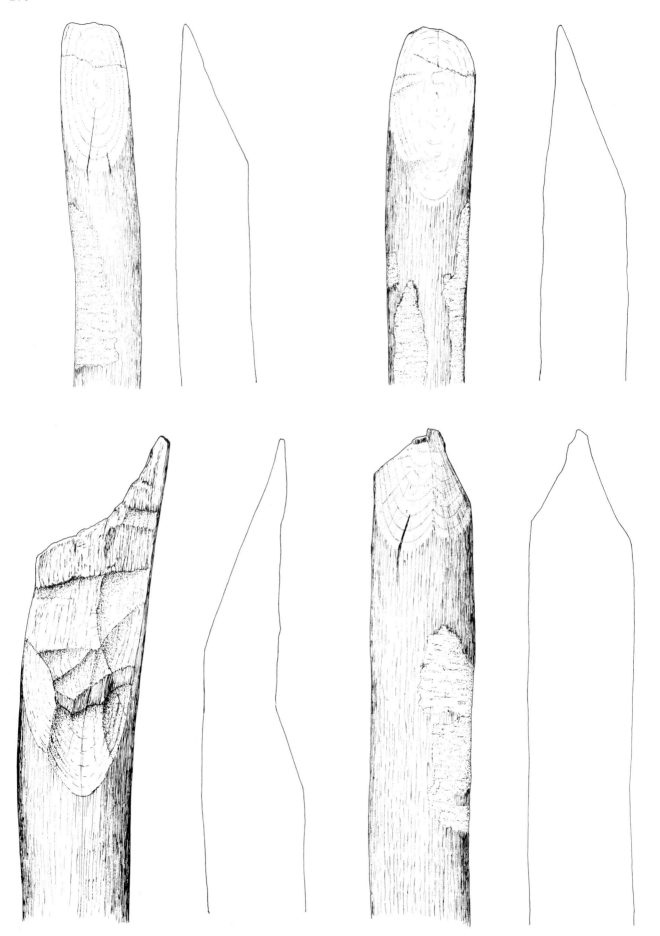

Fig 96   Structure 472: variations in point type. Clockwise from top left: 25885, 25878, 25892, 25877. Scale 1:2

Table 30 Most common wood species by wood category: structure 9014

Species	Roundwood (no working observed)	Worked roundwood	Splitwood (no observed working)	Worked splitwood	Working debris	Timber	Totals
Hazel	288	63	31	7	12	5	406
Ash	28	3	1	1	13	5	53
Oak	14	7	2	1	33	20	79
Blackthorn	16	2	0	0	0	0	18
Alder	17	3	1	0	9	0	30
Hawthorn	14	5	2	1	1	1	24
Subtotals	377	83	37	10	68	31	610

very well preserved, suggesting that the posts were driven into the anaerobic clays soon after their completion. The individual facets on the worked ends tend to be slightly concave in cross-section with facet widths which range in size from fairly narrow examples to wider facets that probably approach the width of the actual axe blades used. These facets can be used to estimate the minimum size of the axes used. The axes were slightly convex in section having blades in excess of 50mm in width, with some larger facet widths (59mm and 69mm) suggesting the use of larger axes.

There is no obvious reason why the posts at one end of the structure required sharper points than the other end, and there is no evidence to suggest two separate periods of construction. Obviously sharpening posts is a fairly prosaic task, so one would be reluctant to over-emphasise stylistic preferences. Nevertheless the working evidence might suggest that two or more individuals were engaged in point production involving slightly different working styles or levels of exertion. The Group 1 posts, being slightly larger, may represent the initial formation of the structure, with wood of a preferred size being lifted from an adjacent wood pile and rather more care taken over the cutting of points. As work moved further along the rows, the size of piles became more variable and generally smaller, while the effort expended in point formation also decreased. The important conclusion to bear in mind is that, to judge from the woodworking information, there is a more significant correlation between the two rows of the structure at the south-western end (Group 1) than between the northern and southern ends of the north-eastern row (Group 2). The lack of any hazel woodworking debris from this phase suggests that the posts were prepared not on the muds but on the adjacent riverbank or beyond.

Yew-wood spread, group 24427 (Phase III, Area E, palaeochannel group E.3.1a)

A dense concentration of 93 yew twigs was recovered from within a dense spread of wood assigned to Phase

III (see Fig 26). They were all narrow, ranging from 4–14mm in diameter, and quite short, the longest being 617mm in length. At least 21 of them have worked ends, occasionally of well-made points. Several of the twigs had been deliberately bent over, quite often half splitting as a result. Several of the smaller fragments exhibit this characteristic split at one end suggesting that they were originally part of larger pieces which did not survive this bending process. The coarseness and irregularity of the roundwood argues against their use in basketry, and they are hard to visualise as part of a fish trap. They could have been used as hoops to peg things down or as some sort of tie, and it should be remembered that the stitching of the boat plank from this phase was made of yew.

Platform / hard, structure 9014 (Phase VI, Area A, palaeochannel group VI)

Over 800 pieces of wood were included in the excavated parts of this large spread of brushwood, woodworking debris, stone and timber, which also included a single line of uprights, the function of which is discussed elsewhere. Roughly one quarter of this assemblage was not lifted, sampled, or analysed for working. Hazel predominated, forming two thirds of the identified wood, with large amounts of oak and ash also occurring in addition to smaller but significant quantities of alder, hawthorn and blackthorn (Table 30).

The majority of the analysed assemblage was roundwood which showed no signs of working. Axe cuts were evidenced on 83 pieces of roundwood, the majority of which were small branches or very young trunks. Woodworking debris was almost as numerous: hazel and alder debris appeared to result from cutting roundwood to a point and this evidence can possibly be related to the on-site finishing of the line of upright posts which were largely of these two species, two oaks being the only exceptions. The oak, ash and lime woodchips and offcuts were more varied in their cross-sections and are more likely to have been derived from the trimming and hewing of

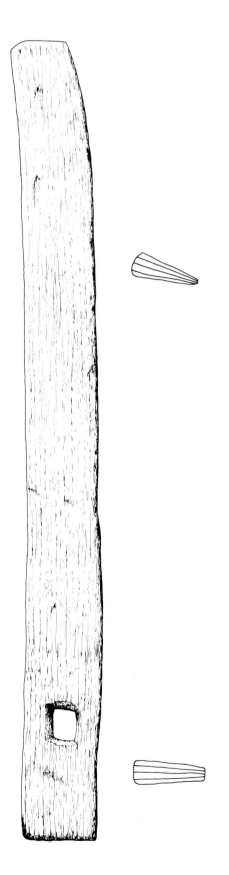

timbers. Numerous timbers of these three species, and especially the oak, were recovered from this context including several well-made planks, three of which had roughly-cut mortises. Two of the latter were radially split oak planks (049, Fig 97, and 332, Fig 98) whilst the other was a half split ash trunk with a mortise hole at either end (197, Fig 98). Some of the smaller pieces of oak and ash 'timber' may be large offcuts from the on-site production of planks or beams (eg 20257).

The row of uprights consisted of fourteen posts, eleven of which were hazel roundwood, and one was alder roundwood. The other two were oak, one remaining in the round (128:012) and the other having been cleft tangentially (128:013, Fig 99). These two were much larger than the other posts with the exception of one of the hazel posts (128: 018) which was a thick trunk retaining a large side branch at the top of its surviving length. Several of the hazel posts had buckled, suggesting that they were driven in whilst still green. This would fit in with the possibility of them being finished on-site.

Trackway structure 473 and hurdle 1401 (Phase VII, Area B, palaeochannel group B.7.1)

Just over 270 pieces of wood can be assigned to these contexts. They consisted of a spread of wood debris and fragmentary hurdle-work running obliquely from the channel edge towards structure 22441. A wide range of species was identified, the vast majority of pieces being hazel with significant quantities of oak and ash but only small numbers of other species (Tables 31 and 32). Unfortunately comments on the working analysis from this structure are made more difficult because many pieces were not retained for analysis.

Broadly speaking, the hazel is mostly either whole roundwood or cleft poles and rods, whilst the ash, oak and lime is cleft or axed woodworking debris. The similarity between the size ranges of hazel whole roundwood and the hazel cleft wood suggests that the selection of raw material was not haphazard. There seems to have been a deliberate attempt to obtain or produce wood of a certain restricted size. There were only four hazel poles with diameters larger than 70mm. Otherwise the hazel roundwood measured in diameter between 13–54mm, with an average diameter of 27mm. In comparison the cleft hazel was only slightly larger measuring 19–70mm in width, with an average width of 38mm. Most of the hazel was cut at very shallow angles (average 12 degrees) to chisel-ends, with only a few examples of simple wedge ends on the larger pieces.

Fig 97 Structure 9014: mortised radial plank 049. Scale 1:10

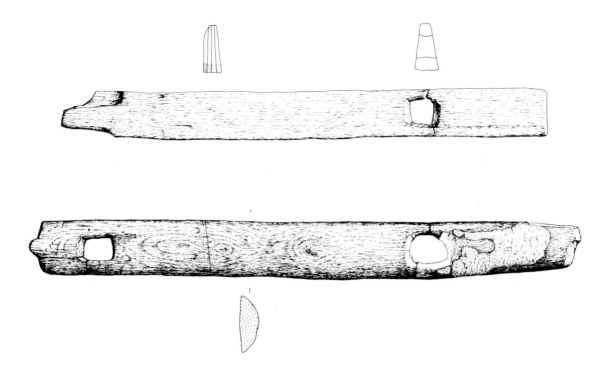

Fig 98   Structure 9014: mortised planks 332 (top) and 197. Scale 1:8

Table 31   Most common wood species by wood category: hurdle 1401

Species	Roundwood (no working observed)	Worked roundwood	Splitwood (no observed working)	Worked splitwood	Working debris	Timber	Totals
Hazel	19	4	1	0	0	0	24
Ash	0	2	0	0	0	0	2
Oak	0	0	0	0	0	0	0
Blackthorn	0	0	0	0	0	0	0
Alder	0	0	0	0	0	0	0
Hawthorn	1	0	0	0	0	0	1
Subtotals	20	6	1	0	0	0	27

Table 32   Most common wood species by wood category: structure 473

Species	Roundwood (no working observed)	Worked Roundwood	Splitwood (no observed working)	Worked splitwood	Working debris	Timber	Totals
Hazel	93	37	20	3	4	0	157
Ash	4	0	2	0	11	4	21
Oak	4	2	3	0	16	12	37
Blackthorn	5	0	1	0	0	0	6
Alder	4	1	3	2	1	1	12
Hawthorn	5	0	0	0	0	0	5
Subtotals	115	40	29	5	32	17	238

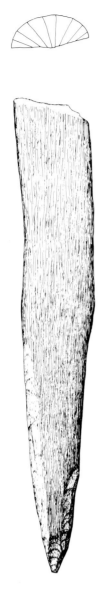

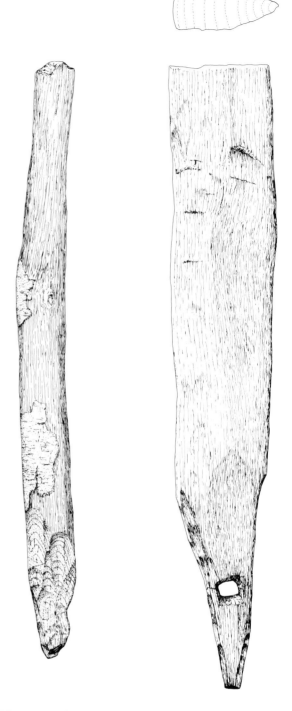

*Fig 99   Structure 9014: split oak upright 128:013.
Scale 1:8*

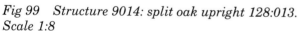

'Bridge / jetty' structure 22441 (Phase VII, Area D, palaeochannel group D.7.1)

In all 101 pieces of wood were examined from structure 22441, which was the most substantial structure from the excavations and may represent a bridge or jetty. It consists of a double post alignment running across a wide, flat-bottomed channel which had slightly silted up. Dendrochronological dating gives a winter felling date for one of the split ash uprights of 990/989 BC. The two parallel rows were roughly two metres apart, and were constructed of pairs of large posts spaced at somewhat irregular intervals. Running between and around the main posts were numerous smaller stakes. Colouration zones on some posts provide an indicator of the exposed areas. Two posts (25860, 25824; Fig 100) have dark surfaces from the point tip up to 550mm and 1310mm in length, probably indicating they had

*Fig 100a   Structure 22441: posts (left to right)
24550, 25824. Scale 1:8*

been driven into the clays to this depth. Thereafter on one post (25860) there is a second colour band between 550–860mm, possibly indicating a variable water mark, while at the very top the badly eroded sapwood may indicate exposure to the air.

Species identified from structure 22441 were hazel (76%), oak (10.9%), ash (7.9%), willow (3.9%) and hawthorn (1%). Clearly hazel was the single most common species used, but a definite pattern of species selection can be seen in the location and function of each of the structural components. The

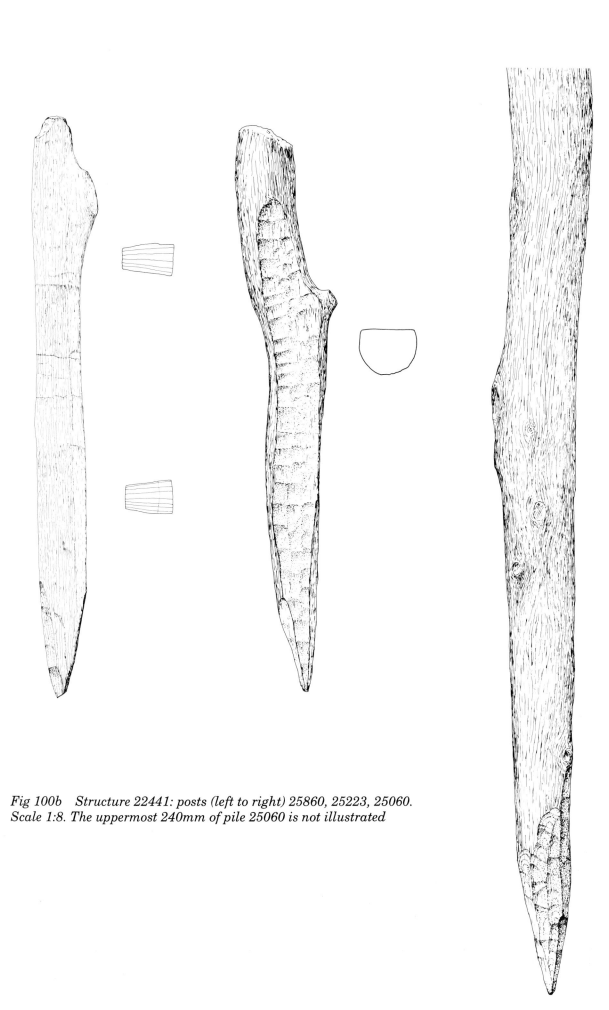

Fig 100b   Structure 22441: posts (left to right) 25860, 25223, 25060. Scale 1:8. The uppermost 240mm of pile 25060 is not illustrated

largest vertical piles were exclusively of oak (9 pieces) or ash (2 pieces). Hazel was only used for the roundwood stakes, whilst the small amount of willow and hawthorn were found only as scattered small roundwood. The eleven main uprights of oak and ash all had diameters of between 120 and 270mm with the exception of the two radially split timbers (25824 and 25860) and one very young oak roundwood (24550, Fig 100). These differences in the wood combined with irregularities in the spacing of the paired posts may suggest some repairs or rebuilding but the evidence from the woodworking provides no definitive evidence. The hazel by contrast has a much smaller diameter, with a range of 17–80mm and an average of 27mm, suggesting that it was not used as a load-bearing part of the structure.

Obviously the choice of species was influenced by the strength and durability of the large oak and ash piles, with the other species used in a secondary role, structurally. The quality of trees taken were variable. The hazel in particular was remarkably free of side-branches and knots, 68% being from straight or very-straight grained trunks. Both the ash and oak were typically of a more mixed quality, there being several instances of forked branches and irregular knotty trunks. Tree-ring and morphological evidence suggests that much of the oak used was taken from immature trees 35–77 years old, topwood or heavy branches. Otherwise straight trunks often had clear evidence for the removal of side-branches. Some of the ash was derived from older trees, timber 25824 being at least 170 years old.

The small hazel stakes were often driven into the clays 'upside-down', ie the opposite way to which they were growing. This may have helped stop sinkage in to the underlying clays. Inserting stakes into the ground against the line of growth, or 'cap down', would prevent the sap rising up the length of the trunk and would prolong the useful life of the upright (Audouze and Buchsenschutz 1991, 52; Mann 1903, 379).

Some evidence existed for the cleaving of the larger wood from this context. There was one radial-split oak post and two cleft ash posts (one quarter-split and one radial-split). One larger hazel trunk was also split to a radial sectioned stake. These split timbers were subsequently hewn along other surfaces. The oak post (25860, Fig 100), after being split to a radial section was trimmed along both sides with an axe to remove both the fragile narrow 'feather edge' and much of the bark. The large ash timber (25824) had been split, hewn, mortised and sharpened. The trunk was finely cleft radially. Thereafter the surfaces were hewn by axe up the length of the timber and a single, square mortise was cut through 173mm from the end. The sharpened end was produced by simply chopping at the side edges of the timber to reduce the width to a point. The mortise is apparently afunctional in this structure indicating the timber may have been reused. Such afunctional mortises near the bottom of stakes have been noted at Flag Fen (Taylor 1992, 482–3), from an undated possible

trackway in Somerset (Bulleid 1945), and from the Neolithic Sweet Track where a board originally prepared as a mortised plank was cut to a point and used as a large 'peg' (Coles and Orme 1984, 16).

However, most of the trunks had been utilised in their natural whole roundwood state. The large oak and ash roundwood posts were all cut to pencil ends, mostly at very shallow cutting angles of 10–15 degrees, leaving narrow, long facets tapering down the point. These facets typically measured 40–50mm wide, but the largest facet measurements encountered were 79mm in facet length, and 53mm in facet width. The toolmarks were concave in cross-section, with a complete jam curve indicating the use of an axe of width 51mm. On occasion these pencil points were achieved by cutting on two adjacent faces before trimming off the back face at a steeper angle to produce a blunted tip. The ash posts were, in contrast, cut in a variety of ways. The smaller ash and hazel posts were generally cut with minimum effort, producing chisel-ends with cutting angles of 15–27 degrees. In a number of examples (eg 25820) the remaining fibres were simply torn with a downward wrench. It is likely that some of these points result from the original tree-felling techniques rather than deliberate sharpening activities.

Discussion

Introduction

In this concluding section we hope to outline briefly the various processes that were involved in the selection, extraction and modification of wood from the Caldicot assemblage. Most wetland sites are actually wetland margin sites, with various economic activities occurring beside rather than in the water. For this reason we know relatively little about the nature of the carpentry that may have been used in the superstructure of houses on the neighbouring dry land. Nevertheless the wood from the Caldicot excavations provides several clues about the woodworking techniques of Late Bronze Age Wales.

Species and wood selection

As described earlier, different species of trees and different parts of trees exhibit varying physical properties which influence their selection by man for various tasks. To determine the nature and degree of selection involved it is necessary to have some idea of the available resource. The exact reconstruction of woodlands from pollen evidence is fraught with difficulties, and it is impossible to estimate accurately the size of the woods or the numbers of each species or their levels of maturity. However, the pollen does indicate the range of species that were present in the local woods.

By far the greater part of the excavated wood was very small, often branch material. The nature and

Table 33 Jam curve types

Curve type	No. of timbers per type	Phase groups represented	Maximum cutting width (mm)	Full width present? (Y/N)
1	6	VI; VII	27 +	N
2	2	VI; VII	44 +	N
3	3	III; VI	54 +	N
4	3	VI; VII	46 +	Y
5	2	VI\VII; VII	36 and 42 +	Y
6	2	III; VI\VII	47	Y
7	4	II; VI\VII; VII	55	Y
8	2	II; VI\VII	42 +	N
9	6	III; VI; VII	50	Y
10	8	VI; VII	51	Y
11	1	III	39 +	N
12	5	VI; VII	36 +	N
13	2	VI\VII; VII	23 +	N

potential origin of this wood is discussed in more detail below, but it is clear that little selectivity was being practised. This is supported by the very broad species range of this material.

Much more thought went into the selection of wood for the various upright structures. The ability of hazel to quickly produce tall, straight, relatively branch-free stems undoubtedly led to its dominant use in structure 472 and for the smaller roundwood in the bridge/jetty (22441), although some of the hazel components of the latter structure were quite knotty with several side branches that had often not been totally removed (eg 25826; 24572; and 25822). Several probable coppiced heels were noted amongst the hazel roundwood (eg 24029; 25765; 24911; and 25471) and on general morphological grounds a minority of pieces of this species could have come from such a source. This is almost certainly due to adventitious coppicing by man or beavers rather than organised woodland management.

For the main load-bearing posts of the bridge/jetty structure, oak and ash were utilised because these trees had larger trunks than the other common species, and were additionally very strong and resistant to rot, especially the oak. However, all these qualities were not realised to the full in this structure. Quite young trees, topwood, or possibly even large branches (eg 24550 only c 12 years old) were used, almost invariably with all their sapwood, as did the mature split ash stake 25824 (Fig 100). Large side branches occurred (eg 24923) and one post was evidently sub-dividing into two at its top surviving end (25060). The utilisation of much young branching oak and ash suggests either a lack of large readily available mature timber trees, or alternatively the ready availability of relatively immature timber trees in the vicinity.

The only other evidence for much selectivity in the

wood assemblage is in the group of yew twigs (24427). Although the exact function of this scatter of cut and bent yew twigs is not readily apparent, they were probably selected for their close-grained strength and flexibility.

The presence of much of the small cut and uncut roundwood may be a by-product of some other form of activity such as the collection of firewood or fodder (hazel, hawthorn, and blackthorn leaves are all edible, Rackham 1990, 179) or the clearance of small areas of scrub woodland. The relatively rare occurrence of species linked with riverside environments such as willow/poplar is notable.

Tools and tool usage

The wood from the Caldicot excavations has clear evidence for the use of axes of various shapes and sizes. The slight curvature in cross-section of the toolmarks generally suggests small, narrow but thick blades. The jam curves can be used to compare blade widths and shapes. Great care has to be exercised in the recording of these features to avoid misinterpretation. A total of 56 separate jam curves were drawn, a figure which could be reduced across the material to thirteen distinct profiles. The jam curves came from a variety of contexts. Eight were from split timbers, 35 from the sharpened ends of posts, eight from the inner surfaces of mortises and five from woodchips. The main types and their phases are shown in Fig 101 and Table 33.

Only six of the thirteen groups contained jam curves which represented the full blade width, and these were mainly derived from mortise holes. This may have introduced a bias into the results if a particular axe type was preferred for this activity. The maximum blade widths may therefore represent

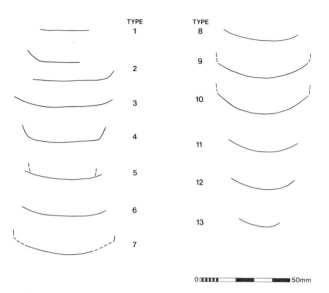

Fig 101   Jam curves

one of the smaller types of contemporary axe, but is just as likely that a general-purpose axe was used for rough mortises as well as for a host of other tasks. Another possible bias is that jam curves are more likely to occur where the cutting angle is acute. It is possible that some tools were only used at very shallow cutting angles and that these would therefore not be represented in the jam curve assemblage.

The largest full blade width is 55mm (type 7) but one type 3 jam curve was at least 54mm in width and had no edges. The most common profiles were of types 9 and 10 which were very similar to each other anyway. Here the full recorded cutting widths were 50mm and 51mm respectively, though of course not all the examples which fitted into these profiles necessarily had the same blade width. None of the other types display widths over 47mm. Some surviving facets exceed the width of the widest jam curve however, including ones of 59mm and 69mm from structure 472. These may suggest the use of wider axes in the early phases but the evidence is too limited to be conclusive. If the effects of wear and re-sharpening are considered we may be looking at only five or six significantly different types of cutting blade. The completely flat jam curves (type 1) may represent a small billhook-type tool but they could equally have been derived from a flat-bladed axe. Types 2, 3, 5, 8, and 11 are all from cut ends on roundwood and are therefore almost certainly made by an axe. No jam curves were derived from the hewn surfaces of split planks where an adze may have been used. Mortise holes were probably cut with an axe rather than an adze, and the angle of the jam curves supports this possibility. The type 13 profile could either represent a very small specialist cutting tool or could have derived from the edge of a much larger blade embedding itself in the wood.

Obviously a range of woodworking tools is indicated by the Caldicot structural and artefactual wood, including various types of axe, gouge, chisel, wedge, mallet and knife. It is possible that this wood can contribute to our understanding of the use of Late Bronze Age tools in South Wales. The first, almost insurmountable, problem that faces such an enquiry is the difficulty in linking the typology of Late Bronze Age metalwork with the absolute chronology produced by scientific dating techniques. There is the further problem that the tools owned by local communities may have been examples of archaic survivals; some tools may have remained functional for centuries after their succession by new types. This discussion of woodworking tools will therefore constitute a brief survey only. It is suggested that experimental archaeology could usefully test the assertions made.

In southern Britain between the calendar dates of 1200–900 BC, the forms of woodworking tools are those of the Penard period (before 1200–mid/late 11th century BC), the Wilburton period (mid/late 11th century–mid 10th century BC), and the earliest years of the Ewart Park period (mid 10th century BC onwards). Penard period metalwork is distributed fairly uniformly throughout Wales and the Marches, but in smaller quantities than in the preceding Taunton period. Within this region the south-east is notable for two of the important hoards of the period, Penard, Glamorgan and Ffynhonnau, Brecon, Powys, both of which include exotic imports (see also Northover p 149). At what some regard as a period of some considerable social and economic stress, the amount of metal available for daily use was restricted, and the market appears to have been increasingly supplied with imported scrap.

An interesting feature of the Penard period is the increasing concentration on deposition of high status or high added-value metalwork in hoards or ritual contexts (high quality weapons, gold torcs, shields, etc) with the axes increasingly recovered as single finds or personal toolkits. The shortage of metal meant better husbanding of the supply and increased recycling. Nonetheless the tools remain of good quality and much the same weight as in the Taunton period, the main change being a reduction in the width of the cutting-edge from around 60mm to nearer 40mm, a value which was retained for the palstaves of the Late Bronze Age and for some socketed axes. Certainly the narrow, curved forms of the palstave cutting-edges could be considered very similar to the edges indicated by the jam curves on the Caldicot wood.

South-east Wales and the southern Marches probably represent the western extent of the distribution of the Wilburton industry, with finds further west then being seen as special imports or scrap. The recovery of Wilburton period material at Caldicot, the long tongue chape and the tin strip, hint at quite complex connections. The Wilburton compositions of the prototype South Welsh axes (Gwithian type) from Cowbridge and Llanthony Abbey show that Wilburton material was re-processed in the region. These axes have a straight cutting-edge that becomes curved with use, and a striking feature of the Caldicot wood jam curves was a form (from Phases III and VII) indicating the use of such straight cutting-edges. Depending on finish, use and re-working, the developed south Welsh axes of the later 10th–8th centuries could have straight or curved edges, unexpanded or expanded, so there would always have been some axes capable of producing the recorded cut marks.

The hafting of these tools for use would have been accomplished in a variety of ways. Some may have been placed on single piece hafts carved from trunk-branch junctions, similar to examples known from Flag Fen (Taylor 1992, Fig 19, 22) and Edenderry, Co Offaly, and the possible handle (1161) from these excavations (see Earwood p 206). Alternatively they may have been of two-piece construction where a straight branch had a hole cut through it near the top which held a wooden peg onto which the tool was hafted. Late prehistoric hafts of this form are known from Flag Fen (Taylor 1992, Fig 20–1), with a well preserved example from Hov, Norway illustrating their likely appearance (Marstrander 1966, 24). Ash wood hafts from Late Bronze Age tools are known from South Wales, from the Breiddin, Montgomeryshire and Penwylt, Breconshire (Green 1978).

The Caldicot toolmarks reflect the patterns exhibited on other Late Bronze Age wetland sites. The toolmarks on the wood from Runnymede Bridge were up to 50mm in cutting width, with both curved and almost straight edges suggested (Heal 1991). Jam curves on timbers from an Iron Age house in the Netherlands also suggested the use of a large number of tool types. At Site Q, Assendelver Polders, there seem to have been two gouges and eight axes used in carving the wood (Therkorn et al 1984, 365–6). Timbers used in a trackway at Derrynaskea, Ireland dated to 974 BC by dendrochronology suggested the use of axes with cutting edges up to 60mm in width (Moloney et al 1993, 35).

Tree-felling, branch removal and burning

The Caldicot wood provides useful insights into tree-felling techniques in Late Bronze Age Wales. Smaller roundwood from all phases was felled by cutting at shallow to medium angles, with hardly more than a couple of blows need to sever the fibres. Chisel-ends, both simple and variant forms, were the points produced reflecting the way in which narrow roundwood can easily be cut down by chopping from one side only. The techniques used to fell the largest trunks have typically been removed by later working. However there is the suggestion from some worked ends that precise techniques were used. In the slightly larger wood which appears to preserve felling-marks, wedge-ends are more common. Often in the larger wedge-ends, most of the chopping was done on one side, with only a small cut at the opposite side. When most of the wood was chopped out of one side, a few blows at the back would have led to the

trunk falling in the direction of that wider cut or 'kerf'. Such techniques of felling trunks in a required direction would be useful when attempting to haul material out from the tangle that is scrub woodland.

There is plenty of evidence for the process of de-branching or 'snedding' of felled trees; for example the larger piles from 22441 had their side-branches removed by very shallow-angled blows, shown by the toolmarks on knots and protuberances. Some of the piles from this structure in fact appeared to be the topwood of larger trees (eg 24550). It is likely that such branch-trimming was carried out close to the woodland, given the awkwardness of hauling an untrimmed branch down to the river.

For the small cut and 'unworked' roundwood, much of the morphological evidence suggests that a lot of the wood is actually the product of branch removal from larger trunks of quite scrubby species such as hawthorn, blackthorn, and potentially hazel. The remarkable uniformity of cut ends, consisting of chisel or basic wedge points formed by a few blows at medium angles seems to reflect felling or trimming techniques, with the points themselves having no apparent function in the deposits.

The barest minimum of working is shown on most pieces, with several examples retaining very large side branches which must have made their transport difficult (eg 25074; 25077; 25809; 24008; and 20324). Much of this roundwood may therefore be a product of some other activity such as the collection of firewood or fodder, or the clearance of areas of scrub woodland. Almost half the charred wood (eg 20288; 20399) retained signs of cutting, raising the possibility that fire was associated with clearance activity. This cut and charred wood was mainly hazel and alder but encompassed a wide variety of other species including a charred split oak fragment (24007). In some cases the charring definitely occurred after the cutting (eg 25338).

Trunk conversion

Oak and ash formed virtually all the larger examples of converted wood. The ash assemblage displays all the different types of conversion but most of the sizeable pieces are in the form of radial splits (eg 24837) or tangentials, like the wide plank 1104 (Fig 102). The oak has a considerable quantity of large converted timbers reflecting the potentially large size of the tree and its ease of splitting. Almost half the oak is radially split (eg 24438; 049; 343) including much material which retains its sapwood (eg 332; 25860). Tangential types form almost another quarter of the oak assemblage, once again including several major timbers (eg 7003 and 128:36). Some intermediate forms appear, including a large timber squared off on all sides (474). Where half or quarter split oaks occur they are usually of a considerable size (eg 991; 128:013).

The hazel, alder, hawthorn and blackthorn are split in a variety of ways, with simple half or quarter

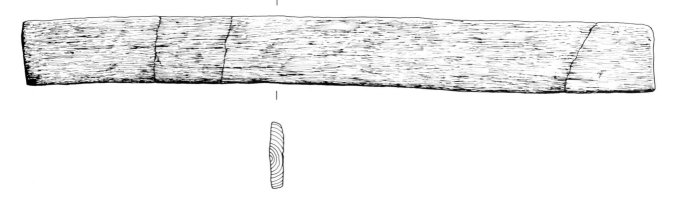

Fig 102   Wood 1104: tangentially converted ash plank. Scale 1:10

splits being by far the most common. With very few exceptions the converted material of these species is very small, and a large part of it may have been caused by the cutting and tearing of branches and especially by natural processes of decay and erosion. Only three pieces are of a large size, comprising a quarter split alder (821), a half split hawthorn (128:200) and a half-split mortised hazel plank (128:38).

This variety of conversion technique between different species is largely due to the difference in trunk, and the greater inherent strength of ash and, in particular, oak wood. Some of the split oak timbers could more readily be called beams rather than planks, such is the narrowness of their widths. These cleft narrow beams were obviously being taken from young trees, probably mostly of small girth. The sizeable oak and ash tangential splits would seem to be an attempt to maximise the size of timber obtainable from a trunk (eg 1104; 128:36). This could be taken to imply the exploitation of secondary woodland rather than wildwood containing frequent very mature timber trees.

The likelihood is that the Caldicot wood was cleft quite soon after felling. Working and cleaving seasoned oak and ash is notoriously difficult (Darrah 1982). There was no on-site evidence for wedges or mallets, although these were undoubtedly used. In addition there were no traces of the compression marks left by such wedges that other authors have noted. These could have been removed by riverine erosion, but it is more likely that they were not present in the first place. It has been suggested that the wood from trees growing in a wetlands margin location might not display these characteristics (Taylor 1992).

Bucking and hewing

'Bucking', or the cutting of trunks and timber to length, is evidenced both on the timbers themselves (eg 24837) and on the woodworking debris produced. A short piece of radially-split alder (24329), which has several steep axe facets on one of its radial faces,

may have been produced from the trimming or shaping of a radial plank to a required length or shape. Similarly, a small radial piece of ash (20257) could be the waste from the trimming of the end of a thin radial plank as it has slight axe or adze marks on one radial face whilst on its outer, tangential face it is cut to a point by several axe blows. Two grooves, 3mm wide and 3mm apart, run transversely across this tangential face. A comparably shaped but much larger (485mm × 60mm × 55mm) piece of oak (25610) may also have been produced as waste when a plank reduced from a radial split was shortened at one end by 48mm. Interestingly, a shallow groove 25mm wide is preserved in the remnant of sapwood which survives on this piece. None of the three grooves preserved on these last two pieces are substantial enough to have been caused by a gouge or chisel and it is hard to visualise a practical binding material which could be thin enough to cause such wear.

Whilst sapwood was usually left on the timbers at Caldicot, there are some examples where both the majority of the outer sapwood and inner pith or 'feather edge' was carefully trimmed off (eg 25860). The waste from trimming a feather edge can be seen in a triangular shaped oak offcut (20608). Apart from this trimming on the sides, there are also surfaces of timbers which have been carefully flattened by hewing, a practice not generally common on prehistoric timbers. One ash plank (25824) had been carefully trimmed along its surfaces with narrow-bladed tools. Hewing of a radial plank may be indicated by four items, three of which are radial fragments of oak 8mm, 24mm and 78mm in thickness, the former retaining some sapwood. Another oak fragment of intermediate cross section (80mm × 20mm × 4mm) may derive from similar activity, whilst a poorly preserved radial-split lime fragment (210mm × 34mm × 6mm) suggests planks of this species may also have been finished nearby. This fine trimming was most likely carried out with the timber supported on its side edge, with the craftsperson standing vertically over it and cutting down diagonally.

Evidence for the finishing of split timbers can also be seen on a thin tangential ash woodchip 143mm in length (128:057). On its outer tangential face are preserved the partial remains of five very shallow adze cuts the largest of which is the same width as the woodchip itself, 61mm. This probably represents waste from the dressing of a tangentially-split ash plank.

Sharpening

Most of the sharpening carried out was on the post structures 472 and 22441. A number of pegs pinning split and mortised timbers to the muds were also sharpened. One large maple roundwood (475, Fig 103) seems to have been used as a sharpening block. In the middle of the trunk, on one surface only, there are numerous cut-marks running across the length-axis of the trunk. This is mostly unintended damage resulting from points being repeatedly trimmed on top of this log. This would be a sensible option, providing a stable surface for the worked ends to be placed on while they were being prepared. More importantly it would have protected the axe blades; contact with the ground or gravel surfaces quickly dulls a sharpened metal edge. It is likely that prehistoric woodworkers were careful with their

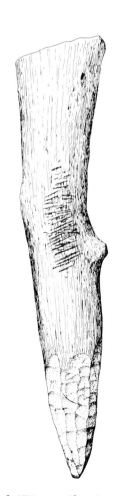

Fig 103   Wood 475: pencil-pointed maple with cut marks indicating its use as a 'chopping-block'. Scale 1:8

tools, excessive re-grinding would quickly wear down an axe blade making it soon fit only for re-casting.

The largest roundwood posts were typically sharpened to tapered pencil-ends. However the worked surface is typically near the end of the timber, only more rarely did the worked surface continue up its length. In contrast the sharpened cleft and round-wood oak piles from the Late Bronze Age settlements of Cortaillod-Est (Arnold 1986, 98–119) and Au-vernier-Nord (Arnold 1982, fig 6.9) on Lake Neuchâtel, Switzerland were sharpened to much finer tapering points, with the worked surface often up to 3m in length. The obvious reason for this contrast is that the Swiss posts had to be driven through compact, thixotropic lake sediments, whereas the Caldicot piles were driven into softer estuarine clays or river silts. In this regard the Caldicot sharpened points are more like the stubbier Late Bronze Age piles at Runnymede Bridge (Heal 1991, 140–1). The indifferent attitude towards preparation of points for driving is emphasised by a number of uprights which still retained substantial side branches which would have made driving impossible in more consolidated sediment. Neverthe-less many of the Caldicot piles were buckled due either to impact with lower harder clays or later compression: if the latter were the case this might suggest they were driven in while still green.

The smaller pieces of roundwood were invariably cut to simple chisel or wedge-shaped points with the minimum of effort expended. However, some inter-esting differences were observed in structure 472 where rather more care was taken over the prepara-tion of uprights in the structure, including pencil-points on the larger roundwood.

Woodworking debris

Numerous woodchips and small offcuts provide evidence for the trimming and dressing and sharp-ening of roundwood and split timbers in the immediate vicinity of the palaeochannels. Only hazel, alder, oak and ash produced sizeable quanti-ties of excavated working waste. A large number of woodchips can be produced from working a single timber so chance factors play an important role in the recovery of such items. However, it is apparent that oak and ash timbers were being finished on site, including bucking, hewing and sharpening, and possibly the cutting of mortises as well. Experimen-tal woodworking, specifically designed to study woodworking debris, would help to extend the infor-mation which can be gained from such material.

Two large groups of ash woodchips (20323 and 25595, Fig 104), occurred in Phase III, numbering 66 in total. The vast majority had radial cross-sections, suggesting they derived from finishing cleft planks. The smaller number of tangentials may have formed from the trimming of plank edges, the cutting of mortises or the sharpening of stakes. All this activity must have taken place very close by, to leave such

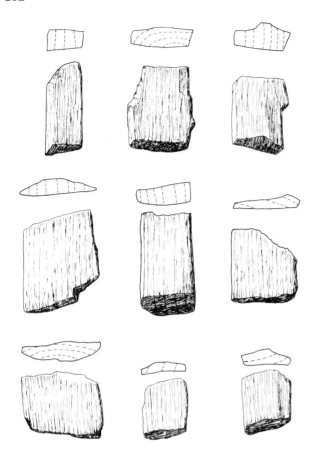

Fig 104   Woodchips 25593: a selection from a concentration of ash woodworking debris. Scale 1:2

dense concentrations of material behind, but no ash timbers have been found from this phase to provide a possible source for this material.

Excluding oak and ash, the remaining species are mainly roundwood which required little or no dressing on site and therefore produced few woodchips. What examples there are seem largely to derive from the cutting of stakes to points. This seems especially true of the woodchips from the platform structure 9014 where the hazel and alder waste recovered can be linked to the line of uprights of the same species.

Mortises, notches, tenons and fastenings

Simple notches occur on several split planks, including two which are diagonally opposed on a tangential oak plank (7003, Fig 105). Another occurs on one edge of a radial ash plank (24837) which also has two mortise holes. These rough-cut notches may have been designed to assist pegging the timbers in place, or even as crude joinery in the structures from which they were reused. Another possibility is they assisted in the hauling or towing of these planks to site.

Mortise holes were recorded on eight split timbers (Fig 106, and see Figs 97, 98 and 100) although only two of them actually appeared to be held in place by roundwood stakes passing through the holes. One of these timbers was a split ash upright (25824) in the

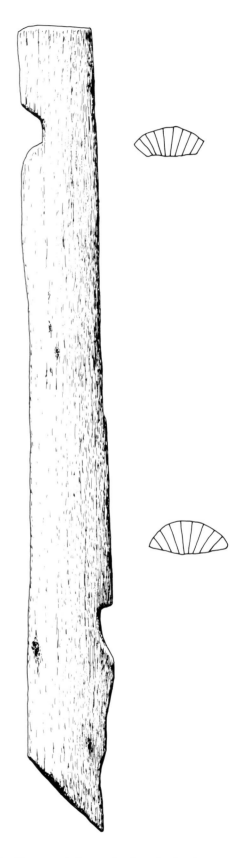

Fig 105   Tangential, notched, oak plank 7003. Scale 1:10

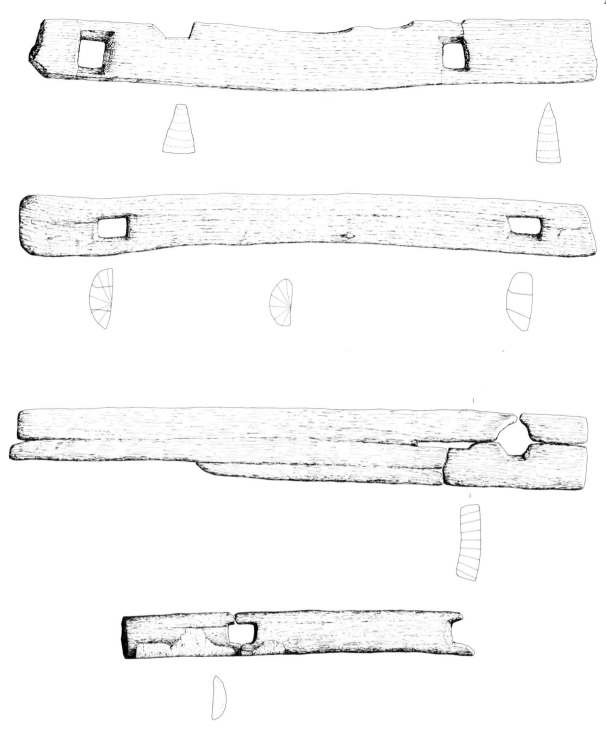

Fig 106   Mortised planks: (top to bottom) 038, 036, 1066, 24837. Scale 1:8

bridge (22441) which had an afunctional mortise near its cut end. This is discussed more fully in the section on that structure. All the remainder were horizontal planks. Three of these (128:049; 128:036; 128:332) had a single mortise at one end. All three were oak, two being cleft radially and the other tangentially. The other four planks had a mortise hole near both ends. Three of these were half-split planks retaining some bark on the outside. One of these was oak (1066), whilst the other two were hazel

(128:38) and ash (128:127). The other double mortise occurred on a radially split ash plank (24837) which had been pegged down, possibly as part of a repair to structure 22441.

The toolmarks on the inner surfaces of the mortises make it possible to reconstruct the process of production (Fig 107). The mortises are almost always roughly square in shape, and were first cut at the two ends to about the width of the axe before the inner waste was cut or levered out with the blade. Hour-

Fig 107 *Toolmarks in plank mortise.*

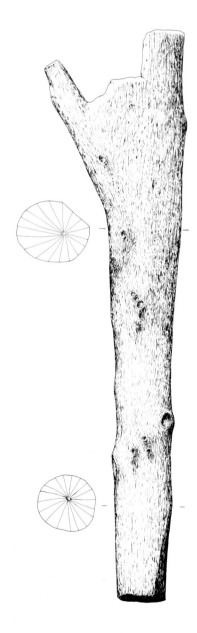

Fig 108 *Wood 20846: possible reused oak upright with cross-cut ends. Scale 1:8*

glass sections indicate that they were cut from both sides of the plank. The mortised upright (25824) in the bridge structure 22441 displayed a different technique however. Here two opposite ends of the mortise were cut from different sides of the plank, each eventually removing a roughly triangular piece of wood. This resulted in a slightly inclined mortise hole with two stepped ends formed by the axe blows, the 'steps' at each end going in different directions. Palstaves have been shown to be eminently suitable for such mortising work.

There are two timbers with possible tenons, not generally found on prehistoric timbers and often misinterpreted (eg Taylor and Pryor 1990). One is exhibited on an oak trunk (20846) measuring 1.19m long and 0.15m in diameter (Figs 40 and 108). It was cross-cut at both ends; the toolmarks are quite bruised, suggesting it was worked after seasoning, implying it was a reused timber. At one end a notch was taken from the trunk leaving a protruding tenon, measuring 105mm × 80mm. Beside this tenon is a truncated secondary branch stump which was not fully removed from the trunk. Little other modification has been done to the trunk and the sapwood remains in some places. The suggestion is that this timber was once a supporting upright in a large structure.

Another important piece of structural wood is a trimmed stake (20909, Fig 109) which may have been used as a mooring post, although it had subsequently collapsed to a horizontal position in the channel. It measured 1.63m in length and 61mm by 43mm in cross section. It was hewn from a quarter-split piece of oak with the edges trimmed to give it a roughly square cross section, the sapwood having been removed from its entire length. Great trouble had been taken at one end to produce a fine pencil-shaped point, with as many as 40 small facets still surviving on the timber at this end. At the other end a step had been cut all around the stake 155mm from the end, above which the timber had been carefully reduced to a circular cross section measuring 26mm to 28mm in diameter. The presence of extensive wear all around the base of this circular projection suggests that the timber may at one point have been used to hold ropes. If this was so, then the care taken in producing a smooth edge for the top projection might have reduced the wear on the ties which were used. The projecting 'tang' at the end of this piece could be described as a tenon; it is possible that this timber had a previous structural role.

A single wooden tie (24777, Fig 110) was found in association with mortised plank 24837 (see palaeo-channel group D.7.2, p 55). This was a hazel rod, twisted and coiled into a circle by interweaving either end. Twisted wood fibres make strong ties, although it is uncertain what load-bearing capacity they have. It may be that such fibres were used as fastenings in wooden structures, possibly either in the place of joints or to strengthen them. More prosaically, the twisted hazel tie could also have been used to bind a collection of faggots or rods for dumping onto the

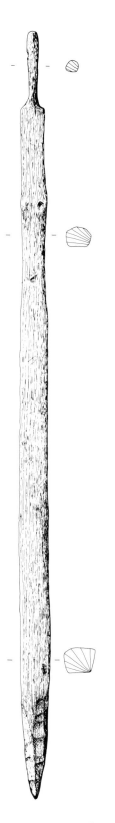

*Fig 109   Wood 20909: quarter-split oak with
pencil-shaped point and 'tenon'. Scale 1:8*

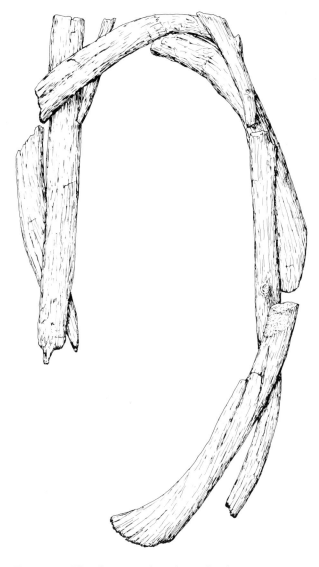

Fig 110   Wood 24777: hazel tie. Scale 1:4

shore. Similar wooden ties have been recovered from
a palaeochannel feature adjacent to a sub-rectangular Iron Age building at Goldcliff (Bell 1993, Fig 40).
Smaller wooden ropes of yew and hazel are known
from the Late Bronze Age boat at North Ferriby,
Humberside (Wright 1990, 156). Twisted withies
were also found in the Late Bronze Age ritual shaft
or well at Wilsford, Wiltshire (Ashbee *et al* 1989).
Iron Age woody ties are known from the Welsh
Marches at the Breiddin hillfort (Britnell and Earwood 1991, 164).

Fine finishing

From the last two phases, six pieces of wood showed
signs of having been cut into round cross-sections to
make pegs, dowels, or rods. Four were oak heartwood, one ash and one spindletree. The ash example
was apparently cut into the round at one stage but
had since split in half. The same appeared to have
occurred to one of the oak pieces (25047) which was
also in a poor state of preservation.

Five further pieces had been shaped into round
rods utilising wood split from much larger trunks.
One piece (20136) is a 0.30m long fragment of a

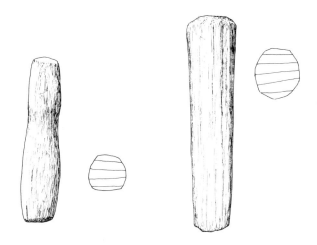

Fig 111 Finely finished oak pieces 20721 (left) and 20834. Scale 1:2

Fig 112 Roundwood with beaver teeth marks. Scale interval 100mm

radially split length of spindletree which has been cut into a round profile, of 20mm diameter. The item is very eroded and incomplete at one end but toolmarks can be seen at the other end. Two other pieces (20280 and 20721, Fig 111) are both small split oak fragments from a much larger tree, containing seven and twelve growth rings respectively. Object 20280 appears to have been cut into the round with a diameter of 21mm, and then split on one side. One end is incomplete so it is not possible to say whether it was just a peg or a longer rod. The other piece (20721) is 0.86m long and cut flat at both ends. It is round in cross section, but widens towards the top from a diameter of 16mm to 18mm. It may have been turned, but a long axe facet is preserved on one side, possibly to make it fit into a perforation. Another small piece of oak (20834, Fig 111) measured 120mm in length and had a diameter which tapered from 23mm to 31mm. It has been split from a much larger trunk and then cut on all sides to produce a round cross-section, both ends being cut at right angles to the grain.

The other interesting piece of finishing occurs on a stem of bird cherry (Earwood p 206) which was cut neatly at top and bottom, but also retained the stub of a side branch. This appears to be a small handled implement with the tip of the side branch forming the working end.

Beaver-gnawed wood

Seventeen pieces of wood from the Caldicot assemblage display the characteristic teeth-marks of European beaver (*Castor fiber*). The Caldicot beaver-gnawed wood derives from Phase III (5 pieces) and Phases VI and VI/VII (12 pieces). Because of the small size of the overall sample it is discussed here as a whole. The wood is all whole roundwood, either young saplings or side-branches, there being no indication that beavers were exploiting humanly felled wood. The identified wood species are mostly of hazel (14 pieces) with single examples of hawthorn and dogwood/guelder rose. The maximum length of the roundwood is 1m, and it ranges in diameter from 22–80mm, with an average diameter of 39mm. The beaver-gnawed wood comprised either chewed ends (10 pieces), chewed and de-barked roundwood (eg 1014, 8255) or chewed side-branches (eg 202). The beaver's 'felling technique' is clearly exemplified on one large piece (1014, Fig 112). The wood was removed by chewing at a shallow angle of 15 degrees, then with much of the outer wood removed, the bulk of the heartwood was cut through at an increasingly steeper angle of cut. The teeth-marks consist of a pair of parallel concave grooves, each 7mm wide, separated by a narrow ridge which reflects the gap between the two front incisor teeth. The smaller rods were chewed through from one side only, in the manner of axe cut chisel-ends. The entire bark was chewed off on the larger roundwood (6 pieces), presumably for food. In one example (8255), a piece of roundwood has been chewed at both ends.

The beaver practice of storing prepared lengths of roundwood underwater in their ponds, prior to chewing off the bark over the winter would lead to this wood being preserved in the anaerobic environment. The Caldicot material may derive from such food stores, and may have been washed downstream when spring floods damaged a dam. However there is some uncertainty as to whether the European beaver habitually builds dams. Modern evidence from Poland suggests it may not always do so (Coles 1992) and the few excavated examples of possible dams are far from convincing (Van de Noort 1993, 57).

Beaver-gnawed wood is known from various other prehistoric structures, from the Mesolithic platform at Star Carr, Yorkshire (Coles and Orme 1983) from the Baker site, a Neolithic platform in the Somerset

Levels (Coles and Orme 1982) and from the Late Bronze Age wooden causeway at Flag Fen, Cambridgeshire (Taylor 1992). Although beavers are no longer present in Britain, the ability of this industrious animal to effect large-scale transformations in the woodland landscape are becoming increasingly appreciated by archaeologists (Coles 1992). Beaver bone has been identified from the Caldicot faunal assemblage and they seem to have been present in Wales at least until the 12th century AD, when they are mentioned by the contemporary historian Giraldus Cambrensis. Beavers fell trees and bushes for food and may create dammed lakes in which to situate their lodges. Branches are suspended in the water for food during the winter, whilst the parts protruding above the water level are often eaten first. It is highly likely that such material would find its way into structural layers, either from deliberate collection by humans or more probably given its small size, as driftwood during flooding.

The activities of beavers in the locality could have had a profound effect on the woodland composition and thus on the wood available for structural purposes. This is because their tree-felling activities would have left large numbers of cleared stumps on the dry land, while their flooded ponds effectively clear-fell an area of woodland. When drained such large areas would have been then open for colonisation by such aggressive species as birch and hazel (Coles 1992). When one considers that beavers may have been living in the area throughout the period studied, it is obvious that they may have been the single most dominant force in shaping the local hydrotopography and woodland environment.

Conclusion

The wood from the Caldicot excavations gives a valuable insight into Late Bronze Age woodworking in South Wales. The local woodland was diverse in species and was affected by human activity, beaver industry and natural processes. A variety of structures and spreads of wood were encountered. There is some evidence for species selection in the choice of timbers for each structure. Trees were felled using a variety of techniques, cleft or hewn, sharpened and mortised according to their function. Woodworking debris testifies to riverside activity. A range of tool types were used, the cutting blades of which can be reconstructed to some extent. Experimental woodworking would be a valuable test for some of the issues raised.

Dendrochronology
Jennifer Hillam

Introduction

A total of 55 structural timbers and wood chips, of both oak (*Quercus* spp.) and ash (*Fraxinus excelsior*), were sampled for dendrochronology and examined at Sheffield over the period 1990–94. Of these, 38 proved suitable for measurement. All but four of the measured samples were from Phases VI and VII. Most of them were from three contexts: eleven from Area A (Phase VI and VII); eight from the possible 'trackway' 473, and seven from the bridge structure 22441 (full details are set out in Table 34). The other four measured samples were from Phase III; three were pieces of woodworking debris from context 22375 (20534, 24401, 24409) and the fourth was a sample through the boat strake 6001.

Methodology

The cross-sections of samples which were to be returned for conservation were pared with a razor blade along an edge or radius. The remainder were prepared by freezing them for at least 48 hours and then cleaning their cross-sections with a surform plane. Freezing consolidates the wood so that all the cross-section can be surfaced rather than just a thin radius. The ring widths were measured to an accuracy of 0.01mm on a travelling stage which is connected to an Atari microcomputer. The Atari uses a suite of dendrochronology programs written by Ian Tyers (pers comm 1993). The measured ring sequences were plotted as graphs using an Epson HI–80 plotter, also connected to the Atari. Crossmatching was carried out first visually by comparing the graphs on a light box, and then using a computer program to measure the amount of correlation between two ring sequences. The crossmatching routines are based on the Belfast CROS program (Baillie & Pilcher 1973; Munro 1984), and all the *t* values quoted in this report are identical to those produced by the first CROS program (Baillie & Pilcher 1973). Generally *t* values of 3.5 or above indicate a match provided that the visual match between the tree-ring graphs is acceptable (Baillie 1982, 82–5). For oak samples, a *t* value greater than 10 is taken to indicate an origin in the same tree. Comparisons of sequences from different trees rarely produce *t* values above 10, although ring sequences from the same tree sometimes give values less than 10. It is not yet known what minimum value should be applied to ash ring sequences thought to derive from the same tree.

After measurement, the oak and ash sequences were processed separately and a master chronology produced for each. These were then crossmatched against each other. From work on oak and ash samples from modern woodlands (eg Groves & Hillam 1988), it is known that oak and ash growth is sufficiently similar for their ring sequences to be crossmatched.

Dating is achieved by averaging the data from the matching sequences to produce a site master curve, and then testing that master for similarity against dated reference chronologies. A site master is used for dating whenever possible because it enhances the

Table 34 Details of the tree-ring samples. ARW – average ring width; HS – heartwood-sapwood transition; '+' – unmeasured rings

Wood number	Palaeo-channel group number	Context number	Species	No of rings	Sapwood rings	ARW (mm)	Dimensions (mm)	Comments
11	D.7.1	22441	oak	100	–	1.10	175 × 160	pile
12	A.6.1	9014	oak	47	–	1.51	140 × 135	upright
13	A.6.1	9014	oak	56	–	1.67	170 × 75	upright
27	B.7.1	473	ash	120	–	0.84	145 × 65	
50	A.7.1	175	ash	48	–	1.16	75 × 15	timber
56	A.7.1	175	ash	75	–	0.98	75 × 10	debris
57	A.7.1	175	ash	34	–	1.03	60 × 10	debris; insufficient rings
60	A.7.1	175	ash	50	–	0.69	55 × 10	timber
65	A.7.1	175	ash	–	–	–	70 × 15	timber; broken; c42 rings
92	A.7.1	175	ash	54	–	0.79	45 × 10	debris
98	A.6/7.1	175	oak	35	–	1.60	60 × 60	upright; insufficient rings
199	A.6.1	9014	oak	42	–	1.00	45 × 40	timber; insufficient rings
332	A.6.1	9014	oak	127	26	0.82	105 × 35	plank; felled winter; conservation sample
336	F.6/7.1	176	oak	40	–	2.20	95 × 20	timber; insufficient rings
474	B.7.1	473	oak	87	–	1.33	150 × 145	upright
813	B.7.1	473	ash	51	–	0.86	60 × 20	debris
815	B.7.1	473	oak	47	3?	1.27	65 × 60	upright
822	B.7.1	473	oak	57	–	1.06	65 × 45	stake
830	B.7.1	473	ash	88	–	0.89	85 × 15	debris
991	A.6.1	9014	oak	89	–	1.02	190 × 165	
1028	A.6/7.1	175	oak	73	–	0.61	50 × 25	debris
1084	A.6/7.1	175	oak	53	42	0.60	60 × 30	debris; bark edge
1184	B.7.1	473	ash	48	–	1.27	60 × 15	lath
1197	B.7.1	473	ash	50	–	0.68	40 × 15	debris
1200	B.7.1	473	oak	43	–	1.05	55 × 40	debris; insufficient rings
1259	A.6.1	9014	oak	50	–	1.01	50 × 45	debris
1350	A.6/7.1	175	oak	40	–	0.63	25 × 10	debris; insufficient rings
6001	B.3.3	7019	oak	107	–	2.33	690 × 120	boat strake; 2 radii conservation sample

Table 34 (cont.)

Wood number	Palaeo-channel group	Context number	Species	No of rings	Sapwood rings	ARW (mm)	Dimensions (mm)	Comments
7001	D.7.1	22441	oak	72	–	1.45	190 × 170	pile
8151	A.6/7.1	175	oak	75	HS?	0.80	145 × 140	upright
8346	B.3.3	7089	ash	–	–	–	35 × 10	debris; broken
20534	E.3.1	22375	oak	53	–	1.03	55 × 10	debris
20813	E.7.2	22308	oak	24	–	2.80	70 × 65	debris; insufficient rings
20835	E.7.2	22308	oak	39	–	2.26	75 × 30	timber; insufficient rings
24223	E.6.1	22330	oak	46	11	1.43	85 × 65	stake?
24401	E.3.1	22375	oak	50	–	0.99	55 × 25	debris
24409	E.3.1	22375	oak	60	–	0.96	60 × 25	debris
24435	H.7.1	22278	oak	88	–	0.56	70 × 15	debris
24438	E.6.1	22330	oak	48	–	3.76	180 × 70	debris?
24478	H.7.1	22295	oak	59	–	0.67	40 × 25	debris?
24560	D.7.1	22241	oak	61	–	1.48	120 × 90	stake
24837	D.7.2	22436	ash	66	–	2.01	135 × 75	plank; felled summer conservation sample
24852	D.7.1	22433	ash	51	–	0.69	40 × 15	debris
24856	D.7.1	22433	oak	38	–	1.32	50 × 20	debris; insufficient rings
25041	D.6.2	22440	oak	–	–	–	50 × 45	debris?; narrow rings - unmeasurable
25048	D.6.2	22443	oak	31	–	1.68	55 × 25	debris?; insufficient rings
25060	D.7.1	22441	oak	73	HS	1.12	180 × 60	pile
25130	D.6.2	22443	oak	54	23	1.28	150 × 105	debris?; felled summer
25223	D.7.1	22441	ash	67	–	1.06	110 × 85	stake; bark edge; felled winter
25553	D.4.1	22447	oak	28 +	16 +	1.42	90 × 75	c 5 rings to bark edge; rejected
25554	D.4.1	22447	oak	–	–	–	–	wood chip; broken; c46 rings
25613	A.6/7.1	22541	oak	19	–	2.63	85 × 50	insufficient rings
25726	C.3.2	22574	oak	–	–	–	35 × 10	debris; narrow rings
25817	D.7.1	22441	oak	70	1	1.10	205 × 200	stake
25824	D.7.1	22441	ash	180	–	1.26	235 × 75	stake; bark edge; felled winter
25846	D.6/7.1	22433	ash	41	–	1.17	50 × 10	debris; insufficient rings

general climatic signal at the expense of the background noise from the growth characteristics of the individual samples. Any unmatched sequences are tested individually against the reference chronologies. All potential tree-ring dates are then checked by examining the quality of the visual match between the graphs.

If a sample has bark or bark edge, the date of the last measured ring is the year in which the tree was felled. If the outer ring is complete, the tree was felled during the period from late autumn to early spring. For convenience, this is termed 'winter felled'. Where the ring is incomplete, the tree was felled during late spring to early autumn; this is known as 'summer felled'. Often, particularly where rings are narrow, it is not possible to distinguish between winter and summer felled trees.

In the absence of bark edge, felling dates of oak timbers are calculated using the sapwood estimate of 10–55 rings. This is the range of the 95% confidence limits for the number of sapwood rings in British oak trees over 30 years old (Hillam et al 1987). Where sapwood is absent, oak felling dates are given as *termini post quem* by adding 10 years, the minimum number of missing sapwood rings, to the date of the last measured heartwood ring. In the absence of bark edge, the *terminus post quem* for the felling of the ash timbers is the date of the outer ring since sapwood rings on ash are not identifiable. The actual felling date of both oak and ash timbers could be much later than the *terminus post quem* depending on how many heartwood rings have been lost.

Results

Of the 55 samples sent for analysis, 25 oak samples and 13 ash proved suitable for dating purposes. Most of the rejected samples had insufficient rings for their ring patterns to be unique. Although 50 rings is usually taken as the minimum number of rings needed for reliable dating (Hillam *et al* 1987), any of the Caldicot samples with more than 45 rings were measured because some of the wood chips might be cut from the larger timbers. Other samples were rejected because they were either broken or had unmeasurable narrow rings.

Details of the tree-ring samples are given in Table 34. The size and age of the trees used at Caldicot are described elsewhere in the wood studies report (Morgan p 194). The measured samples had 46–180 rings: the oak had 46–127 and the ash 48–180 rings. Most of the oak samples were without sapwood although three samples had bark edge. The season of felling of one is indeterminable; another was from a winter-felled tree, and the third from a summer-felled tree. A further three oak samples had some sapwood rings and two had possible heartwood-sapwood boundaries. Bark edge was present on four of the measured ash samples; three of these came from winter-felled trees and one from a tree felled in summer.

The tree-ring analysis shows that the average ring widths of the oak and ash samples have similar ranges (Table 35). The average ring widths of the oak varies between 0.6mm and 1.7mm, except for the boat strake 6001 (2.3mm) and 24438 from E.6.1 (context 22330) (3.8mm). The average width of the ash rings varies between 0.7mm and 1.3mm, except for 24837 from context 22436 (2.0mm). Not all the average ring widths are directly comparable since some represent more of the tree's lifespan than others, and the growth rate can vary depending on the age of the tree. The older rings, for example, are often much narrower than those at the centre of a tree. Nevertheless, the results suggest that many of the timbers were taken from very slow-grown trees. Their growth was obviously limited by one or more factors: possibly competition from other trees or perhaps an ecological factor such as exposed site. Other environmental evidence from the site might throw some light on this.

Dating

When the tree-ring curves were tested against each other, three oak sequences from E.3.1 (context 22375), crossmatched to give an 80-year master sequence (Tables 36a and Table 69a). No match was found between this master and the 107-year sequence from the boat strake 6001. Six oak and seven ash ring sequences crossmatched from Phases VI and VII (Fig 113; Table 36b). As well as inter-species crossmatching, several *t*-values over 3.0 were also obtained between the oak and ash sequences. When master sequences were constructed from the oak and ash curves to give a 134-year oak chronology and a 180-year ash chronology, they were found to crossmatch with a *t* value of 6.33. The mean ring-width data for these chronologies are held in archive.

The three master curves, and any unmatched ring sequence, were tested against reference chronologies of prehistoric date. Apart from a single Neolithic ash chronology from the Somerset Levels (Hillam *et al* 1990), these are currently all constructed from oak timbers. No significant match was found for the Phase III master or the sequence from the boat strake, but consistently high *t* values were obtained for the oak and ash chronologies from Phases VI and VII (Table 37). The oak chronology spans the period 1131–998 BC and the ash 1169–990 BC.

Interpretation

Area A. Two timbers were dated from this area (Fig 113; Table 38). The oak timber 332 associated with structure 9014 was felled in the winter of 998/997 BC, whilst the ash chip 92, from the later palaeochannel group A.7.1, was felled after 991 BC.

'Trackway' 473. None of the six dated ash and oak samples had bark edge. 1197 gives a *terminus post quem* of 991 BC for this group.

Table 35 Summary of the average ring widths

Wood number	Context number	Phase	No of rings	Average ring width	Species
50	Area A	VII	48	1.16	ash
56	Area A	VII	75	0.98	ash
60	Area A	VII	50	0.69	ash
92	Area A	VII	54	0.79	ash
1028	Area A	VI/VII	73	0.61	oak
1084	Area A	VI/VII	53	0.60	oak
8151	Area A	VI/VII	75	0.80	oak
27	473	VII	120	0.84	ash
474	473	VII	87	1.33	oak
813	473	VII	51	0.86	ash
815	473	VII	47	1.27	oak
822	473	VII	57	1.06	oak
830	473	VII	88	0.89	ash
1184	473	VII	48	1.27	ash
1197	473	VII	50	0.68	ash
6001	7019	III	107	2.33	oak
12	9014	VI	47	1.51	oak
13	9014	VI	56	1.67	oak
332	9014	VI	127	0.82	oak
991	9014	VI	89	1.02	oak
1259	9014	VI	50	1.01	oak
24435	22278	VII	88	0.56	oak
24478	22295	VII	59	0.67	oak
24223	22330	VI	46	1.43	oak
24438	22330	VI	48	3.76	oak
20534	22375	III	53	1.03	oak
24401	22375	III	50	0.99	oak
24409	22375	III	60	0.96	oak
24852	22433	VII	51	0.69	ash
24837	22436	VII	65	2.01	ash
11	22441	VII	100	1.10	oak
7001	22441	VII	72	1.45	oak
24560	22441	VII	61	1.48	oak
25060	22441	VII	73	1.12	oak
25223	22441	VII	67	1.06	ash
25817	22441	VII	70	1.10	oak
25824	22441	VII	180	1.26	ash
25130	22443	VI	54	1.28	oak

Table 36 *t* value matrix showing the level of agreement between matching ring sequences from a) Phase III and b) phases VI and VII. Values less than 3.0 are not printed; \ – overlap less than 15 years

a)

	20534	24401	24409
20534	*	9.3	6.6
24401		*	7.3
24409			*

b)

				ash						oak				
	27	92	813	830	1197	24852	25824	11	332	474	822	7001	25060	
27	*				3.5		4.1	4.5	5.8					
92		*		3.0	4.4	3.5	3.1	\		\	\			
813			*	4.5		5.2	3.2							
830				*	3.9	4.4	5.1		3.2					ash
1197					*	4.7	4.0	\		\	\			
24852						*	4.2	\		\	\			
25824							*	3.4	5.1		3.1		3.2	
11								*	5.5	4.9		4.1	5.4	
332									*	3.4	3.9		3.3	
474										*		5.7	3.1	oak
822											*			
7001												*	5.4	
25060													*	

Table 37 Dating the Caldicot oak and ash chronologies: t values with dated reference chronologies. Values less than 3.0 are not printed

Chronology	Ash (t = 6.3)	Oak
Belfast long chronology (Brown *et al* 1986)	3.8	4.4
Croston Moss 2, Lancs (Baillie & Brown pers comm)		4.0
Flag Fen/Fengate, Cambs (Neve 1992)	3.8	4.5
Germany (Becker pers comm)	3.8	
Goldcliff boat, Gwent (Hillam unpubl)	5.7	4.8
Leyland, Lancs (Baillie & Brown pers comm)		3.1
Skinners Wood, Somerset (Hillam 1993)	3.0	4.3

Bridge 22441. The ash stake 25824 was felled in the winter of 990/989 BC. The three dated oak timbers do not have bark edge but could be contemporary with 25824 (Fig 113). A felling date of winter 990/989 BC was also obtained for a piece of woodworking debris (24852) from 22433.

Dendrochronology therefore provides precise dates for some of the Phase VI and VII contexts. The bridge 22441 was constructed in, or very soon after, the winter of 990/989 BC. The 'trackway' could be the same date, or even a little earlier, whilst in Area A, timbers felled over the period 998 BC to at least 991 BC were deposited. There is no indication from the tree-rings that any of the timbers or woodworking debris came from the same tree.

Caldicot is currently one of four sites in England and Wales with Bronze Age timbers which have been dated by dendrochronology, and all have timbers which were felled around 1000 BC (Fig 114). At nearby Goldcliff, although the structural timbers so

Table 38 Summary of the tree-ring dates. In the absence of bark edge, oak felling date ranges are calculated using the sapwood estimate of 10–55 rings (Hillam et al 1987)

Context number	Wood number	Function	Phase	Date span of rings (BC)	Felled (BC)	Species
Area A (A.7.1)	92	debris	VII	1044–991	991 +	ash
473 (B.7.1)	27		VII	1125–1006	1006 +	ash
473 (B.7.1)	474	upright	VII	1119–1033	1023 +	oak
473 (B.7.1)	813	debris	VII	1072–1022	1022 +	ash
473 (B.7.1)	822	stake	VII	1103–1047	1037 +	oak
473 (B.7.1)	830	debris	VII	1080–994	994 +	ash
473 (B.7.1)	1197	debris	VII	1040–991	991 +	ash
9014 (A.6.1)	332	plank	VI	1124–998	998/997winter	oak
22433 (D.7.1)	24852	debris	VII	1040–990	990/989 winter	ash
22441 (D.7.1)	11	pile	VII	1131–1032	1022 +	oak
22441 (D.7.1)	7001	pile	VII	1096–1025	1015 +	oak
22441 (D.7.1)	25060	pile	VII	1098–1026	1016–971	oak
22441 (D.7.1)	25824	stake	VII	1169–990	990/989 winter	ash

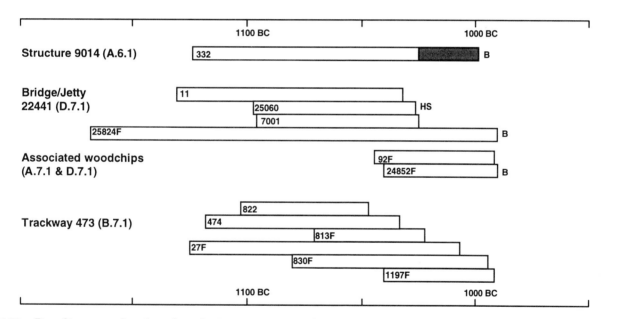

Fig 113   Bar diagram showing the relative positions of the dated ring sequences. White bars – heartwood rings; hatching – sapwood; HS – heartwood-sapwood transition; B – bark edge. Ash samples are labelled 'F' after the wood number; all other samples are oak

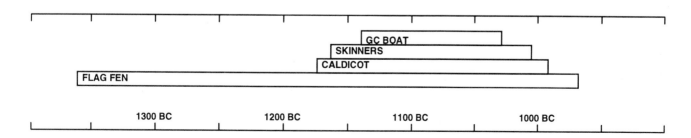

Fig 114   Bar diagram showing the relative positions of chronologies from other sites with Bronze Age timbers dated by dendrochronology. GC BOAT – boat fragments from Goldcliff, Gwent (Hillam unpubl); SKINNERS – Skinners Wood, Somerset Levels (Hillam 1993); FLAG FEN – Flag Fen platform / Fengate post alignment (Neve 1992)

Table 39 Species summary of all roundwood samples examined for tree-ring counts

Phase/ context	Unphased	II 472	III	VI/VII Area A	VII 1401	VII 473	VII 22441	Total	Approx %
Alnus glutinosa (L.) Gaertner			1	29		2		32	3
Cornus spp.	2	1	3	8		1		15	1
Corylus avellana L.	45	54	111	524	19	121	70	944	77
Fraxinus excelsior L.	6		3	41	2	3	5	60	5
Ilex aquifolium L.				1				1	
Ligustrum vulgare L.			2	2				4	
Pomoideae	3		9	27	1	4		44	4
Prunus avium (L.) L.				3				3	
Prunus spp.	1		5	1				7	
Prunus spinosa L.	3		20	32		3		58	5
Quercus spp.		1	1	23		2	1	28	2
Rhamnus cathartica L.				1				1	
Rosa spp.			1					1	
Salix spp.				3		1	4	8	
Sambucus nigra L.			1	2				3	
Taxus baccata L.			1	2				3	
Ulmus spp.			1	2				3	
Viburnum spp.				2				2	
Unidentified				7	2	1	1	11	1
Total	60	56	159	710	24	138	81	1228	

far dated are Iron Age, fragments from Bronze Age boat planks were felled after 1017 BC (Hillam unpubl). In the Somerset Levels, timbers from a trackway at Skinners Wood were felled after 993 BC (Hillam 1993). Finally in Cambridgeshire, the Bronze Age platform at Flag Fen and the adjacent Fengate post alignment also have timbers felled around 1000 BC, although here timbers were felled over a much longer period (Neve 1992).

Roundwood studies
Ruth Morgan

Introduction

Following identification to wood genus/species in Lampeter, some 1230 cross-sections of the brushwood and piles were microscopically examined. The aim of the roundwood study has been to determine the character and composition of the woodland cover growing in the area, which was exploited by those using the channels. The age, growth features and even the season of felling of trees and shrubs can be characterised through the study of the full cross-section of roundwood; split wood from the site was usually too compressed for study and was not examined. As the roundwood represented only a proportion of the wood from the site, this report should be read in conjunction with the species summary (Johnson p 158) and pollen analysis (Caseldine p 83), as well as the reports on the worked wood (Brunning and O'Sullivan p 163) and dendrochronology (Hillam p 187).

Whilst the process and nature of tree growth has been well studied in oak, most of the other wood species have never been subjected to detailed and rigorous research of their growth rates, and any conclusions reached here must take this lack of clear understanding into account.

The brushwood slices (which had been kept wet) were deep-frozen and their transverse surfaces cleaned with a surform plane, which revealed the boundaries of the rings clearly in most species, especially the lighter coloured ones such as alder. Records were made of:

- number of rings or age (assuming annual increment)
- diameter (average if compressed to an oval section)
- character of the rings (classified into five groups of generally wide, narrow, wide declining to narrow, uniform and variable)

• relative width and character of the outermost ring under the bark, if present, to suggest the season of felling.

The ring-widths of a group of mature hazel piles from structure 472, Phase II, were recorded using a calibrated graticule in the microscope, in an attempt to establish whether they were contemporary or even cut from the same stems, and whether they were cut at the same time.

Wood species

The species range of the samples examined in this study is shown in Table 39. Hazel (*Corylus avellana*) dominated the assemblage in all phases with about 77%. Ten percent of the remainder included the Pomoideae family (*Sorbus*, *Crataegus* and *Pyrus* among others), and species of *Prunus* – mostly *Prunus spinosa* (blackthorn), with several samples of *Prunus avium* (cherry). Ash (*Fraxinus excelsior*) comprised 5% and alder (*Alnus glutinosa*) 3% of the assemblage examined, and very small amounts of eleven other wood species were present in Phases III and VI in particular.

Description of the wood by phase

Phase II: Pile structure 472 (palaeochannel group C.2.1, see Fig 16)

The structure contained three possibly distinct groups of piles:

Group 1

The wood of this first group consisted of 22 piles placed in two parallel lines oriented south-west to north-east. The eight piles along the north-westerly line, all of hazel except one of dogwood, were clustered in the age range 20–35 years and 50–63mm in diameter (Fig 115a). The 14 piles along the south-easterly line include two lying further to the south-east (908 and 953). This group of piles ranged in age from 28 to 35 years and 53–74mm in diameter, with the exception of four piles outside the main group. Three of these were 11 years old (25877/891/8304) and one 14 years old (953); two of the piles (891/8304) were also smaller than the rest of the group at 33–46mm, while one (953) was significantly larger at 78mm.

On plan, the smaller than average piles give the impression of being tucked behind or between the other piles, and could be reinforcements or repairs – they correspond better with the general age, size and length of the group 2 wood and the horizontals described below and it may be more appropriate to consider them with that group.

With the exception of the outlying piles, the majority look from Fig 115a to have been selected for their suitable size of 50–65mm in diameter. Ages are also quite uniform at 25–35 years, but not in any way as to suggest coppicing -a system of management unlikely perhaps in hazel wood of such maturity.

The ages and sizes are consistent with more than one pile being cut from the same stem, a conclusion which is supported by the almost identical growth patterns in the rings of a number of the piles. For example, pile 890 at 35 years old and 62mm across could be the upper length of the same stem as pile 889 (lying adjacent to it), also 35 years old and 74mm in diameter (depending on the estimated original length of the piles). A hazel bush, growing in satisfactory conditions as these were, despite apparent setbacks and recovery shown in the rise and fall of their ring-widths, could support two or three such mature stems.

Growth rates were variable, with only a quarter of the stems demonstrating wide rings, a further quarter starting out with fast growth which declined, and around half growing at a variable rate throughout their life.

At least half the stems used for the group 1 piles may have been cut in winter.

Group 2

From group 2 to the north-east came 13 hazel piles (see Fig 16), all but one cut in winter, and all but two wide-ringed, many with uniform growth rates. The average age of these piles was just under 10 years (6–16) and average diameter 33.5mm (25–50mm) (Fig 115a). They were clearly different in age, size and growth rate from the wood used in group 1, and a different source of woodland growing in relatively stable and favourable conditions is suggested.

Outlying piles

Four piles located to the north-east of the main groups were again winter cut and wide-ringed; in size and age they were intermediate to the other two phases, at 11–18 years and 40–53mm.

Horizontals

Three horizontal pieces (8309/8310/8321) lay between the piles, all cut in winter, aged 7–9 years and around 30mm in diameter (Fig 115a). All were wide-ringed or fast grown. All these characteristics suggest they were part of the group 2 piles.

Phase III

Around 160 wood samples were analysed from this phase. Hazel again was dominant with 70%, *Prunus* spp. was also very important (16%), and small

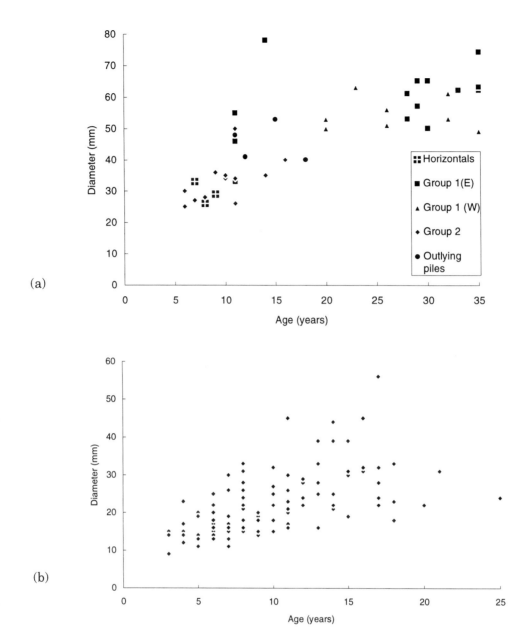

Fig 115   Distribution by age and size of the hazel stems used in (a) the pile structure 472, Phase II and (b) in all contexts in Phase III. There is a notable difference not only in the size and age range of the material collected but also in the growth rate

amounts of ten other woods were identified (Table 39).

The hazel stems almost all fell within a diameter range of 10 to 35mm (Fig 115b). In age they peaked at 5–18 years, and only two exceeded 20 years. The scatter indicates the compact and regular distribution which might be expected from the natural growth of hazel. Over half the stems were wide-ringed or fast-grown, and had enjoyed good conditions of growth.

Around 72% were cut in winter and a possible 11% in summer, suggesting relatively varied cutting seasons according to need.

The 25 *Prunus* samples were probably all *P. spinosa*, aged under 20 years and 10–43mm in size (peaking at 15–30mm). The scatter mirrors that of the hazel (see Fig 120). At least one third of the

blackthorn stems may have been cut in winter and almost half were wide-ringed.

The Pomoideae stems from the same contexts were faster-grown – of similar size but younger in age (see Fig 120), while the ash stems were much slower-grown.

Phase VI or VI/VII

This phase is represented by basal spreads of wood and stone in the main channels, dating to around 3050–2850 BP, located in areas A, D, E and G.

The spreads of brushwood were originally separated into areas, with earlier and later material; however, the time scale of deposition has now been demonstrated by dendrochronological dating and

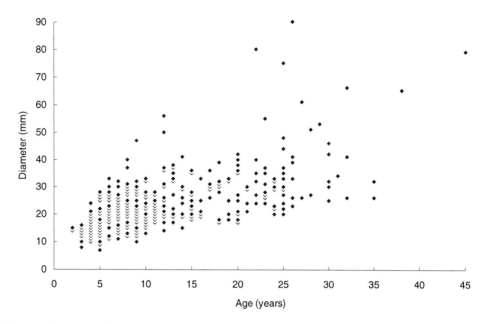

Fig 116   Distribution by age and size of the hazel stems from Phase VI

other means to have been very short, only a matter of a few years. Thus the material has been combined and comprises 710 samples. The assemblage included 74% hazel, 6% ash, 5% blackthorn, 4% each of alder and Pomoideae, 3% oak and 1% dogwood; there were also small quantities of 11 other species (Table 39).

The size of the hazel stems ranged from 7 to 90mm, peaking at 10–30mm (Fig 116 and 117); clearly this was the most useful dimension but occasionally larger stems were needed for strength and consolidation. The range in diameter closely resembles that from Phase III hazel and Phase VII, track 473 hazel (see Fig 117).

In age the stems peaked at 4–10 years (Figs 116 and 118), but there was a consistent appearance of stems up to 30 years old and a few were even more mature. There was no indication of any clustering of age or size – no indication of any previous cutting or management – and the hazel appeared to originate in the cutting of natural woodland. Around 65% was identified as winter cut, with a possible 6% summer cut. Over half the wood was wide-ringed, with only 13% demonstrating uniform growth (Table 40).

Phase VII

Bridge/jetty 22441 provided 81 samples, almost all (86%) hazel with some ash and willow (Table 39). The hazel revealed fast and uniform growth in almost all cases, and stood out as the only assemblage of wood with such high growth levels (Table 40), suggesting a unique source of very fast-grown wood. It was also the most consistent in size at 15–30mm, and in age at 3–14 years (Figs 119, 117 and 118) suggesting that it had been more carefully selected than the other groups of wood.

About one quarter of the wood had probably been cut in summer (Table 40), which is a high proportion compared to the other assemblages on site; it may indicate construction or even repairs during drier periods, when water levels were low.

Trackway 473 was represented by 138 samples of which 88% were hazel, with very small amounts of 7 other species (Table 39). As in other phases, the hazel fell into two groups in age; a younger group of under 15 years and a small more mature group of 20–25 years (Figs 118 and 119). In size the 'track' wood was very varied, peaking at 10–30mm but spreading up to more than 70mm (Figs 117 and 119).

Around 70% of the wood was identified as possibly winter cut with only a few stems suggesting summer cutting. Growth rates were very varied with about half the stems fast-grown (Table 40).

Hurdle 1401 produced only 24 samples with 79% hazel and small amounts of ash and Pomoideae (Table 39). The hurdle wood gave the only likely evidence of some previous cutting of the hazel stools, since almost all the stems were 5 years old, although they varied in size from 5 to 20mm (Figs 118 and 119).

Description of the major wood species

Corylus avellana

Hazel was represented overall by 77% of the wood samples, and between 70 and 96% of the wood in each phase; details are summarised in Table 40.

The age range was consistent in all phases – Fig 118 demonstrates that most of the wood is aged between about 3 and 15 years, with Phase VI having a significant amount of more mature wood. In most

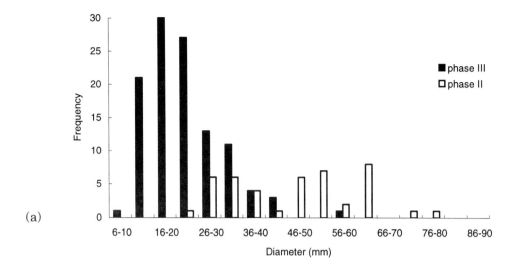

(a)

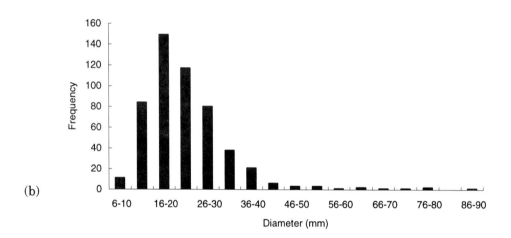

(b)

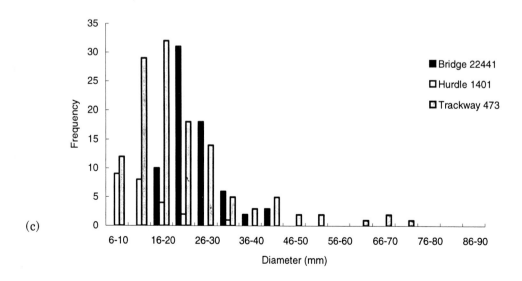

(c)

Fig 117   Histograms showing the size distribution of hazel stems from (a) Phases II and III, (b) Phase VI and (c) Phase VII

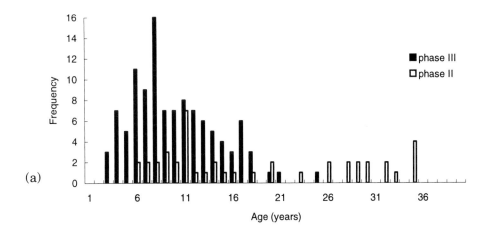

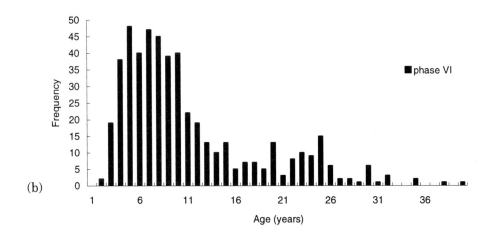

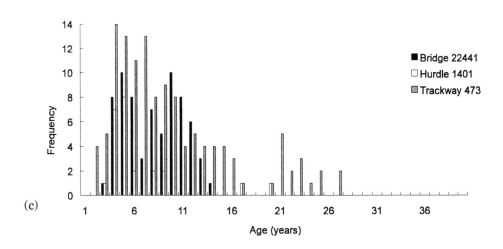

Fig 118   Histograms showing the age distribution of hazel stems from (a) Phases II and III, (b) Phase VI and (c) Phase VII

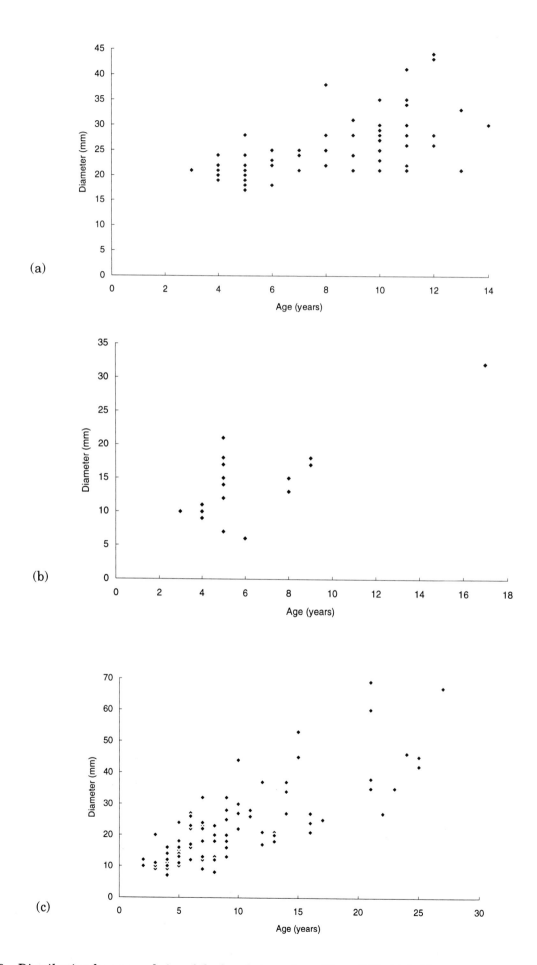

Fig 119   Distribution by age and size of the hazel stems from Phase VII: (a) bridge structure 22441, (b) hurdle 1401 and (c) 'trackway' 473

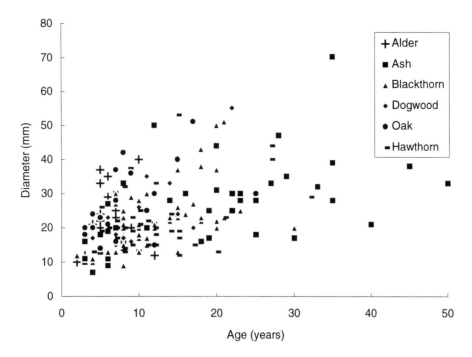

Fig 120 Distribution by age and size of stems of six other wood species – oak, ash, alder, blackthorn, dogwood and the Pomoideae group (probably hawthorn) – which made up a significant part of the assemblage, especially in Phase VI

cases there is a dip in the wood aged around 17–21 years, instead of a gradual reduction in age.

In size, the wood is concentrated between 10 and 30mm (Fig 117) throughout the period of use on the site, with a group of smaller stems in Phase VII and a group of larger stems in Phase II. Invariably, about 70% of the wood was considered to have been cut in winter, but small amounts of summer-cut wood occurred in all phases to supplement the supply.

Prunus spinosa

Blackthorn was the identification of 58 samples, with a further seven not firmly identified to species. Blackthorn hardly occurred in Phase II and only in very small quantities in Phase VII; but was largely concentrated in Phases III and VI, totalling 5% overall (Table 39).

Most stems were around 10–30mm in diameter, and ages ranged mainly from 5 to 20 years (Table 40, Fig 120), although it was difficult to record the precise number of rings because of the very faint ring boundaries, and the figures are approximations. About 40% of the stems were probably cut in winter, and a similar proportion were classified as wide-ringed.

Pomoideae

This group, which may represent one or more of a range of species but is thought most likely to have been hawthorn, was likewise present in most phases

and contexts in small amounts (Table 39), with the exception of Phase II structure 472 and Phase VII jetty/bridge 22441. It represented 4% of the total.

The age range spanned 5 to 20 years, the diameter 10 to 25mm (Fig 120). The wood was fast-grown and larger in size in Phase III, slower-grown and more concentrated in size at 15–25mm in Phase VI/VII (Fig 120, Table 40).

The Pomoideae samples were very pale in colour compared to the other waterlogged woods, and the rings were characteristically clear and wide, indicating rapid growth.

Fraxinus excelsior

Ash occurred mostly in Phase VI/VII, but was present in all phases except Phase II (pile structure 472), up to a total of 5% (Table 39). No split pieces from mature trees were examined, but the roundwood reached up to 50 years old and was generally very slow-grown by comparison with the other species. Age varied greatly, from 4 to 65 years (the ash were the most mature stems in this study), but size was concentrated in the 10–40mm diameter range (Fig 120, Table 40). Generally the young stems were wide-ringed and fast-grown, whilst the older stems tended to have zones of uniformly wide or narrow rings. Ash growth is frequently insensitive (ie apparently unresponsive, in terms of ring-width, to climatic variation).

About half the samples had clear bark surface (the remainder having suffered surface damage or were too narrow-ringed to determine the cutting season),

Table 40 Summary of the hazel samples divided by phase and context. The character of the ring patterns of samples are classified into five groups of generally wide, narrow, wide declining to narrow, uniform and variable

Phase	Context	No. Samples	% Total	Age Range	Age Peak	Diameter Range	Diameter Peak	% Cut Winter	% Cut Summer	Wide rings	Narrow rings	W–N	% Unif	Var
II	472	54	96	6–42	5–15	22–78	25–35	78	2	59	–	20	30	24
					25–35		50–65							
III	All	111	70	3–25	4–18	9–56	10–25	72	11	54	–	26	16	22
VI or VI/VII	Area A	524	74	2–45	4–10	7–90	10–30	65	6	54	4	23	13	16
VII	473	121	88	2–27	4–15	7–73	5–30	70	7	49	4	22	24	15
VII	1401	19	79	3–9	4–5	5–32	5–20	63	47	37	10	58	26	10
VII	22441	70	86	3–14	5–12	17–44	20–30	71	24	86	–	–	74	14

and revealed around 35–40% winter cutting with occasional examples of summer cutting. This species gives a clearer indication of cutting season than woods like hazel, because its ring-porous structure allows the two zones of spring and summer growth to be identified with certainty.

Alnus glutinosa

Alder was represented by 3% of the total sample, almost all from Phase VI (Table 39). Most were 3–7 years old, and there were signs of uniformity in age possibly relating to previous cutting. The majority of the stems varied in size from 10 to 40mm (Fig 120). Those from Phase VI were especially fast-grown. At least half the samples were probably winter cut.

Quercus spp.

Oak provided around 2% of the wood samples mostly from Phase VI (Table 39), and mostly fast-grown roundwood. The stems were 3–15 years old and 10–40mm in size (Fig 120, Table 40). The wood structure near the bark surface indicated that 13 (out of 28) had been cut in winter and one in summer – the figure of 46% winter cut is very similar to that for ash and blackthorn but much lower than the 70% determined for hazel.

Cornus sanguinea

Dogwood occurred in tiny amounts in all phases, totalling 1% (Table 39). The stems were generally 15–25mm in size and varied in age from 4 to 20 years (Fig 120)

Other Species

The ten other species occurred in such small quantities, often only of one sample, as to be largely uninformative, except to note their presence (Table 39). However, it should be mentioned that three out of four young willow stems from Phase VII structure 22441 were almost certainly cut in summer, whilst around half these samples from the minor species were probably winter-cut. A split radial piece of fast-grown elder (*Sambucus nigra*) (showing signs of fungal attack) came from a trunk in excess of 200mm across. A series of slow-grown yew (*Taxus baccata*) samples was supplemented by a group of tiny yew twigs from group 24427 (Phase III, see palaeochannel group E.3.1a, p 30); 56 fragments were 3–12 years old (averaging 7 years) and 5–13mm in diameter (averaging 8mm). Twenty-five stems had an off-centre pith which may be suggestive of branching.

The wood of these minor species fell into two distinct groups relating to typical growth rate – one of very fast-grown stems up to 15 years old and 10–60mm in size, including willow, elder, cherry, rose and guelder rose, and a second group of slow-grown wood 12 to 30 years old and 10–40mm in diameter which included yew, holly, elm, buckthorn and privet.

Discussion

Species range

It is suggested that the wide range of species present in most phases reflects the nature of the local underwood, and that little or no selection of specific wood species was being practiced. The predominant hazel and the range of trees preferring slightly acid and well drained soils (cherry, ash) points to a source away from the low-lying riverside, a theory supported by the very small amounts of wetland-typical alder and willow.

Blackthorn prefers woodland margins and does not like being overtopped. The shrubby and very spiney nature of blackthorn would have made it an unpleasant wood to handle, but its wood has a reputation for toughness. Blackthorn spreads by suckering and has been common on woodland margins since Mesolithic times (Rackham 1980); the frequent mention of thorns in charters and place-names (Rackham 1980, 17) indicates its importance, as fencing, firewood and a food source. It is on record as a source of fodder, and it is unfortunate that the colour and condition of the Caldicot wood did not always allow determination of the felling season of the blackthorn stems, which, if summer, might have suggested collection for fodder.

The almost complete absence of birch wood may suggest collection from natural primary woodland, which was not being managed or regularly exploited, though the evidence from the wood and other environmental sources indicates some interference with the local woodland cover had been taking place. Birch is an early coloniser of cleared woodland. If present in the woodland, at least one or two fragments might have been identified among the brushwood, even if it had been generally avoided owing to its poor quality as structural wood.

From the roundwood size and the species mix, the wood appears to represent the understorey trees and shrubs of a predominantly hazel woodland, mixed with a little blackthorn and ash. Few timber trees are represented (oak and ash are the only woods in this sample which grow to substantial timber size) within the subset of wood examined for this study. It should be noted in this context that hazel does not favour shading by timber trees, and its dominance and good growth may indicate that larger trees were relatively sparse.

Growth rates

Most of the roundwood examined in this study was probably collected originally because it was the correct size for the purpose – in all species this was between 10 and 30mm in diameter. Stems of this size were usually aged under 15 years depending on the rate of growth. Much of the Caldicot wood is fast-grown and therefore reached a suitable size quickly; growth rings were consistently wide in 50–60% of stems, the only exceptions being narrower-ringed wood in the Phase VII hurdle (1401) and wider-ringed wood used in the Phase II pile structure (472) and the Phase VII bridge/jetty (22441). Assuming a local source, the soils and degree of moisture must have suited woodland dominated by hazel, which clearly thrived for a period of time.

Around 15–25% of stems revealed uniform rates of growth, indicating that the trees grew in an area which maintained constant conditions and suffered little year-to-year variation in water levels and temperature. The only exception was the wood of jetty 22441 in which 74% of the wood had uniform ring-widths – they were also wider than average. It is surmised that this wood was carefully selected for its strength in the evenness of growth.

Only 10–25% of the stems were classified as having variable ring-widths, referring to wide year to year variations in growth and more marginal conditions.

Stem Size

In most contexts the stem size peaked at 10–30mm; the largest wood was used for the Phase II pile structure 472 and the Phase VII structure 22441, the smallest for the Phase II hurdle 1401. Within this broad range, little selection for size is apparent.

Stem age

Generally the spread in age was wide, from 2 years up to almost 100 years. In all phases the majority of the stems fell in the 5–15 year range, with smaller peaks at 20–25 years in some phases/structures where larger stems were required. The range appears to indicate a natural situation with no indication of any regular coppicing or management, except possibly the hurdle 1401 wood – a hurdle requires long even-sized flexible rods, usually grown by cropping the hazel stools whether on a regular basis or as required. A number of examples of heels found on the ends of the hazel rods support the evidence for previous cutting.

The most concentrated age range was found in the bridge 22441 (4–12 years) and the hurdle 1401 (4–5 years).

Cutting season

Assuming that the wood assemblage is the result of human felling and deposition (see p 158), the season of death of samples can be equated with the season of felling. Overall, around 70% of the hazel stems (Table 40) showed evidence of winter cutting (bearing in mind the uncertainties of interpreting growth in diffuse-porous woods). Around 6% of the rough brushwood was probably cut in summer, but the structural wood for the hurdle 1401 and bridge 22441 showed a higher proportion of summer cutting at 47% and 24% respectively, and 11% of the Phase III brushwood may have been summer cut. These figures suggest that, while winter was traditionally the most appropriate time to cut wood, the supplies were also supplemented by varying amounts of material cut during the summer, probably to take advantage of lower water levels.

Hazel wood from other sites

A number of assemblages of hazel wood from bronze age contexts have now been excavated and examined. The Eclipse and East Moors hurdle tracks in the Somerset Levels (Morgan 1988, 169) were constructed of wood of similar age and size to that of 'track' 473, although more contemporary with Phase II. The slightly earlier fuel supplies for the Mount Gabriel copper mines in Co Cork (O'Brien pers comm) consisted of hazel 10–45mm in size and aged up to 100 years. Hazel hurdle tracks across Nor Marsh in

Kent (Jackson pers comm; Morgan unpub), dated to around 3050 BP, produced hazel 5–15 years old and 15–30mm in size. This wood was much slower-grown than the Caldicot Phase II wood, but the scatter closely resembled that for the Phase VII bridge/jetty 22441. Gradually, as such assemblages are analysed, it will be possible to gather a clearer impression of the woodland cover and its exploitation in these low-lying areas.

Conclusions

Detailed study of a large assemblage of roundwood from Caldicot has suggested the collection of wood of a range of species and size from areas of predominantly hazel woodland in the vicinity. This has resulted in a variety (by species composition, age and size) of assemblages representing different patterns of use in different periods of time. In almost all phases and contexts, the size of wood selected or collected was generally around 10–30mm, and aged under 20 years; while there is little or no indication of any form of regular cropping or management of the nearby woodland, there is some indication that previous cutting had taken place.

The wooden artefacts
Caroline Earwood

Introduction

The quantity of wooden artefacts recovered from the excavation is not great. Items of a domestic nature include a fragmentary bowl, a ladle and a stave. Many of the other objects are more difficult to classify but include a variety of sword-shaped tools, beaters and a peg. This report does not include the remains of boats which are discussed elsewhere (McGrail p 210).

The majority of the items were recovered from deposits assigned to Phases VI and VII. Judging from their condition, which is generally neither weathered nor abraded, they represent debris from an adjacent settlement or working area. There is little evidence to indicate that they were subjected to extensive movement in the former river channel.

Discussion

The more easily classified domestic objects include the fragmentary remains of a number of wooden containers and a nearly complete ladle. The only wooden bowl (009), which was made from alder (*Alnus glutinosa*), is unfortunately in too fragmentary a state for reconstruction to be attempted. Comparison with contemporary wooden wares is therefore difficult although a similar bowl fragment is known from the late Bronze Age occupation at

Ballinderry crannog 2, Co Westmeath (Hencken 1942, Fig 7). The smooth appearance of the Caldicot bowl may be the result of deliberate polishing to remove toolmarks. The lack of toolmarks and the smallness of the fragment make it impossible to determine if the bowl was carved or turned.

The ladle (5406) shows similar evidence of polishing, resulting in the total removal of all toolmarks. In this respect, and in its general appearance, it is directly comparable to a ladle from Flag Fen, Cambridgeshire (Taylor 1992, 492–3). This also has a large, deep bowl with a handle curving up from it in an unbroken line. It is slightly larger than the Caldicot ladle, the bowl portion being approximately 170mm in length. A similar but smaller ladle, also of Late Bronze Age date, was recorded from Runnymede, Surrey (Needham and Longley 1980, 407). Such ladles are common finds from Alpine lake sites from both the Neolithic period (Muller-Beck 1965, Figs 237 and 239) and the Bronze Age (Perini 1987, plate 37.74).

The best-preserved fragment of a container from Caldicot is a short stave cut from ash (20074). It is difficult to ascertain whether the stave has been used; there are no marks of fittings or hoops. It was intended for a small tub or bucket 162mm in height with a diameter of approximately 250mm. The stave, which is 92mm in width, is directly comparable in its form to examples from the Wilsford Shaft, Wiltshire (Ashbee *et al* 1989, 51–67). Although no complete staves were preserved at Wilsford it has been estimated that they were between 75–100mm in width. Fragments of twisted withy suggest that the containers were bound with wooden hoops. The grooves of the Wilsford staves were made in a similar fashion to the Caldicot example, being cut by strokes directed straight into the wood which would have then been prised out. The profile of the Caldicot stave is typical of staves of Late Bronze Age/Early Iron Age date and has much in common with many carved two-piece cylindrical wooden vessels of this period. In the latter the purpose of the flange above the groove was to strengthen the vessel at the point of greatest stress. However such strengthening is unnecessary in the case of stave-built vessels where the base is inserted into the groove and the staves are then drawn tightly together (Earwood 1993, 161–2, 172–3).

The only other wooden container discovered at Caldicot is the remains of a heavily damaged alder (*Alnus* sp.) trough (20836). Its overall length is difficult to determine as it is damaged at both ends. The maximum length is 546mm, the greatest width is approximately 198mm. At one end there is the remains of a rectangular handle. A small circular hole had been cut in the base. Although generally in poor condition the exterior surfaces of the trough show signs of crude tooling, possible with an axe or adze. No attempt has been made to smooth the surfaces of the trough.

The remainder of the wooden artefacts are more difficult to classify and their function is uncertain.

They include four sword-shaped objects, two possible beaters, a possible spatula, two hooked sticks and a peg.

The four sword-shaped artefacts (272, 541, 940, 8457) have no obvious function. Three were made from oak (*Quercus* spp.), the fourth from ash (*Fraxinus excelsior*). It is unlikely that they could have been used as beaters as they would have had insufficient strength. They have some similarity to weaving swords used in Scandinavia during the Viking period and others of more recent date (Hoffman 1964, 47, Fig 14 and 138, Fig 60). No directly comparable weaving swords are known from late prehistoric, European contexts although there are a variety of sword-shaped objects some of which may have been copies in wood of metal types. Published examples include an early Bronze Age example from Robenhausen, Switzerland (Johl 1917, Fig 81) and another Bronze Age implement from Randers Fjord, Denmark (Bronsted 1939, 121; Capelle 1982, Fig 16). Such wooden swords sometimes show signs of use as fighting weapons: the Roman practice of using wooden swords during training indicates one possible function (Earwood 1990, 155). Wooden swords may have also been made as ritual substitutes for metal swords. Such objects, often made in miniature, are known from Cappagh, Co Kerry (Lucas 1960, Fig 12) and from the Breiddin, Powys (Britnell and Earwood 1991, 164–5).

The two beaters are not especially similar in appearance. One (256) has close similarities to beaters used in the early stages of flax preparation. The beater is 660mm in length with a width across the blade of 100mm. Beaters of this type, with blades either round or sub-rectangular in section, were used in Europe until the mechanisation of flax production during the 19th and 20th centuries (Earwood 1993, 127). Similarly shaped beaters from archaeological contexts have been noted from early historic sites in Ireland including Ballinderry crannog 1, Co Westmeath (Hencken 1936, Fig 8C) as well as from sites at Walthamstow probably dating to the late prehistoric period (Earwood 1990, 108). Although similar in size and shape these beaters are not identical to that from Caldicot. The second beater (8209), which is damaged, is smaller (maximum surviving length 410mm). It is crudely made with sharp angles on one face. Although there are no definite indications of wear on the blade the size and shape of this artefact would suggest use as some form of heavy-duty beater. Both beaters are made from oak (*Quercus* spp.)

A crudely-made rectangular object (832) could have been used as a spatula or stirring stick. It has no direct parallels although more finely-made spatulae are recorded from Neolithic contexts including the Sweet Track, Somerset (Coles and Orme 1976, Fig 41) and from Ehenside Tarn, Cumbria (Darbishire 1874).

It is unclear what the function of the hooked stick (1161) may have been. Its shape suggests use as some form of hook or handle. The use of side branches to form handles, hooks and tool mounts is not unusual. Such forms were used from early prehistoric times in mounting stone tools such as axes and adzes. There is however no indication that this is the case in this instance; the top of the side branch is untrimmed and its curving surface would make the mounting of any tool difficult. Other hooked sticks of unknown function have been identified from a variety of prehistoric and early historic sites, including examples from Feddersen Wierde, Germany (Haarnagel 1979, Fig 31.21) and Deer Park Farms, Co Antrim (Earwood forthcoming). Ethnographic examples from eastern Europe have been used as hooks to which ropes were attached. These were used as an aid to climbing trees during honey-gathering. Similar hooks, which were stuck into house walls, were used for hanging up clothing and domestic utensils. The former use might be relevant to the mooring of boats.

A single peg was identified (1136). It is 246mm in length, tapering to a pencil point. It might have had various functions including securing joints, pegging down wooden structures or in boatbuilding.

Catalogue

009 Fragment of container, probably a bowl (Fig 121). The fragment is from the side of the vessel and does not include any part of the rim or base. It is not possible from the curvature of the surviving fragment to estimate the size of the original container. The thickness varies from 1mm to 6mm; height of fragment 81mm; length 110m.

The surface of the wood, both internally and externally, is very smooth, suggesting polishing. There are no toolmarks visible on any surface and no indication that the vessel was manufactured by turning. If it had been, it is highly likely that at least some slight concentric scoring would be visible particularly on the interior. The growth rings of the wood are prominent on the outer surface of the fragment. They are widely-spaced and the patterning indicates that the container was manufactured from a piece of timber of considerable size.

Wood species: *Alnus glutinosa*

Context: Phase VII, Area A, palaeochannel group A.7.1

256 Beater or paddle, broken into two parts, a bladed portion of approximately rectangular shape, and a handle portion. The total length is 740mm. The blade portion is approximately 500mm in length; this then tapers towards a waisted part which connects the blade to the handle which is approximately 160mm in length. The object is split from a piece of large roundwood so that the surface

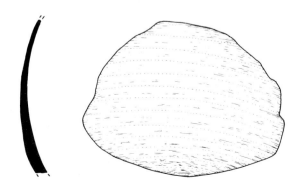

Fig 121 Fragment of a container, probably a bowl, 009. Scale 1:2. Drawing by Caroline Earwood

of the back of the blade is the outer surface of the branch with the centre of the stem forming a slight ridge along the length of the blade. The handle has been further worked into an approximately rectangular section (59mm by 34mm at the end). The maximum width of the blade is 100mm with a maximum thickness of 34mm.

The beater/paddle is slightly decayed and desiccated so that there are no clear toolmarks. It is clear, however, that it was manufactured by radial splitting of a straight-grained stem of large roundwood after removal of the bark. Further processing, probably with an axe, included shaping of the ends which are slightly rounded, and of the handle. The waisted portion between the handle grip and the blade has been deliberately and carefully shaped. It is at this narrow part that the artefact has broken.

Wood species: *Quercus* spp.

Context: Phase VI, Area A, Structure 9014 (palaeochannel group A.6.1)

272 Sword-shaped artefact, broken into two pieces; one end is damaged. The surviving length is 610mm, the maximum width is 55mm and the thickness 18mm. The broken end terminates at the point where a handle might be expected, so that the whole of the surviving artefact forms the blade portion. This appears to be widest towards the middle of the artefact but there is considerable damage towards the broken end. The end tapers towards a blunt point which is also slightly damaged.

The artefact was manufactured from a piece of split timber. There are no clear rays but the rings are visible running in almost parallel lines through the thickness of the blade. The back of the artefact is slightly curved so that the thickest part is approximately in the centre of the width of the blade. The upper surface of the blade has two level surfaces which join near the middle of

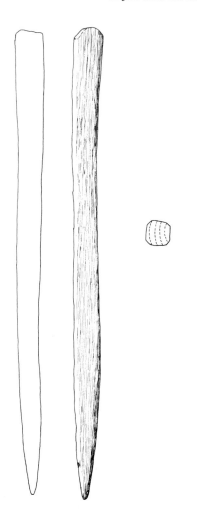

Fig 122   Peg, 1136. Scale 1:2. Drawing by Aidan O'Sullivan

the width forming a slight ridge along the length of the artefact. The wood is slightly decayed and desiccated so that no toolmarks are clearly visible.

Wood species: *Fraxinus excelsior*.

Context: Phase VI/VII, Area F (palaeochannel group A.6/7.1)

541 Fragment of sword-shaped object. The remaining portion of this object is composed of the blade end which is broken into two pieces and incomplete. The surviving length is 245mm, the maximum width is 50mm. It was manufactured similarly to 256, being radially split from a straight-grained roundwood stem. The back of the blade follows the natural curve of the outer part of the stem and there is a slight ridge along the length of the face of the blade which corresponds to the centre of the stem. The end of the blade tapers to a blunt point which is now damaged. No toolmarks are visible although there appears to have been little decay or desiccation.

Wood species: *Quercus* spp.

Context: Phase VI/VII, Area B (palaeochannel group B.6/7.1)

832 Spatula (?), broken into three pieces. The object is 235mm in length, the width varies from 24mm to 48mm. The widest portion is across the blade and the narrowest is towards the handle end. The thinnest part of the object is the handle (6mm). The blade has been roughly shaped to create a slight depression. The artefact was manufactured from a length of split timber: the rays run almost parallel from side to side. No clear toolmarks are visible.

Wood species: *Quercus* spp.

Context: Phase VII, Area B, Structure 473 (palaeochannel group B.7.1)

940 Fragmentary sword-shaped artefact, broken into four pieces, only three of which can be joined together. The maximum length of those parts which can be joined is 302mm, the maximum width (52mm). The thickness of the undamaged part is approximately 7mm. Although both ends are damaged, sufficient remains of one end to show that it tapers towards a blunt point. The object has suffered some decay so that no toolmarks are visible. It was manufactured from a length of split timber with the rays running almost parallel from side to side of the blade.

Wood species: *Quercus* spp.

Context: Phase VI/VII, Area A (palaeochannel group A.6/7.1)

1136 Peg, 246mm in length, with a flat top 13mm by 15mm (Fig 122). The other end tapers to a pencil point which has been trimmed on all sides creating a series of facets. The peg was manufactured from a length of straight-grained split timber (probably radially split): the rings are visible in section curving slightly across the width of the peg. The peg is in good condition with toolmarks on the point which suggest the use of a tool with a wide blade, such as an axe or billhook, rather than a smaller tool such as a knife.

Wood species: either *Alnus* sp. or *Corylus avellana*.

Context: Phase VII, Area B, Structure 473 (palaeochannel group B.7.1)

1161 Hooked stick or handle made from a roundwood stem with part of one side branch left *in situ* (Fig 123). The branch projects from the main stem at approximately 45 degrees and has been trimmed to a blunt point. The top of the stick has been cut across in a number of broad facets. The other end of the stem has been trimmed to a blunt pencil point. The stick is slightly curved although this may be partly the result of distortion due to waterlogging and the pressure of overlying deposits. Apart from where the wood has been trimmed, ie the points, much of the bark remains in situ. The stem is broken towards one end. The total length is 305mm, the diameter varies between 20mm and 24mm.

Wood species: *Prunus padus*

Context: Phase VI, Area B (palaeochannel group B.6/7.1)

1254.1 Bent stick or handle made from a split piece of timber, probably radially split, and further trimmed into an approximately rectangular section (Fig 124). The stick tapers from a section 14mm by 25mm to a broken point. The length is 340mm. From the growth ring pattern it appears that the stick was probably bent into its present curved shape.

Wood species: *Corylus avellana*

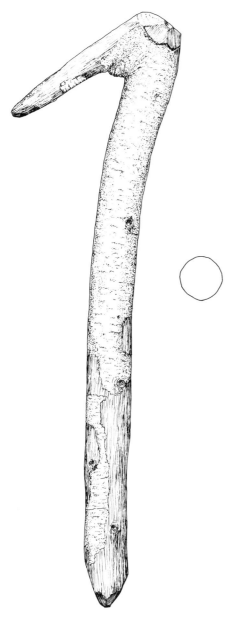

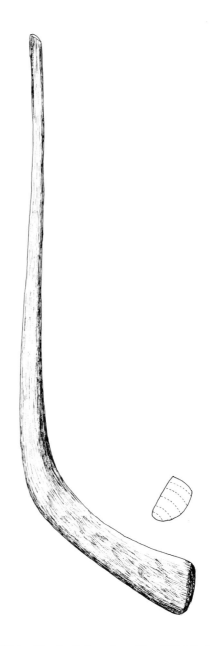

Fig 123   Hooked stick or handle, 1161. Scale 1:2.
Drawing by Aidan O'Sullivan

Fig 124   Bent stick or handle, 1254.1. Scale 1:2.
Drawing by Aidan O'Sullivan

Context: Phase VII, Area B, Structure 473 palaeochannel group B.7.1)

5406 Ladle with large elliptical bowl which is now slightly distorted and broken on one side (Fig 125). Originally the bowl was probably more or less symmetrical with a flat base and sides curving outwards. The length of the bowl part of the ladle is *c* 140mm, with the end being slightly damaged. The width across the interior of the base of the bowl is *c* 45mm. The handle of the ladle is approximately rectangular in section (10mm by 16mm where broken) with a thicker and wider portion where it joins the bowl. The end of the handle is broken.

The ladle is finely finished and was possibly polished so that there are few toolmarks surviving. Its condition makes it difficult to examine the growth pattern but it appears to have been carved from a block of split timber. The ring pattern visible at the break in the handle shows widely spaced rings with little curvature, indicating that the timber was from a tree of some considerable size.
Wood species: *Betula* spp.
Context: Phase VI/VII; found during mechanical excavation of possible midden area between areas F and G

8209 Bat-shaped artefact, possible beater manufactured from a length of radially-split timber. The timber used represents less than a quarter segment of the whole tree. The beater is incomplete; it is broken across the handle end. The surviving length is 410mm. At its widest point the blade is 75mm but this varies considerably as the object was not fully trimmed on its edges so that a number of knots form protuberances. One face of the beater is almost flat while the other has a slight spine along its length. The thickness varies from 19mm to 39mm but with a consistent taper from the broken end to the blunt point. It appears that the bat or beater was made by splitting with little secondary working. There are no clear tool facets remaining.
Wood species: *Quercus* spp.
Context: Phase VI, Area A, Structure 9014 (palaeochannel group A.6.1).

8457 Part of sword-shaped artefact consisting of the blade (Fig 126). The surviving length is 295mm, the maximum width is 56mm. The object was manufactured from a length of radially split, straight-grained timber. Secondary trimming was carried out to form a blunt point at one end. The blade varies little in

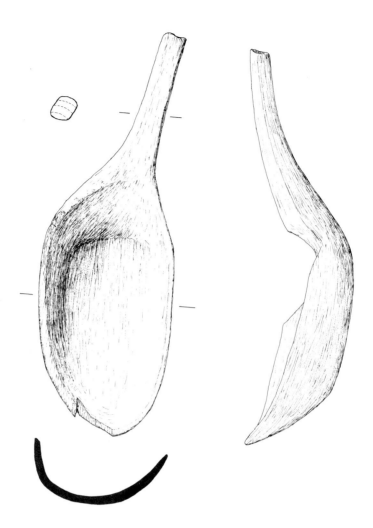

Fig 125   Ladle, 5406. Scale 1:2. Drawing by Aidan O'Sullivan

thickness (c 20mm). Although the artefact is in good condition no toolmarks are visible.

Wood species: *Quercus* spp.

Context: Structure 9014, Area A (palaeochannel group A.6.1)

20074 Stave from small bucket or tub (Fig 127). The stave, which is in almost perfect condition, is 162mm in height with a maximum width of 92mm, across the back at the lower end. It tapers from bottom to top: the thickness at the bottom edge is 10mm while that at the rim is 5.5mm. At about 25mm from the bottom edge the stave thickens into a flange which is 16mm in thickness, below which has been cut a groove in which the base of the container would have rested.

The outer face of the stave has not been smoothly finished, but although the surface is irregular, there are no identifiable toolmarks. The inner face has been more smoothly finished. There is no indication of the type of hoops that were used: no marks of bands can be seen and there are no fastening holes. A crack, running from the rim partly down the stave, passes through two small holes, but these are more likely to be the result of damage than fixing points for hoops.

The curvature of the stave is sufficient to reconstruct the original diameter of the vessel to which it belonged. This vessel would have stood 162mm in height and had an outer diameter of approximately 250mm.

Wood species: *Fraxinus excelsior*.

Context: Phase VI, Area A, 22004 (palaeochannel group A.6.1)

20836 Possible trough, now fragmentary with one end missing (Fig 128). Both sides are damaged and little of the rim remains. It was crudely made; the exterior in particular is roughly finished.

The maximum surviving length is 546mm, the surviving width is 198mm. Across the midline of the vessel the thickness varies from 7mm on one edge, close to the original rim, to 21mm near the centre. However the thickest point is where the vessel curves around at the end, and here the wood is 44mm thick. What remains of the vessel is approximately elliptical with a depth of 64mm. At one end the remains of a handle survives. This is now broken from the body but appears to have protruded from the end at the level of the rim. The handle is approximately rectangular with a length of c 70mm and a width of 48mm. It is 14mm thick in the middle. The only other notable feature of the vessel is a circular man-made hole cut in the bottom and slightly to one side. The hole, which is now damaged, is c 39mm in diameter.

The vessel was cut in such a way that the central part of the tree growth is visible at either end just below the rim. The vessel was therefore made from a log which was first split in half and then carved into shape. The exterior was roughly trimmed to the curvature required but, at what is now the damaged end, little wood was cut away so that in places the original outer surface of the tree is visible. Toolmarks are visible in the vicinity of the surviving handle but they are insufficiently clear for the tool type to be identified. The surface at this point has a dimpled appearance. The exterior surface is better preserved than the interior probably due to the protection of the surrounding deposits. The interior was originally more carefully smoothed but the surface is now partially obscured by a mineral deposit. The wood has also been penetrated by roots.

At the damaged end three pieces of wood were found lying across the vessel. Two of these appear to be fragments from the end but the third does not belong to this artefact as it is of a different wood species (*Fraxinus excelsior*).

Wood species: *Alnus glutinosa*.

Context: Phase VII, Area E, 22308 (palaeochannel group E.7.2)

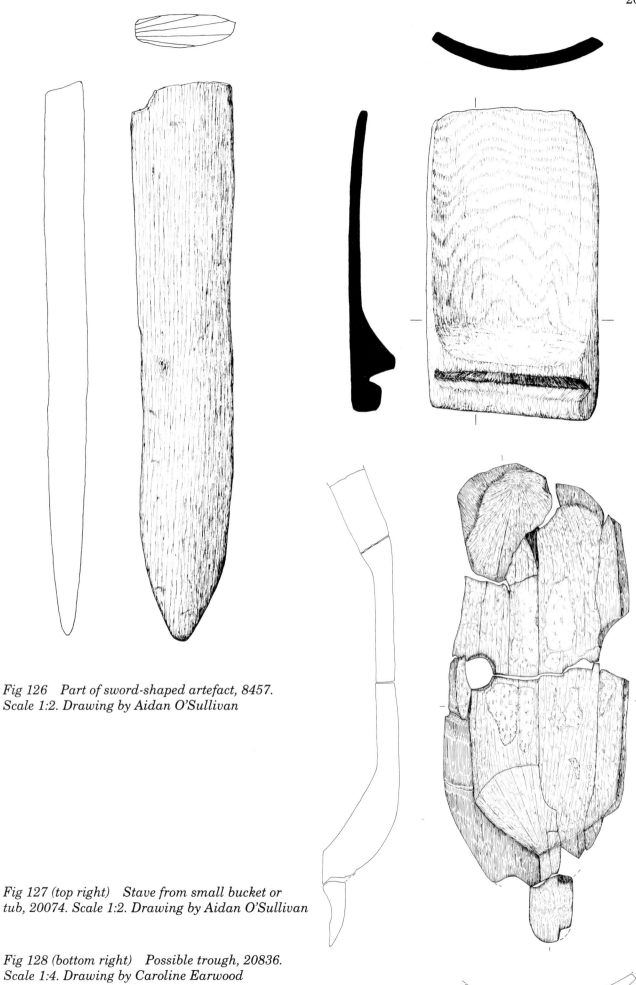

Fig 126   Part of sword-shaped artefact, 8457.
Scale 1:2. Drawing by Aidan O'Sullivan

Fig 127 (top right)   Stave from small bucket or
tub, 20074. Scale 1:2. Drawing by Aidan O'Sullivan

Fig 128 (bottom right)   Possible trough, 20836.
Scale 1:4. Drawing by Caroline Earwood

210

The boat fragments
Sean McGrail

Some of the most important finds from Caldicot were fragments of prehistoric boats. These nautical finds, some certain, some possible, come from three phases of this site:

Phase III

6001 and 20684: a large fragment from a sewn boat plank.

8441 and 8442: two fragments of wooden sewing material (fibre rope).

8440: a possible baler handle.

Phase VI

8331: a possible cleat fragment from a sewn boat plank.

8143: a small fragment from a sewn boat plank.

Phase VII

477: a plank fragment possibly from a sewn boat:

A large fragment from a sewn plank boat: 6001 and 20684 (Figs 129–132)

Context: Phase III, Area B (palaeochannel group B.3.3)

Fragment 20684 was excavated detached from, and to the north of, the main plank fragment 6001 (Fig 129). During post-excavation recording, it was found to match a series of broken holes along the western edge of 6001. In this description, therefore, these two finds are treated as one (Figs 130 and 131).

The raw material

This is a substantial plank of oak (*Quercus* spp.), its overall length being 3.55m, greatest breadth 0.66m,

Fig 129 Oblique photograph of plank 6001 on a plinth during excavation. The bevelled edge is to the right. Fragment 20684 was found in the baulk at the top of the picture. View to north

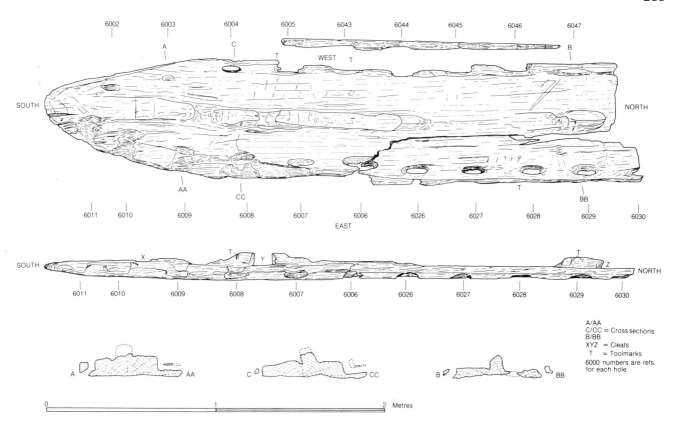

Fig 130 Plan of the upper surface (as found) of plank 6001/20684 with sections. Drawing: GGAT. and Institute of Archaeology, Oxford

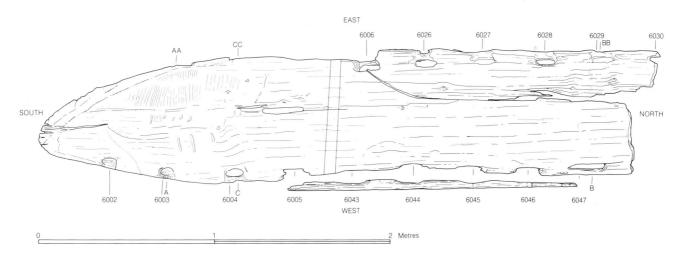

Fig 131 Plan of the underneath surface of plank 6001/20684. The position of the dendro slice is marked by parallel lines. Drawing: GGAT and Institute of Archaeology, Oxford

maximum thickness 0.09m and estimated weight 128kg. As its northern end was broken off in antiquity, it must have been longer when in use. The parent oak of this plank would have had a maximum diameter of at least 0.86m, that is, a girth of *c* 2.70m, and thus was comparable in size with the parent oaks of Ferriby boat 1 (girths > 2m.) and the Brigg 'raft' (girths 2.7 to 3.3m). It was, however, significantly smaller in girth (and possibly in length) than the great oaks used to build such logboats as those from

Brigg (5.70 × 14.78m), Hasholme (5.40 × 12.58m) and Poole (5.40 × 10.01m) (Millett and McGrail 1987, Table 4). With an average ring width of *c* 2.40mm (see Table 34), this Caldicot oak had a moderate growth rate. The alignment of the growth rings and medullary rays in the cross section of this plank (Fig 130) indicate that it had been fashioned from a half log. It has not proved possible, however, to identify the vertical orientation of the plank within its parent tree (by, for example, angle of branch insertion –

Other possibilities → mud sledges, cartwheels.

McGrail 1978, 120), but the shaping and the thickness of the southern end of the plank suggests that this end was nearer the tree's butt or lower end.

Description

Caldicot – less definitely a boat

Preliminary descriptions have been given by Parry and McGrail (1991 A 1991B, 1994). The breadth of this plank, away from its southern end, varies from 0.59m to 0.66m and its thickness is now generally 50mm to 60mm, near the middle line, and 60mm to 90mm towards the edges. The underneath surface (as found) of this plank had been fashioned at its southern end to a curved shape in three dimensions, including chamfering of the edges. The remainder of this surface has been badly eroded, either during use or, more probably, during the early stages of deposition.

wide spacing holes → sewing

The edges and the protruding parts of the upper surface (as found) have also been damaged, probably after primary use and before excavation. Toolmarks (T on Fig 130) can be seen on this surface, evidence for the final dressing of the plank to give it a relatively smooth finish. Projecting from this face are the broken remains of three cleats (X, Y and Z on Fig 130), integral with the plank and on its centreline. Cleats X and Y measure *c* 0.66m in overall length and are *c* 100mm in breadth where they blend into the plank's upper face. The three cleats were probably *c* 100mm in height originally, and the sub-rectangular holes through them probably measured *c* 120mm × 40mm.

The western edge of this plank had been worked square to the plank faces; the other edge has a rabbet cut along its length which generally measures 30mm × 35mm, but which increases markedly in breadth (parallel to the plank face) towards the southern end, to a maximum of *c* 120mm.

Holes have been cut through the plank some 35mm to 55mm in from each edge at a spacing, centre to centre, of 0.33m to 0.38m (mean 0.35m). These holes are generally elliptical in section, with lengths varying from 69mm to 220mm. and widths from 33mm to 60mm. The mean hole dimensions are 134mm × 42mm. The holes near the eastern, rabbeted edge are L-shaped lengthways and run parallel to the two faces of the rabbet, emerging within the plank edge. Most of the holes along the western, squared, edge are similar, but the two holes nearest the southern end (6002, 6003) are angled rather than L-shaped and emerge through the plank's underneath face (Fig 131).

Interpretation

Arguing a tongue + groove joint more likely than a butt joint

The finds from North Ferriby (Wright 1990), Brigg (McGrail 1981; 1985) and Dover (Parfitt and Fenwick 1993) survived to be excavated in an articulated state and they had sufficient recognisable features, including caulking associated with sewn planking, to make their identification as plank boats almost a certainty. The Caldicot find and the recent find from Goldcliff on the Severn foreshore (Bell 1993, 9–11), are both, on the other hand, relatively minor in extent and they do not have all the characteristic features of those finds that are undoubtedly boats. The question must be asked, therefore, whether they are indeed parts of boats. Could there be other Bronze Age artefacts or structures with sewn planks and transverse timbers through cleats: mud sledges, perhaps, or even cartwheels? Such possibilities must be borne in mind; nevertheless, in the case of the Caldicot fragment, its woodworking techniques (the cleats, the fastenings and the scantlings) and its location in a river bed suggest that it was once part of a sewn plank boat of the size and shape of Ferriby 1 (Wright 1990).

The wide spacing (mean 0.35m) of the Caldicot plank's fastening holes suggests that these holes were for individual stitches or lashings as in the Ferriby and Dover boats, rather than the continuous sewing of the Brigg 'raft'. The curved nature of the plank's southern end and its reduced width indicate that it came from near the bow or the stern of a boat where the bottom was rising and the breadth narrowing towards an elongated, rounded end.

The holes along the edges of the Caldicot plank are significantly bigger (mean, 134mm × 42mm) than those of Ferriby 1 (elliptical, 35mm × 25mm; square, 25mm × 25mm). Furthermore, the plank edges of the Caldicot plank are, in section, unlike those on the Ferriby bottom planking: in fact, the rabbet along the eastern edge of the Caldicot plank is the mirror image of the rabbet on the upper edges of the first (lowest) *side strake* of Ferriby boats 1 and 3 (Wright 1990, Fig 4.8f). It seems likely, therefore, that this Caldicot plank was part of a second, or even higher, side strake (Fig 132) which was usually above the waterline where the danger of shipping water through such large holes would have been least. The edge with the rabbet (eastern) would probably have been the lower edge, with the squared edge uppermost. In this alignment, the plank would have fitted on the boat's starboard bow or port quarter where the curvature of its outer (underneath as found) face near the end would have blended into the boat's curving bow or stern and its cleats would have been inboard. Ideally, at least by 20th century standards, this plank should have been broader at the bow or stern end to maintain the horizontal run of the upper edge of this strake; however, the reduced breadth may have been forced on the builder because of insufficient or damaged timber in the chosen log.

Alternatively, it is conceivable that the rabbeted edge of the Caldicot plank was uppermost in the boat. In this case the upper edge of the first side strake would have to match the Caldicot squared edge. Whilst not impossible, a butted joint, with no overlap, seems unlikely with a plank of such breadth as the Caldicot plank: a 'tongue and groove' joint such as on the Ferriby outer bottom plank (Fig 132) would be structurally sounder. Aligning the Caldicot plank this way would bring its non-standard fastening

Dinorora *Erson* *Faraks* *3 cleats* *may have been a keel plane* *side strake* *holes* *Brigg 'raft' → caulking → sewing* *Dover 'raft' → caulking → sewing*

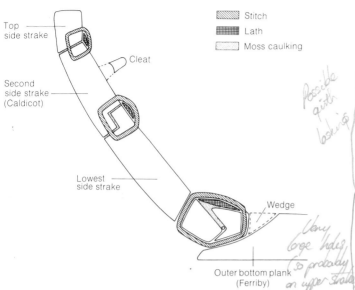

Top side strake

Cleat

Second side strake (Caldicot)

Lowest side strake

Wedge

Outer bottom plank (Ferriby)

▨ Stitch
▦ Lath
▨ Moss caulking

Possible girth lashing

Very large holes so probably on upper strake

Fig 132   Diagram to illustrate the use of plank 6001/20684 as a second side strake in a sewn plank boat. The hypothetical first side strake matches a Ferriby 1 outer bottom plank at its lower edge and matches the lower edge of 6001/20684 at its upper edge. The hypothetical third (top) side strake matches the upper edge of 6001/20684. An actual Ferriby 1 or 3 first side strake would match the rabbet of the Caldicot plank but not the run of its fastening holes. Not to scale. Drawing: Institute of Archaeology, Oxford

Possible 3rd strake

holes (6002, 6003) to a lower level in the boat. At this level, some 0.40 to 0.50m above the bottom of the boat, the risk of damaging the visible, though inset, stitches may well have been unacceptable. The alternative hypothesis, that the rabbeted edge was the lower one (as in Fig 132), is preferred, not least because it more readily matches the Ferriby evidence.

Seen as a 2nd strake. Protective stitching

When in position as part of a second or higher side strake, the fastenings of the Caldicot plank would mainly lie within its thickness (Fig 132) and, although visible inboard, would not be visible from outboard. Thus, when this boat was berthed near the water's edge where the sides (especially near the ends) might be pushed and scraped against river bank or rising ground, the hidden stitching would not be damaged. The fastenings along the upper edge were similarly protected, for although the two holes (6002 and 6003 on Fig 130) nearest the bow emerge in the outer face of the plank, they do so within an inset, and these stitches, though visible from outboard would not have protruded. Figure 132 shows the Caldicot plank fitted as a second side strake in a Ferriby style of boat. It should be emphasised that, although the rabbet along the upper edge of an actual Ferriby 1 and 3 first side strake generally matches the Caldicot rabbet, the Ferriby fastening holes do not match those of Caldicot. Furthermore, the Ferriby side strake rabbets (Wright 1990, Fig 4.4) do not

Hidden stitching so as not to be damaged

appear to have the varying width of the Caldicot rabbet.

Why the two holes, 6002 and 6003, were angled rather than L-shaped is not clear: it may be that girth lashings passed through these holes as well as plank fastenings, although there are no signs of wear or of pressure marks evident on the Caldicot plank. Girth lashings would supplement the plank fastenings and bind the strake ends in place: they have been postulated in hypothetical reconstructions of Ferriby boat 1 (Wright 1990, Figs 5.2, 5.17, 5.20, 5.22).

It is a widespread boat-building principle to minimise the size of holes in the underwater parts of a boat, and it has therefore been argued above that the Caldicot plank was part of a second or higher side strake because of its relatively large holes. Why these holes were so large (c six times the cross section area of the Ferriby holes) is not clear. It may be that hand-size holes near the edges were useful when handling such large and heavy planks during building and during periodic dismantling to renew fastenings. Furthermore, it may have been easier and quicker to cut large rather than small holes within the thickness of the planking.

A third strake must have been fastened to the upper edge of the Caldicot plank. A Ferriby-style 'tongue and groove' joint is theoretically possible here but a butted joint seems more likely; in which case this third, and probably uppermost, strake would have been narrow and in the nature of a capping (Fig 132), except towards the end where it would have had to be broader to fill in the gap left by the downward curving end of the Caldicot plank (see, for example, the hypothetical top strake (SS.3) of Ferriby 1 (Wright 1990, Fig 5.14)).

The form and size of the Caldicot cleats are more like those of the Brigg 'raft' than those of the Ferriby boats. No cleats were found on the fragmentary sides of the Brigg or Ferriby boats; however, they have been used in hypothetical reconstructions of Ferriby boat 1 (Wright 1990, Figs 5.2, 5.17, 5.19, 5.21) where side timbers are shown lashed within gaps in the cleats by fibre ropes which pass through small fastening holes, as found, for example, in the Nydam boat (Åkerlund 1963) and, below the waterline in the early Viking period Oseberg and Gokstad ships (Sjøvold 1969, 24). The Caldicot cleats, however, had mortised holes which are now broken; moreover there are no fastening holes in these cleats. It seems likely, therefore, that side timbers passed through the Caldicot cleats and were wedged there, as were the transverse timbers in the bottom of the Ferriby boats and the Brigg 'raft'. It is relevant to note here that the side strakes of the Dover boat also have cleats with mortised holes rather than cleats with gaps. (Parfitt and Fenwick 1993, Fig 17.3).

Cleats → more like Brigg.

Cleats → no fastening holes → so probably transverse timbers as in Ferriby and Brigg.

Conjectural sequence of manufacture

After the parent tree, which was at least 120 years old, had been felled and the head removed, the trunk

5H   Ferriby + Caldicot fastening holes are very different

Construction

214

was split longitudinally down the middle and one half chosen to become plank 6001/20684. The bark and sapwood were then removed from this half-log and the outer part of the log worked away leaving oversize cleat blanks projecting from the surface of the timber at the required stations. One edge of the plank was then worked square; the other edge was worked to a shape, and given a rabbet, which matched the upper edge of the strake already in position on the boat. The plank face without cleats was then worked to the required thickness and one end shaped in three dimensions to fit approximately the curvature of the bow or stern.

Two or three L-section holes were then cut through this plank near its squared edge and used to hoist and then suspend it in position at one end of a second side strake. The plank was checked for fit against adjacent parts of the boat and marks were made along its lower edge corresponding to the fastening holes in the plank below. After being removed from the boat, the plank was trimmed to shape, the rabbet cut accurately, and further holes cut along both edges; the two upper ones near the curved end being angled rather than L-shaped. The end towards the middle of the boat was fashioned to the shape necessary to join it to the next plank in this strake.

The plank was again hoisted into position and final adjustments made to its lower edge, its ends and its outer surface. If there proved to be gross mis-match at this stage, the plank would have been lowered from the boat for further fashioning.

After being lashed in position, holes were cut through the cleat blanks in line with holes in cleats on the strake below. The oversize cleats were then finished to shape, and a final shaping given to inner and outer faces of the plank.

Importance of this find

There are only six other prehistoric plank boats from Northern Europe, all with sewn planking: the Hjortspring boat of the 4th century BC (Rosenberg 1937), Ferriby boats 1, 2 and 3 of *c* 1300 BC, the Brigg 'raft' of *c* 800 BC and the recently excavated Dover boat of *c* 1400 BC. The Caldicot find, being the oldest of this type, with a calibrated date of 1874–1689 BC at two standard deviations, is thus of international importance, significantly adding to our knowledge of early boats and increasing the data base available for wider studies involving early transport, technology and trade/exchange.

The Caldicot plank is also of importance in a specifically British context. There are several features which the Ferriby and Brigg boats have in common. They were built in the shell sequence (ie their shape came from the shell of planking and not from any framework) from substantial oak planks which were fastened together either by individual lashings or by continuous sewing, with a moss caulking held in position between the planking by longitudinal laths. Special constructional techniques

were used to ensure that, when the boat took the ground (was beached), the plank fastenings were not damaged. The planking was also linked together by transverse timbers wedged within mortises in cleats which were proud of, and integral with, the planks. The two finds which can be hypothetically reconstructed, Ferriby 1 and the Brigg 'raft', seem to have originally been narrow, relatively long boats. The technical details of the Dover boat have not yet been published but this boat appears to have most, if not all these features.

Within this general similarity there are differences of detail. For example, the Ferriby boats were presumably built to ferry passengers and goods across the fast-flowing Humber estuary and had a 'conventional' boat shape: on the other hand, the Brigg 'raft' was built to ferry people and animals across the upper reaches of a relatively quiet Humber creek and thus had a 'box-like' shape. At a more detailed level, in the Brigg 'raft' the plank fastenings were protected from damage by shaping the cross section of each plank so that the sewing holes were well above the bottom (McGrail 1981, 234); whilst the Ferriby sewing holes were worked within the 'tongue and groove' seams (Wright 1990, 65–8). The Caldicot boat plank is different again in details, thus adding to our knowledge of woodworking techniques in the British Bronze Age. Whether these and other differences were regional, temporal, functional or indeed cultural, remains to be investigated.

Although the Caldicot cleats are more like Brigg cleats in shape and size, they are more like Ferriby in being irregularly spaced. The Caldicot plank's date, shape and scantlings, and the use of lashed, rather than sewn, fastenings suggest that its parent boat was generally like Ferriby 1 and that it was probably used in a similar manner in the Severn estuary and in tributary rivers such as the Wye, Nedern and Usk.

The Caldicot plank also demonstrates that, within Britain, sewn plank boats were not solely a speciality of the Humber estuary. This contention is further supported by the recent find of sewn planking at Goldcliff, only 13km away, on the Severn Estuary foreshore (Bell 1993). It seems likely, therefore, that other sewn plank boats will be found in British waters.

Fragments of fibre rope: 8441 and 8442 (Fig 133)

Context: Phase III, Area B (palaeochannel group B.3.3)

8441 and 8442 are split lengths of yew (*Taxus baccata*) withy (244mm × 8mm and 165mm × 11mm) which have been debarked and then twisted upon themselves to form a rope similar in size to the two-stranded rope used to fasten the planking of the Brigg 'raft' (McGrail 1981, 101, 234). These Caldicot stitch fragments are probably too flimsy to have been used with the Caldicot plank (6001/ 20684) but may

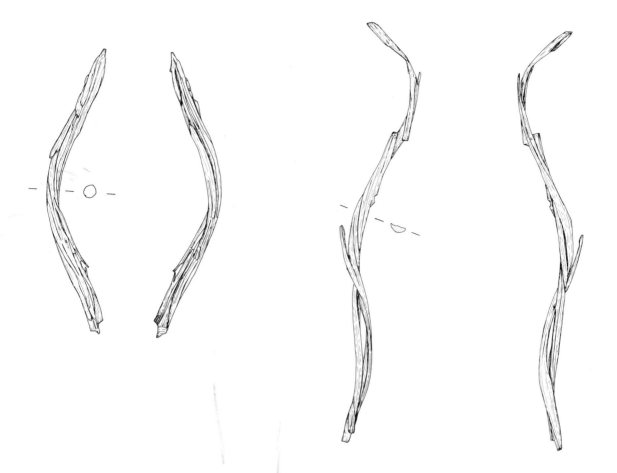

Fig 133 *8441 and 8442: two fragments of wooden sewing material. Scale 1:2. Drawing by Caroline Earwood*

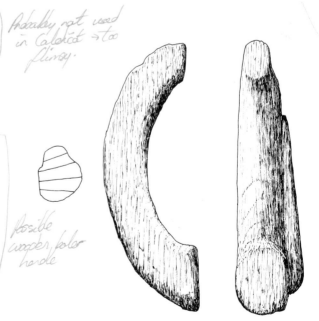

Fig 134 *8440: a possible baler handle. Scale 1:2. Drawing by Aidan O'Sullivan*

have been used in other, less stressed, parts of that boat or in a boat with timbers of different scantlings, similar, for example, to plank fragment 8143 (below) and the Brigg 'raft'.

Possible baler handle: 8440 (Fig 134)

Context: Phase III, Area B (palaeochannel group B.3.3)

A curved timber of oak (*Quercus* spp.) with a rounded cross-section, which has been worked with shortgrain from a radially split board. It has a maximum overall length of 140mm and a diameter of 34mm to 26mm. This fragment is of the right shape and size to have been the handle of a wooden baler, but other, equally likely, uses can be envisaged.

Possible cleat fragment: 8331 (Fig 135)

Context: Phase VI, Area A (palaeochannel group A.6.1)

A fragment of oak (*Quercus* spp.) with an overall length of 160mm which may have broken away from the top of a cleat on a plank of similar dimensions to the Caldicot plank (6001/20684)). Other, equally likely, uses are possible.

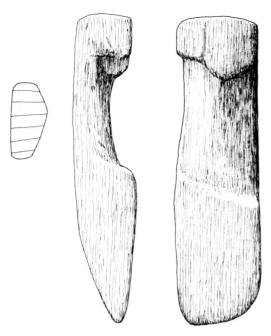

Fig 135 8331: a possible cleat fragment from a sewn boat plank. Scale 1:2. Drawing by Aidan O'Sullivan

Small plank fragment: 8143 (Fig 136)

Context: Phase VI/VII, Area A (palaeochannel group A.6/7.1)

A fragment of oak (*Quercus* spp.) planking, 0.33m in length, worked from a radially-split board. It has features similar to those of the Brigg 'raft' planking: the corresponding Brigg measurements (McGrail 1981, 86) are given in brackets in the following description. The fragment is *c* 14mm (9mm) thick at

its surviving edge, increasing to *c* 21mm (20–30mm) near its other, broken, edge, some 60mm away. Six holes of diameter 5 to 8mm (9 ± 1mm) have been worked 12 to 20mm (18mm) from the surviving edge; their average spacing is 41mm (55 ± 7mm) and the thickness of the planking at these holes is *c* 15.5mm (9mm). The larger, incomplete hole near one end of the fragment is probably secondary, as also found on the Brigg 'raft'. If allowance is made for the tangential and radial shrinkage experienced by the Brigg 'raft' planking during its exposure for at least four months in the summer of 1888 (McGrail 1981, 3), fragment 8143 can be seen to be very similar to an outer section of a Brigg bottom plank. Fibre 'rope', similar in dimensions to that of finds 8441 and 8442 (above), would have been used to fasten this planking to an adjacent plank.

Plank fragment, possibly from a sewn boat: 477 (Fig 137)

Context: Phase VII, Area B, Structure 473 (palaeo-channel group B.7.1)

An oak (*Quercus* spp.) fragment *c* 0.365m in length, and *c* 20mm thick, with two broken edges and a longitudinal ridge which protrudes some 21 to 26mm above the planking. This ridge is 14mm broad at the top, increasing to 37mm where it blends into the planking. Although there are no mortised holes through this ridge it may be compared with the ridges along the centreline of the planks of Ferriby boat 2 (Wright 1990, Fig 4.13). Unlike Ferriby 1, which had individually-shaped cleats, Ferriby 2 had four sets of cleat ridges through which several mortised holes were cut, the average spacing, centre to centre, being *c* 0.26m. The Goldcliff fragments (Bell 1993, Fig 2.2) are similar.

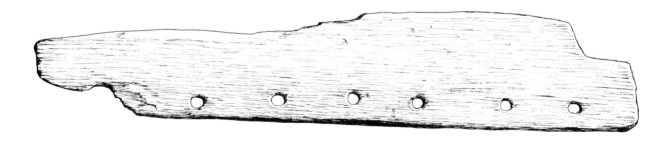

Fig 136 8143: a small fragment from a sewn boat plank. Scale 1:2. Drawing by Aidan O'Sullivan

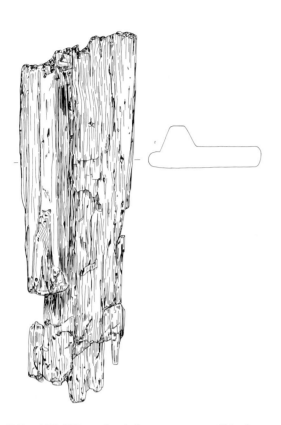

An alternative possibility is that this fragment may be compared with the bottom planks of the Dover boat which have longitudinal ridges with mortised holes, near one edge (Parfitt and Fenwick 1993, Fig 17.3): this potential similarity will be further investigated when the Dover boat is published in detail.

As this fragment has no features, such as sewing holes or worked edges specifically suggesting that it is a plank from a sewn boat, other uses are possible.

But no definite sewn features

Fig 137   137477: a plank fragment possibly from a sewn boat. Scale 1:4

The artefactual evidence

The animal bones
Finbar McCormick, with contributions by Sheila Hamilton-Dyer and Eileen Murphy

Introduction

The animal bones from Caldicot survived in a very good condition owing to the waterlogged nature and neutral pH of the deposits at the site. A wide range of species were represented (Table 41). The bones were from the bed of a series of former river channels and the assemblages are composed of those that owe their presence to anthropogenic processes and those that owe their presence to purely natural factors. In many instances it is difficult to differentiate between the two. The bones of small mammals, predominately water vole but with a few of field vole also, reflect the natural fauna of the area and are unrelated to human activity on the site. The presence of the bones of field vole predators, such as heron and barn owls, are more difficult to interpret. These may represent human food refuse, but at the same time may simply represent the scattered bones of naturally occurring birds.

The status of the fish is also ambiguous. The Phase II semi-complete skeletons of five flatfish, almost certainly flounder, undoubtedly represent natural mortality, as too do the bones of the stickleback and small 'bootlace' sized eels. Only in the case of the single salmon vertebrae (Phase VI) is it likely that human exploitation is being reflected.

Mammal bones

Introduction

The majority of mammal bone was recovered by hand during excavation. In addition to this, some vole bones were recovered from sieved soil samples. These, as well as the hand retrieved vole bones, are not included in the general quantification tables as they reflect natural processes rather than human activity. The animal bones from the different phases are listed in Tables 42 and 43. Those from Phases VI and VII are considered together. Where applicable a minimum and maximum minimum number of individuals (MNI) was estimated. The minimum MNI was based simply on the most frequently recurring bone element of each species without taking bone size or ageing data into consideration. These factors were, however, considered when estimating a modified MNI value which has been used in a few of the contexts. A summary distribution of the species noted in the different contexts is shown in Tables 42 and 43. It is clear that only the Phase VI–VII group was large enough to be of statistical value.

Phase summaries

Phase I

This Neolithic context provided no evidence for human activity. The only bones present were of

Table 41 Species noted at Caldicot. ? = identification uncertain

Mammals	Birds	Fish and amphibians
Cattle : Bos taurus L	goose, Brent? Branta bernicla	Common eel Anguilla anguilla
Pig: Sus domesticus Erxl.	Mallard Anas platyrhynchos	
Sheep: Ovis aries L.	Wigeon? Anas penelope	Stickleback, cf 3-spined
Horse Equus caballus L.	Pintail? Anus acuta	Gasterosteus aculeatus
Dog Canis familiaris L.	Tufted duck Anhya fuligula	Flounder? Platichthys flesus
Red deer Cervus elaphus L.	Crane Grus grus	Salmon Salmo salar
Roe deer Capreolus capreolus L.	Heron Ardea cinerea	
Fox Vulpes vulpes L.	Little grebe Podiceps ruficollis	Common frog? Rana temporaria
Water vole Arvicola terrestris	Barn owl Tyto alba	Common toad Bufo bufo
Field vole Microtus agrestis		
Beaver Castor fiber		

Table 42 Distribution of fragments and MNI percentages from different levels. MNI percentages were not calculated when no value was greater than one. *A near-complete dog skeleton is not included in the fragments values. ** Modified MNI value (see text and Table 60)

	Cattle	Horse	S/G	Pig	Dog	Fox	Red deer	Roe deer	Beaver	No.
Fragments %										
Phase II	83.3	–	–	–	–	–	16.6	–	–	6
Phase III	37.7	–	27.9	19.7	6.6	1.6	6.6	–	–	61
Phase IV	66.6	–	33.3	–	–	–	–	–	–	3
Phase V	50.7	–	43.5	4.3	–	–	–	1.4	–	69
Phase VI–VII	18.6	0.7	57.2	8.9	5.5*	7.7	1.4	–	0.2	586
MNI										
Phase III	1	–	2	2	2	1	1	–	–	9
Phase V	2	–	2	1	–	–	–	1	–	6
Phase VI–VII**	3	2	8	3	3	2	2	–	1	24
MNI %										
Phase VI–VII**	12.5	8.3	33.3	12.5	12.5	8.3	8.3	–	4.1	24

Table 43 Small mammals, birds, fish and amphibians. Those marked x were from flotation and sieving residue. Their presence was noted but they were not quantified

Phase	I	II	III	IV	V	VI–VII
Vole		x	x		x	x
Bird						
Geese	–	–	–	–	–	1
Ducks	–	–	–	–	–	71
Crane	–	–	–	–	–	6
Heron	–	–	–	–	–	1
Grebe	–	–	1	–	–	1
Owl	–	–	1	–	–	–
Unid	–	–	–	–	–	3
Fish						
Eel	–	x	x	x	x	x
Stickleback	–	–	x	x	–	x
Flounder?	–	3	–	–	–	–
Salmon	–	–	–	–	–	1
Unid	–	–	x	–	x	x
Amphibian	x	x	x	–	–	x

amphibians, from a sieved sample, and a fragment of broken red deer tine.

Phase II

A small quantity of cattle was present. The femur fragments appeared to have been split for marrow extraction and displayed evidence of gnawing (see Table 55).

Phase III

It was clear that most of the bones from this phase of occupation constituted discarded food refuse. The fact that some of the unfused bones still had their epiphyses *in situ* suggested that the bones had not been greatly disturbed since their initial deposition. There was evidence for gnawing, indicating that at least some of the bones were not directly thrown into

Table 44 Distribution of fragments and MNI values from Middle and Later Bronze Age sites in Britain and Ireland after (Done 1991, 331–339; Hamilton-Dyer, unpub, Legge 1981; 1992, Levitan 1990, 222; McCormick 1991; 1994). MNI total **The values for Grimes Graves are based on mandibles only

	Cattle	Horse	S/G	Pig	Dog	Wolf	Fox	Red deer	Roe deer	Beaver	No.
Fragments %											
Caldicot Ph. VI–VII	18.6	0.7	57.2	8.9	5.1	0.5	7.7	1.4	–	0.2	586
Great Orme, Viv. Shaft	58.2	–	13.6	27.2	–	–	–	0.9	–	–	448
Runnymede Bridge	29.6	3.3	25.9	34.4	2.4	–	–	P	P	–	2339
Brean Down Unit 4b	47.5	0.9	48.5	2.2	0.6	–	–	0.3	–	–	1759
Grimes Graves MBA	62.8	1.1	26.0	4.5	–	–	–	4.0	1.6	–	1284
Grimes Graves Sh. X	46.8	1.1	45.8	5.1	–	–	–	0.8	0.3	–	3988
Ballyveelish	67.5	3.2	12.9	15.1	0.9	–	–	0.4	–	–	800
Haughey's Fort	65.3	1.8	2.9	24.9	4.6	–	0.2	0.6	–	–	1083
Dun Aonghasa	58.6	0.2	39.1	1.9	–	–	–	0.1	–	–	7700
MNI %											
Caldicot VI-VII	12.0	8.0	32.0	12.0	12.0	4.0	8.0	8.0	–	4.5	24
Runnymede Bridge	27.7	8.5	25.5	38.3	P		–	P	P	–	47
Brean Down Unit 4b											
Grimes Graves MBA**	56.5	0.9	34.5	5.3	–		–	0.9	1.8	–	222
Grimes Graves Sh. X*	53.2	1.1	39.0	5.2	–		–	0.6	0.6	–	267
Ballyveelish	39.1	4.3	15.2	32.6	4.3		–	4.3	–	–	46
Haughey's Fort	53.7	3.7	5.5	25.9	7.4		1.9	1.9	–	–	54
Dun Aonghasa	34.1	1.9	50.6	12.0	–		–	1.3	–	–	158

the river after cooking. The dog sample was unusual in that it consisted exclusively of three mandibulae and a canine tooth from a mandible. The sample was too small to allow useful quantification but it could be suggested that cattle were becoming secondary to the other main species, a pattern that was emphasised in the larger, later samples from Phase VI/VII (see Table 56).

Phase IV

This produced an insignificant bone assemblage (see Table 57).

Phase V

Again there was much fragmentation of the large cattle bones indicative of marrow extraction. There was no gnawing visible on the cattle bones; this coincided with the absence of dogs in the sample (see Table 58).

Phase VI/VII

This, the largest sample, indicated clear predominance of sheep in terms of both fragments and MNI

totals (see Table 59). There are few other extant Middle/Late Bronze Age assemblages from Wales (Caseldine 1990, 64), and the data from southern Britain in general during this period are fairly limited. The largest samples are from Middle Bronze Age abandoned mine-shafts at Grimes Graves, Norfolk (Legge 1981; 1992) but substantial samples have recently been excavated at Runnymede Bridge, on the Thames (Done 1980; 1991), and from Brean Down, on the southern shore of the Bristol Channel (Levitan 1990). In addition to this a small number of Middle/Late Bronze Age deposits from Ireland have produced comparable assemblages. These include Haughey's Fort, Co Armagh, a hillfort dating to about 1100 BC (McCormick 1991); Ballyveelish, Co Tipperary a settlement site dating from around 1000 BC; and Dun Aonghasa, Co Galway, a stone fort with animal bones dating to the first half of the 1st millennium BC (McCormick 1994). The fragments and MNI distribution from Caldicot are compared with contemporary sites in Table 44.

The Caldicot sample shows a clear dominance of the main species by sheep (goats were not present). This is more clearly demonstrated in Fig 138 where only the MNI values of the three main species for a series of the sites are shown. The Caldicot sample, although small, clearly differs from the earlier Grimes Graves sites where cattle are dominant, and Runnymede Bridge where pig is clearly the dominant

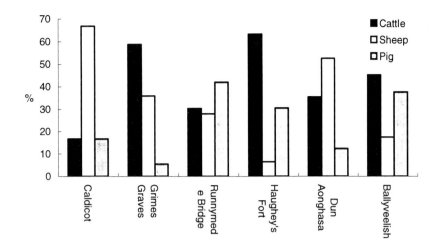

Fig 138   Comparison of MNI values for cattle, sheep/goat and pig after Done (1991, 331–338), Legge (1981; 1982) and McCormick (1991; 1994)

species. Direct comparison with Brean Down is not possible as the MNI values were not estimated at that site. In terms of MNI Caldicot also differs from all the Irish sites except Dun Aonghasa. The high incidence of sheep at Dun Aonghasa may be a product of harsh environmental circumstances as the site is located on the top of a high cliff on a barren windswept island.

The high incidence of sheep at Caldicot, however, anticipates the dominant role that sheep played in southern Britain during the Iron Age. The increase in sheep during this period has been ascribed to different factors. Grant (1984a, 543) has noted that sheep are more suited to the well-drained chalk downland of southern England than cattle. Elsewhere, economic factors are suggested, with Grant (1984b, 116) noting the importance of wool as a factor for the growth, whilst Cunliffe (1978, 184) suggests that it was the demand for dung caused by the expansion of cereal-growing that may account for the expansion of sheep during the Iron Age. It is difficult to evaluate which of these factors might account for the high incidence of sheep at Caldicot. Neolithic sheep were probably too hairy for wool exploitation but the stage at which wool working begun during the Bronze Age is still unclear. Spindle whorls can provide indirect evidence for wools and these appear on Welsh sites from the Neolithic onwards (Grimes 1951, 26). However, the processing of wool may predate the appearance of whorls. In Scandinavia there is a dearth of wool-processing equipment whereas there is plenty of woollen cloth present from much of the Bronze Age (Jørgensen 1991, 118). The earliest actual evidence for the making of wool textiles in Britain apparently comes from an Early Bronze Age barrow at Scale House, Yorkshire, excavated during the last century (Jørgensen 1991, 197) so an expansion of wool production could theoretically account for the high incidence of sheep at Caldicot. This, however, is not supported by the

sheep ageing data which imply that they were primarily kept for meat. Many of the sheep seem to have died during their first autumn/winter and it is possible that this is due to natural mortality rather than deliberate slaughter.

The bones from Phase VI/VII for the most part constituted discarded food refuse. There is, however, an unusually high incidence of canid remains in the sample, consisting of dog, fox and possibly wolf. Caldicot contains the highest incidence of dog and fox remains from any late prehistoric site in Britain (Table 44). Dog is absent from the Middle Bronze Age levels at Grimes Graves although its presence is implied by the presence of gnaw-marks on some of the bones (Legge 1981, 84). Dog bones were also absent from the Welsh Bronze Age copper mine at Great Orme (Hamilton-Dyer unpub). With the exception of Caldicot, the highest incidence of dog found on a late prehistoric site was at Haughey's Fort in Ireland. At a nearby artificial pond, probably contemporary with Haughey's Fort, it has been suggested that the deposition of dog remains constituted part of a ritual process. This pond, known as the King's Stables, is 25m in diameter and 3.5–4m deep, and is surrounded by a low broad penannular bank (Lynn 1977). Whilst the site produced some obvious food remains it also produced an unusually high incidence of dog remains, along with a cache of almost-complete deer antlers and part of a human skull. Lynn (*ibid* 55) concludes that as the pool had no practical function, it was probably constructed for ritualistic purposes, and that the dog, deer and human bone represented ritual deposits in the same tradition as Late Bronze Age hoards in bogs, lakes and rivers.

Although ritual is extremely difficult to demonstrate, it is possible that the canine deposits at Caldicot may represent such activity. These consisted of the near-complete skeleton of a large dog which was scattered over an area of about 1m, as well as other isolated bones found on the former riverbed.

222

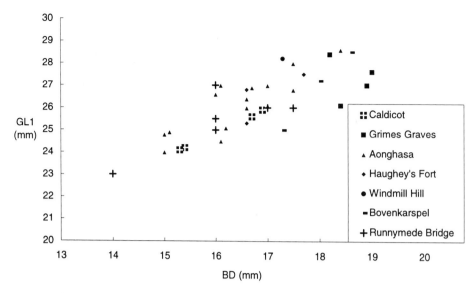

Fig 139   Sheep astragali size after Done 1991 (337), Legge (1992, 73), McCormick (unpub), Ijzereef (1981, 100), Jope (1965, 165). The Bovenkarspel values are the minimum, maximum and mean astragalus size

Phase III also produced an unusual collection of three mandibulae, two from the same individual. The Phase VI/VII fox bones were scattered but seemed to be of two individuals. One isolated dog calcaneus (Phase VI/VII) displayed several knife marks, suggesting that it was skinned before being discarded. A single complete red-deer antler was also present in this sample. Unlike the King's Stables examples, which had been chopped from the skull, the Caldicot example was a naturally shed antler and could have simply been lost when a deer was drinking water at the riverside. On balance, the evidence for ritual deposits at Caldicot is weaker than in the case of the King's Stables, but the high incidence of dog in Phase VI/VII and, indeed, the dog mandibulae from Phase III, cannot satisfactorily be explained in the context of discarded food refuse.

Sheep

As stated before, there was no evidence for the presence of goat at Caldicot, so all the caprovine remains can be regarded as sheep. Goats have, however, been noted in the roughly contemporary site at Brean Down (Levitan 1990, 233) which is also on the Bristol Channel. The metrical data for the Caldicot sheep is presented in Table 45.

The sheep from Caldicot were of an extremely slender lightly-built type. Figure 139 compares the astragali from several British and Irish later Bronze Age sites along with the Dutch Bronze Age site of Bovenkarspel and the British Neolithic site of Windmill Hill. As the size of the astragalus can be related to the weight of the animal (Noddle 1973) the scattergram shows clearly that, in terms of general build, the Caldicot sheep fell at the smaller end of the prehistoric size range.

Only a very small sample of complete metapodials was present, but their dimensions tend to suggest that the sheep were of an extremely long-legged type. The plotting of the few metacarpals and metatarsals in Figs 140 and 141 indicate that they are the longest-legged type in Britain during this period. They also fall at the upper length-limit of large Iron Age assemblages such as those from Danebury (Grant 1984, 506). Why such a slightly-built and long-legged type should be present at Caldicot is unclear. It is thought that this perhaps might have been due to dietary factors.

The ageing data from the sheep at Caldicot is presented in Tables 53 and 54. On the basis of Payne's data as used by Legge (1992, 34), the Caldicot tooth-eruption data indicates that the emphasis is on the slaughter of immature individuals. The small inadequate samples from Phases III and V are all from animals aged between 10 and 20 months old (Stage D) at time of death. During Phase III they tend to be even younger with the great majority being between 3 and 10 months (Stage C). No mature or old sheep were noted amongst the mandibulae but their occasional presence is evidenced by the epiphyseal data. At Grimes Graves too there is an emphasis on the slaughter of 1–2 year olds (*ibid*), but there was also a significant number of older sheep present. A similar pattern was present at Runnymede Down (Done 1991, 337), whilst at Brean Down a large number of older animals were also present (Levitan 1990, 236). The attempted reconstruction of past livestock economies on the basis of age-slaughter patterns is extremely problematical. Payne (1973) suggested that an emphasis on the slaughter of old animals would be consistent with a wool producing economy whilst the emphasis would be on the slaughter of young sheep if they were being kept primarily for their meat. On the basis of this

Table 45 Sheep measurements using the abbreviations of von den Driesch (1976). The *GL1 measurement refers only to astralagus while the *Bt refers to humerus and the Td refers to the metatarsal and metacarpals only. ***The distal epiphysis of this metacarpal was present but not fused

Bone	Phase	GL	Bp	Bs	SD	Bt/Td
Astragalus	VI–VII	24.2		15.4		
Astragalus	VI–VII	25.9		16.9		
Astragalus	VI–VII	24.1		15.3		
	VI–VII	25.6		16.7		
Calcaneus	V	52.4				
	VI–VII	52.9				
Femur	VI–VII			33.3	14.1	
Humerus	VI–VII			30.4		27.3
	VI–VII			28.9		25.9
	VI–VII			28.4		25.4
	VI–VII			26.9		26.0
	VI–VII			23.1		21.6
	VI–VII			23.5		21.8
Metacarpal	VI–VII		19.7		11.1	
	VI–VII		18.4		11	
	VI–VII	135***	21	23.2	12	15.1(Td)
	VI–VII		21.6		13	
	VI–VII		21.6		13	
	VI–VII	135	21	22.8	12	14.4(Td)
	VI–VII		21.6		13.3	
	VI–VII		21.8		12.7	
Metatarsal	VI–VII		19		12	
	VI–VII	148	19.3	22.4	11	15.4(Td)
	VI–VII		18.6		11.6	
	VI–VII		16.5		9.4	
	VI–VII		18.8		11.6	
	VI–VII		17.0?		10	
	VI–VII		14.5		10.3	
Radius	V	152.4	28.5	24	14	
	VI–VII		26.9		14.1	
	VI–VII		27.1		13.9	
	VI–VII		27.1		13.9	
	VI–VII		26.3		14.8	
	VI–VII	152	28.5	26.3	15.5	
	VI–VII		22.4			
	VI–VII		28.6		15	
Tibia	VI–VII			23.8	14	
	VI–VII			24.4	13.6	
Ulna	V	185				

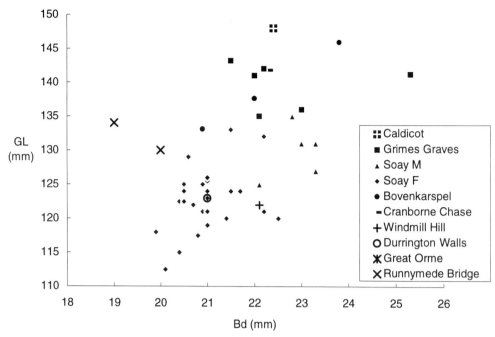

Fig 140   Sheep metatarsal size after Done 1980 (78), Legge (1991, 97; 1992, 74), Jope (1965, 162. The Soay sheep measurements are taken from Legge (1981) Fig 18

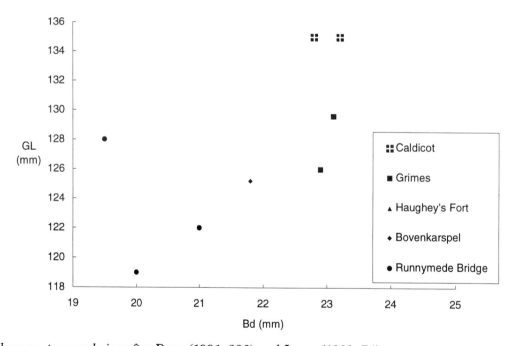

Fig 141   Sheep metacarpal size after Done (1991, 336) and Legge (1992, 74)

model the Caldicot data would suggest that sheep were being kept primarily, if not exclusively, for their meat.

Cattle

The cattle measurements are tabulated in Table 46 whilst the complete metacarpals dimensions are compared with other sites in Fig 142. The Caldicot data are extremely limited, consisting of two examples, but it suggests that the animals were of a lighter build than those found on other prehistoric sites.

Only a limited amount of ageing data was provided by the assemblage and this is presented in Tables 52 and 54. Little can be said except that both young and mature cattle were present. Legge (1981: 1992) argues that dairying was being practised in Britain at this time but others, including the present writer (McCormick 1992), have questioned this hypothesis.

Table 46 Cattle bone measurements after von den Driesch 1976. *GLl

	Phase	GL	Bp	Bd	SD	Bt
Astralagus	VI–VII	63.8*		38.7		
Calcaneus	III	119.6				
Femur	V		106.1			
Humerus	V			80.4		66.8
	V			89.9		75.7
Metacarpal	III	193.5	52.2	52.8	27.8	
	V		45.3		23.1	
	VI–VII		55.5		27.4	
	VI–VII	170	44.9	50.5	26.3	
Metatarsal	III	208	45.1	50.4	24.1	
	VI–VII		41.5			
	VI–VII		41.8		24.4	
Radius	V	258	73.2	62.5	33.1	
Tibia	VI–VII			60.0		
	VI–VII		39.7			

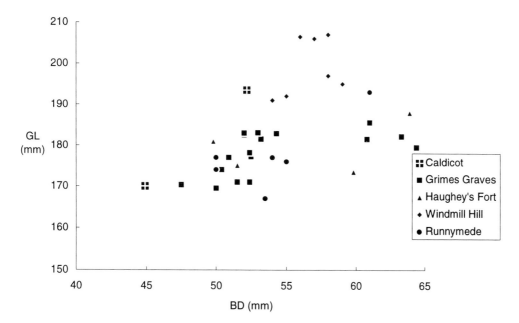

Fig 142   Cattle metacarpal size after Done (1980, 76; 1991, 335), Jope (1965, 156), McCormick 1991, 32) and Legge (1992, 72)

The ageing and sexing data from Caldicot is too limited to contribute to this debate.

Pig

Pig played a relatively minor role in the diet and economy at Caldicot. Metrical data was virtually non-existent. A humerus from Phase VI/VII has a distal width (Bd) of 37.0mm which falls comfortably within the range of domesticated species. At Run-

nymede Bridge the humerus Bd range was between 33 and 48.5mm with an average of 40.4mm (Done 1991, 338). There was no evidence that wild pig was present. Pig thrive well in the presence of woodland and their scarcity at Caldicot may reflect low tree-cover in the site's hinterland.

The pig ageing data is extremely limited and is almost entirely confined to Phase VI/VII. During this phase both young and semi-mature individuals are present. A very small radius was recovered from an animal that cannot be of more than a few weeks of

226

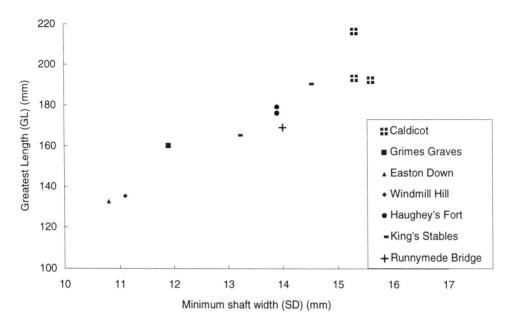

Fig 143   Dog humerus measurements from Caldicot and other early prehistoric sites early prehistoric sites after Burleigh et al (1977, 359), Done (1991, 340) and McCormick (1987)

age, whilst a mandible with its M3 in secondary eruption is of an animal of approximately 19–21 months on the basis of data provided by Higham (1967, 105). Knife marks on pig bones are confined to the distal end of a humerus and the articulation of the same bone, which also displayed gnawing.

Horse

Horse remains were confined to Phase VI/VII (see Table 59). None of the bones display chop-marks but some, especially the femur fragment, display gnaw-ing-marks. The group includes an almost complete scapula and left mandible. The latter is of a ma-ture/old animal but there is no evidence for bit wear on the PM₂. The incisors were missing and no loose examples were found in the vicinity. This implies that the bone had not been thrown directly into the water course after the death of the animal. Gnaw-marks were evident on the mandibular hinge area.

Dog

The unusual nature of the canine assemblage has been discussed above. This included a near-complete skeleton (Phase VII), which is discussed in detail below, and the scattered remains of a few other dogs (Phase III and VI/VII). Some of the Caldicot dogs are characterised by their large size. Figure 143 com-pares the size of dog humeri from Caldicot with those from other Neolithic and Bronze Age sites and the Caldicot animals are the largest in the group. It seems likely that the largest of the Caldicot humeri is of a wolf. It was found that in the case of early

Danish wolves the humerus greatest length range was 201.0–230.0mm with a mean of 216.9mm (Aris-Sørensen 1977, 141), whilst the largest Caldicot humerus has a GL of 216mm. In addition, a large scapula from Phase VI/VII is also probably from a wolf. In Harcourt's (1974, 157) study of early British dog remains, he found that Neolithic humeri had a size-range of about 135–145mm. The Bronze Age material was extremely limited but indicated the presence of larger dogs with humeri of up to 185–190mm in length (*ibid* 158). These are slightly smaller than the Caldicot dogs.

Smaller dogs were also present at Caldicot, al-though these were not represented by complete long bones. Mandibles from Phase III and Phase VI/VII had total lengths (TL) of 125.9mm and 133.6mm respectively; this corresponds to the medium sized Neolithic dogs discussed by Burleigh *et al* (1977, 358). A mandible with a TL of 137.1mm from Phase III is intermediate in size between these and the large near-complete dog from Phase VII. The smaller Caldicot mandibles displayed a high de-gree of crowding of the teeth. This was less pronounced in the case of the large dog but there was still some crowding between the fourth premolar and first molar.

The two smaller of the Caldicot dog humeri in Fig 143 belong to the near-complete skeleton from Phase VII. The skull of this skeleton has a total length of 228mm. This is much larger than British Neolithic dogs (168–168mm) and immediately outside the Bronze Age range of 125–223mm (Harcourt 1974, 157–9). The possibility that the Caldicot skull could be that of a wolf must be considered. Its total length falls immediately below the range (235–283mm) of seventeen modern wolf skulls published by Wagner

(1930, 114) and the range of fourteen Danish fossil wolves (237.0–279.0mm) published by Aaris-Sørense (1977, 140). The upper carnassial has a length of 19.2mm (20.0mm at cingulum) which falls well outside the range for wolf published by Clutton-Brock (1969, Fig 42). The cingular length of the (P[4]) is also smaller than the cingular length of the combined $M^1 + M^2$, thus confirming its identification as a domesticated dog.

The dogs represented by mandibulae were mature or old animals. In all cases wear had exposed some dentine, especially in the Pm[4] and M[1]. Likewise, with one exception, the dog long bones were fused. This all points to the use of the dogs as working animals, either for guarding or hunting or shepherding. The injuries to the large dog, some probably humanly inflicted (below), makes one hesitate at referring to the dogs as 'treasured pets'. There is also a possibility that dogs may have acquired some ritual function at the end of their days (above).

The only bone of a young canine present was that of an unfused calcaneus from Phase VI/VII (4063). It is relatively small and most likely to be that of a dog. The bone displays several fine cut-marks. Knife-marks in such a position are consistent with the skinning of the animal, as one would usually stop removing the pelt immediately above the toes. Whilst the dog may have died of natural causes, it is possible that young dogs were deliberately reared for their pelts and killed as soon as they approached full size. Such a deliberate scheme of killing young animals for their skins has been noted in the case of cats during medieval times (McCormick 1988).

The palaeopathology of the near-complete dog
Eileen Murphy

An almost complete dog skeleton (Fig 144) displaying many pathological lesions was present in the Phase VII contexts (see palaeochannel group E.7.1, p 55). This skeleton is of great interest because complete, or practically complete, skeletons of animals are generally rarely recovered during archaeological excavations. As the skeleton was almost complete it was possible to examine the overall distribution of the lesions and attempt to determine their inter-relationship to each other. A detailed description of each lesion is provided below.

The presence of the os penis indicates that the animal was male. All of the bones were fused indicating that the dog was fully mature when it died. The considerable wear on the teeth and the presence of degenerative joint disease on the vertebrae suggests that the dog was of an advanced age. The measurements obtained from the bones of the animal are presented in Tables 47 to 49. Using measurements obtained from long bones which displayed no pathological lesions, an estimated shoulder height of approximately 0.64 m was calculated (Harcourt 1974, 154).

Trauma

Many parts of the skeleton displayed evidence for injuries and degenerative disorders. Some of these may reflect injuries inflicted by humans. A depressed

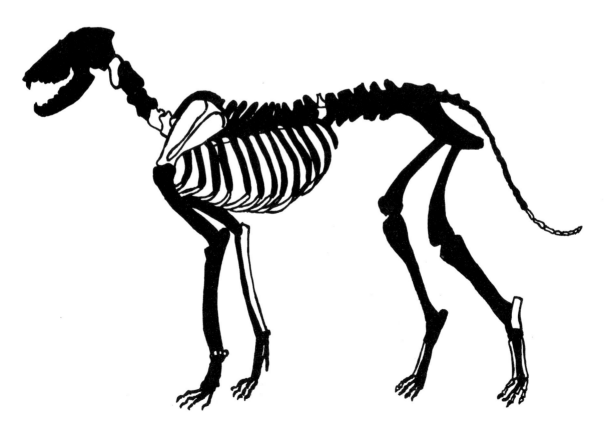

Fig 144   Near-complete dog skeleton (Phase VII): recovered bones

Table 47 Dog post-cranial measurements

Bone	Phase	Gl	Bp	Bd	Sd	Bt
Femur	VI–VII	172		29.8	13.4	
Pelvis	VI–VII	22.2				
Humerus	VI–VII	216	54.2(Dp)	42.1	15.3	30.0
Humerus	VII skeleton	192	44(DP)	37.7	15.6	24.6
		193	47(DP)	38	15.3	25.4
Radius		199	20	27.7	15.1	
Radius		198	19.9	28	15	
Femur (path)		210	43.6		16.2	
Femur	Path	Path	36.8			
Tibia (path)		223		21.1	14.2	
Tibia (path)		222	38.7		14.5	
Calcaneus		49.0				

Table 48 Dog mandibles

Measurement/bone no.		21729	21569	4038	21205*
Phase	von den Driesch no.	III	III	VI	VII
Total length	1	125.9	137.1	133.2	164.6
Height of vertical ramus	18	46.5	60.1	54.6	Path
Height of horizontal ramus behind M1	19	23.1	27.1	27.1	30.9
Length of cheektooth row: M3–P1 along alveolar border	8	71.9	77.5	72.5	85.1
Length of molar row:	10	37.9	37.2	34.9	37.8
length of premolar row P1–P4	11	36.2	41.2	37.1	45.9
Length of Premolar row P2–P4	12	31.2	36.1	32.2	38.8
Length of P1 at alveolus		3.9	4.4	4.1	–
Length of P2 at alveolus		7.9	9.5	9.5	11.5
Length of P3 at alveolus		11.1	11.1	10.9	10.9
Length of P4 at alveolus		11.2	11.6	11.1	11.9
Length of M1 at alveolus		21.1	22.1	19.8	23.5
Length of M1 at cingulum		22.9	23.8	21.1	–
Length of M2 at alveolus		9.2	10.8	7.4	8.5
Length of M3 at alveolus		4.6	4.1	4.5	3.8

fracture was visible on the anterior surface of the right side of the frontal bone in the area immediately adjacent to the orbit (ie by the right eye, Fig 145). The fracture measured c 13mm medio-laterally by c 36mm antero-posteriorly and was oval in shape. The bone surrounding the fracture was smooth lamellar bone which suggests that the fracture was in an advanced stage of healing or even completely healed when the animal died. The morphology of the fracture indicates that it was caused by a blunt object and it is possible that the dog was struck by a blow from either a missile or an implement.

One of the right lower ribs displayed a well-healed fracture. The evidence for this was a small, rounded raised area of bone positioned in the middle third of the rib. There was no evidence of displacement of the bone sections. Radiographic analysis of the bone revealed that the fracture line had almost completely disappeared indicating that the healing process was nearly complete.

Lumbar vertebra two (L2) to lumbar vertebra seven (L7) all had fractured spinous processes. The tip of the spinous process was displaced to the left in L2 to L5 and to the right in L6 and L7. In all cases

Table 49 Dog skull measurement after von den Driesch (1976) and Harcourt (1974). '±' indicates that the measurement was estimated while 'Path' indicates that a pathological anomoly precluded measurement. The skull is of the near-complete Phase VII dog and the *mandible is associated with it. The smaller mandible is from Phase VI

Skull	Harcourt no.	von den Driesch no.	
Total length: Akrokranion-Prosthion	I	1	228
Condylobasal length		2	211.3
Occipital proturerance to nasion	II		120.2
Nasion to alveolare	III	8	112.3
Greatest mastoid breadth		23	76.9
Greatest neurocraniun width		29	64.1
Greatest length of auditory bulla		22	24.6
Palatel length	IX	13a	108.9
Palatel width between P4 and M1	X		67.2
Least palatal breadth		35	43.2
Breadth at canine alveoli	XII	36	48.3±
Length of cheektooth row	XI	15	72.5
Length of P1 at alveolus			6.3
Length of P2 a alveolus			11.5
Length of P3 at alveolus			12.9
Length of P4 at alveolus			19.2
Length of M1 at alveolus			11.9
Length of M2 at alveolus			6.6
Snout index (III x 100/I)			49.2
Snout width index (XII x 100/III)			43.0

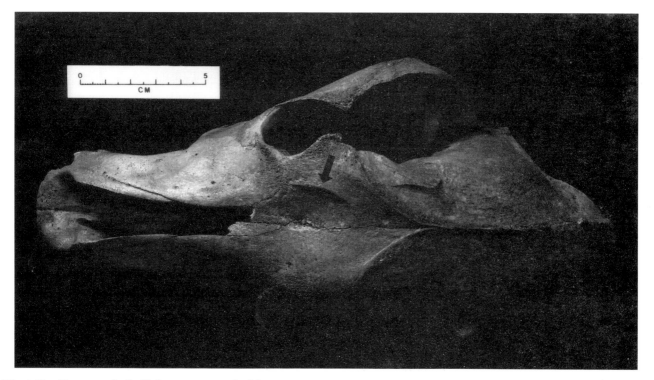

Fig 145   Depressed skull fracture, marked by arrow

230

the fractures appeared to have been well-healed. The median sacral crest also appeared to have been fractured which resulted in its being slightly displaced to the right; again, the fracture was well-healed (Fig 146). This injury is consistent with something heavy falling on the lower back of the animal.

A fracture had occurred at the proximal end of the shaft of the left femur (Figs 147 and 148). It is likely that the fracture was compound, ie affecting the flesh as well as the bone, and radiographic analysis indicated that the bone had been broken obliquely. There was a large amount of callus in the area adjacent to the fracture. In the immediate vicinity of the fracture the shaft was hypertrophied, with the shaft becoming much thicker than in the case of the dog's right femur. The fracture had also resulted in the bone having shortened. It measures approximately 23mm less (187mm) than the right femur (210mm). The proximal area of the shaft is displaced laterally by approximately 20 degrees. Bony exostoses were visible in the areas of attachment of the tibialis posterior muscle, the medial collateral and the inferior transverse ligaments of the left tibia. It is likely that the exostoses are related to straining of these muscles.

Degenerative joint disease

Degenerative joint disease (DJD) can be associated with ageing or physiological wear and tear. It can also develop as a secondary process in functionally or structurally abnormal joints. Many examples were noted in the present dog. DJD was observed on the second metacarpal and second proximal phalanx of the right forefoot. A small area of eburnation was visible on the distal end of the metacarpal. This corresponded to a small patch of eburnation on the proximal end of the phalanx. Degenerative joint disease was also apparent on some of the bones of the left forefoot with osteophytes and eburnation being visible at the distal end of the second phalanx. There was septic arthritis on the second intermediate phalanx and at the proximal end of the second distal phalanx.

The hind feet were also affected. Eburnation on the distal end of the right fifth metatarsal and at the proximal end of the fifth proximal phalanx is indicative of degenerative joint disease. Septic arthritis was visible on the first cuneiform and the cuboid of the left foot. All these lesions could have been caused by cuts to the feet which became infected.

Osteophytes (small bony growths) were present on the articular surfaces of several of the cervical and lumbar vertebra. They were present at the margin of the inferior body of the second cervical vertebra (C2). There were also osteophytes and a small area of eburnation on the left inferior articular process. Corresponding eburnation was apparent on the left superior articular process of C3. Osteophytes were visible at the right margins of the superior and

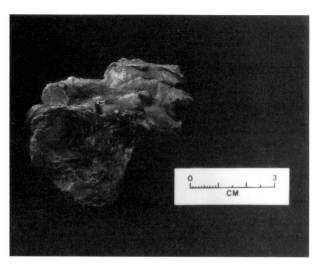

Fig 146   Well-healed fracture of the median sacral crest

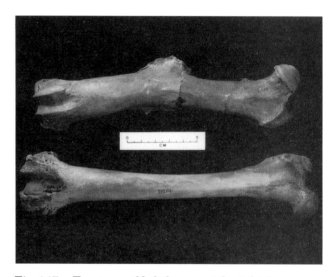

Fig 147   Fracture of left femur with right femur for comparison

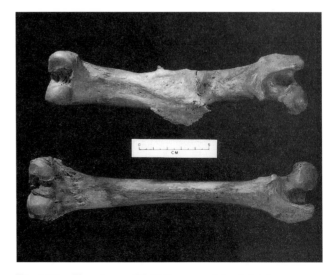

Fig 148   Fracture of left femur with right femur for comparison

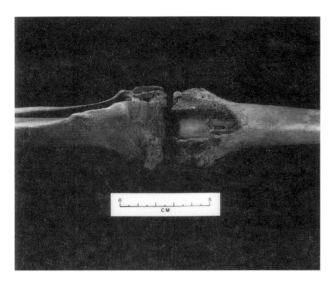

Fig 149 Degenerative lesions on the right knee, probably the result of extra stress as a consequence of the weakened, fractured left femur

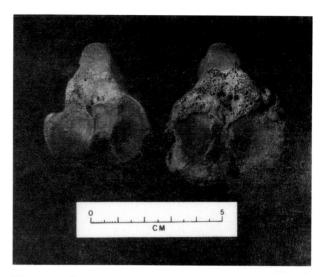

Fig 150 Degenerative joint disease of proximal end of the right tibia with left tibia for comparison

inferior bodies of the second lumbar vertebra (L2). Corresponding osteophytes were also observed around the right margin of the superior body of L3. Large osteophytes were noted at the margin of the inferior body of L7. This may simply have been a product of advancing age in the dog but could also have been a secondary effect of other injuries to the animal (see below).

The pelvic area was also affected. Osteophytes were present around the margin of the superior surface of the first sacral vertebra. Bony exostoses were apparent on both innominates in the area immediately superior to the auricular surface. Both innominates appear to have been almost completely fused to the sacrum at the sacro-iliac joints. It is likely that the fusion of the sacro-iliac joints would indicate that the dog had limited movement of the hip girdle. The fused pelvis coupled with the femoral injuries would have meant that the dog would have displayed a pronounced limping deportment, at least during the early period of its injuries. Finally, there was also osteophytic lipping of the left acetabular rim with corresponding eburnation on a small area of the inferior margin of the rim.

The trauma on the left femur has already been outlined above and it likely that the degenerative lesions on the right knee discussed below are a result of the extra weight and stress exerted on the leg as a consequence of this. Extensive osteophytes were present on the margins of the distal condyles of the right femur (Fig 149). An area of eburnation, which measured c 7mm medio-laterally by c 10mm antero-posteriorly, was visible on the articular surface of the medial condyle. Osteophytes were present at the margin of the left femoral head. These corresponded to the lipping observed on the left acetabulum which was discussed above.

Corresponding degenerative joint disease was visible at the proximal end of the right tibia and fibula. Extensive osteophytes were observed around the margins of the tibial condyles. An area of porosity and eburnation which measured c 5mm medio-laterally by c 5mm antero-posteriorly was present on the medial condyle. The degenerative joint disease of the proximal tibia corresponded to that of the distal femur (Fig 150). A bony tube was observed on the lateral surface of the proximal end of the right tibia. It is possible that the ossified tube was associated with either one of the tibial arteries or the popliteal vein.

Non-specific infection

In non-specific infective diseases the manifestations of disease are common to a wide range of pathogenic organisms. Periostitis, for example, may be a result of trauma or may be also a part of another disease process. This was visible on the left third, fourth and fifth metacarpals. New bone formation was concentrated on the proximal half of the anterior surface of each bone. The new bone was woven bone which was in an advanced stage of remodelling into lamellar bone. This indicates that the animal died in the middle of the healing process.

Periostitis was also apparent on several bones of the right hind foot. This was more acute than in the other paws again probably as a consequence of the additional stress on the right leg for the reasons outlined above. New bone was visible on the lateral surface of the proximal half of the shaft of the third metatarsal. The new bone had the appearance of woven bone which was in the process of remodelling into lamellar bone. A patch of woven bone appeared to have been extending from the area of the shaft where the remodelling was concentrated to the distal end of the shaft. This may indicate that the infection was only healing in part of the bone. The fourth and fifth metatarsals were fused together at the proximal third of their shafts (Fig 151). This fusion appears to

232

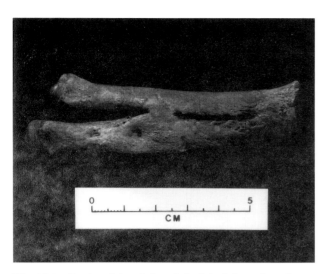

Fig 151   Periostitis of the right hind foot: fused fourth and fifth metatarsals

have been a result of osteomyelitis of the fourth metatarsal. A sinus (perforation) was observed on the bone and a sulcus (an associated drainage channel) was present on the posterio-medial surface of the midshaft. Extensive new bone formation was visible over the entire shaft. The new bone was woven bone in the process of remodelling into lamellar bone; this indicates that the infection was in the process of being healed at the time of death. It is possible that the fourth metatarsal was the originally infected bone and that the infection had spread to the third and fifth metatarsals. On the fifth metatarsal the new bone formation was concentrated on the medial side of the proximal shaft.

Periostitis was visible on the left third and fourth metatarsals. New bone in the process of remodelling was visible on the anterior surfaces of both bones.

Dental disease

Both the maxillary and mandibular teeth displayed extensive attrition. The right mandibular first premolar had been lost ante-mortem.

Discussion

The recovery of the near-complete dog skeleton provided a rare opportunity to examine the distribution of pathological lesions in a Bronze Age dog. The skeleton displayed evidence of trauma to the skull, lumbar vertebrae, sacrum, a rib and the left femur. Degenerative joint disease was apparent on some of the bones in all four of the dog's feet, several of its vertebrae, the innominates (pelvis), and the right femur, tibia and fibula. Evidence of non-specific infection was observed on some of the bones of the feet. The dentition was in good condition though much worn.

It is probable that the dog would have been hindered in its movements. Its left leg would have been shorter than the right, probably causing it to limp. The left leg would have had a swollen appearance in the vicinity of the fracture site. The right knee area would also have been swollen owing to the degenerative joint disease present at this location. It is also likely that there would have been open, infected wounds on all four of the dog's feet.

The evidence of trauma may indicate that the life of a Bronze Age dog was not easy. It is possible that the animal was thumped on the head with some form of implement or had a missile thrown at it. The presence of fractures on practically all of the lumbar vertebrae and the sacrum would imply that the dog was crushed by a heavy object either falling or thrown at it. The back injuries certainly seem as if they were sustained during a single incident. The single fractured rib is not indicative of a crushing injury and it is likely that this injury was caused by a single strike, perhaps from a cattle hoof or a human foot. The fractured left proximal femur was caused by the application of a large amount of force to the animal's leg.

It is likely that the degenerative joint disease (DJD) of the spine is related to the age of the animal or to repeated stress on the vertebrae, with the DJD of the feet probably related to similar factors. It is also possible that these were related to the traumatic injury to the left femur. The altered deportment of the dog caused by the broken leg could have led to stress on the vertebral column. It seems almost certain that the degenerative joint disease of the right knee is a secondary condition to the fracture of the left femur. The result of the fracture to the femur would possibly mean that the dog would not have been able to use its left leg for walking on (at least while the fracture healed), therefore forcing the animal to rely on its right leg for support and propulsion. This could have resulted in strain to the right knee joint and possibly to the muscles of the lower leg. Fusion of the sacro-iliac joint may also have been related to the dog's limp. It is possible that the dog 'carried' its innominates in a constantly fixed position. This would have allowed for no movement between the sacrum and innominates, thereby enabling them to fuse.

The evidence of non-specific infection on the left forefoot and both the left and right feet and septic arthritis on both forefeet and the left foot could have been due to several factors. Although it is possible that the dog did not use its left leg for support and propulsion after its accident, the foot was probably dragged along the ground. Perhaps the more delicate tissues of the superior surface of the foot would have been cut by sharp stones, thereby explaining how the left hind foot also became infected.

Despite its traumatic past the dog survived to an advanced age. With the full use of only three limbs and a weak left leg, restricted movement of its pelvic girdle, a potentially painful right knee and infected cuts on its feet it is probable that the dog would have

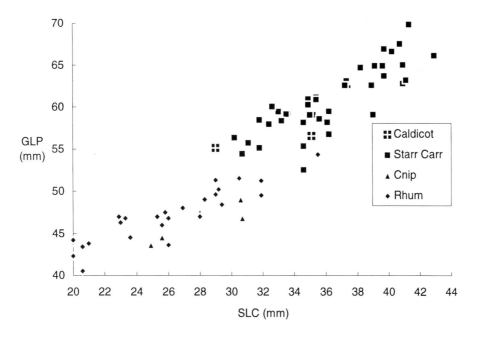

Fig 152   Red deer scapulae after Legge and Rowley-Conway 1988 (126, 141) and McCormick (unpub)

been at a disadvantage when it came to competing for food with the other dogs of the settlement. The animal, however, survived for a period of time after it had obtained its injuries. As these injuries would have presumably left the animal ineffectual at shepherding, hunting or guarding it is possible that it was living in close, and perhaps even amiable, contact with humans.

Wild mammals

Wild mammals were present throughout the phases on the site (see Table 42). The presence of

fox and beaver bones makes it likely that wild animals were hunted for their skins as well as for food. In some instances, as in the case of Phase II, deer were represented by small pieces of antler that may simply reflect the collecting of shed antler for craft purposes. A complete red deer antler was found in the Phase VI/VII river bed and may have been shed by a male during the late spring and be unrelated to human activity. Alternatively, it could represent a ritual deposit. The presence of red deer scapula and pelvis fragments during Phase VI/VII, along with a roe deer pelvis in Phase V, however, make it clear that deer were at least occasionally hunted for their meat.

Table 50 Fox and wolf measurements after von den Driesch 1976

Bone	Phase	GL	Bp	Bd	SD	Bt
Fox						
Humerus	VI–VII	107	21.7(Dp)	18	7	11.3
Radius	VI–VII	96	9.5	12.8	7.1	
	VI–VII		9.5			
Ulna	VI–VII	115				
Tibia	VI–VII	120	19.7	13.2	7.4	
Calcaneus	VI–VII	27.2				
Calcaneus	VI–VII	27.5				
Wolf						
Humerus	VI–VII	216	54.2(Dp)	42.1	15.3	30.0
		GLP	**LG**	**BG**	**SLC**	
?Scapula	VI–VII	41.7	32.2	23.7	39.5	

The beaver remains consisted of a single femur from Phase VI/VII, although beaver gnaw marks were noted on timber from Phase V. Archaeological evidence for beavers in south-west Britain during the later prehistoric period is also provided by beaver bones from Meare and Glastonbury, Somerset (Bulleid and Gray 1917; Gray and Cotton 1966). Their survival in Wales until the medieval period is attested in the 12th century writings of Gerald de Barri (*Giraldus Cambrensis*) who noted that they were still extant but were 'found only in the Teifi river near Cardigan' (O'Meara 1982, 49). The presence of beaver could have had implications for the physical environment of the area (see Hamilton-Dyer below).

Phase VI/VII produced the partial and scattered remains of apparently two foxes, the measurements of which are given in Table 50. Although some of the bones are broken none display any cut- or chop-marks. Both the foxes were mature with all teeth erupted and dentine showing. One calcaneus had developed osteophytes due to slight degeneration of the ankle joint.

The size of red deer has declined in Britain between the early prehistoric period and the present, a reduction which at least in part can be attributed to the decline of their original forest environment. The best evidence for the size of red deer during the earlier prehistoric period are from Starr Carr (Legge and Rowley-Conwy 1988). Figure 152 compares the few Caldicot scapulae dimensions with those of Starr Carr, the diminutive red deer from Cnip, Harris, an Iron Age settlement in the Outer Hebrides and modern deer from the Isle of Rhum. It can be seen that while the Caldicot deer are larger than those from Cnip or Rhum they fall at the lower end of the Starr Carr group. The small size of the Caldicot red deer is confirmed by the dimensions of a single metatarsal present. It has a Bd of 37.8mm while the Starr Carr range is 40.1 – 47.2mm (*ibid* 128). At Grimes Graves Legge (1992, 39) found that the Bronze Age red deer were of a large type similar to those of Starr Carr. He concluded that this indicated that 'environmental conditions were very good' (*ibid*). This might suggest that conditions were less suitable for deer in the vicinity of Caldicot.

Birds, fish amphibians and small mammals
Sheila Hamilton-Dyer

The material was derived both from hand retrieval and from the processing of soil samples from sieving and flotation. The species retrieved are shown in Tables 41 and 43.

Phase I

The only identifiable material was several amphibian bones.

Phase II

At the base of the Early Bronze Age channel, near some piles, the remains of several small fish were discovered (22581). They were extremely well preserved. Some parts were clearly still articulated and must have lain undisturbed since death. These were small flatfish, probably flounder. Measurements of the anal pterygiophore range from 25.1 to 36.9mm indicating fish lengths in the region of 150mm. In addition to this, eel bones and the tooth of a field vole were retrieved by sieving from context 22170.

Phase III

This produced a larger sample than the previous two phases, especially in the case of sieved material. Hand-retrieved material included water and field vole, amphibians, duck, little grebe and barn owl. In addition, sieving produced eel and stickleback.

Phase IV

This group comprised only stickleback and eel all retrieved from sieved samples.

Phase V

Hand retrieval and sieving produced eel and water vole.

Phase VI–VII

The largest sample came from this phase and the material and species present are shown in Table 43. The usual small mammals and fish were present. This phase produced the only salmon bone retrieved during the excavation (5044). It was of a large individual equivalent to a Severn salmon of 0.80m in length.

This phase produced a large sample of bird remains. Most of them were of ducks and it is probable that the majority of these were mallard, some slightly immature. Bones of widgeon are, however, very similar and in the case of some of the smaller individuals of mallard there is a slight overlap. For this reason, the presence of this very similar bird, which overwinters in England and Wales, cannot be ruled out. One bone matched a tufted duck whilst another may be a pintail. Of the probable mallard there is a slight bias towards wing bones. There are the remains of six almost complete wings, four left and two right, providing a MNI of four birds as opposed to two in the case of the leg bones. A mallard carpo-metacarpus had been cut in a position which indicates removal of the end of the wing which contains most of the long flight feathers and no meat.

Other bird bones present include Brent goose, heron, little grebe, some small passerine and several bones of heron and crane. The crane bones consist of a distal tibia, an almost complete ulna, an incompletely ossified femur and a pair of tibiotarsi. The latter are probably all from the same immature individual.

Discussion

Amphibians

It can be difficult to differentiate between the bones of amphibians, especially in the case of immature individuals. Toad were, however, positively identified. These animals require fresh water for breeding, implying that pools or slow running streams were present within a few kilometres of the site. British species will not enter salt or brackish water.

Fish

Apart from the possible flounder skeletons from Phase II and the salmon bone from Phase VI/VII, all the fish bones were retrieved by sieving. Although usually regarded as a freshwater species, some populations of the three-spined stickleback inhabit estuaries and, in Scotland and further north may even be found in coastal waters. This type have distinctive bony plates along the length of the body, some of which were found amongst the Caldicot remains. Eels may be found in both freshwater and marine contexts but, unless transported by humans, need access to the sea as the elvers are hatched in the Sargasso. Many of the remains on the site are of small 'bootlace' eels, only one or two years old. Although these may not represent food waste in the present context, it should be noted that eels of any size make good eating and the Severn Valley is well known for the quality of eels available. They can be caught in almost any small stream by the use of traps, nets or even hook and line.

Flounder also enters brackish streams and may be caught in the same manner, although there is no indication that the partial skeletons present at Caldicot are anything other than natural deaths. Large salmon are unlikely to enter small silty channels. They are often caught in the estuary or in the main river system while returning to the main spawning grounds which are usually far upstream in shallow clean water with a stony bottom. Salmon bones are not frequent in archaeological material as the skeleton in spawning fish is partially de-calcified. The single salmon headbone from Phase VI/VII may not reflect the importance of this fish to contemporary human communities.

There is little comparable evidence concerning the exploitation of fish during the Bronze Age in Wales. Jackson (1915, 78) identified cod and ray in a horizon at Dyserth Castle which is ascribed to the Bronze Age

but the integrity of the stratigraphy is uncertain. There were no fish remains from Brean Down.

Small rodents

Most of the small rodent bones were positively identified as water vole or were of similar size and type. This rat-sized vole swims well and usually makes its burrow in river banks, hence its other name of water rat. It is predominately vegetarian, eating mainly reeds and sedges. Herons and barn owls are important predators. A few bones were of the common field vole.

Beaver

The identification of a complete beaver femur in Phase VI/VII supports the evidence for its presence provided by the chewed wood. An active beaver colony may have a significant effect on the surrounding area (Coles 1992). One side effect of the animals is natural coppicing of trees . If wet coppiced woodland, beaver lawns and ponds were present these would be ideal habitats for the water vole, heron, crane and ducks found at Caldicot. Beaver provide high-quality water-resistant pelts and they may have been hunted specifically for their skins, but the flesh is edible and large amounts of fat may be extracted from the carcass.

Birds

Apart from the barn owl and small passerines (songbirds) the birds present at Caldicot are those which require wetlands to breed and feed. The mallard and the other surface-feeding ducks can be found on almost any open water and marshland and in winter on coastal marshes. The Brent goose also winter on estuaries including the Severn. The little grebe prefers rivers and lakes with heavily vegetated margins. The heron can be found in many wetland habitats where it hunts for eels and other small fishes, frogs and small mammals. The crane is the most specialised in its requirements and has been extinct in Britain as a breeding bird since the 17th century, probably as a result of hunting, disturbance and loss of habitat. Some of the Caldicot bones are of an immature individual, implying that the birds were nesting locally. It breeds today in marshes and wet grassland, nesting on the ground. It was still present in the area in Roman times as evidenced by the discovery of the remains of several birds at Caerleon (Hamilton-Dyer 1993).

Only one bone, that of a mallard, provided evidence of butchery but all the water birds present at Caldicot were edible. Birds can be cooked and eaten without leaving any marks on the bones and it seems likely that most of the bones represent food waste.

Table 51 Red deer measurements

Bone	Phase	GL	Bp	Bd	Sd
Metatacarpal	VI–VII	267.9	38.5±	37.8	21.9
Scapula	VI–VII	GLP	SLC		
	VI–VII	56.5	35.1		
		55.1	29.9		

Table 52 Cattle epiphyseal fusion data

Bone	Age at fusion in months (after Silver 1969)	Fused	Unfused
Phase V			
Humerus D	12–18	2	–
Radius P	12–18	1	–
Radius D	42–48	1	1
Ulna P	42–48	1	–
Metacarpal D	24–30	–	1
Femur P	36	2	–
Tibia P	36–42	1	–
Phase VI–VII			
Humerus D	12–18	1	–
Radius P	12–18	–	1
Radius D	42–48	–	1
Metacarpal D	24–30	1	1
Femur P	42	–	1
Femur D	42–48	1	1
Tibia P	42–48	1	–
Tibia D	24–30	1	–
Metatarsal D	27–36	1	–

Table 53 Sheep epiphyseal fusion data

Bone	Age at fusion in months (after Silver 1969)	Fused	Unfused
Phase V			
Humerus D	10	–	1
Radius P	10	–	1
Radius D	36	–	1
Ulna	30	–	2
Femur D	36–42	–	2
Calcaneus P	30–36	1	–
Phase VI–VII			
Humerus P	36–42	1	–
Humerus D	10	6	1
Radius P	10	1	7
Radius D	36	5	–
Metacarpal D	18–24	1	7
Pelvis	6–10	5	2
Femur P	30–36	–	6
Femur D	36–42	1	7
Tibia P	36–42	–	12
Tibia D	18–24	2	3
Calcaneus	30–36	3	2
Metatarsal D	20–28	1	6

Table 54 Cattle and sheep tooth eruption and wear data. C = crypt of tooth in formation; V = tooth visible through teeth; E = tooth erupting through bone; H = half erupted, unworn U = erupted almost to full height. Lower case letters represent the wear stages of Grant (1982, 93). * After (Legge 1992, 34)

Species	Phase	Higham (1967) stage	Payne stage*	dp$_4$	P$_2$	P$_3$	P$_4$	M$_1$	M$_2$	M$_3$
Cattle	III						c	k	j	g
	VI–VII			k	E	V		g	f	J
				j				f	d	–
							f	k	j	g*
								H		
Sheep	III	12	D	g				f	b	
	III	12?	D	g				f	b?	
	V	12	D	g				f	e	V
	V	12	D	g				f	e	V
	V	12	D	g				f	–	–
	VI–VII	9	C	g				f	E	
	VI–VII	10	C	g				g	H	
	VI–VII	12	D	–				g	f	V
	VI–VII	8	C	g				d	C	
	VI–VII	8	C	g				d	V	
	VI–VII	8	C	g				c	C	
	VI–VII	6/7	C	f				Ub	c	
	VI–VII	5	C	f				H		

Table 55 Phase II: fragments and MNI distribution

	Cattle
Horn	–
Skull	3
Femur	2
Total	5
MNI	1

Table 56 Phase III: fragments and MNI distribution

	Cattle	S/G	Pig	Dog	Fox	Red deer
Horn	–	1	–	–	–	–
Skull	–	1	5	–	–	–
Mandible	1	2	2	3*	–	–
Teeth	–	–	–	1	–	2
Atlas	–	–	–	–	–	1
Cervical V.	–	2	–	–	1	–
Thoracic V.	5	2	–	–	–	–
Lumbar V.	1	–	–	–	–	–
Scapula	1	1	1	–	–	–
Humerus	–	1	–	–	–	–
Ulna	–	–	4*	–	–	–
Metacarpal	1	–	–	–	–	–
Pelvis	–	1	–	–	–	1
Femur	2	3*	–	–	–	–
Patella	–	1	–	–	–	–
Tibia	5	1	–	–	–	–
Astragalus	–	–	1	–	–	–
Calcaneus	1	–	1	–	–	–
Metatarsal	3	1	1	–	–	–
Tarsal/carpal	1	–	–	–	–	–
Phalanx 1	1	1	1	–	–	–
Phalanx 2	–	1	–	–	–	–
Phalanx 3	1	1	–	–	–	–
Total	23	17	12	4	1	4
Total %	37.7	27.9	19.7	6.6	1.6	6.6
MNI	1	2	2	2	1	1

Table 57 Phase IV: fragments and MNI distribution

	Cattle	S/G
Skull	1	–
Pelvis	–	1
Phalanx 2	–	1
Fragments total	1	2
MNI	1	1

Table 58   Phase V: fragments and MNI distribution

	Cattle	S/G	Pig	Roe deer
Skull	8	5	1	–
Mandible	–	3	–	–
Teeth	5	–	–	–
Atlas	1	1	–	–
Axis	1	2	–	–
Cervical V.	2	2	–	–
Thoracic V.	–	1	–	–
Lumbar V.	–	2	–	–
Sternum	1	–	–	–
Scapula	2	1	–	–
Humerus	3	1	–	–
Radius	1	1	–	–
Ulna	2	2	–	–
Metacarpal	1	–	–	–
Pelvis	1	3	–	1
Femur	2	2	–	–
Tibia	2	–	1	–
Astragalus	1	–	–	–
Calcaneus	–	1	–	–
Metatarsal	1	–	–	–
Tarsal/carpal	–	1	–	–
Phalanx 1	1	–	1	–
Phalanx 2	–	1	–	–
Phalanx 3	–	1	–	–
Total	35	30	3	1
Total %	57.7	43.4	4.3	1.4
MNI	2	2	1	1

Table 59 Phase VI/VII: fragments and MNI distribution. **Fragments column for dog does not contain complete dog skeleton

	Cattle	Horse	S/G	Pig	Dog**	Wolf	Fox	Red deer	Beaver
Horn	–	–	2	–	–	–	–	2	–
Skull	20	–	101	16	19*	–	2	–	–
Mandible	6	1	22*	1	3	–	3*	–	–
Teeth	14	1	31	9	14	–	–	2	–
Hyoid	1	–	–	–	–	–	–	–	–
Atlas	3	–	4	–	–	–	2	–	–
Axis	4	–	1	–	–	–	1	–	–
Cervical V.	2	–	7	1	3	–	7	–	–
Thoracic V.	4	–	17	3	1	–	9	–	–
Lumbar V.	3	–	13	3	1	–	–	–	–
Sacrum	–	–	2	–	–	–	2	–	–
Caudal V.	–	–	1	–	–	–	1	–	–
Sternum	2	–	–	–	–	–	–	–	–
Scapula	2	1	9	3	–	1	1	3*	–
Humerus	5	–	14*	3	–	1	1	–	–
Radius	3	–	11	1	–	–	2	–	–
Ulna	2	–	5	1	–	–	3	–	–
Metacarpal	4	–	10	1	1	–	1	1	–
Pelvis	2	–	12	–	1	–	1	2	–
Femur	5	1	22	1	1	–	–	–	1
Patella	–	–	–	–	–	–	–	–	–
Tibia	3	–	25	–	–	–	2	–	–
Fibula	–	–	–	–	–	–	–	–	–
Astragalus	1	–	4	–	–	–	–	–	–
Calcaneus	–	–	6	–	1	–	2	–	–
Metatarsal	6	–	16	3	1	–	3	–	–
Tarsal/carpal	8	–	10	–	1	–	2	1	–
Phalanx 1	1	–	18	3	2	–	3	–	–
Phalanx 2	4	–	4	–	–	–	–	–	–
Phalanx 3	4	–	4	3	–	–	–	–	–
Total	109	4	335	52	30	2	45	8	1
Total %	18.6	0.7	57.2	8.9	5.1	0.5	7.7	1.4	0.2
MNI	2	1	8	2	3	1	2	2	1
Modified MNI	3	2	8	3	3	1	2	2	1
MNI %	9.1	4.5	36.4	9.1	13.6	4.5	9.1	9.1	4.5
Modified MNI %	12.0	8.0	32.0	12.0	12.0	4.0	8.0	8.0	4.0

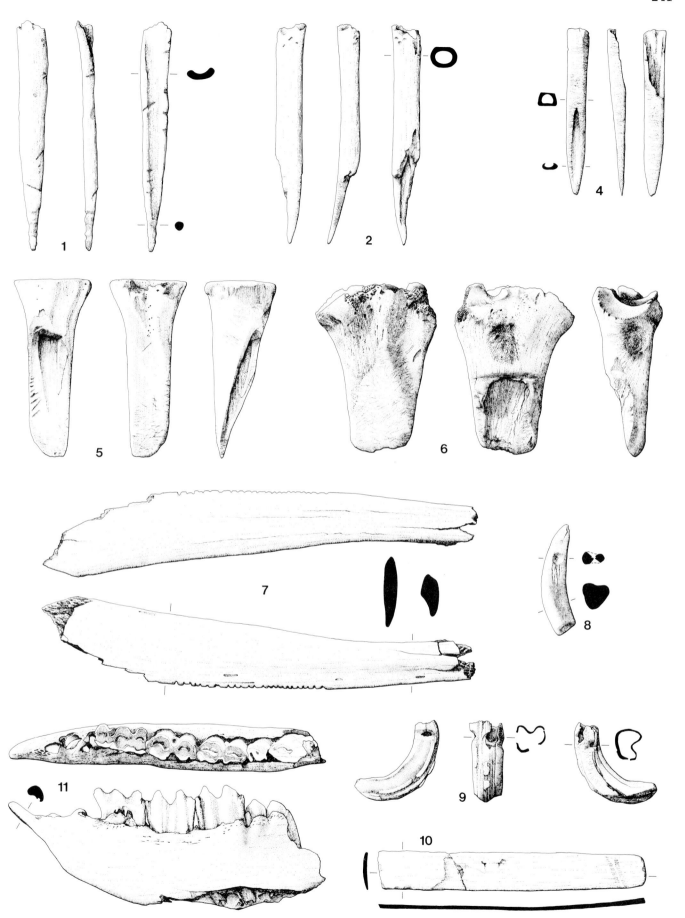

Fig 153 Bone artefacts. Scale: No.1 at 1:1, all others at 1:2

The bone artefacts
Joyce Compton

Out of a total of approximately 1420 individually numbered bone finds from Caldicot only eleven had been utilised (Fig 153). Awls, gouges and points are common finds on most sites but there are also artefacts from Caldicot which are less easily identifiable. The bone identifications were made by Finbar McCormick. The pattern of polish/wear on selected pieces is shown schematically in Fig 154.

1 21566 Awl/pin; very worn. The shaft is flat in section and there is a gradual taper towards the rounded tip. Some striations are visible on the surface. Several similar examples can be found in the Greenwell Collection; the two closest parallels come from Round barrow no 44 Weaverthorpe, North Yorks and no 89 Goodmanham, North Humberside (Kinnes and Longworth 1985, 47 and 82 respectively). Bone unidentified but probably from a small mammal. Weight 2g. Length 61mm.

2 21060 Awl/point roughly fashioned from a split sheep/goat tibia. A tapering spur resulting from the splitting of the bone has been modified to form an awl. Horizontal striations can be seen on both sides of the point and the tip itself bears a polish, probably through use. A selection of awls, also manufactured from sheep/goat tibiae have been recovered from Chapeltump II (Trett forthcoming). Weight 18g. Length 116mm.

3 4056 Pin/needle; very finely made from a splinter of mammal bone. One end tapers to a point; the opposite end is notched and may now be broken, so might once have been pierced. Length 30mm. (Not illustrated).

4 5135 Point, probably from a sheep/goat metatarsal. The implement has been finely worked; the whole surface bears a network of striations and the bone tapers symmetrically and gradually to a flat point. The groove thus revealed by the exposure of the hollow shaft of the bone bears some resemblance to a weaving shuttle and it is possible that the implement was used to make nets. Alternatively, it may have been used in leatherworking, for example to thread thongs. A similarly finely-made point was found in the body of the rampart at Dinorben, Denbighshire, where it was tentatively dated to the Late Bronze Age and given a domestic rather than a military function (Savory 1971, 53 and Fig 14, 7). Weight 4g. Length 88mm.

5 21458 Gouge or chisel fashioned from a cattle metatarsal, with a slight polish and many surface scratches over the tip. The edges where the bone was split are very highly polished. The gouge was probably hafted for use. Similar objects come from Brean Down (Bell, 1990, 162, nos 56–60). Weight 54g. Maximum length 95mm.

6 21577 Gouge formed by making a diagonal cut across the proximal end of a cattle radius. A horizontal cut mark is still visible. The working end is highly polished and covered with a network of striations. The tip has suffered ancient damage, probably through use. There is no polish at the proximal end so the implement must have been hafted for use and it has been suggested that the haft was fixed for use as an axe, hence the damage to the tip. Weight 74g. Maximum length 90mm.

7 5285 Cattle rib with a notched edge. Both ends are broken so it is unclear whether the serrations continued along the edge beyond the breaks, or if there was any other working besides the serrations. There is no evidence of wear except for a slight polish at the proximal end of the rib. There are several longitudinal cracks, but these appear to have been caused after deposition. The serrations are almost U-shaped in profile and seem to be randomly though closely spaced. The deepest groove measures no more than 2mm. The function of this implement remains uncertain, although it may have been used as a comb, in weaving, for instance, or during the manufacture of pottery. The use of ribs as implements

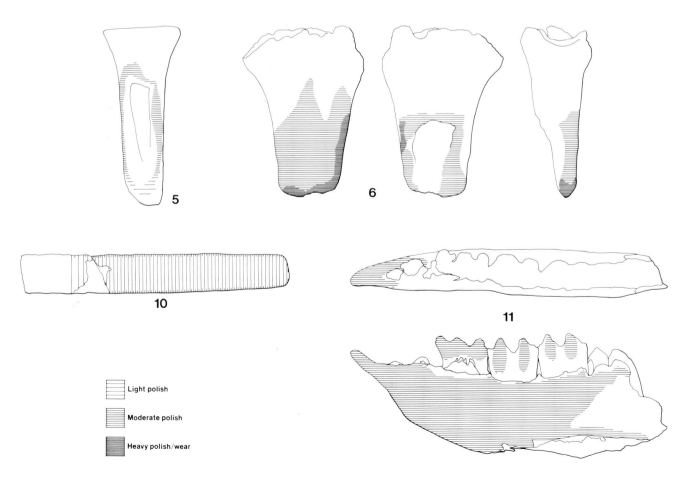

Light polish

Moderate polish

Heavy polish/wear

Fig 154   Wear patterns on selected bone artefacts. Scale 1:2

is discussed by Ijzereef (1981, 132–3), although an exact parallel is lacking. Weight 46g. Maximum length 238mm.

8 21192 Horse incisor pierced for suspension and probably used as an amulet. The hole has been drilled unevenly from either side approximately 19mm from the tip of the root. Most of the surface bears a polish, probably from handling after suspension. Weight 10g. Maximum length 60mm.

9 21184 Canine of a male pig. The tusk appears to be from an old animal as there is very little enamel remaining and the tip is very worn. The root end of the tusk is pierced at both sides, but more as a result of wear rather than deliberately, as if the root had been bound and not pierced for suspension. The object may have been used as an amulet. A parallel can be found in the Greenwell Collection (Kinnes and Longworth 1985, 88), from Round barrow no 117, Goodmanham in the East Riding of Yorkshire, now North Humberside. Weight 14g. Maximum length 70mm.

10 12945 Rib from a medium-sized mammal, split and shaped to form a spatulate implement. The edge and tip are smooth and highly polished through use. The whole of the upper surface bears a light polish and the cancellous tissue of the lower surface is also polished, especially towards the broken end. The rib has been used as a smoother/polisher, probably in the preparation of leather. Rib polishers come from Runnymede Bridge (Needham, 1991, 148, B8 and B9), where the whole rib had been utilised, whereas the Caldicot rib was deliberately split prior to use. Weight 10g. Length 148mm.

11 5037 Utilised cattle mandible. The entire surface, including the teeth, is highly polished. The mandible comes to a smooth point just in front of the unerupted premolars. The underside of the point is so highly polished that the bone has worn away and exposed the roots of the teeth. The mandible has been used as a smoother/rubber and, in addition, the teeth may have been used, possibly to prepare skins for tanning. There was a utilised mandible at Bovenkarspel (Ijzereef 1981) but that had broken teeth and had also been used for striking. Weight 168g. Total length 173mm.

The Bronze Age pottery
Ann Woodward

Although the amount of Bronze Age pottery recovered during excavation was small, the sherds are well-preserved and highly diagnostic. They provide an important addition to the corpus of Later Bronze Age pottery known from South Wales. Most of the pottery was found in stratified deposits belonging to Phases VI and VII, which are well dated by the

radiocarbon and dendrochronological methods. A total number of 36 sherds weighed 1258g; there was also a fragment of a large weight or sinker weighing 585g. The distribution of pottery by phase and fabric type is shown in Table 60.

Five fabric types were recognised. All except the last were characterised by inclusions of a calcareous nature:

Fabric A A moderate scatter of medium-sized to large calcite inclusions.
Fabric B A moderate scatter of medium-sized to large calcite inclusions and fair quantities of mica.
Fabric C A sparse occurrence of small calcite crystals and considerable quantities of quartz sand.
Fabric D A sparse scatter of fragments of fossil shell; soft matrix.
Fabric E A sandy fabric with some grog fragments of varying size; a buff, sandy surface.

Two sherds of Fabric A and four of Fabric C were submitted for microscopic examination by David Williams. His report on their detailed petrology, and notes on their possible areas of origin, is appended.

With the exception of the Fabric E sherds, most of the pottery was reduced, with a dark brown to dark grey hue. Surfaces were generally smoothed and many of the coarser fragments exhibit the traces of finger-smearing or other roughly-wiped surface finishing. Fabric A was the most common, followed by Fabric B and C in roughly equal quantities by weight. It can be seen from Table 60 that Fabric A dominates the Phase VI assemblage whilst in Phases VI/VII and VII, the finer and sandier Fabric C predominates. One sherd from a probable Phase II context (21437, Borehole 3) was a featureless wall sherd in Fabric E; this may be of Early or Middle Bronze Age date.

The rim forms represented at Caldicot Castle are a simple rounded section with a slightly hooked profile, and those with internal rim bevels. The latter occur on the only two decorated vessels which are from Phase VI/VII contexts. A single example of a base appears to possess a simple angle and a slightly

Table 60 The occurrence of Bronze Age pottery by phase and fabric. Weights in kilograms

| | | Fabric | | | | | | | | | | | |
| | A | | B | | C | | D | | E | | Unassigned | |
Phase	No.	Wt	No.	Wt	No.	Wt	No.	Wt	No.	Wt	No.	Wt
0					1	0.002						
II									1	0.006		
V	1	0.003										
VI	10	0.497	5	0.407	1	0.028	1	0.002	1	0.006		
VI/VII	3	0.064			4	0.110					1	0.586
VII	2	0.026			5	0.038						
VII/VIII					1	0.026						
Totals	16	0.590	5	0.407	12	0.204	1	0.002	2	0.012	1	0.586

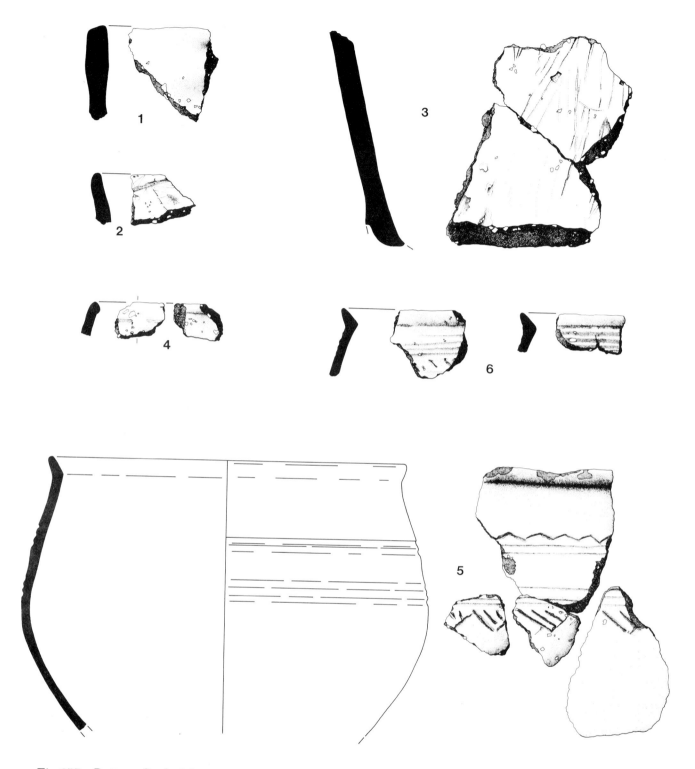

Fig 155   Pottery. Scale 1:2

concave base profile. Although not strictly a form of decoration, the finger-smeared surface found commonly on the coarser sherds is a distinctive characteristic. Many of the sherds from the Phase VI/VII and VII deposits belong to two individual vessels, both of which are decorated with incised motifs including chevrons, filled chevrons, simple diagonal lines and sets of wide shallow horizontal grooves. Both these vessels were black in colour, with carefully-burnished exterior surfaces.

Illustrated sherds (Fig 155)

1 Thick rim sherd with a simple, slightly flattened profile. Fabric A. Find 21468, context 22504, palaeochannel group A.5.1, Phase V.

2 Rim sherd: the simple, rounded profile tapers towards the rim top. Fabric A. Find 5122, context 7068, palaeochannel group B.6/7.1, Phase VI.

3 Joining sherds near base of a large coarse jar; the surface is treated with vertical finger smearing. Fabric B. Find 5050/5052, palaeochannel group B.6/7.1, Phase VI.

4 Simple, rounded rim sherd with a slightly hooked profile. Fabric A. Find 5409, context?, Phase VI/VII.

5 Rim and shoulder of a fine, thin-walled jar with a carefully smoothed surface. The shoulder is rounded and the rim bevelled internally. Above the shoulder there are deeply incised chevrons and two wide grooves. There are two more similar grooves at the shoulder and below, a row of pendant filled triangles. Fabric C. Finds 21103 (right-hand sherd in illustration) and 21175 (uppermost in illustration), context 22259, Phase VI/VII; Find 21240 (left-hand sherd in illustration), context 22317, Phase VII may derive from this vessel or another bearing a similar decorative scheme.

6 Decorated rim from a jar. This vessel is slightly thicker walled than number 5 but displays the same finely smoothed grey-black exterior surface. The rim is internally bevelled. There are four lightly tooled grooves immediately below the rim and a row of incised diagonal strokes below that. Fabric C. Finds 21239 (left-hand sherd in illustration), 21243 (right-hand sherd in illustration) from context 22317, Phase VII.

Discussion

The most common fabrics found at Caldicot Castle are matched fairly closely by those which characterise the Late Bronze Age assemblage from Brean Down Unit 4 (Woodward 1990, fabric 481) and some of the Late Bronze Age and Iron Age pottery from Thornwell Farm, Chepstow (Woodward 1996, fabric 4). The grogged fabric from Phase VI is found in Middle Bronze Age assemblages nearby eg Chapeltump II, Fabrics D and E (Woodward forthcoming) and across the Severn at Brean Down, Unit 5b.

Simple and internally bevelled rims occur in Middle and Late Bronze Age assemblages on both sides of the Severn. Middle Bronze Age examples occur at Coed y Cymdda (Owen-John 1988, Fig 17), Chapeltump II (Woodward forthcoming) and Lesser Garth Cave (Savory 1980, Fig 72). Both rim forms also occur in Post-Deverel-Rimbury groups such as Combe Hay, Avon (Price and Watts 1980, Fig 24), Norton Fitzwarren, Somerset (Woodward 1989, Fig 19, vessels 27 and 28) and Brean Down Unit 4 (Woodward 1990, Figs 93–7). They also occur commonly in Decorated Late Bronze Age assemblages, as at Dinas Powys (Alcock 1963, 124, Fig 24), Thornwell Farm (Woodward 1996) and South Cadbury, Somerset (Ceramic phase 4: Alcock 1980, Fig 12). Vertical finger-smearing is a primary characteristic of Late Bronze Age assemblages and is found at Brean Down (Unit 4), Combe Hay, Norton Fitzwarren, South Cadbury (references as above) and at Rams Hill, Oxon (Barrett 1975).

The finger-tip impressed decoration which is so commonly found on the rims and shoulders of vessels in these Decorated Late Bronze Age assemblages is surprisingly absent at Caldicot. However, the more complex incised motifs can be matched in some of the classic Decorated assemblages such as Rams Hill (Barrett 1975, Fig 3:6, 34), Knights Farm, Berks. (Bradley *et al* 1980, Fig 35) and Potterne, Wilts (Gingell and Lawson 1985, Fig 42). The simple diagonal line motif occurs in Middle Bronze Age groups as well eg Coed y Cymdda (Owen-John 1988,

Fig 17) and Lesser Garth Cave (Savory 1980, Fig 72), and very rough chevrons occur in the Middle Bronze Age Unit 5b groups at Brean Down (Woodward 1990, Fig 91, 36; Fig 92, 55), but the general composition of decorative schemes found on the two Caldicot vessels is best matched in the Decorated assemblages of the Late Bronze Age.

Such comparisons are also in best accord with the absolute dating evidence. The radiocarbon dates from Phase VI correlate with Severn Basin dates for Middle Bronze Age pottery from Chapeltump II (Trett forthcoming), Brean Down Unit 5b (Woodward 1990, 133), and dates relating to Late Bronze Age Post-Deverel-Rimbury assemblages at South Cadbury (Alcock 1980, 709, Table 1) and Aldermaston Wharf, Berks. (Bradley *et al* 1980, 248). On the other hand, the dendrochronological dates *c* 1000 BC obtained for Phases VI and VII match better with the dates for the later Late Bronze Age assemblages which contain Decorated elements, as at Combe Hay (Price and Watts 1980, 25 and 32) and Knight's Farm (Bradley *et al* 1980, 283).

A note on the petrology
David Williams

Introduction

Six sherds of Later Bronze Age pottery were examined in thin-section for a detailed fabric description, which might additionally lead to suggestions as to possible areas of origin.

Petrology and fabric

In the hand-specimen, with the aid of a binocular microscope ($\times$20), all six sherds can quite clearly be seen to contain frequent angular pieces of white calcite. These appear prominently in the weathered sherd 21174, but can also be seen scattered throughout the fabric of the other sherds, most noticeably in fresh fracture. All of the sherds appear in a hard, somewhat burnished fabric, dark grey in colour (Munsell 5YR 4/1 to 10YR 3/1) for sherds 5292, 5002 and 21174, lighter grey surface for 21460 (between 5YR 6/1 and 5/1) and dark buff to grey for 5407.

Thin sectioning and study under the petrological microscope shows that frequent pieces of calcite are a characteristic feature in the fabric of all six sherds, set in a fairly fine-texture clay matrix. Some of the calcite fragments are irregular-shaped while others appear as perfect rhombs. Also present in the sections are grains of quartz, flecks of mica, and a little iron oxide. Occasional argillaceous material which might just possibly be grog (ie crushed up pottery) as opposed to naturally occuring clay pellets or mudstone, was noted in sherds 5292, 5002 and 21174.

Comments

The angularity of much of the calcite in these sherds suggests that it may have been artificially crushed by the potter and added to the clay as a form of temper. With this in mind, a local origin for the pottery making would be entirely feasible, with the Carboniferous Limestone series of the region providing the source for the calcite (Welch and Trotter 1961). It may, however, be worthwhile noting in passing that the Mendip Limestone across the mouth of the Severn has been suggested in the past as the source of similar tempered Iron Age pottery (Peacock 1969).

The stone from the excavations
Steve Howe

The majority of the stones examined from the excavation consist of either yellow to pink coloured sandstones and conglomerates, similar to those found in the local Triassic deposits, or grey to pale grey coloured limestones comparable to those of the local Carboniferous. The sandstones and conglomerates resemble those used in the construction of Caldicot Castle. Many of the conglomerates are quite coarse with substantial rounded white quartz pebbles. Approximately 8% of the rock samples examined are of individual quartz pebbles, some of which appear to be derived from these conglomerates. There appears to be a fairly even use of both the Triassic conglomerates and the sandstones, which accounts for approximately 60% of the rocks examined.

A range of different types of limestone, totalling approximately 24% of the samples examined, occur within the rock samples, all of which are comparable with those to be found within the local Carboniferous succession. A few pieces of limestone contain pieces of fossil coral which confirm that they are derived from the Carboniferous. Many of the samples appear to have been obtained from fresh exposures, but others are strongly weathered and were probably collected from the surface of the outcrops.

Conglomeratic sandstones and limestones similar to those found in the rock samples from the excavations occur locally, ie within 1km of the site. The conglomerates and sandstones appear to have been derived from the Triassic and the limestones from the Carboniferous. It is therefore reasonable to suggest that all of these have been obtained from the local area.

More exotic rock types, from formations that do not occur locally, were identified that accounted for approximately 12% of the samples examined. Most of these are rather small (generally under 50mm), rounded pebbles, some of which have been broken. They consist of quartz, quartzites, flint, feldspathic sandstones and a range of Lower Palaeozoic sediments and seem to have been transported as river pebbles. They appear to be identical to pebbles found within the river terrace gravels seen at outcrop north of Brockwell, near Caerwent. As river terrace gravels cover an extensive area both to the east and west of the site, it seems likely that these pebbles are derived from these deposits.

A number of the blocks of Carboniferous limestone appear to have suffered heating of some kind (specimens 12814, 12848, 12855 and 12870 for example). Some of the surfaces of these blocks are blackened and others coated in a thin veneer of oxidised calcium carbonate.

The flint industry
Stephen Aldhouse-Green

Interpretation

The flint assemblage (Table 61, Fig 156) contains a number of distinctive products both of Mesolithic technology and Neolithic/Bronze Age artefact types. Typical Mesolithic punch-struck blades and blade cores are present. Finds of Neolithic date include the tip of an ogival leaf arrowhead (Green 1980, 98), a flake from a polished axe and a fragment of a possible Late Neolithic 'chisel' arrowhead (Green 1980). A burnt fragment of a 'fabricator', itself made on an older patinated flake, may be of Neolithic or Bronze Age date (Saville 1981, 65; Smith 1965, 108; Wainwright 1971, 176). Finds likely to belong to the earlier Bronze Age comprise a typical 'Beaker' thumb scraper and a plano-convex knife.

All of the above, with the possible exception of the fabricator, are clearly residual. No group of artefacts was detected which, by virtue of typology, differing technology or state of preservation, suggested an age coeval with the sedimentation. Later Bronze Age assemblages (Ford et al 1984; Saville 1977/8) are characterised by a diminished control over the technology of the raw material and by a very

---

Fig 156 (opposite) Examples of flint assemblage. 1: plano-convex knife with bifacially thinned proximal and distal ends, 21478. 2: tip of ogival leaf-shaped arrowhead: 5003. 3: double-sided scraper made on hinge-fractured flake with plain striking platform, 12969. 4: scraper on short thick flake, 5288. 5: thumb scraper, 21016. 6: scraper, 21579. 7: fragment of scraper with steep marginal retouch, 21578. 8: retouched flake fragment, possibly the butt of a chisel arrowhead, 12976. 9: burnt blade-core developed on thick flake with thermal fracture, 12745. 10: burnt fragment of 'fabricator' made on older patinated flake, 5300. 11: burnt bipolar core, 21135. Scale 1:2

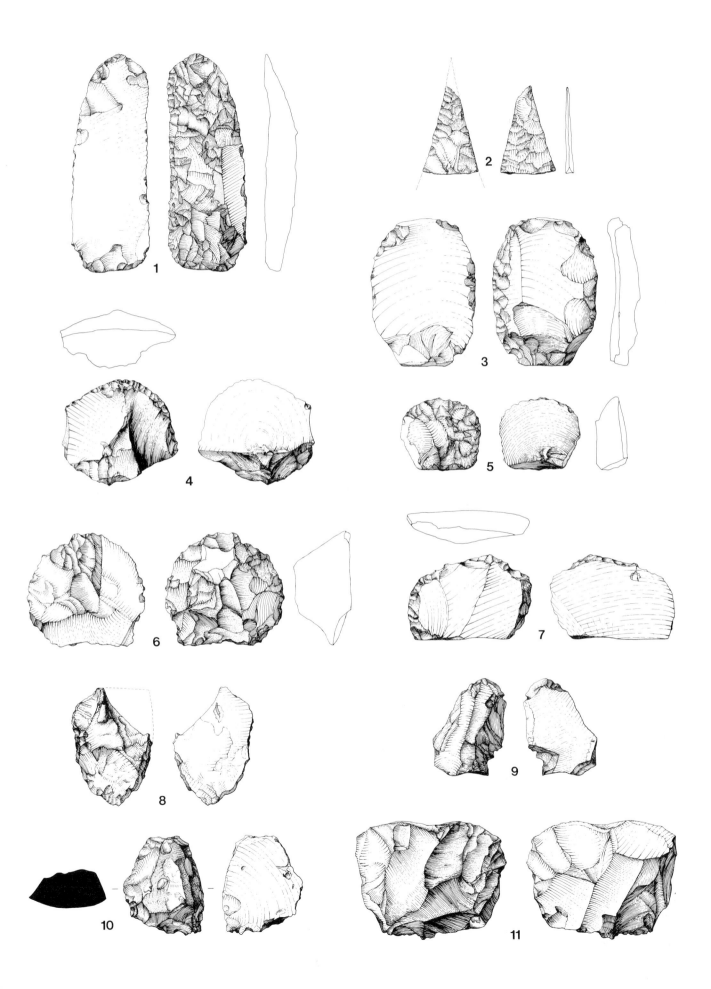

Table 61 Catalogue of the flint assemblage

Find no	Artefact	Probable date	Phase
4018	flake fragment		VI
4020	'punch-struck' blade, patinated	Mesolithic	VI
4027	burnt patinated flake		VI
4121	burnt fragment		VI
4130	proximal fragment of 'punch-struck' blade	Mesolithic	VI
4142	flake fragment		VI
4143	natural rolled gravel		VI
4145	natural rolled gravel (stained)		VI
4220	burnt fragment		VI
5003	tip of ogival leaf-shaped arrowhead	Early Neolithic	VI
5026	flake		VI/VII
5059	exhausted blade core	Mesolithic	VI/VII
5070	flake		VI
5116	flake		VI
5275	flake from polished axe	Neolithic	III
5288	scraper on short thick flake		III
5300	burnt fragment of 'fabricator' made on older patinated flake	? Neolithic	VI/VII
12701	Flake		VII
12745	Burnt blade-core developed on thick flake with thermal fracture	Mesolithic	VI \ VII
12766	'chunk' (?flake or artefact fragment)		VI \ VII
12767	burnt 'punch-struck' blade	Mesolithic	VIVII
12804	utilised flake fragment with crude serrations resulting from use		VIII
12823	spall, possibly from a small scraper		VII
12886	medial blade segment	? Mesolithic	VII
12904	broken fragment of patinated flake		VI
12925	flake fragment		VI
12937	fragment of rolled flint gravel	Natural	VI/VII
12946	flake fragment		VI/VII
12969	double-sided scraper made on hinge-fractured flake with plain striking platform.	Neolithic/Bronze	VI/VII
12976	retouched flake fragment, possibly the butt of a chisel arrowhead	Later Neolithic	VI/VII
21003	'punch-struck' patinated blade	Mesolithic	VI
21016	thumb-scraper	? Beaker	VI
21082	core-trimming flake		VI
21106	medial segment of burnt blade or flake		III
21135	burnt bipolar core	Neolithic	V
21152	flake		III
21277	burnt chip		VII
21237	burnt flake		VII
21391	flake		VII

Table 61 (cont.)

Find no	Artefact	Probable date	Phase
21405	flake		VI
21415	rolled thermally fractured flake		VI
21419	flake		V
21435	fragment, probably artefactual		VII
21444	flake		III
21447	chip		VII
21461	burnt fragment of blade		VII/VIII
21462	natural rolled pebble with utilisation (or natural damage)		VII/VIII
21469	burnt fragment		III
21478	plano-convex knife with bifacially thinned proximal and distal ends	Early Bronze Age	VI
21490	flake		III
21541	patinated 'punch-struck' blade	Mesolithic	VI
21568	flake		III
21578	fragment of scraper with steep marginal retouch	? Neolithic	VI
21579	scraper	Neolithic/Bronze Age	VI
21610	burnt fragment (?natural)		VI
21621	flake fragment		VI
21768	flake		III
21745	outil esquillé made on ? natural patinated piece		III

restricted range of implement types. Indeed, by 1200 BC, only scrapers, awls, rods and fabricators seemed to have remained in regular use. One cannot exclude the possibility that some of the elements present at Caldicot – debitage, scrapers and fabricators – might belong to the later Bronze Age. However, it would be injudicious to make such a claim given both the clearly mixed nature of the assemblage and its very small size.

The presence of the flintwork in the later Bronze Age sediments of the Caldicot sequence can, perhaps, best be explained as naturally derived from reworking by fluvial action or other agency of ancient bank deposits, or as manuports. The latter hypothesis seems to have little to commend it since the flints occurred in a number of different levels and serve no demonstrable function (eg as hardcore to create a firm dry surface in a wet area). The most plausible explanation must lie in the flints being reworked from earlier deposits. It would seem, from the context of the finds, that this reworking may have taken place mostly in Phases VI–VII. The situation has similarities to that at Runnymede Bridge where specifically Mesolithic and Neolithic types were present and none of the flintwork could be assigned 'to the same age as the ceramic and metal finds from the same horizons' (Saville 1991).

The metalwork
Peter Northover

Three pieces of metalwork of Bronze Age date were excavated and all were analysed to determine their composition (see Table 62):

1 A grooved strip of tin
2 A fragment of a long-tongue chape of Wilburton type
3 A miniature chape.

Methodology

All three objects were sampled by drilling with a 1mm diameter bit; the samples were hot-mounted in copper-filled acrylic resin, ground and polished. Analysis was by electron probe microanalysis with wavelength dispersive spectrometry; operating conditions were an accelerating voltage of 25kV, a beam current of 30nA and an X-ray take-off angle of 62°. Thirteen elements were analysed as detailed in Table 62; pure element and mineral standards were used with a count time of 10s per element. Detection limits were 100–200ppm (0.01–0.02%) for most elements, with the exception of 300ppm for gold and

Table 62   Analysis of Bronze Age metalwork

Sample	Find no	Object	Fe	Co	Ni	Cu	Zn	As	Sb	Sn	Ag	Bi	Pb	Au	S
NMW593	12808	Long tongue chape	0.02	0.01	0.29	80.44	0.00	0.31	0.66	8.54	0.25	0.01	9.31	0.02	0.13
NMW497	12821	Short chape	0.02	0.03	0.11	86.42	0.00	0.38	0.06	12.56	0.07	0.01	0.03	0.00	0.31
NMW501	21289	Tin	0.01	0.02	0.02	0.23	0.02	0.50	0.00	99.18	0.00	0.00	0.00	0.00	0.00

0.2% for arsenic. This last is because of the compromises made to avoid the well-known interference between the strongest lines in the lead and arsenic spectra, the lead Lα and arsenic Kα lines while making the analysis in a single pass. It was possible to use the relatively strong Mα line but for arsenic the weak Kβ line had to be used, hence the degradation in performance. More sensitive approaches to the analysis of arsenic exist but they were not thought necessary here.

Three areas, each 50 × 30µm were analysed on each sample; the mean compositions from each sample, normalised to 100% are set out in Table 62.

Results

1. 21289. Grooved strip of tin

Description A curved strip of tin metal with a rectangular cross-section and grooved upper surface; golden iron sulphide patina (Fig 157). Dimensions: 65 × 9 × 2mm.

Analysis The sulphide patina of this piece, typical of those generated under anaerobic conditions in waterlogged sediments, led to a visual identification as bronze. As can be seen from Table 62, it is in fact tin of considerable purity. The electron microprobe is not ideal for the analysis of tin as most trace elements are at very low levels; optical emission spectroscopy has been used with some success on tin (Bollingberg, forthcoming) and it is hoped that future analyses of tin will be by this method and can include a re-analysis of the Caldicot sample.

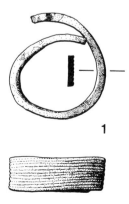

Fig 157   Grooved strip of tin 21289. Scale 1:1

Discussion Until recently objects of metallic tin with a Bronze Age date were extremely scarce in the British Isles. From Ireland there were three rings of 'Late Bronze Age' from Lough Gara and a neck ring from Kilsallagh (Coghlan and Case 1957), and from England Butler (1963) cites some tin beads from Sutton Verney, Wiltshire, now lost. In Wales there is the tin object (possibly a damaged or mis-cast ornament) in the Llangwyllog, Anglesey hoard (Lynch 1991). This hoard can be dated to the Ewart Park period of the Late Bronze Age (late 10th to late 8th centuries BC) and is probably later rather than earlier within this period.

More recently the excavations at Flag Fen and Fengate, Peterborough, Cambridgeshire have produced sixteen tin objects (and at least one other of a tin-lead alloy), of Bronze Age date (Coombs 1992). These include wheel-shaped (*ibid*, Fig 8, nos 16 and 17) and purse-shaped (*ibid*, Fig 6, nos 12–15) ornaments or votive objects, rings (*ibid*, 1992, Fig 6, no 4) and objects which can tentatively be identified as beads (*ibid*, Fig 6, no 16). The wheel-shaped objects are unique in Britain but have very close parallels in Switzerland. The Swiss objects are datable on contextual information to the later Bronze Age, from the end of the 11th century onwards. Recent excavations at Auvernier and Hauterive, both adjacent to Neuchâtel, NE (Rychner 1986; Rychner and Rychner-Faraggi 1993) have increased the range of tin objects from Switzerland whilst confirming their Late Bronze Age dating. These include pieces of wire and strip which provide something of a parallel for the Caldicot strip, but no piece has so far been identified which has the grooved decoration.

In considering tin objects in Britain we should also remember the four wheel-shaped ornaments with curved spokes from Meare Lake Village, Somerset (Gray and Bulleid 1953, 232, pl XLVI, nos Y2–4/6). Although found in ostensibly La Tène contexts at least two, from the foundation of Mound 9, and under the clay of Mound 22, might be residual from Late Bronze Age contexts and had possibly been collected by Iron Age occupants. They obviously require further study.

2. 12808. Long tongue chape

Description Lower part of long tongue chape; hexagonal section with edge and face ribs; stud/washer

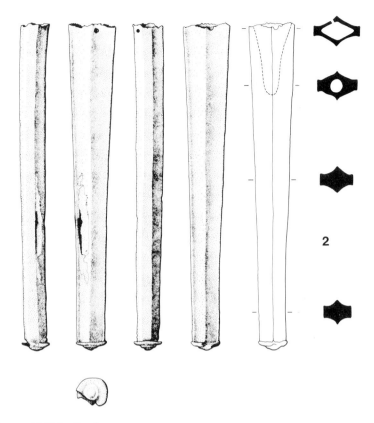

Fig 158 Long tongue chape 12808. Scale 1:2

type foot; fractures just above pin-hole; some core remains; no chaplets visible; black-gold patina (Fig 158). L (present) 172mm.

Discussion This chape fragment is the most straightforward to characterise of the three metal artefacts under discussion here. Typologically and compositionally it is part of a typical long tongue chape of the Wilburton industry, a complex first properly defined by Savory (1958), with the metallurgy later described by Northover (1982). The accumulation of direct and indirect dating evidence would place the Wilburton industry in the 11th century BC, particularly the latter part, and the earliest part of the 10th century. This dating supports the validity of a dating based on the proximity of the chape to a timber with a felling date of 990/989 BC. It should be emphasised that in England and Wales the long-tongue chape is specific to the Wilburton period; there are no antecedents in the preceding Penard period and all tongue chapes assignable to the Ewart Park period (eg Burgess *et al* 1972) are short or diminutive; the same appears to be true of Scottish associations as well (Burgess and Colquhoun 1988, pl 172B, pl 173B, pl 175A).

The Wilburton long tongue chape is marked by its elegant ogival form, U-shaped mouth, flattened hexagonal section with edge and occasional centre ribs, and occasionally complex terminals. The length is generally above 200mm, and can reach an extreme of 380mm with an example in the Guilsfield, Powys hoard (Savory 1965). All these features, with the

exception of the hexagonal section which is more general, are specifically diagnostic of chapes found in England. Chapes in the contemporary and closely related Saint-Brieuc-des-Iffs industry in north-west France have a straight mouth, straight sides, no ribs and a plain termination (Coombs 1988; Northover 1982). The interchange between the two sister industries is indicated, among other things, by the presence of 'French' chapes in English hoards such as Isleham, and 'British' chapes in a Saint-Brieuc-des-Iffs hoard such as that from Clos de la Blanche Pierre, Jersey (Northover 1987). The great majority of Wilburton chapes occur in hoards; indeed, it is the Guilsfield hoard which contains some of the most complete and striking examples of all. Elsewhere in Wales and the Marches long tongue chapes occur only as scattered fragments as in this example from Caldicot Castle, and one from Robeston Wathen in Pembrokeshire.

The composition of the chape is also typical for the Wilburton period (for comparisons see Northover 1982). Two features characterise the Wilburton industry, the first regular use of leaded bronze for castings based on imported low lead bronze scrap with a highly distinctive impurity pattern with arsenic, antimony, silver and nickel, usually with Sb>As>0.5%. The Caldicot chape fits this pattern exactly. Secondly, the chapes were cast in bivalve ceramic moulds with a clay core and sheet bronze chaplets; moulds are known from Dainton in Devon (Needham 1980) and unfinished castings from Isleham supply comprehensive information about manufacture (Northover 1982).

3. 12821. Short chape

Description Intact short chape; straight, slightly oblique mouth; lenticular, sub-hexagonal body section with elliptical bore; straight sides converge towards expanded ellipsoidal foot; large pin or peg-hole for fixing in each face; dark green/bronze patina (Fig 159). L 29mm; width (foot) 20mm; mouth 19 × 12mm.

Discussion This chape, at less than 30mm in length, must be labelled as diminutive. There is a class of diminutive chapes in the British Late Bronze Age. They occur in Ewart Park contexts, often of the Broadward complex (Burgess *et al* 1972). They have a variety of outlines: some, for example in the Broadward, Shropshire hoard itself, appear strongly influenced by continental chapes of the Wilburton period, whilst others, as in the Yattendon, Berkshire, and Pant-y-maen, Pembrokeshire hoards, imitate the features of the British long tongue chape, a U-shaped mouth, ogival outline and mid- or edge-ribs.

This small chape lacks all these features and must therefore be a continental import. There are several widely scattered European parallels which must mainly be assigned to Hallstatt B2–B3, ie contemporary with Ewart Park, although some may be as early as the beginning of that period (Hein 1992). Comparable examples from the British Isles are extremely rare. One of the closest, and also as it happens an exact parallel in terms of composition, is regrettably of uncertain provenance. It was published in 1987 from the collection of Lord MacAlpine of West Green (Northover and Sherratt 1987) as part of an assemblage said to have been found in Gloucestershire. It is now clear that that assemblage is part of a very large find made with metal detectors near Salisbury (Stead 1993); this find contains material from the Middle Bronze Age to the Iron Age including Late Bronze Age material contemporary with the chape. However, the chape differs significantly in patination from the majority of the find and may well not belong to it. There is a reasonable probability, though, that the find was made in Britain but, given the fact that some dealers have attempted to include non-British material with parcels of this assemblage, even this is not certain. Looking further afield one of the closest parallels, at least in terms of the shape of the foot and overall size is as far away as Gr 339 in the north cemetery as Este, near Padua in Italy (Bianco Peroni 1970, Taf 51, No 339a); the principal difference is that this piece has a slight mouth-moulding. Given the European distribution of these small chapes as a whole, it is readily apparent that there is no well-defined type but rather a loosely connected family with considerable variation in shape and decoration but always with small size, lozengic or elliptical section and expanded foot in common. In Ireland there is one piece from near Lisnacrogher, Co Antrim, with a ball-shaped foot (Eogan 1965, 172, no 6b), and another from Sruhagh,

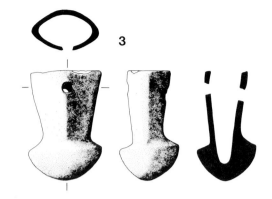

Fig 159   Short chape 12821. Scale 1:1

Co Cavan (Evans 1881, 301–6, esp Fig 367; Eogan 1965, 172, no 8) with a laterally expanded foot. On the European mainland one of the closest connections is in a hoard from Dévill-lès-Rouen, Seine-Maritime, France (O'Connor 1980, 396–8, Fig 63a). This is very much a hoard of Carp's Tongue complex but it also contains the hilt of a *Mörigen* sword, a link with other contexts in Germany and Switzerland where related small chapes may also occur with solid-hilted swords. Interesting examples are from Nächtsenbach, Baden (Sprockhoff 1934, Taf 33.15); Münchenroda, Kr Jena, Thüringen (*ibid*, Taf 21.21) where the organic scabbard to which the chape was attached was wrapped in bronze tape; Hanau-Dunlopgelände, Hessen (Müller-Karpe 1948, Taf 36.20); Mauern, Kr Neuburg a.d. Donau, Bayern (Eckstein 1963), all in Germany; Luissel, Bex, VD (Bocksberger 1964, 78, Taf 28.9); Mörigen, BE (Bernatzky-Goetze 1987, 98, 100, Taf 156.5–6; Auvernier, NE (Rychner 1979, 79, Fig 107.7–9), in Switzerland. Other examples exist but are increasingly removed in type. An important aspect of these parallels is their contexts, which generally date these small chapes to the Carp's Tongue complex/Bronze Final III in France and to Ha B2–B3 in Germany and Switzerland. Thus it is likely that the Caldicot small chape must be contemporary with Ewart Park rather than the Wilburton date of the other pieces.

The composition of the piece is also of interest and may help us in a circumstantial way to look for its origin. The medium-tin unleaded bronze with small arsenic and nickel impurities would, in a British context at least, suggest a Penard period date. There is, of course, no way typologically that this chape can be so early, but we should not forget the existence of a central European import of that date in south-east Wales; this is the Hallstatt A2 tanged Urnfield knife in the Ffynhonnau, Brecon, hoard (Savory 1955; Burgess and Gerloff 1981, pl 133.E). If the chape had been made in Britain in the Ewart Park period it would almost certainly have been made of leaded bronze; the same would apply to the Carp's Tongue regions of France and, probably, to Ireland as well. In Switzerland in Ha B2–B3 there would certainly be significant antimony and silver impurities as well, possibly with Sb>As (Rychner 1990). This leaves Germany as the most likely source area on the assumption that northern Italy is too remote. Unfortunately Germany is largely a blank as far as the published analysis of later Bronze Age metalwork is concerned, but analyses of the contemporary Montelius V period in Denmark, mainly supplied with metal through Germany, suggests that the idea of a German origin may well be correct (Liversage pers comm).

Conclusions

The Caldicot metalwork should be considered in the context of the distribution of Wilburton metalwork in Wales and of exotic imports to the region in Ewart Park times. Wilburton metalwork is here defined as those objects of characteristic Wilburton types, for example long-tongue chapes and Wilburton swords, and locally-developed types with typical Wilburton compositions such as the Gwithian precursors of South Welsh socketed axes from Cowbridge, Glamorgan and Llanthony Abbey, Gwent (Savory 1980, nos 205, 207). The greater part of this material is concentrated in the single hoard from Guilsfield, Powys (Savory 1965), the centre of a concentration of Wilburton objects in the Upper Severn Basin. The only other concentration is in South-East Wales and the southern Marches in a band parallel with the Bristol Channel and lower Severn. The spearheads from Merthyr Mawr (Savory 1980, nos 234–5) and the chape from Pembrokeshire (unpublished) suggest an extension along the south coast, if only as a route for the acquisition of scrap metal. What was happening in the interior at this time is almost invisible to us. Perhaps there was some persistence of Penard metal and forms, and almost certainly there would have been some penetration of Irish types. Almost certainly metal was scarce for the ordinary population and had to be carefully husbanded.

It seems probable the small chape and the tin object from Caldicot, or at least the former, are exotic imports from continental Europe. South-East Wales was always open to such penetration and we can see examples sporadically through the later Bronze Age. In the Penard period there are the Ffynhonnau knife and possibly the conical ferrules as well, together with the arrowhead in the Penard hoard itself (Savory 1980, no 266.6). In the Wilburton period we have the Caldicot tin strip, and in the Ewart Park period there is the small Caldicot chape. Carp's Tongue material is generally lacking but the first occurrence of the classic Carp's Tongue sword blade

and copper ingot fragments has recently been found in Pembrokeshire (Northover, unpublished). The Ewart Park period in southern Wales, though, was generally served by settled local production and exotics are rare. They return finally in the Llyn Fawr period with Armorican socketed axes and classic Hallstatt C types in the Llyn Fawr and Cardiff hoards (Savory 1980, nos 289–321).

The Amber Bead
Joyce Compton

An irregular, round amber bead (21390) with a central perforation, orange in colour when excavated but now darkened to a deep, almost blood red hue following consolidation (Fig 160). The diameter varies from 13–14mm and the thickness varies from 4–5.5mm. The variation in the thickness places the bead in Beck and Shennan's Group 4 (1991, 52, Fig 4.1; 54, Table 4.1; 57). Most British finds of amber beads with a drop-shaped cross section are from later Bronze Age contexts and are thought to have been shaped deliberately in order to hang uniformly on a curved string.

Fig 160   Amber bead 21390. Scale 1:1

Roman Ceramics
Joyce Compton

Two finds of Roman date were made during the course of these excavations. The presence of Roman material here is not surprising given widespread evidence for Romano-British activity in the immediate area, eg pottery kilns in the present town of Caldicot (Barnet *et al* 1990), and adds to the picture of Roman activity on the Gwent Levels.

1 Find no. 5419. An abraded, fragmentary bodysherd of Black Burnished ware. There are no closely datable features. Weight 6g. Unstratified; a surface find from the hedge line (sic).
2 Find no. 21262. A small fragment of tile, probably an imbrex (thickness 14mm), in a pale orange fabric, likely to be from kilns in the Severn Valley. Weight 40g. Found approx. 1.0m below present ground surface during initial cleaning of machined slope in Area H, Phase VIII, context 22281.

Section C: Synthesis

An archaeological and environmental synthesis

Introduction

In this concluding section, an attempt is made to integrate the wide variety of analyses carried out on material recovered from the excavations and then to place the site at Caldicot in its wider regional, environmental, cultural and chronological contexts. Due care is taken to consider the taphonomic and site formation processes touched upon in earlier sections when interpreting assemblages which accumulated in predominantly fluvial contexts. In the first part of this section, the results are integrated within a chronostratigraphic framework to provide an interpretative narrative in which the evidence for vegetation and landscape in the immediate environs of the site and their exploitation by contemporary prehistoric communities are reviewed. Three main zones (watercourse, floodplain and dry land) are identified and used to provide a spatial framework for this narrative.

The evidence from the site is then considered against the wider setting of the Severn Levels and the hinterland of the Nedern catchment and the development of the cultural landscape. Reference is made to recent environmental analyses from Barland's Farm, Caldicot Pill, Goldcliff and Vurlong Reen on the Caldicot Level which provide comparative sequences on vegetational development, and to prehistoric sites and finds from the Gwent Levels and

the site's hinterland. Necessarily, this discussion is constrained by post-depositional and destructive processes which bias the evidence available, particularly with regard to the field archaeology where good archaeological visibility and poor preservational environments in the upland zone (eg the Wentwood Hills) contrast with excellent environmental data but limited archaeological visibility of the alluviated floodplains and levels (cf Evans 1992).

Site narrative

The stratigraphy at Caldicot indicates multiple periods of fluvial erosion, down-cutting and sediment deposition. The resulting channel and valley fills, examined during the excavations and subsequent analyses, reflect the varying sedimentological and environmental conditions. The different lines of environmental evidence examined complement each other, different biota reflecting different source areas and landscape units/blocks (Fig 161). The evidence is largely dominated by aquatic taxa, particularly strongly represented in the diatom, ostracod, mollusc, insect and plant macrofossil assemblages, representing the wet environment of the river channels and adjacent banksides. The nature of this aquatic environment however did not remain constant, with changes in salinity and degree of silting

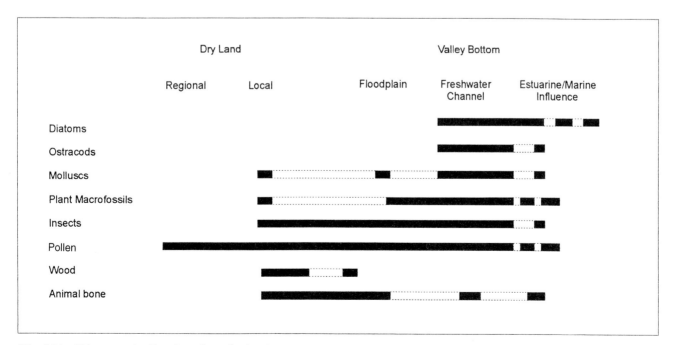

Fig 161   Diagram indicating the relative importance of different biota in reconstructing the environmental history of the landscape blocks at Caldicot

evident in the plant and animal records. The diatoms are the most sensitive indicators of fluctuations/variations in salinity, whilst the molluscs and plant macrofossils, in particular, indicate periods of silting and drying out. Much of the artefactual and structural material recovered reflects specialised and/or localised human activity associated with the prevailing nature of the watercourse. Outside the immediate limits of the channel environment, but merging with it, was an open environment consisting of wet grassland communities, most clearly represented in the plant macrofossil and insect assemblages, which were probably subject to flooding both by fresh and brackish waters at various times. Exploitation of this resource is also demonstrated particularly in the domesticate bone assemblages recovered from the site which stress the value of this zone as a grazing resource. Beyond this floodplain environment, on the drier ground, scrub, woodland, grassland and cultivated areas occurred. This zone, beyond the level of seasonal flooding, is seen as a distinct area, referred to as 'dry land' to denote its independence from changes in contemporary hydrological conditions. The habitats encompassed by this zone can in no way be considered wetlands, but the waterlogged conditions at the site have allowed the preservation of the fullest range of materials gathered from the zone and deposited at the site. This is particularly relevant to the wood assemblage, the majority of which is seen as derivative from woodland communities located off the floodplain.

The integrated results for each site phase are discussed below and summarised in Table 63 within this framework of land blocks.

The Mesolithic and Neolithic environment: Phase I

This phase lacks any direct archaeological evidence and represents a period of rapid aggradation in the valley. The sediments belonging to this phase are characterised by fine sands and silts overlain by a succession of grey clays and intercalated organic horizons, the former reflecting estuarine/marine conditions and the latter periods when fresher waters dominated. Radiocarbon dates bracketing one of the upper horizons are 4670 ± 80 BP (CAR-1323) and 4360 ± 80 BP (CAR-1322) and the period for which there is detailed environmental evidence is approximately middle to later Neolithic.

The residual assemblage of punch struck blades and cores of Mesolithic type point to human activity in the valley bottom at a time for which there is no detailed environmental data from the excavations. It seems probable that much of the present valley floor would have been tidally inundated, with no clearly-defined channel acting as a focal point. The Mesolithic evidence, limited though it is, accords with the view that coastal and sub-coastal environments with their diverse habitats and resources, particularly for fishing and wildfowl hunting, would have been especially attractive to hunter/gatherer communities.

Examination of the upper, organic horizons provides a more detailed picture of the changing environmental conditions in the Neolithic period. Although the evidence is limited, marine and brackish water diatoms indicate a marine influence during deposition of the clays, suggesting the site was below high tide limit. Chenopodiaceae pollen is well represented and demonstrates the close proximity of salt-marsh throughout the phase, the latter condition also suggested by the occurrence of *Spergula*-type pollen. In contrast to the microfossil evidence, macrofossils tend to indicate freshwater, although there are hints of a brackish/marine influence. Most of the plant macrofossils, for example celery-leaved buttercup and duckweed, reflect freshwater conditions though the former can occur in brackish water. Other plants such as false fox-sedge, sea-spurreys, oraches and annual sea-blite may also be found in salt-marsh, brackish ditches or on tidal flats. It is possible the freshwater plant remains derive from upstream, if only a short distance. The sediments are largely sterile of molluscs and ostracods. The absence of molluscs has been noted in intertidal deposits at Goldcliff (Bell p 141) and may imply that similar conditions apply at Caldicot at this time. Although estuarine waters may be largely mixed and brackish with a gradient in average salinity along the estuary, the fresh and saline water masses may be discrete and stratified (see Fig 1.6 Adam 1990) which could help to account for the mixed assemblages recorded in this and later phases.

Diatoms are largely absent from the peaty horizons. Plant macrofossils, ostracods and mollusca indicate freshwater and the presence of reedswamp and fen, though a salt-marsh /brackish water element persists which suggests estuarine conditions were not far away and the site not totally beyond the occasional high tide. *Phragmites* swamp characteristically fringes brackish water. Amphibians are present in the faunal record and British species are only found in freshwater.

To summarise it would seem that the valley was subject to marine inundation for much of Phase I, though probably towards the upper tidal limits. At intervals freshwater conditions prevailed, resulting in organic and peat deposits. Open-water conditions or swamp filled the whole of the valley floor and a floodplain as such did not exist, though plants such as hemp agrimony and great willow herb could have been growing on the drier valley edges.

As with the small Mesolithic flint assemblage, the Neolithic flint and polished stone axe fragment point to some exploitation of the wetland habitats in the valley floor. The evidence for predominantly wetland conditions suggest such activities would have been specialised and limited, perhaps concentrating on exploiting this zone for transport and hunting.

Prior to c 4600 BP on the dry land, from the brief pollen record available, mixed deciduous woodland dominated, mainly oak and hazel, with lime, elm and

Table 63 Human activity and environmental change

Archaeological period	Phase	Dry land	Valley bottom		
			Floodplain	Channel	
Mesolithic	I	* Mixed deciduous woodland. Hunting and gathering		Open water and/or reed swamp. Mudflats. Marine influence. Hunting/fishing and transport.	
Neolithic	I	* 'Elm decline'. Mixed deciduous woodland. Later regeneration of lime. Some clearance activity. Limited pastoralism and cultivation. Funerary monuments.		Open water and/or reed swamp. Mudflats. Marine influence. Hunting/fishing and transport.	
Bronze Age	II	Clearance of lime and expansion of oak. Some pastoralism and cereal cultivation. Woodland exploitation	Development of floodplain. Disturbed ground. Grazing	Down-cutting of channel. Freshwater followed by tidal influence. Possible fish weir. Fishing and transport	
	III	Decrease in oak woodland. Expansion of scrub. Pastoralism and arable activity. Woodland exploitation: craft and by-products. Funerary monuments. ?Settlement	Wet grassland. Disturbed ground. Towards end of phase increase in alder near site. Grazing. ?'Burnt mounds'	Renewed down-cutting and lateral shift. Predominantly freshwater. Occasional tidal influence. Boatbuilding/ breaking. Transport- landing point Focus Crossing	
	IV	Further slight clearance. Similar level of agricultural activity	Wet grassland. Less evidence of disturbance near channel. Grazing.	Freshwater and increasing silting. ?Braiding – main channel elsewhere? ?Residual remains.	
	V	Woodland similar. Increase in grassland – pastoralism. Cereal cultivation.	Wet grassland. Increase in disturbed habitats. Grazing. Increase in alder and then decline – clearance or ?sea level rise.	Renewed down-cutting. Freshwater continues. Refuse.	
	VI–VII	Some clearance of oak and hazel woodland followed by minor regeneration episode. Pastoralism and cereal cultivation. Woodland exploitation – structures, ?coppicing Stone outcrop exploitation. ?Settlement	Wet grassland. Disturbed habitats. Grazing. ?'Burnt mounds' Increase in alder followed by decline – clearance or rise in sea level.	Wide/flat-bottomed channel. Silting. ?Braiding. Later minor channel. Freshwater with increasing marine influence. Ford/weir/hard. Bridge. 'Trackway'. Crossing. Fishing. Transport.	
?Iron Age	VIII	Further clearance activity. Pastoralism and arable cultivation	?Wet grassland	Increase in over-bank sedimentation. Increasing marine influence. Channel shift? Absence of activity.	

* Based on other sites in the area.

alder of less significance However, from *c* 4600 BP there is a marked regeneration of lime and to a lesser degree elm, which seems to have been maintained until the end of the phase. Before *c* 4600 BP there is some slight evidence for agricultural activity which diminishes between 4600–4300 BP. Post 4300 BP the presence of ribwort plantain and cereal-type pollen and an increase in bracken spores suggests renewed agricultural activity within the woodland environment. Although this period is essentially one of regeneration it is possible that a system of 'forest farming' (cf Göransson 1983, 1986, 1987, Edwards 1993), was operating whereby cereal cultivation would occur for a year in axe-cleared coppice, after which the woodland would be allowed to regenerate. Leaf fodder would be provided by the coppice and natural forest would regenerate in marginal areas. However, whether there was any attempt at a formal coppice management system in the Caldicot area is open to debate, and will be returned to later. The cereal-type pollen may reflect other than a cultivated environment (p 101). There are no domesticates recorded from this phase but the limited evidence for red deer in the area is in accord with the evidence for a wooded landscape.

The location of the chambered tomb of Heston Brake (ST 5052 8866, see Fig 163) on the sandstone plateau less than 2km east of the site points to the established presence of Neolithic communities in the area. Differences in the size of the orthostats of the outer and the inner sections of the long passage, the latter section forming a box-like end chamber on a slightly different alignment, have led to the suggestion that the construction is multi-period (Corcoran 1972, 43), emphasising continuity in Neolithic settlement in the immediate vicinity of the site. The absence of other site types should not be seen as evidence for a scarcity of human populations in this period, but rather as the result of post-depositional destruction of less robust structures (cf Evans 1992), a subject which will be returned to in the broader, regional discussion later.

The Bronze Age: Phase II

The very limited excavations of the earliest palaeo-channel deposits on the site and the auger data to the south of the excavations indicate the presence of a substantial channel with water flow running from north-west to south-east with the bed level at *c* 1.8m OD. Its fullest width is unknown as only the partially truncated left edge was encountered. A basal dump of stone and wood provides the first direct evidence of human activity at the site. Following some siltation and concomitant narrowing of the channel, lines of driven hazel piles were constructed across the channel, possibly in two phases. Radiocarbon dates from the piles place this phase in the earlier Bronze Age. The associated sediments were high in silt and low in organic content in comparison with later channel infills.

From the diatom evidence, the environment of the channel is not that different to that existing in the valley during Phase I with brackish/ marine diatoms dominating, although there is some evidence for a mixed freshwater/marine assemblage preceding this brackish/ marine phase, which could indicate either mixing of sediments, the introduction of marine species into a freshwater environment, or freshwater taxa brought downstream into a tidal environment. In the pollen record slightly higher values for the algae *Pediastrum* at this time, compared with later in the phase, confirm a freshwater element. As marine and brackish water diatoms then increase, *Pediastrum* values show a reciprocal relationship and decline. It is likely the benthic diatom species derive from a nearby habitat, whereas the foreshore and open water diatoms were probably brought to the site by incoming tides (Cameron, p 125). Chenopodiaceae pollen is frequent indicating the continued presence of salt-marsh in the area.

Confirmation of estuarine conditions is provided by the presence of the ostracod *Leptocythere lacertosa* and molluscs *Leucophytia bidentata* and *Ovatella myosotis*. However, the occurrence of small instars of the freshwater ostracod *Candona neglecta*, which suggest the latter is *in situ* and breeding, indicates that Caldicot is at the margins of a marine environment, probably only under a marine influence at high tide. Aquatic plant macrofossil taxa are dominated by freshwater species but there is the occasional representative of salt-marsh or species tolerant of brackish water such as orache and grey club-rush.

Similar evidence for contrasting salinity conditions is found in the record for fish and amphibians. The presence of possible flounders points to brackish conditions and supports the diatom evidence. The eels present could live in either brackish or fresh water, but the amphibians are restricted to the latter.

During this phase the evidence seems to suggest that for much of the time the channel environment at the site was subject to frequent inundation by tidal waters, if only at high tide, but this was to some extent counterbalanced by freshwater from upstream. The degree of saline influence would also have varied according to changes in river discharge.

Both the molluscs and ostracods suggest little water movement. *Valvata piscinalis,* which is typically found in moving water and dominates the mollusc assemblages from the other phases, is largely absent. The species that do occur can survive in muddy areas where occasionally there is some drying out, as might have occurred particularly at the edge of the channel.

On balance then, the evidence points to a channel environment subject to regular tidal fluctuation in water level. The sharply-defined interface associated with this phase, and the presence of large clasts of organic sediment reminiscent of Phase I horizons, interpreted as sheered and slumped bank material, supports the environmental evidence for a river channel subject to tidal influences. Channel aggra-

261

dation would appear to be the result of a combination of infill with both riverine and estuarine sediment. During this process of infilling, closely-set piles driven into the bed of the channel created a cross-channel obstruction. The presence of two angled braces on the downstream side of the structure suggests that the major stresses acting on it came from the flow of water from upstream, probably at its greatest during the ebbing tide. Destabilisation of the structure through erosion of the deposits around the piles may have been countered by packing stone, wood and bone around loosened piles. The structure probably functioned as some form of fish weir, possibly in conjunction with nets or baskets, exploiting runs of eels, other migratory fish and resident flatfish. The limited exposure of the contemporary channel bed within the excavations produced no other structural evidence to indicate the presence of landing places or associated occupation, and environmental indicators of flow rates suggest that most types of artefactual material deposited within the soft-bottomed channel would not have been subject to significant transport or erosion. Construction and maintenance of the fish weir required exploitation of resources from beyond the valley bottom, specifically wood and stone from the drier valley sides.

There is a distinct hiatus in the pollen record between Phases I and II. By the beginning of Phase II there had been a marked change in the composition of the surrounding woodland. This is interpreted as clearance, largely of lime dominated woodland, into which oak dominated woodland had expanded. Preferential grazing of more palatable lime foliage could also have led to a relative decline in this tree at the expense of other woodland species. Grass pollen also increases accompanied by ribwort plantain and other taxa indicative of pastoralism. Cereal-type pollen probably indicates the presence of cultivation. As in the previous phase, some farming may have been practised within the wooded environment.

A marked increase in the range of dry-land taxa in the plant macrofossil record confirms the pollen evidence for an increase in open ground dry-land habitats including grassland, particularly damp grassland, disturbed ground and possibly cultivated land. Species such as curled dock and clustered dock frequently occur in damp grassland, as does the mollusc *Vallonia pulchella*, and their occurrence is consistent with the development of a restricted river channel and associated floodplain. Taxa indicative of disturbed ground reflect human activity around the site. The importance of grasslands and pastoralism is further emphasised by the presence of cattle bones, although this is not to say that woodland resources were not also being exploited for leaf fodder at this time.

Blackthorn, hazel, elder and blackberry/raspberry macrofossils indicate the presence of scrub or the understorey of woodland, perhaps on the nearby gravel terraces, while *Alnus* remains suggest alder carr possibly fringing the wetlands upstream. The

former habitats only show up in the pollen record towards the end of Phase II either because there was an expansion in clearance and opening of the forest canopy resulting in increased representation of the understorey species or colonisation of abandoned areas by scrub, or because this activity was occurring closer to the site. The pollen subzone has characteristics of both Phases II and III and there is a possibility that there was some mixing of Phase II/Phase III sediments resulting in transitional assemblages. However, wood from the pile structure confirms the presence of scrubby species and suggests that local woodland/scrub was being exploited. The hazel, which makes up the majority of the wood from the pile structure, was grown under good conditions and is generally more mature than in the later phases. This could be interpreted as evidence for a lower frequency of exploitation and human activity in the area at this time but the structural need here for more substantial wood for piles is probably the determining factor in the choice of materials.

The stone used in the primary dump within the basal fill of the channel and later in association with the pile structure would have been freely available from exposures within 1km of the site (Howe, p 246), on both sides of the valley just beyond the gravel terraces.

Phase III

A further period of downcutting and sedimentation together with limited lateral shift in the channel characterises Phase III. The stratigraphic evidence, particularly from Area C, indicates channel migration to the east and north and Taylor's model of lateral migration of the channel thalweg (the deepest part of the channel) is favoured here. It should be stressed that the channel's position shifts only a matter of a few metres at most and could well have been imperceptible to the contemporary population. Nonetheless, channel migration would have caused some erosion of earlier sediment which presumably contained Mesolithic and Neolithic flints recovered from the Phase III river bed. This erosion also raises the possibility of the incorporation of residual biota from the earlier marine sediments. However, in general the poor preservation of marine diatoms in Phase I deposits, together with the reciprocal relationship between marine diatoms and *Pediastrum* (see below), suggest that the majority of diatoms within the Phase III infill are contemporary. The channel was only investigated in any great detail in the west half of the modern lake and had undergone some truncation by subsequent Phase V downcutting, so its overall morphology is unclear. Water flow would appear to be from north-west to south-east within a sinuous water course which was affected to some extent by the presence of the remains of the Phase II pile structure protruding from the right bank. Human activity at this time included deposition of a wide variety of wood including scrub clearance, woodworking debris and the boat strake. Although some stone and domesticate bone was also deposited, this never reached the densities of material encountered in later Phases VI–VII. Radiocarbon determinations lie in the range 3150–3450 BP. The sediments infilling the channels are clays and silty clays with organic inclusions.

In contrast to the previous phase the overriding evidence for the nature of the channel environment is one of freshwater. However, virtually all the biota display a small element which is ascribable to a brackish/marine environment. This may be due to a variety of reasons, including occasional high tides, storm surges, wind blown salt spray or reworking of estuarine/marine sediments (but see above). Although the diatom record is dominated by oligohalobous (indifferent) taxa, which are interpreted as indicating freshwater conditions, there is a low background count of brackish/ marine taxa and a small but distinct peak in marine taxa in Column 3 (see Fig 86) in sediments preceding the boat strake deposits, which may have some bearing on the navigability and accessibility of the site in relation to the rest of the estuary. The marine species represented are predominantly tychoplanktonic and therefore easily transported, but the evidence does point to an episode(s) of marine incursion or increased tidal influence, perhaps only at the highest tides. Generally in the pollen record there is an increase in freshwater aquatics and a marked expansion in *Pediastrum*, but again there seems to be some evidence for a reciprocal relationship between the frequency of brackish/marine diatoms and *Pediastrum* in Column 3 during Phases III and IV. This is most clearly demonstrated by a marked decline in *Pediastrum* at the same time as the peak in marine diatoms. However, Chenopodiaceae pollen values are low, suggesting salt-marsh communities were further away from the site at this time. The presence of the boat plank, which is interpreted as evidence for nearby boat repair activities, suggests that the channel remained navigable throughout this phase.

The other biota present also demonstrate freshwater conditions, but with occasional indicators of brackish/marine conditions. The brackish water ostracod *Cyprideis* and the estuarine/brackish water mollusc species *Ovatella/Leucophytia* are recorded, while a few Coleoptera species usually found on the sea shore or at the edge of tidal estuaries, including *Bembidion varium*, *B. fumigatum*, *Heterocerus maritimus* and *H. marginatus* occur. Horned pondweed and various sedges can be found in both fresh and brackish water and annual sea-blite and oraches occur in salt marsh. The presence of stickleback largely suggests freshwater but it can occasionally occur in brackish water. Eel can be found in either but amphibians are confined to freshwater. Overall, the dominant conditions in the channel appear to be freshwater but with a background brackish/marine influence, perhaps reflecting only the occasional high tide.

There is close agreement between the pollen, plant macrofossil and beetle evidence for the type of freshwater vegetation growing both within and close to the margins of the channel. For example, the aquatic duckweed (*Lemna*) is represented not only in the pollen and seed records but also by the weevil *Tanysphyrus lemnae*, while *Donacia* species in the beetle record are in accordance with the botanical evidence for sedges, bur-reed, reed-mace and pondweed and *Prasocuris phellandrii* is found on aquatic members of the Apiaceae family.

In terms of the flow rate in the channel the presence of *Limnocythere inopinata* and the range of juveniles to adults in the ostracod evidence indicates still or only sluggishly moving water conditions. By contrast the mollusc evidence is strongly dominated by *Valvata piscinalis*, which is considered to prefer running water but can occur in a range of conditions (see Bell p 139). However, there is a lack of other mollusc taxa indicative of moving water. The insect fauna provides evidence for both types of environment, being made up of a mixture of species which live in still or very slow moving water and others, the Elmidae, which are found in rapidly running water. It has been suggested (Osborne 1988) that the latter require a clean, stony river bottom for greater aeration and are eliminated from slow-flowing rivers where there is an accumulation of fine sediment following forest clearance, ploughing and erosion. Hence at Caldicot they are likely to have been washed down from upstream rather than to have originated locally. Although some of the plant taxa represented can occur in rapidly moving water, the majority favour still or slowly flowing water. Apart from material having been washed down from where there was a more rapid flow rate, it is also probable that a range of micro environments occurred within the channel.

Within a channel flow rates vary: water in contact with the channel boundaries flows more slowly because of frictional forces, and a vertical section through a channel, parallel to the axis of flow, normally reveals a logarithmic distribution of flow velocities. Water flowing around a bend flows more slowly on the inside than the outside of the curve (Spicer 1989, 126). In addition, the growth of vegetation itself would lead to variations in the hydrology across the channel, with the creation of areas where water was still or movement minimal while elsewhere flow rates might increase as a result of the channelling effects of the vegetation. The survival of the concentrations of yew twigs and woodworking debris would tend to support quiet water conditions, and the likelihood of much of the wood being brought in by humans rather than washed in during floods. The range of body parts represented by the bone assemblage from this phase (see McCormick, Table 46) include elements defined by Coard and Dennell (1995) as both stable and unstable in terms of their transportability within a fluvial environment. The presence of *in situ* epiphyses on some of the unfused bone also indicates minimal disturbance. This is interpreted as evidence for an essentially autochthonous faunal assemblage (ie not subject to significant fluvial transport following human deposition into the channel). On the whole the evidence seems to suggest relatively slowly moving water.

No indisputably *in situ* structures were excavated within the channel during this phase and the majority of the artefactual assemblage is interpreted as discarded refuse. The pile structure (472) may have continued in use during the earliest parts of this phase but soon fell into ruin, possibly becoming redundant in the changed hydrological conditions. The wood assemblage is dominated by hazel and *Prunus* roundwood, although localised concentrations of woodworking waste form a significant proportion. The density of wood in the base of the palaeochannel would have consolidated the riverbed and facilitated river crossings and the beaching of boats: whether this was the intention or a chance by-product of discard is unclear although stone deposition is relatively sparse in comparison with the Phase VI structure, 9014. The substantial boat strake, associated fragment and yew ties are also interpreted as discarded material, resulting from the repair of a plank sewn boat: no further boat remains were recovered and the damaged nature of the plank suggests it had become redundant. The concentration of yew withies encountered in Area E might relate to boat repair. The single wooden artefact recovered, a handle or cleat fragment, was also damaged. As yet there is no excavation evidence for the nature of channel further upstream during this period. It may be that the site lay at the limit of navigability for the type of vessels indicated by the boat strake, which would have been more suited to larger rivers and estuarine waters.

There is strong evidence from the beetle and botanical records, and to a lesser extent the mollusc record, for an open environment beyond the immediate environs of the channel, although the pollen suggests a more wooded regional picture. On the floodplain and nearest dry land there was probably grassland, including damp grassland, with plants such as buttercup, knotgrass, thistle, clover and ribwort plantain. As well as open grassland, there are clear indications of disturbed ground attributable to human and animal activity at the site. Representation of the weed greater plantain increases substantially. The presence of species such as fat hen may also reflect trampled areas around the site but along with prickly sow-thistle, nipplewort and black nightshade and the pollen evidence for cereals could indicate cultivation was taking place relatively nearby. However the evidence for agriculture suggests an emphasis on pastoralism in the immediate vicinity of the site rather than cereal cultivation, for which the evidence is more tenuous. The bone assemblage confirms the pollen evidence for pastoral activity. The numerical dominance of sheep over cattle in the small assemblage provides very limited evidence for growth in the importance of sheep in the subsistence economy at a time when the pollen and

beetle evidence suggests the development of a more open grassland environment. Dung beetles, which are most often found in the droppings of large grazing animals such as sheep, cattle or horse, are present in this and later phases. The bone assemblage is seen as discarded food waste with the possible exception of the dog mandibles and the small quantity of bird remains (owl and grebe) which could represent natural deaths. Only a small quantity of stone was encountered and is not seen as functional: it may reflect discard of stone used in some form of 'burnt mound' type of meat preparation. Burnt mounds are often found in close association with water courses: it may be that meat processing was an activity preferentially located on the valley floor (cf Caseldine and Murphy 1989). Alternatively, food waste could have been transported from settlement on the sandstone plateau for discard in the river but the lack of pottery from this phase argues against repeated dumping into the channel of rubbish from occupation sites as well as making the immediate presence of riverside settlement unlikely.

By the beginning of this phase, from the pollen record, there had been a marked reduction in oak woodland and a corresponding expansion in shrubby species such as hazel and blackthorn, presumably into abandoned areas where grazing pressures were relaxed or possibly onto drier parts of the floodplain where the suppressive effects of flooding had become less severe or frequent. The dominance of these species in both the wood and plant macrofossil records from the site would also appear to indicate expansion in scrubland. Alternatively these species could indicate the establishment of hedges (Groenman-van Waateringe 1978). At present it must remain a matter of speculation as to whether naturally occurring areas of scrub, especially of blackthorn and hawthorn, could have become formalised boundaries in the prehistoric landscape during the Bronze Age. Naturally occurring scrub could have acted as buffer zones between established areas of grazing on the valley floor and areas of cleared woodland on the valley sides/dry land exploited for cereal production. Over time, selective clearance may have led to the establishment of some form of hedging made up of grazing resistant species which could have assisted in the control of livestock.

There is some wood from forest trees, notably oak and ash, but this is generally in the form of woodworking debris suggesting exploitation of these species for craft purposes rather than deposition of the by-products of forest clearance. One of the shortcomings of pollen analysis is that although it tells you that clearance has taken place it fails to tell you how that was achieved or for what purpose (Edwards 1979). At Caldicot the wood-working evidence goes some way to rectify the former, providing information about the tree-felling techniques in operation (p 179).

Some species, for example dogwood, privet and yew, could have been growing on outcrops of limestone in the area as opposed to on the sandstones and gravel terraces. Beetle evidence for the local presence of woodland is slight but this may be under-representation because many of the tree-dependent beetles do not have very good powers of dispersal and the woodland may have been beyond the main beetle catchment area. *Scolytus rugulosa*, which lives on the genus *Prunus*, also represented by fruitstones, pollen and wood at the site, is present. It seems likely that the beetles were brought onto the site with the wood but it is also likely that blackthorn was growing quite close to the site. It seems unlikely that wood was transported from very far away, confirmed by the length of some of it – over 4m in some cases. Much of it was fast-grown indicating favourable environmental conditions on the nearby gravel terraces. Most of the wood appears to have been cut in winter and almost all is less than 20 years old. It is quite possible that the same area(s) were being exploited as in the previous phase, though there is no evidence for formal coppice management in terms of identifiable cropping cycles. The morphology of much of the hazel wood, straight and unbranched, and three characteristic coppiced heels could result from deliberate cutting and regeneration but this does not necessarily mean a deliberate coppice cycle was in force (cf Crone 1987). The very occasional occurrence of beaver-chewed wood during this phase means that beaver activity in the area could also have caused some 'natural' coppicing. The oak at the site is relatively immature, suggesting secondary woodland and repeated clearance and regeneration in certain areas, if on a different time-scale. Although the vast majority of the wood was uncharred, partially charred pieces of hazel could reflect craft or domestic activity, or alternatively deliberate burning of clearance debris, possibly to provide ash for cereal cultivation. Towards the end of the phase there is an increase in *Alnus* pollen, reflecting either an expansion in alder carr generally, or the development of carr woodland nearer to the site.

Finally, there is some indication of the nature of wetland environments elsewhere in the region. The occurrence of *Calluna* in the pollen record probably reflects the known development of raised bog at this time in the present Magor/Barland's Farm area and the present intertidal area, for example at Goldcliff.

Phase IV

There is no clear evidence for channel downcutting during this phase: it is characterised by the high organic content and mottled nature of the fills which made this horizon so distinctive during excavation. Artefactual evidence is largely absent and the small amount present may be derived from earlier channel fills. Hence the archaeological evidence points to a reduced level of activity at this time, at least in the area of the site. A radiocarbon determination places the Phase III/ Phase IV interface *c* 3000 ± 60 BP (CAR-1407). The sediments differ from Phase III in a general decrease in bulk densities and percentage carbonate content and an increase in loss on ignition values, corresponding to organic deposition. Frequent mottling in the sediments suggests a lower water level and periods of drying-out, perhaps conditions generally no longer ideally suited for water transport or other activities which took place here during Phase III. Relocation of the river channel to elsewhere on the floodplain, channel braiding and perhaps cut-off could explain these drier conditions.

Throughout the phase the channel environment continued to be predominantly freshwater in character, although low but significant background counts of marine taxa could indicate the occasional high tide. Values for the freshwater algae *Pediastrum* also fluctuate, once again providing a broadly reciprocal relationship with the diatoms. However, overall the evidence suggests the site is generally beyond the reach of tides.

In terms of water flow rates, the evidence is similar to that for the previous phase. The mud and weed growth burrowing ostracods *Candona neglecta* and *Ilyocypris bradyi* continue to dominate the assemblage, but *Limnocythere inopinata* is absent from the later samples. The mollusc record continues to be dominated by moving-water taxa, namely *Valvata piscinalis*, but in the latest sample examined from this phase the slum group mollusc *Anisus leucostoma* predominates, providing support for the sedimentological evidence that conditions were more susceptible to periods of drying out. Plant macrofossils, for example duckweed, largely imply still or slowly-flowing water. High pollen concentration values suggest low sediment accumulation as the channel silted up and was colonised by vegetation.

Outside of the actual channel itself environmental conditions also seem to have remained much the same as in the previous phase, with the pollen record suggesting agricultural activity at a similar, or slightly greater, level. Grassland communities are clearly indicated and pastoralism appears to have continued to play a significant role, though there is some evidence for cultivation. However a distinct reduction in seeds of greater plantain suggests less ground disturbance at the edge of the channel and is consistent with the archaeological evidence for reduced activity at the site itself. A reduction in fat hen, orache and prickly sow-thistle and absence of parsley piert and nipplewort may also reflect a lower level of activity at the site or less cultivation on dry land near to the channel. Fig-leaved goosefoot, which has a similar habitat preference but is also found around manure heaps, is present and possibly points to the continued presence of large herbivores trampling around the channel edge. The very uneven surface of the right bank edge excavated with care during the removal of the baulk between areas B and C (see Fig 27) could support this view. Apart from a further slight decline in arboreal pollen reflecting continued clearance or grazing pressure, there is little change in the woodland communities though field maple and hornbeam are recorded for the first time.

Phase V

The beginning of this phase is marked by renewed down-cutting and is characterised by an apparently round-bottomed, mobile and relatively narrow channel. The site once again seems to have become a focus of human activity with limited deposition of artefacts. Although there are no radiocarbon dates for this phase it probably dates to *c* 3000 BP. The sediments have frequent laminations, indicating changes in the depositional environment. Coarser particles imply intermittent periods of higher energy and flooding and deposition into what was generally a low energy background environment where finer clays were being deposited. A high carbonate content may represent an increase in sediment supply from the limestone areas of the catchment or the effect of rising ground water enriched in calcium carbonate.

The channel environment during this phase continued to be essentially one of freshwater and the diatom assemblage suggests the site was above the high water mark, although compared with the previous phase there is a slight increase in marine and brackish taxa. Similarly the ostracods *Leptocythere* cf *porcella* and *Candona angulata*, the mollusc *Hydrobia ventrosa*, and seeds such as horned pondweed and sea-spurrey hint at a brackish influence. As during previous phases, the presence of *Limnocythere*, dominance of *Candona neglecta* and *Ilyocypris bradyi* and small ostracod instars indicate quiet water conditions. The plant remains also generally reflect slow water movement while the mollusc assemblage continues to be dominated by *Valvata piscinalis*. It could be argued from the sedimentological evidence that there is some evidence during this phase for periods of swifter water movement, and this is discussed further in relation to Phase VI. *Pediastrum* is reasonably well represented. Eel continues to be present indicating either brackish or fresh water, whilst water vole is indicative of fresh water.

There is some evidence to suggest a further expansion of woodland at this time, namely alder carr. However, this then shows a steady decline throughout the phase, which may be due to human interference or other environmental factors (p 114). The wood comprises mainly hazel and blackthorn roundwood reflecting the continued use of scrubland, quite probably from the same area(s) exploited in earlier phases, and much of it is regarded as clearance waste. Whilst it is possible that some of the wood was cut for use at the site, no *in situ* structures were encountered so straightforward disposal may have been the main aim behind its deposition.

The continued importance of pastoralism is reflected in the relatively high representation of ribwort plantain pollen and confirmed by the faunal evidence for sheep and cattle. The presence of pig perhaps points to the use of scrub and woodland in the area for pannage, but the predominance of sheep in the assemblage emphasises the open nature of the immediate environment. The evidence for roe deer may reflect exploitation of the wooded environment further away from the site for hunting.

Cereal-type pollen and other pollen taxa indicate cereal cultivation as do possibly seeds of parsley piert, and perennial and prickly sow-thistles. Fat hen and orache may also reflect cultivation though the latter along with greater plantain may simply represent an increase in disturbed ground near the site as a result of renewed human and animal activity.

Phases VI–VII

Phases VI and VII, which cover the main period of activity at the site, are considered together because, although there are certain structures which can be identified as belonging to one or other phase, it was difficult to assign some evidence with complete certainty. A change in channel cross-profile to a wider (*c* 6.5m) flat-bottomed channel occurs at the beginning of Phase VI. A number of models have been suggested for the change in channel form and the presence of slightly coarser silts in basal fills (Taylor p 77). Relevant variables could include increased run-off and suspended load related to increased clearance and/or rainfall within the Nedern's catchment, and aggradation resulting from increased bed load or background rises in relative sea level. A marked increase in human activity at the site occurs with substantial deposits of stone, wood and artefacts, much of it associated with construction of a ford/hard/weir (9014). Radiocarbon dates lie in the range 3000–2900 BP and a single mortised timber, 332, was dated by dendrochronology to 998/7 BC. The deposits are composed of laminated sediments and Phase VI comprises some of the coarsest sediments, with the lowest density values and carbonate content. Compared with the previous phase there is a possible change in the sediment source, perhaps including erosion of sand from the valley terraces, or a relative decrease in erosion from the limestone area of the catchment in comparison to the area of Devonian sandstone. However, some of the coarser material may be derived from the stone dumped in the channel. This level of activity continues through Phase VII when the wooden bridge (22441) was constructed. Radiocarbon dates range from the middle to late 3rd millennium with dendrochronological dating suggesting construction of the bridge and associated 'trackway' 473 soon after 990/989 BC. A relatively narrow channel (*c* 3m surviving width) and a separate feature (possibly another, braided channel) containing a near-complete dog skeleton, downstream of the bridge is also assigned to Phase VII. The sediments from Phase VII are also laminated silty clays with vertical features mainly from vegetation.

Initially the main channel environment is again basically one of freshwater. The diatom assemblage consists mainly of freshwater oligohalobous taxa with only a background of marine and brackish taxa. *Amphora pediculus* and *Achnanthes* are diatoms that attach themselves to a substrate such as sand grains, rock surfaces, or macrophytes, and given the evidence for stone, sand, and plant macrofossils at the site it seems likely they were deposited *in situ*. Similarly, abundant caddis fly larvae with cases incorporating sand, *Bithynia* operculae and plant material occur at this time. Again the question of to what extent there was water movement arises. *Valvata piscinalis* dominates the mollusc assemblage but operculae, as opposed to shells, of *Bithynia* are also present in quantity. The latter is interpreted as indicative of fluvial sorting. The coarser sediments would also tend to suggest greater water movement at this time. However, the ostracods continue to suggest still or slow water movement although there is a greater proportion of shallow-water swimmers-crawlers as opposed to burrowers present. The stone and possible more rapid water movement would have provided more suitable conditions for the Elmid group of beetles at the site at this time. The possibility of different hydrological conditions across the channel, with perhaps relatively still conditions at the edge but some current movement elsewhere, has already been mentioned. Another possibility suggested by Bell, and supported by Taylor, is that moving water molluscs and ostracods relate to different episodes in the life of the channel.

On balance, the quantity of stone used to secure the structural elements within the basal deposits of the Phase VI channel and the contemporary sedimentary evidence, along with other environmental indicators touched upon above, point to increased flow rates at this time. This should not be over-stressed however and the wood and bone assemblages are probably largely *in situ* with contemporary channel vegetation assisting in artefact capture.

There are hints of marine conditions in the area during Phase VI though the site is generally beyond the upper tidal limit. However a rise in sea-level will affect the ground-water level before there is any change in salinity, and the change in channel cross-profile and increase in alder are perhaps of significance in relation to this. Fragments of marine mollusca, (?) *Littorina*, probably owe their presence to human agency or perhaps birds. In addition species such as sea-spurrey, sea-milkwort, annual sea-blite, grey club rush and possible distant sedge in the plant macrofossil record point towards a marine influence, as does the presence of the near-shore ostracod *Leptocythere*. Later (Phase VI/VII) an increase in marine and brackish diatoms, coinciding with a decline in pollen of freshwater aquatics, suggests the main channel was becoming increasingly tidal. Slightly earlier than this the continuous representation of buck's horn plantain begins in the pollen record. This plant commonly occurs in turf on sandy and gravelly soils near the sea and its presence in the pollen record perhaps reflects the increasingly close proximity of marine conditions. *Pediastrum* values also decline to low levels. Although oligohalobous diatoms remain dominant in Phase VII, the

evidence from both the main channel and the minor channel indicates the trend towards an increasing marine influence continued. Similarly the pollen records from the two channels show an increase in the frequency of buck's horn plantain, particularly in the later channel, which can also be interpreted as reflecting marine conditions nearer to the site. Pollen of sea plantain, which occurs in short turf near the sea and in salt-marshes, is also present, and values for the freshwater algae *Pediastrum* remain low. Throughout this period the other biota basically reflect freshwater conditions though there is the occasional indicator of an estuarine environment such as the molluscs *Ovatella/Leucophytia* and *Hydrobia ventrosa* and plants which can tolerate brackish water. Overall the evidence seems to suggest a return to a periodically tidal environment, which perhaps helps to explain why the bridge was constructed.

In nearly all the Phase VI deposits encountered on the site, especially in basal fills of this broad channel, the density of anthropogenically derived material is far greater than in any other phase. This is particularly the case with regard to structure 9014, where systematic dumping of large quantities of stone, derived directly or indirectly from rock outcrops at the valley sides, combined with the deposition of clearance waste, woodworking debris, substantial timbers, bone waste and even wooden artefacts provided both a consolidated riverbed and protection for a cross-channel line of driven uprights. The structure is interpreted as multi-functional, acting as a hard/ford as well as a fish weir. The presence of a ceramic 'weight' in association with the structure encourages the latter interpretation. Fragments of ridged or holed planking from this phase (see McGrail p 216) suggest continued navigability and the presence of boat forms perhaps similar to the Goldcliff boat find.

Towards the end of Phase VI/VII some changes occur in the plant macrofossil and mollusc assemblages which also may relate to changing environmental conditions elsewhere and/or construction of the bridge. The former suggest the main channel was becoming heavily vegetated by species such as reed canary-grass, bur-reed, common reed and pondweed. The beetle *Donacia clavipes* which is mainly associated with common reed is present. The mollusc assemblage contains a greater percentage of *Bithynia tentaculata*, belonging to the moving water group, and *Anisus leucostoma*, a member of the marsh group. One reason for these changes could be the construction of the bridge which could have impeded flow on the upstream side and resulted in silting and marshy conditions, but at the same time the vegetation and structure itself could also have created channels where there was faster flow such as in the narrower channel (E.7.2) further downstream.

The bridge, 22441, may have been constructed in response to increases in the rate of sedimentation within the channel and possible increases in water depth relating to rising water tables. Such conditions would have made maintenance of a ford/hard increasingly difficult. The associated 'trackway', 473, is interpreted as a temporary means of consolidating the riverbed to facilitate access to the centre of the channel during the bridge's construction. The numerous smaller uprights along both lines of the bridge piles may have extended to sufficient height to provide sails around which rods could have been woven to form hurdle work sides to the structure or alternatively were utilised as fish weirs of some kind. The presence of a pegged, mortised ash plank just downstream of one of the bridge piles points to an attempt at repair before the structure apparently partially collapsed and became incorporated in later sedimentation.

The location of the Wilburton chape, some 4m downstream from the bridge, and the presence of at least two separate, finely decorated vessels, in contemporary deposits downstream could indicate ritual behaviour, although accidental loses cannot be dismissed. The presence of decorative bone objects in close association with one of the pottery vessels, and the single find of an amber bead slightly further downstream are more suggestive of ritual. Other artefact types such as wooden domestic items, and the near-complete dog skeleton could be seen as more prosaic evidence for discard of refuse.

As well as eels, sticklebacks and amphibians there is a large assemblage of birds within the channels, mainly ducks but also Brent geese, heron and crane. All of the latter would have found the range of environments available in the Caldicot area favourable. It is probable that the bird assemblage is present at the site as a result of wildfowling rather than natural deaths.

Apart from the further expansion in alder woodland during Phase VI the woodland communities remain much the same. From a decrease in ribwort plantain pollen there may have been a brief reduction in pastoral activity, but cereal-type pollen continues to be present. This episode is followed by a marked decline in alder pollen, accompanied by falls in oak and hazel pollen, which could reflect either an increase in or clearance activity nearer to the site. Alternatively the decline in alder could result from an increasing marine influence leading to reduction in the available habitat for alder. The majority of pieces of wood at the site seem to represent scrub clearance and it is tempting to see the decline in hazel pollen as reflecting local activity, although the occasional piece of wood with beaver tooth marks serves to remind that not all clearance may be the result of human activity. The hazel from the site was mainly under 15 years old while a second group was more mature around 20–25 years. Coppiced heels of hazel and ash also occur but this probably reflects repeated utilisation of scrubland from the same area on a somewhat haphazard basis rather than a deliberate management system. Oak from the site is also consistent with the pollen evidence for clearance of oak woodland. A slight increase in *Fraxinus* pollen is consistent with opening up of the woodland cover

and an expansion in ash. Partially charred wood could either have resulted from cooking or heating at the site, or from burning during clearance.

Some changes in woodland composition are indicated in Phases VI/VII–VII by the appearance of beech pollen and the occurrence of field maple in wood from the site. Slight increases in hazel, alder and oak pollen indicate a small amount of woodland regeneration during Phase VII. However, as far as the structural components of the bridge from Phase VII are concerned there is a clear case of species selection. Oak and ash were used for the main load bearing posts. Most of these piles came from relatively young trees, suggesting perhaps a limited supply of very mature trees and the largely secondary nature of nearby woodland. Much of the smaller roundwood was hazel. Higher growths rates than the other wood possibly indicate it came from a particular area although it could equally be a function of the young age of this group. Its consistency in size and age suggests careful selection. Twenty five percent was cut in summer, which is a high proportion and perhaps indicates repair during the summer months when water levels would have been lower. Almost all the stems examined for tree-rings from the hurdle structure (1401) were 5 years old, providing the strongest evidence for deliberate coppicing. As in Phase VI, hazel from the possible trackway 473 falls into two age groups: one group under 15 years, the other slightly more mature at 20–25 years. Generally younger hazel was used in this phase perhaps indicating the same area was constantly being exploited and is consistent with continued activity around the site, although the high proportion of wood used in specific structures requiring a consistency in size may be biasing the sample as an indicator of contemporary woodland cover. Some charred wood is present, mainly hazel but with some ash. As previously, this could relate either to clearance activity away from the site or domestic and craft activity at the site.

Throughout Phases VI/VII–VII frequent ribwort plantain and buck's horn plantain pollen indicate an increase in grassland on the drier ground while grassland communities subject to flooding persisted on the floodplain. Trampling of the soils on the adjacent sandy gravel terrace, perhaps where the channel was close to the terrace and stock were coming down to the water would have particularly favoured buck's horn plantain, especially with an increasing maritime influence in the area. Slightly better representation of insects indicative of dry open ground at this time also stresses the open nature of the valley floor. Plant macrofossils and insects support the evidence for wet grassland. The dominance of sheep from the site emphasises the openness of the immediately surrounding area and the generally decreasing woodland environment. This is also supported by the absence of wild pig, low incidence of pig and the reduction in red deer size compared with earlier prehistory. Cattle and dog are present and, for the first time, horse. The large quantities of stone, much of it exhibiting signs of heat damage, and the quantity of bone, much of it cracked open to enable marrow extraction, imply meat preparation possibly through the use of 'burnt mound' type structures, which could have been located in a riverside location with ready access to water.

Cereal-type pollen occurs throughout the period suggesting arable cultivation was taking place on dry land away from the site, though the evidence for the latter is slight. Seeds of plants such as fat hen, knotgrass, slender parsley piert and prickly sow-thistle could reflect cultivation but could equally result from waste ground around the site. Similarly the presence of many-seeded goosefoot and small nettle, which occur for the first time, may be due to arable activity in the area or to people and animals trampling around on the floodplain adjacent to the site. On the whole clearance activity seems to have been primarily aimed at producing grassland for pastoralism, and this is supported by the faunal evidence from the site. However, given that any cereal cultivation would have been taking place on dry land some distance from the site and given the poor transport and dispersal characteristics of cereal pollen, it is probable cereals are underrepresented in the pollen record and that they played a more significant role in the economy than is immediately apparent.

Whilst the quantity of all artefact and wood categories recovered from Phases VI and VI/VII point to increased human activity at the site, together the assemblages do not suggest immediately adjacent riverside settlement. The small ceramic assemblage in particular would argue against this. On balance, given the likely continuing threat of flooding on the valley floor, a problem which probably increased over time, settlement was probably located on the Triassic plateaux nearby.

Phase VIII

This period post-dates human activity at the site and probably dates to the Iron Age. Sedimentologically the deposits are similar to those in the previous phase though there is some evidence for over-bank sedimentation with no clearly defined channel inter-faces or riverbeds. Artefact recovery is low although oxidation and only intermittent waterlogging are contributory factors here.

Possible changes in salinity are indicated by the diatoms. Over 40% of the assemblage is composed of marine taxa but there are similar proportions of oligohalobous taxa. The assemblages are from very different environments and the marine component could derive either from contemporary changes in the salinity regime or from post-depositional sediment mixing. However as there appears to be an increasing marine/brackish element in the previous phase this would tend to support the view that there was a real increase in estuarine/marine conditions. Some additional support for this is provided by the pollen

record. *Pediastrum* values are low, buck's horn plantain is well represented and *Spergula*-type pollen is present. Chenopodiaceae pollen also peaks. This is in agreement with evidence from elsewhere in the estuary for increases in relative sea level rise and a proposed substantial marine transgressive phase during the Iron Age (Rippon 1996, 22)

Preservation of the macrofossil evidence is generally poor and there is insufficient to draw any firm conclusions, but what little there is indicates freshwater. Sedimentation on the valley floor could therefore be the result of increased over-bank flooding in response to rising sea base-level.

The pollen record suggests agricultural activity continued at a similar level, although there is some evidence for renewed clearance following a very slight regeneration episode during the previous phase.

The main archaeological observation associated with this phase is the presumably rapid deposition of sediment around the uprights of the bridge structure and the remnants of the uprights from structure 9014. The survival of even immature roundwood stems to heights of *c* 4.1–4.2m OD suggests rapid and substantial alluviation which sealed the Bronze Age horizons below.

Caldicot and the cultural landscape

The site at Caldicot can be set against a wider background of environmental change and seen in the context of a cultural landscape. As the site comprises a succession of river channels, an understanding of fluvial development of the Nedern valley is fundamental to any interpretation of the artefactual and environmental data recovered from the palaeochannel deposits. The issue of the relative importance of anthropogenic and natural, notably climatic, factors in causing changes in river regimes has been a subject which has received considerable recent attention (eg Macklin & Needham 1992, Bell 1992). Whilst on the one hand it is suggested that the impact of prehistoric cultures on valley fill sedimentation has only comparatively recently been fully recognised and that there is now widespread and increasing evidence to support this, on the other it is argued that sedimentation and erosion in British rivers may have been more directly controlled by climate than previously thought. It has been proposed that, although forest clearance and agricultural practices were important in initiating erosion, it was brief episodes of climatic shift resulting in major changes in flood frequency and magnitude that were responsible for redistribution of the eroded material and widespread alluviation. Eight major phases of alluviation have been recognised during the Holocene (Macklin and Needham 1992, Macklin and Lewin 1993) with phases pertinent to Caldicot occurring between 4800–4200 BP, 3800–3300 BP, 2800–2400 BP, and 2000–1600 BP. The period 8000–5200 BP is regarded as a time of channel incision, slow alluviation or stability. However, it is recognised that phases of increased lateral movement, floodplain incision or erosion, as opposed to accretionary phases, are much more difficult to date.

At Caldicot the fluvial-hydrological regime has clearly been complicated by adjustments to local changes in sea base-level – the fluvial processes modified by sea-level change. During certain periods marine conditions exerted a strong influence whilst at others freshwater predominated but with a subtle marine influence in the background. These fluctuations between marine and freshwater conditions can be related to estuary-wide changes in sea-level, evident in lithostratigraphic and pollen records from other sites in the area, and are discussed in more detail later. However, close comparison with sea-level curves such as that proposed by Heyworth and Kidson (1982) is not attempted here. The uncertain relationship between contemporary mean sea-level and the basal fills of the palaeochannel groups at Caldicot make such an exercise of dubious merit. Sedimentation in the lower fills of the Nedern valley at the site is attributed to marine conditions but later fills are attributed to an increase in net rate of sedimentation from within the catchment resulting in fluvial sediments prograding across marine sediments as sedimentation exceeded local sea-level rise (Taylor p 83).

Whilst changes in channel morphology and sedi-mentation at the site are a reflection of broader landscape evolution, much of the artefactual and structural material contained within the palaeo-channels reflect localised and possibly very site-specific human activity. It is clear from the suite of radiocarbon dates that the site acted as a focus of some sort for at least a millennium. During this period, the site appears to have been used as a crossing-point, a location for the mooring and repair-ing of boats providing communication/transport with the coastal wetlands of raised bog/reed swamp/fen wood/salt-marsh and beyond, a fishing location, and a repository (probably as a by-product of intentional riverbed consolidation) for artefactual material re-lated to activities carried out at other locations. Why prehistoric communities chose a particular site's location over other places in the landscape, and continued to utilise it has been a subject of recent discussion. Tilley (1994) has argued for consideration of perceptual, social factors in addition, if not in place of, more geographically oriented explanations which stress the role of rational decision-making related to factors such as geology, soils, channel development, sea-level change, navigability, vegetation and sea-sonal availability of exploitable resources (cf Fig 162). Certainly many of the physical changes in the nature of the palaeochannels and the contemporary vegetation at Caldicot may have been either imper-ceptible to local communities/individuals or have

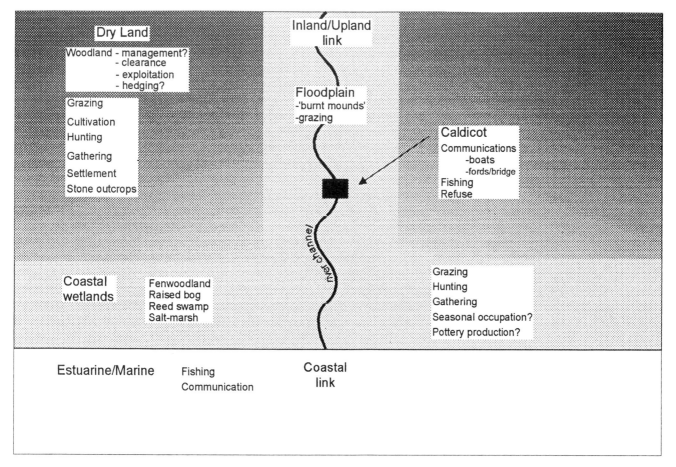

Fig 162   Environmental resources model

held less import than meanings attached to the site as a 'locale' with associations with previous community activities. Similarly, in placing the site in a cultural landscape, we need to be mindful of social factors which may have constrained choices or coloured perceptions regarding the location of both sites and activities including paths/routeways, land use, ritual and settlement. Nonetheless, factors associated with standard approaches to space/landscape description such as topography, vegetational history, and site distribution in the Nedern catchment and its environs (Fig 163) are necessarily utilised here to provide a broad context for the Caldicot data.

Within this area, it is clear that a variety of post depositional processes have created biases inherent in the recorded archaeological and environmental record contemporary with human activity at the Caldicot site. These processes can best be highlighted with reference to three major land blocks defined in terms of topography, land-use, environmental and human history (Evans 1992). The first land-block, the valley sides, plateaux and hills have not been subject to significant alluviation and resultant archaeological preservation. On the contrary, agricultural intensification and enclosure have both radically altered the landscape and eroded more ephemeral archaeological features. An asymmetry in the observed archaeological record should be anticipated with fortified or enclosed settlements and ceremonial/funerary monuments being over-represented. This bias is further compounded by the history of antiquarian and archaeological investigation: interest has concentrated on these visible field monuments and occasional stray finds. The present, mixed agricultural economy with a predominance of improved pasture has predicated against extensive studies of artefact scatters through fieldwalking. Archaeological sites have been identified as a result of quarrying of the Carboniferous Limestone and the development of built-up areas, such as Caldicot and Portskewett, has informed Romano-British and later studies (eg kilns at Caldicot, Barnet et al 1990) but added little to our understanding of Bronze Age activity. Indeed, medieval and later settlement are likely to have destroyed or masked contemporary sites particularly at Caldicot Castle. Its initial construction and subsequent landscaping of its grounds on the Triassic sandstone spur running out into the valley bottom (see Fig 2) will have severely damaged, if not totally destroyed, any Bronze Age remains, in a location which may have been favourable for settlement. The early date of most fieldwork in this land block, the lack of formation of deep stratigraphic sequences, and the aerobic nature of this limited stratigraphy have all mitigated against palaeoenvironmental studies.

The alluviated valley bottom of the Nedern forms a separate land block where both freshwater and estuarine alluvium preserve and mask prehistoric deposits and associated material culture. The apparent paucity of sites is, in part, a function of this lack of archaeological visibility accentuated by a lack, until recently, of appreciation of the zone's archaeological and palaeoenvironmental potential. As much of this zone is also used as permanent pasture this bias is reinforced. The hydrology of the lower reaches of the Nedern have undergone considerable alteration, linked in part to reclamation of the Caldicot Levels. The present course of the river has been extensively canalised and present water table, and hence flow rates, has been lowered by increased abstraction, drainage and pumping to maintain the Severn Tunnel. The presence of relict palaeochannels and cut-offs, visible in the present-day valley floor, reflect the natural evolution of the river system prior to much of this water management.

The river valley bottom merges seamlessly with the alluviated Caldicot Level, the third land block under consideration. It is clear from the presence of a substantial palaeochannel in the intertidal zone at Sudbrook (Gobold and Turner 1993, 4), and the former course of the Nedern fossilised in the parish boundary that during the prehistoric period, the river meandered across the eastern edge of the Level, debouching into the Severn at Sudbrook Point. The exact date when the Nedern was diverted to Caldicot Pill is uncertain, although the mention of a grist mill next to the Common Sea in a manorial survey of 1613 has been interpreted as evidence for the presence of this diversion (Rippon 1996, 77–8).

In some respects, this land block shares characteristics with the river valley bottom: well developed alluvial and peat deposits give good time depth and excellent preservation of palaeoenvironmental and artefactual material, especially organics. Conversely, recovery of prehistoric cultural material has been negligible, with the notable exception of the eroding foreshore, due to alluvial masking and traditional land-use favouring pasture. Environmental and lithostratigraphic data are however available from an increasing number of sites on the Gwent Levels. Four lithostratigraphic units have been identified in the estuary (Allen 1987, Allen and Rae 1987), the first of which, the Wentlooge Formation, encompasses most of the Flandrian deposits, with the exception of about the last 1800 years. The unit consists of sands and gravels followed by up to 12m of estuarine silty clays which are overlain by peats and an upper unit of estuarine, silty clay. The peat deposits have been described at a number of sites (Anderson 1968, Locke 1971, Smith and Morgan 1989, Whittle 1989, Aldhouse-Green et al 1992, Scaife 1993, Scaife 1995, Walker and James 1993, Walker and James unpublished). Dated pollen diagrams (Smith and Morgan 1989, Aldhouse-Green et al 1992, Walker and James 1993, Walker and James unpublished) exist from peat deposits both on the landward and seaward side of the sea wall.

It is evident from the extent of peat deposits beyond the present sea wall, that the shoreline during some prehistoric periods was located considerably further to the south than it is today: the environment of the Caldicot Level during the prehistoric must have been

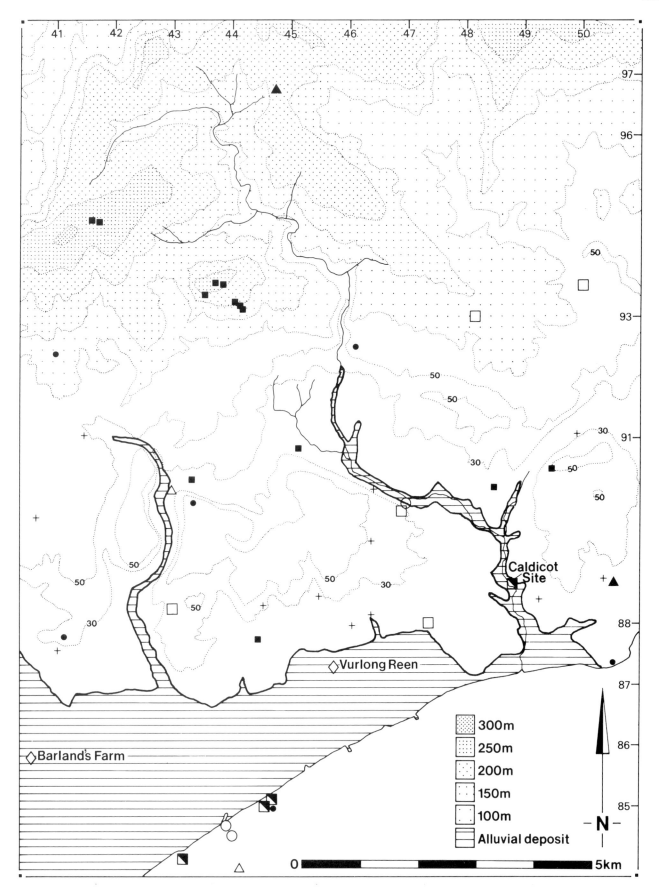

Fig 163   Topography and archaeological site distribution in the Nedern catchment and adjacent coastal wetlands. Based on the Ordnance Survey 1:50,000 series: national grid coordinates are given to allow cross-referencing to sites in the text. Site type symbol conventions are given above. © Crown copyright. Key:
▲ *Neolithic ritual;* △ *Neolithic stray finds;* ■ *Bronze Age ritual;* ◣ *Bronze Age occupation;* □ *Bronze Age stray finds;* ● *Iron Age occupation;* ○ *Iron Age stray finds;* + *Prehistoric stray finds;* ◇ *environmental sampling site*

very sensitive to relative changes in sea-level with episodes of reed swamp, fen, fen carr and raised bog development occurring during periods of relative stability. The Level would have been penetrated by tidal creeks and inlets, evident on the foreshore as palaeochannels cutting peat surfaces. Unlike the landward side of this land block, the intertidal zone, through natural erosion exhibits good archaeological visibility but localised limited time depth. Increased interest in the archaeology of the foreshore has resulted in the recovery of stray finds, particularly of metalwork, and the identification of Bronze Age and later prehistoric sites which are described in the period based discussion which follows.

In placing the site in its cultural landscape and material context, reference is made to sites and environmental data from the catchment of the Nedern and the coastal wetlands which the river crosses on its way to the Severn Estuary.

Mesolithic

The landscape in the Caldicot region during the Mesolithic would have been strongly influenced by a changing sea-level. The movement in sea-level relative to the land in southern Britain has generally been upwards but subject to oscillations (Shennan et al 1983, 1989). In the Severn Estuary during the post-glacial rise in sea-level, at first rapid and then more gradual (Hawkins 1971, Heyworth and Kidson 1982), initially estuarine silty clays were deposited and later the peats developed, at times interrupted by further accretion of minerogenic deposits. At the same time, the valleys of rivers entering the area became drowned (Anderson and Blundell 1965, Williams 1968). This period is represented in the earliest Phase I, silty clay, valley-fill deposits at Caldicot, which suggest that the Nedern valley would have been an inlet of the sea subject to estuarine conditions at this time. A slowing down in sea-level rise appears to have led in other areas, for example Goldcliff and Uskmouth, to extensive freshwater peat development between c 6000–5750 BP. At Caldicot Pill (Scaife 1993; 1995), 2km downstream from Caldicot, oak and alder have given similar dates though these represent later stages in the vegetation succession than the former dates, whereas freshwater muds and peat deposits are dated to 6360 ± 70 BP (Beta-79887) and 6660 ± 80 BP (Beta-79886) respectively. At this time a range of vegetation habitats occurred at Caldicot Pill including freshwater aquatic reflecting either pond or slow flowing riverine, marginal aquatic, and damp oak/hazel fen carr woodland. The possibility of a barrier bar has been considered as a possible reason for the reduction in marine conditions, given the presence of an 'island' evident from sub-sediment contours, but from the occurrence of peats elsewhere in the estuary at this time a regional contraction in marine conditions, perhaps as a result of a reduction in the rate of sea-level rise, is considered more likely (Scaife and Long 1995). Peat development at Vurlong Reen c 4km to the south-west of Caldicot occurred c 5800 BP (Walker and James 1993). The changes on the Welsh side of the estuary also broadly correlate with those on the English side. Radiocarbon dates for peat development in the Somerset Levels range from c 5500–5600 BP and at Stolford in Bridgewater Bay to c 6200 BP. The fresh water hydroseral succession was interrupted at Goldcliff (Smith and Morgan 1989) by a period of marine inundation, giving rise to estuarine conditions, commencing shortly before 5500 BP and ending around 5400 BP. After this date freshwater conditions were again re-established, resulting in reedswamp and fen, and ultimately, c 5000 BP, the development of raised bog. At Caldicot throughout this period estuarine conditions prevailed, although there is an early peat horizon c 1m OD representing a period of relative sea-level stability which predates a later peat/clay regressive contact of 4670 ± 80 BP (CAR-1323).

It is during the period of silt and clay deposition prior to peat formation that there is the strongest evidence for Mesolithic activity, namely human footprints (Aldhouse-Green et al 1992), demonstrating that the tidal mud-flats were being exploited. At the same time mixed deciduous woodland with oak, elm and lime was growing on the dry land inland. Human impact is not easy to identify in these lowland habitats and there is only some tentative evidence for human interference with the landscape before c 5000 BP (Walker et al unpublished). Residual Mesolithic punch-struck blades and blade cores recovered from the Bronze Age horizons at Caldicot imply some exploitation of valley bottom/edge resources where discarded/lost flint could subsequently become incorporated into palaeochannel deposits through channel incision and migration processes.

Neolithic

By c 5000 BP, large areas of the Caldicot Level which had once been estuarine during the earlier Mesolithic and freshwater reedswamp and fen during the later Mesolithic had progressed to raised bog, although in some areas such as Vurlong Reen fen woodland continued to dominate. At Caldicot this period of relative stability is demonstrated by intercalated organic horizons in the upper estuarine clay. A well developed freshwater organic horizon is dated between 4670 ± 80 BP (CAR-1323) and 4360 ± 80 BP (CAR-1322) with further horizons above. These changes therefore seem to correlate with the development of raised bog elsewhere. No Neolithic material has been recovered from the limited excavations on the Caldicot Level but a polished rhyolite axe comes from the intertidal zone near Magor (Green 1989, 196, Fig 4). Auroch skeletons have been retrieved from an number of locations in the intertidal zone (eg Uskmouth and Rumney, Green 1989). More direct evidence for human activity comes from

Goldcliff where fragments of human skull were found within raised bog peat at c 1.5m OD (Bell 1993, 88).

It is around 5000/4900 BP, the 'elm decline', that there is clear evidence of clearance and agricultural activity in the region (Smith and Morgan 1989, Walker and James 1993), although the precise reason for the decline in elm itself remains open to speculation (Chambers 1993; Edwards 1993). At Caldicot, the earliest event that is clearly recognisable and dated is the increase in *Tilia* dated to 4670 ± 80 BP (CAR-1323) and at Goldcliff to 4660 ± 80 BP (CAR-650). At Vurlong Reen and Barland's Farm an increase in *Tilia* is recorded, but at a somewhat later date, 4230 ± 70 BP (BETA-63593) and 4260 ± 70 BP (BETA-63597) at Vurlong Reen and 4480 ± 60 BP (BETA-72508) at Barland's Farm. However, this does agree with an extrapolated date of around 4265 BP for a further increase in representation of *Tilia* at Goldcliff.

Prior to the *Tilia* rise at Caldicot there appears to be a period (site zone CS.1) of clearance activity, though limited. It seems unlikely that this zone commences before c 4800 BP as before this at Goldcliff, Vurlong Reen and Barland's Farm *Tilia* values are high. *Ulmus* is also more frequent, though poorly represented at the latter two sites. From the evidence it is clear that a low level of woodland clearance, particularly affecting lime and possibly elm (the role of elm disease is uncertain but probable), and accompanied by agricultural activity was taking place on the dry land around the edge of the estuary during the 3rd millennium BP. The radiocarbon evidence suggests this phase of activity varied in length locally, registration depending on the location of the pollen site and the proximity and extent of the activity. Similarly, there are differences in the nature of the agricultural activity recorded, with evidence for pastoralism at all sites but cereal type pollen indicating cultivation and mixed farming at Caldicot and Goldcliff but not at Vurlong Reen or Barland's Farm. Again, this may relate to the level of activity, the proximity of the various pollen sites to where cultivation was taking place and how regional or local a record the individual site provides. Archaeological evidence for Neolithic activity on solid geology within the area conforms to the asymmetry anticipated by Evans (1992), being limited to ceremonial monuments and stray finds. The nearby tomb at Heston Brake, previously mentioned, is one of a number of chambered tombs in Gwent located on low hills near the fen edge. Stray finds include a rough preselite axe-head found redeposited in a garden at the Glen, St Brides Netherwent (Burgess 1962) in the valley floor of the misfit stream, probably diverted during the last glacial and a leaf-shaped arrowhead at the interface between the Triassic plateau west of Caldicot and the alluvium.

Though the date of the onset and the intensity of the increase in *Tilia* appears to vary, this event is evident throughout the area. *Tilia* values are markedly higher at Caldicot than at Goldcliff, which is not surprising given the greater extent of dry land in the immediate area of the former site and its poor dispersal characteristics (Greig 1982, Huntley and Birks 1983, Janssen 1966). Similarly at Vurlong Reen exceptionally high *Tilia* values are recorded and, together with the evidence from Caldicot, seem to suggest lime-dominated woodland on the dry land immediately to the north of the two sites. At Barland's Farm higher values than at Goldcliff are recorded but again these seem to represent a more regional picture. Together with reduced frequencies in clearance indicators at most sites, at least initially, the high *Tilia* values appear to demonstrate either a period of reduced human activity in the area or a change in the nature of that activity from a period of forest destruction to one of forest utilisation with coppicing and farming taking place within the woodland environment (cf Göransson 1983,1986, 1987; Edwards 1993).

At Caldicot this episode (site zone CS.2) ends some time after 4360 ± 80 BP (CAR-1322) as two of the local zones, CB.1 and CF.1, on stratigraphic grounds post-date this. Elsewhere the reduction in *Tilia* at the end of this phase is dated to 3950 ± 70 BP (Beta-63592) and 4010 ± 60 BP (Beta-63596) at Vurlong Reen, to 3740 ± 60 BP (Beta-72507) at Barland's Farm and to 3670 ± 70 BP (CAR-646) at Goldcliff. Hence the record from CB.1 at Caldicot may relate to anywhere in the period 4360 ± 80 BP to 3670 ± 70 BP, but taking into account the stratigraphic evidence it could well post-date 4100 BP.

The pattern of clearance activity recorded in the Caldicot area is repeated inland, although the nature of the agricultural activity varies. In south Wales, and the rest of Wales generally, the elm decline is usually accompanied by an increase in *Plantago lanceolata* and other indicators of pastoralism, with relatively few sites yielding cereal type pollen (Caseldine 1990). Apart from Caldicot and Goldcliff (Smith and Morgan 1989) cereal type pollen has been recorded at Llyn Mire in the Wye valley (Moore 1978) and, together with the fact that it is largely absent from upland sites, has prompted the suggestion of a difference in land use between upland and lowland during the Neolithic (Moore 1978, 1981). However, evidence for the nature of Neolithic clearance activity and agriculture in the immediate hinterland of Caldicot, ie the Wentwood Hills, is lacking. The only other identified Neolithic tomb in the Nedern catchment, Gaerllwyd, is situated at over 200m OD in the Wentwood Hills near the source of a feeder stream of the Nedern.

On the English side of the estuary, in the Somerset Levels, the first clear evidence of human impact is Neolithic in date and coincides with the elm decline dated a little later than on the Welsh side, ie at c 4800 BP (Caseldine 1988). Prior to this the composition of the woodland differs in that *Ulmus* is more and *Tilia* slightly less significant. The duration of the clearance episode during the Neolithic also varies, ranging from c 230 to c 460 years, depending on the site. Again, the strongest evidence is for pastoralism but some cereal cultivation is also indicated. Towards the end of the Neolithic, as on the Welsh side of the estuary, there is clear evidence for a regeneration episode but, whereas *Tilia* makes a significant recovery on the Welsh side, in the Somerset Levels it is mainly *Ulmus* and, to a lesser extent, *Tilia* that expand. Dates for the beginning of this episode also show a spread, 4640 ± 70 BP (HAR-4544) to 4278 ± 45 BP (SRR–880), comparable to that in the Caldicot area.

The earlier Bronze Age

The period of comparative sea-level stability recorded during the Neolithic seems to have continued during the earlier Bronze Age, although there is evidence to suggest that some areas were at least intermittently subject to a stronger marine influence than in the Neolithic. While raised bog was maintained in areas such as Goldcliff and Barland's Farm, at Vurlong Reen there is evidence of environmental change *c* 3950 BP when fen woodland was replaced by fen conditions. This may broadly correlate with the development of the Phase II palaeochannel at Caldicot, which at a later stage contains the pile structure. Although the earliest diatom and pollen evidence suggests a mixed estuarine/freshwater environment by the time of the construction of the pile structure *c* 3600/3500 BP the evidence suggests estuarine conditions. This correlates with a peak in *Glaux* pollen at an estimated date of *c* 3600–3500 BP at Vurlong Reen. *Glaux maritima* is usually found in grassy salt-marshes. This phase may have been a period when the site at Caldicot was inundated with saline water only at high tide, but perhaps fairly regularly. A change to predominantly freshwater conditions occurs in Phase III, although there is a very brief episode when there is an increase in halophilous diatom species. Radiocarbon determinations place this phase in the range 3150–3450 BP. The peak in brackish diatoms lies in the earlier part of this phase. Again at Vurlong Reen *Glaux* pollen is recorded at a date *c* 3400 BP and may correlate with this event. This appears to be a much briefer and weaker marine episode than that during Phase II. For most of this period and the later phases at Caldicot it seems that the influx of sediments from the Nedern catchment largely negated the effects of sea-level rise. At Goldcliff a reed swamp peat below estuarine clay is dated to 3130 ± 70 BP (CAR-644) (Smith and Morgan 1989).

From around 4000 BP onwards there seems to be renewed activity in the region, becoming more marked from about 3700 BP. Comparison of the evidence from the palaeochannels at Caldicot with the other sequences is difficult but similarities do occur, the former, because of the greater depth of deposit involved, tending to be a higher resolution of the latter. The earliest pollen evidence from the palaeochannels is that from sequences 23195 and 23010 from the pile structure channel (Phase II).

Radiocarbon determinations of 3620 ± 70 BP (CAR-1317), 3550 ± 70 BP (CAR-1314) and 3430 ± 70 BP (CAR-1415) from the structure imply an Earlier Bronze Age date. Clearly the pollen evidence from 23010 and 23195 Phase II post-dates the second *Tilia* decline in the area. Inevitably, part of the record is missing because the whole depth of this channel was not sampled. However, high *Quercus* values at Caldicot may correlate with a peak in *Quercus* occurring at an estimated date of *c* 3600 BP at Vurlong Reen and 3740 ± 60 BP (Beta-72507) at Barland's Farm. At the same time peaks in cereal type pollen at Goldcliff *c* 3500–3600 BP are in agreement with the evidence from Caldicot that some cultivation was taking place and it seems that while there may have been a short-lived expansion in oak woodland, a certain level of agriculture was maintained. Pollen studies (Brown 1982, 1983, 1987, 1988, Brown and Barber 1985) from the floodplains of the River Severn and its tributaries have demonstrated deforestation of the surrounding terrace woodland from about 3600 BP, similar to that at Caldicot.

For around the next 500 years there seems to be comparatively little change in the landscape, with oak-dominated woodland on the dry land and alder carr and valley woods reduced in extent but accompanied by an expansion in scrubland. Radiocarbon dates for the boat strake channel (Phase III) at Caldicot lie in the range 3150–3450 BP (mid-point 3300 BP) while a mid-zone date of 3380/20 ± 60 BP (Beta-63591) at Vurlong Reen helps to confirm that the low *Alnus* and *Quercus* values evident at both sites are broadly contemporary. Radiocarbon dates of 3130 ± 70 BP (CAR-644) and 3440 ± 70 BP (CAR-645) at Goldcliff bracket an increase in *Plantago lanceolata* and agree well with the evidence from Caldicot and the other sites for the importance of pastoralism at this time, although at both Goldcliff and Caldicot there is also some evidence for cultivation.

However, whereas the regeneration episode ends around 3900–3700 BP on the Welsh side, in the Somerset Levels there seem to be two stages. A distinct decline in *Ulmus* is dated *c* 3900–4200 BP, but with clearance indicator species relatively poorly represented, followed by a further decline in *Ulmus* accompanied by a second decline in *Tilia* and increased representation of clearance indicator species dated *c* 3400–3900 BP, which is broadly consistent with the Welsh evidence. From this time onwards there is clear evidence for pastoralism with some arable agriculture. Further up the Severn, Brown (1982) has identified terrace clearance around 3700–2700 BP, with probable arable activity *c* 3000 BP and clearance of the floodplain much later *c* 2500–1000 BP.

Direct archaeological evidence in the lowland zone surrounding Caldicot is again limited by the presumed lack of enclosed settlement at this time, and alluviation of the river valley bottoms and levels with finds restricted to barrows on the valley sides and terraces, and stray finds. As Savory noted (1940, 169), the lowland area under consideration is not remarkably rich in Bronze Age barrows. Three barrows are located on or adjacent to the valley bottom, of which two have been excavated. In the valley bottom of the misfit stream near St Brides Netherwent (ST433903, see Fig 163), a round barrow, sited on head and terrace gravel deposits, was initially investigated in 1860 (Lee 1862) and later more extensively excavated in response to plough damage in 1973 (Buckley 1975). It is clear that there were at least two phases of construction with a ditch being cut in both cases. A close set kerb of Black Rock Dolomite was probably constructed from rock extracted from an outcrop c 400m to the south. The 'bell' profile of the barrows and the recovery of a grooved ogival dagger in poor condition during the first investigation have led some to argue for links with Wessex (Burgess 1962b). The multiple phases of construction, a small oval mound close to the north edge of the barrow, and finds of a barbed and tanged and a hollow-based lopsided arrowhead all point to several phases of activity at the site.

The excavated barrow at Crick (ST48449025, see Fig 163, Savory 1940) exhibits some traits in common with the St Brides site: there are at least two phases of use, an original bell profile, and a stone kerb derived from a nearby outcrop. The first phase comprised a primary cremation, without grave goods, below a turfed earth mound with a stone kerb and a ditch. Charcoal from the cremation, identified as oak from mature timber implies the use of seasoned oak in the pyre, although the location of the woodland exploited is less clear. Geological examination of the stone kerb led to the hypothesis that 'key' stones had first been erected using immediately available glacial erratics before rock from a nearby outcrop was quarried. Burnt stone, charcoal, flint spalls and a plano-convex knife within the mound were seen as derivative from adjacent settlement, although the material could also reflect funerary practices or other specialised activities. A secondary burial comprised an intrusive cremation with ash and oak charcoal, calcined fragments of a plano-convex knife and a single flake.

The location of barrows on the valley sides and terraces in the lowland reaches of the Nedern Brook and St Bride's Brook catchments could be taken to indicate the siting of funerary monuments at this time in locations visible from relatively open valley bottom grasslands. In addition to providing a valued grazing resource, the valley bottoms may have become established routes for the movement of livestock between seasonal grazing resources on the raised bog/salt-marsh of the Levels and in the uplands of the Wentwood Hills. Barrows of a localised bell form could have defined 'ownership' within seasonally occupied territories, in the valley bottoms, exploited by pastoral groups (cf Fleming 1971). Such a system of transhumance would, to some extent, pre-suppose extensive clearance of the upland zone. Sadly, at the present time there is no contemporary environmental evidence from the upper reaches of

the Nedern in the Earlswood area, although archaeological remains indicate human activity. At Gray Hill (ST438935, see Fig 163), a closely set stone circle 9.6m in diameter and a standing stone located 2.4m to the south-east suggest upland clearance some time during the Late Neolithic/ Earlier Bronze Age on the Old Red Sandstone. A cluster of cairns to the south-east (ST4493) imply continuity of use of this site as a ceremonial centre. To the north-west, near the summit of the Wentwood ridge (ST4195, see Fig 163), two barrows, now enclosed within forestry also point to upland clearance.

In the uplands of south Wales there is considerable evidence for anthropogenic activity during the Bronze Age. At the sites of Waun Fignen-Felen (Smith and Cloutman 1988) the frequency of *Tilia* falls at the same time as a third fall in *Ulmus*. Depending on the site, the date of this event varies between c 4059 BP and c 3750 BP, a range consistent with that from the Caldicot area. Throughout the Bronze Age at these sites there is evidence for sustained human pressure. Elsewhere in south Wales, for example at Coed Taf (Chambers 1983), Cefn Ffordd (Chambers 1982), and sites in the Black Mountains (Price and Moore 1984), there is also evidence for considerable human impact on the landscape during the Bronze Age. Hence this upland activity must have had a substantial effect on run-off and sediment load, reflected in the river systems of the lowlands, and erosion and aggradation of the palaeochannels such as those at Caldicot.

The later Bronze Age

From around 3000 BP there is evidence for an increasing marine influence in the Gwent Levels. At Goldcliff a reed swamp peat below estuarine clay is dated to 3130 ± 70 BP (CAR-644) (Smith and Morgan 1989) and at Barland's Farm (Walker and James unpublished) peat beneath an estuarine clay is dated c 2900 BP. At Caldicot during Phases IV, V and VI freshwater conditions prevail, although it is possible that occasionally high tides might have reached the site. Alder communities appear to expand, particularly in Phase VI, perhaps in response to a rising water-table resulting from a continued rise in sea level. Radiocarbon dates for Phase VI range from 3060 ± 70 BP (CAR-1319) to 2800 ± 70 BP (CAR-1318). A comparable pollen zone with higher *Alnus* values at Vurlong Reen dates from c 3050 to 2700 BP. Phase VI is also marked by a change in channel morphology from a narrower down-cutting channel to a wider flat-bottomed channel in cross-section, which is consistent with a change in base-level and a rising water table. Following the decline in alder at Caldicot (Phase VI/VII), *Plantago coronopus* and Chenopodiaceae are consistently present at more than 1%. Together with an increase in brackish/marine diatoms slightly later in the zone, which is accompanied by a decline in freshwater aquatics, they signify increasingly marine conditions. One possibility for the expansion and decline in alder is that a rising sea-level and corresponding rise in water-table temporarily favoured the spread of alder further inland, ie in the Vurlong Reen/ Caldicot area, until an increasing marine influence had a deleterious effect. Alternatively the decline in alder could represent clearance on the floodplain. Even stronger evidence for estuarine conditions is evident in Phase VII, although freshwater still predominates. Wood from the bridge (structure 22441) is dated c 2580 ± 70 BP(CAR-1408) and at Vurlong Reen peat lying below a probable estuarine clay is dated c 2500 BP. Phase VIII dated c 2400 BP shows the strongest evidence for marine conditions. Stratigraphically these clays appear to be widespread across the valley and would appear to correspond with those deposited at Vurlong Reen though this could have happened slightly later. At Llanwern a radiocarbon date of 2660 ± 110 BP (Q–691) from peat below a clay containing marine diatoms (Godwin and Willis 1964) is also consistent with the Caldicot evidence. The date of 2580 ± 70 BP (CAR-1408) from the bridge is the same as that from the surface of the raised bog peat at the site of structure 2 at Goldcliff, prior to deposition of estuarine clay. It would therefore seem that the construction of the bridge could have been a direct response to rising sea-levels and improved access to the rest of the estuary.

Elsewhere in the estuary later changes in sea-level are also indicated such as in the Avonmouth area where the highest of three peat bands gave a date of 3110 ± 100 BP (laboratory code not quoted) (Murray and Hawkins 1976). Dates of 3100 ± 100 BP, 2900 ± 95 BP, 3350 ± 120 BP and 3510 ± 100 BP (laboratory codes not given) were also obtained from four upper peat bands to the south of the Severn Estuary (Hawkins 1971). Within the Somerset Levels radiocarbon dates from below an estuarine clay in the Glastonbury area range from c 2900 BP to, at its furthest point inland at the Glastonbury lake village site, c 2500 BP(Housley 1988, 1995). A flooding horizon within the raised bog peat, reflecting a higher ground water table, dates to c 2600 BP (Beckett 1978).

Finally, further up the estuary at Longney, below Gloucester, the early Holocene rise in sea-level also caused rapid aggradation represented by blue estuarine clays (Brown 1987b). Wood peats interpreted as a freshwater backswamp development accumulated from c 5090 BP until c 2830 BP when a silty clay unit was deposited which is interpreted as analogous to salt flats only periodically flooded by high tides. It is suggested this flooding by brackish waters may be due to either changing beach barrier configurations and/or increasing storm heights. The evidence is consistent with the evidence from elsewhere in the estuary for a general rise in sea-level. Archaeological evidence (Allen and Fulford 1990) demonstrates that reclamation of the tidal floodplain in the Longney area first occurred during the Romano-British period. Studies of salt-marsh accretion and sediment budget (Allen 1990, 1991) suggest

that the retreat of the inner Bristol Channel-Severn Estuary continues in response to a continuing upward trend in relative sea-level in the region.

With the exception of stray finds of metalwork and flint, evidence for Later Bronze Age occupation within the study area (see Fig 163) is restricted to the present day intertidal zone where natural erosion of the Wentlooge Formation clays has led to the exposure and subsequent investigation of a number of prehistoric wooden structures. These include a cluster of structures near Cold Harbour Pill excavated in the 1980's. At Chapeltump 1 (ST44708514), the remains of a circular structure c 10m in diameter comprised an outer circle of driven oak planks, an inner circle of roundwood posts and a central post (Whittle, 1989). Artefactual material included potsherds, pot-boilers and heat fractured stone. Radiocarbon dates of 2910 ± 70 BP (CAR-402) and 3170 ± 70 BP (CAR-992) place the site firmly in the Bronze Age. Some 80m to the east, a concentration of pottery, charred material and heat fractured stone (Chapeltump 2, Lillie 1991) has been dated to the Later Bronze Age by a radiocarbon date from the only structural timber at the site, an oak post, of 2830 ± 70 BP (CAR-961). Radiocarbon determinations from a possibly residual human femur and a charcoal sample are less securely associated with activity at the site. The quantity of pottery sherds and the recovery of worked or burnt clay lumps encourages interpretation of the finds as a pottery production site, although burnt stone and plant remains are suggestive of other activities implying occupation. Apart from taxa which largely reflect natural plant communities, one fragment of chaff from Chapeltump 1 is assigned to *Triticum dicoccum/spelta* (emmer/spelt wheat) and *Triticum* (wheat) and *Hordeum* (barley) remains are recorded from Chapeltump 2 (Milles 1989).

At Cold Harbour Pill (ST43218420), charcoal concentrations, sharpened stakes, pottery sherds, pot-boilers and fragments of animal bone are associated with a radiocarbon date of 2900 ± 60 BP (CAR-991) (Whittle 1989). West of the Pill, part of an undated longitudinal brushwood trackway may also be Bronze or Iron Age in date (Rippon 1996, 21) on stratigraphic and technological criteria. At Goldcliff, fragments of plank sewn boat had been reused in a trackway crossing a small palaeochannel dated by associated roundwood to 2720 ± 70 BP (CAR-1434) (Bell 1993, 86) and by dendrochronology to after 1017 BC (see Hillam, p 193).

Ongoing observations of eroding peat surfaces in the intertidal zone off the Gwent Levels (Bell and Neumann 1996) continue to emphasise the widespread presence of Late Bronze Age sites, often apparently associated with peat/clay transgressive contacts, where archaeological visibility permits a realistic assessment of occupation density. Sites which await complete excavation include a possible Bronze Age roundhouse near Collister Pill, sites off Rhumney Great Wharf (Allen pers comm), and possible transitional Bronze Age/ Iron Age structures at Redwick. The density of sites implies considerable occupation and exploitation of the coastal plain contemporary with the phases of most intense activity at Caldicot. The presence of quantities of burnt stone, fragmented animal bone and wood species more usually associated with well drained dry-land locations are common features of many of these sites. In addition, many of the intertidal sites are located close to palaeochannel systems which were presumably navigable for considerable distances inland to sites like Caldicot, close to the interface with solid geology. Communication and transport by river seems probable between occupation sites on the levels and possibly more permanent settlement on solid geology, above the threat of seasonal floods and storm surges.

Conclusions

The excavations at Caldicot have produced evidence for human activity on the floodplain and hinterland of the Nedern over a thousand radiocarbon years of the later prehistoric period. Through stratigraphic excavation of the succession of palaeochannel deposits, punctuated by episodes of downcutting and channel migration, it has proved possible to identify the 'multiple associations within stratigraphic sequences' which Macklin and Needham (1992) noted as one of the key features of alluviated sites. In contrast to much of Welsh prehistory, the site has provided true time depth in a deeply stratified sequence. The apparent continuity of human activity in the area throughout the Bronze Age perhaps stresses the importance of the site as a 'locale' in contrast to suggestions of some kind of social hiatus between the earlier and later Bronze Ages proposed by some authors. Radiocarbon has provided the absolute dating framework to enable inter-site comparisons but may be potentially misleading with regard to the longevity of particular phases. Where dendrochronological dates are available, sadly restricted to the latest phases, they suggest the cultural remains are the result of relatively brief periods of activity over decades rather than centuries. As yet, insufficient sites, precisely dated by tree-rings, exist in the immediate region to enable discussions of late prehistoric landscape change and social and economic activity with the degree of precision which the method offers. Further tree-ring dating of prehistoric sites, particularly in the Gwent Levels, offers the possibility of beginning to discuss regional development within a near 'historical' (Baillie 1995, 57) chronological framework.

Whilst the preservation of a wide variety of artefacts and environmental indicators has encouraged the use of a large number of methods of analysis, the interpretation of their results has had to take account of the processes of taphonomy and site formation which make alluvial archaeology such a challenging environment for study. The nature of the contemporary river system at the site, particularly with regard to flow rates, has minimised the problems here. The fluvial system, for the most part a mature, small, freshwater river with substantial emergent vegetation along its banks, contrasts with the relatively high energy systems associated with rivers such as the Trent and Thames which have been subject to considerable archaeological investigation. Nonetheless, study of site assemblages has provided insights into the development of the landscape of the catchment, primarily through combined pollen analysis and assessment of the wood assemblages. Periods of occasional or more persistent estuarine influence which can be correlated with estuary-wide trends in sea-level change have been detectable both in the pollen and diatom assemblages. Hence, even though fluvial transport is not seen as a major barrier to interpretation, palaeochannel sediments have acted as repositories for indicators of wider landscape change. The added dimension of links to estuarine environments and marine transgressions contrasts with recently published excavations of Bronze Age sites on the Thames (eg Runnymede, Needham 1991; Anslow's Cottages, Lobb 1992) where purely freshwater fluvial systems were encountered.

Whilst pollen data and genus identification of the wood assemblage has provided information on woodland composition and clearance, critical examination of the wood assemblages has allowed some assessment of the methods of clearance and the evidence for woodland management. The majority of the wood is consistent with secondary woodland subjected to episodic clearance and regeneration. This is not to say that any formal system of management existed. The age profiles of particular species do not conform to the narrow ranges and skewed distributions proposed for formal coppice rotations. Rather, the assemblages are interpreted primarily as the by-products of clearance of scrub woodland: a process which over centuries, in conjunction with livestock grazing, led to an increasingly open landscape on the valley sides and low hills of the hinterland during the Bronze Age. Structural timbers and woodworking debris highlight cultural/rational preferences for oak and ash, and to a lesser extent alder and occasionally lime, for carpentry purposes in accordance with preferences seen in contemporary British Late Bronze Age assemblages. The high proportions of blackthorn and hawthorn type in the roundwood at Caldicot have also been observed in other Bronze Age palaeochannels. Whilst blackthorn should be anticipated in scrub woodland and woodland edge environments, its presence in such numbers could equally reflect use of grazing-resistant thorn species in hedges as a method of livestock control and even land division. Discrimination between the by-products of hedge management and clearance, however, may never be possible.

The bone assemblage from Caldicot, particularly from the later phases, adds significantly to a very limited set of faunal data from Welsh Bronze Age sites. The proportions of domesticates imply dominance of sheep and, in conjunction with the limited pollen evidence for cereal cultivation, suggest a primarily pastoralist subsistence economy. The fractured nature of much of this material, along with the associated stone, some of which exhibited heat damage, points to meat preparation and disposal of food refuse. If burnt mounds had been located on the floodplain, then they may yet survive preserved but obscured within later alluviation. In contrast to other anthropogenically derived material on the floodplain and within palaeochannels, stone, particularly heated stone, may be detectable using established geophysical techniques. Clearly, the partially excavated remains at Caldicot could be used to assess the efficacy of various remote-sensing procedures.

The artefacts and structures recorded at Caldicot are interpreted as the remains of specialised activities taking place at the river location, rather than riverside settlement. The practice of location of settlements on eyots (river islands) seen in the Upper Thames does not seem an appropriate model for Caldicot. This raises the question of where contemporary settlement was situated. The spur of hard geology on which the medieval castle was built would have had its attractions to prehistoric communities but the extensive landscaping of the castle grounds has probably destroyed any meaningful remains. Certainly no substantial earthworks survive which are not associated with medieval or later construction. East of the floodplain, on the ridge of Farthing Hill overlooking the valley, an undated enclosure approximately 220m long by 40m wide with two internal divisions is now largely covered by an old yew plantation. This site awaits systematic investigation. Certainly the best hope for the identification of Late Bronze Age settlements, in the dry-land zone as against the alluviated landscape, lies in critical examination of known enclosures. It is perhaps surprising that no evidence of Late Bronze Age occupation has been forthcoming from the very limited excavations of Iron Age enclosures/hillforts in the immediate area. Recent rescue excavations at Thornwell Farm, on the south-east outskirts of Chepstow recorded 'settlement debris' and substantial circular structure which probably predate a later Iron Age enclosure (Hughes 1996, 89).

Caldicot provides a 'bridge', through the environmental data incorporated in its palaeochannel sequences, between the late prehistoric, wetland habitats and activities identified in the Gwent Levels through recent investigations and the less well characterised hinterland. As the body of prehistoric data coming from rescue excavations on the Levels continues to grow, so the relative lack of contemporary information from the inland and upland zones becomes more apparent. Clearly, there is a need to address this imbalance through investigation of upland sequences which can provide comparative data on the exploitation and landscape development of the Wentwood Hills and other outlying hills.

The alluviated river valley bottoms of the small rivers of the South Wales coast, including the minor tributaries of the Severn Estuary, are a valuable but vulnerable and challenging archaeological resource. The preservation of a wide range of organic artefact types and environmental indicators within silted palaeochannel features can provide well-resolved and precisely-dated long sequences with the potential to allow multi-disciplinary reconstruction of cultural landscape development. Such a framework provides a meaningful context not only for the artefactual material contained within such channels but also for the surrounding contemporary archaeological resource.

Bibliography

Aaris-Sørensen, K, 1977, The subfossil wolf, *Canis lupus* L., in Denmark, *Vidensk. Meddr dansk naturh. Foren*, **140**, 129–46.

Absolon, A, 1973, Ostracoden aus einigen Profilen spät- und post-glazialer Karbonatablagerungen in Mitteleuropa. *Mitteilung der Bayerischen Staatssammlung für Paläontologie und Historische Geologie*, **13**, 47–94.

Adam, P, 1990, *Saltmarsh ecology*. Cambridge: University Press.

Åkerlund, H,1963, *Nydamskeppen*. Goteborg.

Al-Saadi, R, and Brooks, M, 1973, A geophysical study of Pleistocene buried valleys in the Lower Swansea Valley, Vale of Neath and Swansea Bay, *Proceedings of the Geologists Association*, **84**, 135–53.

Alcock, L, 1963, *Dinas Powys – An Iron Age, Dark Age and Early Medieval Settlement in Glamorgan*. Cardiff.

——, 1980, The Cadbury Castle Sequence in the First Millennium BC, *Bull Board Celtic Stud*, **28**, 656–718.

Aldhouse-Green, S H R, Whittle, A W R, Allen, J R L, Caseldine, A E, Culver, S J, Day, M H, Lundquist, J, and Upton, D, 1993, Prehistoric human footprints from the Severn Estuary at Uskmouth and Magor Pill, Gwent, Wales, *Archaeologia Cambrensis* (1992), **141**, 14–55.

Allen, J R L, 1985, Intertidal drainage and mass-movement processes in the Severn Estuary: rills and creeks (pills), *J Geol Soc Lond*, **142**, 849–61.

——, 1987, Late Flandrian shoreline oscillations in the Severn Estuary: The Rumney Formation at its Typesite (Cardiff Area), *Phil Trans R Soc Lond B*, **315**, 157–74.

——, 1990a, The post-glacial geology and geoarchaeology of the Avon wetlands, *Proc Bristol Naturalist's Soc*, **50**, 28–46.

——, 1990b, The Severn Estuary in southwest Britain: its retreat under marine transgression, and fine sediment regime, *Sedimentary Geology*, **66**, 13–28.

——, 1991, Salt-marsh accretion and sea-level movement in the inner Severn Estuary, southwest Britain: the archaeological and historical contribution, *J Geol Soc, Lond*, **148**, 485–94.

——, 1992, Tidally influenced marshes in the Severn Estuary, southwest Britain, in J R L Allen and K Pye (eds), *Saltmarshes: Morphodynamics, Conservation & Engineering Significance*, 123–47, Cambridge: University Press.

——, and Fulford, M G, 1986, The Wentlooge Level: A Romano-British saltmarsh reclamation in Southeast Wales, *Britannia*, **17**, 91–117.

——, and ——, 1990, Romano-British wetland reclamation at Longney, Gloucestershire, and the evidence for early settlement of the inner Severn estuary, *Antiquaries Journal*, **70**, 288–326.

——, and Rae, J E, 1986, Time sequence of metal pollution, Severn Estuary, southwestern UK, *Marine Pollution Bulletin*, **17**, 427–31.

——, and ——, 1987, Late Flandrian shoreline oscillations in the Severn Estuary: a geomorphological and stratigraphical reconnaissance, *Philosophical Transactions of the Royal Society, London*, **B315**, 185–230.

Andersen, S Th, 1970, The relative pollen productivity and pollen representation of North European trees and correction factors for tree pollen spectra, *Danmarks Geologiske Undersogelse II*, **96**, 1–99.

——, 1973, The differential pollen productivity of trees and its significance for interpretation of a pollen diagram from a forested region, in H J B Birks and R G West (eds), *Quaternary Plant Ecology*, 109–15. Oxford: Blackwell.

Anderson, J G C, 1968, The concealed rock-surface and overlying deposits of the Severn Valley, and estuaries form Upton to Neath, *Proceedings of South Wales Institute Engineers*, **83**, 27–47.

——, 1974, The buried channels, rock-floors and rock-basins, and overlying deposits of the South Wales Valleys from the Wye to Neath, *Proceedings of South Wales Institute Engineers*, **88**, 1–25.

——, and Blundell, C R K, 1965, The sub-drift rock-surface and buried valleys of the Cardiff district, *Proceedings of the Geologists Association*, **76**, 367–77.

——, and Owen, T R, 1979, The Late Quaternary history of the Neath and Afan valleys, South Wales, *Proceedings of the Geologists Association*, **90** (4), 203–11.

Arnold, B, 1982, The architectural woodwork of the Late Bronze Age village Auvernier-Nord, in S McGrail (ed), *Woodworking Techniques Before A.D. 1500*, *BAR Int Ser*, **129**, 111–28, Oxford.

——, 1986, *Cortaillod-Est, un village du Bronze final 1: Fouille subaquatique et photographie aérienne* Saint-Blaise, Editions du Ruau.

Ashbee, P, Bell, M A, and Proudfoot, E V, 1989, *Wilsford Shaft: Excavations 1960–62* English Heritage Archaeological Report **11**, English Heritage, London.

280

Atkinson, M D, 1992, Biological Flora of the British Isles *Betula pendula* Roth (B. verrucosa Ehrh.) and *B. pubescens* Ehrh, *Journal of Ecology*, **80**, 837–70.

Audouze, A, and Buchsenschutz, O, 1991, *Towns, villages and countryside of Celtic Europe*, London: Batsford.

Baillie, M G L, 1982, *Tree-Ring Dating and Archaeology*, London: Croom Helm.

——, 1995, *A Slice Through Time: dendrochronology and precision dating*, London: Batsford.

——, and Pilcher, J R, 1973, A simple crossdating program for tree-ring research, *Tree Ring Bulletin*, **33**, 7–14.

Barber, K E, and Twigger, S N, 1987, Late Quaternary palaeoecology of the Severn Basin, in K J Gregory, J Lewin, and J B Thornes, (eds), *Palaeohydrology in Practice*, Chichester: John Wiley and Sons Ltd, 217–50.

Barnet, C, *et al*, 1990, Romano-British Pottery Kilns at Caldicot, Gwent, *Archaeol J*, **147**, 118–47.

Barrett, J, 1975, The later pottery: types, affinities, chronology and significance, in R Bradley, and A Ellison, *Rams Hill*, BAR, **19**, Oxford.

Battarbee, R W, 1986, Diatom analysis, in B E Berglund, (ed), *Handbook of Holocene Palaeoecology and Palaeohydrology*, Chichester: John Wiley & Sons Ltd, 527–70.

——, 1988, The use of diatom analysis in archaeology: a review, *J Arch Sci*, **15**, 621–44.

——, Scaife, R G, and Phethean, S J, 1985, Palaeoecological evidence for sea-level change in the Bann estuary in the Early Mesolithic period, in P C Woodman, *Excavations at Mount Sandel 1973–77, Northern Ireland*, Archaeological Monographs: No 2, H M S O, Belfast, 111–20.

Beck, C, and Shennan, S, 1991, *Amber in Prehistoric Britain*, Oxbow Monograph **8**.

Beckett, S C, 1978, The environmental setting of the Meare Heath Track, *Somerset Levels Papers* **4**, 42–6.

Beckinsale, R P, and Richardson, L, 1964, Recent findings on the physical development of the Lower Severn Valley, *Geographical Journal*, **130**, 87–105.

Behre, K, -E, 1981, The interpretation of anthropogenic indicators in pollen diagrams, *Pollen et Spores*, **23**, 225–45.

Beijerinck, W, 1947, *Zadenatlas der Nerlandsche Flora*, Wageningen: Veenman.

Bell, M, 1992, Archaeology under alluvium: human agency and environmental process. Some concluding thoughts, in S Needham and M G Macklin (eds), *Alluvial Archaeology in Britain*, Oxbow Monograph **27**, 271–6.

——, 1993a, Field survey and excavation at Goldcliff, Gwent 1993, *Archaeology in the Severn Estuary 1993: Annual Report of the Severn Estuary Levels Research Committee*, 81–101.

——, 1993b, Intertidal archaeology at Goldcliff in the Severn estuary, in J Coles, V Fenwick and G Hutchinson (eds), *A spirit of enquiry*, Exeter: Wetlands Archaeology Research Project, 9–13.

——, and Neumann, H, 1996, Intertidal survey in the Welsh Severn Estuary, *Archaeology in the Severn Estuary 1995: Annual Report of the Severn Estuary Levels Research Committee*.

Bengtsson, L, and Enell, M, 1986, Chemical Analysis, in B E Bergland, (ed), *Handbook of Holocene Palaeoecology and Palaeohydrology*, Chichester: John Wiley and Sons Ltd, 423–51.

Bennett, K D, 1994, *Annotated catalogue of pollen and pteridophtye spore types of the British Isles*, Department of Plant Sciences, University of Cambridge, Cambridge.

——, Whittington, G, and Edwards, K J, 1994, Recent plant nomenclatural changes and pollen morphology in the British Isles, *Quaternary Newsletter*, **73**, 1–6.

Berggren, G, 1969, *Atlas of seeds and small fruits of Northwest-European plant species with morphological descriptions. Part 2. Cyperaceae.* Stockholm.

——, 1981, *Atlas of seeds and small fruits of Northwest-European plant species with morphological descriptions. Part 3. Salicaeae-Cruciferae.* Arlow.

Bernatzky-Goetze, M, 1987, *Mörigen: der spätbronzezeitlichen Funde*, (Bern).

Bertsch, K, 1941, *Früchte und Samen. Handbücher der praktischen Vorgeschichtsforschung. I.* Stuttgart, Ferdinand Enke.

Bianco Peroni, V, 1970, Die Schwerter in Italien, (München: C.H. Beck'sche Verlagsbuchhandlung, *Prähistorische Bronzefunde, IV(1)*).

Birks, H J B, 1989, Holocene isochrone maps and patterns of tree-spreading in the British Isles, *Journal of Biogeography*, **16**, 503–40.

Bocksberger, O-J, 1964, *Age du bronze en Valais et dans le Chablais Vaudois*, Lausanne: Imprimerie Centrale.

Bollingberg, H J, 1995, Copper-alloyed artefacts from Roman imports in Scandinavia, in P B Vandiver, J R Druzik, J L Galvan Madrid, I C Freestone and G S Wheeler, eds, *Materials issues in art and archaeology IV*, Pittsburgh: Materials Research Society Symposium Proceedings, **352**, 621–9.

Boon, B C, 1980, Caerleon and the Gwent levels in early history times, in F H Thompson, (ed), Archaeological and coastal change, *The Society of Antiquaries Occasional Papers*, London, 24–36.

Bradley, R, *et al*, 1980, Two Late Bronze Age settlements on the Kennet gravels: excavations at Aldermaston Wharf and Knight's Farm, Burghfield, Berkshire, *Proc Prehist Soc*, **46**, 217–96.

Britnell, W J, and Earwood, C, 1991, Wooden artefacts and other worked wood from Buckbean Pond, in C R Musson (ed), *The Breiddin Hillfort*, 161–72, *CBA Res Rep* **76**, London.

Bronsted, J, 1939, *Danmarks Oldtid* Volume 2, Gyldendalkse Boghandel Nordisk Forlag, Copenhagen.

Brown, A G, 1982, Human impact on the former floodplain woodlands of the Severn, in M Bell and S Limbrey (eds), *Archaeological Aspects of Woodland Ecology*, BAR Int Ser, **146**, 93–104.

——, 1983, Floodplain deposits and accelerated sedimentation in the Lower Severn Basin, in K J Gregory, (ed), *Background to Palaeohydrology*, Chichester: John Wiley and Sons Ltd, 375–98.

——, 1985, Traditional and multivariate techniques in the interpretation of floodplain sediment grain size variations, *Earth Surface Processes and Landforms*, **10**, 281–91.

——, 1987a, Long-term sediment storage in the Severn and Wye catchments, in K J Gregory, J Lewin, and J B Thornes, (eds), *Palaeohydrology in Practice*, Chichester: John Wiley and Sons Ltd, 307–32.

——, 1987b, Holocene floodplain sedimentation and channel response of the lower River Severn, United Kingdom, *Zeitschrift fur Geomorpologie*, **31**, 293–310.

——, 1988, The palaeoecology of *Alnus* (alder) and the postglacial history of floodplain vegetation. Pollen percentage and influx data from the West Midlands, United Kingdom. *New Phytologist*, **110**, 425–36.

——, and Barber, K E, 1985, Late Holocene palaeoecology and sedimentary history of a small lowland catchment in central England, *Quaternary Research*, **24**, 87–102.

Brown, D M, Munro, M A R, Baillie, M G L, and Pilcher, J R, 1986, Dendrochronology – the absolute Irish standard, *Radiocarbon*, **28** (2A), 279–83.

Buckley, D G, 1975, The Excavation of a Bronze Age Barrow Mound at St Brides Netherwent, Monmouthshire, *Archaeologia Cambrensis* **CXXIV**, 36–51.

Bulleid, A, 1945, Oak piles in King's Sedgemoor, *Proc Somerset Arch and Nat Hist Soc*, **91**, 109.

——, and Gray, St G, 1917, *The Glastonbury lake Village, Vol. II*. Glastonbury Antiquarian Society.

Burgess, C B, 1962, Two Grooved Ogival Daggers of the Early Bronze Age from South Wales, *BBCS* **XX**, 75–94.

——, and Colqhoun, I, 1988, *The swords of Britain*, (München: C H Beck'sche Verlagsbuchhandlung, *Prähistorische Bronzefunde, IV(5)*).

——, and Gerloff, S, 1981, *The dirks and rapiers of Great Britain and Ireland*, (München: C H Beck'sche Verlagsbuchhandlung, *Prähistorische Bronzefunde, IV(7)*).

——, Coombs, D, and Davies, D G, 1972, The Broadward Complex and barbed spearheads, in F Lynch, and C B Burgess, (eds), *Prehistoric Man in Wales and the West* (Bath: Adams and Dart), 211–84.

Burleigh, R, Clutton-Brock, J, Felder, J P, and Sieveking, G de G, 1977, A further consideration of Neolithic dogs with special reference to a skeleton from Grime's Graves (Norfolk), England, *J Arch Sci*, **4**, 353–66.

Burrin, P J, 1985, Holocene alluviation in south-east England and some implications for palaeohydrological studies, *Earth Surface Processes and Landforms*, **10**, 257–71.

——, and Scaife, R G, 1984, Aspects of Holocene valley sedimentation and floodplain development in southern England, *Proceedings of the Geologists Association,* **95**, 81–96.

Butler, J J, 1963, Bronze Age connections across the North Sea, *Palaeohistoria,* **9**, 166.

Butterworth, C A, and Lobb, S J, 1992, *Excavations in the Burghfield Area, Berkshire: Developments in the Bronze Age and Saxon Landscapes*, Wessex Archaeology Report No **1**.

Cameron, N, 1993, Diatom analysis of the Oscar 3 profile, in S Godbold, and R Turner, *Second Severn Crossing, Archaeological Response: Phase 1, the intertidal zone in Wales.* Cadw (Welsh Historic Monuments) 61–4.

Capelle,T, 1982, Erkenntnismöglichkeiten ur- and frühgeschichtlicher Bewaffnungsformen, Zum Problem von Waffen aus organischem Material, *Bonner Jahrbücher* des Rheinischen Landesmuseums in Bonn, 265–88.

Cappers, R T J, 1993, Seed dispersal by water: a contribution to the interpretation of seed assemblages, *Vegetation History and Archaeobotany*, **2**, 173–86.

Caseldine, A E, 1988, A wetland resource: the environmental exploitation in the Somerset Levels during the prehistoric period, in P Murphy and C French, *The Exploitation of Wetlands*, BAR Brit Ser, **186**, 239–65.

——, 1990, *Environmental Archaeology in Wales,* Saint David's University College, Lampeter, Wales.

——, 1993, Plant macrofossils from Vurlong Reen, near Caldicot, South Wales, in M Bell, *Archaeology in the Severn Estuary 1993*, Annual Report of the Severn Estuary Levels Research Committee, 71–2.

——, and Murphy, K, 1989, A Bronze Age Burnt Mound on Troedrhiwgwinau Farm, near Aberystwyth, Dyfed, *Archaeology in Wales*, **29**, 1–5.

Chambers, F M, 1982, Two radiocarbon-dated pollen diagrams from high altitude blanket peats in south Wales, *Journal of Ecology*, **70**, 445–59.

——, 1983, Three radiocarbon-dated pollen diagrams from uplands north-west of Merthyr Tydfil, South Wales, *Journal of Ecology*, **71**, 475–87.

——, 1993, Late Quaternary climatic change and human impact commentary and conclusions, in

282

F M Chambers, (ed), *Climatic Change and Human Impact on the Landscape*, London: Chapman and Hall, 247–59.

Chinery, M, 1986, *Collins Guide to the Insects of Britain and Western Europe*, London: Collins.

Clapham, A R, 1975, *The Oxford Book of Trees*, Oxford: Univ Press.

Cleland, D M, 1954, A study of the habits of *Valvata piscinalis* (Muller) and the structure and function of the alimentary canal and reproductive system, *Proceedings of the Malacological Society*, **30**, 167–203.

Cleve-euler, A, 1951–1955, *Die Diatomeen von Schweden und Finland. Kungliga Svenska Vetenskaps Handlingar* Ser 4, 2(1) 3–163; 4(1) 3–158; 4(5) 3–255; 5(4) 3–231; 3(3) 3–153.

Clutton-Brock, J, 1969, The origins of the dog, in D Brothwell and E Higgs (eds), *Science and Archaeology*, London 303–9, (second edition).

——, and Noe-Nygaard, N, 1990, New osteological and C-isotope evidence on Mesolithic Dogs: Comparisons to hunters and fishers at Starr Carr, Seamer Carr and Kongemose, *J Arch Sci*, **17**, 643–53.

Coard, R, and Dennell, R W, 1995, Taphonomy of some articulated skeletal remains. Transport potential in an artificial environment, *J Arch Sci*, **22**, 441–8.

Codrington, T, 1898, Submerged rock-valleys in South Wales, Devon, and Cornwall, *Quarterly Journal of the Geological Society*, **54**, 251–78.

Coffey, G, 1906, Two finds of Late Bronze Age objects, *Proceedings of the Royal Irish Academy*, **24C**, 119–24.

Coghlan, H H, and Case, H J, 1957, Early metallurgy of copper in Ireland and Britain, *Proc Prehist Soc*, **23**, 91–123.

Coles, B, 1992, Further thoughts on the impact of the beaver on temperate landscapes, in S Needham and M G Mackin (eds), *Alluvial archaeology in Britain*, Oxbow Monograph, Oxford, 93–9.

Coles, J M, 1990, *Waterlogged Wood: guidelines on the recording, sampling, conservation, and curation of structural wood*, English Heritage, London.

——, and Coles, B, 1982, Beaver in the Somerset Levels: some new evidence, *Somerset Levels Papers*, **8**, 67–93.

——, and Coles, B, 1983, Homo sapiens or castor fiber?, *Antiquity*, **57**, 95–102.

——, and Coles, B, 1984, Ten excavations along the line of the Sweet Track, *Somerset Levels Papers*, **10**, 5–45.

——, and Coles, B, 1985, Prehistoric wood-working from the Somerset Levels: 3 roundwood, *Somerset Levels Papers*, **11**, 5–50.

——, and Goodburn, D M, 1991, *Wet Site Excavation and Survey*, WARP Occasional Paper **5**, Exeter.

——, and Orme, B J, 1976, The Sweet Track, Railway Site, *Somerset Levels Papers*, **2**, 34–65.

——, Coles, B J, Morgan, R A, and Caseldine, A, 1988, The Meare Heath track 1988, *Somerset Levels Papers*, **14**, 6–33.

——, Fenwick, V, and Hutchinson, G, 1993, *A spirit of enquiry*, Exeter: WARP.

Collinson, J D, and Thompson, D B, 1989, *Sedimentary Structures*. London: Chapman and Hall.

Condry, W, 1974, *Woodlands*, Collins.

Coombs, D, 1988, The Wilburton complex and Bronze Final II in Atlantic Europe, in P Brun, and C Mordant, (eds), *Le groupe Rhin-Suisse-France orientale et la notion de civilisation des Champs d'Urnes* (Nemours: Éditions A.P.R.A.I.F., *Memoires du Musée de Préhistoire d'Île de France 1*), 575–82 and Type 34.

——, 1992, Flag Fen platform and Fengate Power station post alignment – the metalwork, *Antiquity*, **66**, 504–17.

Corcoran, J X W P, 1972, Multi-Period Construction and the Origins of the Chambered Long Cairn in Western Britain and Ireland, in F Lynch and C Burgess (eds), *Prehistoric Man in Wales and the West*, Bath: Adams and Dart, 31–64.

Cotter, C, 1994, Atlantic fortifications – The duns of the Aran Islands, *Archaeology Ireland*, **8:1**, 24–8.

Crabtree, P J, 1990, Subsistence and ritual: The faunal remains from Dún Ailinne, Co Kildare, Ireland, *Emania*, **7**, 22–5.

Crone, A, 1987, Tree-Ring Studies And The Reconstruction Of Woodland Management Practices In Antiquity, in J C Jacoby, and J W Hornbeck (eds), *Proceedings of the International Symposium on Ecological Aspects of Tree-Ring Analysis*, 327–36.

Culver, S J, and Bull P A, 1979, Late Pleistocene rock-basin lakes in South Wales, *Geological Journal*, **14**, 107–16.

Cunliffe, B, 1978, *Iron Age communities in Britain*, London.

Darbishire, R D, 1874, Notes on discoveries in Ehenside Tarn, Cumberland, *Archaeologia*, **44**, 273–92.

Darrah, R, 1982, Working unseasoned wood, in S McGrail (ed), *Woodworking Techniques before AD 1500*, BAR Int Ser, **129**, 219–30, Oxford.

Denys, L, 1988, Fragilaria blooms in the Holocene of the Western Coastal Plain of Belgium, *Proceedings of the 10th Diatom Symposium*, 397–406.

——, 1992, *A check list of the diatoms in the Holocene deposits of the Western Belgian Coastal Plain with a survey of their apparent ecological requirements: I. Introduction, ecological code and complete list*, Service Geologique de Belgique: Professional Paper No **246**, 41.

Dickson, C A, 1988, Distinguishing cereal from wild grass pollen: some limitations, *Circaea*, **5**, 67–71.

Dodds, J G, 1953, Biological Flora of the British Isles *Plantago coronopus* L, *Journal of Ecology*, **41**, 467–78.

Done, G, 1980, The animal bone, in D Longley, *Runnymede Bridge 1976: excavation on the site of a Late Bronze Age settlement*, Surrey Archaeological Society Research Volume no **6**, Guildford, 74–9.

——, 1991, The animal bone, in S P Needham, *Excavation and salvage at Runnymede Bridge, 1978: The Late Bronze Age Waterfront site*, British Museum in association with English Heritage, 327–44.

Earwood, C, 1990, *Domestic wooden artefacts from prehistoric and early historic periods in Britain and Ireland: their manufacture and use*. PhD University of Exeter.

——, 1993, *Domestic Wooden Artefacts: in Britain and Ireland from Neolithic to Viking Times*. University of Exeter Press.

——, forthcoming, Wooden artefacts from Deer Park Farms, Co Antrim, in C Lynn, (ed), *Deer Park Farms*. Department of the Environment for Northern Ireland.

Eckstein, M R, 1963, Ein späturnenfelderzeitliches Kriegergrab von Mauern, Ldkr. Neuburg a.d. Donau, *Germania,* **41**, 88–92, Abb. 3.6.

Edwards, K E, 1979, Palynological and temporal inference in the context of prehistory, with special reference to the evidence from lake and peat deposits, *J Arch Sci*, **6**, 255–70.

Edwards, K J, 1993, Models of mid-Holocene forest farming for north-west Europe, in F M Chambers (ed), *Climate Change and Human Impact on the Landscape*, London: Chapman and Hall, 133–45.

Ellenberg, H, 1978, *Vegetation Mitteleuropas mit den Alpen,* 2 Auflage. Stuttgart: Ulmer.

——, 1988, *Vegetation Ecology of Central Europe*, Fourth edition. Cambridge: University Press.

Eogan, G, 1965, *Catalogue of Irish Bronze Age swords*, Dublin: National Museum of Ireland.

Esho, R, 1989, Diatom identifications from the intercalated clay layer at Goldcliff site 1. Appendix 1, in A G Smith and L A Morgan, A succession to ombrotrophic bog in the Gwent Levels, and its demise: a Welsh parallel to the peats of the Somerset Levels, *New Phytologist*, **112**, 145–67.

Evans, J, 1992, Molluscs, in C A Butterworth, and S J Lobb, *Excavations in the Burghfield Area, Berkshire: Developments in the Bronze Age and Saxon Landscapes*. Salisbury: Wessex Archaeology Report, **10**, 130–43.

Evans, J G, 1991, Synthesis of the environmental evidence, in S P Needham, *Excavation and Salvage at Runnymede Bridge, 1978*, London: British Museum Press.

——, Davies, P, Mount, R, and Williams, D, 1992, Molluscan taxocenes from Holocene overbank alluvium in central southern England, in S Needham, and M G Macklin, (eds), *Alluvial Archaeology in Britain*, Oxford: Oxbow Monograph **27**, 65–74.

Faegri, K, and Iversen, J, 1989, *Textbook of Pollen Analysis*, 4th edn, (revised by K Faegri, P E Kaland, and K Krzywinski), Chichester: John Wiley & Sons Ltd.

Field, M H, 1992, *A Study of Plant Macrofossil Taphonomy in Lakes and Rivers and its Application for Interpreting Some Middle Pleistocene Assemblages*, PhD thesis, College of St Paul and St Mary, Cheltenham, UK.

Fleming, A, 1971, Territorial Patterns in Bronze Age Wessex, *Proc Prehist Soc*, **37** part II, 138–66.

——, 1988, *The Dartmoor Reaves: Investigating Prehistoric Land Divisions*, London: Batsford.

Flower, R J, (unpubl), Preliminary report on the diatoms in the stratigraphic sequence of sediment samples from the Caldicot sondage, 2pp.

Folk, R L, and Ward, W C, 1957, Brazos River Bar: A study in the significance of grain size parameters, *Journal of Sedimentary Petrology*, **27**, 3–26.

Ford, S, Bradley, R, Hawkes, T, and Fisher, P, 1984, Flint-working in the metal age, *Oxford Journal of Archaeology*, **3**, 157–73.

Fretter, V, and Graham, A, 1978, The Prosobranch Molluscs of Britain and Denmark, Part 3-Neritacea, Viviparacea, Valvatacea, terrestrial and freshwater Littorinacea and Rissoacea. *Supplement 5, Journal of Molluscan Studies*.

Gaillard, M J, Gôransson, H, Hèkansson, H, and Lemdahl, J, 1988, The palaeoenvironment at Skatelhom-JÑravallen (Southern Sweden) during Atlantic and early Sub-Boreal time on the basis of pollen, macrofossil, diatom and insect analyses, in L Larsson, (ed), *The Skateholm Project. I. Man and Environment. Acta Regiae Societatis Humaniorum Litterarum Lundensis LXXIX*.

Gingell, C, and Lawson, A J, 1985, Excavations at Potterne, 1984, *Wilts Archaeol Mag*, **79**, 101–8.

Gobold, S, and Turner, R C, 1993, *Second Severn Crossing Archaeological Response: Phase 1: The Intertidal Zone in Wales*, Brentwood: Westbury Press.

Godwin, H, and Willis, E H, 1964, Cambridge University natural radiocarbon measurements. VI. *Radiocarbon*, **6**, 116–37.

Gôransson, H, 1983, Nar borjar neolititikum? *Popular Arkeologi*, **1**, 4–7.

——, 1986, Man and the forests of nemoral broad-leaved trees during the Stone Age, *Striae*, **24**, 143–52.

——, 1987, *Neolithic Man and the Forest Environment around Alvastra Pile Dwelling*. Theses and Papers in North-European Archaeology, **20**, Stockholm.

Graham, A, 1971, *British Prosobranch and other operculate gastropod molluscs*, Linnean Society

Synopsis of the British Fauna, London: Academic Press.

——, 1988, *Molluscs: Prosobranch and Pyramidellid Gastropods*, Linnean Society Synopsis of the British Fauna NS 2. Leiden: Brill/ Backhuys.

Grant, A, 1982, The use of tooth wear as a guide to the age of domestic ungulates, in B Wilson, C Grigson, and S Payne (eds), *Ageing and sexing animal bones from archaeological sites*, *BAR, Brit Ser*, **109**, 91–108.

——, 1984a, Animal husbandry, in B Cunliffe, *Danebury: An Iron Age hillfort in Hampshire, vol. 2, The excavation 1969–1978, the finds*, *CBA Res Rep*, **52**, London, 496–548.

——, 1984b, Animal husbandry in Wessex and the Thames Valley, in B Cunliffe, and D Miles, *Aspects of the Iron Age in central Southern Britain*, University of Oxford: Committee of Archaeology monograph no **2**, 102–19.

Gray, H St G, and Bulleid, A, 1953, *The Meare Lake Village*, vol **ii** (Taunton: privately published).

——, and Cotton, M A, 1966, *The Meare Lake Village*, vol **iii**. Taunton Castle, Taunton.

Green, H S, 1978, Late Bronze Age wooden hafts from Llyn Fawr and Penwylt and a review of the evidence for the selection of wood for tool and weapon handles in Neolithic and Bronze Age Britain, *Bulletin of the Board for Celtic Studies*, 136–41.

——, 1980, *The Flint Arrowheads of The British Isles*, Oxford: *BAR, Brit Ser*, **96**.

Greig, J R A, 1982, Past and present lime woods of Europe, in M Bell and S Limbrey (eds), *Archaeological Aspects of Woodland Ecology*, *BAR, Int Ser*, **146**, 23–55.

Grimes, W F, 1951, *The Prehistory of Wales*, National Museum of Wales. Cardiff. 2nd edition.

Grimm, E C, 1991, *TILIA and TILIA-GRAPH*, Illinois State Museum, Springfield.

Groenman-van Waateringe, W, 1978, The impact of Neolithic man in the Netherlands, in S Limbrey and J G Evans (eds), *The effect of man on the landscape: the lowland zone, CBA Res Rep*, **21**, 135–46.

Groves, C, and Hillam, J, 1988, The potential of non-oak species for tree-ring dating in Britain, in E A Slater, and J O Tate (eds), *Science and Archaeology, Glasgow 1987*. *BAR Brit Ser*, **196**, 567–79.

Haarnagel, W, 1979, *Feddersen Wierde*. Wiesbaden: Franz Steiner Verlag GmbH.

Håkansson, H, 1988, Diatom analysis at Skateholm-JÑravallen, Southern Sweden, in L Larsson (ed), *The Skateholm Project. I. Man and Environment. Acta Regiae Societatis Humaniorum Litterarum Lundensis LXXIX*.

Hamilton-Dyer, S, 1993, The animal bone, in D Zienkiewicz, Excavations in the *Scamnum Tribunorum* at Caerleon: The Legionary Museum site 1938–5, *Britannia*, **24**, 132–6.

Harcourt, R A, 1974, The Dog in Prehistoric and Early Historic Britain, *J Arch Sci*, **1**, 151–75.

Harris, E C, 1989, *Principles of archaeological stratigraphy*. London: Academic Press, Second edition.

Haslam, S M, 1971, Physical factors and some river weeds, in *Proceedings of the European Weed Research Council 3rd International Symposium Aquatic Weeds 1971*, 29–39.

——, 1982, *River plants*. Cambridge: University Press.

——, Sinker, C A, and Wolseley, P A, 1982, *British Water Plants*, reprinted from *Field Studies* **4**, 2 (1975), 243–51.

Hawkins, A B, 1971, Sea-level changes around south-west England, in D J Blackman (ed), *Marine Archaeology*, 67–87. London: Butterworths.

Heal, S V E, 1986, Recent work at North Ferriby, North Humberside, England, *Proc Prehist Soc*, **52**, 317–8.

Heal, V, 1991, The technology of the worked wood and bark, in S P Needham, *Excavation and Salvage at Runnymede Bridge, 1978: the Late Bronze Age Waterfront Site*, 140–7. London: British Museum Press.

Hein, M, 1991, Eins Scheidenbeschlag vom Heligenberg bei Heidelberg: zur Typologie endbronzezeitlicher und ältereisenzeitlicher Ortbänder (Ha B2/3-Ha C), *Jahrbuch des Römisch-Germanisch Zentralmuseums Mainz*, **36**(i), 301–26.

Hencken, H O N, 1936, Ballinderry crannog 1, *Proc Royal Irish Academy* 34C, No **5**, 103–239.

——, 1942, Ballinderry crannog 2, *Proc Royal Irish Academy* 47C, No **1**, 1–76.

Hendey, N I, 1964, *An Introductory Account of the Smaller Algae of British Coastal Waters. Part V. Bacillariophyceae (Diatoms)*.Ministry of Agriculture Fisheries and Food, Series IV.

Heyworth, A, and Kidson, C, 1982, Sea-level changes in southwest England, *Proceedings of the Geologists Association*, **93**, 91–111.

Higham, C F W, 1967, Flock rearing as a cultural factor in prehistoric Europe, *Proc Prehist Soc*, **33**, 84–106.

Hillam, J, 1985, Theoretical and applied dendrochronology: how to make a date with a tree, in P Phillips (ed), *The Archaeologist and the Laboratory*, *CBA Res Rep*, **58**, 17–23.

——, 1993, Tree-ring dating of oak timbers from site C, Skinner's Wood, Somerset. *Ancient Monuments Laboratory report series 86/93*.

——, Groves, C M, Brown, D M, Baillie, M G L, Coles, J M, and Coles, B J, 1990, Dendrochronology of the English Neolithic, *Antiquity*, **64**, 211–20.

——, Morgan, R A, and Tyers, I, 1987, Sapwood estimates and the dating of short ring sequences, in R G W Ward (ed), *Applications of tree-ring studies: current research in dendrochronology and related areas*, *BAR* **S333**, 165–85.

Hoffman, M, 1964, *The Warp Weighted Loom*, Studia Norvegica 14, Universitetsforlaget, Oslo.

Hopkins, J S, 1950, Differential flotation and deposition of coniferous and deciduous tree pollen, *Ecology*, **31**, 633–41.

Housley, R A, 1988, The environmental context of Glastonbury Lake Village, *Somerset Levels Papers*, **14**, 63–82.

——, 1995, The environment, in J Coles and S Minnitt *'Industrious and Fairly Civilised' The Glastonbury Lake Village*, 121–36.

Hughes, D A, and Lewin, J, 1982, A small-scale flood plain, *Sedimentology*, **29**, 891–5.

Hughes, G, 1996, *The Excavation of a Late Prehistoric and Romano-British Settlement at Thornwell Farm, Chepstow, Gwent, 1992*, *BAR Brit Ser*, **244**.

Huntley, B, and Birks, H J B, 1983, *An atlas of past and present pollen maps of Europe: 0–13000 years ago*. Cambridge: University Press.

——, Bartlein, P J, and Prentice, I C, 1989, Climatic control of the distribution and abundance of beech (Fagus L.) in Europe and North America, *Journal of Biogeography*, **16**, 551–60.

Hustedt, F, 1930–1966, *Die Kieselalgen Deutschlands, Oesterreichs und der Schweiz unter Berücksichtigung der übrigen Länder Europas sowie der angrenzenden Meeresgebiete. In Dr. L. Rabenhorsts Kryptogamen-Flora von Deutschland, Oesterrech und der Schweiz 7*, Parts 1–3.

——, 1957, Die Diatomenflora des Fluß-systems des Weserim Gebiet der Hansestadt Bremen, *Ab natura Ver Bremen*, **34**, 181–440.

Hyde, H A, 1940, Report on plant remains (carbonised wood) from Crick barrow, in H N Savory, A middle Bronze Age barrow at Crick, Monmouthshire, *Archaeologia Cambrensis*, **95**, 186–7.

——, and Harrison, S G, 1977, *Welsh Timber Trees – native and introduced*. National Museum of Wales.

Ijzereef, G F, 1981, *Bronze Age animal bones from Bovenkarspel*, Nederlandse Oudheden, **10**, ROB, Amersfoort.

Iversen, J, 1973, The development of Denmark's nature since the last glacial, *Danmarks Geologiske Undersogelse*, Series V, 7-C, 1–26.

Jack, R I, 1988, Wales and the Marches, in H E Hallam (ed), *The Agrarian History of England and Wales. Vol. II 1042–1350*. Cambridge: University Press.

Jackson, J W, 1915, Notes on the vertebrate and molluscan remains from Dyserth Castle, in T A Glenn, Prehistoric and historic remains at Dyserth Castle, *Archaeologia Cambrensis*, **15**, 47–82.

Jacobson, G L, and Bradshaw, R H W, 1981, The selection of sites for palaeovegetational studies, *Quaternary Research*, **16**, 80–96.

Jansma, M J, 1990, Diatoms from a Neolithic excavation on the former Island of Schokland, Ijselmeerpolders, The Netherlands, *Diatom Research*, **5**, 301–9.

Janssen, C R, 1966, Recent pollen spectra from the deciduous and coniferous-deciduous forests of north-eastern Minnesota: a study in pollen dispersal, *Ecology*, **47**, 804–25.

Johl, C H, 1917, *Die Webstühle der Griechen und Römer*. Borna, Leipzig.

Johnson, S, 1991, Interim report on the Goldcliff wood identifications, *Severn Estuary Levels Research Committee Annual Report 1991*. SELRC, Lampeter, 21–2.

——, 1993m Goldcliff – interim wood identification report, in M Bell, *Archaeology in the Severn Estuary 1993*, Annual Report of the Severn Estuary Levels Research Committee, 103–8.

Jope, M, 1965, Faunal remains, in A Keiller, *Windmill Hill and Avebury*, Oxford: Clarendon Press.

Jørgensen, L B, 1991, *North European textiles until AD 1000*, Aarhus University Press.

Juggins, S J, 1992, *Diatoms in the Thames Estuary, England: Ecology, Palaeoecology, and Salinity Transfer Function*, Bibliotheca Diatomologica 25. Cramer, Berlin.

Kenward, H K, 1992, Rapid recording of archaeological insect remains – a reconsideration. *Circaea*, **9**, no 2: 81–8.

Kerney, M P, 1976a, A list of the fresh and brackish-water Mollusca of the British Isles, *Journal of Conchology*, **29**, 26–8.

——, 1976b, *Atlas of the non-Marine Mollusca of the British Isles*. Monks Wood: Institute of Terrestrial Ecology.

Kinnes, I A, and Longworth, I H, 1985, *Catalogue of the excavated prehistoric and Romano-British material in the Greenwell Collection*. British Museum Press.

Kjemperud, A, 1981, Diatom changes in sediments of basins possessing marine/lacustrine transitions in Frosta, Nord-Trøndelag, Norway, *Boreas*, **10**, 27–38.

Klie, W, 1938, Ostracoda; Muschellkrebse, *Tierwelt Deutschland*. Jena: 1–230.

Kloet, G S, and Hincks, W D, 1977, A check list of British insects (Coleoptera), Handb Ident Br Insects **XI**. *Roy Ent Soc Lond*.

Lee, J E, 1862, *Isca Silurium*, 108–9.

Leeder, M R, 1982, *Sedimentology: process and product*. London: Allen and Unwin.

Legge, A J, 1981, The agricultural economy, in R Mercer, *Grimes Graves, Norfolk: Excavations 1971–72*, Department of the Environment Research Reports **11**, London: H M S O, 1, 79–103.

——, 1991, The animal bones from six sites at Down Farm, Woodcutts, in J Barrett, R Bradley and M Hall (eds), *Papers on the prehistoric archaeology of Cranborne Chase*, Oxbow Monograph **11**, Oxford, 54–100.

——, 1992, *Animals, environment and the Bronze Age Economy*, (excavations at Grimes Graves, Norfolk 1972–1976, Fascicule 4). London: British Museum Press.

——, and P A Rowley-Conway, 1988, *Starr Carr revisited: a re-analysis of the large mammals*. Birkbeck College, University of London, London.

Lennox, P J, 1992, *Caldicot Castle Lake, Caldicot, Gwent. Archaeological Watching Brief.* Glamorgan-Gwent Archaeological Trust.

Levitan, B, 1990, The vertebrate remains, in M Bell, *Brean Down excavations 1983–1987*, English Heritage Archaeological Reports no **15**, 220–41.

Lewis, G,W, 1982, The geomorphology of alluvial cutoffs: Geometry, Processes, Development Rates and Sedimentation. Unpublished PhD thesis, University of Wales.

Lillie, M C, 1991, *Bronze Age Gwent*. BA Hons Dissertation, University of Nottingham.

Limbrey, S, 1978, Changes in quality and distribution of the soils of lowland Britain, in S Limbrey, and J G Evans, (eds), *The effect of man on the landscape, the Lowland Zone, CBA Res Rep* **21**, London, 21–7.

Lindholm, R, 1987, *A practical approach to sedimentology*, London: Allen and Unwin Inc.

Lobb, S J, 1992, Archaeological Investigations at Anslow's Cottages, Burghfield, in C A Butterworth and S J Lobb (eds), *Excavations in the Burghfield Area, Berkshire*, 79–169. Wessex Archaeology Report No 1. Salisbury: Trust for Wessex Archaeology Ltd.

Locke, S, 1971, The post glacial deposits of the Caldicot Level and some associated archaeological discoveries, *Monmouthshire Antiquary*, **3**, 1–16.

Lucas, A T, 1960, Archaeological acquisitions in the year 1958, *Jnl Royal Soc Anti Ireland*, **90**, 1–40.

Lynch, F, 1991, *Prehistoric Anglesey*, 2nd ed. Llangefni: Anglesey Antiquarian Society.

Lynn, C J, 1977, Trial excavations at the King's Stables, Tray Townland, Co Down, *Ulster Journal of Archaeology*, **40**, 42–62.

Macklin, M G, and Lewin, J, 1993, Holocene river alluviation in Britain, in I Douglas, and J Hagedorn (eds), Geomorphology and geoecology, fluvial geomorphology, *Zeitschrift für Geomorpologie*, (Supplement), **85**.

——, and Needham, S, 1992, Studies in British alluvial archaeology: potential and prospect, in S Needham and M G Macklin (eds), *Alluvial Archaeology in Britain*. Oxbow Monograph **27**, 9–23.

Magilligan, F J, 1992, Sedimentology of fine grained floodplains, *Geomorphology*, **4**, 393–408.

Mann, L, 1903, Prehistoric pile-structures in pits in Wigtownshire., *Proc Soc Antiq Scotland*, **37**, 371–405.

Marriott, S, 1992, Textural analysis and modelling of a flood deposit: River Severn, UK, *Earth Surface Processes and Landforms*, **17**, 687–97.

Marstrander, S, 1966, A wooden helve from Hov, on the island of Lokta, Nesna in Helgeland, *Acta Archaeologica*, **37**, 234–41.

McCormick, F, unpub, *The animal bones from Cnip*.

——, 1986, Animal bones from prehistoric Irish burials, *Journal of Irish Archaeology*, **3** (1985–86), 37–48.

——, 1987b, The animal bones, in M Doody, Late Bronze Age settlement at Ballyveelish 2, Co Tipperary, in R M Cleary *et al* (eds), *Archaeological excavations on the Cork–Dublin gas pipeline (1981–82)*, Cork Archaeological Studies No 1, Dept of Archaeology, University College Cork.

——, 1987b, *Stockrearing in Early Christian Ireland*. Unpublished PhD thesis, The Queen's University of Belfast.

——, 1988, The domesticated cat in Early Christian and Medieval Ireland, in P F Wallace and G Mac Niocaill (eds), *Keimilia: Studies in medieval archaeology and history in memory of Tom Delaney*. Galway: University Press.

——, 1991a, The animal bones from Haughey's Fort, *Emania*, **9**, 27–33.

——, 1991b, Evidence for Dairying at Dún Ailinne, *Emania*, **8**, 57–62.

——, 1991c, The effect of the Anglo-Norman settlement on Ireland's wild and domesticated fauna, in P J Crabtree and K Ryan (eds), *Animal use and cultural change*, MASCA research papers in Science and Archaeology, Supplement to Vol 8, 40–52.

——, 1992, Early faunal evidence for dairying, *Oxford Journal of Archaeology*, **11**, 201–9.

——, 1994, Faunal remains from Navan and other late prehistoric sites in Ireland, in J P Mallory and G Stockman (eds), *Ulidia Proceedings of the first International Conference on the Ulster Cycle of Tales*. Belfast: December Publications, 181–6.

McGrail, S, 1978, *Logboats of England and Wales*, *BAR*, Oxford, **51**.

——, (ed), 1981, *Brigg 'raft' and her prehistoric environment*, *BAR*, Oxford, **89**.

——, 1985a, Brigg 'raft' – problems in reconstruction and the assessment of performance, in S McGrail, and E Kentley, (ed), *Sewn Plank Boats*, 165–94. *BAR*, Oxford, **S276**.

——, 1985b, Early Landing places, in A E Herteig (ed), *Conference on waterfront archaeology in northern European towns*, 12–18. Bergen: Historisk Museum.

Megaw, J V S and Simpson, D, 1984, *Introduction to British Prehistory*, Leicester: University Press.

Miles, J, and Kinnaird, J W, 1979, Grazing: with particular reference to birch, juniper and Scots pine in the Scottish highlands, *Scottish Forestry*, **33**, 280–9.

Milles, A, 1989, Plant remains, in A W R Whittle, Two later Bronze Age occupations and an Iron Age Channel on the Gwent foreshore, *Bulletin of the Board of Celtic Studies*, **36**, 209–11.

Millett, M, and McGrail, S, 1987, Archaeology of the Hasholme logboat, *Archaeol J*, **144**, 69–155.

Moloney, A, Keane, M, Jennings, D, and MacDermott, C, 1993, *Survey of the Raised Bogs of County Longford*, Irish Archaeological Wetland Unit Transactions **1**, Dublin.

Moore, P D, 1978, Studies in the vegetational history of mid-Wales, V: stratigraphy and pollen analysis of Llyn Mire in the Wye Valley, *New Phytologist*, **80**, 281–302.

——, 1981, Neolithic land-use in mid-Wales, *Proceedings of the 4th International Conference on Palynology Lucknow*, **3**, 279–90.

——, and Webb, J A, 1978, *An Illustrated Guide to Pollen Analysis*. London: Hodder & Stoughton.

——, ——, and Collinson, M E, 1991, *Pollen Analysis*. 2nd Edition. Oxford: Blackwell Scientific Publications.

Morgan, R A, 1988, Tree-ring studies of wood used in Neolithic and Bronze Age trackways from the Somerset Levels, *BAR*, **184**.

Müller-Beck, H, 1965, Seeburg Bürgäschisee-Süd Volume 5 Holzgeräte und Holzbearbeitung, *Acta Bernensia* II. Verlag Stümpfli, Bern.

Müller-Karpe, H, 1948, Die Urnenfelderkultur in Hanauer Land, *Schriften zur Urgeschichte*, **1**.

Munro, M A R, 1984, An improved algorithm for crossdating tree-ring series, *Tree Ring Bulletin*, **44**, 17–27.

Murrey, J W, and Hawkins, A B, 1976, Sediment transport in the Severn Estuary during the past 8000–9000 years. *Journal of the Geological Society*, **132**, 385–98.

Nayling, N, 1993, Tales from the riverbank: Bronze Age palaeochannels in the alluviated Nedern Valley at Caldicot Castle Lake, Gwent, in J Coles, V Fenwick, and G Hutchinson, (eds), *A spirit of enquiry*. Exeter: Wetlands Archaeology Research Project, 72–6.

Needham, S P, 1980, An assemblage of Late Bronze Age metalworking debris from Dainton, Devon, *Proc Prehist Soc*, **46**, 177–215.

——, 1991, *Excavation and Salvage at Runnymede Bridge, 1978*. British Museum Press, London.

——, 1992, Holocene alluviation and interstratified settlement evidence in the Thames valley at Runnymede Bridge, in S P Needham, and M G Macklin, 1992, (eds), *Alluvial Archaeology in Britain*, 249–60. Oxbow Monograph **27**, Oxbow Books, Oxford.

——, and Longley, D, 1980, Runnymede Bridge, Egham: A late Bronze Age riverside settlement, in J Barrett, and R Bradley, (eds), *The British Later Bronze Age*, 397–46. *BAR*, **83**(ii), Oxford.

——, and Macklin, M G, (eds), 1992, *Alluvial Archaeology in Britain*. Oxbow Monograph **27**.

Neve, J, 1992, An interim report on the dendrochronology of Flag Fen and Fengate, *Antiquity*, **66**, 470–5.

Nichols, M,M, and Biggs, R B, 1985, Estuaries, in R A Davies, Jr, (ed), *Coastal Sedimentary Environments*. Springer-verlag, New York, 77–186.

Noddle, B A, 1973, Determination of the body weight of cattle from bone measurements, in J Matolchi (ed), *Domestikationsforschung und Geschichte der Haustiere*, Akadémiai Kiadó, Budapest.

Northover, J P, 1982, The metallurgy of the Wilburton hoards, *Oxford Journal of Archaeology*, **1**(1), 69–109.

——, 1987, Analysis of the hoard from Clos de la Blanche Pierre, Jersey, *Annual Bulletin of the Société Jersiaise*, **24**(3), 363–79.

——, and Sherratt, A, 1987, Hoards and other groupings represented in the catalogue, in A MacGregor, ed, *Antiquities from Europe and the Near East in the collection of Lord MacAlpine of West Green*. Oxford: Ashmolean Museum, 17–19, 42, also 110, No. 11.78

O'Connor, B, 1980, *Cross-Channel relations in the later Bronze Age*, BAR, Int Ser, **91** (*i & ii*).

O'Meara, J J, (ed), 1982, *The history and topography of Ireland by Gerald of Wales*. Harmondsworth: Penguin.

Orme, B J, and Coles, J M, 1983, Prehistoric woodworking from the Somerset Levels: 1 timber, *Somerset Levels Papers*, **9**, 9–43.

——, and ——, 1985, Prehistoric woodworking from the Somerset Levels: 2. Species selection and prehistoric woodlands, *Somerset Levels Papers*, **11**, 7–24.

Osborne, P J, 1988, A Late Bronze Age Insect Fauna from the River Avon, Warwickshire, England: Its implications for the Terrestrial and Fluvial Environment and for Climate, *J Arch Sci*, **15**, 715–27.

O'Sullivan, A, 1991, *Prehistoric woodworking techniques: the evidence from excavated trackways in the raised bogs of County Longford*. Unpublished MA thesis, University College, Dublin.

Owen-John, H, 1988, The Hill-slope Enclosure in Coed y Cymdda, near Wenvoe, S Glamorgan, *Archaeologia Cambrensis* **CXXXVII**, 43–98.

Pannet, D, and Morey, C, 1976, The origin of the Old River Bed at Shrewsbury, *Shropshire Conservation Trust Bulletin*, No **35**, 7–12.

Parfitt, K, and Fenwick, V, 1993, Rescue of Dover's Bronze Age boat , in J Coles, V Fenwick, and G Hutchinson, (eds), *A spirit of enquiry*. Exeter: Wetlands Archaeology Research Project, 72–6, *et al*, 77–80.

Parry, S J, 1989, Caldicot Castle Lake, in P Crew (ed) *Archaeology in Wales*, **28**, *1988*, 55–6. Porthmadog: Council for British Archaeology Group 2: Wales.

——, and McGrail, S, 1991a, Sewn plank boat and

288

a hard from Caldicot Castle Lake, Gwent, *Newswarp*, **10**, 9–10.

——, and ——, 1991b, Prehistoric plank boat fragment and a hard from Caldicot Castle Lake, Gwent, *Int Journal of Nautical Archaeology*, **20**, 321–4.

——, and ——, 1994, A Bronze Age Sewn Boat Fragment from Caldicot, Gwent, Wales in C Westerdahl (ed), *Crossroads in Ancient Shipbuilding*, Oxford: Oxbow Monograph 40, 21–28.

——, and Parkhouse, J, 1990, Caldicot Castle Lake, in P Crew and S Crew (eds), *Archaeology in Wales*, **29**, *1989*, 47–8. Porthmadog: Council for British Archaeology Group 2: Wales.

Paterson, D M, and Underwood, G J C, 1990, The mudflat ecosystem and epipelic diatoms, *Proc Bristol Naturalist's Society*, **50**, 74–82.

Payne, S, 1973, Kill off patterns in sheep and goats: the mandibles from Asvan Kale, *Anatolian Studies*, **23**, 281–303.

Peacock, D P S, 1969, A contribution to the study of Glastonbury ware from south-western Britain, *Antiq J*, **49**(1969), 41–61.

Pearson, G W, and Stuiver, M, 1986, High-precision calibration of the radiocarbon timescale, 500 BC–2500 BC. *Radiocarbon*, **28**, 839–62.

Peck, R M, 1973, Pollen budget studies in a small Yorkshire catchment, in H J B Birks and R G West (eds), *Quaternary Plant Ecology*, 43–60. Oxford: Blackwell.

Penn, C, 1977, An osteological analysis of the animal remains from the King's Stables, in C J Lynn, Trial excavations at the King's Stables, Tray Townland, Co Down, *Ulster Journal of Archaeology*, **40**, 42–62.

Perini, R, 1987, *Scavi archeologici nella zona palafitticola di Fiave- Carera Part II: Reste della cultura Materiale*. Servizio Beni Culturali della Provincia Autonoma di Trento.

Pigott, C D, 1983, Regeneration of oak-birch woodland following exclusion of sheep, *Journal of Ecology*, **71**, 629–46.

——, and Huntley, J P, 1980, Factors controlling the distribution of *Tilia cordata* at the northern limits of its geographical range. II. History in north-west England, *New Phytologist*, **84**, 145–64.

——, and ——, 1981, Factors controlling the distribution of *Tilia cordata* at the northern limits of its geographical range. III. Nature and causes of seed sterility, *New Phytologist*, **87**, 817–39.

Praeger, R L, 1913, On the buoyancy of the seeds of some Britannic plants, *Proceedings of the Royal Dublin Society*, **14**, 13–62.

Price, M D R, and Moore, P D, 1984, Pollen dispersion in the hills of Wales: a pollen shed hypothesis, *Pollen Spores*, **26**, 127–36.

Price, R, and Watts, L, 1980, Rescue excavations at Combe Hay, Somerset, 1968–1973, *Somerset Archaeol Natur Hist*, **124**, 1–49.

Primas, M, 1984, Bronzezeitlicher Schmuck aus Zinn, *Helvetia Archäologica*, **15**, 33–42.

——, 1985, Tin objects in Bronze Age Europe, in *xxxxx*, ed, *Studi di Paletnologia in onore di Salvatore M Puglisi*. Roma: Università di Roma 'La Sapienza', 554–62.

Pryor, F M M, 1992, Discussion: the Fengate/Northey landscape, *Antiquity*, **66**, 518–31.

Rackham, O, 1980, *Ancient Woodland – its history, vegetation and uses in England*. London: Arnold.

Ranwell, D S, 1974, The salt marsh to tidal woodland transition, *Hydrobiological Bulletin (Amsterdam)*, **8**, 139–51.

Renberg, I, 1990, A procedure for preparing large sets of diatom slides from sediment cores, *Journal of Paleolimnology*, **4**, 87–90.

Richardson, C, 1887, The Severn Tunnel, *Proceedings of the Bristol Naturalist Society*, **5**, 49–81.

Rippon, S, 1996, *The Gwent Levels: The Evolution of a Wetland Landscape*, CBA Res Rep **105**.

Robinson, M A, and Lambrick, G H, 1984, Holocene alluviation and hydrology in the upper Thames Basin, *Nature*, **308**, 809–14.

Rodwell, J S, 1991a, *British Plant Communities. Volume 1: Woodlands and scrub*. Cambridge: University Press.

——, 1991b, *British Plant Communities. Volume 2: Mires and heaths*. Cambridge: University Press.

——, 1992, *British Plant Communities. Volume 3: Grasslands and montane communities*. Cambridge: University Press.

——, 1995, *British Plant Communities. Volume 4: Aquatic, swamp and tall herb fen communities*. Cambridge: University Press.

——, forthcoming, *British Plant Communities. Volume 5: Salt-marsh, maritime cliff and weed communities*. Cambridge: University Press.

Rosenberg, G, 1937, *Hjortspring fundet*. Copenhagen.

Rotnicki, K, and Borowka, R K, 1985, Definition of subfossil meandering palaeochannels, *Earth Surface Processes and Landforms*, **10**, 215–25.

Roy, P S, Thom, B G, and Wright, L D, 1980, Holocene sequences on an embayed high-energy coast: an evolutionary model, *Sedimentary Geology*, **26**, 1–19.

Rychner, V, 1979, *L'âge du Bronze final à Auvernier: typologie et chronolgie des annciennes collections conservées en Suisse, 1–2*. Lausanee: Bibliothèque Historique Vaudoise, *Cahiers d'Archéologie Romande, 15–16*.

——, 1990, Recherches sur les cuiveres et les alliages du l'âge du Bronze moyen et final en Suisse, *Prähistorische Zeitschrift*, **65**(2), 204–17.

Rychner-Faraggi, A M, 1993, *Hauterive-Champréveyres*, Vol 9, *métal et parure au Bronze Final*. Neuchâtel: Musée Cantonal de Neuchâtel, *Archéologie Neuchâteloise* **17**.

Sagar, G R, and Harper, J L, 1964, Biological Flora of the British Isles *Plantago major* L., *P. media* and *P. lanceolata* L., *J Ecology*, **52**, 189–221.

Salisbury, E J, 1942, *The reproductive capacity of plants*. London: G Bell and Sons.

——, 1976, Seed output and the efficacy of dispersal by wind, *Proceedings of the Royal Society of London*, B **192**, 323–9.

Saunders, G E, Burrin, P J, and Wood, S J, 1986, Floodplain and valley fill development in South Wales: some initial findings from the Ilson tributary of the Pennard Pill Valley, Gower, *Cambria*, **13** (2), 189–96.

——, ——, and ——, 1989, Late-glacial and Holocene environmental change in the Gower Peninsula, South Wales: evidence from the alluvial valley fill of the Ilston River, *Quaternary Newsletter*, **59**, 14–23.

Saville, A, 1977/78, Five flint assemblages from excavated sites in Wiltshire, *Wiltshire Arch Mag*, 72–3, 1–27.

——, 1981, The Flint Assemblage in R J Mercer (ed), *Grimes Graves, Norfolk: Excavations 1971–72* Vol II London: Dept. Of the Environment Archaeological Reports, **11**.

——, 1991, The flintwork: Mesolithic, Neolithic and Bronze Age in S P Needham, *Excavation and salvage at Runnymede Bridge, 1978: The Late Bronze Age Waterfront* site, British Museum in association with English Heritage, 327–44.

Savory, H N, 1940, A middle Bronze Age barrow at Crick, Monmouthshire, *Archaeologia Cambrensis*, **95**, 169–91.

——, 1955, Prehistoric Brecknock, *Brycheiniog*, **1**, 79–125.

——, 1958, The Late Bronze Age in Wales: some new discoveries and new interpretations, *Archaeologia Cambrensis*, **107**, 3–63.

——, 1965, The Guilsfield hoard, *Bull Board Celt Stud*, **21**, 179–96.

——, 1971, *Excavations at Dinorben, 1965–9*. Cardiff: National Museum of Wales.

——, 1980, *A Guide Catalogue to the Bronze Age Collections*. Cardiff: National Museum of Wales.

Scaife, R G, 1993, The palynological investigations of the peats and sediments, in S Godbold, and R Turner, *Second Severn Crossing, Archaeological Response: Phase 1, the intertidal zone in Wales*. Cadw (Welsh Historic Monuments), 51–9.

——, 1995, Pollen analysis and radiocarbon dating of the intertidal peats at Caldicot Pill. *Archaeology in the Severn Estuary 1994: Annual Report of the Severn Estuary Levels Research Committee*, 67–80.

——, and Burrin, P J, 1983, Floodplain development in and the vegetational history of the Sussex High Weald and some archaeological implications, *Sussex Archaeological Collections*, **121**, 1–10.

——, and ——, 1992, Archaeological inferences from alluvial sediments: some findings from southern England, in S Needham and M G Macklin (eds), *Alluvial Archaeology in Britain*. Oxbow Monograph **27**, 75–91.

——, and Long, A, 1995, Evidence for Holocene sea-level changes at Caldicot Pill, *Archaeology in the Severn Estuary 1994: Annual Report of the Severn Estuary Levels Research Committee*, 81–6.

Schoch, W H, Pawlik, B, and Schweingruber, F H, 1988, *Botanical macro-remains*. Berne and Stuttgart: Paul Haupt.

Schweingruber, F, 1978, *Microscopic Wood Anatomy*.

Shennan, I, 1983, Flandrian and Late Devensian sea-level changes and coastal movements in England and Wales, in D E Smith, and A G Dawson, (eds), *Shorelines and Isostasy*. London: Academic Press, 255–83.

——, 1989, Holocene crustal movements and sea-level changes in Great Britain, *Journal of Quaternary Science*, **4**, 77–89.

——, Tooley, M J, Davis, M J, and Haggart, B A, 1983, Analysis and interpretation of Holocene sea-level data, *Nature*, **302**, 404–6.

Sherrod, B L, Rollins, H B, and Kennedy, S K, 1989, Subrecent intertidal diatoms from St Catherines Island, Georgia: Taphonomic Implications, *Journal of Coastal Research*, **5**, 665–77.

Shotton, F W, 1978, Archaeological inferences from the study of alluvium in the Lower Severn-Avon valleys, in S Limbrey, and J G Evans, (eds), *The effect of man on the landscape, the Lowland Zone, CBA Res Rep* **21**, London, 27–32.

Silver, I A, 1969, The ageing of domestic animals, in D Brothwell and E Higgs (eds), *Science and Archaeology*, London, 283–302 (2nd edition).

Sjøvold, T, 1969, *Oseberg find*. Oslo: Universitetets Oldsaksamling.

Smith, A G, and Cloutman, E W, 1988, Reconstruction of Holocene vegetation history in three dimensions at Waun-Fignen-Felen, an upland site in south Wales, *Philosophical Transactions of the Royal Society of London*, B **322**, 159–219.

——, and Morgan, L A, 1989, A succession to ombrotrophic bog in the Gwent Levels, and its demise: a Welsh parallel to the peats of the Somerset Levels, *New Phytologist*, **112**, 145–67.

Smith, I F, 1965, *Windmill Hill and Avebury*. Oxford: Clarendon Press.

Sparks, B W, 1961, The ecological interpretation of Quaternary non-marine Mollusca, *Proceedings of the Linnean Society of London*, **172**, 71–80.

290

Sprockhoff, E, 1934, *Die Germanischen Vollgriffschwerter der jüngeren Bronzezeit*, Berlin: de Gruyter, *Römisch-Germanische Forschungen*, **9**.

Stace, C, 1991, *New Flora of the British Isles*, Cambridge: University Press.

Stead, I M, 1993, Many more Iron Age shields from Britain, *Antiq Journ*, **71**, 1–35.

Straub, F, 1990, *Hauterive-Champréveyres, 4. Diatomées et reconstitution des environnements préhistoriques*, St Blaise, Editions du Ruau, Archéologie neuchâteloise, **10**.

Stuiver, M, and Pearson, G W, 1986, High-precision calibration of the radiocarbon timescale AD 1950–500 BC, *Radiocarbon*, **28**, 805–38.

Tansley, A G, 1968, *Britain's Green Mantle*, 2nd edn. Allen and Unwin.

Tauber, H, 1965, Differential pollen dispersion and the interpretation of pollen diagrams, *Danmarks Geologiske Undersogelse* Series II, **89**, 1–69.

——, 1967, Investigation of the mode of pollen transfer in forested areas, *Review of Palaeobotany and Palynology*, **3**, 277–87.

Taylor, M, 1981, *Wood in Archaeology*. Aylesbury: Shire Archaeology.

——, 1992, Flag Fen: the wood, *Antiquity*, **66**, 476–98.

——, and Pryor, F, 1990, Bronze Age building techniques at Flag fen, Peterborough, England, *World Archaeology*, **21** (3), 425–34.

Taylor, M P, 1993, *Holocene Sedimentation in River Severn Catchments*. Unpublished PhD thesis, University of Wales, Aberystwyth.

——, and Lewin, J, in press, River behaviour and Holocene alluviation: the River Severn at Welshpool, mid-Wales, UK, *Earth Surface Processes and Landforms*.

Therkorn, L L, Brandt, R W, Pals, J P, and Taylor, M, 1984, An Early Iron Age Farmstead: Site Q of the Assendelver Polders Project, *Proc Prehist Soc*, **50**, 351–73.

Thompson, M T, and Walsh, J N, 1983, *A handbook of inductively coupled plasma spectrometry*. London: Blackie and Son Ltd.

Tilley, C, 1994, *Phenomenology in the Landscape: Places, Paths and Monuments*. Oxford: Beug.

Trett, R, forthcoming, Excavations at Chapeltump II, Gwent.

Turner, J, 1962, The Tilia decline: an anthropogenic interpretation, *New Phytologist*, **61**, 328–41.

——, 1964, The anthropogenic factor in vegetational history I Tregaron and Whixall Mosses, *New Phytologist*, **63**, 73–90.

Underwood, G J C, 1994, Seasonal and spatial variation in epipelic algal assemblages in the Severn Estuary, *Diatom Research*, **9** No 2, 451–72.

——, and Paterson, D M, 1993a, Seasonal changes in diatom biomass, sediment stability and biogenic stabilization in the Severn Estuary, *J Mar Biol Ass*, U K, **73**, 871–87.

——, and ——, 1993b, Recovery of intertidal benthic diatoms after biocide treatment and associated sediment dynamics, *J Mar Biol Ass*, U K, **73**, 25–45.

——, and Yallop, M L, 1994, *Navicula pargemina sp.nov.*- a small epipelic species from the Severn Estuary, U K, *Diatom Research*, **9** No 2, 473–8.

Van de Noort, R, 1993, *Wetland Heritage*, Humber Wetland Project. Hull.

van Wijngaarden-Bakker, L H, 1986, The animal remains from the Beaker settlement at Newgrange, Co Meath: Final report, *Proceedings of the Royal Irish Academy*, **86C**, 17–111.

Vos, P C, and de Wolf, H, 1988, Methodological aspects of palaeoecological diatom research in coastal areas of the Netherlands, *Geologie en Mijnbouw*, **67**, 31–40.

Wade, A E, 1970, *The Flora of Monmouthshire*. Cardiff: National Museum of Wales.

Wagner, K, 1930, Rezente hunderassen, *Skrifter Norske Videnskab*, Akademi Oslo, **3**, 1–157.

Wainwright, G J, 1971, *Durrington Walls: Excavations 1966–68* London: Research Report of the Society of Antiquaries XXIX.

Walden, H W, 1976, A nomenclatural list of the land Mollusca of the British Isles, *Journal of Conchology*, **29**, 21–5.

Walker, M J C, Bell, M, Caseldine A E, Smith, D N, Hunter, K, and James, J H, unpublished, *Palaeoecological investigations of mid- and late Holocene buried peats on the Caldicot Levels, South-east Wales*.

——, and James, J, 1993, A radiocarbon dated pollen record from Vurlong Reen, near Caldicot, South Wales, in M Bell, *Archaeology in the Severn Estuary 1993*, Annual Report of the Severn Estuary Levels Research Committee, 65–70.

——, and ——, unpublished, Pollen records from Barland's Farm, Magor, South Wales.

Waller, M, 1994, Paludification and pollen representation: the influence of wetland size on Tilia representation in pollen diagrams, *The Holocene*, **4**, 430–4.

Welch, F B A, and Trotter, F M, 1961, *Geology of the Country around Monmouth and Chepstow*. Memoirs of the Geological Survey, H M S O, UK.

Werff, A, Van Der, and Huls, H, 1957–1974, *Diatomeenflora van Nederland*, 10 volumes.

Westlake, D F, 1971, Water plants and the aqueous environment, *Biology of Human Affairs*, **36**, 23–32.

Wheeler, E A, and La Pasha, C A, 1986, *Computer Assisted Multiple Entry Key for Computer Assisted Wood Identification (GUESS)*, N Carolina State University.

——, Pearson, R G, La Pasha, C A, Hatley, W, and

Zack, T, 1986, *North Carolina Agriculture Station Bulletin*, **474**.

Whitten, D G A, and Brooks, J R V, 1972, *Dictionary of Geology*. Middlesex: Penguin.

Whittle, A W R, 1989, Two Later Bronze Age occupations and an Iron Age channel on the Gwent foreshore, *Bulletin of the Board of Celtic Studies*, **36**, 200–23.

Williams, G J, 1968, The buried channel and superficial deposits of the Lower Usk, and their correlation with similar features in the Lower Severn, *Proceedings of the Geologists Association*, **79**, 325–48.

Williams, J T, 1963, Biological Flora of the British Isles *Chenopodium album*, *Journal of Ecology*, **51**, 711–25.

Wills, L J, 1938, The Pleistocene development of the Severn from Bridgnorth to the sea, *Quarterly Journal of the Geological Society*, **94**, 161–242.

Woodward, A, 1989, The Prehistoric Pottery, in P Ellis, Norton Fitzwarren Hillfort: A Report on the Excavations by Nancy and Philip Langmaid between 1968 and 1971, *Somerset Archaeol Natur Hist*, **133**, 39–53.

——, 1990, The Bronze Age pottery in M Bell, *Brean Down Excavations 1983–1987*, English Heritage Arch Report no **15**. London.

——, 1996, The prehistoric and native pottery, in G Hughes, *The Excavation of a Late Prehistoric and Romano-British Settlement at Thornwell Farm, Chepstow, Gwent, 1992, BAR Brit Ser*, **244**.

——, forthcoming, The Bronze Age pottery, in Trett, forthcoming.

Wright, E V, 1990a, *The Ferriby Boats: Seacraft of the Bronze Age*. London: Routledge.

Appendix I: Plant Macrofossil Tables

Table 64 Plant macrofossils from sample Column 1. 250µm fraction: Rare, r ≤ 4; Occasional, oc = 5 < 24; Moderate, m = 25 < 49; Frequent, f = 50 < 99; Abundant, a ≥ 100

Phase			I	I	V	V–VI	VI	VI/VII	VI/VII	VII	VIII
Sample number			2078	2074	2070	2068	2066	2062	2058	2054	2050
Depth (cm)			140–145	120–125	100–105	90–95	80–85	60–65	40–45	20–25	0–5
Height + (m) OD			2.373 -2.423	2.573 -2.623	2.773 -2.823	2.873 -2.923	2.973 -3.023	3.173 -3.223	3.373 -3.423	3.573 -3.623	3.773 -3.823
Sample weight (g)			1000	1000	1000	1000	1000	1000	1000	1000	1000
RANUNCULACEAE											
Ranunculus repens type	(Creeping buttercup)		–	–	5	4	6	4	35	1	–
R. sceleratus L.	(Celery-leaved buttercup)		132	6	16	23	40	6	3	8	5r
R. cf. *flammula* L.	(Lesser spearwort)		–	–	–	–	–	–	3	–	–
R. Subgenus *Batrachium* (DC) A. Gray	(Crowfoots)		3	1	1	32oc	55	5	1	3	r
Ranunculus spp.	(Buttercups)		–	–	–	–	3	–	2	–	–
URTICACEAE											
Urtica dioica L.	(Common nettle)		20r	150oc	9r	22oc	55r	19r	18r	20	4r
U. urens L.	(Small nettle)		–	–	–	–	–	–	1	–	–
BETULACEAE											
Betula spp.	(Birch)		–	–	–	1	–	1	1	–	–
Alnus glutinosa (L.) Gaertner	(Alder)		–	1	2	11	6	16	13	–	–
Corylus avellana L. frags	(Hazel)		–	–	–	1	–	–	–	–	–
CHENOPODIACEAE											
C. polyspermum L.	(Many-seeded goosefoot)		–	–	–	–	2	1	–	–	–
C. ficifolium Smith	(Fig-leaved goosefoot)		–	–	–	–	–	–	–	2	–
C. cf *ficifolium* Smith			–	–	1	–	–	–	–	–	–
C. album L.	(Fat-hen)		–	–	11	3	5	7	8	6	–
Atriplex prostrata Boucher ex DC.	(Spear-leaved orache)		–	–	–	–	4	–	–	–	–
Atriplex spp.	(Oraches)		–	2	43	16	23	–	8	7	–
Suaeda maritima (L.) Dumort.	(Annual sea-blite)		–	1	–	–	2	–	–	–	–

294

Table 64 (cont.)

		I	I	V	V–VI	VI	VI/VII	VI/VII	VII	VIII
Phase										
Sample number		2078	2074	2070	2068	2066	2062	2058	2054	2050
Depth (cm)		140–145	120–125	100–105	90–95	80–85	60–65	40–45	20–25	0–5
Height + (m) OD		2.373 -2.423	2.573 -2.623	2.773 -2.823	2.873 -2.923	2.973 -3.023	3.173 -3.223	3.373 -3.423	3.573 -3.623	3.773 -3.823
Sample weight (g)		1000	1000	1000	1000	1000	1000	1000	1000	1000
PORTULACEAE										
Montia fontana L.	(Blinks)	–	–	–	–	–	–	1	–	–
CARYOPHYLLACEAE										
Stellaria media (L.) Villars	(Common chickweed)	–	–	1	3	5	1	2	–	–
S. palustris Retz.	(Marsh stitchwort)	–	–	1	–	–	–	1	–	–
S. cf. *palustris* Retz.		–	–	–	–	1	–	–	–	–
S. uliginosa Murray	(Bog stitchwort)	–	–	–	2	3	2	7	1	–
Stellaria sp.	(Stitchworts)	–	–	–	1	–	–	1	–	–
Cerastium sp.	(Mouse-ears)	–	–	r	–	r	–	oc	–	–
Sagina sp.	(Pearlworts)	–	–	–	oc	–	–	r	–	–
Spergularia spp.	(Sea-spurreys)	r	–	–	oc	–	r	r	–	–
Lychnis flos-cuculi L.	(Ragged robin)	1	–	–	1	12	2	–	–	–
Silene sp.	(Campions)	–	–	–	–	–	–	2	–	–
Caryophyllaceae indet.		–	–	–	oc	–	–	1	–	–
POLYGONACEAE										
Persicaria maculosa Gray	(Redshank)	–	–	–	–	–	–	1	1	–
P. lapathifolia (L.) Gray	(Pale persicaria)	–	–	–	–	–	1	–	–	–
P. hydropiper (L.) Spach	(Water-pepper)	–	–	–	4	2	–	–	–	–
Persicaria spp.	(Knotweeds)	–	–	–	–	1	–	1	1	–
Polygonum aviculare L.	(Knotgrass)	–	–	6	1	1	2	–	2	–
Rumex acetosella L.	(Sheep's sorrel)	–	–	–	–	2	1	–	4	1
R. hydrolapathum type	(Water dock)	–	–	3	–	–	–	–	1	–
R. cf. *crispus* L.	(Curled dock)	–	–	–	1	–	–	–	–	–

295

Table 64 (cont.)

		Phase	VIII	VII	VI/VII	VI/VII	VI	V–VI	V	I	I
		Sample number	2050	2054	2058	2062	2066	2068	2070	2074	2078
		Depth (cm)	0–5	20–25	40–45	60–65	80–85	90–95	100–105	120–125	140–145
		Height + (m) OD	3.773 / –3.823	3.573 / –3.623	3.373 / –3.423	3.173 / –3.223	2.973 / –3.023	2.873 / –2.923	2.773 / –2.823	2.573 / –2.623	2.373 / –2.423
		Sample weight (g)	1000	1000	1000	1000	1000	1000	1000	1000	1000
R. conglomeratus Murray with perianth	(Clustered dock)		–	7	–	9	4	4	–	–	–
R. cf. *conglomeratus*			–	6	3	2	3	5	8	–	·
R. cf. *sanguineus* L.	(Wood dock)		–	–	–	–	–	–	2	–	–
R. cf. *obtusifolius* L.	(Broad-leaved dock)		–	2	–	–	–	–	–	–	–
R. cf. *palustris* Smith	(Marsh dock)		1	–	–	1	–	–	1	–	–
Rumex spp.	(Docks)		3	4	2	2	5	19	4	–	–
Rumex sp. perianth frags.			–	4	–	–	–	3	–	–	–
CLUSIACEAE											
Hypericum sp.	(St. John's-worts)		–	–	–	oc	oc	oc	r	–	–
MALVACEAE											
Malva sylvestris L.	(Common mallow)		–	5	33	–	–	3	1	–	–
Althaea officinalis L.	(Marsh mallow)		–	6	27	1	5	–	1	–	–
BRASSICACEAE											
Rorippa nasturtium-aquaticum (L.) Hayeck	(Water-cress)		–	–	–	–	–	1	–	–	–
Rorippa cf. *nasturtium-aquaticum* (L.) Hayeck			–	–	–	–	–	–	r	–	r
R. palustris (L.) Besser	(Marsh yellow-cress)		–	–	–	–	1	–	–	–	–
R. cf. *amphibia* (L.) Besser	(Great yellow-cress)		–	–	1	–	–	r	–	–	–
Brassicaceae indet.			–	–	1	–	–	–	–	–	–
PRIMULACEAE											
Glaux maritima L.	(Sea-milkwort)		–	–	3	–	1	1	–	–	–
ROSACEAE											

296

Table 64 (cont.)

Phase				VIII	VII	VI/VII	VI/VII	VI	V–VI	V	I	I
Sample number				2050	2054	2058	2062	2066	2068	2070	2074	2078
Depth (cm)				0–5	20–25	40–45	60–65	80–85	90–95	100–105	120–125	140–145
Height + (m) OD				3.773 -3.823	3.573 -3.623	3.373 -3.423	3.173 -3.223	2.973 -3.023	2.873 -2.923	2.773 -2.823	2.573 -2.623	2.373 -2.423
Sample weight (g)				1000	1000	1000	1000	1000	1000	1000	1000	1000
Rubus fruticosus L. agg.	(Bramble)			–	4	2	–	5	5	8	4	–
Rubus cf. *idaeus* L.	(Raspberry)			–	–	–	–	1	–	–	–	–
Rubus sp.	(Brambles)			2	–	–	r	1r	1r	2	–	–
Potentilla anserina L.	(Silverweed)			–	16	30	2	–	9	1	–	–
Aphanes arvensis L.	(Parsley piert)			–	–	–	–	–	2	1	–	–
A. inexspectata Lippert	(Slender parsley-piert)			–	1	1	1r	–	–	–	1	1
Prunus spinosa L.	(Blackthorn)			–	–	–	–	2	1	1	–	–
Crataegus monogyna Jacq.	(Hawthorn)			–	–	–	–	–	–	–	–	–
Rosaceae thorn				–	–	–	–	–	r	–	–	–
cf. Rosaceae				1	–	–	–	–	r	–	–	–
LYTHRACEAE												
Lythrum sp.	(Purple-loosestrifes)			–	r	–	1	oc	oc	–	oc	–
ONAGRACEAE												
Epilobium hirsutum type	(Great willowherb)			oc	–	–	r	4	3oc	r	–	1
APIACEAE												
Berula erecta (Hudson) Cov.	(Lesser water-parsnip)			–	1	–	–	–	–	–	–	–
Apium graveolens L.	(Wild celery)			–	1	–	–	4	2	–	–	–
A. nodiflorum (L.) Lag.	(Fool's water-cress)			–	–	1	–	–	1	1	–	–
A. nodiflorum / inundatum	(Fool's water-cress/lesser marshwort)			–	–	–	–	–	5	2	–	–
Apium sp.	(Marshworts)			–	–	–	–	1	–	–	–	–
Peucedanum sp.	(Hog's fennels)			–	–	1	–	–	–	–	–	–
Apiaceae indet.				–	–	2r	r	–	–	–	–	–
SOLANACEAE												

Table 64 (cont.)

Phase	I	I	V	V–VI	VI	VI/VII	VI/VII	VII	VIII
Sample number	2078	2074	2070	2068	2066	2062	2058	2054	2050
Depth (cm)	140–145	120–125	100–105	90–95	80–85	60–65	40–45	20–25	0–5
Height + (m) OD	2.373 –2.423	2.573 –2.623	2.773 –2.823	2.873 –2.923	2.973 –3.023	3.173 –3.223	3.373 –3.423	3.573 –3.623	3.773 –3.823
Sample weight (g)	1000	1000	1000	1000	1000	1000	1000	1000	1000
Solanum nigrum L. (Black nightshade)	–	–	2	–	1	–	–	1	–
S. dulcamara L. (Bittersweet)	–	3	–	2	–	–	6	–	–
LAMIACEAE									
Stachys cf. *palustris* L. (Marsh woundwort)	1	–	–	–	1	–	–	–	–
Prunella vulgaris L. (Selfheal)	–	–	–	–	–	–	2	–	–
cf. *Clinopodium acinos* (L.) Kuntze (Basil thyme)	–	–	–	–	–	–	2	–	–
Lycopus europaeus L. (Gypsywort)	1	–	–	5	3	–	–	2	–
Mentha arvensis / aquatica (Corn/water mint)	111r	2	7	19	28	2	–	–	–
HIPPURIDACEAE									
Hippuris vulgaris L. (Mare's-tail)	–	–	–	–	2	–	–	–	–
CALLITRICHACEAE									
Callitriche spp. (Water-starworts)	–	–	2	11	1	1	1	7	–
PLANTAGINACEAE									
Plantago major L. (Greater plantain)	6	–	18r	38oc	8	–	2r	4oc	–
SCROPHULARIACEAE									
Veronica beccabunga L. (Brooklime)	–	r	oc	oc	r	oc	oc	m	oc
CAPRIFOLIACEAE									
Sambucus nigra L. (Elder)	1	–	1	8	15	–	2	–	1f
ASTERACEAE									
cf. *Carduus* sp. (Thistles)	–	–	–	–	1	–	–	–	–
C. cf. *palustre* (L.) Scop. (Marsh thistle)	–	–	–	1	3	–	–	–	–
C. cf. *arvense* (L.) Scop. (Creeping thistle)	–	–	1	16	3	–	1	3	–
Cirsium sp. (Thistles)	–	–	–	–	2	–	–	1	–

Table 64 (cont.)

Phase		VIII	VII	VI/VII	VI/VII	VI	V-VI	V	I	I
Sample number		2050	2054	2058	2062	2066	2068	2070	2074	2078
Depth (cm)		0–5	20–25	40–45	60–65	80–85	90–95	100–105	120–125	140–145
Height +(m) OD		3.773 -3.823	3.573 -3.623	3.373 -3.423	3.173 -3.223	2.973 -3.023	2.873 -2.923	2.773 -2.823	2.573 -2.623	2.373 -2.423
Sample weight (g)		1000	1000	1000	1000	1000	1000	1000	1000	1000
Lapsana communis L.	(Nipplewort)	–	1	–	1	–	–	–	–	–
S. arvensis L.	(Perennial sow-thistle)	–	–	–	–	–	3	–	–	–
S. asper (L.) Hill	(Prickly sow-thistle)	–	1	–	3	3	–	2	–	–
Eupatorium cannabinum L.	(Hemp agrimony)	–	–	–	–	–	3r	1	77	–
Asteraceae indet.		–	–	–	–	–	r	–	–	–
ALISMATACEAE										
Alisma spp.	(Water plantain)	–	3	3	1	6	10	3	–	36
POTAMOGETONACEAE										
P. berchtoldii Fieber	(Small pondweed)	–	–	203	–	17	–	–	–	–
P. cf. *berchtoldii* Fieber		–	–	–	–	–	1	–	–	–
Potamogeton sp.	(Pondweed)	–	–	8	–	–	1	1	–	–
cf. *Potamogeton* sp.		–	–	3	–	–	–	–	–	–
ZANNICHELLIACEAE										
Zannichellia palustris L.	(Horned pondweed)	–	1	–	–	–	1	–	–	–
LEMNACEAE										
Lemna gibba L.	(Fat duckweed)	–	1	3	–	–	–	–	–	6
L. trisulca L	(Ivy-leaved duckweed)	–	–	1	–	–	–	–	–	–
Lemna spp.	(Duckweeds)	–	oc	–	–	–	–	–	–	–
JUNCACEAE										
Juncus spp.	(Rushes)	f	f	oc	oc	1m	a	oc	oc	oc
CYPERACEAE										
Eleocharis palustris /uniglumis	(Common/slender spike-rush)	–	4	–	2	6	5	–	–	–

299

Table 64 (cont.)

Phase	I	I	V	V-VI	VI	VI/VII	VI/VII	VII	VIII
Sample number	2078	2074	2070	2068	2066	2062	2058	2054	2050
Depth (cm)	140–145	120–125	100–105	90–95	80–85	60–65	40–45	20–25	0–5
Height + (m) OD	2.373 -2.423	2.573 -2.623	2.773 -2.823	2.873 -2.923	2.973 -3.023	3.173 -3.223	3.373 -3.423	3.573 -3.623	3.773 -3.823
Sample weight (g)	1000	1000	1000	1000	1000	1000	1000	1000	1000
Bolboschoenus maritimus /Schoenoplectus lacustris (Sea/common club-rush)	–	–	1	1	1	–	1	–	–
S. tabernaemontani (C. Gmelin) Palla (Grey club-rush)	–	–	2	2	4	–	–	1	–
Cladium mariscus (L.) Pohl (Great fen-sedge)	–	–	–	–	–	1	1	–	–
Carex paniculata L. (Greater tussock sedge)	–	–	–	1	2	1	1	1	–
C. otrubae Podp. (False fox-sedge)	3	2	–	4	4	4	6	–	–
C. pseudocyperus L. (Cyperus sedge)	–	–	–	–	3	–	–	–	–
C. cf. *rostrata* Stokes (Bottle sedge)	–	–	–	–	–	1	–	–	–
C. cf. *vesicaria* L. (Bladder-sedge)	–	–	1	–	–	–	–	–	–
C. cf. *distans* L. (Distant sedge)	–	–	–	–	4	2	–	–	–
C. cf. *hostiana* DC. (Tawny sedge)	–	–	–	–	–	2	1	–	–
C. cf. *pallescens* L. (Pale sedge)	–	–	–	1	10	4	–	1	–
C. cf. *digitata* L. (Fingered sedge)	–	–	–	–	1	–	–	–	–
Carex sp. - trigonous	–	–	2	–	–	–	–	–	–
Carex spp. (Sedges)	–	–	–	–	–	5	3	2	–
Carex sp. utricle	–	–	–	–	–	1	3	–	–
POACEAE									
Poa annua L. (Annual meadow-grass)	–	–	–	–	–	–	1	–	–
Poa cf. *annua* L.	–	–	–	–	–	1	–	–	–
Phalaris arundinacea L. (Reed canary-grass)	–	–	1	–	–	1	52	6	–
Phragmites australis (Cav.) Trin. ex Steudal (Common reed)	–	–	–	–	–	–	5	–	–
Poaceae indet. <2mm	2	–	–	10	9	16	7	2	–
Poaceae indet. >2mm	–	–	4	7	4	1	22	5	–

Table 64 (cont.)

Phase		I	I	V	V-VI	VI	VI/VII	VI/VII	VII	VIII
Sample number		2078	2074	2070	2068	2066	2062	2058	2054	2050
Depth (cm)		140–145	120–125	100–105	90–95	80–85	60–65	40–45	20–25	0–5
Height + (m) OD		2.373 -2.423	2.573 -2.623	2.773 -2.823	2.873 -2.923	2.973 -3.023	3.173 -3.223	3.373 -3.423	3.573 -3.623	3.773 -3.823
Sample weight (g)		1000	1000	1000	1000	1000	1000	1000	1000	1000
cf. Poaceae indet. >2mm		–	–	–	–	–	1	2	–	–
SPARGANIACEAE										
Sparganium cf. natans L.	(Least bur-reed)	–	–	–	–	2	–	–	–	–
Sparganium sp.	(Bur-reed)	–	–	–	1	6	4	22	–	–
OTHER REMAINS										
Bud scales		–	–	–	1	–	–	–	–	–
Tree buds		–	–	–	–	1	–	–	1	–
PTEROPSIDA										
Pteridium aquilinum (L.) Kuhn leaf frags	(Bracken)	–	–	–	6	–	–	–	–	–
CHAROPHYTA										
Chara sp.	(Stoneworts)	oc	r	oc	oc	r	–	–	–	–
POLYZOA										
Plumatella sp. statoblasts		–	–	r	–	r	r	r	oc	r
CLADOCERA										
Daphnia sp. ephippia		r	–	–	oc	r	r	r	oc	r
No. of items (quantified)		325	249	181	349	417	141	581	162	18

250µm fraction: rare, r ≤ 4; occasional, oc = 5 < 24; moderate, m = 35 < 49; frequent, f = 50 < 99; abundant, a ≥ 100

301

Table 65   Plant macrofossils from sample Column 2 and spot sample 23166 (Column 4)

Phase		II	II	III	III	III
Sample number		23061	23059	23057	23055	23166
Depth (cm)		40–45	30–35	20–25	10–15	0–5
Height + (m) OD		2.39–2.44	2.49–2.54	2.59–2.64	2.69–2.74	2.85–2.90
Sample weight (g)		250	250	250	250	250
RANUNCULACEAE						
Ranunculus repens type	(Creeping buttercup)	–	2	4	–	11
R. sceleratus L.	(Celery-leaved buttercup)	–	6	15	5	11
R. Subgenus Batrachium (DC) A. Gray	(Crowfoots)	–	1	4	2r	67
Ranunculus spp.	(Buttercups)	–	–	5	1	–
URTICACEAE						
Urtica dioica L.	(Common nettle)	1	4	13r	7r	4r
BETULACEAE						
Betula spp.	(Birch)	–	–	1	–	–
Alnus glutinosa (L.) Gaertner	(Alder)	–	1	1	–	4
A. glutinosa (L.) Gaertner	cone-scale	1	–	–	–	–
Corylus avellana L. frags	(Hazel)	1	1	–	–	–
CHENOPODIACEAE						
C. ficifolium Smith	(Fig-leaved goosefoot)	–	–	–	1	–
C. album L.	(Fat-hen)	–	–	13	4	3
A. patula L.	(Common orache)	–	2	4	2	1
Atriplex spp.	(Orache)	1	4	41	1	8
Suaeda maritima (L.) Dumort.	(Annual sea-blite)	–	–	2	–	–
Chenopodiaceae indet.		2	1	–	–	–
PORTULACEAE						
Montia fontana L.	(Blinks)	–	–	–	1	–
CARYOPHYLLACEAE						
Stellaria media (L.) Villars	(Common chickweed)	–	1	1	1	2
S. palustris Retz.	(Marsh stitchwort)	1	–	1	1	–
S. uliginosa Murray	(Bog stitchwort)	–	1	–	1	–

Table 65 (cont.)

	III	III	III	II	II
Phase	III	III	III	II	II
Sample number	23166	23055	23057	23059	23061
Depth (cm)	0–5	10–15	20–25	30–35	40–45
Height + (m) OD	2.85–2.90	2.69–2.74	2.59–2.64	2.49–2.54	2.39–2.44
Sample weight (g)	250	250	250	250	250
Stellaria sp. (Stitchworts)	2	1	–	–	–
POLYGONACEAE					
Polygonum. aviculare L. (Knotgrass)	8	1	–	–	1
Rumex acetosella L. (Sheep's sorrel)	–	2	–	–	1
R. hydrolapathum type (Water dock)	4	14	17	5	4
R. cf. *crispus* L. (Curled dock)	12	–	11	3	1
R. conglomeratus Murray with perianth (Clustered dock)	20	16	38	–	1
R. cf. *conglomeratus* (Clustered dock)	8	8	72	11	-
R. cf. *palustris* Smith (Marsh dock)	–	1	1	1	1
Rumex spp. (Docks)	2	7	52	3	1
Rumex sp. perianth frags.	–	–	3	–	–
CLUSIACEAE					
Hypericum sp. (St. John's-worts)	1oc	1	r	r	–
MALVACEAE					
Malva sylvestris L. (Common mallow)	–	1	–	–	–
Althaea officinalis L. (Marsh-mallow)	–	–	1	–	–
BRASSICACEAE					
Rorippa nasturtium-aquaticum (L.) Hayeck (Water-cress)	r	–	–	–	–
Rorippa cf. *nasturtium-aquaticum* (L.) Hayeck	–	–	r	r	–
R. palustris (L.) Besser (Marsh yellow-cress)	1r	–	–	–	1
PRIMULACEAE					
Anagallis minima /Samolus valerandi (Chaffweed/Brookweed)	–	r	–	–	r
Glaux maritima L. (Sea-milkwort)	1	–	–	–	–
ROSACEAE					

Table 65 (cont.)

Phase		III	III	III	II	II
Sample number		23166	23055	23057	23059	23061
Depth (cm)		0–5	10–15	20–25	30–35	40–45
Height + (m) OD		2.85–2.90	2.69–2.74	2.59–2.64	2.49–2.54	2.39–2.44
Sample weight (g)		250	250	250	250	250
Rubus fruticosus L. agg.	(Bramble)	8	4	–	–	–
Rubus sp.	(Brambles)	1r	r	3	3	–
Rubus sp. thorn		–	2	2	–	–
Potentilla anserina L.	(Silverweed)	3	3	1	2	–
A. inexspectata Lippert	(Slender parsley-piert)	–	1r	1	–	–
Prunus spinosa L.	(Blackthorn)	3	–	–	1	–
Prunus sp.	(Cherries)	1	–	–	–	–
C. monogyna Jacq. thorn		1	–	–	–	–
Rosaceae thorn cf. Rosaceae		1	–	–	–	–
LYTHRACEAE						
Lythrum sp.	(Purple-loosestrifes)	r	–	–	–	–
ONAGRACEAE						
Epilobium hirsutum type	(Great willowherb)	r	1r	2r	–	–
APIACEAE						
Conium maculatum L.	(Hemlock)	–	–	1	–	–
Apium graveolens L.	(Wild celery)	2	3	14	–	–
A. nodiflorum (L.) Lag.	(Fool's water-cress)	–	1	6	–	–
A. repens (Jacq.) Lag.	(Creeping marshwort)	–	–	1	–	–
Apium spp.	(Marshworts)	1	2	3	–	–
Apiaceae sp. indet.		r	3r	–	–	–
SOLANACEAE						
S. dulcamara L.	(Bittersweet)	–	2	1	1	–
LAMIACEAE						
Lycopus europaeus L.	(Gypsywort)	1	–	1	1	–
Mentha arvensis/aquatica	(Corn/water mint)	1	2	1	–	–

Table 65 (cont.)

Phase		II	II	III	III	III
Sample number		23061	23059	23057	23055	23166
Depth (cm)		40–45	30–35	20–25	10–15	0–5
Height + (m) OD		2.39–2.44	2.49–2.54	2.59–2.64	2.69–2.74	2.85–2.90
Sample weight (g)		250	250	250	250	250
HIPPURIDACEAE						
Hippuris vulgaris L.	(Mare's-tail)	–	–	1	–	–
CALLITRICHACEAE						
Callitriche spp.	(Water-starworts)	–	r	–	1r	2oc
cf. *Callitriche* sp.		–	–	–	–	1
PLANTAGINACEAE						
Plantago major L.	(Greater plantain)	3r	7r	44r	27r	41oc
P. lanceolata L.	(Ribwort plantain)	–	–	–	–	1
SCROPHULARIACEAE						
Veronica beccabunga L.	(Brooklime)	r	–	–	oc	oc
CAPRIFOLIACEAE						
Sambucus nigra L.	(Elder)	1	1	1	–	–
ASTERACEAE						
cf. *Carduus* sp.	(Thistles)	–	–	–	–	1
Carduus/Cirsium		–	–	–	1	–
Cirsium cf. *vulgare* (Savi) Ten.	(Spear thistle)	–	–	1	3	2r
C. cf. *palustre* (L.) Scop.	(Marsh thistle)	1	–	–	–	–
C. cf. *arvense* (L.) Scop.	(Creeping thistle)	1	5	5	4	3
Cirsium sp.	(Thistles)	–	1	1	–	2
S. arvensis L.	(Perennial sow-thistle)	–	–	–	1	–
S. asper (L.) Hill	(Prickly sow-thistle)	–	1	5	2	1
Sonchus sp.	(Sow-thistles)	–	1	–	–	–
Aster tripolium L.	(Sea aster)	–	–	1	–	–
Senecio sp.	(Ragworts)	–	–	2	–	–
Eupatorium cannabinum L.	(Hemp agrimony)	1	1	1	–	r

Table 65 (cont.)

		Phase	II	II	III	III	III
		Sample number	23061	23059	23057	23055	23166
		Depth (cm)	40–45	30–35	20–25	10–15	0–5
		Height + (m) OD	2.39–2.44	2.49–2.54	2.59–2.64	2.69–2.74	2.85–2.90
		Sample weight (g)	250	250	250	250	250
ALISMATACEAE							
Alisma spp.	(Water plantain)		1	2	4	7	2
ZANNICHELLIACEAE							
Zannichellia palustris L.	(Horned pondweed)		–	–	–	1	–
LEMNACEAE							
Lemna gibba L.			–	–	–	–	1
JUNCACEAE							
Juncus spp.	(Rushes)		oc	oc	m	oc	m
Luzula sp.	(Wood-rush)		–	–	1	–	–
CYPERACEAE							
Eleocharis palustris/uniglumis	(Common/slender spike-rush)		–	–	2	3	5
Bolboschoenus maritimus/Schoenoplectus lacustris	(Sea/common club-rush)		2	4	1	–	2
S. tabernaemontani (C. Gmelin)Palla	(Grey club-rush)		–	1	2	–	1
Schoenoplectus sp.			–	–	1	–	–
Carex paniculata L.	(Greater tussock sedge)		–	1	1	–	1
C. otrubae Podp.	(False fox-sedge)		1	2	4	1	2
C. pseudocyperus L.	(Cyperus sedge)		–	–	–	2	–
C. cf. *distans* L.	(Distant sedge)		–	–	–	–	1
C. cf. *hostiana* DC.	(Tawny sedge)		–	–	–	2	–
C. cf. *pallescens* L.	(Pale sedge)		–	–	1	–	1
Carex spp.			3	–	1	–	–
POACEAE							
cf. *Festuca* sp.	(Fescues)		–	–	5	–	2
Poa annua L.	(Annual meadow-grass)		1	1	1	–	–

Table 65 (cont.)

Phase		III	III	III	II	II
Sample number		23166	23055	23057	23059	23061
Depth (cm)		0–5	10–15	20–25	30–35	40–45
Height + (m) OD		2.85–2.90	2.69–2.74	2.59–2.64	2.49–2.54	2.39–2.44
Sample weight (g)		250	250	250	250	250
Poa cf. annua L.		–	–	1	1	–
Poa sp.	(Meadow-grasses)	6	–	1	–	–
cf. Poa sp.		1	–	–	–	–
Phalaris arundinacea L.	(Reed canary-grass)	1	11	2	–	–
Phalaris cf. arundinacea L.		1	–	–	–	–
Phragmites australis (Cav.) Trin. ex Steudal	(Common reed)	–	1	–	–	–
Poaceae indet. <2mm		12	21	9	4	–
Poaceae indet. >2mm		13	32	18	7	–
cf. Poaceae indet. >2mm		1	–	–	–	–
SPARGANIACEAE						
Sparganium sp.	(Bur-reed)	3	1	1	1	–
OTHER REMAINS						
Bud scales		11	–	–	–	–
Tree buds		22	2	11	1	3
Leaf scars		2	–	–	–	–
PTEROPSIDA						
Pteridium aquilinum (L.) Kuhn leaf frags	(Bracken)	–	6	3	5	–
BRYOPHYTA						
Moss leaves		+	+	+	–	+
POLYZOA						
Plumatella sp. statoblasts		–	oc	–	–	–
No. of items (quantified)		338	232	468	102	35

Table 66 Plant macrofossils from sample Column 3

		IV	IV	IV	IV	III	III	III	III	III
Phase										
Sample number		23017	23019	23021	23023	23026	23027	23028	23030	23032
Depth (cm)		0–5	10–15	20–25	30–35	45–50	50–55	55–60	65–70	75–80
Height + (m) OD		3.33 -3.38	3.23 -3.28	3.13 -3.18	3.03 -3.08	2.88 -2.93	2.83 -2.88	2.78 -2.83	2.68 -2.73	2.58 -2.63
Sample weight (g)		250	250	250	250	250	250	250	250	250
RANUNCULACEAE										
Ranunculus repens type	(Creeping buttercup)	–	1	7	2	1	2	1	1	3
R.bulbosus L.	(Bulbous buttercup)	–	–	–	1	–	–	–	–	–
R. sceleratus L.	(Celery-leaved buttercup)	3	12	23	11	10	20oc	28r	6	7r
R. Subgenus Batrachium (DC) A. Gray	(Crowfoots)	r	4	15r	25	29	113	101r	57	61
Ranunculus spp.	(Buttercups)	–	–	–	–	–	–	–	1	2
URTICACEAE										
Urtica dioica L.	(Common nettle)	–	2	15r	9oc	3	12	4r	1	6
BETULACEAE										
Betula spp.	(Birch)	–	2	1	–	–	–	–	1	–
Alnus glutinosa (L.)Gaertner	(Alder)	1	–	4	5	1	6	–	–	5
A. glutinosa (L.)Gaertner	cone scale	–	–	1	–	–	–	–	–	1
CHENOPODIACEAE										
Chenopodium rubrum L.	(Red goosefoot)	–	–	1	–	–	–	–	–	–
C. ficifolium Smith	(Fig-leaved goosefoot)	–	–	1	–	–	–	–	–	–
C. album L.	(Fat-hen)	1	–	1	–	2	12	4	–	1
Chenopodium sp.	(Goosefoots)	1	–	–	–	–	–	–	–	–
Atriplex prostrata Boucher ex DC.	(Spear-leaved orache)	–	–	–	1	–	–	1	–	–
A. patula L.	(Common orache)	–	–	–	1	4	16	2	6	6
Atriplex spp.	(Orache)	1	–	1	3	8	13	7	–	21
Salicornia spp.	(Glassworts)	–	–	–	–	–	1	–	–	–
Chenopodiaceae indet.		–	1	–	–	–	–	1	–	1

Table 66 (cont.)

Phase		III	III	III	III	III	IV	IV	IV	IV
Sample number		23032	23030	23028	23027	23026	23023	23021	23019	23017
Depth (cm)		75–80	65–70	55–60	50–55	45–50	30–35	20–25	10–15	0–5
Height + (m) OD		2.58 –2.63	2.68 –2.73	2.78 –2.83	2.83 –2.88	2.88 –2.93	3.03 –3.08	3.13 –3.18	3.23 –3.28	3.33 –3.38
Sample weight (g)		250	250	250	250	250	250	250	250	250
CARYOPHYLLACEAE										
Moehringia trinervia (L.)Clairv.	(Three-nerved sandwort)	–	–	1	1	–	–	–	–	–
Stellaria media (L.) Villars	(Common chickweed)	–	1	–	–	–	–	–	–	–
S.holostea L.	(Greater stitchwort)	1	–	–	–	–	–	–	–	–
S. palustris Retz.	(Marsh stitchwort)	–	–	1	2	–	–	–	–	–
S. uliginosa Murray	(Bog stitchwort)	–	1	–	–	–	–	–	–	–
Stellaria sp.	(Stitchwort)	–	–	1	–	–	–	–	–	–
POLYGONACEAE										
P. hydropiper (L.) Spach	(Water-pepper)	–	–	–	1	–	2	1	–	1
P. laxiflora (Weihe) Opiz	(Tasteless water-pepper)	–	1	–	–	–	–	–	–	–
Persicaria spp.	(Knotweeds)	–	–	–	–	–	–	3	1	1
Polygonum aviculare L.	(Knotgrass)	1	–	2	–	–	–	1	1	–
Rumex acetosella L.	(Sheep's sorrel)	–	–	1	5	2	1	2	–	–
R. hydrolapathum type	(Water dock)	5	–	1	16	11	1	–	–	1
R.cf. crispus L.	(Curled dock)	5	–	1	1	4	–	–	–	–
R. conglomeratus Murray with perianth	(Clustered dock)	5	1	6	7	8	10	1	2	–
R. cf. conglomeratus		6	8	10	34	4	3	4	1	–
R. cf. obtusifolius L.	(Broad-leaved dock)	–	–	4	–	–	–	–	–	–
R. cf. palustris Smith	(Marsh dock)	1	–	2	–	–	–	–	–	–
Rumex spp.	(Docks)	6	–	6	16	4	9	–	–	1
Rumex sp. perianth frags.		3	–	3	–	–	2	–	1	–
CLUSIACEAE										
Hypericum sp.	(St. John's-worts)	r	–	oc	oc	r	–	oc	r	–

Table 66 (cont.)

		IV	IV	IV	IV	III	III	III	III	III
Phase										
Sample number		23017	23019	23021	23023	23026	23027	23028	23030	23032
Depth (cm)		0–5	10–15	20–25	30–35	45–50	50–55	55–60	65–70	75–80
Height + (m) OD		3.33 / −3.38	3.23 / −3.28	3.13 / −3.18	3.03 / −3.08	2.88 / −2.93	2.83 / −2.88	2.78 / −2.83	2.68 / −2.73	2.58 / −2.63
Sample weight (g)		250	250	250	250	250	250	250	250	250
MALVACEAE										
Malva sylvestris L.	(Common mallow)	–	1	–	–	–	–	–	2	–
Althaea officinalis L.	(Marsh-mallow)	–	–	–	–	–	–	–	–	1
BRASSICACEAE										
Rorippa nasturtium-aquaticum (L.) Hayeck	(Water-cress)	1	r	4r	–	–	–	–	–	–
Rorippa cf. nasturtium-aquaticum (L.) Hayeck		r	–	–	–	–	–	–	–	r
R. palustris (L.) Besser	(Marsh yellow-cress)	–	4oc	3oc	1r	–	1	–	–	–
PRIMULACEAE										
Anagallis minima /Samolus valerandi	(Chaffweed/Brookweed)	–	–	–	r	r	–	r	–	–
Glaux maritima L.	(Sea-milkwort)	–	–	–	–	–	1	–	1	–
ROSACEAE										
Rubus fruticosus L. agg.	(Bramble)	1	1	3	3	13	17	9	–	17
Rubus sp.	(Brambles)	·	1	–	r	3	–	14	–	2
Rubus sp. thorn		–	–	2	6	–	2	–	–	3
Potentilla anserina L.	(Silverweed)	–	2	1	2	2	2	1	–	2
Potentilla sp.	(Cinquefoil)	–	–	–	–	–	–	–	–	1
Aphanes arvensis L.	(Parsley piert)	–	–	–	–	–	1	–	1	–
A. inexspectata Lippert	(Slender parsley-piert)	–	–	–	–	–	–	–	–	–
Rosa sp.	(Rose)	–	–	1	–	–	–	–	–	–
Prunus spinosa L.	(Blackthorn)	–	–	–	–	–	6	–	–	5
Prunus sp.	(Cherries)	–	–	–	–	1	–	1	1	–
Crataegus monogyna Jacq.	(Hawthorn)	–	–	–	–	–	1	–	–	–

Table 66 (cont.)

	III	III	III	III	III	IV	IV	IV	IV
Phase									
Sample number	23032	23030	23028	23027	23026	23023	23021	23019	23017
Depth (cm)	75–80	65–70	55–60	50–55	45–50	30–35	20–25	10–15	0–5
Height + (m) OD	2.58 / −2.63	2.68 / −2.73	2.78 / −2.83	2.83 / −2.88	2.88 / −2.93	3.03 / −3.08	3.13 / −3.18	3.23 / −3.28	3.33 / −3.38
Sample weight (g)	250	250	250	250	250	250	250	250	250
C. monogyna Jacq. thorn	–	–	1	2	1	–	–	–	–
Rosaceae thorn	4	–	–	–	1	1	2	–	–
LYTHRACEAE									
Lythrum sp. (Purple-loosestrifes)	–	–	oc	oc	oc	oc	oc	–	r
ONAGRACEAE									
Epilobium hirsutum type (Great willowherb)	7r	–	1oc	1oc	oc	11oc	19oc	3r	1
APIACEAE									
cf. *Berula erecta* (Hudson) Cov.	–	–	–	–	–	1	–	–	–
Apium graveolens L. (Wild celery)	1	–	2	–	1	14	8	–	3
A. nodiflorum (L.) Lag. (Fool's water-cress)	–	–	–	4	–	1	–	–	–
A. nodiflorum/inundatum (Fool's water-cress/lesser marshwort)	–	–	–	–	–	–	–	–	2
A. repens (Jacq.) Lag. (Creeping marshwort)	–	–	–	–	2	2	–	2	–
Apium spp. (Marshworts)	–	–	–	1	–	3	3	–	1
Apiaceae sp. indet.	1r	–	r	–	r	oc	r	r	r
SOLANACEAE									
Solanum nigrum L. (Black nightshade)	–	–	1	2	1	–	–	–	–
S. dulcamara L. (Bittersweet)	1	–	1	–	–	–	–	–	–
BORAGINACEAE									
Myosotis sp. (Forget-me-not)	–	2	–	–	–	–	–	1	–
LAMIACEAE									
Prunella vulgaris L. (Selfheal)	–	–	1	–	–	–	–	–	–
Lycopus europaeus L. (Gypsywort)	1	–	–	–	2	1	2	–	–
Mentha arvensis/aquatica (corn/water mint)	2	1	3	5	2	5	9	3	1

311

Table 66 (cont.)

	IV	IV	IV	IV	III	III	III	III	III
Phase									
Sample number	23017	23019	23021	23023	23026	23027	23028	23030	23032
Depth (cm)	0–5	10–15	20–25	30–35	45–50	50–55	55–60	65–70	75–80
Height + (m) OD	3.33 -3.38	3.23 -3.28	3.13 -3.18	3.03 -3.08	2.88 -2.93	2.83 -2.88	2.78 -2.83	2.68 -2.73	2.58 -2.63
Sample weight (g)	250	250	250	250	250	250	250	250	250
HIPPURIDACEAE									
Hippuris vulgaris L. (Mare's-tail)	–	–	–	–	–	–	–	1	–
CALLITRICHACEAE									
Callitriche spp. (Water-starworts)	2	3	32r	23oc	6	13oc	11oc	1	–
PLANTAGINACEAE									
Plantago major L. (Greater plantain)	–	–	6	3r	8r	39	8oc	22r	29r
P. lanceolata L. (Ribwort plantain)	–	–	1	–	–	–	–	–	–
SCROPHULARIACEAE									
Veronica beccabunga L. (Brooklime)	oc	oc	oc	oc	oc	oc	oc	r	m
Veronica sp. (Speedwells)	1	–	–	–	–	–	–	–	–
RUBIACEAE									
Galium palustre L. (Common marsh-bedstraw)	–	–	–	1	–	–	–	–	–
CAPRIFOLIACEAE									
Sambucus nigra L. (Elder)	–	–	2	–	1	6	2	1	4
ASTERACEAE									
cf. Carduus sp. (Thistles)	–	–	–	–	–	1	–	–	–
Cirsium cf. vulgare (Savi) Ten. (Spear thistle)	–	–	–	1	–	–	–	–	–
C. cf palustre (L.) Scop. (Marsh thistle)	1	–	–	–	8	2	–	1	1
C. cf. arvense (L.) Scop. (Creeping thistle)	1	–	1	–	1	6	6	2	5
Cirsium sp. (Thistles)	–	–	–	1	–	–	–	4	–
Lapsana communis L. (Nipplewort)	–	–	–	–	1	1	–	–	–
Picris hieracioides L. (Hawkweed oxtongue)	–	–	–	–	1	1	–	–	1
Sonchus cf. palustris L (March sow-thistle)	1	–	–	–	–	–	–	–	–
S. oleraceus L. (Smooth sow-thistle)	–	–	–	–	–	–	–	2	–

Table 66 (cont.)

Phase		IV	IV	IV	IV	III	III	III	III	III
Sample number		23017	23019	23021	23023	23026	23027	23028	23030	23032
Depth (cm)		0–5	10–15	20–25	30–35	45–50	50–55	55–60	65–70	75–80
Height + (m) OD		3.33 / –3.38	3.23 / –3.28	3.13 / –3.18	3.03 / –3.08	2.88 / –2.93	2.83 / –2.88	2.78 / –2.83	2.68 / –2.73	2.58 / –2.63
Sample weight (g)		250	250	250	250	250	250	250	250	250
S. asper (L.) Hill	(Prickly sow-thistle)	–	–	2	2	5	2	5	6	16
Taraxacum sp.	(Dandelions)	–	–	–	2	–	–	–	–	–
Aster tripolium L.	(Sea aster)	–	–	–	–	–	–	–	–	1
cf. *Chamaelum nobile* L.All.	(Chamomile)	–	–	–	–	–	1	–	–	–
Eupatorium cannabinum L.	(Hemp agrimony)	–	1	6	1	1r	2r	2r	–	1r
ALISMATACEAE										
Alisma spp.	(Water plantain)	–	16	6	12	3	6	1	1	2
POTAMOGETONACEAE										
Potamogeton lucens L.	(Shining pondweed)	–	–	–	1	–	–	–	–	–
P. praelongus Wulfen	(Long-stalked pondweed)	–	–	–	–	–	1	–	–	–
P. berchtoldii Fieber	(Small pondweed)	–	–	1	–	–	–	–	–	–
Potamogeton sp.	(Pondweed)	–	–	–	1	–	1	–	–	–
ZANNICHELLIACEAE										
Zannichellia palustris L.	(Horned pondweed)	–	–	–	–	–	3	–	–	–
LEMNACEAE										
Lemna gibba L.	(Fat duckweed)	–	4	–	1	–	–	–	–	–
L. minor L.	(Common duckweed)	–	–	1	–	–	–	–	–	–
L. trisulca L	(Ivy-leaved duckweed)	–	–	–	1	–	–	–	–	–
Lemna sp.	(Duckweeds)	–	oc	–	–	–	–	–	–	–
JUNCACEAE										
Juncus spp.	(Rushes)	oc	oc	f	f	m	oc	oc	m	f
CYPERACEAE										
Eleocharis palustris luniglumis	(Common/slender spike-rush)	2	4	1	1	–	4	2	3	23

Table 66 (cont.)

		III	III	III	III	III	IV	IV	IV	IV
Phase		III	III	III	III	III	IV	IV	IV	IV
Sample number		23032	23030	23028	23027	23026	23023	23021	23019	23017
Depth (cm)		75–80	65–70	55–60	50–55	45–50	30–35	20–25	10–15	0–5
Height + (m) OD		2.58 -2.63	2.68 -2.73	2.78 -2.83	2.83 -2.88	2.88 -2.93	3.03 -3.08	3.13 -3.18	3.23 -3.28	3.33 -3.38
Sample weight (g)		250	250	250	250	250	250	250	250	250
Bolboschoenus maritimus/Schoenoplectus lacustris	(Sea/common club-rush)	3	–	–	2	2	–	–	2	–
S. tabernaemontani (C. Gmelin) Palla	(Grey club-rush)	–	–	2	1	–	1	–	–	–
cf. *Cladium mariscus* (L.) Pohl		–	–	1	–	–	–	–	–	–
Carex paniculata L.	(Greater tussock sedge)	3	–	–	–	–	1	–	–	–
C. otrubae Podp.	(False fox-sedge)	5	–	3	3	3	4	1	1	–
C. cf. *distans* L.	(Distant sedge)	1	–	1	1	–	2	1	–	–
C. cf. *extensa* Gooden.	(Long-bracted sedge)	–	–	–	1	–	–	–	–	–
C. cf. *hostiana* DC.	(Tawny sedge)	–	–	–	–	1	–	–	–	–
C. cf. *pallescens* L.	(Pale sedge)	–	–	–	1	–	–	–	–	–
Carex spp.	(Sedges)	–	–	–	–	–	1	5	1	–
Carex sp. utricle		–	–	–	–	1	–	–	1	–
POACEAE										
cf. *Festuca* sp.	(Fescues)	1	–	–	–	–	1	1	–	–
Poa annua L.	(Annual meadow-grass)	–	–	–	–	1	2	2	–	–
Phalaris arundinacea L.	(Reed canary-grass)	1	–	–	2	1	–	1	1	1
Agrostis cf. sp.	(Bents)	–	–	1	–	–	–	–	–	–
Phragmites australis (Cav.) Trin. ex Steudal	(Common reed)	–	–	1	–	–	–	2	–	–
Poaceae indet. <2mm		12	3	3	5	6	5	8	1	5
Poaceae indet. >2mm		1	5	–	2	3	3	5	3	5
cf. Poaceae indet. >2mm		–	–	–	–	–	–	1	–	–
SPARGANIACEAE										
Sparganium cf. *natans* L.	(Least bur-reed)	1	–	–	–	–	–	1	–	–

Table 66 (cont.)

		III	III	III	III	III	IV	IV	IV	IV
Sample number		23032	23030	23028	23027	23026	23023	23021	23019	23017
Depth (cm)		75–80	65–70	55–60	50–55	45–50	30–35	20–25	10–15	0–5
Height + (m) OD		2.58 −2.63	2.68 −2.73	2.78 −2.83	2.83 −2.88	2.88 −2.93	3.03 −3.08	3.13 −3.18	3.23 −3.28	3.33 −3.38
Sample weight (g)		250	250	250	250	250	250	250	250	250
Sparganium sp.	(Bur-reed)	3	–	5	–	–	–	3	2	1
OTHER REMAINS										
Bud scales		–	–	–	–	10	1	3	–	–
Tree buds		31	–	2	19	6	–	4	–	–
Leaf scars		–	–	–	1	–	–	–	–	–
PTEROPSIDA										
Pteridium aquilinum (L) Kuhn leaf frags	(Bracken)	–	–	–	5	–	2	–	–	–
BRYOPHYTA										
Moss leaves		–	–	–	–	–	+	+	–	–
CHAROPHYTA										
Chara sp.	(Stoneworts)	–	–	r	–	r	oc	–	–	oc
POLYZOA										
Plumatella sp. statoblasts		oc	–	r	–	r	r	–	r	r
CLADOCERA										
Daphnia sp. ephippia		–	–	–	–	–	–	–	–	–
No. of items (quantified)		339	144	279	456	187	210	236	86	40

315

Table 67 Plant macrofossils from sample Column 5. Habitat preferences: B = brackish; salt-marsh; A = Aquatic; Bs = Bankside; M = fen, swamp, marsh; Ht = heathland; G = grassland; D = disturbed; Da = disturbed agricultural; H = hedges; S = scrub; W = woodland; d = damp; Cst = coastal

Phase		IVI	VI	VI	VII	VII	VII	Habitat Preferences
Sample number		23260	23259	23258	23257	23253	23251	
Height + (m) OD		3.11	3.127	3.20	3.21	3.336	3.466	
Sample weight (g)		250	250	250	250	250	250	
RANUNCULACEAE								
Ranunculus repens type	(Creeping buttercup)	–	2	2	–	–	–	M,Gd,D,Da,W,Cst
R. bulbosus L.	(Bulbous buttercup)	–	–	–	–	–	–	G,Cst
R. sceleratus L.	(Celery-leaved buttercup)	16oc	10	12	3r	1	2	B,A
R. cf. *flammula* L.	(Lesser spearwort)	–	–	–	–	–	–	A
R. Subgenus *Batrachium* (DC) A. Gray	(Crowfoots)	16r	17oc	9r	2	–	1	B,A
Ranunculus spp.		–	–	–	–	–	–	B,A,M,Gd,D,Da,W,Cst
PAPAVERACEAE								
Papaver rhoeas / dubium	(Common/long-leaved poppy)	–	–	–	–	–	1	D,Da
URTICACEAE								
Urtica dioica L.	(Common nettle)	19r	12oc	22oc	3oc	2r	2	M,G,D,Da
U. urens L.	(Small nettle)	–	–	–	–	–	–	D,Da
BETULACEAE								
Betula spp.	(Birch)	2	–	2	–	–	–	M,W
Alnus glutinosa (L.) Gaertner	(Alder)	25	19	25	1	–	–	Bs,M,W
A. glutinosa (L.) Gaertner cone-scale		3	–	1	–	–	–	
Corylus avellana L. frags.	(Hazel)	–	–	–	–	–	–	H,S,W
CHENOPODIACEAE								
Chenopodium rubrum L.	(Red goosefoot)	–	–	1	–	r	–	B,D,Da
C. polyspermum L.	(Many-seeded goosefoot)	–	–	–	1	–	–	D,Da
C. ficifolium Smith	(Fig-leaved goosefoot)	–	–	1	–	–	–	D,Da
C. cf. *ficifolium* Smith		–	–	–	–	–	–	
C. album L.	(Fat-hen)	4	6	4	8	1	1	D,Da

Table 67 (cont.)

Phase	I/VI	VI	VI	VII	VII	VII	Habitat Preferences
Sample number	23260	23259	23258	23257	23253	23251	
Height + (m) OD	3.11	3.127	3.20	3.21	3.336	3.466	
Sample weight (g)	250	250	250	250	250	250	
Chenopodium sp. (Goosefoots)	–	–	–	–	–	–	B,D,Da
Atriplex prostrata Boucher ex DC. (Spear-leaved orache)	–	–	–	–	–	–	B,D,Da
A. patula L. (Common orache)	–	–	–	–	–	–	B,D,Da
Atriplex spp. (Orache)	9	6	8	12	–	–	B,D,Da
Salicornia spp. (Glassworts)	–	–	–	–	–	–	B
Suaeda maritima (L.) Dumort. (Annual sea-blite)	–	–	–	–	–	–	B
Chenopodiaceae indet.	–	–	–	–	–	–	
PORTULACEAE							
Montia fontana L. (Blinks)	1	1	–	–	–	–	Bs,Gd,Da
CARYOPHYLLACEAE							
Moehringia trinervia (L.) Clairv. (Three-nerved sandwort)	–	–	–	–	–	–	W
Stellaria media (L.) Villars (Common chickweed)	–	–	2	3	–	1	B,G,D,Da
S. holostea L. (Greater stitchwort)	–	–	–	–	–	–	H,W
S. palustris Retz. (Marsh stitchwort)	–	–	–	–	–	–	M
S. cf. *palustris* Retz.							
S. uliginosa Murray (Bog stitchwort)	–	–	–	–	–	–	Bs,W
Stellaria sp. (Stitchworts)	–	–	–	–	–	–	B,Bs,M,G,D,Da,H,W
Cerastium sp. (Mouse-ears)	–	–	–	–	–	r	G,Cst,Da
Sagina sp. (Pearlworts)	–	–	–	–	–	r	B,Bs,G,D,Da,Cst
Spergularia spp. (Sea-spurreys)	–	–	–	–	–	r	B,Cst
Lychnis flos-cuculi L. (Ragged robin)	5	7	1	1	–	–	M,Gd,Wd
Silene sp. (Campions)	–	–	–	–	–	–	B,Bs,G,D,Da,H,W
Caryophyllaceae indet.	–	–	–	–	–	–	
POLYGONACEAE							
Persicaria maculosa Gray (Redshank)	–	–	–	–	–	–	A,D,Da

Table 67 (cont.)

Phase		I/VI	VI	VI	VII	VII	VII	Habitat Preferences
Sample number		23260	23259	23258	23257	23253	23251	
Height + (m) OD		3.11	3.127	3.20	3.21	3.336	3.466	
Sample weight (g)		250	250	250	250	250	250	
P. lapathifolia(L.) Gray	(Pale persicaria)	–	–	–	–	–	–	A,D,Da
P. hydropiper (L.) Spach	(Water-pepper)	1	–	–	–	–	–	A
P. laxiflora (Weihe) Opiz	(Tasteless water-pepper)	–	–	–	–	–	–	A
Persicaria spp.	(Knotweeds)	–	–	–	–	–	–	
Polygonum aviculare L.	(Knotgrass)	–	–	–	2	1	3	B,D,Da,Cst
Rumex acetosella L.	(Sheep's sorrel)	–	–	1	–	2	4	M,G,Da,Ht
R. hydrolapathum type	(Water dock)	1	–	–	–	–	1	A,Bs,G,M
R. cf. *crispus* L.	(Curled dock)	–	2	–	–	–	–	B,G,D,Da,Cst
R. conglomeratus Murray with perianth	(Clustered dock)	–	–	–	1	1	2	Gd,W,Bs
R. cf. *conglomeratus*		2	4	–	–	–	3	G,D,W,H,Bs
R. sanguineus L.	(Wood dock)	–	–	2	–	–	–	D,H,G
R. cf. *obtusifolius* L.	(Broad-leaved dock)	–	–	–	–	–	–	A,Gd
R. cf. *palustris* Smith	(Marsh dock)	–	–	–	–	–	–	
Rumex spp.	(Docks)	1	4	7	2	2	2	B,A,Bs,G,Gd,D,Da,H,W
Rumex sp. perianth frags.		–	–	–	–	1	1	
CLUSIACEAE								
Hypericum sp.	(St. John's-worts)	oc	oc	r	oc	–	–	Bs,G,Wd,Bs,W,Ht
MALVACEAE								
Malva sylvestris L.	(Common mallow)	–	–	–	–	–	–	D
Althaea officinalis L.	(Marsh mallow)	–	–	–	–	–	–	B,Bs,G,Cst
BRASSICACEAE								
Rorippa nasturtium-aquaticum (L.) Hayeck	(Water-cress)	–	–	–	–	–	–	A

Table 67 (cont.)

Phase		I/VI	VI	VI	VII	VII	VII	Habitat Preferences
Sample number		23260	23259	23258	23257	23253	23251	
Height + (m) OD		3.11	3.127	3.20	3.21	3.336	3.466	
Sample weight (g)		250	250	250	250	250	250	
Rorippa cf. *nasturtium-aquaticum* (L.) Hayeck		r	–	r	r	–	–	A
R. palustris (L.) Besser	(Marsh yellow-cress)	1	–	–	–	–	–	A,Dd
R. cf. *amphibia* (L.) Besser	(Great yellow-cress)	–	r	–	–	–	–	A
Brassicaceae indet.,		–	–	–	–	–	–	
PRIMULACEAE								
Anagallis minima / *Samolus valerandi*	(Chaffweed/Brookweed)	–	r	–	–	–	–	B,Bs,Ht,W,Cst
Glaux maritima L.	(Sea-milkwort)	–	–	–	–	–	–	G,Cst,B
ROSACEAE								
Rubus fruticosus L. agg.	(Bramble)	2	2	2	2	1	–	Ht,D,H,S,W
R. cf. *idaeus* L	(Raspberry)	–	–	–	–	–	–	Ht,D,W
Rubus sp.	(Brambles)	1r	1r	1r	1r	–	–	Ht,D,H,S,W
Rubus sp. thorn		–	–	–	–	–	–	
Potentilla anserina L.	(Silverweed)	–	1	1	2	2	–	B,Gd,D
Potentilla sp.	(Cinquefoil)	–	–	–	–	–	–	B,M,Ht,Gd,D,Cst,H
Aphanes arvensis L.	(Parsley piert)	–	–	–	–	–	–	D,Da
A. inexspectata Lippert	(Slender parsley-piert)	–	·	·	–	r	4	D,Da
Rosa sp.	(Rose)	–	–	–	–	–	–	H,S,W,Cst
Prunus spinosa L.	(Blackthorn)	–	–	–	–	–	–	H,S,W
Prunus sp.	(Cherries)	–	–	–	–	–	–	H,S,W
Crataegus monogyna Jacq.	(Hawthorn)	–	–	–	–	–	–	H,S,W
C. monogyna Jacq. thorn		–	–	–	–	–	–	
Rosaceae thorn		–	–	–	–	–	–	
cf. Rosaceae		–	–	–	–	–	–	

Table 67 (cont.)

Phase	I/VI	VI	VI	VII	VII	VII	Habitat Preferences
Sample number	23260	23259	23258	23257	23253	23251	
Height + (m) OD	3.11	3.127	3.20	3.21	3.336	3.466	
Sample weight (g)	250	250	250	250	250	250	
LYTHRACEAE							
Lythrum sp. L. (Purple-loosestrifes)	1r	oc	oc	r	·	–	Bs,M
ONAGRACEAE							
Epilobium hirsutum type (Great willowherb)	1r	–	1	r	–	–	Bs,M
APIACEAE							
Berula erecta (Hudson) Cov. (Lesser water-parsnip)	–	–	–	–	–	–	A,Bs,M
cf. *Berula erecta* (Hudson) Cov.	–	–	–	–	–	–	Bs,d,D
Conium maculatum L. (Hemlock)	–	–	–	–	–	–	B,A
Apium graveolens L. (Wild celery)	1	–	1	–	–	–	A,Bs,M
A. nodiflorum (L.) Lag. (Fool's water-cress)	–	–	–	–	–	–	A,Bs
A. nodiflorum /inundatum (Fool's water-cress/lesser marshwort)	–	–	–	–	–	–	A,Bs
A. repens (Jacq.) Lag. (Creeping marshwort)	–	–	–	–	–	–	A,Bs
Apium sp. (Marshworts)	–	–	1	–	–	–	A,Bs,M
Peucedanum sp. (Hog's fennels)	–	–	–	–	–	–	B,Bs,M
Apiaceae indet.	r	r	–	–	–	r	
SOLANACEAE							
Solanum nigrum L. (Black nightshade)	1	–	–	2	–	2	D,Da
S. dulcamara L. (Bittersweet)	2	2	3	1	–	–	D,H,W,M,Cst
BORAGINACEAE							
Myosotis sp. (Forget-me-not)	1	–	–	–	–	–	A,Bs,M,Gd,Cst
LAMIACEAE							
Stachys cf. *palustris* L. (Marsh woundworts)	–	–	–	–	–	–	Bs,D
Prunella vulgaris L. (Selfheal)	–	–	–	–	–	–	G,D

Table 67 (cont.)

Phase	I/VI	VI	VI	VII	VII	VII	Habitat Preferences
Sample number	23260	23259	23258	23257	23253	23251	
Height + (m) OD	3.11	3.127	3.20	3.21	3.336	3.466	
Sample weight (g)	250	250	250	250	250	250	
cf. *Clinopodium acinos* (L.) Kuntze (Basil thyme)	–	–	–	–	–	–	G
Lycopus europaeus L. (Gypsywort)	5	6	3	1	–	–	Bs,M,Gd
Mentha arvensis/aquatica (Corn/water mint)	18	20r	5r	2	–	–	A,Bs,M,Da,Wd
Mentha sp. (Mint)	–	–	–	1	–	–	A,Bs,M,Da,Wd
HIPPURIDACEAE							
Hippuris vulgaris L. (Mare's-tail)	1	4	1	–	–	1	A
CALLITRICHACEAE							
Callitriche sp. (Water-starworts)	6	4	4r	–	–	15r	A
cf.*Callitriche* sp.	–	–	–	–	–	–	
PLANTAGINACEAE							
Plantago major L. (Greater plantain)	2	–	1r	oc	2r	8r	D,Da
P. lanceolata L. (Ribwort plantain)	–	–	–	–	–	–	G
SCROPHULARIACEAE							
Veronica beccabunga L. (Brooklime)	oc	oc	oc	m	oc	oc	A,M,Bs
Veronica sp. (Speedwell)	–	–	–	–	–	–	Bs,M,G,Gd,H,W
RUBIACEAE							
Galium palustre L. (Common marsh-bedstraw)	–	–	–	–	–	–	M,Gd,Bs
CAPRIFOLIACEAE							
Sambucus nigra L. (Elder)	4r	3r	1	2	–	–	S,W,H
ASTERACEAE							
cf. *Carduus* sp. (Thistles)	–	–	–	–	–	–	Bs,G,D,Cst
Carduus/Cirsium	–	–	–	–	–	–	
Cirsium cf.*vulgare* (Savi) Ten. (Spear thistle)	–	–	–	–	–	–	G,D,Da
C. cf. *palustre* (L.) Scop. (Marsh thistle)	–	–	–	–	–	–	Gd,H,W,M,Bs
C. cf. *arvense* (L.) Scop. (Creeping thistle)	–	4	2	2	1	–	G,D

Table 67 (cont.)

Phase	I/VI	VI	VI	VI	VII	VII	VII	VII	Habitat Preferences
Sample number	23260	23259	23258	23257	23253	23251			
Height + (m) OD	3.11	3.127	3.20	3.21	3.336	3.466			
Sample weight (g)	250	250	250	250	250	250			
Cirsium sp. (Thistles)	1	–	–	–	1	–			G,Gd,D,H,W,Da
Lapsana communis L. (Nipplewort)	–	1	–	–	–	–			D,Da,H,W
Picris hieracioides L. (Hawkweed oxtongue)	–	–	–	–	–	–			G
Sonchus cf. *palustris* L. (Marsh sow-thistle)	–	–	–	–	–	–			Bs,M
S. arvensis L. (Perennial sow-thistle)	–	–	–	–	–	–			Bs,Da,Cst
S. oleraceus L. (Smooth sow-thistle)	–	–	–	–	–	–			D,Da
S. asper (L.) Hill (Prickly sow-thistle)	1r	–	5	–	–	–			D,Da
Sonchus sp. (Sow-thistles)	–	–	–	–	–	–			Bs,M,D,Da
Taraxacum sp. (Dandelions)	–	–	–	–	–	–			G,Cst,Gd,M
Aster tripolium L. (Sea aster)	–	–	–	–	–	–			B
cf. *Chamaemelum nobile* (L.)All. (Chamomile)	–	–	–	–	–	–			G
Senecio sp. (Ragworts)	–	–	–	–	–	–			M,G,D,Cst
Eupatorium cannabinum L (Hemp agrimony)	–	r	–	oc	-	1r			Bs,M,G
Asteraceae indet.	–	–	–	–	–	1			
ALISMATACEAE									
Alisma spp. (Water plantain)	5	4	3	–	–	1			A
POTAMOGETONACEAE									
Potamogeton lucens L. (Shining pondweed)	–	–	–	–	–	–			A
P. praelongus Wulfen (Long-stalked pondweed)	–	–	–	–	–	–			A
P. berchtoldii Fieber (Small pondweed)	1	–	1	–	–	–			A
P. cf. *berchtoldii* Fieber	–	–	–	–	–	–			A
Potamogeton sp. (Pondweed)	1	–	–	–	–	–			A
cf. *Potamogeton*	–	–	–	–	–	–			A
ZANNICHELLIACEAE									
Zannichellia palustris L. (Horned pondweed)	–	1	–	–	–	5			B,A

322

Table 67 (cont.)

Phase	I/VI	VI	VI	VII	VII	VII	Habitat Preferences
Sample number	23260	23259	23258	23257	23253	23251	
Height + (m) OD	3.11	3.127	3.20	3.21	3.336	3.466	
Sample weight (g)	250	250	250	250	250	250	
LEMNACEAE							
Lemna gibba L. (Fat duckweed)	–	–	–	–	–	–	A,B
L. cf. gibba L.	1	–	–	–	–	–	
L. minor L. (Common duckweed)	–	–	–	–	–	–	A
L. trisulca L (Ivy-leaved duckweed)	–	–	–	–	–	–	A
Lemna spp. (Duckweeds)	–	r	r	–	–	–	A
JUNCACEAE							
Juncus spp. (Rushes)	oc	m	m	m	oc	–	Ht,G,D,d,M,B,Cst
Luzula spp. (Wood-rush)	–	–	–	–	–	–	Bs,Ht,H,W,G
CYPERACEAE							
Eleocharis palustris luniglumis (Common/slender spike-rush)	2	1	2	–	–	1	B,M,Bs
Bolboschoenus maritimus/Schoenoplectus lacustris (Sea/common club-rush)	2	1	–	1	–	–	B,M,A
S. tabernaemontani (C. Gmelin) Palla (Grey club-rush)	2	–	–	–	–	–	B,M,A
Schoenoplectus sp. (Club-rush)	–	–	–	–	–	–	B,M
Cladium mariscus (L.) Pohl (Great fen-sedge)	–	–	–	–	–	–	Bs,M
cf. Cladium mariscus (L.) Pohl	–	–	–	–	–	–	Bs,M
Carex paniculata L. (Greater tussock sedge)	3	2	1	1	–	–	M,Wd,Bs
C. otrubae Podp. (False fox-sedge)	2	4	4	–	–	2	B,Bs,Gd
C. pseudocyperus L. (Cyperus sedge)	–	–	–	–	–	–	Bs,M
C. cf. rostrata Stokes (Bottle sedge)	–	–	–	–	–	–	Bs,M
C. cf. vesicaria L. (Bladder sedge)	–	1	1	–	–	–	Bs,M
C. cf. distans L. (Distant sedge)	5	–	–	–	–	–	B,M
C. cf. extensa Gooden. (Long-bracted sedge)	–	1	1	–	–	–	B

Table 67 (cont.)

		Phase						Habitat Preferences
Phase		I/VI	VI	VI	VII	VII	VII	
Sample number		23260	23259	23258	23257	23253	23251	
Height + (m) OD		3.11	3.127	3.20	3.21	3.336	3.466	
Sample weight (g)		250	250	250	250	250	250	
C. cf. *hostiana* DC.	(Tawny sedge)	–	–	–	–	–	–	B,M
C. cf. *pallescens* L.	(Pale sedge)	–	3	1	–	–	–	Bs,Gd,S,W
C. cf. *digitata* L.	(Fingered sedge)	–	–	–	–	–	–	W,S
Carex sp. - biconvex		–	–	2	1	–	–	
Carex sp. - trigonous		–	1	–	–	–	–	
Carex spp.	(Sedges)	1	1	–	–	–	–	B,Bs,M,Gd,S,W
Carex sp. utricle		–	–	–	–	–	–	
POACEAE								
cf. *Festuca* sp.	(Fescues)	–	–	1	–	–	–	B,G,W,H
Poa annua L.	(Annual meadow-grass)	–	–	–	–	–	1	G,D,Da
Poa cf. *annua* L.		–	–	–	–	–	–	G.D,Da
Poa sp.	(Meadow grasses)	–	–	–	–	–	–	G,D,Da,Cst
cf *Poa* sp.		–	–	–	–	–	–	
Phalaris arundinacea L.	(Reed canary-grass)	–	–	–	1	1	–	B,Bs,M,Gd,D
Phalaris cf. *arundinacea* L.		–	–	–	–	–	–	
Agrostis sp.	(Bents)	–	–	–	–	–	–	G,Gd,D,Da,M,Cst
Phragmites australis (Cav.) Trin. ex Steudal	(Common reed)	–	–	–	–	–	4	B,Bs,M
Poaceae indet. <2mm		12	–	7	–	–	–	
Poaceae indet. >2mm		1	–	3	2	–	4	
cf. Poaceae indet. >2mm		–	–	–	–	–	–	
SPARGANIACEAE								
Sparganium cf. *natans* L.	(Least bur-reed)	–	–	1	–	–	–	A,Bs,M
Sparganium sp.	(Bur-reed)	24	22	16	–	–	–	A,Bs,M
OTHER REMAINS								
Bud scales		2	1	2	–	–	–	

Table 67 (cont.)

Phase	I/VI	VI	VI	VII	VII	VII	Habitat Preferences
Sample number	23260	23259	23258	23257	23253	23251	
Height + (m) OD	3.11	3.127	3.20	3.21	3.336	3.466	
Sample weight (g)	250	250	250	250	250	250	
Tree buds	–	2	–	–	–	–	
Leaf scars	–	–	–	–	–	–	
PTEROPSIDA							
Pteridium aquilinum (L.) Kuhn (Bracken) leaf frags	1	–	2	–	–	–	Ht,W
BRYOPHYTA							
Moss leaves	–	–	–	–	–	–	M,G,D,Da,H,S,W
CHAROPHYTA							
Chara sp. (Stoneworts)	oc	oc	–	oc	–	–	A
POLYZOA							
Plumatella sp. statoblasts	r	–	r	–	–	–	A
CLADOCERA							
Daphnia sp. ephippia	–	oc	r	r	-	–	A
No. of items (quantified)	219	184	180	61	19	74	

Table 68 Plant macrofossils from the stitch-hole samples. + = present

Taxa	6020	6022	6025	6032	6034	6036	6038	6040	6042	6049	6050
Sample weight (g)	272	190	769	469	425	186	192	273	235	569	322
RANUNCULACEAE											
Ranunculus repens type (Creeping buttercup)	–	–	+	–	–	+	+	+	+	–	–
R. sceleratus L. (Celery-leaved buttercup)	+	+	+	+	+	+	+	+	+	–	+
R. Subgenus *Batrachium* (DC) A. Gray (Crowfoots)	+	+	+	+	+	+	+	+	+	+	+
Ranunculus spp. (Buttercups)	–	–	–	–	–	–	–	–	–	–	+
URTICACEAE											
Urtica dioica L. (Common nettle)	+	+	+	+	+	–	+	+	–	–	+
BETULACEAE											
Alnus glutinosa (L.)Gaertner (Alder)	–	+	+	–	–	+	+	+	–	–	+
CHENOPODIACEAE											
C. album L. (Fat-hen)	+	+	–	–	–	–	–	–	–	+	+
Atriplex spp. (Oraches)	+	–	–	–	–	+	–	+	–	+	–
Suaeda maritima (L.)Dumort. (Annual sea-blite)	–	–	+	–	–	–	–	–	–	–	–
CARYOPHYLLACEAE											
Stellaria sp. (Stitchworts)	–	–	+	–	+	–	–	–	–	–	–
Sagina sp. (Pearlworts)	–	–	–	–	–	–	–	–	–	–	+
Silene sp. (Campions)	–	–	+	–	–	–	–	–	–	–	–
Caryophyllaceae indet.	–	–	–	+	–	–	–	–	–	–	–
POLYGONACEAE											
P. hydropiper (L.) Spach (Water-pepper)	–	+	–	–	–	–	–	–	–	–	–
R. conglomeratus Murray with perianth (Clustered dock)	+	–	+	+	–	+	+	+	–	–	–
R. conglomeratus	–	–	+	+	+	–	+	–	–	+	–
Rumex spp. (Docks)	+	–	–	–	+	+	–	+	–	–	–
CLUSIACEAE											
Hypericum sp. (St. John's-worts)	+	–	+	+	+	+	–	–	–	–	+

Table 68 (cont.)

Taxa		6020	6022	6025	6032	6034	6036	6038	6040	6042	6049	6050
Sample weight (g)		272	190	769	469	425	186	192	273	235	569	322
BRASSICACEAE												
Rorippa nasturtium-aquaticum (L.) Hayeck	(Water-cress)	–	–	+	–	–	–	–	–	–	–	–
R. palustris (L.) Besser	(Marsh yellow-cress)	–	–	+	–	–	–	–	–	–	–	+
Brassicaceae indet.		+	–	–	–	–	–	–	–	–	–	–
PRIMULACEAE												
Glaux maritima L.	(Sea-milkwort)	·	–	–	+	–	–	–	–	–	–	–
ROSACEAE												
Rubus fruticosus L. agg.	(Bramble)	+	–	+	+	+	+	+	+	–	+	+
Rubus sp. thorn		–	+	+	–	–	–	–	–	–	–	–
Potentilla anserina L.	(Silverweed)	–	–	+	–	–	–	–	–	–	–	–
Prunus spinosa L	(Blackthorn)	–	–	+	–	+	–	–	+	–	+	+
Prunus sp.		–	+	–	–	–	–	+	+	–	–	+
Crataegus monogyna Jacq.	(Hawthorn) thorn	–	–	–	+	–	–	+	–	–	–	–
Rosaceae thorn		+	–	–	–	–	+	–	–	–	–	–
LYTHRACEAE												
Lythrum sp.	(Purple-loosestrifes)	+	–	+	+	+	–	–	+	–	–	+
ONAGRACEAE												
Epilobium hirsutum type	(Great willowherb)	+	+	+	–	–	+	–	+	–	–	+
APIACEAE												
Apium graveolens L.	(Wild celery)	+	–	–	+	+	–	+	+	–	–	–
A. nodiflorum (L.) Lag.	(Fool's water-cress)	–	+	–	–	–	–	–	–	–	–	–
Apiaceae indet.		–	–	–	–	–	–	–	+	–	–	–
SOLANACEAE												
Solanum spp.	(Nightshades)	+	+	–	+	+	+	–	+	–	–	–
LAMIACEAE												
Lycopus europaeus L.	(Gypsywort)	–	–	+	–	+	–	–	+	–	+	–
Mentha arvensis./aquatica	(Corn/water mint)	–	+	–	–	–	–	+	–	+	–	–

Table 68 (cont.)

Taxa		6020	6022	6025	6032	6034	6036	6038	6040	6042	6049	6050
Sample weight (g)		272	190	769	469	425	186	192	273	235	569	322
CALLITRICHACEAE												
Callitriche spp.	(Water-starworts)	+	+	+	–	–	–	–	–	+	–	–
PLANTAGINACEAE												
Plantago major L.	(Greater plantain)	+	–	+	–	–	+	+	+	–	+	+
SCROPHULARIACEAE												
Veronica beccabunga L.	(Brooklime)	+	+	+	–	–	+	–	–	+	+	–
CAPRIFOLIACEAE												
Sambucus nigra L.	(Elder)	–	+	+	+	+	+	–	+	+	–	–
ASTERACEAE												
C. arvense (L.) Scop.	(Creeping thistle)	–	–	–	–	–	–	–	–	–	+	–
Cirsium sp.		–	–	+	–	–	+	–	–	–	–	–
S. asper (L.) Hill	(Prickly sow-thistle)	–	–	+	–	–	–	–	+	–	–	–
Eupatorium cannabinum L.	(Hemp agrimony)	+	+	–	–	–	+	–	–	+	+	–
ALISMATACEAE												
Alisma spp.	(Water plantain)	–	–	+	–	–	+	–	–	–	+	–
POTAMOGETONACEAE												
Potamogeton berchtoldii Fieber	(Small pondweed)	+	–	+	–	–	–	–	–	–	–	+
JUNCACEAE												
Juncus spp.	(Rushes)	+	+	+	+	+	+	+	+	+	+	+
CYPERACEAE												
Eleocharis palustris / uniglumis	(Common/slender spike-rush)	–	–	+	–	–	–	–	–	–	–	–
Bolboschoenus maritimus/ Schoenoplectus lacustris	(Sea/common club-rush)	+	–	+	–	–	–	–	+	–	–	+
Carex paniculata L.	(Greater tussock sedge)	–	–	+	–	–	+	–	–	–	–	–
C. otrubae Podp.	(False fox-sedge)	+	+	+	+	+	–	+	+	–	+	–
POACEAE												
Phalaris arundinacea L.	(Reed canary-grass)	–	+	+	–	–	+	+	+	–	–	–
Poaceae indet.		+	+	+	+	+	+	+	+	+	+	–

Table 68 (cont.)

Taxa		6020	6022	6025	6032	6034	6036	6038	6040	6042	6049	6050
Sample weight (g)		272	190	769	469	425	186	192	273	235	569	322
SPARGANIACEAE												
Sparganium spp.	(Bur-reed)	–	–	+	+	–	–	+	–	–	+	–
OTHER REMAINS												
Tree buds		–	–	–	–	–	–	–	+	–	–	–
PTEROPSIDA												
Pteridium aquilinum (L.) Kuhn leaf frags	(Bracken)	–	–	–	–	–	–	–	+	–	–	–
BRYOPHYTA												
Moss leaves		–	–	+	–	–	–	–	–	–	–	–
CLADOCERA												
Daphnia sp. ephippia		–	+	+	–	–	–	–	+	–	–	–

Appendix II: Ring-width Tables

Table 69 Ring widths data from a) the Phase III master, b) the Phase VI/VII oak chronology, c) the Phase VII ash chronology, and d) the boat strake 6001

a) 80-year 3 undated master – phase III

year	ring widths (0.01mm)										number of samples									
1	139	93	138	93	77	114	150	69	92	89	1	1	1	1	1	1	1	1	1	1
	98	108	87	93	103	149	104	122	150	144	1	1	1	1	1	1	1	1	1	1
	81	125	87	94	134	97	126	140	95	139	2	2	2	2	2	2	2	2	2	3
	131	137	92	94	124	90	73	85	89	92	3	3	3	3	3	3	3	3	3	3
	109	110	62	93	55	79	94	108	106	87	3	3	3	3	3	3	3	3	3	3
51	98	128	92	74	99	134	108	95	66	88	3	3	3	3	3	3	3	3	3	3
	109	92	66	106	84	95	111	90	54	81	2	2	2	2	2	2	2	2	2	2
	84	102	74	118	100	113	123	116	116	112	1	1	1	1	1	1	1	1	1	1

b) oak chronology, 1131–998BC

date	ring widths (0.01mm)										number of samples									
1131BC										193										1
	137	207	160	134	96	65	72	88	178	117	2	2	2	2	2	2	2	2	2	2
	141	114	125	86	126	106	111	115	81	111	3	3	3	3	3	3	3	3	3	3
	163	144	91	83	146	154	102	126	172	130	3	3	3	3	3	3	3	3	3	3
1100BC	114	86	119	126	157	171	126	106	126	166	3	3	3	3	3	3	3	4	3	3
	119	63	69	123	137	127	142	129	165	176	5	5	5	5	5	5	5	5	5	5
	96	93	123	119	182	139	151	131	137	177	5	5	5	5	5	5	5	5	5	5
	128	134	115	142	120	111	106	107	91	114	5	5	5	5	5	5	5	5	5	5
	106	91	84	115	126	86	65	90	65	123	5	5	5	5	5	5	5	5	5	5
1050BC	133	149	135	128	80	102	94	134	117	95	5	5	5	5	5	5	5	5	5	5
	76	96	80	69	82	98	106	110	98	95	5	5	5	5	5	5	5	5	5	3
	82	72	80	94	104	94	123	69	73	84	3	3	3	3	3	3	3	3	2	1
	74	53	71	99	62	87	104	80	57	64	1	1	1	1	1	1	1	1	1	1
	77	101	81	62	57	62	67	81	61	82	1	1	1	1	1	1	1	1	1	1
1000BC	57	43	57								1	1	1							

Table 69 (cont.)

c) ash chronology, 1169–990BC

date	ring widths (0.01mm)										number of samples
1169BC	94	215	216	257	181	172	146	107	94	72	1 1 1 1 1 1 1 1 1 1
	122	114	94	114	74	148	182	173	147	84	1 1 1 1 1 1 1 1 1 1
1150BC	194	140	157	148	100	172	173	199	151	186	1 1 1 1 1 1 1 1 1 1
	159	304	210	253	122	224	191	196	218	251	1 1 1 1 1 1 1 1 1 1
	191	241	158	186	221	167	235	221	275	218	1 1 1 1 1 1 1 1 1 1
	125	147	103	94	94	107	105	117	116	97	2 2 2 2 2 2 2 2 2 2
	119	112	87	83	113	172	146	141	143	123	2 2 2 2 2 2 2 2 2 2
1100BC	85	92	110	130	118	124	116	122	119	87	2 2 2 2 2 2 2 2 2 2
	104	65	79	86	106	109	96	118	141	137	2 2 2 2 2 2 2 2 2 2
	88	104	116	117	131	124	103	73	78	91	2 2 2 2 2 2 2 2 2 2
	121	70	93	135	142	137	121	150	112	129	3 3 3 3 3 3 3 3 3 3
	90	101	90	119	92	90	92	105	75	117	4 4 4 4 4 4 4 4 4 4
1050BC	89	93	84	101	80	82	83	103	112	93	4 4 4 4 4 4 4 4 4 4
	66	81	68	66	60	74	77	74	70	74	4 4 4 4 4 4 4 4 4 4
	74	63	56	62	70	75	98	77	62	76	7 7 7 7 7 7 7 7 7 7
	58	80	93	96	76	70	81	82	78	69	7 7 7 7 7 7 7 7 7 7
	54	64	79	74	83	57	64	79	71	59	6 6 6 6 6 6 6 6 6 6
1000BC	129	48	61	53	52	59	59	73	85	122	5 5 5 5 5 5 5 5 5 5
											2

Table 69 (cont.)

d) boat strake 6001 – 107 years, undated

ring widths (0.01mm)

year										
1	143	285	234	223	251	297	221	164	197	224
	252	271	241	224	222	248	306	274	151	257
	286	233	294	187	246	185	214	231	389	313
	373	322	450	397	369	308	338	294	350	298
	257	289	315	295	314	218	305	261	211	261
51	300	368	283	282	187	218	255	316	296	283
	227	230	169	193	190	208	234	158	214	225
	162	177	203	163	224	168	212	184	250	241
	242	240	145	113	146	174	177	210	296	274
	165	150	116	128	126	142	121	116	194	146
101	147	152	218	179	158	144	223			

Index

by Jill Halliday

Note: page numbers in *italics* refer to figures and tables